The Law in Context Series

Editors: William Twining (University College London)
Christopher McCrudden (Lincoln College, Oxford) and
Bronwen Morgan (University of Bristol)

Since 1970 the Law in Context series has been in the forefront of the movement to broaden the study of law. It has been a vehicle for the publication of innovative scholarly books that treat law and legal phenomena critically in their social, political and economic contexts from a variety of perspectives. The series particularly aims to publish scholarly legal writing that brings fresh perspectives to bear on new and existing areas of law taught in universities. A contextual approach involves treating legal subjects broadly, using materials from other social sciences, and from any other discipline that helps to explain the operation in practice of the subject under discussion. It is hoped that this orientation is at once more stimulating and more realistic than the bare exposition of legal rules. The series includes original books that have a different emphasis from traditional legal textbooks, while maintaining the same high standards of scholarship. They are written primarily for undergraduate and graduate students of law and of other disciplines, but most also appeal to a wider readership. In the past, most books in the series have focused on English law, but recent publications include books on European law, globalisation, transnational legal processes, and comparative law.

Books in the Series

Anderson, Schum and Twining: *Analysis of Evidence*
Ashworth: *Sentencing and Criminal Justice*
Barton and Douglas: *Law and Parenthood*
Beecher-Monas: *Evaluating Scientific Evidence: An Interdisciplinary Framework for Intellectual Due Process*
Bell: *French Legal Cultures*
Bercusson: *European Labour Law*
Birkinshaw: *European Public Law*
Birkinshaw: *Freedom of Information: The Law, the Practice and the Ideal*
Cane: *Atiyah's Accidents, Compensation and the Law*
Clarke and Kohler: *Property Law: Commentary and Materials*
Collins: *The Law of Contract*
Cranston: *Legal Foundations of the Welfare State*
Davies: *Perspectives on Labour Law*
Dembour: *Who Believes in Human Rights? The European Convention in Question*
de Sousa Santos: *Toward a New Legal Common Sense*
Diduck: *Law's Families*
Elworthy and Holder: *Environmental Protection: Text and Materials*
Fortin: *Children's Rights and the Developing Law*
Glover-Thomas: *Reconstructing Mental Health Law and Policy*

Freedom of Information

The Law, the Practice and the Ideal

Fourth Edition

PATRICK BIRKINSHAW

CAMBRIDGE
UNIVERSITY PRESS

CAMBRIDGE UNIVERSITY PRESS

Cambridge, New York, Melbourne, Madrid, Cape Town, Singapore,
São Paulo, Delhi, Dubai, Tokyo

Cambridge University Press
The Edinburgh Building, Cambridge CB2 8RU, UK

Published in the United States of America by Cambridge University Press, New York

www.cambridge.org
Information on this title: www.cambridge.org/9780521888028

© Patrick Birkinshaw 2010

First edition first published by Weidenfeld and Nicolson 1988
Second edition first published by Butterworths 1996
Third edition first published by Butterworths 2001
This edition first published by Cambridge University Press 2010

Printed in the United Kingdom at the University Press, Cambridge

A catalog record for this publication is available from the British Library

ISBN 978-0-521-88802-8 Hardback
ISBN 978-0-521-71608-6 Paperback

Contents

Preface

In the Introduction to this book I give an outline of some of the developments in the law relating to freedom of information since the last edition. My discs were sent to the publishers early in May 2009 but I was able to incorporate some developments until October 2009. I would like to thank Dan Metcalfe who, as the Law School's research assistant, provided invaluable work on examining the decisions and appeals of the Information Commissioner and the Information Tribunal.

October 2009

Table of statutes

Table of cases

UK cases - Information Tribunal

Introduction

Most introductions for previous editions of this book have been written in periods of high drama, crisis and feverish activity relating to secrecy or scandals connected to the release of information. The episode concerning MPs expenses' claims, which commenced with a freedom of information (FOI) request, continues that tradition. In May 2009, the promise of major constitutional change was uppermost in the minds of political leaders. A problem that had not been properly addressed by the authorities – what should MPs be paid for being an MP? – led to a disreputable system for expenses that was ill conceived, effectively un-policed and in which greed and cynicism were encouraged. I cannot recall the reputation of Parliament being at a lower ebb. Ministers and celebrated parliamentarians were standing down or faced de-selection. The affair led to the resignation of the Speaker, the first such resignation since 1695. Widespread reform was being promised including efforts to spread power more widely, reinvigorating local government, encouraging independent minded individuals to stand for Parliament, reforms of MPs expenses and independent audit and monitoring of those claims for expenses. The sights quickly moved to empowering MPs and select committees in their scrutiny of the executive (see chapter 9), proportional representation, an elected upper chamber, fixed-term parliaments and reining in the prerogatives of the prime minister (see chapter 9). That old chestnut, a written constitution, soon emerged. The latter would confront two shibboleths of the British constitution: the Crown and parliamentary sovereignty. The MPs saga has undoubtedly damaged the institutional sovereignty of Parliament. We shall see. It is in all our interests that Parliament is effective in its roles and comprises trustworthy members and peers.

MPs' expenses involving travel and the second home allowances' scheme (the former additional cost allowance (ACA) and presently the personal additional accommodation expenditure) has been the biggest news item concerning the Freedom of Information Act (FOIA). MPs and the Speaker and political leaders including the prime minster, had been slow to realise what living in a FOI environment meant – MPs do not know what juggernaut is coming their way, Jack Straw is reported to have said.[1] When it became apparent what that

---

[1] C. Mullin, *The Secret Diary of the Minister for Folding Deckchairs* (2009) p. 284.

environment meant for a cosy club-land existence at public expense, the reaction was tawdry. From January 2005 until January 2006, the parliamentary authorities received over a hundred FOI requests for information on MPs expenses most of which were refused on data protection grounds (see chapter 8).[2] In January 2007, the Information Tribunal (IT) ruled in favour of release of MPs' travel expenses – there had been publication of Scottish MPs expenses in Scotland. A Conservative MP, David Maclean introduced a Private Members' Bill into the Commons. This sought to remove Parliament from the ambit of FOIA. After various procedural manoeuvres, the bill failed in the Lords when it could not attract a sponsor. While conducting an enquiry into MPs expenses, the Speaker became embroiled over published stories of his and his wife's use of expenses. In February 2008, the IT rejected an appeal by the House of Commons concerning ACA allowances and ruled that the information that should be disclosed was in fact more extensive than in the decision of the Information Commissioner (IC) (see chapter 8, p. 309). This decision of the IT was upheld by the High Court. In January 2009, the government drafted an order that, in respect of Members of Parliament, would remove most expenditure information held by either House of Parliament from the scope of the Act. The order was dropped. Then in May 2009, ahead of the July deadline for release of the information to the public, the data were sold via a director of an intelligence company to the *Daily Telegraph*. In June the information was released by Parliament under FOIA – heavily redacted!

Loathed as the FOIA may be by parliamentarians, they had passed the bill after the government accepted the case by the Public Administration Committee to extend its provisions to Parliament. The Act has facilitated the righting of an aspect of 'old corruption'. The Committee on Standards in Public Life began a wide-ranging review of MPs' allowances in the spring of 2009. Political scientists and commentators often ask whether FOI has increased the public's trust in government and Parliament. Surely a question should be: has FOI increased your confidence in wrongs being outed and in appropriate action to remedy serious shortcomings?

On 10 June 2009, Prime Minister Brown announced to the Commons that there would be a new independent statutory Parliamentary Standards Authority to regulate allowances and a statutory code of conduct for MPs. The details are in the Parliamentary Standards Act 2009. Details of expenses would be publicly available. Legislation would cover sanctions for misconduct of Lords. A special all-party Parliamentary Commission will advise on parliamentary reforms including making select-committee processes more democratic, scheduling more and better time for non-government business in the House, and enabling the public to initiate directly some issues for debate. The prime minister announced that FOIA would be extended to a broader range of

[2] O. Gray, The Freedom of Information (Amendment) Bill, Bill 62 of 2006–7, House of Commons Research Paper 07/18.

bodies – private bodies performing public tasks (see chapter 4, p. 122) – and that following the Dacre Review (see chapter 9, p. 352), while there would be greater protection for 'particularly sensitive material' such as those relating to the royal family and Cabinet documents (see chapter 6, p. 205), the thirty-year rule would be relaxed to twenty years for other documents. It is not clear whether this means 'sensitive' documents will be given greater exemption or exclusion from FOIA or whether they will be subject to the thirty-year rule, or both. There would be greater access to government information on the Internet. He also announced steps for further reform of the Lords and its membership, a 'wide debate' on a written constitution, greater devolution and engagement of people in their local communities, proposals for taking the debate on electoral reform forward and increasing public engagement in politics. The plea was for 'integrity and democracy'. There was nothing specific on reforming prerogatives or fixed term Parliaments. (see http://www.number10.gov.uk/ Page19579). The Committee on Standards in Public Life's report, *MP's Expenses and Allowances* is Cm. 7724 (Nov. 2009). There are sixty recommendations. Just a week later, he announced that an enquiry would be established into the war in Iraq. It was to sit in private. Widespread criticism led to concessions.

Chapters six and eight detail the investigations by the IC and the appeals to the IT on requests under FOIA including personal data. Chapter 7 deals with the Environmental Information Regulations. Together with MPs expenses there have been disclosures on meetings between Rupert Murdoch and the prime minister before the Iraq war; and requests leading to eventual disclosure of the Attorney General's advice on the legality of that war and on numbers of missing sex offenders, and advice on reform of the pensions framework to Chancellor Brown in 1997 which had an adverse effect on pensions provision following a request in 2005. Disclosures led to the resignation of Ian Paisley Jr from office in Northern Ireland after he was shown to have lobbied on behalf of a close associate, and disclosures revealed the extent of Prime Minister Blair's involvement in exempting Formula One from the tobacco advertising ban after a donation was given to the Labour Party. The veto under s. 53 FOIA has been exercised in relation to the minutes of Cabinet meetings (see chapter 6, and see HC 622 (2008–9)).

Besides the sensational and state-shaking requests, there is a vast majority of mundane requests all of little importance to those other than the requester. Figures are given in chapter 6. However, the IC has stated that until May 2009 there had been a half million FOI requests, 11,500 complaints to the IC, 1,225 decision notices, 415 appeals to the IT.[3] For the vast majority of these requests, requesters now have a largely free and effective information service where before there was grace and favour – sometimes, perhaps, a very benevolent grace and favour, but one dependent on discretion and length of foot! With the increase

---

[3] Private Data, Open Government: Questions of Information, Conference, QEII Centre, 13 May 2009.

in numbers there comes an attendant delay in IC investigations, a matter on which the press have complained because of the damage to 'hot news items'.[4]

It came too late to include in the text that the plan to have secret inquests (see chapter 2, p. 64) had been modified, and that the government was to outlaw 'black lists' for employment purposes (see chapter 8, p. 272). Also the notification fee for data controllers has been increased to £500 for controllers with a turnover of over £29.5 million *and* over 250 staff (see chapter 8, p. 310) (SI 1677/2009).

The publication of the Intelligence and Security Committee's (ISC) Report into the London bombings (see chapter 2, p. 50) brought home the importance of data sharing and the dangers of such sharing where there is not in existence a secure framework of data retention and sharing. Sharing is beneficial where it prevents serious crime, assists in law enforcement, improves public service, protects the vulnerable and is used in the public interest for research and statistics. The public concern is over a lack of agreed and specific purposes for building databases. Two problems attend the practice: human negligence in failing to devise safe data systems and the inability of the Data Protection Act now to provide a reliable and appropriate framework of protection. A study commissioned by the Office of the Information Commissioner has made recommendations for a revision to the European Community Data Protection Directive on which the UK legislation for data protection is based.[5]

In June 2009, the IC retired from office to be replaced by Christopher Graham, head of the Advertising Standards Authority (see Justice Committee, *The Work of the Information Commissioner* HC 146 and Reply HC 424 (2008–9)). Relevant official reports cover *Protecting the Public in a Changing Communications Environment* (Home Office Cm. 7586) (see chapter 2, p. 58) a consultation on communications data and the government response to the House of Lords Constitution Committee's report on *Surveillance, Citizens and the State* (Cm 7616) (see chapter 8, pp. 271, 313). The latter report, in discussing numerous recommendations, did not accept an extension of investigation of private-sector data controllers without their consent by the IC as will be the case with public-sector data controllers. Private-sector controllers may be designated as public authorities. In the government Reply to the Public Administration Committee's report *Mandarins Unpeeled* (HC 428 (2008–9)) the Government did not accept the case for an independent body (the IC) to arbitrate disputes concerning publication of memoirs by former ministers or officials. The Committee recommended that contractual duties of confidentiality and assignment of copyright should apply to advisers and civil servants and the Radcliffe principles and the Ministerial Code should apply to ministers (see chapter 9, p. 326).

---

[4] J. Hayes, *A Shock to the System: Journalism, government and the Freedom of Information Act 2000* (2009).

[5] N. Robinson *et al.*, *Review of the European Data Protection Directive* (2009).

In *Secretary of State for the Home Department v AF(FC) and another* [2009] UKHL 28, the House of Lords in an *en banc* committee of nine judges unanimously overruled (with obvious reluctance) the Court of Appeal's majority decision in *AF* (see chapter 11, p. 437) ruling that such a judgment was not consistent with the European Court of Human Right's (ECtHR) decision in *A v United Kingdom* (see p. 437). The committee declined to consider 'closed evidence' (see p. 432). The judgments of the House 'must be open to all' said Lord Hope (para. 88). To comply with Art. 6 rights to a fair trial the subject of a control order must have sufficient information to allow his special advocate to make an effective challenge to an allegation on which the Secretary of State relies. As Lord Hope said 'in two vitally important sentences [the ECtHR] made it clear that the procedural protections can never outweigh the controlled person's right to be provided with sufficient information about the allegations against him to give effective instructions to the special advocate' (para. 81). The procedures were not criminal trials so sources, methods and complete evidence may not have to be disclosed but providing sufficient information of an essential allegation to make an effective challenge may make it difficult at times to avoid this. The choice for the Secretary of State is then a stark one: proceed but disclose; don't disclose, orders will be quashed. The Law Lords believed that the majority in the Court of Appeal in *AF* had interpreted *MB* correctly so *MB* decided that an *irreducible minimum of evidence* did not have to be disclosed in every case but this holding was not consistent with the ECtHR's judgment in *A*, the Law Lords have now ruled. The Prevention of Terrorism Act 2005 could however be read down as the majority accepted in *MB* so that its provisions did not lead ineluctably to the imposition of a control order in a procedure requiring a breach of Art. 6 and the Human Rights Act and a declaration of incompatibility. What life remains in control orders we shall have to see. Lord Brown believed that the ruling in *AF* would make no difference to the procedures of the Special Immigration Appeals Commission (SIAC) in deportation cases and *RB* (see p. 435) where no other Convention rights applied apart from an effective remedy under Art. 13 (para. 113). Other procedures involving special advocates and closed material, such as forfeiture orders under the Counter Terrorism Act 2008, where Convention rights are in play requiring Art. 6 protection, will be affected.[6] It was emphasised that what was 'fair' would be for the judges at first instance with only an appeal on a point of law to the Court of Appeal.

Following the ECJ decision in *Kadi* (see chapter 11, p. 438) the Court of First Instance ruled in *Othman v Council* (Case T-318/01: 11 June 2009) that financial restrictive measures in Council Regulation EC 881/2002 (27 May 2002) which implemented UN Security Council Resolutions, and in which Othman was named, were unlawful for depriving the applicant of an effective

---

[6] They are also used in The Proscribed Organisations Appeals Commission, Pathogens Access Appeals Commission, planning inquiries, s. 57 Race Relations Act, in Northern Ireland, Parole Board hearings, judicial review, criminal proceedings and the Security Vetting Appeals Panel. Cf. *A v HM Treasury* [2008] EWCA Civ 1187.

right of challenge. He was given no opportunity to challenge the evidence. The Regulation was annulled.

The IT judgment *Guardian News and Media Ltd v IC and MoJ* EA/2008/0084 upheld the IC's decision (FS50145985 – chapter 8, p. 299) and ruled that details of disciplinary action against judges were rightfully refused under s. 40 FOIA and s. 31. The judgment has interesting details on procedures involved. The IC's annual report for 2008–9 is HC 619 (2008–9).

The House of Lords select committee on the EU published a report on access to EU documents (HL 108 (2008–9) (see chapter 10). Proposals for making the office of Attorney General more independent were dropped from the Constitutional Reform and Governance Bill in July 2009 (see chapters 2, p. 38, and 3, p. 116). A *Protocol between the Attorney General and Prosecuting Authorities* was published in July 2009 and the AG's consent for prosecutions will be retained where required by law (as in the Official Secrets Act) or where national security is involved (see www.attorneygeneral.gov.uk/attachments/ Protocol%20between%20the%20Attorney%20General%20and%20the%20 Prosecuting%20Departments.pdf).

The Public Administration Select Committee published its report on *Leaks and Whistleblowing in Whitehall* and recommended a greater role for the Civil Service Commissioners (HC 83 (2008–9)) (see chapter 9, p. 348). The Joint Committee on Human Rights published its report on *Allegations of UK Complicity in Torture* which included criticisms of a lack of accountability structures for intelligence and security (HL 152/HC 230 (2008–9)) (see chapter 2 and the Foreign Affairs Committee HC 557 (2008–9)).

In two cases the High Court has found the IT and IC in error in relation to information held by the BBC for the purposes of 'journalism, art or literature' (p. 142 below). The court ruled that the 'predominant purpose test' for holding information was not a part of the statutory language and that the expression 'journalism etc' was not to be construed narrowly as the IC and IT had done (*BBC v Sugar and IC* [2009] EWHC (Admin) 2349 and *BBC v IC* [2009] EWHC (Admin) 2348). The IT's decisions were reversed.

The decision in *Binyam Mohamed v Secretary of State* (see chapter 2, p. 33 and chapter 11, p. 426) was reopened in [2009] EWHC 2549 (Admin). In a redacted judgment, the court ordered release, pending appeal, of the seven paragraphs relating to interrogation of BM from the documents supplied by US intelligence to the UK. No details of any intelligence factors would be released by the order. 'We consider that, viewed objectively, a decision by a court in the United Kingdom to put the redacted paragraphs into the public domain in the circumstances of this case would not infringe the principle of [US] control over [US] intelligence . . . The information related to matters of great public importance' (para. 73). Evidence from the CIA and Secretary of State Clinton did not reveal a 'real risk' to national security in so far as future intelligence may not be given to the UK by the USA, the court believed. The court was not persuaded that co-operation would not continue. A different context now operated in the USA. The seven paragraphs were of historical significance but no longer secret intelligence. The court made observations about the absence of a 'systematic archive' for closed judgments as well as any procedure to apply for access.[7]

The enforcement notices upheld by the Information Tribunal in *Chief Constable of Humberside etc. v IC* (pp. 13 and 287 below) were quashed by the Court of Appeal ([2009] EWCA Civ 1079) and the Tribunal's decision reversed.

Hansard HC vol. 496, col. 64 WS (16 July 2009) has a statement on a revised code under s. 46 FOIA, a reduction of the period of thirty years to twenty years under the Public Records Act and the designation of private bodies as public authorities under s. 5 FOIA (see chapter 4, p. 122). The Prime Minister has announced a programme to make public sector information available via the web to assist in service delivery: www.data.gov.uk following the White Paper Putting the Frontline First: Smarter Government Cm 7753 (2009) (see pp. 14 et seq infra).

Finally, chapter 2 has been significantly extended as a chapter in its own right covering national security, secrecy and information. Chapter 1 focuses on the contextual and theoretical context of freedom of information. A sobering thought on the contemporary information age is that the World Wide Web now contains a trillion pages growing at the rate of 3 billion per day.[8] Chapters 6, 7 and 13 are completely new and chapter 8 is significantly amended and extended. Chapter 9 is new but is based on chapters 4 and 5 from previous editions. All remaining chapters have been fully revised.

[7] See further [2009] EWHC 2973 (Admin).
[8] Peter Fleischer, Google Global Privacy Council, note 3 above.

1

Persistent themes and novel problems

The popular phrase 'Information Society' was coined to describe the essence of the computerised world. From globalised financial markets to government, from national and international security to education, from multinational corporations to small employers, from police to social welfare, medical treatment and social services, we are confronted by information repositories and retrieval systems whose capacity to store and transmit information is staggering. A moment's thought should make us appreciate that we have always been an information society. Anyone who has studied the constitutional history of Britain will appreciate that a major factor in the struggle between Crown and Parliament was the latter's desire to be informed about who counselled and advised the monarch in the formulation of policy. That monumental work in the history of our public administration, the Domesday Book, was basically an information exercise to assess the wealth and stock of the nation.[1] Our process of criminal trial by law constitutes an attempt to exclude unreliable evidence and to establish by rules of evidence a more reliably informed basis of fact on which to establish guilt or innocence. Lawmaking itself 'confessedly needs to be based on an informed judgment' requiring 'the widest access to information'.[2] The spread of information in the form of fact, opinion or ideas has variously been repressed, exhorted, victimised or applauded to advance the ideologies of those whose moment of power is in the ascendant. In this general sense, we can see previous societies as information societies. What is novel in our society, however, is the heightened awareness of the use, capability of collection, dissemination or withholding of information. Such functions are facilitated by artificial intelligence systems, advanced information technology and the opportunities which exist to influence public opinion through ever-more sophisticated telecommunications, information technology and information dissemination networks.

Many *causes célèbres* have involved information in the form of the giving or keeping of confidences. Socrates would have been in his element in discussing

---

[1] See Cm. 7022, HM Treasury on the National Assets Register with details of public assets worth over £1 million to a total in 2008 of £338 billion.

[2] R. Berger, *Executive Privilege* (1974), p. 3

the case of a civil servant deliberately leaking information to 'advance' the public interest (PI); the nature of informed consent before medical treatment;[3] the extent of the duty to inform parents of advice by doctors to their children;[4] a leak of a difference of opinion between the head of state and the prime minister on government policies;[5] the failure to inform those affected of the extent of nuclear accident and disaster;[6] seeking to prevent disclosure of information that would reveal the Government knew that defendants in a criminal trial were wrongfully indicted;[7] the use of allegedly unreliable information to support a case for armed invasion;[8] the loss of information about sensitive details on millions of individuals stored in electronic retrieval systems. For a Socrates, the details would be novel; there would, however, be a persistence in the nature of the problems they pose. The 'problems' surround the 'use' and 'abuse' of information. 'Use' and 'abuse' in this context are evaluative terms, and ones which I hope will be clarified in the course of this book. They are also relative terms. We may consider that a government abuses information when, without apparent justification, it refuses individuals access to information in its possession. This would not be the case in a system geared towards traditional representative democracy – where our representatives govern on our behalf and account to a collective assembly. It would certainly not be the case where government is absolutist and is accepted as such by those whom it governs.

A further comparative aspect of the terms 'use' and 'abuse' is present in two other features. One concerns the changing nature of the role of government not simply as an agent protecting and defending the realm from external and internal strife, but as a shaper of people's lives in almost every conceivable way. Government intervenes more and more in our society, whatever its political hue and whether to defend us or to influence us. Different roles require different sorts and amounts of information. The administrative regulatory state is the most acquisitive. In addition, the sophistication of information technology has made the collection, storage and retrieval of information not simply a national and corporate preoccupation, but a global one. The speed and ease with which

---

[3] *Sidaway v Board of Governors of the Bethlem Royal Hospital etc.* [1985] AC 871; *Bolitho v City and Hackney Health Authority* [1997] 4 All ER 771; *Pearce v United Bristol Healthcare NHS Trust* [1999] PIQR P53.

[4] *Gillick v West Norfolk and Wisbech Area Health Authority* [1985] 3 All ER 402, HL, concerning contraception for girls under 16; *R (Axon) v Secretary of State for Health* [2006] EWHC (Admin) 37.

[5] Resulting from a leak by the Queen's Press Officer: *The Times*, 8 July 1986.

[6] And secret post mortems on bodies of former workers at the Sellafield plant, *The Times*, 19 April 2007.

[7] See A. Tomkins, 'Public interest immunity after Matrix Churchill' (1993) Public Law 650, and *The Constitution after Scott: Government unwrapped* (1998); these were the events behind the Matrix Churchill inquiry by Sir Richard Scott. See P. Birkinshaw, (1996) JLS 406; B. Thompson and F. Ridley, *Under the Scott-light* (Oxford University Press, 1997); (1996) Public Law Autumn Issue dedicated to The Scott Report.

[8] *Review of Intelligence on Weapons of Mass Destruction* under Lord Butler, HC 898 (2003–4).

information may be transferred across national boundaries, by governments or private concerns, or matched by computers for different purposes from those for which the information was collected, is seen by many as an abuse in itself. The 'abuse' would be in the creation of information systems which are incapable of effective regulation at a price that treasuries would be prepared to tolerate. Privacy protection has not traditionally been afforded a high political priority in the United Kingdom; the developments which I have referred to diminish it even further. The impact of the Data Protection Act 1998 (DPA) and Human Rights Act 1998 (HRA) will be examined but their contribution to privacy protection is qualified.

Things must be seen in perspective. The UK Government is a holder of vast amounts of manual (i.e. documentary) information, much of it on individuals.[9] But the movement towards a 'paperless environment', as IBM's administration was described over twenty years ago during the passage of the Access to Personal Files Act in 1987, is a distinct characteristic of our age. The characteristics of information technology, however, require further elaboration.

Computers and information

Information technology is often described in exceptional and dramatic terms. The following from more than twenty years ago and before the emergence of the Internet and its staggering implications is a vivid example:

> In the last hundred years, we see the rapidly accelerating advent of a technology so powerful, novel, widespread, and influential that we may indeed call it the Second Industrial Revolution. Its basis is electromagnetic, in many interconnected forms: photography, photocopying, cinematography, and holography; telegraphy, telephony, radio communication, radar, sonar, and telemetry; sound and video recording and reproduction; vacuum tubes, transistors, printed circuits, masers, lasers, fiber optics, and (in rapid succession) integrated circuits (IC), large-scale integration (LSI), and very large-scale integration (VLSI) of circuitry on a tiny semiconducting 'chip'; and, finally, the bewildering variety of electronic digital computers. All these devices are intimately interrelated, and any advance in one tends to generate advances in all of them.

> The progress has been truly amazing. In only about 40 years, electronic communications and news media have become commonplace and indispensable; computers have proliferated, becoming increasingly fast, powerful, small and cheap, so that now there is scarcely a human activity in which they are not to be found, bearing an increasing share of the burden of repetitive information processing, just as the machines of the First Industrial Revolution have taken over the majority of heavy and unpleasant physical labor (we may say, energy processing).

---

[9] www.ancestor-search.info/NAT-NatArchives.htm and see ch. 9, p. 351.

Now, information can not only be stored, retrieved, communicated, and broadcast in enormous quantities and at phenomenal speeds; but it can also be rearranged, selected, marshalled, and transformed.[10]

Since that was written there has been an advance in digital systems sweeping away remaining distinctions between data processing and telephony. We have witnessed a growing convergence of computer and telephone systems and a wholesale shift to computer networking. The mobile or cell phone has proliferated. The obvious progeny has been the internet – a network of computers which works like a combined telephone and postal service – and the creation of the World Wide Web. Broadband has facilitated easy access. We are moving towards a protocol for communications via the Internet. In 1988 there were 1 million users of the internet. By 2009, the number of users is approaching 1.5 billion, 21.9 per cent of the world's population, and a 305.5 per cent increase since 2000. Who controls the internet and what is the wealth of networks are central questions.[11] Access brings all the benefits of instantaneous search engines, libraries and services. Cyberterrorism, cybercrime and cyberpornography pose major threats to government and society. China and Iran have sought to censor by various devices the information that can be retrieved on line. The blogosphere and Twitter have the capability to thwart the most restrictive of injunctions issued by courts against the press (*Financial Times* 14 October 2009). Governments have increasingly taken steps to prevent the transmission of 'obscene' material via the internet. In the US, the president signed into law the Communications Decency Act 1996 which the Supreme Court ruled unconstitutional.[12] In the UK, over fifteen sets of regulations deal with emails. Policing the net has become a global preoccupation. There is no global policeman. The Internet Governance Forum is a group of stakeholders of carriers; academics; Internet Service Providers; and civil society, government and international governmental organisations. It meets annually dealing with subjects like openness, security, e-criminals, diversity and access. It advises ICANN – the International Corporation for Assigned Names and Numbers. It is an independent not-for-profit organisation based in California which originally reported to the US Department of Commerce. It now reports to the 'Internet community'.

---

[10] J. Halton, 'The anatomy of computing' in T. Forrester (ed.), *The Information Technology* (1985). On the Internet and law, see: L. Edwards and C. Waelde, *Law and the Internet*, 2nd edn (2000); C. Reed, *Internet Law: Text and materials*, 2nd edn (2004); M Ihusuki (ed.), *Transnational Cyberspace Law* (2001); Y. Akdeniz and C. Walker, *Internet Law and Society* (2001); M. Gould, *Foundations of Internet Governance* (2001). A. Fung, M. Graham, and D. Weil, *Full Disclosure: The perils and promise of transparency* (Cambridge University Press, 2007).

[11] J. Goldsmith and T. Wu, *Who Controls the Internet?* (Oxford University Press, 2007); Y. Benkler, *The Wealth of Networks: How social production transforms markets and freedoms* (Yale University Press, 2006).

[12] *ACLU v Reno* 929 F Supp 824, 117 S Ct 2329 (1997); US Communications Decency Act 1996, 47 USC 230.S.

Decades ago, the Lindop Committee[13] offered a thoughtful and informative account of the problems posed by data accumulation and protection. It noted that the electronic computer was 'only a part of any information system' and that the rest of the system will perform 'the functions of collecting and preparing the data for the computer, devising its instructions, and transferring the information produced to those who need it'. All of this would require human control and 'often human intervention' and the creation of 'at least some manual records'.

The report spoke quite correctly of the dangers of abuse of information that would come with centralisation of information on electronic systems. Shock-horror stories of MI5's access to millions of electronic files have been generated for decades. For over twenty years, computer network contracts have specified how a free flow of information can pass between the major government departments contrary to existing legislative requirements.[14] An increasing number of statutes has facilitated such transfer. [15] Now data matching and data transfer are widespread and the government plans to introduce comprehensive authorisation for transfer in the Coroners and Justice Bill 2009 (see chapter 8, p. 272).[16] The National Health Service has developed an Electronic Patient Records database hoping to achieve a comprehensive national digital database of all personal health records. The national identity card programme introduced under the Identity Cards Act 2006 will establish a national database and one in six people may not be able to use their cards because of 'failure to enrol' problems.[17] There was a constant criticism that security aspects on the data retention would not be adequate. All ID systems use biometric data such as fingerprints, iris scans, facial topography and hand scans. They can be used to obtain geographical/locational information through RFID, global positioning systems, smart cards, transponders or radio signals. ID cards would be used to secure the 'efficient and effective provision of public services'.[18] There was also widespread criticism that data would be used for 'social sorting' which could determine preferential access to public services, exclusive or selective marketing, sorting people for preferential treatment according to status. What of those without access to e-services and public services, employment and recruitment? Closed-circuit TV, mobile phones and automatic number-plate recognition have all facilitated location of individuals and their movements. The House of Lords Constitution Committee's major report into *Surveillance* will be examined in chapter 8.

---

[13] Cmnd 7341 (1978), following *Computers and Privacy*, Cmnd 6353 (1975).

[14] *The Guardian*, 7 January 1987.

[15] R. Thomas and M. Walport, *Data Sharing Review Report* (2008) containing recommendations and information on public surveys.

[16] A wide ranging inquiry is in *Surveillance: Citizens and the State*, House of Lords Constitution Committee HL 18-I–II (2008–9). The Ministerial Committee on Data Sharing is MISC 31.

[17] A. Grayling, *In Freedom's Name: The case against identity cards* (Liberty, 2005). See *Report on the Surveillance Society* by the Surveillance Studies Network September 2006.

[18] Commons Science and Technology Committee, *Sixth Report*, HC 1032 (2006–7).

Data controllers responsible for the Police National Computer (PNC) have been the subject of enforcement notices issued by the Information Commissioner (IC) and upheld by the Information Tribunal (IT).[19] The legal framework for the PNC is 'permissive' not mandatory and is not comprehensive.[20] Following the Bichard inquiry into events surrounding the murder of two young girls by Ian Huntley,[21] a new code of practice was produced in 2005 by the Association of Chief Police Officers (ACPO) entitled *Management of Police Information.* Guidance was also published on retention and erasure and in 2006 guidance was issued on retention of nominal records (linked to a named individual) on the PNC. The 2006 guidance was 'not endorsed' by the IC. Data is pooled by chief constables and they are the controllers of data placed on the PNC. These data concern conviction data although they are much wider than court convictions (hard data) and guidance may be kept until the data subject is one hundred years old! The 2006 retention guidelines include cautions, warnings, reprimands and penalty notices for disorder or arrests for 'recordable offences' and data on charges is kept ('soft data'). It may be 'stepped down' over time, which means only police have access, but practices are not clear and there is discretion to remove certain data that are subject to variable application by different chief constables. The PNC can read external databases such as the Driving and Vehicle Licensing Centre and has links to 30,000 terminals.[22] The Serious Organised Crime Agency (SOCA) established by the Serious Organised Crime and Police Act 2005 absorbed the National Criminal Intelligence Service Authority responsible for disseminating criminal intelligence to police forces and law enforcement agencies. SOCA also absorbed the HM Revenue and Customs unit on serious drug trafficking as well as the Immigration Services intelligence for organised crime. The National Police Improvement Agency maintains the PNC. ACPOs Criminal Records Office provides operational support for records management, fingerprints and DNA records. Like the secret intelligence and security services and General Communications Headquarters (see below) SOCA is excluded from the Freedom of Information Act 2000 (FOIA). National security and policing are given wide grounds for exemption from Data Protection Act provisions (see chapter 8). Lindop was all too aware of the dangers of excessive secrecy attaching to the operation of police computers and their potential abuse. He saw a useful model in the case of

---

[19] *Chief Constable of Humberside etc. v IC* EA/2007/0096.

[20] *Ibid.* S. 27(4) Police and Criminal Evidence Act 1984 and SI 2000/1139.

[21] HC 653 (2003–4).

[22] The Criminal Justice Act 2003 allowed police retention of fingerprints and DNA of all arrested persons and records are kept on the PNC: see chapter 8 note 22. There were 6 million sets of prints in 2006. The national DNA database was set up in 1995 and by December 2005 3.45 million individuals were included. The 2005 Drugs Act gave police the power to test all people arrested for specified offences. The Criminal Justice Exchange System allows information to be shared across all agencies of criminal justice and a cross-regional information-sharing project will create a single national police data base.

Sweden.[23] For 'national security' data the authority should have an officer with a security clearance sufficiently high to enable him to operate in effect as a consultant to the Home Office and the security services and to establish with them the appropriate rules and safeguards for their systems. None of these recommendations was accepted. Versions of such a scheme are operational in Sweden and France.

Chief Constables disclose to the Criminal Records Bureau (CRB – an executive agency of the Home Office: see SI 460/2009) through the National Identification Service conviction details on data subjects in response to requests for 'standard' and 'enhanced' certificates. These certificates contain details on convictions, cautions, and other information held for the use of forces generally under Pt V Police Act 1997 and regulations (SI 2002/233 reg. 9). The information is given to the applicant for employment (the data subject) and a prospective employer (a 'registered person'). Records are not made public. A code issued under s. 122 Police Act 1997 seeks to ensure fair and reasonable behaviour by registered employers and compliance with the code is a condition of registration. CRB commenced operations in the summer of 2001 and provides checks on those working with children and vulnerable adults. These constitute exemptions to 'spent convictions' under the Rehabilitation of Offenders Act 1974. The Commons Home Affairs Committee expressed concerns over the accuracy of data on the PNC from which checks will be made. Error rates were between 15 and 65 per cent.[24] Details of entry on 'barred lists', i.e. being barred from working in education with children or vulnerable adults, must also be given. Appeal against barring lies to the Care Standards Tribunal. The Safeguarding Vulnerable Groups Act 2006 will replace the barred lists with new forms, and decisions on barring will be made by the Independent Barring Board.

The use of such information technology (IT) can have a potent impact on centralising and co-ordinating information, facilitating centripetal administrative tendencies within organisations and between hierarchical levels of bureaucracy, and it can increase dramatically the dangers of improper use or storage. There are dangers in over-sensationalising. Government, in whatever form, will have to exploit new technology. The Office of Government Commerce (OGC) is responsible for central government IT procurement. OGC draws up security terms and conducts 'gateways reviews' of projects which have been subject to freedom of information (FOI) requests (see p. 193 below). The E-Government Unit in the Cabinet Office (formerly Office of the e-Envoy) is responsible for assisting and improving the e-delivery of government services and information.

---

[23] In Sweden, codes are negotiated between the Data Protection Authority and the police. As seen above, the 2006 guidance from ACPO on data retention of data was not endorsed by the Information Commissioner. The European Court of Human Rights has held that there was no breach of Arts. 8 or 10 of the Convention on Human Rights when the Swedish Government refused access to a register containing personal information relating to national security: *Leander v Sweden* (1987) 9 EHRR 433. See also *Rotaru v Romania* (2000) 8 BHRC 449 (ECtHR). See I. Cameron, *National Security and the ECHR* (2000).

[24] *Criminal Records Bureau*, HC 227 (2000–1).

The Treasury has incorporated delivery targets in Public Service Agreements.[25] *Transformational Government* (2005)[26] sets out the agenda for the development of e-government and public service which are to be achieved by Service Transformation Agreements (2007). Many government websites were closed in 2007 leaving government to concentrate on two sites: direct.gov.uk and businesslink.co.uk[27]

The Central Sponsor for Information Assurance is a unit within the UK Government's Cabinet Office providing a focus for Information Assurance activity across the UK in the public and private sectors. It works closely with the National Technical Authority for Information Assurance (in General Communications Headquarters – GCHQ – which provides advice on areas of 'vital interest' in the security of communications and data) and the Centre for the Protection of National Infrastructure. The latter reports to the director of MI5 and is concerned with critical infrastructure. SOCA and the Home Office provide advice on security in relation to criminal information and data.[28] The Cabinet Office has published detailed guidance on information and data security adding to manuals and management codes on security.[29] This sets out the following requirements on data security and was driven by the spate of episodes in which sensitive data on millions of data subjects was lost through inadvertence and negligence.[30] It sets out core standards on security; information charters are to be published by departments which will define standards setting out what to do if things go wrong; departments should publish specific information assets on the information they hold and how it is used – these are known as the Information Asset Registers and are to be viewed on the Office of Public Sector Information's website;[31] and the Cabinet Office will publish core standards. There will be scrutiny by the National Audit Office of IT contracts; spot checks by the IC; targeted intervention by departments or a special unit of GCHQ via the National Technical authority (above); and use of new powers amending the Data Protection Act 1998 (s. 55A–E) which make it a criminal offence for failure to take reasonable steps not to breach the data-protection principles (see p. 289).[32]

For over thirty years the benefits of computerising governmental administration have been celebrated. As stated above, the Government set out its agenda in *Transformational Government – Enabled by Technology* (Cm 6683) which stated

---

[25] HC 94 (2000–1) and see *Government on the WEB* from the National Audit Office: HC 87 (1999–2000). On PSAs, see www.cabinetoffice.gov.uk/about_the_cabinet_office/publicserviceagreements.aspx.

[26] www.cio.gov.uk/transformational_government/index.asp (2 March 2009).

[27] *Financial Times*, 28 March 2007 on company websites.

[28] The Department for Business and Regulatory Reform and the IC are also part of the network.

[29] *Data Handling Procedures in Government: Final Report* (2008, Cabinet Office).

[30] *Surveillance, Citizens and the State* HL 18 (2008–9).

[31] www.opsi.gov.uk/advice/crown-copyright/copyright-guidance/information-asset-register-and-freedom-of-information (2 March 2009).

[32] See *Personal Internet Security*, HL 165-I–II (2006–7) and Government Reply, Cm 7234.

that in 2005, £14 billion was spent on IT and related activity, 50,000 people were employed directly by government in the IT field and the UK Government was one of the largest customers of the IT industry although originally there was reluctance to use systems in the private sector. This reluctance has, however, long been overtaken by events.

The Power of Information sets out the advantages to government and the governed of e-democracy.[33] The government has suggested the use of the 'highway to democracy'[34] for e-government, transformational government, e-voting, e-petitions, video links, chat rooms and emailing the prime minister. There is greater availability of scientific and medical research on-line. IT was at the centre of Prime Minister Blair's wish for joined-up government in his plans for *Modernising Government*.[35] In early 1996, the Government relaxed the copyright laws where statutory provisions allowing access to information were concerned to facilitate access.

As far back as 1995, the US Office of Management and Budget launched an ambitious programme or 'electronic open meeting' entitled 'People and their Governments in the Information Age'. Use of the 'information superhighway' in the USA by government is at its most advanced in terms of interfacing the government with the people and providing public-service information to citizens.[36] Numerous details on the US FOI laws may be obtained from the internet and such publications have not been protected by copyright. In the UK, *Hansard* and official bills were protected by copyright and, absent libraries, were only available where high fees were expended. Paper and paid-for copies still exist but the former documents, select committee reports, statutory instruments and government papers are available through the Internet. The availability, revolutionary just several years ago, is now taken for granted. These have been accompanied by fuller and more helpful explanatory material for legislation, regulations and decisions.

Reuse of public-sector information

Access to government-held information has been widely accepted. What of allowing the reuse of that information for commercial and wealth creating opportunities? In the EU, the European Commission Green Paper of 1999 *Public Sector Information in the Information Society*[37] was sensitive to the use of government-held information to improve the quality of government service, to make it easier for individuals and business to relate to government and to generate increased wealth and industrial competition. The EU Council of Ministers, the Commission and European Parliament have operated an electronic register of documents held as will be seen in chapter 10. In December 2003 a Directive

---

[33] E. Mayo and T. Steinberg, *The Power of Information* (Cabinet Office, 2007) and Government Reply, Cm. 7157.

[34] K. Oakley, *The Highway to Democr@cy* (CoE, 2003)   [35] Cm. 4310 (1999).

[36] *Government Information Quarterly*, Issue 2 (2009).   [37] COM (1998) 585.

on the Reuse of Public Sector Information was promulgated (2003/98/EC OJ L 345, 31.12.03 p. 90) and this was implemented into UK law by SI 2005/1515 the Reuse of Public Sector Information Regulations (see Cm 7672 (2009)).

These regulations have as their main objective the establishment of methods ensuring and encouraging:

- the ready identification of public-sector documents that are available for reuse
- that documents are generally available for reuse at marginal cost
- that public-sector bodies deal with applications to reuse in a timely, open and transparent manner
- that the process is fair, consistent and non-discriminatory
- that best practice is shared across the public sector.

Regulation 3 defines the public bodies covered by the regulations. The document has to be identified by the public body as being available for reuse (reg. 5(2)) and this seems to be subject to no obvious form of control. It covers documents supplied to an applicant for re-use under, e.g., FOI laws or otherwise available. Conditions may be imposed on reuse. Charges may be made including a reasonable return on investment for the authority. A commercial rate for the reuse of documents may be charged where appropriate. This will be particularly applicable to public-sector bodies that are required to operate in a commercial manner in order to cover their costs. This includes government trading funds. Where applicable, the charges should cover the costs of collection, production, reproduction and dissemination, together with a reasonable return on investment, based on normal accounting cycles.

Some documents are excluded from the scheme. This covers documents that are exempt from disclosure under FOI legislation. It covers those cases where a particular interest needs to be demonstrated by an authority, e.g. its own commercial interests; documents in which the copyright and/or other intellectual property rights are owned or controlled by a person or organisation other than the public-sector body; documents that fall outside the scope of the public task of the public-sector body. This covers situations where a public-sector body produces documents that are not directly related to the core responsibilities of the public-sector body. This may cover documents that are of a value added or commercial nature; documents that are held by public service broadcasters and other bodies or their subsidiaries for the fulfilment of a public-service broadcasting remit; documents held by educational and research establishments such as schools, universities, archives, libraries and research facilities; documents held by cultural establishments, including museums, libraries, archives, orchestras, theatre and performing-arts establishments.

All public-sector bodies should operate an effective, transparent complaints procedure to deal with rejected applications for reuse. The following Office of Public Sector Information (OPSI) guidance on the dispute resolution process, which is described as 'independent', constitutes best practice:

- The dispute process will be managed by the OPSI. Complainants will be expected to specify the basis of their complaint and how a public sector body is failing to comply with the Regulations.
- The complaint will be investigated by OPSI. A Decision will be issued within thirty working days. 'Complex' cases may be subject to a non-refundable payment of £500.
- Both parties can appeal to the specially constituted panel of the Advisory Panel on Public Sector Information (APPSI). The Chair or the Deputy Chair of APPSI will convene an appropriately independent and balanced panel of experts (the Panel). The Panel will investigate and reach a decision within sixty working days.
- Generally evidence will only be considered in written form. The Chair of the Panel will have the discretion to co-opt individuals who are not existing members of APPSI.
- Complaints about OPSI will be referred to APPSI so as to maintain an equivalent level of independence.
- A summary of each case and all Decisions will be published.
- Compliance with decisions will be monitored by OPSI (or APPSI in the case of complaints made against OPSI).
- Non-compliance will be referred to the Minister to the Cabinet Office who will consider issuing a Ministerial Letter of direction.

The importance of information

At this stage the focus will be upon a theoretical analysis of information, its importance in human relationships and its treatment in state/civil society compacts. The argument will be advanced that citizens have a right to expect more information from their government than is currently the case in the UK notwithstanding initiatives from 2000 onwards, which I discuss in detail subsequently. Legislation, it will be argued later in the book and depending obviously upon its content, can go some way to redressing the current imbalance. It can help to a certain extent in creating a better-informed public and establishing the basis of fuller participation of individuals and groups in the process of rule. But we need to understand why the provision of information is limited. Are there justifications for limiting it? Does current practice represent an implicit theory of state/individual relationships which the overwhelming majority are happy to accept? If so, are they misguided? Claims and counterclaims about freedom of information are couched in terms of a theory of democracy by their respective proponents, often unwittingly. An attempt must be made to unpack and analyse these claims. Ironically, freedom of information could make us a very undemocratic and very unprincipled – indeed a more callous – society.

Our capacity as human beings to acquire, use and store information is essential for our survival. This might appear a tall claim for something that in English law cannot be the object of theft.[38] At a practical level disasters are avoided, accidents prevented and sustenance provided by our use of information. Hamlet's tragedy was that he was accurately informed; Othello's that he was not. While information itself is important, our ability to discern the degree of the reliability of the information provided is essential in the exploitation of resources or relationships, or in the exposure of sham. Information acquired through scientific inquiry establishes that it is irrational to believe that consulting the auspices, the stars or the tea leaves is a reliable indication of future events. Information is necessary to make sensible choice or wise judgement. Moral and ethical evaluation depends upon information acquired through our own and our predecessors' experience. Information in the form of facts constitutes the basis of order in our lives, of community, regularity and knowledge. Are 'facts' nothing more than the haphazard ascription of names or categories to phenomena impinging on our consciousness, however? And if there are no facts, is it possible to know anything? In order to think or make decisions we apply categories of thought such as quantity, substance and causality, or 'a priori intuitions' such as space and time, to myriad phenomena which we encounter. These are categories or intuitions which, according to Kant, inhere in the working of the mind itself. They are the starting point, he argued, of our organisation of confused data. They are the most basic forms of information. Their existence, Kant reasoned, is a basic fact.

Without the application of these categories and intuitions we would be incapable of achieving judgement or making decisions. We would be incapable of existence beyond that of a vegetable. Such intuitions and categories, Kant believed, are inescapable in the human predicament. But the information to which we apply our faculties of judgement and decision-making is far from immutable. It is subject to change, historical development, inaccuracy, distortion or imprecision, and so on. This is why we normally set a high premium on telling the truth, faithful and accurate recording of events, care in the provision of information; and why we punish cheats and frauds or censure liars, or hold as culpable the negligent transmission of information that causes harm.[39] These examples illustrate the importance of the mutual and implicit acceptance of certain ground rules in the use of information and its employment in human

[38] *Oxford v Moss* (1978) 68 Cr App Rep 183; *R v Absolon* (1983) The Times, 14 September. See now, however, Computer Misuse Act 1990 as amended by the Police and Justice Act 2006, ss. 35–8 on computer hacking and *AG's Ref (No. 1 of 1991)* [1992] 3 All ER 897, CA; *R v Bow Street Stipendiary Magistrate, ex p. United States Government* [1999] 4 All ER 1, HL; and *Mckinnon v Government of the USA* [2008] UKHL 59. Use of data is 'processing' under the Data Protection Act (see ch. 8). Intellectual property law is by nature proprietary and on confidentiality see R. Toulson and C.Phipps, *Confidentiality*, 2nd edn (2006), pp. 29 *et seq.* Plagiarism is not a breach of intellectual property law per se: *Baigent and Leigh v Random House Group Ltd* [2006] EWHC 719 (Ch) and the *Da Vinci Code*.

[39] For references negligently compiled see: *Spring v Guardian Assurance plc* [1994] 3 All ER 129, HL.

communication. Rather like the categories of thought, they are an inescapable feature of existence, in particular of communication.

These are commonsensical observations. Can they be given a theoretical, explanatory framework? A theory of communication that might assist has its most developed expression in the work of Jürgen Habermas.[40] Habermas has sought to establish that the process of communication between human beings, of which information is an essential if not exclusive component, is only possible on the basis that certain ground rules representing an underlying consensus are accepted. These will cover such obvious features as: assertions are made on the basis that they are believed to be true, or that the facts that we allude to in our speech are correct. Rational discourse is premised upon norms such as these. Even if we rejected the norms, we would still have to accept them implicitly to communicate. If I operate on the basis that deception is the fundamental truth of communication, I will set out to deceive. But a corollary of what I accept as a fundamental truth is that others may operate on the same basis. If they are attempting to deceive me, how can I assume that what they are uttering is not in fact the truth – for they will deceive me by telling the truth, which I will not believe since I will accept it as lies. More importantly, in order to deceive, I must have an idea of the concept of truth. Deception implies truth or the concept of truth. If the consensus of the claims inherent in communicative competence is challenged, then its validity, correctness or acceptability can only be tested by debate and argument.[41]

Habermas argues that through discourse, as he calls it, the only form of pressure that is allowed to operate is the force of the better argument. Discourse is a 'special form of communication', but all communicative action implies that those 'interacting in it are discursively justifying their beliefs and norms through the giving of reasons'. As a practical reality, this is very often not the case; but communication must take place on the basis that the 'conditions constituting communicative competence are true'. If not, communication in any meaningful sense of the word would be impossible. What discourse presupposes, Habermas believes, is 'an ideal speech situation'. In this situation all participants must be given the same opportunity to debate and justify according to reasoned argument without external pressure or domination. All assertions and norms and claims are subject to examination and appraisal in discussion. By this method, norms will only be found to be justified when grounded in 'generalisable interests' and not simply on the power of those asserting the norms. The 'ideal speech situation' is precisely that – an ideal, although it is a fulfilment of the conditions which enable meaningful communication. It is forever frustrated as a matter of practice by 'systematically distorted communication' – by, for instance, manipulation of public opinion, misinformation,

---

[40] J Habermas, *Toward a Rational Society* (1971), esp. chs. 5 and 6, and *Communication and the Evolution of Society* (1979). See T. Prosser, 'Towards a critical public law' (1982) 9 JLS 1.

[41] 'Discursive examination' free from domination, per Prosser, 'Towards a critical public law'.

a lack of full information on which to exercise a proper freedom of choice, or ideologies legitimating class, economic or political domination. Habermas argues that a fundamental question of practical philosophy today 'has been . . . a question of the procedures and presuppositions under which justifications can have the power to produce consensus'.[42] This will be a point to which I shall return.

The attempt to convey correct information is the basis on which communication is premised. We are all regular providers of information, and we know the consequences of providing false information if we are caught out. There is a converse side to the provision of information. This is the control of information: that pursuit of secrecy or confidentiality or that quest for privacy that is essential to our full development as human beings. How can this be reconciled with the 'ideal speech situation' advanced by Habermas?

It can be reconciled by accepting that there are spheres of our personal and public lives that are a legitimate object of secrecy or privacy. Without adequate protection for justifiable secrets our integrity can be compromised, our identity shaken, our security shattered. Details of legitimate intimate relationships, medical facts, of prolonged sensitive negotiations, extremely delicate investigations in the PI, development of strategic or commercial plans, often require secrecy; likewise the long-term development of products requiring constant experimentation and creative thought or the protection of ideas. Without the guarantee of secrecy, there would be no protection for their development. The law has come to recognise this by the enactment of copyright and patent laws, the burgeoning area of intellectual property law, the law of confidentiality and specific privacy laws such as those that have been enacted in America and parts of the Commonwealth and Europe or which English judges have been developing in

---

[42] Habermas, *Communication*, p. 205. In *The Theory of Communicative Action* (1981) Habermas developed a dual level social theory namely an analysis of communicative rationality that is embedded in speech with a theory of modernisation and modern society. The argument constitutes a theory of the justification for rational and free collective action in 'systemic coordination', i.e. markets and bureaucracies. Law is seen as an essential part of the solution as citizens make laws ensuring improvement in democratic practice. Clearly there are strong elements of idealism in this theory: full information, rational debate and fully reasoned conclusions, but the theory does provide a powerful rationale for socio-political coexistence. There are problems for moral choices and the application of his theory. People often will not accept 'unacceptable' choices even after a reasonable discourse because it clashes with their moral predisposition. The unbiased observer will see the morally superior argument after a critical evaluation of 'formal dialogues', Habermas argues. Private autonomy is best guaranteed when equal citizens participate in making laws for their governance: but what of laws developed through common-law techniques that are judicially developed? Reasonable political discourse must operate on the basis that one right legal answer is possible to a legal problem, or at least a set of answers on which a fair compromise, acceptable to all parties, is possible. At the global level, Habermas builds on the importance of 'international public law'. See further, *The Philosophical Discourse of Modernity* (1996), *Between Fact and Norm: Contributions to a discourse theory of law and democracy* (1998), *The Inclusion of the Other: Studies in political theory* (2001) and *The Post-national Constellation: Political essays* (2000).

the twenty-first century.[43] Some American states have gone further and made unauthorised appropriation of industrial secrets a crime.

In other respects secrecy is essential for and between participants to make sense of a situation; there would be little point in playing cards or chess if one constantly revealed one's future plans. This illustrates a deeper theme. 'What is at issue', argues Bok, 'is not secrecy alone but rather the control over secrecy and openness.'[44] It is very often a question of the timing of the release of information so as not to prejudice legitimate interests. Financial information whose release may allow unconscionable profiteering or undermine market rescue initiatives, or examination papers are obvious examples. But with information comes power and, with the exclusive control and use of information, power is augmented. The problem then becomes one of establishing when secrecy operates not only to protect or advance the interests of those possessing or sharing secrets, but to subvert the interests of those not privy to such secrets. A lack of transparency in the way power is exercised invariably, but not inevitably, prejudices those without access to full information. To a lawyer this is familiar territory: a balancing of interests, protection of proprietorial or quasi-proprietorial rights, reasonable behaviour. But the law can only play a minimal role in opening-up closed societies or secret relationships given the strength of the attraction of secrecy and confidentiality in business relationships, professional associations, bureaucracy whether private or public, political groups, government, police and Freemasonry.[45] The problem concerning the exclusive use of information is at its most acute when we have a state or an official institution speaking on behalf of the collective or public interest that accumulates unimaginable amounts of information and which carries out its operations, whether by design, stealth or accident, in secrecy or at best under significant limitations on openness and access.

Information and the state

The position that a ruling body adopts towards the provision of information about its activities to a representative chamber or the civil society at large will

---

[43] As well as actions for wrongful invasion of privacy developed after the seminal article of S. Warren and L. Brandeis, 'The right of privacy' (1890) 4 HLR 193. See the Younger Report on Privacy, Cmnd 5012 (1972); R. Wacks, *Personal Information: Privacy and the law* (1993) and *Privacy and Press Freedom* (1995); P. Birks (ed.), *Privacy and Loyalty* (1997); R. Singh and J. Strachan, *The Law of Privacy* (2001); D. Feldman, *Civil Liberties and Human Rights*, 2nd edn (2002); M. Tugendhat and I. Christie, *The Law of Privacy and the Media* (2004); H. Fenwick and G. Phillipson, *Media Freedom under the Human Rights Act* (2006); A. Kenyon and M. Richardson (eds.), *New Dimensions in Privacy Law: International and comparative perspectives* (2006).

[44] S. Bok, *Secrets* (1984). Bok's work has numerous references to theoretical works on secrecy.

[45] See the Home Affairs Committee, *Freemasonry in the Police and Judiciary*, HC 192 (1997–8), and Government Reply, HC 578 (1997–8). See Home Office Press Release 233/2000 on the consultation by the Home Office with police on registering masonic membership. The police were not registering on a voluntary basis to the same extent that judges and magistrates were.

inevitably be coloured by considerations about the proper role of government, as well as sheer political expedience.

When government was in the personal household of the monarch, the words of King James I expressed the 'private nature' and arcane mysteries of state business by warning that 'None shall presume henceforth to meddle with anything concerning our government or deep matters of state.'[46] Francis Bacon was more subtle in his justification of state secrecy and in his presaging of a Leviathan, an almighty state:

> Concerning government, it is a part of knowledge secret and retired in both these respects in which things are deemed secret; for some things are secret because they are hard to know, and some because they are not fit to utter. We see all governments as obscure and invisible.

In Leviathan, the all-powerful state, citizens have no need of governmental information and nor do those who purport to speak on their behalf. Government is absolute. It is absolute because it needs absolute power to defend society. Too much information about state activity will demystify the process of government.

When government is limited, however, in the nature of a trust on behalf of the community, such assumptions of absolutism which inform the relationship between state and society, government and the community, can no longer prevail. The nature of the bond between the state and its citizens, and between citizens *inter se*, is formulated in an implied contract, not an unalterable status. Breach of its terms by the government justifies its removal. John Locke saw the supreme power of the state residing in a legislature, and behind the legislature the people. The people governed, but they were not government. Nor were they the legislature, although they were represented in it. In matters of government, claims for information could not be made by the community directly, but via their representatives. Part of Locke's philosophy also justified acquisitive individualism and the rights of citizens to own what 'they have mixed their labour with' deriving from a natural right of property antecedent to the existence of government. When property is extended of information we have the joinder of issue with which we are still engaged – the conflict between a representative democracy and a democratically elected government and its preserve upon information on the people's behalf. The force of the argument posed on behalf of society is political not legal.

The growth of governmental power, quite simply, necessitated greater safeguards against abuse. 'Secrecy, being an instrument of conspiracy', said Bentham, 'ought never to be the system of a regular government.'[47] His appeal

---

[46] Cited in Bok, *Secrets*. See also W. Eamon, *Science and the Secrets of Nature: Books of secrets in medieval and early modern culture* (1994). In spite of his belief in state secrecy, Francis Bacon advocated promulgation of scientific knowledge beyond a 'privileged few'.

[47] J. Bentham, 'On Publicity' in J. Bowring (ed.), *Works of J Bentham* (1843), vol. 2, pp. 310–17; see also F. Rosen and J. H. Burns (eds.), *The Collected Works of J Bentham: Constitutional code*

is to a political morality to which government must adhere and which, for all Bentham's apprehensions on extending the franchise,[48] is sympathetic to representative democracy, and especially publicity 'in matters of government'. 'Without publicity, no good is permanent; under the auspices of publicity no evil can continue.' Secrecy was the climate in which, at worst, those placed in government would abuse the power which had been given to them. It protected misrule. Publicity, regular elections and a free press were needed to safeguard the electorate from their chosen governors – from the excesses of 'bullies, blackguards and buffoons'. The risk that mistake or perversity in the electors' choice would increase as the franchise was extended was the dilemma Bentham found. Much has been made of this dilemma in analysis by political theorists.[49] But elsewhere Bentham represented that rational impulse which insisted on the goodness of publicity, of knowing. He quoted enthusiastically from Pope's *Essays on Man*: 'What can we reason but from what we know?' It was a theme that was to be developed in the liberal tradition.

With the extension of the franchise, liberal democracy proclaimed its strength as a political system in which individuals were given the greatest opportunity for self-development and self-fulfilment, especially under the influence of John Stuart Mill. The author of *On Liberty* would have approved of the words of Adam Smith who, in postulating the example of the 'ideal observer', said it was one who could infer that a moral principle for human guidance was correct after pursuing a mental procedure that was dependent upon such valuable human characteristics as being 'fully informed, free, imaginative, sympathetic, calm, impartial, fair, willing to universalise, acting on principle, considering the good of everyone alike, and so forth'.[50] The emphasis is upon being fully informed and rational. Within limits, modern pleas for freedom of information would have struck a chord of sympathy in Mill's breast, and later liberal philosophers came to realise more keenly that sharing of information was an essential component of democracy itself. Democracy had to be extended to ensure the greater informed participation of citizens in the process of government. It was a representative participation. The questions would be put by elected representatives, and information would filter through the system to the citizens. In spite of Mill's desire for an informed society in which maximum opportunity was available for self-improvement and the development of individuals, he prevaricated upon the extension of the franchise. Freedom was one thing, irresponsibility another. Other notes of caution must be sounded.

(1983), vol. 1, esp. pp. 162–8, 283–93; and F. Rosen, *Jeremy Bentham and Representative Democracy* (1983), esp. ch. 7.

[48] Rosen, *Jeremy Bentham*, notes now the *Code* stipulated that no one could be a member of the legislature who had not been admitted and successfully examined in the system of education prescribed for judges and senior civil servants.

[49] C. B. Macpherson, *The Life and Times of Liberal Democracy* (1977).

[50] A. Gewirth, *Reason and Morality* (1978), p. 20. See generally J. S. Mill, *Considerations on Representative Government*.

Bentham, however, would have seen it as proper for government to have restricted a free flow of information about its activities. Bentham argued for three exceptions to a prohibition on government secrecy: where publicity would assist an enemy of the state, where it would harm the innocent, or where it would inflict unduly harsh punishment on convicted persons. I cannot envisage arguments which would establish and successfully support the need for no restriction on freedom of information. The difficulty lies in allowing government prerogative alone to call the tune.

Secondly, liberal philosophers of a different school have frequently urged caution insofar as the well-informed individual wishes to use information, or to keep information secret, not only to advance his own position but to distort equality of opportunity or effectively deny a like liberty for all. In administering a state, Kant argued, there is a problem in knowing how 'to organise a group of rational beings who together require universal laws for their survival, but of whom each separate individual is secretly inclined to exempt himself from them'. Possibly the most influential of present-day liberal theorists, John Rawls, has argued that a fully informed individual *cannot* make the decision to deduce what principles *ought* to govern the operation of social institutions and government. Rawls argues for a method whereby individuals will achieve a state of 'reflective equilibrium' to establish through consensus the basic principles of justice that will be applied in their relationships as individuals and collectively.[51] He imagines rational men and women coming together in a temporary state of ignorance of their own personal strengths and weaknesses to form a compact in which the 'principles of justice', as he calls them, will be arrived at. The individuals will be rational – they will know how to reason and they will have information allowing them to argue on a general rather than a personal level. They will also be self-interested. They will be equipped to assess what their reaction as rational human beings would be to particular situations and what principles justify their decisions. The principles would allow them to assess moral priorities; they are 'constitutive of justice'.[52] As Rawls sees it, the temporary lack of information by each individual of their personal abilities, strengths and weaknesses is an essential ontological feature of the method of establishing 'principles with independent moral appeal'. If they knew of their strengths and weaknesses, they would load the dice to achieve an outcome that would be in their individual interest and not in the collective interest of all or of the whole in which they have an equal part. Rawls's device is a fiction; it is a method to capture an objective analysis required in moral philosophy. Apart from establishing the principles of justice, Rawls would not argue that a lack of information is a good thing per se; the principles of justice would be given full publicity in their existence, interpretation and application so that individuals

---

[51] J. Rawls, *A Theory of Justice* (1971).
[52] See R. Dworkin, *Taking Rights Seriously* (1977), ch. 6.

would not misunderstand how they work.[53] But this does not tell us how much they are entitled to know.

> It is one aspiration, that social and ethical relations should not essentially rest on ignorance and misunderstanding of what they are, and quite another that all the beliefs and principles involved in them should be explicitly stated. That these are two different things is obvious with personal relations, where to hope that they do not rest on deceit and error is merely decent, but to think that their basis can be made totally explicit is idiocy.[54]

It is ironic that Rawls chose for his tableau individuals in a 'veil of ignorance'. To simplify a Marxist critique of liberal philosophy and practice one need only address a Marxist belief that liberalism as an ideology perpetuates a veil of ignorance in as much as it is a legitimating device for capitalist accumulation and exploitation. The class structure is not seen for what it is: an organised enterprise bent on the exploitation of the economically weak by the economically powerful who manage to cloak the partial nature of the exercise of power with the ideologies of equality and liberty emanating from and supporting the material relations of production. The true nature of liberal society will be concealed by providing no information, disinformation or misinformation. Even in its more humane manifestations, the critique continues, it is elitist. In liberal society, information given by the government only serves to mystify because it is either intentionally false or it is part of a matrix in which systemic distortion is generated.

The last note of caution on democracy and information concerns power groups that are not ostensibly governmental, but which may be private and professional or trade associations and unions, and which are often protected by oaths, duties, or a culture, of confidentiality. There are arguable reasons why confidentiality must be maintained or not maintained in various relationships. These relate to individual respect and integrity. A problem arises when the private body in question exercises considerable influence in public life but insists on confidentiality in its operations to such an extent that it is effectively its own master. The movement to government by contract for more than two decades illustrates the problem. The common expectation of contractors is that their work for a public task, or many aspects of it, will be conducted in secrecy or confidentiality. To what extent can these expectations run counter to a greater PI? A lack of information facilitates a lack of accountability for the exercise of power and influence and the impact these forces have upon the public welfare where democratic controls are absent. The credit crunch commencing in 2007 resulted from opacity, complexity and a lack of reliable information.

---

[53] Rawls, *A Theory of Justice*, p. 133, refers to this as 'publicity'. Bernard Williams calls it 'transparency' in *Ethics and the Limits of Philosophy* (1985). See also A. M. S. Piper, 'Utility, publicity and manipulation' (1978) Ethics 88, 189.

[54] Williams, *Ethics and the Limits of Philosophy*, p. 102.

Information and communication

It will be recalled that Habermas maintained that an 'ideal speech situation' is one where there is no distortion of discourse by contained inequalities or ideologies concealing inequality and that the 'ideal speech situation' was nothing more than the fulfilment of what is presumed in the effort of communication.[55] At the political level, he continues, legitimacy – justification for the exercise or non-exercise of power on the public behalf – can only properly be achieved under certain conditions. These are satisfied where decision-making processes are organised in such a way that arrangements can be found in which the institutions and political decisions would meet with the unforced consensus, if not approval, of the members of society *if they had been allowed* to participate as free and equal in policymaking.[56] The issue then becomes one of organising decision-making processes that provide information about their operations in as full and timeous a manner as possible as well as establishing the most appropriate procedures, organisations and mechanisms which 'are in each case better suited to bring about procedurally legitimate decisions and institutions'. Attempts to arrange a society democratically can only be perceived as 'a self-controlled learning process'[57] for all its members, not simply governmental or other elites.

One response to Habermas's attempt to extend his theory of communicative competence to political institutions and collective decision-making is to assert that it is all visionary and idealistic, that the world does not and cannot work like that. On the other hand, there is a link with the liberal tradition which has argued for liberalism as the system for the encouragement of individual development and achievement for all. Participation in government and publicity about the working of government have been consistent themes in the liberal tradition. Where Habermas differs fundamentally is in insisting upon an assessment and reassessment of the procedures and the information that are available so that legitimation can be achieved only after a participation of all as free and equal or, most importantly, who *would agree as such persons* if they had participated in policy and decision-making, i.e. if the process were seen to be even-handed and above-board. Habermas here accepts, it seems, certain realities of governmental decision-making. The decisions are made by government or elected chambers or elsewhere, and the 'elsewhere' poses particular problems. We cannot all be there in the chamber, in the Cabinet, in the department. But what does go on in those places we would agree to, if not in terms of the substantive outcome, then at least on the basis that decisions were made on a rational assessment of the information which was not perverted by ideology, or distorted by influence and domination which is tangible or subliminal.

But if we are not in the chamber or elsewhere, how do we know the debate was rational? Experience may lead us to believe it is anything but. The point

---

[55] See L. Fuller, *The Morality of Law* (1969), pp. 185–6 on 'communication'.
[56] Habermas, *Communication*, p. 186.   [57] *Ibid.*

is that the more irrational the process, the more governors will want to conceal, the more they pervert the conditions of legitimacy. It must be accepted, however, that we cannot know everything about a government's operations and decision-making whenever we want. Such a restriction is consistent with Habermas's theory. The reasons for not imparting information, however, must satisfy the test that would justify an unforced consensus which would constitute a sure basis for legitimation. As long as we accept as inescapable that people exercise power on our behalf, then the exercise of power in whatever form must satisfy those ultimate criteria. Where I find strength in Habermas's analysis, which is lacking in the work of much of liberal theory, is his attempt to establish the ontology, the pure conditions of legitimation for the exercise of power through institutional frameworks whose arrangement is only justified to the extent that it facilitates discussion, information, reasoned decisions and supporting evidence. It is not a liberalism which assumes the inherent inequality of the social condition around which the agenda is set. Nor is the *tabula rasa* of Habermas contingent upon material forces of production distorting the information which shapes its inscriptions, as Marxists believe. Economic inequality is a distorting feature of domination preventing true consensus. It must be seen for what it is, and the interests of the economically weaker must be equally represented, *and represented with equal efficacy*, *as* other interests. Examples from over thirty years illustrate the point: a government does not wish to publish its Cabinet proposals for changes in child benefit;[58] it makes nineteen changes in the formula for calculating the number of unemployed;[59] it provides information on the increase of poverty and its effects in a manner designed to attract as little attention as possible,[60] or in a form which is incomprehensible; it does not publish figures for deaths from hypothermia among pensioners until after the November 2000 Budget Forecast announced increases for fuel allowance; it distorts the truth about the safety of food production;[61] it becomes obsessed by the 'packaging' of its policies. One can see the forces of domination perverting the discussion. The Treasury Select Committee criticised government plans to make the Office for National Statistics independent – the criticism was that the plans did not make the office sufficiently independent. The select committee wanted a clearer separation between delivery and supervision. It also wanted any arrangements to cover 1,450 sets of government statistics databases and not just the 250 sets produced by the Office of National Statistics.[62]

---

[58] The revelations by Frank Field in 1976.   [59] HC Debs., 25 July 1986.

[60] HL Debs., 30 March 1987 – a controversy surrounding the alleged suppression of the Health Education Council's Report *The Health Divide* on poverty and sickness, two hours before it was due to be published.

[61] See the Bovine Spongiform Encephalopathy Inquiry Report, HC 887-I–IX (1999–2000).

[62] HC 1111 (2005–6), Government Reply, HC 1604 (2005–6) and HC 934-I–II (2006–7). The Statistics Commission welcomed the report. The government's proposals were published in *Independence for Statistics* HM Treasury (2006) and are now in legislation, see ch. 9, p. 353. The *Financial Times*, 26 July 2006 reported a former national statistician commenting that the government's proposals did not follow 'best international practice'.

Freedom of information, open government and transparency[63]

Freedom of information means access by individuals as a presumptive right to information held by public authorities. Reasonable and clearly defined time limits for the right must be in operation. In some regimes it is restricted to citizens or residents within a legal regime. The right must be defined in law to be a right. It imposes duties on others. The right is invariably limited by exemptions to protect the public welfare or safety, or to protect items such as commercial secrecy or individual privacy. The tests for establishing the exemptions are invariably demanding and the onus is on the public authority to justify its claim. Very frequently there are PI tests allowing disclosure where a greater PI is served by disclosure and even though the information is exempt. The right covers access to information, records, papers or computerised files – in short information, however stored – held by public authorities. More recent laws have moved the target of attention to private bodies that perform public functions or which are designated as 'public' by a minister (UK) or to private bodies that interfere with human rights of individuals (South Africa). Exemptions to the right of access typically include national security, personal privacy, commercial secrecy, defence, international relations and interference with the criminal investigation and prosecution or law enforcement processes. There is inevitably an independent arbiter in the form of a court or a Commissioner to determine contested claims. The specific details of regimes differ, as one would expect.

Transparency has a much wider meaning. It gained popular appeal within the EC from the early 1990s where it was seen as a useful device to combat claims of democratic deficit and complexity in the operations of the EC – the EC was shortly to become a more complicated and even less perspicuous three-pillar structure at Maastricht in 1993. Access to information is a component of transparency but the latter also entails conducting affairs in the open or subject to public scrutiny. It means keeping observable records of official decisions and activities (for subsequent access). It also means making public processes and lawmaking as accessible and as comprehensible as possible. Transparency entails ensuring that conduct is as open and accessible as possible allowing comprehension and involvement of interested parties. Complexity, disorder and secrecy are all features that transparency seeks to combat.[64]

Openness is very similar to transparency. It goes beyond access to documents to cover such items as opening up the processes and meetings of public bodies. The Government in the Sunshine Act and the Federal Advisory Committee Act of the USA are examples of 'openness' as they are of transparency. 'Openness' means concentrating on processes that allow us to see the operations and activities of government at work – subject again to necessary exemptions. Local

---

[63] See C. Hood and D. Heald (eds.), *Transparency: The key to better governance?* (2006) for a general discussion.

[64] Funding of political parties has been a huge problem re transparency: Political Parties etc. Act 2000 and Electoral Administration Act 2006.

government in the UK has to conduct its affairs under conditions of openness as a legal requirement – far more so than central government because access to meetings is provided for. Even with the UK FOI laws, which came into effect on 1 January 2005 to give individual rights of access to requesters, much of the proceedings of the Cabinet and departments will remain as secret as ever. This party committee has obscure origins in the Privy Council and is invariably a one-party committee of Parliament. It is the governing body of the UK, is not organised or established by law; its proceedings are protected by the law of confidentiality[65] and its deliberations are covered by a variety of wide exemptions under the UK FOIA.[66] But 'openness' has also been used in a pejorative sense in the UK. It has been seen as the term used by government in the UK to avoid legal obligations of access to information. 'Open government', it has been claimed, means in this sense providing access to information under non-legally binding codes which do not create rights. The Commons Public Administration Committee in its report on the Freedom of Information Bill (UK) used the expression 'open government' in a critical manner and followed the viewpoint of the detractors of 'open government'.[67] I prefer to use the term in the wider sense outlined above and not the pejorative sense. The concept of openness has featured in the Commission White Paper on European Governance (COM (2001) 428 final) and in discussions concerning the 'open method of co-ordination' involving governance in the EU.[68] Criticism has been made that these developments involve 'soft' provisions and not ones that are backed by legal rights.

Freedom of information – the good, the bad and the ugly

The 'information society', or its members, are making increasing claims for freedom of information, open government and transparency. Such claims are easily made, but more difficult to justify if one has not established what theory of democracy one accepts. Information is inherently a feature of power. So too is its control, use and regulation. Government, to repeat, is the organisation of information for the use, effective or otherwise, of power in the PI. Take away a government's preserve on information, and its preserve of when and what to release, and take away a fundamental bulwark of its power. This may be desirable or it may not. It is undeniable, however, that its impact is profound. Such

---

[65] *AG v J. Cape* [1975] 3 All ER 484: relationships between Ministers in Cabinet are protected by the law of confidentiality as emphasised by the convention of collective responsibility. This also covered advice by officials to Ministers. However, the duty was not absolute and could evaporate over time as the case itself illustrated. See ch. 9, p. 325. S. Low, *The Governance of England*, 14th impression (1927), ch. 2.

[66] Exemptions relating to formulation of government policy, collective responsibility or prejudice to the effective conduct of public affairs in particular. See ch. 6, p. 205 on the use of the FOIA veto to protect Cabinet minutes from disclosure: EA/2008/0024 and 0029 *Cabinet Office v IC and C. Lamb.*

[67] HC 570-I (1998–9).   [68] P. Craig, *European Administrative Law* (2006), ch. 6.

developments could establish new centres of power and organisation outside government, where 'government' would be 'all inside and no outside', to rearrange Woodrow Wilson's snappy phrase. Making government all outside could make government powerless in the face of those intent on economic exploitation, abuse of dominant position and who are beyond effective regulation. It could facilitate an even more acquisitive and inquisitive and captious society, or an oppressive one. One has only to remember that the president who coined the phrase 'executive privilege' in 1958 to circumscribe Congressional investigations was the same president who refused to hand over executive documents to Senator McCarthy in his witch-hunt of Un-American 'activists'. An investigative press or unregulated broadcasting system could do untold damage to individuals in a freedom-of-information state; hence the development of privacy protection, albeit largely by the courts in the UK. Chat rooms on the Internet can do permanent and unjustifiable damage to individuals although here we are moving into the realm of freedom of speech. Any responsible advocate for open government and freedom of information must accept that there are subjects that we do not all need to know and be informed on and that we cannot insist on knowing as of right. The question then becomes: what kind of information is this and, if I do not know, is someone entitled to know on my behalf and to what extent are they entitled to know to oversee the protection of our interests?

Information and institutional structure

This leads us to the question of institutional structure. How do we best organise our institutions that are responsible for making decisions affecting the public and the PI? How can they be structured to ensure that the debate over our welfare is carried on in as informed a manner as possible? What allows unjustifiable domination in present institutions? On what, if any, issues should information be the preserve of the prime minister and one or two others? Is it wrong that it is so restricted, and why? When should information be exclusive to the Cabinet? When should it go to an assembly of elected members and how should it go – to the whole chamber or to specific committees? When is there a need for wider public debate at either inquiries or other public meetings, and how well informed will the public be? When is a subject appropriate for a judicial body or tribunal, and how widely should such bodies, especially courts, range in seeking information?[69] Too frequently in cases concerning national security, the courts accept that they have no alternative but to accept the evidence of the executive where a defendant lacks any means of challenging that evidence.[70] Should there be a difference between litigation between private individuals according to law,

---

[69] *R (MT) v Secretary of State for the Home Department* [2008] EWHC 1788 (Admin) and the line of cases concerning alleged involvement of MI5 officials in torture of suspected terrorists overseas.

[70] *R (Gilllan) v Com'r Met. Police* [2006] UKHL 12.

which is therefore a matter of PI, and litigation about the PI itself? When do we need to present information for the assessment of outside experts who will assist either ministers, the elected and representative chambers or the nation at large? The reaction of British governments to such questions as these has been a tinkering at the edges and an insistence on the maintenance of the status quo. This is not simply because of the power of tradition and confidentiality. It is because in the British tradition, unlike the American or Scandinavian traditions that provided the prototype of FOI legislation, political power and survival have been inextricably bound up with control of information.[71] Any information is used by the Opposition to make political capital out of the Government's position – hence the increasing concern of successive governments to put 'spin' on the presentation of policy; to put their policies in their best light, which is often assisted by the timing of disclosures.[72] However, there is evidence of secrecy in the operation of the Council and Commission of the EC where political power is not so dependent upon the control of information. FOI laws have also emerged when traditional constraints on representative government have been eroded or weakened by new forms of governance and contracting arrangements. These points can be more conveniently discussed in chapters 9, 10 and 11 respectively.

What might be the cost for institutional structures of governance of FOI laws? 'Cost' may take a variety of forms. There is the sheer financial cost. Allow access and everyone will want to see everything. This will entail indexing, and staff to deal with requests, to provide reviews, to check that exempt material is not included, to deal with challenges to refusals, to check that filing and recording are carried out correctly. There is the cost of a loss of candour in advice when the giver or the referee knows that it may be published or shown to the subject. There is the fear of perpetual intervention when policymakers are constantly exposed or challenged and have to justify their every move. In such a situation individuals may not wish to take risks or make innovative decisions. The cost could be a reduction in professionalism. There is the cost of inertia. There is also the possible cost of creating greater secrecy: the spectre of the file behind the file, the meeting behind the meeting, the state behind the state. There is the possible cost of 'the paperless environment' where record-keeping is minimised. It is now time in the next chapter to move from the general and fairly abstract to the particular and to examine a problematic area which poses significant political, legal and practical difficulties in relation to information control and its regulation and to see how the government has responded to the competing claims of security and accountability.

[71] K. G. Robertson, *Public Secrets* (1982).
[72] See *Government Communications* HL 7 (2008–9), ch. 9, p. 354 below.

2

Information and national security[1]

National security poses the most difficult of practical problems in respect of information. 'Information Warfare' has become an important aspect of the agencies that defend national security.[2] National security concerns what many regard as the quintessential function of the state. It involves the most developed form of information technology – most highly secret and according to renegade security agent David Shayler much of the intelligence is unreliable, an accusation that was vigorously denied.[3] The allegation resurfaced in relation to the use of intelligence to justify the war in Iraq.[4] The subject covers the most intrusive of information-gathering exercises conducted on behalf of government agencies. National security is also a virtually unanswerable plea to immunity and confidentiality, preventing access by individuals to information upon themselves. As we shall see in chapter 11, the courts have long shown themselves sensitive to executive assertions of national security precluding judicial investigation of an individual grievance. Although there are indications of increasing unease where the plea is put to a strained use, the courts have nonetheless reminded themselves of their limited role when assessing questions concerning executive judgements involving national security.[5] Many of the most controversial cases concerning information in recent years have related to national security. The peculiar potency of the subject must be fully realised. It is not characteristic of all areas of government activity. However, it will provide an interesting area of

---

[1] I. Kearnes and K. Gule, *The New Front Line Security in a Changing World* IPPR (2008): I. Cameron, *National Security and the ECHR* (2000); Venice Commission, *The Democratic Oversight of the Security Services*, CDL – AD (2007) 016.

[2] See Intelligence and Security Committee, *Annual Report 2000*, Cm. 4897 (2000), pp. 28–9 and successive annual reports, www.cabinetoffice.gov.uk/reports.aspx.

[3] Cm. 4897, p. 18.

[4] *Review of Intelligence on Weapons of Mass Destruction*, HC 898 (2003–4).

[5] *Rehman v Secretary of State* [2002] 1 All ER 122 (HL). In *R (B. Mohamed) v Secretary of State for Foreign and Commonwealth Affairs* [2008] EWHC 2048 (Admin), *ibid.* [2008] EWHC 2100 (Admin), [2008] EWHC 2519 (Admin) and [2009] EWHC 152 (Admin), the Divisional Court ordered disclosure of documents by the UK government concerning details of torture on the claimant which were held by the US government subject to public interest certificates which the UK government was asked to clarify. The US government alleged that disclosure would prejudice intelligence relations between the US and the UK (see ch. 11, p. 426 and Introduction, p. 6). See *Canada (Minister of Justice) v Khadr* [2008] SCC 28 and *Khadr v AG of Canada* [2008] FC 807.

human activity in which some of the theoretical points in chapter 1 above may be tested. This is because the subject poses the most difficult of questions about executive action and its relationship to effective accountability and informed public opinion. The culture of government secrecy owes much of its inspiration to this responsibility of government.

Is distortion of the truth allowable for the greater public good? Is this an area which is appropriately colonised by the powers of 'democratisation', as Habermas advocated? If so, with what necessary concessions to the claims of responsible and efficient government? Is distortion permissible in the conduct of trials where a relevant defence may not be invoked because of public-interest immunity (PII) protection for vital information (see chapter 11) or to prevent publication of the identity of witnesses?[6] Does distortion make such trials unfair? The answer from the courts on this last question has been 'Yes'.

On national security, the UK approach has meant that the assessment of such an important matter and what the interests of national security require are for the executive alone.[7] The courts lack the necessary expertise and information to make decisions on such sensitive matters. Any judicial body undertaking to question such a judgement is going beyond its proper remit.[8] In 2007, the director of the Serious Fraud Office ordered the cessation of inquiries into alleged bribery in armaments contracts involving BAE systems and Saudi Arabia because of threats by the Saudi Arabian Government not to assist in the war on terror and the transfer of intelligence. The Divisional Court ruled the decision unlawful and an affront to the rule of law. The House of Lords overruled that decision. The action was prompted by the request for information from BAE systems and enquiries into a Swiss Bank account.[9] There had been intervention by the prime minister and the Attorney General who had fully represented the seriousness of the threats from the Saudi Government. The Law Lords were

---

[6] Sir Richard Scott answered with a categorical 'no' in Matrix Churchill: HC 115-I–V (1995–6), and index. On secrecy for witnesses, see *R v Davis* [2008] UKHL 36 (engaging in practices to ensure anonymity of witnesses in a murder trial was unlawful) reversed by Criminal Evidence (Arrangement of Witnesses) Act 2008; and *R v Lord Saville of Newdigate, ex p. A* [1999] 4 All ER 860, CA. See Cameron, *National Security and the ECHR*, n 19, p. 28 and *McCann v UK* (1995) 21 EHRR 97 following the 'Death on the Rock' shootings involving IRA terrorists. Failure to conduct proper investigations into shooting of terrorists has been ruled a breach of Art. 2, ECHR: *Hugh Jordan v UK* (2003) 37 EHRR 52.

[7] On the judiciary, see ch. 11, p. 420. Note *A v Secretary of State for the Home Department* [2004] UKHL 56.

[8] *Rehman v Secretary of State*.

[9] *R (Corner House Research) v Director SFO* [2008] UKHL 60 This concerned the Al Yamanah contract for the sale of arms between Saudi Arabia and the UK the contracts for which contained confidentiality clauses. The Divisional Court ruling is [2008] EWHC 714 (Admin). OECD Convention on Bribery Art. 5 (an 'unincorporated rule of international law' per Lord Bingham) prohibits national economic considerations or relations with a foreign state from influencing a decision on prosecution. The director stated he had not breached that Article – the Law Lords refused to rule on this because it was not a matter for a municipal court. The director was faced with an 'ugly and unwelcome threat' per Lord Bingham but he exercised his power responsibly and lawfully in relation to the threat to national security. See p. 363 below.

clearly heavily influenced by the perceived enormity of that threat to national security.[10] The United States has also threatened not to share intelligence on the war against terrorism if UK ministers disclosed documents and information to a litigant setting out US involvement in torture. The court accepted it could not enforce disclosure (see Introduction, p. 6).[11] Residual grounds of review will remain to ensure basic fairness and no irrationality and the courts have intervened where detention of a non national on grounds of national security was not established under Art. 15 European Convention on Human Rights (ECHR). Derogation orders were irrational, disproportionate and discriminatory. The power of executive detention in s. 23 Anti-terrorism, Crime and Security Act 2001 breached Arts. 5 and 14 ECHR.[12]

The definition of security of the state and community against threats to their wellbeing is hopelessly expansive, and has in fact assumed more of an international-security dimension in the global war on terror[13] as well as counter-espionage, counter-terrorism and counter-subversion dimensions. This latter feature, which is notoriously broad, still survives in the legislation setting out the powers of the security service even though the anti-subversive unit of the security service was wound up in 1992.[14] Should national security not involve some objective assessment of well-being on the basis of political and civil rights, open democracy, and participative processes of rule? Surely these are features of a 'secure nation' moving towards a more secure international order?[15] Or are these features satisfied by existing safeguards? The courts have shown that while they should respect judgements on security assessments including a declaration of a state of emergency they will not allow powers of detention to be used for discriminatory and disproportionate purposes.[16] Nor would the courts allow intelligence or evidence obtained by torture overseas to be used in judicial proceedings before the Special Immigration Appeals Commission (see chapter 11, p. 430).[17] However, the person alleging that the evidence was obtained by torture would have to establish that the evidence was so obtained – in reality a virtually impossible task. What ought we to know about decisions on national security, the security and intelligence services, their general operations and those of the

---

[10] They found no evidence of unlawful pressure being exerted on the director. See EA/2006/0044 *Campaign against the Arms Trade v IC* before the Information Tribunal ch. 6, p. 185.

[11] See note 5 above.

[12] *A v Secretary of State for the Home Department* [2004] UKHL 56. For the ECtHR see *A v UK* App. 3455/05.

[13] *Rehman v Secretary of State.* The EComHR has stated that 'national security' cannot be defined 'exhaustively': *Hewitt and Harman* v *UK* (1992) 14 EHRR 657 and *Esbester v UK* (1993) 18 EHRR *CD* 72.

[14] See R. Norton-Taylor, 'National security' in R. Blackburn and R. Plant (eds.), *Constitutional Reform* (1999).

[15] See Cameron, *National Security and the ECHR*, note 1, p. 28; and L. Lustgarten and I. Leigh, *In From the Cold: National security and parliamentary democracy* (1994).

[16] *A v Secretary of State for the Home Department* [2004] UKHL 56.

[17] *A v Secretary of State for the Home Department* [2005] UKHL 71 and see *RB v Secretary of State for the Home Department* [2009] UKHL 10, ch. 11 below.

police in security work or indeed on the extent to which the security service is assuming the role of a police force? What should we know of their techniques for obtaining and dealing with information, and what safeguards exist, and should exist, to prevent abuse?

The answer given by the Freedom of Information Act 2000 (FOIA) to these questions is negative. Security and Intelligence bodies (and the Serious Organised Crime Agency) are excluded from the Act and information from such bodies or about such bodies held by public authorities is given an absolute exemption. National security is not given an absolute exemption under the Act. A ministerial certificate may certify conclusively that it is information protected by the absolute exemption or it is protected by national security. This is subject to a very limited challenge in the IT.[18] Where records from the security and intelligence services are placed in the National Archives or the Northern Ireland Public Records Office, they lose their absolute exemption after 30 years (see p. 350 below). However, those records not placed in the National Archives will retain their exclusion when possessed by the secret intelligence services.[19]

Accountability and information

Two questions are particularly pertinent for this study. The first concerns our information, or lack of it, about the security and intelligence services (MI5,[20] MI6 and GCHQ (General Communications HQ) and related bodies) and their accountability.[21] MI5 is the secret security service and was established in 1909.[22] MI6 is the secret intelligence service.[23] GCHQ is the intelligence-gathering organisation at Cheltenham. The Regulation of Investigatory Powers Act 2000 refers to them as 'the intelligence services'. At common law, the services have no executive powers. Legislation (below) now provides them with a variety of intelligence-gathering powers under warrant. The 'arms and legs' are provided by the Special Branch (SB) – there are 53 SBs in the UK and they are described as an 'executive partner', a 'major extension' of intelligence capability (Cm. 5837, para. 69) – and occasionally by the SAS as events in Gibraltar indicated in 1988

---

[18] See ch. 5, p. 159 *et seq.* Under DPA, s. 28: see ch. 8.   [19] FOIA 2000, s. 64.

[20] Whose director reports to the Joint Intelligence Committee of the government on the Joint Terrorism Analysis Centre which analyses terrorism intelligence and levels of risk. The Centre is overseen by an Oversight Board chaired by the Cabinet Office seeking to ensure it meets the needs of its 'customer departments'. The system for assessing threat levels is published as is *Countering Terrorism: the UK's Strategy* (2006).

[21] H. Born *et al.* (eds.), *Who's Watching the Spies? Establishing intelligence service accountability* (2005).

[22] Walsingham was regarded as the head of Elizabeth I's secret service in the sixteenth century. MI5 has a director general, MI6 a chief and GCHQ a director as chief officer.

[23] See S. Dorril, *MI6: Fifty years of special operations* (2000). The Defence Intelligence is a part of the Ministry of Defence. See S.Twigge *et al.*, *British Intelligence* (2009).

when three IRA terrorists were shot by that service.[24] MI5 has 'close relations' with chief constables. Since the end of the first cold war, the security and intelligence services have engaged in new fields of activity and investigations and organised crime, money laundering, narcotics and international fraud have become their targets as have, allegedly, environmental and animal rights groups. The emergence of the Serious Organised Crime Agency (SOCA) has allowed the services to withdraw from some of their non-counter-terrorism activities and in 2007, MI5 assumed the lead role for national security in Northern Ireland. The war on terror has brought about a rapid expansion in the services – so much so that the Parliamentary Intelligence and Security Committee has expressed concern that counter-terrorism may undermine efforts in other areas including a possible re-emergence of the cold war. A large expansion in the numbers of officials also caused security problems in themselves, the Committee felt, especially in relation to quality assurance (CM 7299, 2008). The services are co-ordinated through the Joint Intelligence Committee and Security and Intelligence Co-ordinator who is a permanent secretary. The official website publishes information about the services (www.intelligence.gov.uk) and the last ten years have seen considerable developments in terms of removing the complete secrecy attaching to the services, as we shall see. But problems remain.

The second question concerns the methods the services adopt to extract information from individuals or institutions and the use which they make of such information.

The 'covert' ethos of the security services has undoubtedly formerly helped to present an extraordinary picture of botched amateurism and eccentricity.[25] The whole question of accountability of these services in a democratic state was given dramatic, not to say sensational, prominence by the events in a Sydney courtroom, and later in English courts, when the British Government sought to restrict publication of the memoirs of the former MI5 agent Peter Wright. There were allegations of the infiltration by foreign spies at the highest level in the service, and a catalogue of 'dirty tricks' regularly practised by security officials, which involved their role in the resignation of a prime minister and the undermining of British governments in the past as well as assassination plots on a foreign head of state, President Nasser of Egypt. There was also the

---

[24] Lord Windlesham and R. Rampton QC wrote a report, *Report on Death on the Rock* (1989), on the affair. In July 1995, the ECttHR ruled that the shootings were in breach of Art. 2 ECHR: *McCann v UK*.

[25] See C. Andrew, *Secret Service: The making of the British intelligence community* (1985) and also *Defence of the Realm: The authorized history of MI5* (2009). A particularly useful study written by lawyers is Lustgarten and Leigh, *In From the Cold*, with a very helpful bibliography. Renegade agents going public for highly dubious reasons have carried on that ethos (how rigorously are they assessed for employment?) and the use of a ten year old thesis as the basis of a major plank justifying the war on Iraq caused disbelief. See Hutton *Inquiry into the Circumstances Surrounding the Death of Dr David Kelly CMG*, HC 247 (2003–4), the Butler Report on *Review of Use of Intelligence on Weapons of Mass Destruction*, HC 898 (2004–5); the Intelligence and Security Committee's report on *Weapons of Mass Destruction*, Cm. 5972, and Government Reply, Cm. 6118 (2004).

question of an eccentric and highly questionable individual being placed in such a sensitive position as Wright occupied. Suppressing Wright's memoirs became a worldwide drama. It was an extraordinary episode in which the public caught a glimpse of the machinations of British government at the highest level. One of the most dramatic moments was the rare scenario of a Cabinet Secretary upon oath under hostile cross-examination in a court of law both in Australia and in England. Such a picture re-emerged albeit less dramatically in the case of former MI5 officer David Shayler who was charged with offences under the Official Secrets Act 1989 (OSA) in the autumn of 2000 after revealing various alleged malpractices about the services. These cases precipitated further calls for reform of the security services in the UK, which had been not only distant but isolated from any form of democratic oversight or accountability commensurate with their power and influence.

Until 1989, one statute, Robin Cook has claimed, named the secret service: the Civil List and Secret Service Money Act of 1782, which restricted the issue of public money to the service to £10,000 per annum.[26] When the statute was repealed in 1977 expenditure was estimated at £30 million per annum and by 2001–2 expenditure on the intelligence services was forecast at £867 million.[27] By 2007–8, it was £1,867.6 million. By 2010–11, the budget (the Single Intelligence Account: figures are not given for the separate services) will increase to £3,500 million.[28] The Cabinet Secretary is the accounting officer for the services and their accounts are audited by the National Audit Office who has criticised incomplete reports and accounts (Cm 7299, p. 13).

The services owe their origin and operations to the murkier side of the Crown prerogative. Nor should we forget that the Crown possesses a prerogative power not to prosecute charges, and to stop criminal proceedings, as was evidenced by the 'shoot to kill' policy practised by the RUC in Northern Ireland which was originally investigated by John Stalker.[29] The prime minister announced plans to reform the powers of the Attorney General in the 2008 White Paper on Constitutional Renewal which included the removal of the *nolle prosequi* power as it is known. However, the bill that introduced these powers gave the Attorney General power to order the cessation of any inquiries by the director of the Serious Fraud Office or to order the cessation of any institution of a prosecution or a prosecution in England and Wales in the interest of national security. The BAE episode, above, was clearly in mind. The direction may be withdrawn. A

---

[26] However, cf. Government of Ireland Act 1920, s. 23 and sch. 6.

[27] See Cm. 4897 (2000) p. 20. In 1997, the services were subject to a Treasury-driven comprehensive spending review from a zero base. The details were not published. The 1782 Act was repealed by the Statute Law (Repeals) Act 1978, s. 1 and sch. 1, Pt II. See p. 51 *et seq.* below on the Comptroller and Auditor General's remit under the Intelligence Services Act 1994.

[28] www.mi5.gov.uk/output/P76.html and Cm. 7299, p. 7. See HC 480 (2008–9)

[29] See HC Debs., 25 January 1988. See J Stalker, *Stalker* (1988). Cf. the Stevens Inquiry into security forces, collusion and murders in Northern Ireland 17 April 2003: http://news.bbc.co.uk/1/shared/spl/hi/northern_ireland/03/stephens_inquiry/pdf/stephens_inquiry.pdf.

ministerial certificate certifying that the direction was necessary is conclusive evidence. The Attorney General has to report to Parliament on any direction with the omission of information for which public-interest immunity (PII) could be maintained or withheld because of national security or serious damage to international relations, or which could prejudice investigations or court proceedings (Cm 7342, 2008 I and II – and see Introduction p. 6 above).

The public has witnessed a growing body of information – including publication of the identities of the heads of the services and official publications about them[30] – and speculation about the security services and its operations. Scandals and revelations throughout the late 1970s, 1980s and 1990s coincided with the prolonged dispute surrounding the introduction of polygraph 'lie detectors' at GCHQ (see p. 422 below), the subsequent banning of trade unions at GCHQ and the Peter Wright, David Shayler and Richard Tomlinson affairs among others.

The Security Commission made intermittent appearances to examine breaches or suspected breaches of security and to advise on security procedures.[31] This body was established in 1964 following the famous Denning Report on the Profumo scandal.[32] Its chairman is a senior judge and it has four members. The prime minister, traditionally, after consulting the Leader of the Opposition, refers cases to the Commission. In 1982, the Commission, then under Lord Diplock, recommended a relaxation of positive vetting in the civil service,[33] and a relaxation of the rules governing release of classified information

---

[30] E.g., Home Office, *MI5: The Security Service* (1998). The former director general of MI5, Stella Rimmington gave the Dimbleby Lecture as director on TV and the director Stephen Lander gave a public lecture in March 2001. The services have websites, and MI6 has advertised recruitment on BBC Radio 1 and has featured on BBC's The ONE Show (23/9/08). The *Financial Times* reported on 23 April 2008 that Stella Rimmington was prevented from giving evidence to the standing committee on the Counter Terrorism Bill. Former director general Dame Eliza Manningham Buller spoke out against features of the bill.

[31] See, e.g., Cm. 4532 (2000).

[32] Cmnd 2152. He described its functions as 'the Defence of the Realm, from external and internal dangers arising from attempts at espionage and sabotage' or actions 'subversive of the State'.

[33] Government Statement on the Recommendations, Cmnd 8540. A procedure to 'purge' communists and fascists from vital security-sensitive operations was revised in 1957: HC Debs., vol. 563, cols. 152–6 (WA) (29 January 1957). A procedure involving the 'Three Advisers' advised the Secretary of State and heard the civil servant, though s/he was not allowed to cross-examine government witnesses. 'Positive vetting' was introduced to confirm the reliability of a candidate for a post involving access to 'top secret' information in 1952: see HC 242 (1982–3) and the memorandum from the MoD. Vetting policy guidelines were revised in 1990 and 1994 (HC Debs., vol. 177, cols. 159–61, and HC Debs., vol. 251, cols. 764–6) and overt references to communism or fascism have been erased although no one should be employed in work which is vital to the security of the state where they have been engaged in espionage, terrorism, sabotage or actions intended to overthrow or undermine parliamentary democracy by political, industrial or violent means. Where they have connections with such organisations or are susceptible to pressure from such bodies or foreign agents or have defects of character which render the person susceptible to blackmail they are likewise not to be employed. A Defence Vetting Agency was established in 1997 to take responsibility for national security vetting. A Security Vetting Appeals Panel was established in 1997 for vetting decisions, HC cols. 243–4 (19 June 1997). Applicants have no 'right of appeal' to the latter. There are

especially where it was held back to prevent possible political embarrassment. A report in 1985, however, recommended an extension of positive vetting in the security service following the case of the spy in the service, Michael Bettaney.[34] The Commission found faults in the management of the services, but the prime minister ruled out any parliamentary oversight. It has also recommended the use of polygraph or lie detectors for security vetting. In 2000, the Intelligence and Security Committee (ISC), which is discussed below, conducted an inquiry into the Mitrokhin episode that formerly would have been investigated by the Commission.[35] However, the Commission did investigate the vetting of royal households in the 2003–4 session (Cm. 6177).

The essential position of the security services in the defence of the realm means that neither the prime minister nor the Home Secretary will answer *detailed* questions about the services in Parliament. Since 1992, there has been a wider dissemination of information about the services and the services have their own web pages (www.securityservice.gov.uk/, www.sis.gov.uk and www.gchq.gov.uk).[36]

At present, 'national interest' demands that *operations* relating to the services are not discussed in Parliament.[37] Home Secretary Jack Straw was prepared not to seek judicial orders preventing publication of newspaper disclosures by David Shayler provided that no information about operations was contained. In July 2000, the former Secretary of State for Northern Ireland admitted that she had authorised the bugging of vehicles carrying *Sinn Fein* leaders.[38] Harold Macmillan described how security matters were for discussion between the prime minister and the Leader of the Opposition[39] – a convention which Mrs Thatcher threatened not to follow in 1986. The House of Commons was told as little as possible. The Denning Report revealed in 1963 that responsibility for security had rested with the prime minister until 1952. A recommendation

---

various levels of vetting including 'counter-terrorist checks', 'security checks' which allow access to secret and sometimes top secret information and is reviewed every ten years. The highest level is 'developed vetting' allowing uncontrolled access to top-secret information and which is reviewed after five years and thereafter every seven years. Between 150,000 and 160,000 vetting cases and checks are carried out each year. There are also basic identity checks and criminal-records checks. See Lustgarten and Leigh, *In From the Cold*, ch. 6 and Cameron, *National Security and the ECHR*, pp. 215 *et seq.* and K. McEvoy and C. White, 'Security vetting in Northern Ireland: Loyalty, redress and citizenship' (1998) 61 Mod LR 341. See further the *Trestrail* case, HC 59 (1982–3) and the *Prime* case, Cmnd 8876. The government introduced polygraph (lie-detector) security screening, HC Debs., vol. 42, cols. 431–4 (12 May 1983); Cf. *Council of Civil Service Unions v Minister for the Civil Service* [1984] 3 All ER 935, HL.

34   HC Debs., 3 December 1986. The Bettaney report is Cmnd 9514. See also HC Debs., vol. 78, col. 897 (9 May 1985). No reference was made to Sir Maurice Oldfield, former head of MI5 who had been a hyper-active 'rough trade' homosexual.

35   Cm. 4897, p. 25.

36   This contains details of the MI5 Phoneline which has been in existence since 1998 for those who wish to provide information to the Service to assist in its work.

37   See Lustgarten and Leigh, *In From the Cold*, for references.

38   BBC, *You Only Live Once*, July 2000; *The Guardian*, 21 November 2000.

39   *At the End of the Day* (1973), p. 434.

from Sir Norman Brooke, the Cabinet Secretary, resulted in a directive from the Home Secretary of that year to the director general of the security service – MI5. This stated:

> in your appointment . . . you will be responsible to the Home Secretary personally. The Security Service is not, however, a part of the Home Office. On appropriate occasions you will have the right of direct access to the Prime Minister.[40]

The prime minister continues to answer questions on 'broad issues of security' and has 'ultimate responsibility' for intelligence and security agencies[41] but, as Drewry suggests,[42] formal ministerial responsibility is rendered largely irrelevant by keeping Parliament uninformed of the detail. Indeed, the question of how far the prime minister is informed by the services has been a major imponderable.[43] In their 2000 report, the Parliamentary Intelligence and Security Committee (ISC) noted that the Ministerial Committee on Intelligence which the PM chairs had met very infrequently in the past two administrations. The ISC recommended it meet at least 'annually' (Cm. 4897 (2000), p. 9). Successive reports criticised the absence of formal meetings of the Ministerial Committee noting:

> The current system for setting requirements and priorities is almost entirely based on decisions and recommendations from officials, which are then endorsed by CSI members out of committee. As a result, we believe that CSI Ministers are not sufficiently engaged in the setting of requirements and priorities for secret intelligence, nor do they all see the full capability of intelligence collection. [Para 56, Cm. 5837]

After an eight-year adjournment, the committee met in 2003 but ISC's complaint of lengthy adjournments re-emerged. It has also noted subsequently that the committee was not used as a forum for ensuring ministerial co-ordination on intelligence and security (Cm. 7299 (2008)). The ISC noted the appointment of a new ministerial committee which would meet to discuss these matters. Apart from the inner caucus, traditionally 'ministers do not concern themselves with the detailed information which may be obtained by the Security Service' and receive only such information as is necessary for them to provide guidance. Legislative developments which are discussed below may have altered the picture – but the position is oblique.

Following the Butler Report into use of intelligence on Iraq (below) the ISC believed that the value of the Joint Intelligence Committee (JIC) chairman as an independent arbiter of intelligence analysis has decreased as a result of the

---

[40] Cmnd 2152. There is a responsibility of the Foreign Secretary for the operation of MI6 and its chief reports to the former.

[41] Chairman, Intelligence and Security Committee, *Annual Report* Cm. 4897; G. Drewry, 'The House of Commons and the security services' (1984) Public Law 370.

[42] Drewry, 'The House of Commons and the security services'.

[43] As evidenced by the Anthony Blunt affair: see generally C. Pincher, *Too Secret Too Long* (1984); and J. Callaghan MP, HC 92-II (1985–6), p. 223. See R. Thomas, *Espionage and Secrecy* (1990).

merger of his role with that of the Security and Intelligence Co-ordinator (SIC), and it did not consider that 'the amalgamation is consistent with the core message of the Butler Review, which stressed the need to strengthen opportunity for challenge and dissent at all levels across the intelligence community' (Cm. 6864 (2006)). In its reply (Cm. 6865 (2006)) the government pointed out the Committee's apprehension that the independent role of the JIC chairman to provide unbiased advice to ministers would clash with the SIC role of representing the views of the intelligence community to the prime minister. The government sought to assure the Committee that the SIC works closely with the agencies but is required to provide ministers with independent, unbiased advice about the effectiveness of that work. The SIC is not appointed to represent the agencies' views and interests. It follows that the government sees no clash between these roles. They are in fact 'mutually reinforcing'.

Parliamentary questions on 'matters, of their nature secret, relating to the secret services and to security' are not in order, although national security is not listed as an automatic block on questions in Erskine May[44] and there has been a relaxation to a limited extent since the beginning of the 1990s.[45] Ministerial prerogative has allowed ministers to decline to answer specific questions.[46]

Select committees of the House of Commons in theory are likely to meet the same barriers although there has been movement and a special Joint Committee on Intelligence and Security has been appointed. This committee is examined below but it noted with apprehension the fact that the government refused to give the committee documents requested over several years on an important matter. Refusal initially was because they were documents created under a previous administration. When the former Foreign Secretary was approached, he stated he had no objection to the present Foreign Secretary or Committee seeing the documents. Refusal has persisted. The Committee regretted that given the Prime Minister's desire to strengthen the Committee, the documents had not been forthcoming (Cm. 7299 and Government Reply Cm. 7300 (2008)).

The Employment Committee was not allowed to question certain officials when it investigated the background to the government's decision to ban trade union membership at GCHQ. D notices (now DA notices)[47] and positive vetting[48] have been examined by the Defence Committee, and the Home Affairs Committee has investigated aspects of the administration and accountability of

---

[44] *Erskine May*, 23rd edn (2004), pp. 339 *et seq.* and 345–53 sets out the principles on blocked PQs. Only refusals in the same session are now noted by the Table Office to determine whether a PQ is inadmissible. A refusal to answer a PQ on the grounds of the public interest cannot be raised as a matter of privilege, although responses will be consistent with FOIA exemptions. For the position of national security previously, see *Erskine May*, 21st edn, p. 292.

[45] Lustgarten and Leigh, *In From the Cold.*

[46] Drewry, 'The House of Commons and the security services' for 'guarded PM written answers'.

[47] See p. 357 *et seq.* below.   [48] See note 33 above.

the Special Branch.[49] The Home Affairs Committee has examined the subject of accountability of the security services[50] and in its review of the Consultation Paper and Draft Freedom of Information Bill the Public Administration Committee heard evidence from a former member of the security service.[51] The director of GCHQ appeared before the Public Accounts Committee in December 2003 together with the SIC. The Foreign Affairs Committee examined the decision to go to war in Iraq.[52] The House of Commons has debated the services with reference to the ISC's (see below) annual report and the government reply.[53] The Speaker of the House has ruled, however, that MPs could not see in the confines of Parliament a proposed TV programme allegedly endangering national security.[54] The House of Commons Committee of Privileges upheld the temporary ban until a full debate in the Commons could be held. The Committee rejected any removal of MPs' existing immunity from prosecution under the OSA, or any restraint upon MPs by court injunction from disclosing information damaging to national security in the course of parliamentary proceedings.[55] It further rejected any prohibition by ministers (through the Speaker) of an MP's right to publicise information in the House which he or she believed should be available. We shall see in the following chapter that Claire Short MP disclosed information about the bugging activities of MI6 at the UN based on her knowledge as a former minister and only faced censure from the party whips, not a prosecution under the OSA.

The most prominent inquiries involving intelligence were those conducted by Lord Hutton and Lord Butler into *The Circumstances Surrounding the Death of Dr David Kelly CMG* (HC 247 (2003–4) and *Review of Intelligence on Weapons of Mass Destruction* (HC 898 (2003–4)) respectively.[56] Lord Hutton took evidence from the chief of MI6, Sir Richard Dearlove, but the report failed to assuage public anxiety about the use of intelligence in the war on Iraq and Lord Butler conducted a further inquiry which heard evidence from the heads of the services, and from witnesses who asked to remain anonymous. Discussion of intelligence and related materials by Butler was in closed session; only conclusions were published. The latter report is the most detailed investigation into the use of intelligence that has been conducted. Lord Saville chairing the inquiry into the Bloody Sunday inquiry in Northern Ireland ruled that intelligence reports should be seen for limited purposes.[57]

---

[49] HC 71 (1984–5); and see Home Affairs Committee, *Accountability of the Security Service*, HC 265 (1992–3) and the Trade and Industry Committee, *Exports to Iraq*, HC 86 (1991–2). Sir Richard Scott took evidence from members of the intelligence agencies in closed session.

[50] HC 291 (1998–9) and Government Reply, Cm. 4588.

[51] HC 570-v (1998–9), 6 July 1999.   [52] HC 813 (2002–3).

[53] HC Debs., vol. 532, col. 470, 22 June, 2000.

[54] 22 January 1987. An unsuccessful application for a ruling had been sought from the High Court.

[55] HC 365 (1986–7).

[56] Government Reply, Cm. 6492 (2005); W. R. Runciman (ed.), *Lifting the Lid on the Workings of Power*, (Br. Acad/Oxford University Press 2004). Hutton, (2006) Public Law 807.

[57] www.bloody-sunday-inquiry.org.uk/index2.asp?p=4.

The potential for abuse by security service officials has been exemplified by accounts of former officials which support the claims of informed, speculative or privileged 'outsiders'. As we shall see in chapter 11, the government successfully obtained an *interim* injunction in the Court of Appeal and House of Lords against the reporting in newspapers of a former security official's allegations of abuse by officials, on the basis that a breach of confidence to the Crown would be perpetrated, even though a similar publication of the information had been made.[58] The court believed that the confidentiality owed to the Crown by employees and former employees of the service outweighed any public right to know alleged shortcomings in the security service, whose papers were never put into the Public Records Office[59] and whose activities were of the 'highest sensitivity'. These arguments did not prevail before Mr Justice Powell in the Supreme Court of New South Wales, nor when the government sought to restrict publication of *Spycatcher* in New Zealand. Indeed Powell's judgment was devastating in its critique of the government's behaviour and actions.[60] They were also rejected in the English High Court by Mr Justice Scott, as will be explained in chapter 11 (p. 438). By that time the publication of the book in the USA and elsewhere had rendered protection meaningless. In a later case involving publication of a former security official's memoirs, the House of Lords established that the only ground on which publication could be prevented was where there was evidence of damage or additional damage to national security. This could take place even though the 'facts' had already been published or where the fact that it was a former official might give additional credence to the disclosures causing damage to the reputation of the services in the eyes of foreign allies.[61] In reality, numerous former security and intelligence officers, including a former director general, have published or have sought to publish their memoirs. This in spite of a lifelong prohibition on disclosures by such officers under s. 1 OSA 1989 (see chapter 3).

After some initial setbacks for the government in their efforts to prevent publication the House of Lords has maintained a strict and absolute ban on unauthorised stories or publications where the courts have some power of control. In the next chapter we shall see that in *Shayler*, the Law Lords left no scope for Art. 10 freedom-of-speech rights in relation to ss. 1 and 4(3) OSA 1989 which impose what are essentially absolute prohibitions against disclosure against members of the services.[62] In *AG v Punch Ltd* the Law Lords ruled that publication of articles by Shayler by a journal in breach of a court order was a

---

[58] See p. 438 *et seq*. below: the *Spycatcher* episode.

[59] See now, however, ch. 4, p. 135 below and FOIA 2000, s. 64(2) concerning records transferred to the PRO and s. 2(3)(a) Intelligence Services Act 1994.

[60] Especially the 'inconsistent' failure to restrict publication of C. Pincher, *Their Trade Is Treachery* (1982) and *Too Secret Too Long* (1984) and Channel 4's programme, *MI5's Official Secrets* (1985).

[61] *Lord Advocate v Scotsman Publications Ltd* [1989] 2 All ER 852, HL. See, however, *AG v Blake* App. No. 68890/01 (2006).

[62] *R v Shayler* [2002] UKHL 11.

contempt. Intent to harm national security on the part of the editor did not have to be proved.[63] However, where a publication by a former intelligence officers has not been approved and where the work has been published elsewhere or on the internet and was therefore in the public domain the Court of Appeal would not issue an injunction preventing publication of extracts.[64] Section 12 Human Rights Act (HRA) also provides an obstacle to the award of injunctions as we shall see in chapter 11 (see pp. 401, 444 *et seq.*). However, in *AG v Blake*[65] the House of Lords imposed a duty to account for profits from his book, *No Other Choice*, on the spy George Blake, a former member of MI6. This was a novel development for an equitable remedy for a breach of contract but conventional damages were not available and Blake was outside the jurisdiction and so beyond the reach of the OSA. An account was ordered for payment of the profits realised from the 'very thing he had promised not to do' in his signed undertaking on entering the service. He undertook not to disclose information acquired in office, during or after his service, in book form or otherwise. 'An absolute rule against disclosure, visible to all, makes good sense', said Lord Nicholls, seeming to support a lifelong duty of confidentiality.[66] The Law Lords also disapproved the judgment of the Court of Appeal that the Attorney General could prevent Blake receiving his royalties by 'public-law process' and injunction. Interestingly, in spite of the lifelong duty of confidentiality imposed on such agents under statute and common law Blake was not a 'fiduciary' because the information was no longer confidential – it was widely known. Lord Steyn believed that Blake was 'in a position very similar to a fiduciary' and an account was therefore appropriate.[67]

In spite of repeated Opposition requests for an 'external' inquiry into the allegations of treasonable and criminal conduct of MI5 agents beyond those adverted to above, Mrs Thatcher categorically refused to authorise such inquiries, stating that she was content with the *internal* review by the head of MI5. However, in an attempt to assuage official anxiety, in November 1987 the prime minister announced that a former senior civil servant was to be appointed as a 'staff counsellor' to security and intelligence personnel where their disquiet or grievances about their work could not be assuaged through 'conventional

---

[63] [2003] 1 All ER 289 (HL) overruling the Court of Appeal.

[64] The work was written by former MI6 officer Richard Tomlinson: *The Big Breach: From top secret to maximum security*. He had been dismissed by MI6 and left the jurisdiction. He claimed that MI6 had a close association with Nelson Mandela – vigorously denied by Mandela – and that MI6 was planning to assassinate Slobodan Milosevic: *AG v Times Newspapers Times*, [2001] EWCA Civ 97.

[65] [2000] 4 All ER 385. See *Blake v UK* App. No. 68890/01 (2006) – the ECtHR ruled that proceedings had not been pursued by the UK with the diligence required and there was a breach of Art. 6 ECHR.

[66] As under the OSA 1989, s. 1 and see *Scotsman Publications*, note 61 above.

[67] See *Snepp v US*, ch. 12, p. 477, note 85. The Law Lords assumed there was a contract in existence between Blake and the Crown vis-à-vis the non-publication agreement even though at the time the contract was made, civil servants were not thought to be in a contractual position re employment by the Crown.

ways', i.e. an interview with superiors. He is to have access to all documents and all levels of management and the Cabinet Secretary. He is to report not less than once a year to the Home Secretary, the Foreign Secretary and the prime minister. The counsellor can make recommendations to heads of MI5 and MI6, but the prime minister refused to accede to a request that he be allowed to sit on meetings of the Directorate.[68] The Intelligence and Security Committee's annual report (Cm. 7542 (2007–8), para. 66) noted the appointment of an ethical officer (EO) for the security service and that twelve persons had been to see the EO since 2006 – the EO was a former deputy DG of the service.

Some changes and questions

Following the Butler Report, a businessman was to be appointed to the Board of MI6 to add management expertise and an internal official from MI6 was to head a new internal watchdog reporting service on intelligence to assess reliability. The management of reports' officers and operations staff had been separated. In 2002, MI6 was allowed to obtain advice from the First Division Association, a civil servants' trade union and this was extended to MI5 in 2008 via their staff association. The Public Interest Disclosure Act 1998 (see chapter 3, p. 116) does not apply to these agents[69] so they do not get the protection of that Act. As the Law Lords have emphasised: their secrets go with them to their graves.[70]

We know of our security-conscious world. Global terrorism, the possible re-emergence of a cold war, and the globalisation of organised crime dictate the necessity. The existence of a security and intelligence service is not the point. The point is to what extent should such services be rendered accountable? Who should know of their activities and responsibilities and call them to account? It is frequently claimed that simply leaving the information as a preserve of the prime minister and a few trusted ministers and aides is inadequate. This can allow improper influence on a prime minister or by a prime minister as in the case of the Iraq dossier,[71] or pressure upon the security services only to

[68] HC Debs., 2 November 1987 (WA) and 3 November 1987.
[69] Employment tribunals now cover security and intelligence officers: 1999 Employment Relations Act, sch. 8; Intelligence and Security Committee, *Annual Report 1999–2000*, Cm. 4897, and The Employment Tribunals (Constitution and Rules etc.) Regulations SI 2004/1861 contain special procedural provisions for the protection of national security where that falls for consideration: see para. 54 and sch. 2; and see Northern Ireland Act 1998, ss. 90–1 and appeals against certificates of the Secretary of State that an act was done against an individual to safeguard national security – this followed the decision in *Tinnelly & Son Ltd v UK* (1998) 27 EHRR 249. Note also the Special Immigration Appeals Commission Act 1997 and the procedures to replace the advisory panel which heard 'appeals' from those who were subject to an order of deportation conducive to the public good on the grounds of national security. The legislation followed *Chahal v UK* (1996) 23 EHRR 413 (see ch. 11, p. 425 below).
[70] Dame Stella Rimington was about to publish *A Life of Surprises* about her role as DG of MI5 in April 2009 accompanied by an official ministerial statement of disapproval.
[71] Concerning intelligence on weapons of mass destruction; or in relation to Harold Wilson's mysterious resignation.

provide the information the government wishes to hear. In the 1960s, GCHQ and MI6 informed the government of how Rhodesia was able to break trade sanctions after its unilateral declaration of independence, only to be told by the government that it did not want to know.[72] Both the British prime minister and the president of the USA used completely and suspiciously unreliable intelligence to commence a war leading to large loss of life and destruction. In the USA, the 9/11 Commission[73] investigating the events on that fateful day when planes were flown into the World Trade Centre in New York and the Pentagon found serious faults in the operation of security and intelligence in the USA despite the fact that in the States there are powerful Congressional committees surveying the executive in this sphere of activity.[74] In the absence of FOI laws in this area, who should know of the activities of the UK security services in order to vouchsafe to the UK public that those activities are conducted according to proper mandates and the law? Who should know of the degree of interrelationship between GCHQ and the US National Security Council[75] or the Central Intelligence Agency?

Do we need to know whether MI6 have plotted to kill Colonel Gaddafi, President Nasser, Sadam Hussein, or Slobodan Milosevic or of the 'dirty tricks' of our agents and their involvement in torture?[76] The answer is 'we do'; if not directly then there should certainly be a more extensive report and oversight than exists within the present privileged circle of communication. By insisting on too much secrecy the government will invariably engage in efforts which are counterproductive or destructive of democratic values themselves. For example, in the 1980s GCHQ, after the union-banning fracas, was raised from 'useful obscurity' to become the most notorious government HQ outside Whitehall.[77] The frequency of catastrophe within the services, from spies to internal mismanagement, makes the public expect the worst in the absence of appropriate accountability mechanisms. The brevity of past Security Commission investigations does not enhance their reports – but they have been replaced by statutory structures. What safeguards are there for the operations of the services?

[72] H. Wilson's comment on the prime minister and national security in *The Governance of Britain* (1976) consisted of one page of text!

[73] *9/11 Commission Report*, National Commission on Terrorist Attacks on the United States of America (2004).

[74] And note the 'Irangate' episode and Congressional committees of inquiry into the role of the president, his advisers and the National Security Council. The Congressional Committee's majority report of November 1987 recommended direct notification by the president of covert actions to the Congressional Committees, and the appointment of an independent inspector general for the CIA.

[75] N. West, *GCHQ: The secret wireless war* (1986) claims that at that time there was a 95 per cent exchange of information' and an exchange of staff.

[76] P. Stiff, *See You in November* (1986) and R. Tomlinson, *The Big Breach*.

[77] H. Young, *The Guardian*, 18 March 1986.

The security and intelligence services legislation and Regulation of Investigatory Powers Act (RIPA) 2000

The most important pieces of legislative reform have been the Security Service Act 1989, which accompanied the OSA 1989, and the Intelligence Services Act 1994.[78] To these have been added the Security Service Act 1996, the Regulation of Investigatory Powers Act 2000 (RIPA) and amendments under terrorism legislation.[79] As we shall see, the OSA did provide for a lifelong prohibition on unauthorised disclosures by security and intelligence officials and those purporting to be such officials as well as by notified persons.[80] Judicial decisions have confirmed this position under civil law. The other legislation requires a further analysis at this stage. The first two statutes do place the security and intelligence services on a statutory basis and they do provide for some form of parliamentary oversight. In addition they set out in very broad terms the powers of the services, the necessity for warrants from the Secretary of State[81] for otherwise illegal activity or activity contravening the ECHR. They provide in each case for a commissioner to oversee their activities and a tribunal to deal with complaints about service activities. These have now been brought within RIPA 2000. The 1996 Act extended the remit of the security service as we shall see. However, compared with developments in Canada and Australia in relation to their own democratic oversight of the services, they leave a good deal to be desired. What do the statutes provide?

First of all, the 1994 Act introduced what had been rejected in 1989, namely a Parliamentary Intelligence and Security Committee (ISC) which has already been referred to. This is a joint committee of both Houses and is charged with examining the expenditure, administration and policy of the security and intelligence services and GCHQ. It takes evidence from the heads of the services and all relevant figures. There are nine members and membership must exclude ministers. Members are appointed by the prime minister after consultation with the Leader of the Opposition. The prime minister may also exercise unlimited power of dismissal.[82] Members of ISC are 'notified persons' under s. 1(b) OSA 1989 (see chapter 3, p. 102). The Committee reports annually to the prime minister and may report at other times on the discharge of its functions. The annual report is laid before both Houses subject to exclusions of information which in

---

[78] *Christie v UK* 21482/93 EcomHR, 78A DR 119 (1994). The Commission rejected a plea that the security and intelligence Acts contravened the ECHR.

[79] Under the Anti-terrorism, Crime and Security Act 2001, s. 116 – the Act has wide provisions on disclosure of information to the security services, see ss. 17–20 and sch. 4; Terrorism Act 2006, s. 31 and Counter Terrorism Act 2008, ss. 19–21.

[80] Ch. 3, p. 103 *et seq.* below.

[81] Or officials under certain circumstances, see e.g. Security Service Act 1989, s. 3.

[82] S. 10(3) and sch. 3, para. 1(d). The first annual report of the Committee is Cm. 3198 (1996). And see: Cm. 4073 (1997), Cm. 4532 (1999) and www.cabinetoffice.gov.uk/intelligence/annual_reports.aspx for annual reports. The 2007–8 report was sent to the prime minister in December 2008 for clearance which took several months.

the prime minister's opinion would be prejudicial to the continued discharge of the functions of the services. This subjection to ministerial veto in publication is not shared by other committees. The only safeguard against prime ministerial abuse is a duty upon the prime minister to consult the Committee about exclusions and a statement relating to the exclusion has to accompany the report. The published components of reports are frequently censored in relation to names, details and functions and other items. The Committee has power to determine its own procedure but not to decide if and when it goes into open session, as are other committees. It cannot compel the attendance of witnesses and in this respect its powers are weaker than a Commons select committee. It may request information which shall be provided subject to exemptions discussed below and 'subject to and in accordance with arrangements approved by the Secretary of State'. It will receive the key policy document setting out intelligence priorities and identifying key intelligence heads and officials. It has criticised the fact that it does not receive the 'confidential annexes' to the Commissioners' reports under interception and services legislation.[83] The Committee meets in the Cabinet Office, not in Westminster, and is not open to the public. Some modifications to the committee's procedures were set out in Prime Minister Brown's White Paper and draft Constitutional Renewal Bill outlined above. The White Paper suggested some reforms to the ISC including nomination by the usual select committee process, public briefings where possible, reappointment of an investigator to assist the Committee, and changes in Parliament's debating procedure for reports including the possibility of a Lords debate. The committee's 2007–8 report discussed and approved these proposals which have been agreed by Parliament (Cm. 7542 (2009); GR Cm. 7543). The Committee also criticised the abandonment of the SCOPE IT project seeking to secure more effective communications for the agencies (para. 147 *et seq.*) and noted that the agencies employ 350 'consultants' (para. 70 *et seq.*).

Where the Committee requests presentation of information it may be refused by the relevant director/chief on several grounds, i.e. where it is:

- sensitive information – although the director may disclose it if he considers it safe to disclose it (it is sensitive information where it might lead to the identification or provide details of sources of information, other assistance or operational methods available to the services)
- information about particular operations which have been, are being, or are proposed to be undertaken by those bodies
- information provided by, or by an agency of, the government of a territory outside the UK where the government does not consent to the disclosure of the information.

The relevant director may nonetheless allow disclosure where the director etc. considers it safe to disclose it.

---

[83] Cm. 4897 (2000), p. 14.

Information may also be refused where the Secretary of State has determined that it should not be disclosed. He may only so decide where he would be justified in not disclosing information to a departmental select committee of the House of Commons. The Secretary of State shall disclose such information if he considers it 'desirable in the public interest'. The Committee does complain about not receiving information it believes it should. As well as annual reports it publishes special reports.[84] The government has hinted at the possibility of oversight in the future by a conventional select committee.

In May 2009, the ISC published its *Review of the Intelligence on the London Terrorist Attacks on 7 July 2005* (Cm. 7617). The Committee believed the report contained an 'exceptional level of operational information' (para. 17) noting that only 6 per cent of the overall known terrorist threat had a 'reasonable level of intelligence coverage'. Although the two major targets fell off MI5's radar, the ISC pointed to 'the constraints on resources' (para. 143) and the many limits to intelligence (para. 155). To have applied 'consistent surveillance' to all who fell into the same category as the three who had meetings with the two major targets, MI5 'would have needed to be a very different organisation, both in terms of its size and how it operates, which would have huge ramifications for our society and the way we live' (para. 143). The report noted problems about retrieving information from older records (legacy databases), about sharing and receiving intelligence from the police, the regionalisation of MI5 and the non-use of existing data from court records. The intelligence operations of MI5 prior to the bombings were exonerated by the ISC.

The Intelligence and Security Committee was a welcome addition, but lacking the investigatory powers of select committees might, on the surface, appear a serious handicap. The general contribution of select committees has been limited although useful investigations have included the Department of Trade and Industry inquiry into the Iraqi supergun affair. Leigh and Lustgarten for instance claim that although much of the crucial evidence only emerged when a minister let slip vital information under defence cross-examination in subsequent criminal proceedings and PII certificates were lifted in the trial, the committee had played a crucial role in helping to publicise vital if apparently unsensational evidence.[85] The movement to greater openness concerning the services has been noted. Even so, information has not always been forthcoming to the Intelligence and Security Committee. Specific items linked to operations

---

[84] These include: *Rendition*, Cm. 7171 (2007) with a Government Reply, Cm. 7172 which also includes sections on specific cases and intelligence sharing; the *London Terrorist Attacks*, Cm. 6785 (2006) and Government Reply, Cm. 6786; *Handling of Detainees by UK Intelligence Personnel in Afghanistan, Guantánamo Bay*, Cm. 6469 (2005) and Government Reply, Cm. 6511; *Weapons of Mass Destruction*, Cm. 5972 and Government Reply, Cm. 6118. On the limits of the ability of the committee to investigate allegations of British collusion in torture overseas, see *R (B. Mohamed) v Secretary of State for Foreign and Commonwealth Affairs* [2009] EWHC 152 (Admin). In September 2009, the police investigated a file on MI6 members concerning allegations of their participation in torture.

[85] Lustgarten and Leigh, *In From the Cold*, p. 454.

are rarely given. The Committee will examine the expenditure of the services and will require access to their budget and there are provisions whereby information may be disclosed to the Comptroller and Auditor-General (CAG) for him to carry out his scrutiny of their expenditure. The Committee has frequently expressed its misgivings about accounts, particularly GCHQ whose accounts were not qualified by the National Audit Office for three years although they were subsequently.

Statutory oversight of the intrusion by the services became necessary both because of judicial prompting in England and pressure applied through the ECHR. The legislation manifested the 'Government's policy to be as open as possible about security and intelligence matters without prejudicing national security, the effectiveness of the security and intelligence services or the safety of their staff'.[86] In the passage of the bill on MI5 in 1989, the government accepted no amendments to the bill and the committee stage of the bill was a committee of the whole House. Both the 1989 and 1994 Acts (s. 1) provide for the continuation of the respective services under the authority of the Secretary of State. This would appear to indicate the potential authorisation of secretaries of state other than the Home or Foreign Secretary. Under the 1989 Act no reference is made to the use by the service of the Special Branch or other forces despite the services' growing remit. The Security Service Act 1996, makes acting in support of prevention and detection of a serious crime a function of the service and this has been taken to include computer security in Whitehall along with drug trafficking, illegal immigration rings, international trafficking in prostitutes and avoidance of excise. Arrangements will allow M15 to act in co-ordination with the police and 'other law enforcement agencies'. These now include SOCA. The ISC has expressed concern about the interrelationship between the police and the service, a concern repeated by the Security Commissioner, especially as police surveillance techniques were at that time non-statutory. They are now under the Police Act 1997 and RIPA 2000 (below). No reference is made to co-operation between British and overseas security and intelligence services or to the use of 'private' contractors or agents.

In addition to the 1996 extensions, the functions of the security service according to the 1989 Act shall be the protection of national security and in particular its protection against threats from espionage, terrorism and sabotage, from the activities of agents of foreign powers and from actions intended to overthrow or undermine parliamentary democracy by political, industrial or violent means (s. 1(2)). This leans heavily upon the erstwhile Harris definition of 'subversion' which was criticised for being far too broad.[87] 'National security' concerned 'matters related to the survival or well being of the nation as a whole, and not to party political, sectional or lesser interests'.[88] It was seen above how *Rehman* extended the definition of national security to include

---

[86] Lord Chancellor, HL Debs., vol. 550, col. 1023.
[87] HL Debs., vol. 375, col. 947.   [88] HC Debs., vol. 143, col. 1113.

threats against foreign governments. The 1989 Act contains provisions prescribing that the service shall not take action to further the interests of any political party. However all the weaknesses of the previous Harris definition survive from the perspective of civil liberties and there is nothing to prevent a prime minister condemning trade unionists as the 'enemy within' as occurred during the miners' strike in 1984, thereby rendering their actions 'subversive' and therefore an appropriate object of MI5 attention.[89] The same could apply to the farmers and road hauliers in their fuel protests in the autumn of 2000 and subsequently. What are we to make, for instance, of animal rights activists engaging in mass non-violent protests? In the debates on the bill, the Home Secretary refused to define 'parliamentary democracy'. As Leigh and Lustgarten express the point:

> It is easy to imagine many in the service, and indeed many ministers, treating parliamentary democracy as the subjects' right to vote once every few years and their obligation to obey the rest of the time. Civil disobedience therefore becomes subversion. This unsatisfactory state of affairs is compounded by the use of the term 'undermining' which imparts no limitation of immediacy or directness.[90]

The Act contains no explicit safeguards against improper instructions from ministers, apart from those of a party-political nature, although the role of the staff counsellor or ethical officer should be recalled. The 1952 directive authorised non-compliance with ministerial requests requiring a misuse of the service. In Australia, where the Attorney General instructs an inquiry to commence or discontinue in circumstances where the director general feels that the instructions are improper, the instruction must be in writing and copies have to be sent to the prime minister and the inspector general who oversees the service and deals with complaints. MI6 also has its functions set out in the statute e.g. 'to obtain and provide information relating to the actions or intentions of persons outside the British Islands (NI)' as well as 'other tasks' relating to such persons and such functions are exercisable only in the interests of national security 'with particular reference to the defence and foreign policies of HMG in the UK' in the interests of the economic well being of the UK – which under the 1989 Act is not qualified in any way – and in support of the prevention or detection of serious crime which is again undefined and is not jurisdictionally limited.

Both the 1989 and 1994 statutes[91] provide for the continuation of a director general of MI5 and chief of MI6 and director of GCHQ and it is their responsibility to ensure that only relevant information is collected by their services which is 'necessary for the proper discharge of its functions' and that information is not disclosed except for itemised functions.[92] The question of data

---

[89] S. Milne, *The Enemy Within: MI5, Maxwell and the Scargill affair* (1995).

[90] Lustgarten and Leigh, (1989) MLR 807.

[91] They have been amended by provisions outlined in note 79 above.

[92] E.g. 1994 Act, ss. 2(2)(a) and 4(2)(a).

transfer, and the Criminal Records Bureau, have been outlined above. The Data Protection Act provides a virtual exclusion of data held for national security purposes from the safeguards in the Act. The directors etc. are responsible for ensuring the party political neutrality of their services' activities. They report on their services' activities to the prime minister and Secretary of State annually and they may report at any other time.

Section 3 of the 1994 Act outlines the powers of GCHQ to monitor or interfere in intelligence operating electronically. Section 7 of the 1994 Act empowers authorisation by the Secretary of State of acts done outside the UK which would otherwise be crimes within the UK. The authorisation is subject to safeguards. The 1996 Act makes clear that neither the intelligence service nor GCHQ may engage in property-intrusive activities (burglary, trespass) within the British Islands. The security service may engage in such activities in relation to what became s. 3B of the 1994 Act. This relates to warrants authorising intrusive action in relation to property where it concerns one or more offences involving the use of violence, results in substantial financial gain, or is conduct by a large number of people in pursuit of a common purpose. Section 5 states that no entry is unlawful if authorised by the Secretary of State'. No authority means it is unlawful. Alternatively, the offence, or one of the offences, is an offence for which a person over twenty-one with no previous convictions could reasonably expect a custodial sentence of three years or more. The government said, under the first part, the 'conduct' would relate to serious crime – 'industrial disputes cannot and do not constitute organised crime'.[93]

Both statutes also provided for Commissioners to oversee the exercise of the powers in each statute by the Secretary of State and the services, departmental officials and members of HM forces. These must give whatever information or documents to the Commissioners as they may require to discharge their functions. These have now become the Intelligence Services Commissioner under s. 59 RIPA. Under RIPA, the Commissioner's primary responsibility is to examine the issue of warrants by the Secretary of State which authorise entry or interference with property or in the 1994 Act wireless telegraphy in addition to obtaining information to carry out their functions. Without the warrant such interference would be unlawful. The Commissioner established to oversee interceptions (see below) will keep interceptions of communications under review where he is required to do so under Pt I RIPA – oversight of interception is largely that Commissioner's responsibility and not that of the ISC.

The Commissioner's remit also covers the performance by the Secretary of State in connection with, or in relation to, the activities of the intelligence services and of officials of the Ministry of Defence (MoD) and HM forces, other than in NI, of the powers and duties conferred on him by RIPA, Pt II and III. These involve authorisations (warrants) for surveillance and covert human intelligence sources (see below) and investigation of electronic data protected by

---

[93] HC Debs., vol. 271, col. 1054.

'encryption' or secret keys.[94] The remit also covers the exercise and performance by members of the intelligence services (and MoD officials etc.) of other powers and duties conferred on them by the same provisions. The Commissioner has to ensure the adequacy of safeguards to prevent keys obtained for understanding data from being put to wrongful use. Further responsibilities were added by the Identity Cards Act 2006 and the Prevention of Terrorism Act 2005. The Commissioner also has to give the tribunal, created by RIPA and which deals with matters arising under the Act, such assistance as the tribunal may require in the investigation by it of any matter or otherwise for the consideration or determination by the tribunal of any matter (see below). 'Assistance' may include the Commissioner's opinion. The Commissioner's brief does not cover review of subordinate legislation.

The Commissioner is a person of high judicial office. He makes an annual report to the prime minister who must lay a copy of such reports before each House of Parliament subject to exclusion of any matter 'contrary to the public interest or prejudicial to national security, the prevention or detection of serious crime, the economic well-being of the UK or the continued discharge of the functions of any public authority subject to the Crown' (HC 902 (08-09)). Exclusions include details on numbers of warrants or authorisations issued to the services although the numbers of errors are reported.[95] The excluded details are in a confidential annex which the ISC has complained about not seeing. A statement referring to such exclusion must be made to Parliament. Separate tribunals were established under the 1989 and 1994 legislation to deal with complaints by persons aggrieved by anything done to them or their property by the services and there was no power of cross-reference.

A single tribunal is now established by RIPA. In relation to the intelligence services (including MI5) any person may complain to the tribunal if they are complaining about a matter under s. 7 of the HRA 1998 – a breach of a Convention right, especially one might add, Art. 8 – by the services or persons acting on their behalf. The tribunal is the 'only appropriate' forum for such matters (s. 65 RIPA). Under the tribunal's rules (SI 2000/2665) there is no obligation to hold an oral hearing (r. 9(2)). Any such hearing must be held in private (r. 9(6))[96] and no person can be compelled to give evidence (r. 11(3)). The Administrative Court allowed a claimant to proceed by way of judicial review, against a service challenge, where as a former officer of MI5 he was denied permission to publish details of his work in the service allegedly in breach of Art. 10 ECHR protecting freedom of speech. This decision was reversed by the Court of Appeal which ruled that the tribunal was the appropriate forum.[97]

---

[94] Encryption, which involves the use of 'keys' of a private and secret nature and a public key to maintain confidentiality in communications: See House of Commons Research Paper 00/25 3 March 2000, p. 47 *et seq.*

[95] See e.g. *Annual Report Intelligence Services Commissioner 2007*, HC 948 (2007–8).

[96] See App. Nos. IPT/01/62 and IPT/01/77 (23 January 2003), ruling 9(6) ultra vires insofar as it required in camera proceedings.

[97] *A v B* [2009] EWCA Civ 24.

The tribunal's jurisdiction is not restricted to surveillance, interception, use of covert services and encryption. The Administrative Court made the following points:

> It is difficult to envisage circumstances in which such claims [surveillance etc] would properly be dealt with by the court since Parliament has clearly intended that the Tribunal should deal with them. Nothing I have said should encourage anyone who is concerned that his rights have been infringed by any such matters to seek redress through the court rather than the Tribunal. Any such attempts are likely to fail. But the circumstances of this case are somewhat different and, although the tribunal undoubtedly has jurisdiction, its procedures are less satisfactory and the issues are wider than those for which RIPA specifically required it to be established.[98]

As noted, this decision was overruled by a majority in the Court of Appeal ruling that the tribunal was appropriate for this case. The tribunal also deals with a variety of matters for which it is the 'appropriate forum' and other matters allocated to it by the Secretary of State. This refers, inter alia, to non HRA proceedings against the intelligence services or those acting on their behalf.

The tribunal is also the appropriate forum for any cause for complaint which the complainant believes took place in relation to him, his property, any communication sent by him or intended for him, or to his use of any postal or telecommunications service or system, and was carried out by or on behalf of the intelligence services and where the complaint is about their conduct. The tribunal's jurisdiction is much wider than its predecessors and covers the breadth of activities under RIPA and complaints about those activities. Proceedings may be allocated to the tribunal to the exclusion of courts or other tribunals – although they may be remitted to a court or tribunal. In making an order for a tribunal hearing, the Secretary of State has to consider the need to secure that information is not disclosed to an extent or in a manner which would be contrary to the PI or prejudicial to national security or other matters.

The complaint is to be investigated according to relevant schedules unless the complaint is considered 'vexatious or frivolous' by the tribunal. Considering the obvious difficulty a complainant will have in obtaining relevant information, such a barrier becomes more formidable than might appear at first. Under s. 23 FOIA 2000, information from the intelligence services held by a public authority is given an absolute exemption as will be explained in chapters 5 and 6 and under s. 24 information relating to national security is subject to a ministerial certificate which can only be overturned by the Information Tribunal (IT) on very limited grounds. The RIPA Tribunal has power to award interim orders. The tribunal may refer to the Commissioner any case under RIPA requesting the assistance of the Commissioner or his opinion on any relevant issue. The tribunal also keeps the Commissioner informed of complaints referred to it where relevant to the Commissioner. The tribunal may report its conclusion

---

[98] *A v B* [2008] EWHC 1512 (Admin) para. 26.

to the prime minister where an authorisation given by the Secretary of State was involved. The tribunal has power to order to disclosure of documents and information from a wide range of bodies under s. 68(7). In making its determination on alleged breaches of the Convention, the tribunal applies principles applicable by a court on judicial review,[99] i.e. mistake of law, failure to consider all factors, irrationality, disproportionality and so on. A similar provision applies to other complaints but as the Convention is not involved in those complaints, proportionality may not be applicable, though whether this would make much difference to the jurisprudence of the tribunal is a moot point.[100] Remedies where a breach of the Act has taken place include quashing or cancelling of warrants, destruction of records obtained under warrant or held by any public authority in relation to any person and compensation.[101]

The decisions of the tribunal, and this is formulated in the broadest sense, are not questionable in any court of law.[102] The Secretary of State may provide otherwise by order under s. 67(8). The Secretary of State has to provide for appeal for some complaints to a court under s. 65. Where the Secretary of State makes an order under s. 67(8), he may also establish another special tribunal to hear appeals. This will be in relation to cases where the tribunal is the 'only appropriate' or the 'appropriate' tribunal (as above). This is a very interesting example of administrative justice and a circuitous device to comply with the requirements of the ECHR while removing the regular courts.[103] Rules may provide for the giving of reasons for its decisions (SI 2000/2665).

To sum up, the 1989 and subsequent legislation still leave a great deal to be covered by custom and practice. The working relationship of the prime minister with the services is not explained and no reference is made to direct access to the prime minister by the director general in particular. In terms of service officials, the legislation only deals with reports by the heads of services and not their servants. Nor does the legislation dwell on the amount of information given to the Secretary of State or the independence of the director etc. from ministers, in spite of restrictions on action on party political grounds. How much of the convention survives that ministers are only informed in outline and are not given 'detailed information' but only that as may be 'necessary for the determination of any issue on which guidance is sought'? (Maxwell-Fyfe Directive).

---

[99] These principles have developed since this formula was first used to embrace matters such as proportionality, substantive legitimate expectation and fundamental rights and not simply *Wednesbury* unreasonableness etc.

[100] *R v Chief Constable of Sussex, ex p. International Trader's Ferry Ltd* 1999] 1 All ER 129, HL, though see Lord Steyn's classic statement in *R (Daly) v Secretary of State for the Home Department, ex p. Daly* [2001] UKHL 26.

[101] In relation to complaints about the services, it is reported that an answer to a Parliamentary Question in 2005 stated that out of 'around 1,100 complaints' no complaint had been upheld: Harry Cohen MP, PQs 13170 and 13171, July 2005.

[102] See s. 67(8).   [103] See s. 67(10)(c), however. And note *Al Rawi* p. 458 below.

It could be argued that, from a constitutional point of view, one of the most glaring omissions is the absence of a precise statutory code covering the powers of the services. The Acts set out their functions in very broad terms. The government would argue, understandably, that such a code would inhibit the effectiveness of the services, especially the covert operations of MI6. 'Tight' internal controls operate so that, for instance, in the case of MI6, any matter of political sensitivity would require the permission of the Secretary of State if a warrant were not necessary. Such a response would be more acceptable if adequate procedures existed for grievance resolution. RIPA is an improvement and far more attention has been paid to complaints but procedures remain uncertain in their scope, and they do not cover complaints relating to events before the schedules of the Acts came into effect. In any event, the 'system' – by which I mean the service and all those within and without the service who serve or assist it – is likely to seize up if there is unlawful action, in contravention of, or without, a warrant and an injured victim wishes to sue. Section 1 RIPA provides for a tort of unlawful interception of communications, for instance. But where will the evidence come from? Where the source of information to a third-party complainant is a security official, the latter will run the risk of prosecution under s. 1 OSA 1989. The identity of such an official will not be kept confidential from government by investigating authorities.

It is also important to realise that these Acts, given the breadth and vague nature of their contents, may not be the exclusive source of authority and power of the services. In *R v Secretary of State for the Home Department, ex p. Northumbria Police Authority*[104] the Court of Appeal accepted that a prerogative power, in this case maintaining the peace, could survive a statutory enactment covering the same subject area. Traditional doctrine has it that where a statute is passed on a subject hitherto under the prerogative, the statute takes precedence unless Parliament indicates the contrary intention. There was no such intention behind the Police Act 1964, the court held. Were this reasoning to apply in the present context of security and intelligence then an ancient prerogative would be rattling its chains once more down the centuries.[105] The legislation hardly constitutes a constitutional code. The *Northumbria* decision renders uncertain the extent of the service's authority. The Home Secretary insisted that the 1989 legislation was 'taking an area of public policy out of the realm of the prerogative and putting it into the realm of statute'.[106] The process may have continued but the assessment may be over sanguine.

---

[104] [1988] 1 All ER 556, CA.

[105] *See R v Secretary of State for the Home Department, ex p. Fire Brigades Union* [1995] 2 All ER 244, HL. In this case, it was established that a Secretary of State could not use prerogative powers to put a programme of criminal injuries compensation into effect in a manner which was inconsistent with statutory powers to introduce a statutory scheme under existing statutory provisions.

[106] HC Debs., vol. 145, col. 213.

Interception of communications, surveillance and RIPA

Interception of communications has been performed by the executive since correspondence began, although until 1985 there was no legislative basis for such action. The Birkett Report of 1957 thought that the position of the law could be stated to recognise the power of the Crown to intercept letters and telegrams, and 'it is wide enough to cover telephone communications as well'.[107] In *Malone v Metropolitan Police Comr*[108] the power of the Secretary of State to authorise telephone taps was judicially recognised absent any other tort or criminal act. Birkett described the authority of the Secretary of State as 'absolute', although authorisations were in practice issued to a limited number of listed agencies. When the European Court of Human Rights (ECtHR) held in *Malone v UK* that the British Government's guidelines on tapping were in contravention of Art. 8 ECHR protecting privacy,[109] the government produced a bill intending to secure compliance with our obligations under the Convention. *The Times* spoke of the bill as an act of 'dumb insolence' attempting to achieve the absolute minimum to comply with the Court ruling in *Malone*.[110]

The Interception of Communications Act 1985 was repealed by RIPA 2000. The 1985 Act covered interception of communications by post or public telecommunications systems, which includes cell phones, Email and fax.[111] Between 1985 and 1999, the number of telecommunications companies offering fixed-line service had increased from 2 to about 150. Mobile phones had increased in a way that was unforeseen; new services were introduced such as international simple resale. There has been a rapid development of the satellite telephone market and correspondence via the Internet.[112] The government believed that the powers of interception had to be increased to cover these developments. Furthermore, the decisions of the ECtHR on breaches of the Convention had created difficulties for the UK in relation to private telephone networks[113] and the HRA, which incorporates much of the Convention, had to be addressed in the context of interceptions.[114] The government wished to make statutory provision for interceptions on all these forms of communications as well as to obtain 'communications data' which means information about the use of a communications service, i.e. the number and frequency of communications but not their content. Within the next five years, most communications

---

[107] Cmnd 283.   [108] [1979] Ch 344, Sir Robert Megarry VC.
[109] ECHR, Series A, No. 82, Judgment of 2 August 1984.
[110] *The Times*, 6 March 1985. See I. Cameron (1986) NILQ 126. Note also the report of the European Parliament of 29 May 2001 on the Echelon spying network and global eavesdropping.
[111] Cm. 108, para. 5 and mobile phones.
[112] Ed Richards, Robin Foster, and Tom Kiedrowski (eds.), *Communications in the next Decade* (Ofcom, 2006).
[113] *Halford v UK* (1997) 24 EHRR 523.
[114] As well as the EC Telecommunications Data Protection Directive (97/66/EC) and successors on confidentiality of telecommunications communications made (ch. 8, p. 279). See Art. 5(2). S. 4 RIPA incorporates Art. 5(2) of the Directive.

within the UK will be delivered using the Internet Protocol. By 2016, the Home Office predict that discrete communications events per year will double to 450 billion in the UK.[115] RIPA is already out of date.

RIPA makes interception without a warrant from the Secretary of State a criminal offence. Interception without lawful authority is also made a tort under s. 1(3). Under s. 1(6), controllers of private communications' services are excluded from criminal liability where they make an unauthorised intercept but their action will remain a tort unless parties are put on notice that their calls are likely to be monitored. The Secretary of State has issued regulations under s. 4(2) RIPA which authorise for the purposes of RIPA the interception of telecommunications in the widest of terms for the purposes, inter alia, of monitoring business calls.[116] All reasonable steps have to be taken to inform those affected. Authority can be given by the consent of the person who made or received the communication, or where reasonable grounds exist to believe consent has been given, or by the warrant of the Secretary of State. It is very rare for the Home Secretary to reject a request for a warrant,[117] the highest incidence of refusals occurring in foreign affairs. The government rejected the need for prior judicial approval for a warrant.[118]

A warrant must not be issued unless necessary for one of four specified grounds: the interests of national security; preventing or detecting serious crime; safeguarding the economic wellbeing of the UK; or, under the second ground (serious crime) in order to give effect to an international mutual assistance agreement (see ss. 20 and 32 Terrorism Act 2006). The Secretary of State has to believe that the conduct authorised by the warrant is proportionate to what is sought to be achieved by that conduct. Consideration must be given to whether the information could be obtained by other means before a warrant is issued, and there are limits set for the duration and premises and persons intercepted.[119] The Secretary of State has to make arrangements to secure that disclosure of information obtained and copying of the information is limited to the minimum necessary to comply with the criteria given above, and that uncertified material obtained on an interception is not regarded or examined. Section 6 covers those who may make applications for warrants, and as well as the intelligence chiefs and police (largely through SOCA which now includes immigration and Revenue and Customs intelligence) they include competent foreign authorities under mutual-assistance schemes. Warrants must contain

---

[115] *Privy Council Review of Intercept as Evidence,* Cm. 7324 (2008), para. 109; see HC Debs., vol. 487, col. 89 WS.

[116] The Telecommunications (Lawful Business Practice) (Interception of Communications) Regulations 2000, SI 2000/2699: see *Chand v Met. Police Com'r* [2006] PLR 301 (IPT) on the scope of the regulations. See the ECHR decision in *Copland v UK* App. No. 62617/00, *The Times,* 24 April 2007 on monitoring employees.

[117] Lustgarten and Leigh, *In From the Cold,* p. 59. In 'urgent' cases, and following statutory conditions, a senior civil servant may issue the warrant.

[118] Executive authorisation was approved in *Christie v UK* (1994) ECtHR.

[119] 'External' interceptions are far broader than 'internal' ones.

various details and may be modified. The Secretary of State may by order require a public postal or telecommunications service to maintain assistance in interception warrants. A Technical Advisory Board was established. Unauthorised disclosure of information obtained through intercepts is a criminal offence under s. 19. Codes may be issued under the Act.

An Interception of Communications Commissioner is appointed by the prime minister to keep under review the exercise of powers of warrant by the Secretary of State. The Commissioner has to assist the tribunal in a manner similar to the ISC (above). He also is a senior judge. Those regulated by the Commissioner must co-operate by providing information and documents. An Investigatory Powers Commissioner is established for Northern Ireland. Scotland has its own legislation and there are various dovetailing provisions. The Commissioner publishes annual reports (see HC 901 (2008–9)).[120] Warrants are examined by the Commissioner 'largely at random' (HC 252 (2007–8), para. 7). In 2007, there were ten Communications Service Providers which were those 'most engaged in interception work' (HC 947 (2007–8)). Details of warrants issued by the Foreign Secretary or for Northern Ireland are not given and remain in a confidential annex. Home Secretary warrants in force were 754 (2006) and 929 (2007); issued 1,333 (2006, 9 months) and 1,881 (2007).There were also 'modifications' which means a change in address or number and prior to 1998 this would have meant a new warrant: 3,489 (2006) and 5,577 (2007). Errors are mainly 'procedural' and the staff for whom the Commissioner has a high regard seek his advice in cases of doubt or difficulty.

Material obtained from intercepts may not be admitted in evidence in court hearings although it may be admitted in proceedings before the Investigatory Powers Tribunal, the Special Immigration Appeals Commission, for control orders before courts and the Proscribed Organisations Appeals Commission. It may be used for proceedings involving offences under the RIPA itself. Intercepts in foreign countries under foreign laws are not excluded in English courts.[121] The prosecution has to review the material to see what a fair prosecution requires. The guidance of the trial judge may be sought and a statement of fact may be made in exceptional circumstances.[122] But the evidence is not disclosed to the defence. Material covered by legal professional privilege and confidentiality is dealt with by a code but, at best, use of such material is dealt with on a self-denying ordinance basis. Making intercept evidence admissible would not in itself contravene the ECHR and many countries do allow it to be admitted in criminal proceedings. The security and intelligence services in the UK are against its admissibility because of what the material may reveal about their

---

[120] www.official-documents.gov.uk/document/hc0708/hc09/0947/0947.pdf.

[121] *Privy Council Review of Intercept as Evidence*, Cm. 7324 (2008), para. 22: *R v P* [2001] 2 All ER 58, HL. Conversations recorded with the consent of one of the parties or recorded by hidden microphone are not covered by the exclusion.

[122] *Ibid.*, para. 21.

methods. A Privy Council review recommended in 2008 conditional support for the admissibility of intercept evidence in criminal proceedings.[123]

The House of Lords has ruled that RIPA authorises the use of secret electronic surveillance in a police station to obtain evidence from discussions between a lawyer and his clients.[124] Evidence obtained by authorised bugs and property-intrusive warrants is admissible in court hearings unless otherwise privileged.

Authorisations must be given in order to obtain access to communications data. 'Communications data' as we have seen means information about the use of a communications service including information held by a service provider: contacts, dates, times, addresses, duration, location, Internet access. It does not concern their content as with an intercept. The necessary grounds for obtaining such data are considerably broader than for obtaining an interception warrant. Authorisations are given by designated persons within the relevant authorities. A notice may also be given to postal or telecommunications operators to obtain or disclose data. The conduct authorised must be proportionate to the objectives of seeking the data. Regulations have been approved implementing an EU directive on data retention (EC Directive 2006/241/EC). These cover fixed line and mobile phones and public communications providers (SI 2199/2007). Internet related communications data (internet telephony and internet email) will be covered by regulations by March 2009 (SI 859/2009). The regulations will allow the government to work co-operatively with the industry to ensure that appropriate retrieval mechanisms are in place; make provisions to avoid duplicative retention of communications data; and require communications data to be retained for a period of twelve months.[125] A Home Office proposal to establish a national database for communications data was dropped in April 2009. The 2008 report of the Interception Commissioner (HC 252 (2007–8)) listed the authorities empowered to acquire and disclose communications data. As well as security and intelligence and police, it includes 474 local authorities and 110 'other authorities' such as the Financial Services Authority, SFO and the Independent Police Complaints Authority.[126] Of 253,577 data requests in 2006, about 0.4 per cent contained errors – on which the Commissioner stated 'further information would not be necessary' (HC 252 (2007–8), para. 58). In the following period, there were 519,260 requests for data – a huge increase in

---

[123] *Privy Council Review of Intercept as Evidence*, Cm. 7324 (2008). See the ISC 2008 AR, Cm. 7542, p. 43 *et seq.*

[124] In *Re McE* [2009] UKHL 15 despite the express provision in the Police and Criminal Evidence Act 1984, s. 58 of *private* consultation and Terrorism Act 2000, sch. 8. The surveillance was wrongly classified as 'directed' however.

[125] See also the Anti-terrorism etc. Act 2001, Pt 11 and see SI 3335/2005 (Further Extensions Order).

[126] A chief inspector and five inspectors conduct oversight in this area. There have been shock-horror stories of local authorities using these powers to establish the home address of a schoolchild for school admission purposes and other relatively trivial purposes such as defecating dogs and owners not stooping to scoop!

requests but the number of errors decreased significantly because changes in 2007 meant only privacy-intrusive errors were reported.

Part II RIPA regulates the use of covert surveillance in three forms: 'directed', i.e. planned following of targets;[127] 'intrusive' which involves the use of an individual or the use of surveillance devices in any residential premises or vehicle; and the conduct and use of 'covert intelligence sources' which involves the cultivation of individual 'sources' to supply information. These definitions of directed and intrusive surveillance may be changed by order under s. 47, and under s. 71 codes may be issued covering covert surveillance and covert human intelligence sources. The three forms of covert surveillance have to be authorised by designated authorities on specified grounds. The authorised conduct has to be proportionate. The designated authorities for intrusive surveillance are listed in s. 32[128] those for directed and covert intelligence sources authorisations are in s. 30. The Surveillance Commissioner and Chief Surveillance Commissioner possess various regulatory and appeal powers. Special provisions cover intelligence services' authorisations under Pt II. The provisions under Pt II add to those in the Police Act 1997, Pt III and the Intelligence Services Act 1994 which regulate entry on or interference with property, or with wireless telegraphy and which were necessitated by the anticipation that use of secret listening devices without legal regulation was in breach of Art. 8 ECHR. The decision of the ECtHR in *Khan v UK* established that there was such a breach and *legal* not *administrative* regulation was necessary.[129] This came after the House of Lords ruled evidence obtained by 'bugs' was admissible against the defendants and on the basis of which they were convicted of importation of prohibited drugs.[130] The Lords' judgment came before the HRA incorporated the Convention.

Part III RIPA empowers authorities to demand that encrypted material – computerised and protected by a secret code – be rendered intelligible or that a key allowing it to be decrypted be handed over. It applies to such material that has come into a person's possession as a result of a statutory power of search and seizure, e.g. Police and Criminal Evidence Act 1984, or some other lawful means. A power may be exercised by one with the 'appropriate permission' under sch. 2. A notice requiring disclosure may be served on the person who is believed to be in possession of the key. It must not be given for speculative reasons. A notice may not be required where its purpose would be defeated by being given. A disclosure request must be necessary on stated grounds and proportionate.

---

[127] See *C v Com'r Met. Police* [2006] PLR 151 (IPT).

[128] Or otherwise listed in SI 2000/2417.

[129] *Khan v UK* (2000) The Times, 23 May. *R v P* [2001] 2 All ER 58, HL.

[130] *R v Khan* [1996] 3 All ER 289, HL. Article 8 was not at that time a part of our domestic law. Under s. 17 RIPA, evidence obtained from intercepts is not admissible in any legal proceedings with some exceptions in s. 18 including proceedings before the tribunal. This prohibition does not apply to the other parts of the Act although intercepted material for which keys are obtained under Pt III will be covered. S. 78 PACE 1984 will govern the use of such material that is not covered by the prohibition.

Stricter controls apply where the key itself is required.[131] Non-disclosure when requested, as well as tipping off another person about a notice where secrecy is required, are punishable offences. Defences are available and a duty is imposed to safeguard keys. Breach of the duty is actionable.

RIPA establishes a tribunal which is appointed by the Crown to hear complaints not only from victims of interception of a communication either by or to them but also on a variety of topics under s. 65 involving security and intelligence details of which were outlined above. Complaints cover conduct concerning data communications, covert surveillance under Pt II, complaints concerning Pt III notices and disclosure and use of keys, entry or interference with property or interference with wireless telegraphy. As well as being the tribunal for complaints about the intelligence services which do not fall within the HRA, the tribunal is also the appropriate tribunal for conduct under the Act which has taken place in challengeable circumstances. This means not only where there is, or purports to be, a warrant, authorisation, notice, a permission under sch. 2, or an authorisation under s. 93 Police Act 1997.[132] It also includes circumstances where there is no warrant etc. but 'it would not have been appropriate for the conduct to have taken place without it' or without proper consideration of that factor. In other words, unlike the 1985 Act, the tribunal may hear complaints where action is not authorised. The Tribunals and Inquiries Act 1992 applies to the tribunal.

Rules may be made concerning the form of the hearing, the provision of information about any determination, or order etc., to be given to the complainant and on legal or other representation for complainants. Rules may provide for the giving of summaries of evidence to the complainant and giving of reasons in a manner that does not compromise sensitive information (SI 2665/2000). The Secretary of State must have regard to the need to protect information from disclosure which is against the PI, or prejudicial to national security, the prevention or detection of serious crime, the economic wellbeing of the country or the continuing discharge of the functions of any of the intelligence services. Until November 2006, only four decisions of the tribunal had been published on its website – all others remained secret.

RIPA is a remarkable illustration of administrative justice within the inner recesses of the state. It seeks to maintain the ideals of legality and of the Convention while securing as little interference from the legal order as possible. Some of the worst features of previous legislation have gone – although much has to be provided by way of regulations and orders to realise the improved safeguards. In their place is a statute with sweepingly intrusive powers. Monitoring of private communications systems will be standard practice and authorised under regulations or by notice where users will have no choice but to use the

---

[131] *R v S* [2009] 1 All ER 716: although requesting a key leading to a criminal charge may be self-incriminatory, it is fair and proportionate. See *Jalloh v Germany* (2006) 20 BHRC 575 ECtHR.

[132] This covers authorisations to interfere with property.

systems. Powers are so wide that they are going to be extremely difficult to breach. Unauthorised intercepts are an offence and actionable. How is one to obtain necessary evidence when the perpetrators are likely to be cliques in the intelligence services or police? Other unauthorised action under the Act is not made 'lawful' but is not a statutory offence under RIPA. It may be actionable if tortious or an offence if otherwise criminal. It will also have to be consistent with the HRA. The Interception Commissioner and the Intelligence Services Commissioner report errors in warrants and authorisations but only numbers of cases going before the tribunal are reported – no details and not the outcome. Nor are innocent targets to be notified after the intercept etc. that they have been the subject of such action. This is the practice in Germany, Finland and Denmark but was felt to be too difficult in our jurisdiction.[133] The tribunal will operate like a court hearing a judicial review and is not meant to become involved with the merits of warrants and authorisations although in HRA cases it can apply proportionality. To assist the services and law enforcement agencies, a '24 hour' National Technical Assistance Centre has been established. This will provide a central facility for complex processing and will include internet services. It will be operated by the SOCA.

In April 2009, the government announced a review of RIPA because of widespread concerns over the use of the Act.

Inquiries and national security

National security has found its way into the Inquiries Act 2005. Section 19 restricts public access to inquiries on a number of grounds including national security. Orders may be indefinite. Section 23(2) reverses the PI test under FOIA in relation to the order of information by an inquiry chair which risks damaging the UK economy. Under s. 25 material in reports may not be published where a wide range of harm may be caused including damage to national security. The Coroners and Justice Bill 2009 has provisions for inquests into deaths to be conducted by a High Court judge without a jury and not by a coroner where matters are raised that should not be public. These include national security, international relations, preventing crime, preventing harm to a witness or otherwise in the interests of justice. These matters are certified by the Secretary of State. A possible concession might provide that a judge issues the certificate with an appeal against that decision (see Introduction p. 4). The provisions follow highly publicised events when coroners have been critical of the non-production of information by the US authorities concerning episodes of death by friendly fire of UK military personnel. The courts had decided cases introducing greater powers into the scope of coroners' inquiries and conclusions.[134]

---

[133] See I. Cameron, (1985) Mod LR 201.
[134] Cm. 6849, Coroner Reform: The Government's draft bill.

Reform – some food for thought?[135]

Here it is pertinent to note that a 1981 Canadian report from the Commission of Inquiry Concerning Certain Activities of the Royal Canadian Mounted Police[136] (the McDonald Commission) has affirmed that the principle 'of the Rule of Law and of responsible, government in a liberal democracy' should govern the organisation of security intelligence work and policing generally. The report is voluminous, and exhaustive in its investigations, which took place over a three-and-a-half-year period. It found numerous breaches of the law by security officers and deliberate withholding of relevant or significant information' from the ministers who were responsible. A crucial recommendation of the McDonald Commission was that a security agency's mandate must be 'clear and public' and must be stated in the legislation which would establish the agency. The agency's activities in relation to security and its responsibilities should be defined in statute and not 'diffuse and ambiguous' sources arising as they did from a 'melange of Cabinet directives, ministerial correspondence and unstated RCMP assumptions'. As well as arguing for more ministerial and judicial involvement in surveillance and information acquisition, the report also proposed an independent review body with complete access to the new agency's records, and a Security Appeals Tribunal to hear appeals against decisions in security-screening procedures. The review body would be advisory, not executive, and would report to the Solicitor General and to a parliamentary joint standing committee on security and intelligence.

The Canadian Security Intelligence Services Act 1984 created the Canadian Security Intelligence Service. The director is 'under the direction of the minister'. The minister has power to give written directions to the director, copies of which are given to the Security Intelligence Review Committee (SIRC) which was established under the Act. It has been argued that the Act falls short of the McDonald Commission's recommendations, though the service's mandate is spelt out in statute[137] and it has to report to and advise the Canadian Government. Members of the SIRC are privy councillors (but not current senators and MPs). A complaints procedure is established for individuals concerning the activities of the security intelligence service, together with an inspector general (IG) who has powers of monitoring and review, though not as wide ranging as the SIRC's. Cabinet secrets are precluded from investigation by either the IG or the SIRC. The SIRC differs markedly from the McDonald proposals as it is not a joint parliamentary committee. It nevertheless has full powers of access to agency records, reports annually to Parliament, and reports to the minister.

---

[135] See G. Hannah, K. O'Brien and A. Rathmell, *Intelligence and Security Legislation for Security Sector Reform* (Rand Europe, 2005).

[136] Ottawa: Minister of Supply, 1981. The report was in three volumes; see A. Goldsmith (1985) Public Law 39; I. Cameron (n. 133 above).

[137] Which directs the service to 'collect, by investigation or otherwise, to the extent that it is strictly necessary, and analyse and retain information and intelligence respecting activities that may on reasonable grounds be suspected of constituting threats to the security of Canada'.

The Commission under Mr Justice McDonald reported that while the security services of other liberal democracies are not a matter of public record, he doubted whether they were completely innocent of the kind of excesses the Commission recorded in the Canadian security service. Britain is a case in point.

The Canadian Department of Public Safety and Emergency Preparedness Act 2005 was a significant addition to statutory changes to the intelligence framework in Canada since 1981. Under this statute all of the entities concerned with national security in the Canadian Government became part of the new Department of Public Safety and Emergency Preparedness Canada. The aim of this was to centralise the intelligence network under a singular command; in that respect it is similar to the creation of the Department of Homeland Security in the US. Apparently the Sub-Committee on National Security in Canada's Parliament have expressed the desire to include elements of oversight and accountability for Canada's security and intelligence in their eventual mandate.[138]

Serious thought does need to be given to the following points: do the complaints procedures in the UK legislation need strengthening; should oversight be allowed of operational activities; should there be publication – at ten-year intervals – of details of the major activities of the services? Information (redacted) is provided on interception warrants, numbers of complaints referred to the tribunal, numbers of positive vetting referrals handled. Should there be more information on the services' opinion on threats and priorities in the relevant period; a case history relevant to the services' work from each branch; and a statement from each director etc. relating to any significant changes in practice?[139] Few citizens would accept that they as individuals have a need to know the details of security operations. But that does not mean that knowledge and oversight would not be more effective, and thereby a greater safeguard for civil liberties, if they were more widely established as suggested. Such a development has taken place in Australia.[140] This followed a Royal Commission under Mr Justice Hope. Australia has a joint parliamentary committee to oversee the activities of the Security and Intelligence Organisation, and an inspector general (IG) to hear complaints from officers. A charter spells out the powers and responsibilities of the organisation, and its director general reports to the minister, and has to obtain the approval of the Attorney General for phone taps and other sensitive operations. The relevant Australian legislation – the Australian Security and Intelligence Organisation Act 1979 – is fifty-six pages long; the UK legislation, excluding RIPA, is under half that length. The Act provides for legal assistance for complainants, costs, witnesses' fees and so on before the Security Appeals Tribunal, which deals with security clearance. The IG of intelligence

---

[138] A National Security Committee of Parliamentarians: A Consultation Paper to Help Inform the Creation of a Committee of Parliamentarians to Review National Security (2004), ww2.ps-sp.gc.ca/publications/national_security/nat_sec_cmte_e.asp.

[139] Suggested by Conservative MP, R. Shepherd, HC Debs., col. 245 (16 January 1989).

[140] See below.

and security acts as an ombudsman for the public and has unlimited powers to obtain information. An agreed report may be shown to a complainant. All ministerial directions on security and intelligence must be shown to the IG.

In Australia, the Intelligence Services Act 2001[141] is a key piece of legislation which establishes a statutory footing for the Australian Secret Intelligence Service (ASIS) and confirms its remit. The relevant minister may direct the actions of ASIS so long as he has consulted other relevant ministers and is satisfied that there are satisfactory arrangements to ensure that the actions do not go beyond what is necessary and that the consequences are reasonable. The remit of the DSD (essentially Department of Defence) is defined and ministerial oversight is provided for, with the DSD and ASIS having to obtain authorisation before commencing activities. Limits are placed on the agencies' functions and activities. The statute provides for co-operation between agencies.[142]

The responsible minister in relation to ASIS, and the responsible minister in relation to DSD, must make written rules regulating the communication and retention by the relevant agency of intelligence information concerning Australian persons. The appointment of the director general is provided for and his role is to control and manage ASIS – he is under the relevant minister. Provision is also made for an oversight committee on ASIO (ASIO is the security service), ASIS and DSD. Its functions are as follows:

(a) to review the administration and expenditure of ASIO, ASIS and DSD, including the annual financial statements of ASIO, ASIS and DSD
(b) to review any matter in relation to ASIO, ASIS or DSD referred to the Committee by:
  (i) the responsible minister or
  (ii) a resolution of either House of the Parliament
(c) to report the Committee's comments and recommendations to each House of the Parliament and to the responsible minister.

There are also some provisions on the communication of intelligence information. Further amendments are in the ASIO Legislation Amendment (Terrorism) Act 2003 and the Intelligence Services Amendment Act 2004.

The 9/11 attacks caused major changes to the US intelligence network. A CIA Office of Inspector General's Report on CIA Accountability with Respect to the 9/11 Attacks[143] was finalised in June 2005 but remained secret until its public release in August 2007. It was conducted by the CIA's Office of Inspector General at the request of the Senate Select Committee on Intelligence and the House Permanent Select Committee. The report comments on the various failings of the CIA leading up to the 9/11 attacks. This report led to the downfall of CIA director, George Tenet. The main areas for concern were: senior leadership,

---

[141] www.comlaw.gov.au/ComLaw/Legislation/Act1.nsf/0/9CCEEBDEDDD27800CA25741000056 C26/$file/1522001.pdf. See also ASIS website, www.asis.gov.au/.
[142] Obviously, sharing of intelligence is vital but not always practised.
[143] www.cia.gov/library/reports/Executive%20Summary_OIG%20Report.pdf.

management of resources, information-sharing, strategic analysis, operations, covert action, and technology.

The Senate Select Committee on Intelligence's Report on the US Intelligence Community's Prewar Intelligence Assessments on Iraq[144] noted a number of failures by the security services, mainly regarding the methods of intelligence analysts and general accountability.

The US legislative response to the 9/11 events involved the Homeland Security Act 2002[145] which introduced the critical infrastructure and information security provisions – basically providing widespread exclusions to the US FOIA, an information directorate for security analysis and information-sharing provisions. The Act introduced a comprehensive framework for ensuring the effectiveness of information security controls over information resources that support Federal operations and assets and security controls for federal information. The Protect America Act 2007 introduced powers (under sunset provisions) to obtain evidence without warrant by electronic surveillance to legitimise a practice that had been going on for some time. Finally, the Foreign Intelligence Surveillance Act 1978 Amendments Act 2008 liberalises the wiretapping laws (intercepts) and protects phone companies from legal liability for wiretapping activities.

The cost of freedom of information to national security

National security, and the activities and oversight of those responsible for national security, is a difficult but instructive testing ground for problems associated with freedom of information. It is an area where government has made concessions to provision of more information if not openness. Cutting through the arguments supporting or undermining the existing state of operations, there is one factor implicit in this or any government's reckoning. That is cost. The cost of opening up the world of security operations, it argues, even on the scale suggested above, would be destructive of our security. Giving more information, even to limited numbers of elected representatives, would increase the risk of leaks and treasonable use of information. The consequences would affect all of us. It is a constant conflict zone between executive efficacy and democratic accountability. Before we can examine freedom of information we have to analyse the wider legal framework for controlling information.

[144] www.gpoaccess.gov/serialset/creports/iraq.html.
[145] www.dhs.gov/xlibrary/assets/hr_5005_enr.pdf.

3

Government and information: a historical development

Government control of information in Britain did not first emerge as a problem for government in 1889, when the first Official Secrets Act was passed.[1] Control of information had been a central preoccupation of government since government first assumed responsibility for defence, taxation and administration, and even before. The King's household, until the Tudor monarchy, was characterised by personal government on the advice of trusted counsellors who remained bound by allegiance and confidence to the Crown. Serious breaches of confidence might involve a charge of treason in the form of adhering to the King's enemies under the Act of 1351, which was extended well beyond the terms of the statute by judicial decisions.[2] High treason 'was regarded as a final denial of the divine order of things as established in the body politic and defined in the oath of allegiance'.[3]

Breaches of confidence were not always problematic in the absence of widespread printing and publishing facilities. More pressing for the power in existence was the control of the spread of seditious ideas or movements which could threaten its position. This point is vividly illustrated by the breach with the Church of Rome and the accumulation of statutes extending treason to punish *inter alios* those who:

> shall by writing, printing, preaching, speech, express words or sayings, maliciously, advisedly and directly publish, set forth, and affirm that the Queen our said sovereign lady Queen Elizabeth is an heretic, schismatic, tyrant, infidel or an usurper of the Crown of the said realms or any of them . . . [4]

Even before the advent of the Tudor dynasty, the procedure for treason trials was weighted heavily in favour of the Crown.[5] What was novel about the Tudor dynasty was the revolution in government which took place.[6]

---

[1] As first drafted, it was entitled Breach of Official Trust Bill. For a contemporary analysis of secrecy see A. Roberts, *Blacked Out: Government secrecy in the information age* (2006).

[2] G. R. Elton, *The Tudor Constitution*, 2nd edn (1981), p. 59; Cf. J. Bellamy, *The Tudor Law of Treason* (1979).

[3] Elton, *The Tudor Constitution*.   [4] 13 Eliz. I, c. I (1571).

[5] Elton, *The Tudor Constitution*, though see his *Policy and Police* (1972).

[6] G. R. Elton, *The Tudor Revolution in Government* (1953).

After 1530, there was:

> a rejection of the medieval conception of the kingdom as the King's estate, his private concern properly administered by his private organisation; it conceived its task to be national, its support and scope to be nationwide, and its administrative needs, therefore, divorced from the King's household.[7]

On governmental administration, the change is characterised by the individual assertion of King's advisers as opposed to the 'anonymity' of the medieval period. Almost all the available state papers from 1530–40 are those of Thomas Cromwell, Henry VIII's minister of state. A fastidious keeper of records, he also presided over an Act of 1536 'concerning the Clerkes of the Signet and Privie Seale' which enacted that no manner of writing was to pass the great seals[8] of England, Ireland, the Duchy of Lancaster and the Principality of Wales, or 'by process out of the Exchequer', unless it had first been examined by the King's principal secretary or a clerk of the signet.[9]

From the mid-1530s onwards, the Privy Council developed as an institution whose name signified 'the special "secretness" or closeness to the King of his more intimate advisers', a 'special and more important branch of the Council' based upon the exclusiveness of its nineteen or so members.[10] Nevertheless, although the Council established its right to information, particularly on foreign affairs, Cromwell 'knew and insisted that serious business should be transacted in conversations with the King and himself'.[11] He acted, according to Elton, 'in practice like a somewhat despotic Prime Minister presiding over a Cabinet of comparative mediocrities'. The period witnessed the emergence of national departments of state, bureaucratically organised and independent of the King's household, but responsible to the Crown. Responsibility to Parliament had yet to come, but we should note that proceedings in Parliament itself were secret, breach of secrecy constituting a serious contempt. By Elizabethan times, parliamentary affairs were 'the common talk of tavern life',[12] however, in spite of the injunction that 'Every person of the Parliament ought to keep secret, and not to disclose, the secrets and things done and spoken in the Parliament house'.[13] Freedom of debate, and freedom from the monarch's intervention, required secrecy. In 1628, it was confirmed that speeches would not be printed in the *Journal*, but by 1641 the House decided to print various notes and minutes of its proceedings to gain support in the City against Charles I.[14] In 1771, the House commenced proceedings against John Wilkes, who had published details of parliamentary proceedings.[15] The House of Commons won its legal case, but press

---

[7] *Ibid.*, p. 4.   [8] See ch. 3 of Elton, *The Tudor Constitution* for a discussion of the seals.

[9] The fine for disobedience was £10 – half to the Crown and half to the informer

[10] Elton, *The Tudor Revolution in Government*, p. 316 *et seq.*   [11] *Ibid.*, p. 355.

[12] J. E. Neale, *The Elizabethan House of Commons* (1949), p. 416 *et seq.*

[13] Cited in D. Englefield, *Parliament and Information* (1980).

[14] *Ibid.* Note, C. Parry, 'Legislatures and secrecy' (1954) 67 Harv LR 737.

[15] The House still maintains its right to secure the privacy of its debates, e.g. in wartime. The Parliamentary Papers Act 1840 gave the protection of absolute privilege to parliamentary

reporting developed informally in ensuing years. Such reporting was assisted by the growing practice of Parliament publishing its reports which brought the subject of parliamentary privilege into conflict with the legal right right not to be defamed,[16] most famously in *Stockdale v Hansard* and subsequent litigation.[17]

Crown, mace and information

Parliament saw secrecy for its proceedings as a necessary protection against the Crown's absolutist tendencies. An astute monarch had other ways of rendering Parliament compliant. His advisers, by courtesy of sympathetic MPs, would know what was what.

In 1641, Pym's Ten Propositions to the Lords included as number three that the King commit 'his own business, and the affairs of the Kingdom, to such councillors and officers as the Parliament may have cause to confide in'. The Nineteen Propositions of Parliament of 1 June 1642 proposed that privy councillors and ministers be approved by both Houses of Parliament. Further:

> the great affairs of the Kingdom may not be concluded or transacted by the advice of private men, or by any unknown or unsworn councillors, but that such matters as concern the public, and *are proper for the High Court of Parliament*... may be debated, resolved and transacted only in Parliament, and not elsewhere[18]

and the King should act only on the public behalf on the advice of a majority of privy councillors. Parliament wanted to know who advised the King, so that they could be made accountable to Parliament. How had this come to pass?

Information and accountability – the struggle

In a system of government that is monistic – that is, one that is assembled around one power base – accountability is achieved by protection of the status quo through the power of tradition, the force of custom, the influence of an unquestioned hierarchy reflecting a naturally ordained harmony: 'Take but degree away, untune that string / And, hark! what discord follows.'[19] When government is arranged around pluralistic competing forces, any assertion of a status quo maintaining the natural supremacy of one branch of public power

papers. For the position of command papers, see HC 261 (1969–70) and Cmnd 5909, p. 55. Press and broadcast reports are protected by qualified privilege: see P. Leopold on 'live' broadcasting (1987) Public Law 524.

[16] Unless authorised by *legislation*.

[17] *Stockdale v Hansard* (1839) 9 Ad & El 1 in which the claimant successfully sued Hansard for publishing a libel in a report published by order of Parliament; *Case of Sheriff of Middlesex* (1840) 11 Ad & El 273. An order of the House of Commons could not override the common law of defamation. However, the courts in the second case were powerless to intervene by habeas corpus in the face of a statement from the House that Stockdale and two sheriffs had been committed by the House for contempt when attempting to enforce the earlier judgment. The impasse led to the Parliamentary Papers Act 1840.

[18] My emphasis.   [19] *Troilus and Cressida*, I, iii, 109.

over another is less readily justified by appeals to tradition. The emerging conflict between competing forces inevitably centres on the *nature* of accountability itself – what form does it take, to whom and by what process? Accountability is impossible in any real sense unless the body exercising power accounts to whoever asserts the right to expect an explanation, a justification for action or inaction, for acts of prerogative and for policy. Knowing who did what, and why, is the first step to rendering an institution or person accountable.

In the English tradition, the King escaped personal liability in law – the King can do no wrong.[20] Bracton wrote that the King was beneath God and the law. There was no legal machinery of enforcement. Five important factors emerge on the route to constitutional monarchy: the Crown must act through a servant; a servant cannot plead in defence an unlawful command of the King; the King must be advised by councillors acceptable to Parliament; the King's will must be a matter of record; and the Commons has the power of inquiry as a necessary prelude to impeachment of the Crown's ministers.[21] Honoured as much in the breach as in the observance, these principles, their development and scope taxed the minds of the finest constitutional and legal experts of the seventeenth century as well as, with necessary modifications, their counterparts in America in more recent times.[22]

By the beginning of the seventeenth century, the problem facing Parliament in controlling the King concerned control over his policies, which meant, in turn, the problem of who should advise on those policies. The claim that the Crown had a prerogative right to choose its own advisers without parliamentary interference fell increasingly on deaf ears when the Commons from 1604 'sought to superintend a public, not a personal, administration' of the Crown.[23]

Equally important was the emergence of the Commons as *the* force in Parliament with an established political and corporate identity. The English Revolution began in a constitutional, if not material, sense when the Commons insisted on being informed of who advised the Crown so that they could be made accountable for any 'unlawful, injurious or hateful' advice and policies. Unlike the barons of previous centuries, who were content to bloody the King's nose on individual occasions by punishing his high advisers, the Commons was embarking on a process that would lead to oversight of public administration. On the eve of the Civil War in 1642, what most members wished for was 'the right to vote impeachments against ministers whose faults they could declare to be crimes, and the right to vote censures against counsellors whose advice to the King they could read in Council books'.[24] Parliamentarians and pamphleteers realised that it was of cardinal importance to discover who provided the King

---

[20] Although events as far back as 1215 testified to the view that the King could do wrong, see Art. 61 *Magna Carta*.

[21] C. Roberts, *The Growth of Responsible Government in Stuart England* (1966), ch. 1.

[22] The Watergate and Irangate, or Snoozegate, episodes, for instance and Clinton's sexual peccadilloes. See R. Berger, *Impeachment* (1973).

[23] Roberts, *The Growth of Responsible Government*, p. 9.   [24] *Ibid.*, p. 118.

with 'evil counsel', not simply to punish those who followed his 'tyrannous' orders. Publicity of advice was the universal desideratum. Its realisation, of course, would run counter to every tradition of government.

The Commons wanted to know, not necessarily to nominate. The interregnum of 1649–60 was seen by many as an illustration of the undesirability of placing the executive within the legislature so that both were part of an indiscriminate whole. In that period, however, there were:

> [by] the right of inquiry, of the right of interrogation, of the right of surveillance, of the right of criticism, and of the right of censure inculcated in MPs habits not even the Restoration could erase. [MPs] . . . questioned ministers of state. They clamoured for information. They objected to oaths of secrecy taken by their own committees. They sent committees of inquiry into the counties. They examined accounts and appropriated revenues. They investigated military failures and criticised naval designs. They opposed, condemned, criticised and censured those whom they found remiss in the performance of their duties.[25]

By 1667, Charles II had to accept a statutory commission with power to subpoena any royal servant and cross-examine him under oath and with access to all records vis-à-vis the public accounts. There was a regal reaction. Increasing use was made of special committees of the Privy Council to deal with confidential matters, e.g. the Committee of Intelligence and the 'Cabinet Council'. Charles promised to discuss affairs of public importance with the Privy Council at all times. A small group of confidential ministers acted as 'an informal quorum' of the Council, a trend which James II continued and reinforced:

> Throughout this century, behind the formal apparatus of councils, cabinets, committees and camarillas lay the simple, usually quite easy, relationship between the King and one or two trusted ministers . . . The really important decisions were taken in complete privacy, without surviving records.[26]

A royal proclamation of 1674 forbade Charles's subjects to 'intermeddle in private discourse with state affairs, or the persons of the King's ministers'. By that date, however, the Commons had questioned his ministers on 'the innermost secrets of state', and had voted addresses to the Crown for their removal, refusing to grant supply until they were. To extract advice given to the King in his Cabinet Council, his advisers had to be brought before the Commons and intimidated. If that failed, the Commons had to resort to common fame: if a minister was known to be a party to the Council which advised the King and of which the Commons disapproved, this could form the basis of an address from the Commons that he be removed from office – but it could not form the basis of an impeachment. The enduring legacy of Court and parliamentary battles between the years 1674 and 1681 was the voting of addresses against the King's ministers, not the voting of impeachments, which were dilatory and clumsy affairs. Having secured freedom of speech, debate and proceedings in

[25] *Ibid.*, p. 153.   [26] J. P. Kenyon, *The Stuart Constitution*, 1st edn (1966), p. 479.

1689,[27] Parliament, in the Act of Settlement of 1701, insisted that important business was to be conducted in the Privy Council and councillors were to sign all resolutions to which they assented. This solved the problem of identity, but it was unworkable and was repealed in 1706.

Also repealed in 1706 was the clause of the 1701 Act which stipulated that 'no person who has an office or place of profit under the King . . . shall be capable of serving as a member of the House of Commons'. As the eighteenth century unfolded, it became increasingly obvious that a most commodious partnership between Crown and Parliament could be built around an arrangement whereby the King appointed as leading ministers those who could control the Commons but the Commons, on their side, knew who they were. That did not mean they were entitled to know what ministers knew. Ministers might be forced to resign because of a lack of confidence among members of Parliament, but the Commons has rarely questioned ministers' right to keep confidential the innermost secrets of the Cabinet, the closet or even, in the absence of an untoward event, the department of state. The Commons in its collective identity might not expect this, but others, including individual MPs, the press and the public, have. The Commons is generally content to be informed on terms laid down by the executive. At that moment when the power of the Commons to inquire into Crown business was unequivocally established, it was only operable to the extent that the power of a minister controlling a majority party in the Commons allowed it. The implications for his own position, should an inquiry cause embarrassment, were obvious enough. In a parliamentary system of government, the emergence of collective and individual responsibility of ministers seemed inescapable. The irony is that the doctrines our forebears chanced upon to gain information on who was responsible for what, came to constitute the greatest barrier to a wider parliamentary and public access to information.

By the early 1700s it was established that Parliament could inquire, investigate and criticise; but ministers initiated. And what is more, they selected the materials for investigation:

> this enquiry, Sir, will produce no great information if those whose conduct is examined, are allowed to select the evidence.[28]

Throughout the later stages of the eighteenth century and into the nineteenth century there was a growth of interest among ordinary MPs in every aspect of executive activity, initiated by concern over expenditure. With an increasing interest in social and economic problems it was inevitable that the Grand Inquest of the Nation would:

---

[27] Bill of Rights, I Will. and Mary, Sess. 2, c. 2.

[28] William Pitt, *Parl. Hist. England* (1741), II, p. 1009, cited in R. Berger, *Executive Privilege* (1974). Berger believes that Parliament asserted an unqualified right: 'it is our duty', said Pitt, 'to inquire into every step of publick management, either abroad or at home, in order to see that nothing is done amiss' (pp. 169–71). Berger's own choice of examples does not support this see p. 170.

inquire into everything which it concerns the public well to know; and *they themselves* I think, are entrusted with the determination of what falls within that category.[29]

As we shall see, this is a high-water mark, for they may inquire into what they want but they do not always get what they want. We should not think that the desire for a greater dissemination of information was restricted to Parliament, however.

Information and censorship

Although the demands for information and accountability formed the constitutional centrepiece of the seventeenth century, a wider audience was also involved. It was a period of prevalent censorship, although this had existed since 1408 and Archbishop Arundel's *Constitutions*. Henry VIII imposed religious censorship in 1530 before the breach with Rome, and this was augumented by royal proclamations, injunctions, Privy Council orders and Star Chamber decrees. The Star Chamber decree of 11 July 1637 was 'the most elaborate instrument in English history for the suppression of undesired publication; nothing was unforeseen except the determination with which it was defied'.[30] It became a general offence to print, import or sell 'any seditious, scismaticall or offensive Bookes or Pamphlets', and no book could be printed unless licensed, or relicensed if previously printed, and entered into the Stationers' Register.[31] The abolition of Star Chamber in 1641 left the press virtually without regulation, confirming Selden's remarks that there is 'no Law to prevent the printing of any Bookes in England, only a decree in Star Chamber'. The control over printing had been an exercise of royal prerogative. The public might write of the benefits on the alternatives of who should counsel the King in a way they had never done before, but such publication was short-lived. By June 1643, Parliament passed an order which Milton described as the 'immediate image' of the decree of 1637. This order stimulated his *Areopagitica* containing his famous defence of freedom of the press and, excluding Catholics, religious toleration. The order established 'licensing, registration, signature, copyright, import control, search and seizure, arrest, imprisonment by order of Parliamentary committee and association of the Stationers in administering the order'.[32] Except for short periods in the Commonwealth, the Puritan Revolution maintained a continuous licensing of printing in England. The preoccupation of censors turned more and more to the prohibition of obscene, scandalous or scurrilous literature, which in the hands of a Walpole could be moulded into a pervasive form of political censorship, even though general censorship of the press under law

[29] *Howard v Gosset* (1845) 10 QB 359, at 379–80, per Coleridge J. Unqualified acceptance of this dictum by Berger seems a little incautious.

[30] *Complete Prose Works of John Milton* (Yale University Press, 1958), vol. 2, p. 159.

[31] The Stationers' Company owned a monopoly of book publishing in England.

[32] Berger, *Executive Privilege*, p. 163.

by the Stationers' Company ceased in 1694.[33] The Spycatcher episode in the second half of the 1980s, which I examine elsewhere, at one stage threatened to resurrect a wide form of legal censorship from the seventeenth century.[34]

The executive and Parliament – the die is cast

From 1670 onwards, the Commons 'became immensely sensitive to the tactics used by the Court to circumscribe their activities or reduce their capacity for independent criticism. Naturally, they feared secret influence and they called time and time again for a statement about expenditure from the Secret Service Fund.'[35] Sir Robert Walpole was, by the 1720s, the controller of the Secret Service money and, in that capacity, was rightly regarded as the head of the government's patronage system and thus the 'chief figure in the Ministry'.[36] He dedicated his efforts to an obsessive anti-Jacobite campaign, building up a 'vast web of counter-espionage with his own spies in all capitals and ports in Europe'.[37] He preferred to use ad hoc meetings of an inner Cabinet, meeting in the houses of the chief secretaries, instead of the full Cabinet which was large and unwieldy, or to have secret discussions with 'his tried and loyal supporters' or private individual interviews. 'He preferred the closet to the Cabinet', or at best a small efficient Cabinet in which he could secure a majority.[38] All the while his 'love of administration, his desire to see it based efficiently on knowledge [and information] was very much in tune with the more advanced opinion of his age'.[39] It is hardly surprising that it was Walpole's use of Secret Service money for covert purposes which activated some of the most heated exchanges between Parliament and government in this period on Parliament's right to be informed.

By the second half of the eighteenth century, the Commons could exercise its right to information in a variety of ways. A member could move that 'a return should be made to the House providing statistical or other information about a specific subject',[40] such as the collection and management of the tax revenue, public expenditure and general statistics. 'But information about the exercise of the prerogative, e.g. treaties with foreign powers, dispatches to and from Governors of colonies, and returns connected with the administration of justice or the activities of one of the Secretaries of State could be obtained only by an address to the Crown.'[41] The House could not demand this information; it had to request politely.

---

[33] W. S. Holdsworth, 'Press Control and Copyright in the Sixteenth and Seventeenth Centuries' (1920) 29 Yale LJ 841. For censorship and obscenity law, see G. Robertson, *Obscenity* (1979).

[34] P. 438 *et seq.* below.

[35] J. H. Plumb, *The Growth of Political Stability in England 1675–1725* (1967), p. 47

[36] J. H. Plumb, *Sir Robert Walpole* (1956), vol. 1, p. 348.   [37] *Ibid.* (1960), vol. 2, p. 41.

[38] *Ibid.*, p. 330.   [39] *Ibid.*, p. 234.

[40] Sir Norman Chester, *The English Administrative System 1780–1870* (1981). I am indebted to Chester's work for information on the following six pages.

[41] *Ibid.*, p. 99.

The government also provided information by way of reports and papers circulated by command of the Crown. This was the usual arrangement for the reports and evidence of Royal Commissions. An increasing number of reports were ordered to be printed by the Commons, not the least of which were the reports of the factory inspectors to the Home Secretary, a point seized on by Karl Marx in *Das Kapital*. These were published every six months, and 'They therefore provide regular and official statistics of the voracious appetite of the capitalists for surplus labour.'[42] However, 'let us note that England figures in the foreground here because it is the classic representative of capitalist production, and it is the only country to possess a continuous set of official statistics relating to the matters we are considering', viz. capitalist economic exploitation.

Sir Norman Chester remarked how a requirement to provide returns and annual reports became a regular feature of Acts of Parliament. 'As early as 1787 an Act[43] placed an obligation on the Treasury to lay before Parliament annually an account of the produce of the duties of Customs, Excise, Stamps and the Expenses.'[44] From 1803, the Treasury had to submit each year an account of the total revenues of Great Britain, together with an account of the Consolidated Fund and other financial details. Information was required on a regular basis on the activities of the executive in areas of current concern.[45] The requests produced an increasing workload for departments, necessitating the creation of specialised officers. In 1832, a statistical branch in the Board of Trade was agreed to by the Treasury.

Special agencies, boards or even local councils created by Parliament inevitably had to report back to Parliament, sometimes directly, more usually via a minister. Inspectors of Prisons appointed under an Act of 1835 are an example of the latter, and the Registrar of Joint Stock Companies reported back via the Board of Trade. Even where a statute remained silent on the duty of publication, practice often dictated that reports would be submitted to Parliament via the minister, e.g. reports of inspectors of schools and factories.

Committees of MPs could take evidence and report with recommendations, providing 'a mass of information not only to Parliament but also for the Press and general public'.[46] However, these committees existed only for one session, and often could not complete their inquiries. They were not peripatetic, so witnesses had to be summoned to London. Nor was there a guarantee that a government would do anything about their recommendations. Between 1832 and 1862, 'Some 190 Royal Commissions were appointed to deal with subjects such as: Poor Relief; Municipal Corporations; Education; Military Promotions and County Courts.' They were appointed and had their terms of reference drawn up by the government. Departmental committees, though not popular

[42] Pelican edition (1976), vol. 1, p. 349.   [43] 27 Geo. III, c. 13.

[44] Chester, *The English Administrative System*, p. 101.

[45] E.g., the numbers employed by public departments and in public offices, as well as their salaries, 50 Geo. III, c. 117: Chester, *The English Administrative System*, p. 100.

[46] *Ibid.*, pp. 102–3.

before 1870, were used. They comprised two or three officials, but were under no obligation to publish their reports. The Northcote-Trevelyan Report of 1854 on the civil service is a famous example of such a report which was in fact published and formed the basis of civil service reform for well into the twentieth century.

Nor were changes in government administration the only development. In 1803 the House recognised the right of the press by reserving special seats in the public gallery for the use of reporters. *Hansard* reports of debates commenced in the same year. Published debates became far more detailed; official division lists were published in 1836, thereby making it clear how particular MPs had voted. 'This made Members more consciously answerable to their constituents or to the outside groups interested in the outcome of their vote.'[47] More frequent publication of parliamentary materials and greater availability of information became increasingly common. Parliamentary questions became more ordered and routinised, as did MPs' questioning of ministers on the floor of the House.

However, government still had ultimate control over what became public. Certain areas, while not arousing a great deal of public interest, were sensitive; these included police special branch, aliens, subversives and foreign policy. In foreign policy, dispatches and 'blue books'[48] were doctored before publication, or correspondence was simply not acknowledged. The Reform Acts of 1832 and 1867 helped to dismember the old consensus which had developed throughout the previous century between government and parliamentary elites. The growth of the press, the emergence of strong political parties and organised party political conflict, the development of interest group politics[49] all contributed to a wider group beyond the two above which wished to be informed of public business. Until the 1830s, the battle for information had largely been fought out in a constitutional struggle between Crown and Commons, and between court and country. The reforms of the nineteenth century acted as a midwife to a prolonged labour for a fuller democracy. It was time for power-holders not only to set the agenda for Parliament but to take active steps to prevent an unwished-for dissemination of information from departments of state.

Make no mistake, we have witnessed an enormous growth in the information business until the 1870s; government could not resist that. But information was provided on terms. The moment that compact was threatened by forces beyond the control of government and Parliament, the government felt the necessity for legislation to maintain the culture of secrecy. 'As newspapers . . . became almost as much a part of the political arena as the chamber of the House of Commons so most permanent officials learned to keep away from them.'[50] But not all officials or citizens wanted this isolation. Even in the eighteenth century,

---

[47] *Ibid.*, pp. 107–9.
[48] These were despatches between the British Government, its embassies and foreign governments. I am grateful to Bernard Porter for this information.
[49] S. H. Beer, *Modern British Politics* (1982).
[50] Chester, *The English Administrative System*, p. 108.

societies aimed at the spread of public opinion were legion[51] and included the Society for Constitutional Information. Trade and work associations emerged alongside older corporatist groups such as the church, aristocracy, country gentry, the Inns of Court and the universities.[52] Throughout the nineteenth century, however, a problem was developing within government departments. What if servants of the Crown broke their trust of confidentiality?

Officials and secrecy in central government

The Northcote-Trevelyan Report of 1854 recommended competitive entry to the civil service based upon examination. Sir George Cornewall Lewis wrote:

> One of the first qualities required in the clerks of a public office is trustworthiness . . . The honourable secrecy which has distinguished the clerks of our superior offices . . . cannot be too highly commended. But this discreet reserve depends on qualities which cannot be made the subject of examination.[53]

Much had changed in the previous years. In 1780, the typical 'Cabinet minister had the assistance of only a few clerks. The Home Office contained only four rooms and sometimes handled less than twenty letters a day.'[54]

The Treasury and Admiralty Boards, with 'satellite and subordinate departments', were much larger. Most of the departments had a small staff, who were largely engaged in copying documents and letters and other routine tasks.

By 1870, developments in administrative practice had altered departments beyond recognition. In the Treasury, the number of registered papers averaged between 2,500 and 3,000 a year in the period 1783–93; by 1800 it was 4,812. By 1820, the figure had risen to 22,288 and by 1849 it was 29,914. The Home Office was handling over 13,500 letters per annum.[55] The increasing number and routinisation of parliamentary questions and the increasing workload of departments meant that a minister could no longer answer all questions about his department impromptu. Notice of questions was required and permanent staff prepared the answers. The Home Secretary was particularly busy.[56]

As departments grew in size, the problem of confidentiality became more acute. Older clerks steeped in the traditions of Crown service were invariably able to maintain a discreet silence about their work. The increasing number of 'outsiders' appointed to senior posts were less tractable. It was not unknown for such senior officials to espouse a cause openly, e.g. free trade, or to liaise with MPs, to encourage the establishment of select committees and feed them

---

[51] E.g. Society for Supporting the Bill of Rights, the Society of the Freedom of the People (1792), the London Corresponding Society (1792).

[52] Beer, *Modern British Politics.*   [53] Chester, *The English Administrative System*, p. 158.

[54] *Ibid.*, p. 282 *et seq.* The Colonial Office in nine months in 1775–6 used 2,000 pens; it employed nine officials!

[55] *Ibid.*

[56] The Home Secretary was responsible for prisons, the police in a general sense, poor relief, factory conditions and local government.

with evidence. They advised in private and advocated in public. Reform, says Chester, was what they advocated.[57]

It was difficult for ministers to perceive how such behaviour was compatible with individual ministerial responsibility. It could reveal antagonisms; it could pressurise a minister into a course of conduct which he did not favour. Peel as prime minister referred to Trevelyan as a 'consummate fool' for publishing departmental information in a letter to the *Morning Chronicle*. What *was* expected is caught in the following lines of Sir James Stephen:[58]

> Be assured that...my office is, and, ought to be, that of a mere Subordinate...[an] effective and submissive Servant to its Head...he sustains the undivided responsibility for every decision taken here and that I am responsible only for supplying him...with all the necessary materials for forming such decisions.

Reports to departments by their inspectors and agencies often hit a controversial tone which governments found embarrassing and which was 'inconsistent with the character such reports ought to bear'. The Home Office instructed inspectors not to publish correspondence with the department or information outside the strict terms of their duties. The education minister censored and threatened to refuse to publish reports critical of government policy: 'It would be a mischievous principle, to lay down that the heads of each Department...should be compelled to print indiscriminately at the public cost everything sent into them by their subordinate agents.'[59] This problem would increase as departments syphoned off executive or regulatory functions to an ever-widening range of bodies.

Parliament had expressed its desire to be informed of the contents of reports from inspectors and agencies to departmental heads. The thrust of the argument was that Parliament had a right to be kept fully informed about the administration which it was responsible for financing, and this included the ungarbled comments of those who had direct oversight over aspects of that administration. The president (Secretary of State) of the Education Department expressed a point of general principle in 1863 when he stated that it was an issue of general importance 'whether in the Education Department there shall or shall not be that discipline which exists, and is found necessary, in every Department of the State'.[60] Administration was impossible without the loyalty of 'these gentlemen':[61]

> If the House chooses to say that the Inspectors are to report directly to it of course we shall instruct them to obey the order; but if the reports are to pass through our hands, I hold it to be the first principle of official duty to enforce that sort of reticence and reserve which all official men are bound to practise...no public Department...can be expected to carry on its Operations with success, if it is

---

[57] Chester, *The English Administrative System*, p. 312.   [58] *Ibid.*, p. 315.
[59] The Vice President of the Privy Council; Chester, *The English Administrative System*, p. 318.
[60] Chester, *The English Administrative System*, p. 320.
[61] See K. G. Robertson, *Public Secrets* (1982), ch. 4.

obliged to print controversies maintained against itself by the very persons whom it employs to carry out the objects entrusted to its charge.[62]

Inspectors were thus neutered in the fashion of other officials. A select committee investigated the question of ministerial censorship and reported that ministers had exercised their powers fairly and that no objection was made by ministers to *statements of facts*. This loophole was finally to be sealed in 1911.

Legal control of information

Franz Kafka wrote that 'Official decisions are as shy as young girls.' The government did not find them as shy as it would have liked. Legislation, it asserted, was necessary and justified to protect official secrets.

A series of events from the 1830s onwards highlighted particular problems for ministers and senior civil servants over unauthorised disclosure of official information. One concerned the sale and publication of diaries and memoirs kept by officials and diplomats and the government's attempts to prevent publication by court injunction.[63] The legal question concerned the right of property in the memoirs – usually concerning foreign affairs – and the Foreign Office was pressing for right of ownership and delivery to it of the papers. According to the records, the first case of this kind occurred in 1833, and judgment was entered for the Foreign Office. The government was successful in other cases. Establishing a right of property in the information that was in question in these cases was bound to cause legal complexity. Absent larceny or treason, and departments could find the position heavy going. Such was the case in 1847 when *The Times* published correspondence relating to the Congress of Vienna. The Foreign Office was advised that property rights were difficult to establish and publication was not prevented, in spite of the FO's rule that materials after 1760 were not available for public inspection. In other cases larceny was charged but an essential ingredient of the offence – permanent deprivation of the article in question where there had merely been a temporary removal and copying – was missing.[64] There was no legal concept of 'official information' which was protected by the law against unauthorised dissemination thereby rendering it an 'official secret'.

By the 1870s, the large anonymous government department had been established; ministerial responsibility was faithfully accepted and party loyalty and pressure would prevent parliamentary majorities pressing for information which could make them a nuisance. But could the ministers' servants be trusted?

---

[62] Chester, *The English Administrative System*, p. 320.

[63] See Robertson, *Public Secrets*, for examples from the public records.

[64] D. G. T. Williams, *Not In the Public Interest* (1965). The civil law of confidentiality was in an elementary state: *Prince Albert v Strange* (1849) 1 Mac. & G. 25.

In 1873 a Treasury minute, *The Premature Disclosure of Official Documents*, was issued.[65] It expressed concern at what today we would refer to as civil service 'leaks' to the press. Dismissal was threatened by the Lords Commissioners of the Treasury in cases where officials were guilty of these offences which were of 'the gravest character'. The minute appealed to the civil servants' sense of honour, fidelity and trustworthiness – in short, their bureaucratic professionalism. A further minute of 1875 warned civil servants of the serious consequences of close links with the press, and a Treasury minute of 1884 prohibited the publication of 'official information' without authority.[66] But neither the circulars nor minutes, nor an amendment to the law of larceny in 1861, plugged the holes. Home Office circulars of 1884 and 1896 to its factory inspectorates warned them not to disclose information to parliamentary committees or to courts where privilege could be claimed. Robertson has shown how by 1914 Treasury minutes, memoranda and rules covered diverse matters. These included the production of information before select committees of Parliament, the political activities of civil servants, restriction of publication by officials of works from official sources, and standardisation of the rules governing publication by departments of their documents. Exceptions were made for 'internal documents, foreign relations, privacy of the individual, secret service and "scalping" and other such atrocities in war'.[67] These remained completely secret.

The Treasury assumed responsibility from the Admiralty for drafting a bill making it an offence 'improperly [to] divulge official information'. This would cover the whole public service. After one abortive attempt, it passed into law as the Official Secrets Act 1889. The statute provided for the prosecution and punishment of unauthorised disclosure of official information by penalty of the criminal law. Details of this legislation are provided elsewhere.[68] By 1903, however, it was clear to the War Office that the legislation had incurable defects as it placed on the state the burden of proving both *mens rea* and that it was not in the interest of the state that such communication take place. Newspapers which published leaked information were not punished, and convictions could only be secured where the government testified to the truth of the information published. An official report of 1909 recommended greater powers of arrest and search and seizure.[69] The most persuasive evidence to the committee had related to German spies, about whom there were numerous cases. Not one case had been reported by the police, although information had been provided by

---

[65] Robertson, *Public Secrets*, p. 53 *et seq.*   [66] *Ibid.*

[67] *Ibid.*, p. 61. Hitherto, the Treasury allowed no publication of materials after 1759; the War Office after 1830; and the Home Office after 1778.

[68] Williams, *Not In the Public Interest.*

[69] A sub-committee on Foreign Espionage of the Committee of Imperial Defence conducted the investigation.

'private individuals', fuelling speculation as to their identity and motives and whether they in fact existed.[70]

The committee's recommendations were aimed at espionage, and so it recommended that the bill should be introduced by the Secretary for War and not the Home Secretary. This must rank as one of the most notable postures of disingenuousness by any government.

The Act of 1911

The Official Secrets Act which finally emerged in 1911 did not simply strengthen the anti-espionage provisions to assist national security in s. 1. Section 2 imposed the widest prohibition, on pain of criminal prosecution, on unauthorised dissemination of official information. And yet, s. 2 was not mentioned once in the parliamentary debates, nor did the government give a full explanation of the bill. Parliament was anxious to pass the bill to protect the security of the nation. 'There was no doubt, however,' believed Franks in his 1972 departmental report on s. 2, 'that the Bill had, and was intended by the Government to have, a wider scope.'[71] Franks's own account of the circumstances surrounding the enactment of the 1911 Act is succinct, but eloquent testimony:

> It was in these circumstances that the 1911 legislation passed through Parliament with little debate. The country was in crisis and it was late summer. The debates on the Bill in the House of Lords were brief and the House of Commons passed it in one afternoon with no detailed scrutiny and virtually without debate. The debates give a clear impression of crisis legislation, aimed mainly at espionage. Closer study, and reference to official sources, reveal a different story. This legislation had been long desired by governments. It had been carefully prepared over a period of years. One of its objects was to give greater protection against leakages of any kind of official information whether or not connected with defence or national security. This was clear enough from the text of the Bill alone. Although s. 2 of the Act was much wider in a number of respects than s. 2 of the 1889 Act, the files suggest that the Government in 1911 honestly believed that it introduced no new principle, but merely put into practice more effectually the principle of using criminal sanctions to protect official information. At all events, the Government elected not to volunteer complete explanations of their Bill in Parliament. And Parliament, in the special circumstances of that summer, did not look behind the explanations offered.[72]

The provisions of the Act require some general explanation. Franks pointed out that misapprehension was common; that many 'leaks' were not leaks at all,

---

[70] There were 47 allegations of espionage or suspicious activities by Germans in 1908, and 31 in the first three months of 1909: Robertson, *Public Secrets*, p. 64; see also D. French, 'Spy fever in Britain, 1900-1915' (1978) 21 The Historical Journal 355.

[71] Lord Franks, *Departmental Committee on Section 2 of the Official Secrets Act 1911*, Cmnd 5104, vol. I (1972), para. 53.

[72] *Ibid.*, para. 50.

but authorised; that the signing of a declaration of notice by all civil servants and government contractors, research workers and others does not mean that express prior authorisation for dissemination is *always* required; and the declaration does not mean that it covers *all* official information. The drafting was, however, ambiguous and misleading – one must suspect deliberately so. It was often referred to as a 'catch all' provision – that it covered leaks that were harmful to the public interest (PI) and those that were harmless. Franks also indicated that s. 2 did not stand alone; it supported the culture of secrecy and confidentiality that was inherent in the working of our constitution which we have examined along with vetting for sensitive posts, security classifications[73] and privacy markings. Security classifications until 1994 were: *Top Secret* – publication or disclosure would cause exceptionally great damage to the nation; *Secret* – publication, etc., would cause serious injury to the interests of the nation; *Confidential* – publication, etc., would be prejudicial to the interests of the nation; *Restricted* – publication, etc., would be undesirable in the interests of the nation. Privacy markings cover *Commercial – in Confidence; Management – in Confidence* and *Staff – in Confidence.* 'Confidential means secret.' As we shall soon see, security classifications were redrafted after the introduction of new official secrecy laws. The 'D notice' (now DA notice) system covering the press and media will be examined in chapter 9, together with other devices protecting secrecy.

In 1972, Franks found the case for change 'overwhelming'. But s. 2 survived until 1989. It had a remarkable durability. In December 1987, the Home Secretary, however, announced he was preparing a White Paper on 'reform'. Only once before, in 1939, had Parliament 'back-pedalled' on Official Secret Act (OSA) legislation when it legislated that s. 6 of the 1920 OSA, which concerned powers to obtain information in connection with offences under the OSAs, would only cover s. 1 offences and not s. 2 offences.[74] Section 1 is headed by the legend 'Penalties for Spying'.[75] In *Chandler v DPP*,[75] the House of Lords held that s. 1 was not restricted to spying, as was commonly thought, but also covered conspiracy to commit sabotage or enter a prohibited place intentionally, regardless of motive. In *Chandler* protestors had entered a US air base in England to demonstrate against the presence of nuclear weapons whose presence was not in the PI, they argued. In matters of defence, the PI was determined by the government not by protestors.

The OSA has mistakes in its drafting; its various bill stages in Parliament have been characterised by incomplete information and erroneous explanation. It has been used to threaten an MP.[76] The legislation was among the most widely

---

[73] The Radcliffe Report found that substantial amounts of documents were over-classified and should be downgraded, Cmnd 1681 *Security Procedures in the Public Service.*

[74] S. 6 OSA 1920.

[75] [1964] AC 763; and D. Thompson, 'The Committee of 100 and The Official Secrets Act 1911' (1963) Public Law 201.

[76] Duncan Sandys MP and HC 101 (1938–9) and HC 173 (1937–8). See an interesting note by A. I. L. Campbell, 'Ponting and privilege' (1985) Public Law 212. According to Middlemas, Lloyd

discussed of all laws in Britain and the current laws are still widely discussed.[77] Indeed, prosecution of and inability to prosecute former military, security and intelligence personnel in the late 1990s and into 2000 brought renewed attention.[78] Section 2 has now been consigned to history and repealed and its detailed provisions need not detain us but it operated to create a culture of apprehension and caution among civil servants. Such an ethos is likely to survive all but a genuine and complete relaxation of unnecessary secrecy laws.

Attempts at reform were made, including that by Mrs Thatcher shortly after taking office in 1979. This attempt was, however, sabotaged by the revelations of the Anthony Blunt affair when it was reported that the Queen's personal artistic adviser was a Russian spy and part of the unending Philby, Burgess and Maclean saga. Had the proposed bill been law, the press would not have been allowed to report these events prompting widespread accusations that the bill was in fact more repressive than s. 2. But change was forced upon the government by three events that threatened to take matters out of their control.

Nevertheless use of the Acts was not abated. Before Franks reported, there had been thirty prosecutions with twent-six convictions under s. 2 of the Act.[79] Since 1946 there had been twenty prosecutions under s. 1 of the Act for spying.[80] There were nineteen convictions. By 1 August 1978, a further five prosecutions had been brought under s. 2.[81] These involved three cases, one of which was concluded. In the same period there were six prosecutions under s. 1, with four convictions, and a fifth under s. 7.[82] Between 1 August 1978 and 9 February 1983, there were eleven prosecutions leading to ten convictions under s. 2.[83] There were five completed cases under s. 1, three of which led to prosecution. One further case led to a conviction under s. 2 alone, and another to a conviction under just s. 7 of the Act. In an additional case to the five, the police charged under s.

George was threatened in 1932 for using a Cabinet document in Parliament – (1976) Pol Q 39, citing CAB 63/45.

[77] D. Hooper, *Official Secrets: The use and abuse of the Act* (1987). Atomic Energy has special provisions under: the Atomic Energy Act 1946, ss. 11, 13; Atomic Energy Authority Act 1954, sch. 3, s. 6(3), covering prohibited places; Nuclear Installations Act 1965, s. 24 and sch. 1, and European Communities Act 1972, s. 11(2), covering Euratom institutions; and Radioactive Substances Act 1993, ss. 34 and 39 and Radioactive Materials (Road Transport) Act 1991, s. 5. See Nuclear Safeguards Act 2000; Anti-terrorism, Crime and Security Act 2001, Pt 8; and SI 403/2003. For specific statutory provisions prohibiting the disclosure of information acquired from citizens, see *Open Government*, Cm. 2290 (1993) App. B; and P. Birkinshaw, *Government and Information: The law relating to access, disclosure and their regulation*, 3rd edn (2005), Annex B.

[78] The cases of David Shayler and Richard Tomlinson former MI5 and MI6 agents respectively and their publications of life inside the services: see *AG v Times Newspapers Ltd* [2001] ECWA Civ 97, [2001] 1 WLR 885.

[79] Many s. 2 cases were tried by magistrates.

[80] And also in *Chandler v DPP*, see note 75 above.

[81] I am grateful to the Attorney General's office for the following figures.

[82] Of the 1920 Act which deals with attempts, incitement etc.

[83] HC Debs., 9 February 1983.

1, but the Attorney General did not consent to prosecution. From 10 February 1983 until 24 April 1986, there were nine cases under s. 2, leading to five convictions, though one of these was subject to a successful appeal. In one further case, the Solicitor General had authorised a prosecution. There were three prosecutions under s. 1, and one authorised prosecution under section 7.[84] In 1987 and 1988 following Clive Ponting's trial there were twenty-three prosecutions under s. 2 before the courts bringing seven convictions. Between 1991 and 1993, there were five prosecutions under the 1989 Act with one conviction and seven under the s. 1 of the 1911 Act with three convictions. Between 1994–8, there were three prosecutions under the 1989 Act at magistrates' courts – two convictions and two sentences of immediate custody.[85] These figures would include the Shayler prosecution. These figures do not, of course, cover cases where confessions have been given *and* resignations tendered *in return for immunity*, as in the case of Ian Willmore.[86] Between 2001–7 there were three convictions under the 1989 Act, and one case was 'proceeded with', and one conviction under s. 1 of the 1911 Act.[87] There were several high-profile prosecutions and convictions in 2008–9.

The OSAs are designed to operate *in terrorem*. If the government miscalculated the public sentiment badly in the case of Ponting, it is doubtful whether the acquittal in that case would influence more than a handful of individuals to act as he did where they had a sincere, well-motivated and morally felt duty, not simply to their political overlords but to Parliament and the nation. The OSAs should be seen for what they are: the legal framework of a tradition of government which is steeped in secrecy and confidentiality which have been used 'viciously and capriciously by an embarrassed executive'.[88] In fact, it could be argued that there is now a more effective regime for imposing secrecy in the government's interests and not in the PI (see below).

---

[84] See HC Debs., vol. 108, col. 13 (12 January 1987).

[85] Figures supplied by the Home Office 18 July 2000.

[86] R. Pyper, 'Sarah Tisdall, Ian Willmore and the civil servant's "right to leak"' (1985) 56 Pol Q 72.

[87] Office for Criminal Justice Reform letter, November 2008 and March 2009. Figures for 2008 were not available until November 2009.

[88] See Caulfield J's memo to Franks (n 71 above), vol. II, p. 350. On the Act's effects upon civil servants, see Franks (n 71 above), vol. 1, p. 17; Clive Ponting, *The Right to Know* (1985), pp. 36–42; see also J. Ward, 'The impact of freedom of information legislation on senior civil servants' (1986) 1 Public Policy and Admin. 11; and L. Chapman, *Your Disobedient Servant* (1979). Note, minister-to-be J. Aitken, *Officially Secret* (1971) on *R v Aitken and Others*. The absence of high judicial authority on almost any aspect of s. 2 was amazing, although see *Galvin* [1987] 2 All ER 851 where the Court of Appeal quashed a conviction where a jury was not asked to consider the defence of prior dissemination of information which might have authorised its use. The courts have generally taken a strict line on information under the OSA still being secret, although in the public domain: A. Nicol, 'Official secrets and jury vetting' (1979) Crim LR 284; *R v Crisp and Homewood* (1919) 83 JP 121, though Canadian cases differ: *Boyer v R* (1948) 94 CCC 195, per Marchand J and *R v Toronto Sun Publishing Ltd* (1979) 47 CCC (2d) 535.

The Ponting trial

The law had been thrown into more than its usual state of uncertainty by the acquittal of the former assistant secretary at the Ministry of Defence (MoD), Clive Ponting. Ponting's trial was a sensational event. He was a civil service 'high flier' who had responsibility for 'the policy and political aspects of the operational activities of the Royal Navy'. Ponting was concerned with drafting replies and answers on the sinking of the Argentinian warship *Belgrano* by the Royal Navy during the Falklands campaign.[89] He disagreed with his colleagues on what, and how, information on the sinking should be published. His belief that the government was positively and deliberately misleading the Commons, a select committee[90] and the public caused him to send two documents to Tam Dalyell MP. They were duly handed to the chairman of the Select Committee on Foreign Affairs, who, in turn, handed them back to the Secretary of State at the MoD. Ponting was subsequently prosecuted for breach of s. 2(1)(a). This section made it a criminal offence for a person holding office under Her Majesty to communicate official information to any person other than a person to whom he is authorised to communicate it, or a person to whom it is his duty *in the interest of the state* to communicate it. In the course of the trial 'interest' and 'interests' were used interchangeably.[91]

Both prosecution and defence accepted that Dalyell was not a person authorised to receive official information under the terms of the Act. Was an MP a person to whom it was Ponting's duty in the interest of the state to pass such information?[92] This issue was central to Ponting's defence. In the trial,[93] McCowan J consulted *Chandler v DPP* where Lord Reid observed that the term 'state' did not mean the government or the executive but 'the realm' or the 'organised community'. Lord Reid also believed that a minister or a government did not *always* have the final say on what was in the PI, although *in cases concerning the defence of the realm* a different approach would be necessary. *Chandler* was such a case.[94] McCowan J directed the jury that '*interests* of the state' (*sic*) were synonymous with the interests of the government of the day, adopting Lord Reid's narrower interpretation regarding defence. The offence indicted in *Chandler* was a conspiracy to commit an act of sabotage within a prohibited place 'for a purpose prejudicial to the interests of the state' under s. 1. In the context of national defence, the state was the 'organised community', 'the organs of government of a national community' and responsibility for armed forces and defence fell to the Crown, viz. the government of the day

---

[89] C. Ponting, *The Right To Know* (1985). He worked with the 'Crown Jewels', which were top secret documents setting out the details of the events leading to the sinking of the *Belgrano*. Inclusion of this information meant that the jury had to be vetted.

[90] The Committee reported in July 1985 and, while critical of the government's reticence, it did not think the government had sought to mislead it.

[91] See R. Thomas, HC 92-II (1985–6), App. 26, for an informative analysis.

[92] Cf. Ponting, *The Right to Know*.   [93] [1985] Crim LR 318.

[94] [1964] AC 763; see above.

advising the Crown. This military necessity as Lord Devlin suggested, was not a blueprint to suggest that the interests of the state were *always* the same as those of the government of the day.[95] The 'duty' referred to in s. 2(1)(a), McCowan J ruled, is an official duty under the terms of an office and authorised chain of command. It did not refer to a moral or 'public' duty. But surely this begs the question. There was ample scope to argue that this interpretation constituted a misconstruction of the provision and indeed the prosecution accepted that Ponting's leak had not adversely affected national security.

Until 1998, it remained a severe criticism of our system of government that there is no equivalent of the US Civil Service Reform Act 1978 – as amended – which protects civil servants who 'blow the whistle' in the PI from punishment by administrative disciplining. The UK Public Interest Disclosure Act 1998 seeks to protect disclosures by employees in the PI but it does not apply to those whose work is certified by a minister as safeguarding national security. Security and intelligence officers are not covered by this Act. An amendment brought the police under the protection of the Act. The US Act protects those servants who leak information which they reasonably believe reveals violation of the law or regulations or 'mismanagement, a gross waste of funds, an abuse of authority, or a substantial and specific danger to public health or safety'. Where the disclosure concerns foreign intelligence and counter-intelligence, it must be made to designated officials who have to inform the appropriate Congressional Committee. Similar protection covers FBI agents and other officials. Reports of investigations are submitted to Congress, the president and the complainant. These provisions were extended in 1989 following the Oliver North episode[96] (note the existence of an inspector general for CIA). In the previous chapter the reforms post 9/11 in the USA were noted. The 1989 Act provides a safeguard against administrative reprisals, but not against a criminal prosecution where a crime is committed.

Additional difficulties related to the question of the *mens rea* necessary to secure a conviction and whether *proof* of intent was required, i.e. intent to leak *and* prejudice the safety etc. of the state.

Stated in fairly dispassionate academic terms, the position might seem relatively straightforward. But when the OSA is put into practice and prosecution is attempted before a jury, then unless a confession is forthcoming, as in the case of Sarah Tisdall, who leaked documents to *The Guardian* relating to the arrival of cruise missiles, or concerns straightforward allegations of fact, it can prove to be impossible to secure a conviction. In the case of *Ponting*, failure to convict no doubt related to a jury refusing to be browbeaten by a judge, the

---

[95] Thomas, (n 91 above) p. 371. And see N. MacCormick, 'The interests of the state and the rule of law' in P. Wallington and R Merkin (eds.), *Essays in Memory of FH Lawson* (1986).

[96] 5 USC, ss. 1206–8, 2302. See Y. Cripps, 'Disclosure in the public interest: The predicament of the public sector employee' (1983) Public Law 600; Cf. use of the Espionage Act in the USA. Note the Inspector-General for the CIA and the IG's role: *Inspector-General in the CIA Compared to Other Statutory Inspectors-General*, F. Kaiser CRS Report 89–679 GOV (1989).

prosecution handling the case less adroitly than it should, a feeling that the government was actively involved in manipulating an outcome, and the Attorney General appearing to prejudge guilt in a radio broadcast.[97] And Ponting's lawyers mounted a very successful campaign outside the courtroom.[98] Yet *all* the vital rulings in law went against Ponting. In law, the Crown (government?) could not have asked for more, and no judge could have provided such, since juries were last imprisoned before *Bushell's* case[99] in 1670 for returning verdicts against the judge's direction. Ponting's acquittal was a resounding death knell for s. 2.

The Spycatcher litigation

A former member of the British security service and somewhat embittered by his lack of recognition and paltry pension, Wright sought to publish his memoirs in Australia – outside the criminal jurisdiction of s. 2 – and these contained well-rehearsed allegations concerning the activities or 'dirty tricks' of the security service. The novel feature in this case was that Wright was a former 'insider', a fact which might give added credibility to his allegations. This episode and its ramifications are examined in greater detail in chapter 11 but the eventual refusal to award permanent injunctions by Scott J to prevent reporting of the allegations in *Spycatcher* and of the proceedings relating to its attempted publication, and the judge's belief that some of the original allegations deserved to be published in the PI[100] forced the government's legal advisers to accept that the law of confidentiality would not always fill the hole left by the deficiencies in s. 2 and that 'prior restraint' may not always be lightly imposed by an English court. In generally ringing terms, Scott J spoke of the strengthening of British law by the influence of Art. 10 European Convention of Human Rights (ECHR) which guarantees freedom of speech and dissemination of information and how the courts must hold the balance between public security and freedom of speech in a manner which did not automatically accept the *ipse dixit* of the government of the day. The courts were not justified in restraining newspaper or media reports concerning unauthorised disclosures unless there was a risk of further damage to national security. As the European Court of Human Rights (ECtHR) subsequently established, a court may take a different attitude at different stages of the interlocutory and permanent hearings for an injunction – for that Court ruled that the original injunctions restraining newspaper coverage of events in Australian proceedings and details of the book were justified because of the possible danger to national security but that the injunctions imposed after the publication of the book in the USA were no longer justified.[101] This is actually narrower than the judgment of Scott J who

---

[97] Bernard Ingham, the Prime Minister's press secretary, opined that he hoped a 'severe' judge would try the case!

[98] *The Times*, 12 February 1985.   [99] (1670) 6 State Tr. 999.   [100] See p. 438 *et seq.* below.

[101] *Observer and Guardian v UK* (1991) 14 EHRR 153.

felt that some of the original allegations were justified, although on this point he was *obiter*. In chapter 11, I shall examine more closely the role of the courts in protecting government confidences and secrets by injunction and the extent of the PI defence under our civil jurisdiction. This topic has now to address s. 12 Human Rights Act 1998 (HRA) which seeks to protect freedom of expression under the ECHR Art. 10, as well as Art 8. As we shall see in chapter 11 (see p. 444) interim injunctions preventing publication are not to be granted unless the party seeking the relief, the Attorney General, establishes to the satisfaction of the court that he is likely to succeed in his claim at the final hearing that publication should not be allowed. Various other items have to be addressed in the case of 'journalistic, artistic and literary material' in balancing relevant interests.

Nonetheless, Scott J's decision, basically upheld in its entirety in the higher courts, indicated a new and more rational approach by the courts where government could not assume that judges would be happy to perform the executive's work on its behalf and that the only way to redress the damage was by reform of s. 2.

The Shepherd Bill

In November 1987, a Private Member's bill sought to repeal s. 2. It bore the same title as the government's discredited Protection of Official Information Bill of 1979, although it differed in important respects.

Under the bill, six classes of information or 'articles' would have been protected by the criminal law insofar as unauthorised dissemination might lead to criminal prosecution with the consent of the Attorney General or, in some cases, the consent of the Director of Public Prosecutions. The areas covered were: defence, international relations, security or intelligence 'the unauthorised disclosure of which would be likely to cause serious injury to the interests of the nation or endanger the safety of a British citizen' (cl. 1(1)(a) and 1(2)(a) information). Further specified classes were covered. *Mens rea* had to be proved. A defence that the information had been publicly available in the UK *or* elsewhere was provided. A PI defence to a criminal charge was also available.

A three-line whip and invocation of the pay-roll on Tory MPs helped to kill the bill in January 1988. The government was emphatic that such an important subject was not suitable for backbench reform.

The White Paper on reform

The fourteen pages of White Paper took fourteen months to complete. It agreed with Franks that s. 1 OSA does not provide full protection for official information and that the criminal law needs to punish leakage as well as espionage where there is a sufficient degree of harm to the PI. The White Paper said 'nothing about the separate issue' of freedom of information because this did not arise directly out of the reform of s. 2. It is therefore difficult to square with the Home Secretary's subsequent announcement that his bill represented a 'substantial unprecedented thrust in the direction of greater openness' that it was an 'essay in openness . . . unprecedented since the Second World War'.

The government ultimately decided not to follow Franks but to 'look afresh at the issues', taking into account the criticisms of its 1979 bill and the development of parliamentary and public thinking in recent years. A closer look at such thinking would suggest that the Government had been treating it less than sympathetically. Six specific areas of information were to be protected against unauthorised disclosure where the disclosure was damaging. Damaging disclosures by unauthorised recipients would be covered, but the mere receipt of official information without authority was not to be a crime unless, presumably, aiding and abetting, incitement or encouraging or assisting in crime,[102] or conspiracy could be charged. However, the White Paper dropped the idea of ministerial certificates which specified that the information was properly classified as information the disclosure of which was considered likely to cause serious injury to the interests of the nation. The new requirement that a disclosure be 'damaging' was less onerous than the 'serious damage' requirement of the 1979 bill, although in that bill serious injury was to be established by a ministerial certificate. The White Paper stipulated that there was to be no PI defence as had been present in the Shepherd Bill, nor a defence of prior publication, even though one had been present in cl. 7(1) of the 1979 bill.

Although disclosures had normally to be proved to be damaging by the prosecution, there were four areas where the disclosure would *ipso facto* be deemed damaging, and where UK interests abroad were concerned the disclosure only had to jeopardise or seriously obstruct those interests. The first covered leaks by security and intelligence officials and 'notified persons' (see below) of security and intelligence information. The second absolute offence concerned the disclosure of information obtained or information concerning activities under the Interception of Communications Act 1985 and what was to be the Security Service Act 1989, i.e. burglary and 'investigations' by MI5 and subsequent legislation (see chapter 2). These would cover Clive Ponting, Peter Wright and Cathy Massiter, the former MI5 official who disclosed that the Campaign for Nuclear Disarmament's telephone lines and those of its members were being tapped.[103] The third area covered information relating to international relations. Fourthly, information obtained in confidence from other governments would be protected – it seemed absolutely as any disclosure without authority would be harmful. Information would also be protected when given in confidence to a foreign government, but only where it was leaked without authority in that state and subsequently published in the UK. The Act provided for the

---

[102] Serious Crime Act 2007, Pt 2.
[103] *R v Secretary of State for the Home Department, ex p. Ruddock* [1987] 2 All ER 518

protection of information relating to defence and that which would be useful to criminals if disclosed without authority. These were the fifth and sixth
categories of protected information.

> The government . . . proposes that, when it is necessary for the courts to consider
> the harm likely to arise from the disclosure of particular information, the pros-
> ecution should be required to adduce evidence as to that harm and the defence
> should be free to produce its own evidence in rebuttal. The burden of proof would
> be on the prosecution in the normal way. [Cm. 408: para. 18]

In other words, no ministerial certificates would dictate to the jury a finding of
guilt. A free trial before one's peers, lauded by the remnants of the liberal press
during Ponting's acquittal prompting the White Paper, was to be preserved
in all its integrity. The fact that the ground rules determined that no likely
defence was available for certain disclosures was beside the point. It is also a
little disingenuous to state, as we shall see, that ministerial certificates have not
been introduced.

There were, nevertheless, certain improvements. Large areas of official information would no longer be covered by the OSAs. For example, Cabinet documents were not to be protected as a class unless they fell within one of the
above protected categories. Economic information was not to be protected as
a class (e.g., the budget), and information given to government in confidence
was not to be protected per se. The information would have to fall within one
of the six categories. The White Paper indicated that, at the same time, civil
service rules and departmental rules would be amended to make new provision
for internal disciplinary punishment to protect information not covered by the
OSAs.[104] New statutes would also provide for criminal offences for unauthorised disclosure as and when required. In 2004, the number of such statutes and
regulations extended to over 240 statutes including NI orders and over sixty-five
regulations.[105] However, it is deceptive, therefore, to assert as the White Paper
does that the 'result of implementing the Government's proposals would be
that only small proportions of the information in the hands of Crown servants
would be protected by the criminal law' (para. 71).

Classification of information for security purposes still remains, even though
classification at a particular grade of secrecy is not, of itself, evidence of likely
harm or damage in a court of law. Classification will continue to play an 'essential
administrative role in the handling of information' within government itself
and will also be relevant for internal disciplinary offences. In a criminal trial,
a classification will not be evidence of the causing of damage; but the grade
may be relevant 'as evidence tending to show that the defendant had reason
to believe that the disclosure of the information was likely to harm the public

---

[104] Note the current provisions under the *Civil Service Management Code* (April 2008), ch. 4,
www.civilservice.gov.uk/iam/codes/csmc/index.asp.
[105] Birkinshaw, *Government and Information*.

interest'. The causation of damage will have to be proved by separate evidence. Classifications, which are reviewable internally, are as follows:[106]

- 'Top secret': the compromise of this information or material would be likely to threaten directly the internal stability of the UK or friendly countries; to lead directly to widespread loss of life; to cause exceptionally grave damage to the effectiveness or security of the UK or allied forces or to the continuing effectiveness of extremely valuable security or intelligence operations; to cause exceptionally grave damage to relations with friendly governments (but what of revelations of torture in those countries?); or to cause severe long-term damage to the UK economy.
- 'Secret': this covers information or material where compromise would be likely to raise international tension or damage seriously relations with friendly governments; to threaten life directly, or seriously prejudice public order, or individual security or liberty; to cause serious damage to the operational effectiveness of security in the UK or allied forces; or to cause material damage to national finances or economic and commercial interests.
- 'Confidential': this is where compromise as above would be likely materially to damage diplomatic relations, i.e. cause formal protests; to prejudice individual liberty or security; to cause damage to the operational effectiveness or security of UK or allied forces or the effectiveness of valuable security or intelligence operations; to work substantially against national finances or economic or commercial interests; substantially to undermine the financial viability of major organisations; to impede the investigation or facilitate the commission of serious crime; to impede seriously the development or operation of government policies; to shut down or otherwise substantially disrupt significant national operations.
- 'Restricted': this is where compromise etc. would be likely to affect diplomatic relations adversely; cause substantial distress to individuals; make it more difficult to maintain the operational effectiveness or security of UK or allied forces; cause financial loss or loss of earning potential to or facilitate improper gain or advantage for individuals or companies; to prejudice the investigation or facilitate the commission of crime; to breach proper undertakings to maintain confidentiality from third party communications; to impede the effective development or implementation of government policies; to breach statutory restrictions on disclosure of information; to disadvantage government in commercial or policy negotiations with others; to undermine the proper management of the public sector and its operations.

Within government these classifications are often accompanied by descriptors which indicate the nature of the sensitivity – for example, 'Appointments',

---

[106] HC Debs., 23 March 1994, cols. 259–60 (Written Answers). The aim was to give departments and agencies greater responsibility for assessing the nature of the risks they face and for making decisions about the security measures they need to put in place. See ch. 1 p. 13 above on IT security.

'Budget', 'Commercial', 'Contracts', 'Management', 'Policy', 'Medical', 'Regulatory', 'Staff'. Departments may add to this list to cover types of information specific to their organisation.

The burden and quantum of proof would vary as between civil servants, government contractors and civilians. Among civil servants, where the offence related to security and intelligence information, a distinction was drawn between security and intelligence officials and 'notified' persons under s. 1 OSA 1989 (below) in one group and other civil servants in another. Unauthorised disclosures by the former group are, in the absence of one unlikely defence which I will discuss below, an absolute offence. For other offences, a distinction was drawn between civil servants, government contractors and civilians.

The test of liability would depend upon the state of knowledge of the discloser, and in the case of Crown servants it is reasonable to assume that they know the value of the information received in official duties. *Mens rea* is also a component of the offence. It would be open to the civil servant or contractor to plead that they could not reasonably have been expected to realise the harm likely to be caused by the disclosure. In the case of civilians, the opposite presumption would be made, and the prosecution should have to prove that harm was likely to follow and that the discloser knew, or could be reasonably expected to know, that harm would be likely to result. The constituents of the prosecution case differ according to the category of defendant. In the case of civil servants and contractors, *mens rea* is presumed unless proved otherwise; in the case of civilians, knowledge of the damaging quality has to be established by the prosecution. In the case of information obtained under interception or security warrants, once the prosecution has established that a non-civil servant knew, or had reasonable cause to believe that, it was such information and that it was disclosed unlawfully under the Act, the offence is made out.

Reference must be made to the special treatment of classes of security and intelligence information. Because it would normally be necessary for the prosecution to present additional evidence that such disclosures were damaging to secure a conviction, the government declared that further and possibly greater damage could be caused by adducing such information. To counter such difficulty, it was proposed that the prosecution could show that the information disclosed was of a class or description the disclosure of which would be likely to damage the operation of the services. 'This would allow the arguments to be less specific.'[107] The prosecution would simply assert that the information belongs to a class of information the disclosure of which is damaging. No *specific* supporting evidence would have to be produced although the less specific the evidence the less convincing the case. It is difficult to interpret this as anything other than a ministerial certificate by default which the White Paper had appeared to rule out. Leigh and Lustgarten have argued that this is not the same

---

[107] Cm. 408, para. 40.

as conviction on the say-so of a minister.[108] Granted that this is restricted to one category of information, nevertheless the continued classification of documents and the secret lists of ministerially designated and 'notified' officials who work in close proximity with the security and intelligence services have to be appreciated.

Public-interest disclosure

The White Paper adverted specifically to the defences of prior publication and PI disclosure. The Shepherd Bill had contained a PI defence where the defendant had a reasonable cause to believe crime, fraud, abuse of authority, neglect, or other misconduct had been perpetrated. The judicially developed law of confidentiality has long recognised that there cannot be a confidence in an iniquity.[109] A duty cannot be owed to maintain as a secret that which ought, in the PI, to be disclosed. The courts have come to accept that a disclosure may be justified not because there is an iniquity but because there is an item of information the disclosure of which is justified on the facts.[110] The PI defence was dramatically invoked by Scott J in *Spycatcher* when he argued that the revelations of Wright's allegations, concerning the attempts to undermine the Wilson Government and the plot to assassinate President Nasser of Egypt by MI5 and MI6 officials, respectively, were protected by a PI defence (see chapter 11). Correspondingly, the press were justified in publishing this information, at least in its essentials. This was information which the concept of democracy demanded should be placed before the public. Scott J suggested that revelations by an official may also be so protected, in spite of the lifelong duty of confidentiality, a point supported by the higher courts. When the question of an agent's confidentiality was most recently tested in the *Shayler* case, the lifelong and complete confidentiality of security and intelligence officers was emphasised although Lord Scott expressed some doubt on its absolute nature.[111] However, since the security allegations formed a minute part of the book, Wright had been culpable in publishing the book in that particular form. What this amounted to was that, in examining the PI defence, the court will look very carefully at the manner and method of

---

[108] L. Lustgarten and I. Leigh question whether this amounts to conviction on the 'say so' of the minister and believe the case is overstated: *In From the Cold: National security and parliamentary democracy* (1994), pp. 238–40.

[109] *Gartside v Outram* (1856) 26 LJ Ch 113.

[110] *Lion Laboratories v Evans* [1985] QB 526. See also *Ashdown v Telegraph Group Ltd* [2001] 2 All ER 370: Art. 10 ECHR could not on the facts provide a defence to a breach of copyright (a breach of confidence was also claimed) concerning reports based on a minute taken by the former Liberal Democrat leader of a meeting with the prime minister. Defences under ss. 30 and 171(3) of the Copyright etc. Act 1988 were no defence to the newspaper. Protection of property was necessary in a democratic society and an injunction preventing publication was allowed notwithstanding s. 12 HRA 1998. See *Ass. Newspapers Ltd v HRH Prince of Wales* [2006] EWCA Civ 1776.

[111] *R v Shayler* [2002] 2 All ER 477, para. 120.

disclosure, and the motives of the discloser. Financial gain and widespread publication may undermine the defence so that the prudent course of action might
be to inform the police or Solicitor General rather than the press. This latter
point has been emphasised by Lord Donaldson MR on a variety of occasions,
as well as by Lord Griffiths and Lord Goff in *Spycatcher*.

In Canada, public servants at the federal level may successfully invoke the
PI defence against disciplinary hearings.[112] The Public Interest Disclosure Act
1998 offers some protection to UK civil servants and other employees (see
p. 116 *et seq.*) but none at all to security and intelligence officers. In the case of
intelligence and security officers, the House of Lords has ruled that an 'absolute
ban on disclosure' makes good sense[113] and this was the conclusion in *Shayler*.
This does not seem to countenance a PI disclosure at common law or disclosures
of trivia or useless information or that already published under authority of
the government as supported by Scott J. The House of Lords had to focus
on the fact that Blake was seeking to profit from his wrongdoing rather than
making a PI disclosure. Shayler unsuccessfully pleaded that s. 1 OSA 1989 was a
disproportionate interference with his right to free speech under Art. 10 ECHR.
Where the Public Interest Disclosure Act does not apply, a PI defence is only
a defence against a civil action for breach of confidence, and the confider still
retains his or her rights under the law of employment.[114] Whistle-blowers tend
to fare very badly.[115]

The government refused to countenance a PI defence which would allow
juries to consider and balance the benefits of the unauthorised disclosure of
information, the motives of the discloser and the harm it was likely to cause.
Several attempts to introduce such defences in the Commons and Lords failed. It
was the government's line that the object of reform of s. 2 had been to introduce
clarity and that such a defence would subvert this aim. Further, the reforms
would concentrate on protecting areas of information which demonstrably
require the protection of the criminal law 'in the public interest'. The government
argued: 'It cannot be acceptable that a person can lawfully disclose information
which he knows may, for example, lead to loss of life simply because he conceives
that he has a general reason of a public character for doing so.'[116] This seems
to confuse an assertion of such a defence by a defendant with its acceptance
by a jury. Expressed in the government's terms, the claim sounds startling. The
PI defence allows a defendant to plead that the disclosure has been a positive
benefit to the PI is not a licence for the mischievous, the woolly headed and
loose-tongued. The idea is to let the jury decide where there are arguments of

---

[112] *Quigley v Treasury Board* (1987) Public Service Staff Relations Board 166–2–16866.
[113] *AG v Blake* [2000] 4 All ER 385, HL; see also *AG v Times Newspapers* [2001] EWCA Civ 97,
       [2001] 1 WLR 885.
[114] *R v Civil Service Appeal Board, ex p. Bruce* [1989] 2 All ER 907; *R v Lord Chancellor's
       Department, exp Nangle* [1991] ICR 743 and see p. 116 *et seq.* below on whistle-blowing and
       protection.
[115] Y. Cripps, *Disclosure in the Public Interest*, 2nd edn (1994).
[116] Cm. 408, para. 60.

damage and benefit. Yet the government would not facilitate such a contest: 'the effect of disclosure on the PI should take place within the context of the proposed damage tests where applicable'.[117] The government's one assurance, binding in honour only, was that the Act would not be used to punish those who had embarrassed the Government. Katherine Gun was not prosecuted in 2004 for disclosing details of MI6 bugging of UN delegates before the Iraq war, but her defence would have included cross-examination of the prime minister on the legality of that war. That prospect was too embarrassing. However, if an offence has been committed there is no provision for juries to be instructed according to the government's assurance. Would it be a 'perverse' jury, therefore, that saved a defendant who had acted in the PI out of conscience? The jury that acquitted Ponting was not, arguably, perverse in that it felt, presumably, that he had acted 'in the interests of the state'. A powerful argument can be made out to the effect that for a jury to acquit in such circumstances is not a perverse action but a rational one motivated by integrity.[118] However, such a defence is no longer available. It is merely a question of the prosecutor's discretion, a matter which highlights the long-running problem over the Attorney General's independence from government colleagues (below).[119] It should also be recalled that some disclosures are *ipso facto* damaging.

The government's continued claim that a PI defence had no respectable precedent in our criminal law is also unfounded. As well as a generic defence of 'necessity' and duress, specific statutes may contain such defences. The government has suggested that reform of the 1989 Act may be necessary in order to clarify the position in relation to necessity and duress, i.e. to remove them as possible defences.[120]

Prior publication

The White Paper ruled out the necessity of a prior-publication defence, arguing that the inclusion of such a defence in the 1979 bill was 'flawed'.[121] The government's case, also argued with success before the courts,[122] was that a further publication of information already in the public domain might be damaging, possibly even more damaging than the original publication. A newspaper story about a certain matter may carry little weight in the absence of firm evidence of its validity. But confirmation of that story by, say, a senior official of the relevant government department would be very much more damaging and deserving of prosecution. So would publication of details of 'persons in public life' in one list, even though the names and addresses were publicly, albeit not

---

[117] *Ibid.*, para. 61.   [118] MacCormick, 'The interests of the state and the rule of law'.
[119] See Ponting, *The Right to Know* and Nicol, 'Official secrets and jury vetting'.
[120] The Intelligence and Security Committee has reported that the Home Secretary believed, in the light of case law, that the need for reform was 'less urgent' Cm. 7542 p. 43.
[121] Cf. s. 180(l)(r) Financial Services Act 1986 which allowed a defence of prior publication.
[122] *Lord Advocate v Scotsman Publications Ltd* [1989] 2 All ER 852 HL

conveniently, available elsewhere.[123] Prior publication would be relevant to assess the degree of harm, and it is therefore possible to argue that the damage alleged had already been perpetrated. But prior publication would not be conclusive for the defence. In some cases, viz. security and intelligence and interception and security warrant cases, prior publication would be irrelevant as the offences are 'absolute'. Case law suggests that prior publication without preventative government action may indicate that disclosure has been authorised, even though the information is still technically 'secret'.[124]

The House of Lords[125] accepted the thrust of government thinking when it acknowledged that the test for awarding an injunction to prevent publication in the law of confidentiality was that if an injunction were not awarded there would be damage or further damage to the PI. If the test is satisfied, an injunction may be awarded even where the information or document has been published on a limited basis. In the case in question it was only the government admission that all the damage had already occurred that prevented the award of the injunction. On the other hand, government attempts to stifle what had already been widely published had met with the rebuke from Lord Griffiths, then chairman of the Security Commission, that such awards would make the law appear an ass. As Scott J put it in December 1987, it would be part of the case for the 'absolute protection of the security services that . . . could not be achieved this side of the Iron Curtain'. The metaphor maintains its potency. In 2001, the Court of Appeal refused to issue an injunction preventing publication of extracts of a book by a former MI6 officer which had been published in Russia.[126] It had entered the public domain. However, the House of Lords did uphold a conviction for contempt by the editor of *Punch* who published articles authored by Shayler and which contained information which had been prohibited by injunction from publication. The editor had deliberately interfered with the effectiveness of the court's order. Furthermore, it was perfectly in order for the Attorney General to specify in the order sought what could be published. This did not make the Attorney a censor and his view as set out in the order could be varied by the court, and in future those enjoined should be advised of the power of variation.[127]

In Parliament

The bill was a faithful replica of the White Paper with one significant development concerning information relating to international relations. Although

---

[123] Cm. 408, para. 62.   [124] *R v Galvin* [1987] 2 All ER 851, CA.

[125] *Lord Advocate v Scotsman Publications Ltd* [1989] 2 All ER 852, HL; and in *AG v Blake* (above) the duty of absolute secrecy was supported in relation to seizing profits from sales of the book. There was no question of banning a book already published.

[126] *AG v Times Newspaper Group Ltd* [2001] EWCA Civ 97, [2001] 1 WLR 885.

[127] *AG v Punch Ltd* [2003] 1 All ER 289. Some misgivings were expressed about orders being drafted in too wide a formulation.

several minor amendments were made to the bill in its parliamentary passage, the government refused to cede ground on any of its major objectives.

The Home Secretary rejected accusations that only allowing six days on the floor of the House to debate all sixteen clauses of the bill was 'niggardly'. Furthermore, the committee stage was a committee of the whole House. After a two- and then a three-line whip, the guillotine was imposed, an amendment to the bill in committee was not incorporated for consideration at report stage, and inconsistent answers were given on crucial points. 'The effect of the guillotine was that, while some topics received thorough discussion, others were barely considered at all.'[128] Indeed, s. 5, as we shall see, contains what could be a fatal flaw. In seeking to amend the bill by introducing a PI defence, Richard Shepherd reminded the Commons that, while Parliament might often pursue abuses of authority, it rarely raised them. In the Lords, Lord Hutchinson of Lullington, counsel in many OSA cases, challenged the government view that the reform was a liberalising measure. The six areas of information saw 'even greater restrictions' introduced, and in the past thirty years all prosecutions involving leaks to the media had involved the six areas. The statutory definitions of 'damaging' were wide and vacuous, with 'weak, inexact and unreliable' criteria, 'far removed from the central issue of the security of the state'.[129]

And so it was that after seventy-eight years, s. 2 had been reformed. Reform was, of course, needed. Of that there was no doubt. Now, the government assured us, there was to be no more talk of catch-all provisions with well over 2,000 offences. The Act would target six specific areas. Civil-service codes and statutes would be used to plug other gaps as we shall see. There would be no prosecution of those who had caused only embarrassment or distress to ministers by their leaks; nor would pensions be stopped unless a conviction under the criminal law had been secured. To what extent, however, would prosecutors turn to common-law offences built on 'misconduct in public office' as witnessed in the Damian Green MP episode in 2008–9 (see p. 348 below)?

The Official Secrets Act 1989

The Act, which came into force on 1 March 1990, extends, with minor exceptions, to Northern Ireland and to offences committed abroad by British citizens and Crown servants (s. 15). Prosecutions may only be brought with the consent of the Attorney General or Lord Advocate, except for offences under s. 4(2). This safeguard has been claimed, on numerous occasions, to be more apparent than real, as the Attorney General is, severally, protector of the PI, lawyer, elected politician, member of the government, government legal adviser, and Crown, i.e. government, prosecutor. Given the judicial endorsement, per McCowan J, in *R v Ponting* of the interests of the state as synonymous with the interests of

---

[128] B. Winetrobe, *The Official Secrets Bill 1988–89* (1989), Res. Note 437, HC Library.
[129] HL Debs., vol. 504, col. 1632 (9 March 1989).

the government of the day, it is hardly surprising that decisions of the Attorney General have not infrequently been perceived as partial. Although ministers may be consulted, 'the final decision is his alone' on prosecutions.[130] The prime minister announced plans to bring changes to the office of the Attorney General in 2008 which were contained in the Constitutional Renewal Bill of 2008 (see Introduction and also p. 116 below).[131]

Authorised disclosures

The distinction between an authorised and an unauthorised disclosure is central to the whole structure of the 1989 Act. The concept is also crucial for the operation of the civil service codes. Some explanation is therefore required.

Throughout the 1990s and into the 2000s, it became evident to the government that the relationship between ministers and civil servants was in need of reformulation. Civil servants had long abandoned the veil of anonymity with which their work was traditionally shrouded. A huge change in culture had taken place in the civil service brought about by the financial management initiative, a significant reduction in manpower, agencification and targeted performance. There were other causes and effects. The role of civil servants in leaking the Solicitor General's letter to Michael Heseltine in the Westland saga, the confusion into which the Ponting trial and acquittal threw the government, greater trade union activity and industrial unrest at GCHQ,[132] were all contributory factors. However, the deliberate placing of civil servants in the front line of media and press attention by ministers was not without importance. Furthermore, by the end of the 1980s, the wholesale devolution of managerial responsibility to executives and line managers running executive agencies outside the ministerial/departmental structure, the increasing emphasis upon commercial enterprise and contracting out[133] and the attenuation of ministerial responsibility, all helped to place the minister/civil servant relationship under strain. So too did the use of special advisers by ministers. The formal relationship was expressed in memoranda and Cabinet Office guidelines from Sir Robert Armstrong in 1985 and 1987 respectively. In these, he stated that civil servants were servants of the Crown. He added that the 'Crown' means, and is represented by, the government of the day whose ministers are answerable to Parliament. A civil servant's primary duty is to the minister in charge of the department in which they are serving and whom they must serve 'with complete integrity and to the best of their ability'. The maintenance of trust between ministers and civil servants, and the efficiency of government, required that the

---

[130] Franks (n 71 above), para. 37.
[131] Cm. 7342-II; the White Paper was Cm. 7342-I (2008).   [132] See ch. 2, p. 36 *et seq.*
[133] Government Trading Act 1990; Civil Service Management Functions Act 1992; Deregulation and Contracting Out Act 1994.

latter kept the confidences to which they become privy in their work.[134] This definition has been amended but its spirit remains intact.[135] The Constitutional Renewal Bill of 2008 (see p. 100 above) set out proposals to place the Civil Service Commission on a statutory basis although it excluded the security and intelligence services and GCHQ. Codes of practice for civil servants and special advisers will be made under statutory powers if the reforms come to realisation (see Introduction, p. 6).

I shall deal with civil service codes and disciplinary proceedings later. From the above, however, and excluding any developments under the bill, it is clear that the release of information operates under the authority of the minister. Ministers are, therefore, to a large extent, self-authorising; they do not leak, they brief. Senior civil servants are in substantially the same position,[136] the extent to which they are self-authorising depending upon their position and seniority, the context of the disclosure and what is necessary for the performance of their duties. Section 2 of the 1911 Act created an offence if Crown information was disclosed to someone 'other than a person to whom [the civil servant] is authorised to communicate it, or a person to whom it is in the interests of the state [the civil servant's duty] to communicate it'. The Act did not explain the meaning of these words. In *Ponting*, McCowan J directed the jury that the 'interests of the state' were synonymous with the interests of the government of the day. He expressed no qualification. In so instructing, he wrenched from their context dicta of the Law Lords in *Chandler v DPP* which could be used to support Ponting's case where national security was not at stake.

At the root of the problem is an inherent conflict between the governing of a country by a particular government which may abuse its powers, and the idea of the state, or specifically the Crown, as representative of a larger collective weal which is bigger than any government. 'Those whose prime loyalty is to the government of the day look to the Crown as a more enduring expression of their position within the constitution.'[137] The First Division Association of Civil Servants (FDA) has argued that loyalty to the Crown included the Crown in Parliament, thereby creating a special relationship between MPs and civil servants. It is probably more accurate to look upon the 'Crown in Parliament', however, as a legislative device, not an all-pervasive functional relationship although in a sense it does describe the confusion of the executive and the legislature in both Houses.

To avoid what must have seemed to any government as metaphysical meanderings, lawful authority for a disclosure by a Crown servant or a person notified under s. 1 of the 1989 Act means 'if, and only if, it is made in accordance with

---

[134] See ch. 9 p. 343 below.

[135] See ch. 9 p. 343 *et seq.* and note the former Civil Service Department's *Legal Entitlement and Administrative Practices* HMSO (1979) on compliance with the law.

[136] Franks (n 71 above), para. 18 and Treasury and Civil Service Committee, *Civil Servants and Ministers: Duties and responsibilities*, HC 92-I–II (1985–6), p. 5.

[137] HC 92-I–II (1985–6), para. 3.2.

[an] official duty'. The established view would see an official duty emanating solely from within the official chain of command, going up to, and including, the permanent secretary and minister as adviser to the Crown.

The 1989 Act provides that a disclosure by a government contractor is, tautologically, made with lawful authority if, and only if, it is made in accordance with an official authorisation, or for the purposes of the functions by virtue of which they are a government contractor without contravening an official restriction (s. 7(2)). Disclosure of protected information by any other person is made with lawful authority if, and only if, it is made:

(a) to a Crown servant for the purpose of his or her functions as such
(b) in accordance with an official authorisation (s. 7(3)).

The mysteries of self authorisation will remain. A party charged with an offence under ss. 1–6 of the 1989 Act may prove, with the onus on that party, that at the time of the alleged offence they believed that they had lawful authority to make the disclosure in question and had no reasonable cause to believe otherwise. Their simple belief is not enough, even if mistaken.

An authorised disclosure under the Freedom of Information Act (FOIA) (see p. 134) will be protected under this provision. Under s. 44 FOIA, the relevant statutory prohibition is the OSA which makes a proviso for lawfully authorised disclosures.

Security and intelligence information

Section 1 protects security and intelligence information, which is defined in s. 1(9). The provision stipulates that members and former members of the services – MI5 and MI6 respectively and GCHQ employees – and 'notified' persons are guilty of an offence if without lawful authority they disclose any information, document or other article relating to security and intelligence acquired by virtue of their position as such a member/person.

In the Commons it was stated that 'carefully selected and mainly senior officials', as well as members of the armed services working in a 'few government departments' assessing intelligence information of the highest sensitivity and assisting ministers, would be notified. Also proposed for notification would be those who work on providing the services with regular professional support for their operation and activities. These will usually be Crown servants. Members of the armed forces who undertake technical communications and work alongside the services in various parts of the world will be notified, as will ministers and others 'with particular responsibilities or public duties in respect of the services'.[138] The government insisted that a notification would be secret, so no reasons would be given though, after denial and equivocation, it was accepted by the government that a notification would be judicially reviewable. Even with

---

[138] HC Debs., vol. 145, cols. 1128–9 (25 January 1989).

reasons, however, the possibility of a successful judicial review involving a matter of security and intelligence is extremely rare.[139] Notification will be in force for five years from the day on which it is served, though it may either be revoked within that period or indeed extended.

Section 1(2) also covers statements purporting to be security or intelligence disclosures; i.e. vacuous 'big talk' or idle boasts by security and intelligence officers or former officers and notified persons. The position under common-law confidentiality was discussed above where there is a defence for trivia and a PI defence. This is not so under the OSA. Any disclosure within s. 1(1)–(2) under the 1989 Act is presumed damaging. The Law Lords believed that the OSA 1989 and the law of confidentiality are on a par in relation to such officers.[140] This was discussed above. Presumably editors would be able to plead such a defence under the law of confidentiality.

It seems that the offences of attempting, aiding, abetting, encouraging or assisting crime in s. 7 OSA 1920 do not apply to the 1989 Act. Section 7 applies to the 1920 Act and the 'principal Act', i.e. s. 2 of the 1911 Act. Nothing in the 1989 Act refers to it being included in the expression 'principal Act'. But there are common-law offences and statutory provisions of attempting, aiding, abetting and encouraging crime. If these offences were invoked by a prosecutor then it would add considerable uncertainty to the position of, e.g., a newspaper editor or publisher. The formless offence of conspiracy should also be kept in mind from the point of view of the recipient. Having said that, the common law and statutory inchoate offences have not been resorted to and there must be a serious risk that they would fall foul of the HRA and Art. 10 ECHR if brought against reputable editors. Arguably, they would also run counter to Parliament's intent in removing these statutory inchoate provisions under the 1920 Act.

For Crown servants, other than members of the security services and notified persons, and for government contractors, which are defined in s. 12, an unauthorised disclosure is punishable as an offence if it is 'damaging'. By s. 1(4) a disclosure is deemed to be damaging if 'it causes damage to the work of, or any part of, the security and intelligence services'. No specific allowance is made for trivia or the PI so that, for example, damage would be caused if a disclosure revealed that the service was engaged in murder.[141] In August 2000, when David Shayler, formerly of MI5, was prosecuted on his return to England under the OSA, he was not prosecuted in relation to revelations of alleged MI6 plots to arrange the assassination of Colonel Gaddafi. The government also legislated via the back door for analogues of ministerial certificates to be introduced, in

---

[139] *Council of Civil Service Unions v Minister for the Civil Service* [1985] AC 374, HL; *R v Secretary of State for the Home Department, ex p. Ruddock* [1987] 2 All ER 518; *R v Director GCHQ, ex p. Hodges* (1988) The Times, 26 July. On this latter case – dismissal of a homosexual from GCHQ – see p. 424 *et seq.* below.

[140] *Lord Advocate* v *Scotsman Publications Ltd* [1989] 2 All ER 852, HL And see *AG v Blake* [2000] 4 All ER 385, HL.

[141] See Lord Donaldson MR [1988] 3 All ER 545, at 603–6, esp. 605d-e.

spite of their contrary claims – although this point has been criticised.[142] This was achieved as follows. Section 1(4) allows damage to be presumed where the disclosure is of information the unauthorised disclosure of which:

> would be likely to cause such damage [viz. to security or intelligence] or which falls within a class or description of information, documents or articles the unauthorised disclosure of which would be likely to have that effect.

I have already described the impact of this provision. It will allow arguments to be 'less specific'. There would still have to be arguments and some supporting evidence but details are likely to kept exiguous. The prosecution will simply have to show that the information was classified under s. 1(4). Once that is established, the offence is made out. The classification will be that of a minister and is evidence of its damaging quality, unlike the security classifications discussed above. Under s. 8(4) OSA 1920, the public and press may be excluded from a trial under the 1989 Act (s. 11(4)). Such an order excluding the press will prevent the public being informed of details.

Although the above provision has been described as an absolute offence, a defence is nonetheless available. The defence allowable under s. 1(5) involves the security or other relevant officer proving that at the time of the alleged offence they did not know, and had no reasonable cause to believe, that the information or documents related to security or intelligence. One might be tempted to think that they would have to be singularly unintelligent intelligence officers to plead ignorance successfully in this context. Where the offence is not absolute, non-notified Crown servants have to prove that they did not realise that the disclosure would be damaging.

In the case of recipients, such as newspaper editors, news media or publishers, s. 5 covers their unauthorised receipt and damaging disclosure of information, although I referred above to the danger of the use of common law offences of aiding and abetting offences under s. 1. 'Damaging' is established in the same way as for non-notified Crown servants under s. 1(4). However, the prosecution must prove in addition that the defendant made the disclosure knowing, or having reasonable cause to believe, that it is protected against disclosure under s. 1. In other words, *mens rea* has to be specifically established vis-à-vis the recipient's disclosure; it is not presumed as in the case of Crown servants. The relevant disclosure to the recipient will, under s. 5(1), be made by a Crown servant or government contractor without authority. Alternatively, it will be made after the servant or contractor has entrusted the information 'in confidence', either expressly or implicitly, and there was then an unauthorised disclosure. There are also offences covering situations where it was received by a third or fourth party and the disclosure to that party was made without authority by a person to whom it was entrusted 'in confidence'. A necessary condition for the offence is that the recipient is not committing an offence

---

[142] Lustgarten and Leigh, *In From the Cold.*

under ss. 1–4 (which only cover Crown servants or government contractors). Section 5 creates the possibility of a chain ad infinitum from the perspective of recipients. However, *mens rea* (or a criminal intent) must be established in the case of each recipient[143] and where the disclosure without lawful authority is by a government contractor or by a person to whom it was entrusted in confidence by a Crown servant or government contractor, the relevant disclosure must be by a British citizen, or it must take place in the UK, Channel Islands, Isle of Man or a colony. In other words a limitation to the territorial extent of the offence is introduced.

The Government accepted that, as s. 5 only applies to disclosures by Crown servants or government contractors, former servants and contractors and their disclosures were not included. It should be noted that this shortcoming, from the government's perspective, is not remedied by s. 5(1)(a)(iii), which only covers a situation where an intermediary receives information in confidence. The government may be forced to use the civil law of confidentiality in such cases. This could be a substantial flaw in the 1989 Act, since it was aimed at circumstances similar to those at stake in the Peter Wright affair. Where a newspaper does not receive information from a person who received it in confidence, such as a former security official, a prosecution under s. 5 may well flounder. And, it would not be possible to obtain an injunction under the civil law where a newspaper intended to report information received from a source not bound by confidentiality.[144]

As a concluding comment on this section it has been well observed that when everything is secret, nothing is secret. The offence under s. 1 covering security officials seeks to achieve such total secrecy. It is a case of overkill and its very breadth may well prevent it meeting its objectives. Quite rightly, the question has been raised whether s. 1 contravenes Art. 10 ECHR guaranteeing freedom of speech. By July 2000 *The Guardian* correspondent reported that eight books had been published in recent years by former MI6, MI5, SAS or military officers and publications have continued.[145]

---

[143] The position on *mens rea* and s. 2 (1)–(2) of the 1911 Act was never satisfactorily concluded. On the position of newspaper editors and court orders to produce documents and evidence under s. 9 and sch. 1, para. 4 PACE 1984, see *R v Central Criminal Court, ex p. Bright* [2001] 2 All ER 244 (n 145 below).

[144] Unless it could be established that the disclosure would damage the national interest and this would be on the usual test of the balance of convenience – inevitably on the government's side in such matters.

[145] 27 July 2000. Approval is given by the Cabinet Secretary. The Divisional Court has also spoken of the importance of fundamental rights to freedom of speech in refusing to award orders to the police to seize evidence of correspondence with David Shayler because of the stifling impact this would have on such a right and legitimate press investigation and freedom of speech. There is also discussion of the dangers of self-incrimination in allowing orders under s. 9 and sch. 1 PACE 1984: *R v Central Criminal Court, ex p. Bright, Alton and Rushbridger* [2001] 2 All ER 244. The court was not prepared to accept the 'bare assertion' of the police on evidence of national security. In relation to *The Observer's* reporter, his letter from Shayler had not been the subject of a wrongful order of access under the Act. See *A v B* [2009] EWCA Civ

Shayler's trial

David Shayler was a former MI5 officer. Shayler, who at that time lived in Paris, had sent a letter to *The Guardian* which was published after being edited. *The Observer* also published an article about the allegations made by Shayler. These included allegations and knowledge of names of British agents (these were not disclosed) who had conspired to assassinate Colonel Gaddafi of Libya. Shayler returned to England in August 2000, was arrested, charged with offences under s. 1 and also s. 4 (see p. 111 below). In a preparatory hearing under s. 29(1) of the Criminal Procedure and Investigations Act 1996 the court ruled that no PI defence was available to Shayler under those sections and that ss. 1 and 4 were compatible with Art. 10 ECHR guaranteeing freedom of speech. The judgment was upheld in the Court of Appeal[146] and House of Lords[147] . Article 10 ECHR provides:

1. Everyone has the right to freedom of expression. This right shall include freedom to hold opinions and to receive and impart information and ideas without interference by public authority and regardless of frontiers. This article shall not prevent States from requiring the licensing of broadcasting, television or cinema enterprises.
2. The exercise of these freedoms, since it carries with it duties and responsibilities, may be subject to such formalities, conditions, restrictions or penalties as are prescribed by law and are necessary in a democratic society, in the interests of national security, territorial integrity or public safety, for the prevention of disorder or crime, for the protection of health or morals, for the protection of the reputation or the rights of others, for preventing the disclosure of information received in confidence, or for maintaining the authority and impartiality of the judiciary.

Despite glowing endorsements of the common-law fundamental right to freedom of speech, ss. 1 and 4 OSA 1989 afforded the defendant no opportunity to show that the disclosure was in the PI and imposed on the prosecution no obligation to prove that the disclosure was not in the PI. It was clear to the Law Lords that in the context of the Act a defendant was not entitled to be acquitted if he showed it was, or believed it was, in the public or national interest to make the disclosure in question. Nor was he entitled to acquittal if the jury believed it was in the PI to make the disclosure. Sections 1 and 4 did not breach Art. 10. The European Court and Commission on Human Rights had recognised the need to preserve the secrecy of the security and intelligence information.[148] The test to be applied was whether in all the circumstances an interference with the right to freedom of expression prescribed by national law was excessive

---

24, p. 54 above to the effect that challenges to refusal to allow publication of memoirs have to be made to the Investigatory Powers Tribunal and not by way of judicial review.

[146] *R v Shayler* [2001] 1 WLR 2206 (CA).   [147] [2002] 2 All ER 477 (HL).

[148] See the case law cited by Lord Bingham at para. 26.

to meet the legitimate object that the state was seeking to achieve. The Law Lords did not believe that the ban was absolute because a lawful disclosure could be made. Under s. 7(3)(a) a former or acting member of those services could make a disclosure *internally*. These included the staff counsellor (see chapter 2, p. 45 above), the Attorney General, the Director of Public Prosecutions, the Commissioner of the Metropolitan Police or the prime minister or other ministers 'if s/he had concerns about the lawfulness of conduct, or concerns about misbehaviour, irregularity, maladministration, waste of resources or incompetence'. Where such internal report had 'no appropriate action', under s. 7(3)(b) the officer could seek official authorisation from a 'wider audience'. The request would have to be responded to consistently with the importance attached to freedom of speech; any restriction would need to be 'necessary, responsive to a pressing social need and proportionate'. A request should not be considered in a 'routine or mechanical' way (para. 30). A refusal to disclose could be subject to a judicial review.[149] The careful application of all these procedures 'provided sufficient and effective safeguards'. It was not open to a defendant to argue that in effect these procedures would have provided no safeguard or would have been of no avail. If the information posed no danger to security or intelligence interests a court's reaction is likely to be very different to a disclosure of highly classified information which could lead to identification of agents or informers. Because it is a Convention right, the court will engage in a 'rigorous and intrusive review' of a decision not to authorise publication.[150]

In the Court of Appeal decision in *Shayler*, the court indicated that the common-law defence of duress of circumstances would in theory be available as a defence against a charge under the Act. The government considered this may require legislative reform to remove such a defence. Since then, the courts have indicated that the duress would need to be direct and imminent to succeed. It would comprise a real and immediate threat to the defendant or someone for whom he is directly responsible. The need for legislative reform was not pressing.[151]

Defence

Section 2 OSA 1989 covers defence information and damaging disclosures by existing and former civil servants and defence contractors. Damage is not presumed as under s. 1. The defendant can establish the defence that at the time of the alleged offence they did not know, and had no reasonable cause to believe, that the information related to defence or that its disclosure would be

---

[149] *A v B*, note 144 above. On the shortcomings in some of these safeguards, see *R (B. Mohamed) v Secretary of State for Foreign and Commonwealth Affairs* [2009] EWHC 152 (Admin).

[150] Para. 33, per Lord Bingham, and see *R (Daly) v Secretary of State for the Home Department* [2001] 3 All ER 433.

[151] See Cm. 7543 paras. 162–3; *R v Hassan* [2005] UKHL 22.

damaging.[152] 'Damaging' is defined in s. 2(2). It is a disclosure which damages or is likely to damage the capability of the armed forces of the Crown, or any part of them, to carry out their tasks. It also covers a disclosure which leads to loss of life or injury to members of those forces, or to serious damage to the equipment or installation of those forces. Last of all, it covers those disclosures which otherwise endanger the interests of the UK abroad, seriously obstructs the promotion or protection by the UK of those interests, or endangers the safety of British citizens abroad.

There were fears that the section would include within its embrace disclosures about unnecessary wastage, inefficient production and substandard products, especially if these affected UK economic interests abroad, or defence cuts causing forces to be poorly armed and equipped in time of conflict. Section 2(4) defines 'defence', however, to include:

(a) the size, shape, organisation, logistics, order of battle, deployment, opera-tions, state of readiness and training of the armed forces of the Crown;
(b) the weapons, stores or other equipment of those forces and the invention, development, production and operation of such equipment and research relating to it; [This would need to be a damaging disclosure, so the jury would be correct to consider factors which diminish the damage to UK military interests abroad by, for example, revealing extravagant waste.]
(c) defence policy and strategy and military planning and intelligence;
(d) plans and measures for the maintenance of essential supplies and services that are or would be needed in time of war.

For a party who is not a civil servant or a government contractor, s. 5 provides that their unauthorised receipt, or receipt in confidence, and subsequent unau-thorised disclosure, is an offence where that person knows, or has reasonable cause to believe, that it is protected against disclosure by s. 2 and that it has come into that person's possession as under s. 5(1). The prosecution must establish *mens rea*, and that the disclosure was damaging, and that the defendant knew, or had reasonable cause to believe, that it would be damaging. Similar limits apply to a potential chain of recipients as applied in the discussion on the receipt of security and intelligence information above.

This section would cover the notorious episode involving Duncan Sandys MP who used leaked information to reveal Britain's ill-prepared war defences prior to 1939. Apart from parliamentary privilege for MPs, no defence would obtain to protect those who originally disclosed the information. The Sandys case prompted Sir Winston Churchill to denounce the use of the OSA to shield ministers who have strong personal interests in concealing the truth about matters from the country.

---

[152] *R v Keogh* [2007] EWCA 528 Crim holds that ss. 2–3 OSA do not reverse the burden of proof but the defendant is under an evidentiary burden to make out the defence.

International relations and information received in confidence from states and international organisations

Section 3 is concerned with unauthorised disclosures of information relating to international relations by Crown servants and government contractors. Section 5 is concerned with the damaging disclosures of such information by others who have received the information within the terms of s. 5(1). For the former defendants, knowledge of the damaging nature of the disclosure will be presumed; for the latter (others) it has to be proved. Offences under this section include the disclosure of information relating to international relations. It also covers 'any confidential information . . . obtained from a state other than the United Kingdom or an international organisation, which is, or was, in the servant or contractor's possession by virtue of their position as such'. Section 3(5) defines international relations as relations between states, international organisations (IO), or between one or more states and one or more such organisations, and 'includes any matter relating to a State other than the United Kingdom or to an international organisation which is capable of affecting the relations of the United Kingdom with another State or with an international organisation'. IO would include the European Community (EC) and Union and the UN, although Douglas Hurd as Home Secretary expressed the view that the bulk of information from the EC was 'not confidential', and that most information received in confidence would fail the damage test.[153]

In spite of Mr Hurd's assurance, if a journalist revealed information leaked by a civil servant that subsidies were being paid to companies purchasing privatised concerns which contravened EU law, then this would concern international relations and it may well be damaging to such relations. Or, once again, a disclosure which revealed Cabinet discussions and pejorative comments about the national characteristics of our EU partners and allies may be treated likewise. It could also cover the disclosure of information concerning inhumane treatment by an ally or trading partner of political opponents or minority groups. Where the broad test of 'damaging' is made out, the offence is established. Such information about security and intelligence and information obtained by torture is likely to be protected by s. 1.

The test of damaging is to be found in s. 3(2). A disclosure damages, first, if it endangers the interests of the UK abroad, seriously obstructs the promotion or protection by the UK of those interests or endangers the safety of British citizens abroad and, secondly, if it is a disclosure of information that is such that its unauthorised disclosure would be likely to have any of those effects. The breadth of this latter category can be illustrated by an example. If a document was stamped 'confidential', or was obtained in circumstances making it reasonable for the state or international organisation to expect confidentiality, which is readily presumed in international relationships, then it will be treated

---

[153] HC Debs., vol. 147, col. 429 (15 February 1989). This is not true of the EU's second and third pillars pending reform under the Treaty of Lisbon.

as confidential for the purposes of the OSA, even if it would not be considered confidential under our civil law as judicially developed.[154]

In the White Paper, it seemed that the government had created an absolute offence under this category. In fact, the Home Secretary and ministers were at pains to point out that the confidentiality or nature of documents might, but would not necessarily, be crucial.[155] Even though otherwise innocuous information is stamped 'confidential', a jury may infer, but is not constrained to infer, that its unauthorised leak is damaging.

Crime

Existing and former Crown servants and government contractors are guilty of an offence where they make an unauthorised disclosure of information which is or has been in their possession because of their official position, and which results in one of the following:

(a) the commission of an offence (Events in Northern Ireland concerning security leaks of information on individuals have dramatically illustrated the sensitivity of information in the possession of the police and security forces, the disclosure of which has led to the murder of IRA suspects.[156] The government has argued that the defence available in s. 4(4) (below) would protect disclosures about, for example, inefficient security systems.)

(b) an escape from legal custody or the doing of any other act prejudicial to the safekeeping of persons in legal custody (One wonders about the situation where a prison officer reveals that a prison is at breaking point, or that inmates have been inhumanely treated and in consequence are on the point of insurrection.)

(c) impeding the prevention or detection of offences or the apprehension or prosecution of suspected offenders.[157]

There is a general defence to these charges where the defendant can prove that at the time of the alleged offence they did not know and had no reasonable cause to believe that the disclosure would have any of those effects.[158]

Furthermore, by s. 4(2)(b), unauthorised disclosures of information which are such that they are likely to have any of the above consequences are also an offence. A defendant may, however, show that they did not know, and had no reasonable cause to believe, that it was information to which the section applied.[159]

---

[154] IC and IT cases on confidentiality, ch. 6, p. 242 below.

[155] HC Debs., vol. 147, cols. 426–7.

[156] Stevens, *The Times*, 18 May 1990. The Stevens Inquiry, Overview and Recommendations (2003), into collusion between the police and security services in Northern Ireland leading to murder and other abuses: http://cain.ulst.ac.uk/issues/collusion/stevens3/stevens3summary.htm.

[157] S. 4(2)(a).   [158] S. 4(4).

[159] S. 4(5) but note this defence does not apply to s. 4(2)(b).

It is important to appreciate that police records are not given blanket protection by the OSA, although police officers are prescribed as 'Crown servants' for the purposes of the Act.[160] Where information is sold or disclosed, the law of corruption, data protection, and disciplinary offences may have to be invoked against officers. The role of the Criminal Records Bureau and Police National Computer were examined in chapter 1, p. 13.

Where 'other persons', i.e. non-civil servants and government contractors, receive information that is covered by the above provisions of s. 4, it is an offence when they make an unauthorised disclosure of information protected by s. 4 where they know, or have reasonable cause to believe, that it is protected against disclosure by s. 4(2). As in the other areas of information, the prosecution must prove, and cannot simply presume, the defendant's state of knowledge.

Information relating to special investigation powers

Section 4 also applies to any information obtained under 'special investigation powers'; viz. information which is obtained by warrant under the Interception of Communications Act 1985 and any related information, documents and articles, or obtained by warrant under the Security Service Act (SSA) 1989 or the Intelligence Services Act 1994. To this legislation has now been added the interception powers under Regulation of Investigatory Powers Act 2000 (RIPA) as well as those matters which are carried out by the intelligence services under Pt II of that Act and which require a warrant, or authorisation (see chapter 2, p. 58). These Acts authorise what had hitherto been practised under the prerogative powers of national security and preservation of the peace.[161] The powers of mail interception, and more latterly 'phone tapping', had always been assumed to exist, and that was felt to be sufficient justification until one plaintiff invoked Art. 8 of the European Convention on Human Rights (ECHR) to challenge a telephone tap. We saw the consequences in chapter 2. The provisions of the legislation were examined in that chapter.

The provisions relating to intrusive surveillance powers and encryption under RIPA and the powers under the Police Act 1997 which are not covered by this present provision may well be relevant to the preceding provision concerning crime where unauthorised disclosures are made which contravene the relevant provision, viz. they impede the prevention or detection of offences, their prosecution etc.

Section 4(3) OSA 1989 makes it an absolute offence for information, as described, obtained under the Acts to be disclosed without lawful authority by a Crown servant or government contractor. In fact, 'absolute' is not strictly accurate since a defendant can make out a defence similar to the one available for security and intelligence officers under s. 1 and described earlier.

---

[160] S. 12.   [161] Lord Birkett, *Interception of Communications*, Cmnd 283 (1957).

Under s. 5, a person, for example a newspaper editor, who received information obtained under such warrants and who knowingly discloses it without authority, is guilty of an offence. The prosecution must prove that they knew or had reasonable cause to believe it belonged to such a category to establish a criminal offence. Actual knowledge of the nature of the information has to be proved. Once proved, and in most cases it will be glaringly obvious what its nature is, the offence will be made out no matter how trivial the information is and without reference to any PI being served by its being made public. This is the strictest provision of all for third party recipients as no damage has to be proved.[162]

The existence of this offence means that there would be no difficulty in prosecuting a Cathy Massiter, the former MI5 officer who revealed the targeting and intercepting of CND campaigners by the security service. This would also appear to be the case regarding Katherine Gun outlined above. In the latter case, a prosecution would have proved too embarrassing (see p. 97 above). This measure is particularly draconian and dangerous. It refuses to allow for the possibility that the rot is operating at such a high level that it is impossible to deal with it by internal devices. The investigatory and tribunal procedures under these two Acts, which seek to protect 'victims', are judicial-review proof; that is to say that they cannot be reviewed by the courts. A revelation of a phone-tap without a warrant or other unauthorised invasion of privacy would not be covered by s. 4 OSA, but it may well be covered by s. 1 where perpetrated by security, intelligence or other notified officials.

Information entrusted in confidence to other states

The government plugged a loop-hole by providing in s. 6 OSA 1989 that the unlawful disclosure of information relating to security, intelligence, defence or international relations which has been communicated in confidence by or on behalf of the UK to another state or IO, will be an offence if two conditions are satisfied: first, if it has come into the discloser's possession, whether originally disclosed to them or another, without the authority of the state or IO, or a member of the latter; secondly, if the disclosure is not already an offence under the previous sections of the Act. Section 6 is aimed at punishing a disclosure of information which has been leaked abroad, even if already published abroad, without the authority of the state or IO to whom it was entrusted, or where the discloser otherwise has no authority. In other words, publishing a story in the UK which satisfies the above criteria, and even though widely published abroad without authority, will constitute an offence. Publication with the authority of the overseas state prior to disclosure is a defence. The prosecution must prove that the defendant made a damaging disclosure knowing, or having reasonable

---

[162] See Lustgarten and Leigh, *In From the Cold*, ch. 10.

cause to believe, that it is information as described in s. 6 and that its disclosure would be damaging.

Disclosure by recipients under s. 5

We have seen how receipt of information within the terms of s. 5, which is information protected by ss. 1–4, and its subsequent unauthorised disclosure by the recipient, will be an offence, and how a chain of offences may be committed. We also noted the limitations and exceptions concerning an unauthorised disclosure by a Crown servant or government contractor and those to whom such disclosures are made. An offence is not committed where such a disclosure is made by a person who is not a British citizen or takes place outside the UK, the Channel Islands, the Isle of Man or a colony.

Finally s. 5 refers to s. 1 of the 1911 Act which concerns 'espionage' and which has already been discussed. Section 5 stipulates that it is an offence to disclose any information without lawful authority and which the discloser knows, or has reasonable cause to believe, came into his or her possession as a result of a contravention of s. 1 of the OSA 1911.

Safeguarding information

Section 8 creates a variety of offences relating to the following. Crown servants (including a notified person under s. 1(1) whether or not 'a Crown servant', or government contractors, commit an offence if they have in their possession information which it would be an offence under the Act to disclose without lawful authority and, being a Crown servant etc., they retain the document or article contrary to their official duty. A defence is available where they believe, and have no reasonable cause to believe otherwise, that at the relevant time they were acting in accordance with an official duty. Offences also cover the failure of a government contractor to comply with an official direction for the return or disposal of a relevant document, and the failure by a Crown servant or contractor to take such care to prevent the unauthorised disclosure of the document or article as a person in his or her position may reasonably be expected to take. This latter offence criminally punishes negligence. No prosecution but a resignation followed in April 2009 when Assistant Commissioner Bob Quick, who was head of Scotland Yard's specialist operations wing involving anti terrorism, unwittingly revealed outside No. 10 papers with details of an anti terrorist operation marked 'secret'.

Any person, including a past Crown servant or government contractor, who has information that it is an offence to disclose without lawful authority under s. 5, is guilty of an offence if they fail to comply with an official direction for the return or disposal of the information. Such persons are also guilty of an offence if they, in simple parlance, are negligent in looking after information entrusted to them in confidence by a Crown servant or contractor. A person is also guilty where they fail to comply with an official direction for the return of information protected by s. 6. Offences also cover disclosures which facilitate unauthorised access to protected information (s. 8(6)).

Miscellaneous

Offences under the Act are triable on indictment or summons, although some offences under s. 8 are triable by summons only. 'Trial by summons' means trial without a jury before magistrates who tend to be more sympathetic to the prosecution than juries and to be more conviction-minded. Under guidelines issued by the Attorney General, juries may be vetted for OSA trials. The Act contains arrest-and-search provisions. Although these are more extensive than under the PACE 1984, the latter Act now applies to legally privileged, excluded and special procedure material.[163] By s. 11(4), the provisions of earlier secrecy legislation, allowing the public[164] to be excluded from a trial on the grounds of national security, apply to offences under the 1989 Act, although there are minor exceptions under s. 8. Such orders will have to be consistent with the HRA and Art. 10.[165]

Under the Act, the term 'Crown servant' includes ministers, civil servants, members of the armed forces, police officers and any other person employed or appointed in or for the purposes of any police force.[166] The Secretary of State may prescribe as Crown servants office-holders and some or all of their staff, and the Comptroller and Auditor General and employees of the National Audit Office have been so prescribed.[167] Orders are subject to the affirmative resolution procedure of the House of Commons. The Secretary of State may also prescribe some or all of the members of staff of a range of bodies. 'Government contractor' is defined as a person other than a Crown servant who provides goods or services for the purposes of a minister or body of Crown servants. The Act extends to Northern Ireland and to offences committed abroad by British citizens and, with minor exceptions, Crown servants.

The OSA and privilege

There are bound to be problems of practical importance concerning the question of disclosures in contravention of the Act and privilege. The privileges in question are of two kinds. The first is that of an MP who cannot be prosecuted under the criminal law for statements made or actions in the House or for those which are made or performed in the course of parliamentary proceedings. The second concerns the privilege between a lawyer and client and the giving of legal

---

[163] See *R v Central Criminal Court etc.* above note 145, p. 105. S. 11(3) of the OSA 1989 applies PACE, s. 9(2) and sch, 1 para. 3(b) to s. 9 OSA 1911.
[164] *Re Crook* (1989) 93 Cr App Rep 17.   [165] See *Leander v Sweden* (1987) 9 EHRR 433.
[166] *Lewis v Cattle* [1938] 2 KB 454; *R v Loot* [1985] Crim LR 154.   [167] SI 1990/200 and s. 12.

advice during which a disclosure of information protected by the 1989 Act is made.

The Act does not add to, or diminish, parliamentary privilege. An MP will be protected as before, though the government resisted an attempt to allow a member of the public to be given immunity in passing protected information to an MP. The current position is that the privilege is that of the MP and no one else.[168] In November 2008, an Opposition front-bench spokesman, Damian Green MP, was arrested under the common-law offences of 'conspiring to commit misconduct in public office and aiding or abetting, counselling or procuring misconduct in public office' after Home Office immigration papers were leaked to him by a civil servant Christopher Galley. The police investigation and arrest followed a request to them from the Cabinet Office to investigate a series of Home Office leaks. The charges against Green were subsequently dropped, but the episode raised many questions about the extent of parliamentary privilege. Mr Green's premises in Parliament were searched without a warrant by the police with the Serjeant at Arms' permission.[169] Similarly, the 1989 Act does not affect the operation of the law relating to legal professional privilege, contrary to the views of the Law Society as represented by the Shadow Home Secretary.[170] Where the disclosure is made with a view to obtaining legal advice on, e.g., whether disclosure constitutes an offence, it is protected. It will not be protected where the disclosure was made to facilitate a crime in which the lawyer has become involved.

The Attorney General

The role of the Attorney General – whose *fiat* is required for a prosecution under the Act – has been described as invidious inasmuch as the decision to prosecute is his. Franks found no evidence of political interference with Attorneys General in the past. Events since Franks cast doubts on the continuing accuracy of that view,[171] and in the Peter Wright episode an embarrassed Cabinet Secretary was forced to admit in open court in Australia, by the Attorney General himself, that certain decisions on prosecuting, or not prosecuting, had

---

[168] See HC 173 (1937–8) and HC 101 (1938–9) for the Select Committee on Official Secrets and MPs.

[169] Home Affairs Committee, *Policing Process of Home Office Leaks Inquiry*, HC 157 (2008–9). A Speaker's committee set up to investigate the process leading to permission for a police search had not met by April 2009. The Speaker issued a protocol stating that, in future, police searches of MPs' offices in Parliament would require a warrant.

[170] HC Debs., vol. 147, col. 503 (16 February 1989).

[171] Suspicion has attended both Labour and Conservative Government interference: see Ponting, *The Right to Know*, ch. 6 and Nicol, 'Official secrets and jury vetting'. For breaches of confidentiality proceedings and the Attorney General's role, see HC Debs., cols. 619–20 (1 December 1986). As with the Lord Chancellor, the problem attaches to a multiplicity of roles in one person: law officer, MP, minister, prosecutor etc. See *AG v BBC* [2007] EWCA Civ 280.

not been the responsibility of the Attorney General.[172] The proximity of the Attorney General to the government makes it very difficult for the office-holder to argue persuasively that he is an 'honest broker', regardless of his identity. The performance of the Attorney General in the Matrix Churchill affair bestowed little credit upon the holder of the office.

Franks found that s. 2 was saved from absurdity by the 'sparing exercise of the Attorney General's discretion to prosecute', although the matter still gave rise to 'considerable unease'. Even after reform, Franks still envisaged a central place for the Attorney General, who would retain control of prosecutions in the major areas where Franks recommended the law should operate and hopefully apply judicious discretion. An 'appropriate alternative' to legislation to protect official secrecy outside the area of espionage was difficult to conceive, the government argued in 1972, and Franks accepted that over-reliance on voluntary forms of internal restraint by the press and media would be undesirable. They may have a 'responsibility' to publish what is in the PI, but government has a constitutional responsibility to protect the nation, which cannot be 'abdicated on the basis that a failure to exercise them will be made good by the responsible behaviour of others'. And, as we all know, the press in particular do not always act with the requisite degree of responsibility.[173]

In 2008 the prime minister published proposals to amend the prosecution powers of the Attorney General (see Introduction, p. 6 and chapter 2, p. 49). The bill will remove the requirement of the consent of the Attorney General in relation to prosecutions, but s. 9 OSA 1989 is not included. This section requires the consent of the Attorney General. A decision on beginning summary proceedings is to be taken by the Director of Public Prosecutions.

Public Interest Disclosure Act 1998 (PIDA)

The PIDA seeks to provide a 'framework for whistleblowing across the public, private and voluntary sectors'.[174] It amends the Employment Rights Act 1996. Where a qualifying disclosure (QD) is made, the whistle-blower raising a matter of genuine concern in good faith will be protected against victimisation. A QD does not include a disclosure which is an offence, e.g., in contravention of the Official Secrets Acts. Victims are entitled to enhanced compensation where they are not reinstated and there are no qualifying periods of employment for such rights. Interim protection orders may be sought. QDs are specified in the Act and include those made in a reasonable belief that there are actual or apprehended breaches of law, miscarriages of justice, dangers to health, safety and the environment, and include concealing such malpractice. The Act will

---

[172] Sir Robert gave evidence that the decision not to prosecute Chapman Pincher for revelations in *Their Trade is Treachery* was taken by the Attorney General, Sir Michael Havers. Sir Michael took no part in the decision.

[173] Especially on unjustified invasion of privacy. See ch. 8.

[174] G. Dehn, 'Public Interest Disclosure Act', *Current Law Statutes* (1998).

encourage whistle-blowing procedures and will, believes Dehn, have the effect of encouraging employers to publicise employees' rights in order to minimise such disclosures.[175] Disclosure may be made internally, e.g. to a minister where a civil servant is involved, employer or manager, or to an external regulator. A list of authorised (permitted) disclosees is contained in orders (SIs 1999/1549, 2003/1993 and 2008/531). Where a disclosure is made externally, additional safeguards must be satisfied for the disclosure to be protected. Where a cover up has been attempted, a disclosure to the press is more likely to be protected. The Act allows disclosures to others, but there must be no question of gain in such disclosures and disclosure must be reasonable in all the circumstances and other conditions must be satisfied. This will be particularly important where a disclosure is made to the press and an order is sought seeking the identity of the source.[176] 'Reasonable' may be interpreted with regard to the identity of the person to whom the disclosure was made and the seriousness of the matter and other factors. Exceptionally serious matters may be disclosed and protected in less restricted circumstances. Confidentiality clauses seeking to prevent QDs are void. A QD may be made to a legal adviser while seeking legal advice and there is no good-faith requirement in this case – the only disclosure afforded such a concession. The unavailability of the Act to the secret and intelligence services was noted in chapter 2 as well as to civil servants engaged in national security work. The position of contractors is not referred to. Police are now protected by these provisions by virtue of s. 37 Police Reform Act 2002. The *Financial Times* noted that in 2003 £10 million had been paid in compensation for whistle-blowing.[177] The Financial Services Authority saw whistle-blowing as an important element in combating financial irregularity. In September 2008, Marks and Spencer's dismissed an employee who had disclosed confidential plans to change the company's pension scheme for employees to a less favourable scheme. This disclosure was not in the PI, the company argued.

[175] *Ibid.*   [176] See ch. 11, p. 413 *et seq.* below.   [177] 30 April 2003.

4

The Freedom of Information Act 2000[1]

On 30 November 2000, the Freedom of Information Bill was given Royal Assent to become the Freedom of Information Act 2000 (FOIA). Section 1 of the Act has been described by the Information Tribunal (IT) as a 'new fundamental right to information'.[2] The bill had been before Parliament for over a year. Prior to that, the White Paper on Access to Information and then a draft bill and consultation paper, had been scrutinised by the Select Committee on Public Administration in the Commons as well as, in the case of the latter, by a special committee of the House of Lords.[3] In 1966, the Fulton report had recommended ways of removing unnecessary secrecy from public life. Since 1974, and throughout the long years of opposition, the Labour Party had supported numerous Freedom of Information (FOI) bills.[4] These would have created a right for an Information Commissioner to enforce the disclosure of information and would also have amended the Official Secrets Act (OSA).

Reluctant support was given to a Private Member's bill in 1979 by Prime Minister Callaghan immediately before the loss of office to Mrs Thatcher. Neil Kinnock stated in 1992 that a FOI Bill would be among the first bills of an incoming Labour Government. For Tony Blair FOI legislation was essential to bring about a culture change in British government. It would be a signal of a 'new relationship' between the people and government. This fundamental and vital change in the relationship between government and governed[5] would be at the heart of his reforms on access to information. The new government was over two years into power before a FOI Bill was published; its publication had been subject to numerous delays – in spite of the fact that many Western democratic

---

[1] J. Macdonald *et al.* (eds.), *The Law of Freedom of Information*, 2nd edn (2009); P. Coppel, *Information Rights*, 2nd edn (2007).

[2] *DFES v IC and Evening Standard* EA/2006/0006 para. 61.

[3] For the Commons Committee: HC 398-1–II (1997–8), HC 570-1–II (1998–9) and HC 78 (1999–2000); for the House of Lords a special committee of the House of Lords: HL 97 (1998–9); the proposals had also been before the Lords Deregulation Committee to consider powers delegated under the bill – HL 79 (1998–9).

[4] See ch. 8 of the second edition of this work and also P. Birkinshaw and A. Parkin 'Freedom of information' in R. Blackburn and R. Plant (eds.), *Constitutional Reform: The Labour Government's constitutional reform agenda* (1999), ch. 8.

[5] *Your Right to Know: Freedom of information*, Cm. 3818 (1997), Preface by the prime minister.

states had models which could act as inspiration for the British model. A wealth of experience had been acquired on FOI regimes overseas.

There was a prevailing sense of disappointment, indeed outrage, on the publication of this bill in May 1999. Why should this be so? There was a widespread and pervasive sense that underlying the provision of a right to information held by public bodies, the bill was characterised by numerous devices whose targeted objective was the maintenance of secrecy. After two years in power the initial declarations of building a new constitution fit for a new millennium had been tempered by caution, even defensiveness. The Government had suffered embarrassing leaks and publications of sensitive information.[6] More particularly, the bill, which was part of a consultation package, was seen as a wholesale abandonment of the liberal principles contained in the White Paper *Your Right to Know*[7] which was published along with an enthusiastic endorsement by the prime minister in December 1997. The White Paper was widely acclaimed for offering a completely new vista on how government should be run in the future, turning its back on unnecessary secrecy in British public life: the White Paper would introduce a legal right of access to information across the public sector, a sector which was to be broadly defined. 'This will be a radical change in the relationship between citizens and their government', it proclaimed. Too radical, it seems, for the minister responsible for the White Paper was sacked in the Cabinet reshuffle in July 1998 after press revelations of his being humbled by senior ministers and responsibility for the bill was handed to the Home Office, never a ministry to experiment with radical innovation in government.[8]

The White Paper promised that there would be a legally enforceable right to information, which included documents,[9] held by public bodies. The IT has stated on several occasions that the right is a right to information and this point will be returned to later.[10] In particular, the White Paper stated that in all but one area – policy formulation – the test for withholding information would be where its disclosure would cause 'substantial harm' – a more demanding test than any other FOI statute. The Information Commissioner (IC) would have power to decide on where the greater public interest (PI) lay – in publication or in withholding information. The Commissioner's decisions would be enforced through the courts. There would be no ministerial override to prevent disclosure. Exempting interests would number seven and not fifteen as under the 1994 Open Government Code on Access of John Major (see chapter 9). While

---

[6] These included the Ecclestone affair; events surrounding publicity for the arrest of Jack Straw's son; the McPherson Report on the death of Stephen Lawrence, Cm. 4262-I–II (1999) published in Scotland by the press before official publication and then the discovery that addresses of witnesses had wrongly been published; press publication of Cabinet minutes of the Dome project; the press story about Mandelson and the Hinduja brothers' passports and so on.

[7] See note 3.   [8] The Home Office has long been subject to leaks, ch. 3, p. 115.

[9] The 1994 code only covered information not documents although the ombudsman has suggested that the easiest manner in which to comply with the code may well be by supplying documents.

[10] See pp. 146, 180 below.

almost universally acclaimed, the White Paper had possessed some problems at its core. The relationship between access to personal documents and to other official documents was not clearly thought through. The subject of access to personal records under FOIA and other provisions is taken up in chapter 8. In the case of personal documents the law would have to conform with the provisions of the EU directive on data protection, implemented by the Data Protection Act 1998 (DPA).[11]

Several areas of information were excluded from the bill – meaning the proposed law would have no application whatsoever to those items of information. These included the security and intelligence services and also functions relating to the investigation, prosecution or prevention of crime or the bringing of civil or criminal proceedings by public authorities (PAs). Parliament was excluded. PAs would be excluded from provisions allowing access to their personnel records by employees beyond those rights contained in the DPA. Legal advice and that protected by legal professional privilege were to be excluded.[12]

As well as these difficulties, which were criticised by the advocates of open government, there were criticisms of a different persuasion. It was also felt by some that the tone of the White Paper was hopelessly optimistic especially for instance in setting the damage test as one of 'substantial harm' and that safeguards were inadequate to prevent administrative overload, especially given the wide range of bodies covered by the White Paper many of whom would have no expertise in dealing with access to information claims.[13] This is a wonderful White Paper, opined one eminent Australian judge, but, he added, it won't see its way into law! The White Paper also had its detractors in influential circles among the senior ranks of the civil service although others were supportive.

The Act and its contents

The draft bill was amended considerably to remove some of the more objectionable features and the government modified its position on a variety of features as the bill progressed. The IC was established although he would succeed to the office of the Data Protection Commissioner. He can issue decision notices (DNs), enforcement notices (ENs) and information notices (INs). From his DNs an appeal may be made to the IT by either party. Only the PA can appeal to the IT against an EN or IN. The Act, which also deals with amendments to the public-records legislation, makes information held by PAs available as a legal right unless it is exempt or otherwise access is qualified, or where the PA is excluded from the Act's provisions, i.e. it is not named in the schedule or only named in respect of certain functions. Notable exclusions include the Queen

---

[11] EC Council Directive 95/46 ([1995] OJ L281/31). See ch. 7.
[12] The report of the Commons Select Committee on Public Administration on the White Paper is HC 398-I–II (1997/8).
[13] See the evidence of Professor Hazell to the Select Committee, HC 570-v (1998/99), Q. 485.

and royal family; the security and intelligence services; the Serious Organised Crime Agency; nationalised banks; and the Bank of England in relation to (a) monetary policy, (b) financial operations intended to support financial institutions for the purposes of maintaining stability, and (c) the provision of private banking services and related services but not otherwise. The BBC is also excluded in relation to its functions of journalism, art or literature and this question has been a constant source of complaint.[14]

Authorities must respond 'promptly' to requests, which have to be in writing, and in any event within twenty working days (originally it was forty).[15] There is no undertaking to produce indexes of information held by authorities, a reform introduced in 1996 in the USA (see chapter 12). The law relating to EU documents allows for the establishment of a register (see chapter 10). Full indexes would help the task of requesters enormously. They would assist them to establish what documents they wished to see. As seen in chapter 1 there are now Information Asset Registers (IARs). The IAR is a catalogue of unpublished information resources that anyone with web access can search through its web interface inforoute at www.inforoute.hmso.gov.uk in order to identify: 'what information the government holds: how useful that information is, and importantly, a contact point to whom requests for the underlying information may be made; requests would be subject to the . . . FOI Act.' Guidance on the IAR may be found at: http://www.opsi.gov.uk/advice/crown-copyright/copyright-guidance/information-asset-register-and-freedom-of-information

Public authorities

The Act, following the White Paper, covers an extremely wide range of public bodies making it unique initially in the world FOI landscape. A very large corpus of non-departmental public bodies and advisory bodies is included in sch. 1 FOIA. It includes the ombudsmen and the IC. It covers all government departments, the House of Commons and House of Lords (unlike the USA where Congress is not included), the Northern Ireland and Welsh Assemblies and the armed forces of the Crown.[16] The FOIA covers local government, the meshing of existing and new local government provisions was given better effect in 2006 (see chapter 9), the NHS, educational bodies funded by the state including universities, and the police including British Transport and Ministry of Defence police. The Act provides that bodies created by the royal prerogative or enactment or by ministerial fiat or by a government department or the

---

[14] *Sugar v BBC* [2009] UKHL 9.
[15] The period in the 1994 code was twenty days for 'simple requests'. Reforms in 1996 in the USA to its FOIA have set a time limit of ten days to respond to expedited requests in two subject areas.
[16] But not the special forces or those assisting GCHQ; see ch. 2.

Welsh Assembly and whose members are appointed by the Crown, a minister, a government department or the Welsh Assembly may be included.[17]

The minister may designate private bodies as public bodies for the purposes of the bill where they are performing public functions as well as bodies under contract with PAs to deliver public services. By 2009, not one body had been so designated (see Introduction, p. 7). The Ministry of Justice launched a consultation in 2007 on designation of additional bodies.[18] In the case of the former, privatised utilities spring to mind although not all their functions are public. It covers 'publicly owned companies'.[19] PAs may be listed as bodies to which the Act has limited application. It will not apply to non-public affairs. This was of particular concern to privatised industries. Bodies not included in the schedule or which are not designated or otherwise covered are excluded as explained above.

Because of this breadth of coverage, the Act's provisions did not have to be implemented for five years in order to allow those bodies who have no expertise in access requests to acquire that expertise. Initially it was reported that central government would be brought under the Act within eighteen months – they had been used to operating under the 1994 Code on Access. Provisions on access to personal documents would be effective from October 2001. In March 2001, it was reported that the Act would not come into effect in relation to government departments until at least July 2002 because many files were missing or unlocated.[20] But this date would only cover publication schemes; rights of individual access would come later. The date of individual access rights was finally set for 1 January 2005.

Publication schemes

Authorities will have to draw up publication schemes detailing the information that they will publish and the manner in which it will be published and whether it is available free of charge or for a fee. The scheme may be published in such manner as the authority thinks fit. Schemes are to be approved by the Commissioner who may produce model schemes. While these give significant powers of influence to the Commissioner, the Commissioner is not given any power to compel the inclusion of specific items. He may simply refuse to approve the scheme or he may revoke approval given – with notice and reasons. The publication schemes could be of enormous value if, for instance, they published information about internal manuals, guidelines, rules and procedures which are used to determine individual cases. In the USA, information requested on two previous occasions is automatically published under mandatory provisions as is that for which there is likely to be a substantial demand. It was envisaged at

---

[17] They do not have to be scheduled. Could the IC presume they were public authorities?

[18] Consultation Paper CP 27/07, *Freedom of Information Act 2000 Designation of Additional Authorities*, Ministry of Justice.

[19] Ss. 3(1)(b) and 6.   [20] *The Guardian* 7 March 2001.

an early stage that information about government decisions and the facts and analysis behind them would be made available under such schemes. Schemes could usefully include information about government contracts (contract price, unit prices, performance targets) or returns to a consultation document and information about specific contracts. The PI in making information available would have to be considered by authorities as well as a general provision on giving reasons for decisions. Originally, it was envisaged that the IC could award a practice recommendation against an authority that was not complying with its scheme but this now appears unlikely as such recommendations are linked to matters covered in a code of practice and the draft code says practically nothing about schemes. An EN may be served by the IC to ensure compliance by an authority with a scheme (see below). The Ministry of Justice (formerly Department for Constitutional Affairs (DCA)) and the IC have published guidance on Publication Schemes.[21] The Campaign for Freedom of Information published a report entitled *Central Government Publication Schemes Good Practice* in 2004. The IC launched a programme of revision of schemes to be brought into effect in 2009. The IC offers a model publication scheme for all authorities covering seven different categories of information.[22] Despite all the effort involved in producing the schemes public awareness was low. The argument that MPs had a reasonable expectation that the details of their expenses that would be published would be that in the publication schemes was rejected by the High Court (see chapter 8, pp. 305, 309 and Introduction, p. 1).

Disclosure logs often set out details of requests received and information disclosed under the Act. A good practice guide was published by the DCA in December 2005. A MySociety website, http://www.whatdotheyknow.com/, allows searches by listed PAs and is designed for requesters to make requests to PAs, allowing the responses to be published automatically on the website. Questions of copyright have been raised by some authorities.[23]

Public-interest disclosures, exemptions and the veto

Section 2 deals with the PI in releasing exempt information. This provision was subject to considerable amendment as it progressed through Parliament. It was a barometer of the changing nature of the bill: was it becoming a true measure of openness with ultimate power in the Commissioner, or was it yet a further grace and favour measure under the ultimate control of the executive? The end result is a mixture of both of these positions. Although, in the original bill, authorities have to have regard to the PI when exercising this discretion (see below), the decision on disclosure was *their* decision and there was no PI

---

[21] IC, www.ico.gov.uk/what_we_cover/freedom_of_information/publication_schemes.aspx; and MOJ, www.justice.gov.uk/publication-scheme.htm.

[22] www.ico.gov.uk/upload/documents/library/freedom_of_information/detailed_specialist_guides/generic_scheme_v1.0.pdf.

[23] House of Commons Library, *Freedom of Information Requests*, SN/PC/02950 October 2008.

override in the bill enforceable by the Commissioner. This was considered to be a substantial compromise of the spirit of the White Paper. In the case of a minister, s/he can account to Parliament for a refusal to disclose. For public bodies not headed by a minister, this option was not available.

The bill was subsequently amended to allow the Commissioner to order the disclosure of information but this was subject to what amounts to a veto power in various parties to stop disclosure. The veto power which the White Paper rejected was therefore resurrected in various respects (see below). It is contained in s. 53 FOIA. The veto power was exercised for the first time in February 2009 in relation to the ruling from the IT that the minutes of Cabinet meetings discussing the possibility of commencing hostilities in Iraq should be published.[24] Just before the access provisions became operative in 2005, the then Lord Chancellor, Lord Falconer, announced that the veto would have to be agreed to by the Cabinet and was not one for an individual minister – although this was based on an interview with *the Guardian* published on 1 January 2005, not an official statement. Veto would be 'very, very exceptional'. In exercising the veto in 2009, the Justice Secretary announced he had *consulted* the Cabinet.[25]

But this failure to give the Commissioner final power of decision in PI disclosures was just one of numerous alleged compromises contained in the Act. It has to be said, however, that several of the excluded categories were brought in as exemptions. First of all, the number of exemptions had grown from seven in the White Paper to over twenty-three in the Act.[26] The test for withholding information in those areas where a contents exemption applied is where disclosure 'prejudices' or 'is likely to prejudice' one of a number of identified interests. The qualifying use of 'substantial' has gone. Many exemptions are class based, i.e. they do not have to be justified by a claim of prejudice or any other form of harm although most of these are still subject to the discretionary test of PI disclosure.[27] However, as well as these exemptions, and the exclusion of those bodies not listed in the schedule,[28] there are also eight exemptions

---

[24] See EA/2008/0024 and 0029 *Cabinet Office v IC and C. Lamb*.

[25] 24 February 2009. In the Lords Lord Falconer used the term 'consulted': HL Deb., c. 441, 25 October 2000. In Australia, the government planned to remove the veto power from ministers. This was a part of the Labour manifesto in the 2007 Australian elections.

[26] This does not include subdivisions of exemptions within sections. Excluding retrospective exemptions, the Campaign for Freedom of Information numbered all of them at thirty-one: *FOI Briefing* 20 April 2000.

[27] Those which are not so subject include security service etc. information, court records and information relating to legal proceedings as well as, arguably, national security information when correctly certified. The Act does not apply to courts' records. The contents/class basis of withholding information resembles the position in public-interest immunity although following the Iraqi supergun report (the Scott Report) the government undertook not to make class claims and this was supported by the incoming Labour Government: HC Debs., vol. 287, col. 949 and HL Debs., vol. 576, col. 1507 (18 December 1996) and HC Debs., vol. 297, col. 616 (11 July 1997). It had been held that police may make such claims in certain cases: *Taylor v Anderton (Police Complaints Authority Intervening)* [1995] 2 All ER 420 distinguishing *R v Chief Constable of the West Midlands Police, ex p. Wiley* [1994] 3 All ER 420, HL.

[28] See p. 120 above and bodies which are private in form and not within ss. 4–6 FOIA and so on.

which are 'absolute'. There is in the case of absolute exemptions, in other words, no discretion to allow a PI disclosure by the authority and the Commissioner cannot order (even though subject to the veto) disclosure. Therefore, a PA's decision is final, subject to an exemption being inapplicable. If inapplicable, the IC can rule on this, e.g. the information in question is *not* protected by the law of confidentiality. I deal with these in detail below.

Some of the exemptions as originally drafted were outrageously broad, e.g. those covering policy advice and policy formulation and criminal and civil investigations and commercial interests. These clauses were again subject to considerable amendment. Authorities are given widespread powers allowing them not to be covered by (excluded from) the duty to confirm or deny the existence of documents under s. 1 covering numerous exemptions – 'we neither confirm nor deny that we hold the information'.[29] In other words, they are allowed not only to deny access but to play the deadest of bats in response to a request. The response of the 'inscrutable face of the Sphinx'!

Novel features

The original bill had many disquieting features in relation to exemptions which parliamentary pressure removed. There is no need to revisit these suffice to say that the inspiration for some of these was to be found in the DPA 1998. But the novel developments included a provision (cl. 37) which allowed the authority to deny access to information where that information when pieced together with other information, which may not even be disclosable under the bill or otherwise, could make the information as a package fall within one of numerous exemptions.[30] This provision known as the 'jigsaw' provision has its provenance in the USA where the courts developed the possibility of a 'mosaic' basis to deny access initially to security and intelligence information. It was extended by administrative *fiat* in 1986 to law enforcement information although whether this would be successfully invoked has never been tested in the courts.[31] In other words its use in the United States has been strictly confined and is subject to judicial control. After searing criticism from the Commons

---

[29] In the USA, this is restricted to intelligence and law enforcement information; Exec. Order No. 12,958 s. 1.8(e) and 5 USC s. 552(b)(7) especially (C). Aspects of criminal law investigations may be excluded totally from the USFOIA: S USC s. 52(c)(1)–(3).

[30] Cll. 21(1) defence, 22(1) international relations, 23(1) relations within the UK, 24(1) the economy, 26(1) law enforcement, 28(3) collective responsibility, 30(1) health and safety and 34(2) commercial interests. It is interesting that it did not apply against cl. 25 (s. 30 on investigations and proceedings), presumably because that clause is so extensive it does not require a jigsaw. A broad swathe of investigations were removed from what was cl. 25 on amendment including investigations into accidents. This information may be protected under other provisions.

[31] *Halperin v CIA* 629 F 21, 144 (DC–1980) and *FOI Guidance and Privacy Act Overview*, US Department of Justice, May 2004, p. 142 *et seq.*

select committee and from the Lords' committee, this clause, and others, were removed.[32]

We have seen that where a damage test has to be satisfied to withhold information, the test in the White Paper of substantial harm had been reduced to prejudice. The test in the White Paper had met with almost universal support.[33] The test introduced in the bill met with universal criticism but was explained away by the Home Secretary who, in Parliament, stated that the prejudice would have to be 'real, actual or of substance' and it referred to a probability of prejudice not a possibility and that in interpreting 'prejudice' in specific cases, officials could invoke his statement in support of such an interpretation under the rule in *Pepper v Hart*.[34] This is problematic for a variety of reasons. First of all, if the provision is one requiring *real* prejudice why not say what the law means in the legislation? Secondly, the reference to the case is misleading: it only applies where there is an ambiguity in a statutory provision which the reference to Hansard may clarify. There is no need to seek elucidation on the word 'prejudice' – its meaning is clear enough. It is certainly not the same as 'serious' or 'substantial' prejudice. Lastly, the people who will be most in need of guidance are officials making decisions on access at the coal face as it were. They, unlike courts of law, do not need to seek authorisation under the rule in *Pepper v Hart* to refer to the Home Secretary's words. Guidance is provided by the Ministry of Justice and IC.

Arguably, what officials need is a purpose clause to give the necessary support for greater openness. The absence of such a clause was a further criticism in the bill: it contained no purpose clause setting out the pursuit of greater openness and provision of information as an overriding statutory objective to influence the decisions of officials who have to interpret the eventual Act. Such provisions are common in other FOI statutes: in Australia, Canada, New Zealand and in Ireland.[35] Indeed they are not uncommon in domestic provisions. An outstanding example is seen in the Civil Procedure Rules 1998, r 1.1.[36] This states that the rules are a new procedural code 'with the overriding objective of enabling the court to deal with cases justly'. What this means is spelt out in r. 1.2 and includes ensuring the parties are on an equal footing, saving expense, dealing with cases in a manner which is proportionate, expeditiously and fairly and that it receives a proper allocation of a court's resources. Lord Woolf, the

---

[32] One further provision denied access to information where it would lead to self-incrimination by a public authority. See the 3rd edn of this book, p. 297, note 4, for a discussion on this remarkable provision.

[33] See for instance Richard Shepherd MP cross-examining the Home Secretary at HC 570 (1998–9), p. 5 *et seq.*

[34] [1993] 1 All ER 42, HL.

[35] See respectively: s. 3 of the Australian Act, s. 2 of the Canadian Act, s. 4 'Purposes' of the New Zealand Act and the long title of the 1997 FOIA (Ireland). Purpose clauses are well known in an English context: s. 1(1) Children Act 1989, s. 37(1) Crime and Disorder Act 1998, and Civil Procedure Rules 1998, SI 1998/30 r. 1.1. See HC 570-1 (1998–9) paras. 55 *et seq.*

[36] SI 1998/3032.

inspiration for the rules, in his evidence to the select committee examining the bill supported the case for a purpose clause saying:

> As I understand it, one of the things that the Government is seeking to do, and on which they should be complimented, is that they are seeking to change the culture with regard to freedom of information and I think that in that sort of situation a signpost at the beginning as to the general intent of the legislation can be very important.[37]

The official response was that such a clause would cause confusion and the solution, as provided in the bill it was felt, was in a clear expression of rights and exemptions which are set out clearly. The clause setting out the right to information (originally cl. 8, now s. 1), proclaimed Jack Straw, *was* a purpose clause. As the Select Committee on Public Administration pointed out, however, a purpose clause would colour attitudes generally in favour of access and openness at every level of discretion. It has to be said that the IC and IT have regarded s. 1 as a declaration on openness and access.

The difficult question of 'third-party rights' is also dealt with in a problematic manner. This concerns the situation where a requester seeks access to information about another person or body. It most often applies to commercial information but can also cover personal information.[38] The government were disinclined to build in legal duties to consult such parties; it would be too onerous. A code of practice under s. 45 (below) would set out good practice on consultation. The law of confidentiality, it was felt, would protect those whose legal interests were being infringed. This is all rather happenstance and is reminiscent of the situation in the USA before a special procedure was introduced by executive order to notify third parties of claims for information covering, most often, their businesses (see chapter 12, p. 468). The order was necessitated by the chaos caused by the absence of any safeguards. Nor will the law of confidentiality be adequate where all that can be claimed is damages after an allegedly wrongful disclosure where consultation did not take place.[39]

The White Paper's promise of a duty to give reasons for administrative decisions has not resulted in a full-blown provision in the Act but was placed in an authority's publication scheme.[40] The authority is to 'have regard to the public interest . . . in the publication of reasons for decisions made by the authority'. This is another example of how what would best be placed in statutory duties has been reduced to a discretionary practice. The Commissioner will have to be vigilant in approving schemes to ensure among other things that appropriate provisions apply to the giving of reasons for administrative decisions

---

[37] Lord Woolf, Q. 889, HC 570–ix (1998/9).

[38] Personal information may well be covered by the Data Protection Act 1998.

[39] The Act seeks to give an immunity for breaches of the statute, but this would not cover breaches of confidentiality or negligence: see now s. 56.

[40] In the 1997 edition of John Major's code, bodies covered by it had to give reasons for decisions except in those few areas such as certain monopoly and merger cases and enforcement action where there was a well-established authority against giving reasons.

and that the authority comply with its own schemes. The clause and the bill originally said nothing about duties on authorities to give reasons for decisions either to unsuccessful applicants for information or to the Commissioner on an investigation where exempt information has not been forthcoming. If the Commissioner is not told the reasons for refusal and how the PI is exercised, her position is otiose. Amendments did provide for the giving of reasons as we shall see. More will be said on this point under 'enforcement' below.

Many of the essential administrative practices under the FOI regime are in a code of practice issued by the Secretary of State under s. 45 which sets out desirable practice for them to follow on, inter alia, the provision of advice to requesters and complaint-handling (and also third parties as noted above).[41] Breaches of the code may result in the award by the Commissioner of a practice recommendation to the authority.[42] A code has also been issued, originally by the Lord Chancellor, under s. 46 in relation to public records (see Introduction, p. 7). Many essential details on practice are contained in the codes and publica-tion schemes, provisions which elsewhere would be in law.[43] At the report stage in the Lords, an amendment was added (now s. 16) that stated that PAs were under a duty 'so far as it would be reasonable to expect the authority to do so' to provide advice and assistance to requesters. This was satisfied by complying with the code under s. 45.[44]

Basically, it was felt that the bill had been the outcome of a pact between forces of darkness in government and an extremely clever, if somewhat context-blind in terms of openness, draftsman. This pact had undermined the major principles of the White Paper by removing the power of the Commissioner to make binding decisions on bodies covered by the bill so that release of information should be enforced where a greater PI was served by disclosure than by secrecy, confidentiality or privacy. There were rumours of enormous lobbying by commercial and utility interests. It was reported that the bill was given the particular support of Tony Blair in that it made various concessions for the first time to legal rights of access, but it left absolute control with ministers in every crucial area. The Select Committee in the Commons believed that what the bill sought to introduce was a discretionary Open Government framework in the tradition of successive British governments starting with the Croham Directive of 1977 and culminating in John Major's 1994 code. All good intent but no real substance. This was in contradistinction to a FOI statutory regime

---

[41] *Code of Practice on the discharge of public authorities' functions under Part I of the Freedom of Information Act 2000*, Issued under s. 45 of the Act, November 2004.

[42] The Home Office stated a practice recommendation is enforceable by judicial review. Breaches are subject to public law controls of legitimate expectation and the contents of the code are relevant criteria to address in exercising a discretion.

[43] In the States for instance, manuals, decisions, formal and informal procedures etc. are all provided for in primary legislation. Under the 1996 reforms, where information has previously been requested on a certain number of occasions, it will automatically be published: see p. 465 below.

[44] See n 41 above.

proper where information was available as a right and where exemptions were subject to independent scrutiny and arbitration so that the *ipse dixit* of the minister did not prevail. It has to be said of course that 'open government' elsewhere does not have this meaning but means opening up a wider range of official decision-making processes to external scrutiny under legal constraint (see chapter 1, p. 29 *et seq.*).

Civil servants and ministers were both blamed for the about-turn and the Cabinet committee which deliberated the bill was the only such committee to have more members than the Cabinet. Everybody wanted to attend to protect their patch.[45] This was reflected in the numerous class exemptions which protect information on a blanket basis, although in most cases it will be subject to a PI test, as well as the other unusual aspects of a FOI provision.

Open points

The Home Secretary expressed surprise at the hostility to the bill.[46] Wasn't any praise due for allowing a legal right of access? There were indeed some good points to the bill. It removed all but one of the exclusions that were in the White Paper. It is retrospective unlike the Whiter Paper. It provides a legally enforceable right to information via the powers of the Commissioner who may impose a series of notices ordering disclosure under s. 1, and enforcing obligations under Pt I of the Act or enforcing access by himself to contested information by an IN – including to that where an absolute exemption is claimed.[47] Where the Commissioner challenges the basis for claiming whether such an exemption is established (see below) access will be crucial. A memorandum of understanding, dated 24 February 2005, between the Department for Constitutional Affairs and IC records a set of procedures for dealing with the situation where the IC requires information from a department. An IN will be preceded 'wherever possible' by an advance notice. Where the IC requests information withheld under ss. 23 or 24 covering information from the security or intelligence services or that exempt by virtue of national security, the department does not commit itself to providing withheld information to the IC but considers requests on a case by case basis.[48]

There are other non-statutory developments apart from the veto under-taking. These include the establishment of a central clearing house (see http://www.justice.gov.uk/guidance/foi-procedural-referring.htm).[49] The Clearing House provides expert advice on complex, sensitive, or high-profile

---

[45] See Peter Hennessy's evidence to the House of Lords committee: HL 97 (1998/9), Q. 391.

[46] For a critical account see the evidence of the Campaign for Freedom of Information: HC 570–i (1998/9), p. 15 *et seq.*

[47] The IC may issue an information notice to obtain access. The relevant section, s. 51, does not exclude absolute exemptions. A notice may be subject to appeal to the IT.

[48] Annex 2 Information to which ss. 23 and 24 FOIA and reg. 12(5)(a) Environmental Information Regs. apply. See EA/2006/0039 *FoE v IC and DTI.*

[49] See FS50087614.

requests for information; ensures consistency across central government in the handling of these types of request; and works to develop, through litigation, the boundaries of the legislation in accordance with government policy.

The Act applies to a wide range of public bodies and covers functions and services as was indicated above. Unlike the 1994 code, contractual and commercial matters of PAs are not excluded by virtue of the governing statute of the Parliamentary Commissioner for Administration (PCA, also known as the Parliamentary Ombudsman (PO)).[50] Guidance has been issued by the Office of Government Commerce in *Civil Procurement Policy and Guidance*.[51] The Act unifies the Data Protection and Information Commissioner in one person – the IC – thereby seeking to avoid the confusion of roles between the two Commissioners that the White Paper seemed to offer, although the result is very technical and can be very difficult for officials to deal with.[52] It covers the police and is not restricted to their administrative functions but the exemptions involving investigations and law enforcement are excessively broad (see chapters 5 and 6). The government has included the power to repeal unnecessary secrecy clauses in previous statutes[53] and has made alteration etc. of documents to prevent disclosure a criminal offence. The government in 1999 left open the possibility of including Parliament itself in the bill's coverage and both Houses were subsequently included in amendments.[54] In 2007 there was an attempt to exclude Parliament because of IC and IT rulings on disclosure of MPs expenses. The bill to effect this could not attract a sponsor in the Lords. The fees structure is liberal and is dealt with below.[55] The cost of the Act in 2006 was calculated to be around £11.1 million for central government and about £8 million for local government.[56] There was also an attempt to amend the fees regulations in 2007 following a review by a private consultant but the initiative was unsuccessful.[57]

---

[50] The ombudsman is prohibited from investigating complaints about commercial or contractual matters. This is by virtue of the Parliamentary Commissioner for Administration Act 1967, sch. 3, para. 9. Public services delivered by private contractors are within the scope of the Act where maladministration is present in delivery. The *Guidance on Interpretation* on the code stated: '[Para. 9] should not impair his ability to investigate complaints about non-disclosure of information relating to the functions delivered through contractors.' Pt IV. See e.g. HC 572 (1998–9), p. 17. For the local ombudsmen see Local Government etc. Act 2007, s. 173.

[51] www.ogc.gov.uk/documents/OGC_FOI_and_Civil_Procurement_guidance.pdf.

[52] Basically, access by data subjects to their own files etc. is via the DPA. Access to files on another is via the FOIA. See ch. 8.

[53] The White Paper, *Open Government*, Cm. 90 (1993), Annex B, Pt I contains a list of statutory prohibitions on disclosure. Pt II has a list of statutory provisions conferring powers to disclose. See Annex D on release of papers especially intelligence papers and also courts martial.

[54] There was a feeling that imposing a duty on other public bodies but excluding Parliament itself might look like hypocrisy. How prophetic!

[55] SI 2004/3244 FOI and DP (Appropriate Limit and Fees) Regs. See FS50106800 on the IC's guidance on what may be included in assessing fees (below).

[56] See Frontier Economics, *Independent Review of the Impact of the Freedom of Information Act* (2006).

[57] *Ibid.*

Regulations also provide for multiple requests from one person or from different persons who appear to the authority to be acting in concert or in pursuance of a campaign (below).

As the bill progressed, concessions were made by the government although the need for a purpose clause was not conceded. Both the Commons and Lords select committees made important contributions although the committees differed on certain points.[58] The government responded.[59] There is no doubt that the bill gained enormously from the scrutiny of the White Paper and the draft bill particularly in the case of the input from the Commons committee which alone scrutinised the White Paper.

Progress was clearly being made. But a major weakness in the bill concerned the central question of independent enforcement and its absence where the government wished to resist disclosure under s. 53.

Denying the Commissioner the ultimate say

The failure to provide a power for the Commissioner to enforce his or her decisions where disclosure is discretionary on PI grounds, i.e. where it is protected by an exemption but not an absolute exemption, and where the veto is exercised, was one of the most criticised aspects of the bill. Although the White Paper was widely, indeed enthusiastically, praised by many, under it the Commissioner did not possess an overriding power on the PI that she could enforce directly. She had to go to the High Court seeking a contempt order for failure to comply with a disclosure order. Her decision on 'disclosure' was subject to judicial review. This was not a very coherent approach.

Under the 1994 code, the PO effectively seized an opportunity and claimed the power to disclose which had not been spelt out and the then Prime Minister acquiesced.[60] Although the PO could not enforce his recommendation he could say to an authority:

> nevertheless my judgement is different from yours; it is that the balance of advantage in the public interest is thus rather than thus, and that has been accepted.[61]

Under the Act, the IC can enforce the production of information requested under s. 1 which, presumably, it is 'not otherwise unlawful to disclose'.[62] Section

---

[58] On purpose clauses and national security, the Lords differed from the Commons committee.

[59] Public Administration Committee, *Fifth Special Report*, HC 831 (1998–9) and see HC 925 (1998–9) and HC 78 (1999–2000).

[60] See Case A 12/95 para. 8 and evidence of William Reid to the Select Committee on the Parliamentary Commissioner for Administration, 8 March 1995, HC 84 (1995–6), Q. 41.

[61] HC 570–ii (1998/9), Q. 101. Under s. 11(3) of the PCA Act 1967, the minister has the power to prevent the PO handing information to anyone else.

[62] The original cl. 14 included these words but they were omitted from s. 2. The lawfulness of the IC's decision may be challenged before the IT and then before the courts. S. 78 states that nothing in the Act takes away existing powers to disclose information. The biggest barrier to

58 DPA, which extends to FOIA, prevents any legal barrier to disclosure in other legislation or rule of law precluding an individual disclosing information to the IC. The OSA cannot be prayed in aid, for instance where the information is necessary to fulfill duties under the DPA or FOIA. An exemption would have to be claimed. Section 34 DPA (s. 72 FOIA) does not allow the FOIA to override the protection of data under the DPA – this is to make the DPA dominant in relation to FOIA but as will be shown the DPA does not have complete domination (see chapter 8).

The IC can, according to the Home Office, enforce the steps that are to be taken by authorities in producing their publication schemes although she cannot write the schemes for authorities. If an authority fails to publish information as set out in its schemes, can the IC respond to a complaint on such a matter and issue a decision or EN? These notices may be subject to appeal to the IT. The FOIA appears not to confer power to award a DN in relation to a scheme as notices seem related to 'requests for information' under s. 1 and other matters. An EN may be served where the IC is satisfied that an authority has failed to comply with any of the requirements in Pt I which includes s. 19 dealing with publication schemes. Where the code of practice issued by the Secretary of State is not followed by an authority, that can be remedied by a practice recommendation. Quite what this will do is not clear. The ability of the IC to issue a variety of notices to authorities to make decisions and to enforce them is backed up by a power to issue INs under s. 51 that allow the IC to gain access to the information. The memorandum of understanding on this was referred to above. The IN is also subject to exclusions concerning legal professional privilege.[63] The Commissioner also has considerable powers of entry, inspection and seizure under a warrant issued by a circuit judge, which again are subject to excluded items.[64]

The role of the IC was also assisted by the addition of duties on PAs to provide reasons for claiming that the PI in either maintaining the exclusion of the duty to confirm or deny (see below) it holds information or withholding information outweighs the duty to disclose that it holds the information or to disclose the information. The balance is in favour of disclosing where the scales are even; this reversed the position in earlier versions of the bill and is fully examined in chapter 6. In either case, the authority under s. 17 has to

---

disclosure would be the OSA 1989; see s. 58, as amended by FOIA, in the text. Some of the wording of the exemptions leans heavily on the 1989 Act. The IC could not give information obtained from an information notice to a claimant, it is submitted and acting pursuant to a notice will be deferred pending exhaustion of any appeal. Under s. 59 DPA as amended by sch. 19 FOIA the IC is prohibited, along with former IC's and staff and former staff and agents, from disclosing information about an identified or identifiable individual or business unless made under lawful authority: see s. 59(2) DPA for lawful authority.

[63] s. 51(5) FOIA – this covers the advice to a public authority in relation to its obligations under FOIA; see EA/2007/0016 *Ministry of Justice v IC*, ch. 6, p. 209.

[64] Information exempt by virtue of ss. 23(1) and 24(1), i.e. the intelligence services and national security and matters protected by legal professional privilege arising under the Act: sch. 3.

provide reasons for its decision and as we have seen, the IC will have access to all relevant documents. Both the IC and IT have provided detailed guidance on PI factors which I examine in chapters 5 and 6. Gaps in reasoning will be quickly exposed. In refusing information under s. 1(1), the authority must not only state which exemption applies, but also state why the exemption applies. Reasons also have to be given where an absolute exemption is claimed but not so as to compromise the exemption. The duties to provide reasons have been spelt out in the decisions of the IT and IC (see chapter 6).

Responding to a request

Requests have to be made in writing and this may include in electronic form providing it is clear. The s. 45 code advises on assistance where a request is not in writing. The authority is under a duty to inform in writing the requester for information whether it holds information of the type specified in the request. If they do then they must communicate the information – which means information recorded in any form – by means of a copy in permanent form, or another form acceptable to the requester. Communication may be made by allowing inspection or by providing a digest or summary of the information in permanent form. The right is a right of access to *information* and this has been emphasised by the IT (see p. 146 below). However, a request may be made to see a specific file or document and, subject to redactions and fee levels, this should be complied with. The authority must, as far as reasonably practicable, adopt the chosen means of communication although the authority may have regard to the question of cost involved in a chosen means of communication. An authority may reasonably request further information from a requester in order to identify and locate information. The information is that held at the time of the receipt of the request although amendments or deletions may be made where they would have been made regardless of the request. They must not be made *because of* the request. A request does not have to be complied with until any fee in a fees notice served on the applicant has been paid. The requester has three months from the date the notice is given to pay the fee. Regulations have waived fees in prescribed cases and set maximum fees (see below) as well as providing for their manner of calculation. The authority must comply with the request promptly and in any event within twenty days of receiving the request. This period may be extended to sixty days by regulations and may also prescribe different days in relation to different cases and confer a discretion on the IC. However, any period during which a requested fee is not paid delays the computation of the twenty-day, or presumably other, period.

There is no specific power to redact or censor papers or documents before handing them over but an applicant may request information in summary form. An authority may comply with a request by communicating information by any means which are 'reasonable in the circumstances'.

Fees

Government departments, Houses of Parliament and bodies listed in sch. 1, Pt 1 are to make no charge up to a limit of £600 for time taken to locate, sort, redact or edit material. This is the 'marginal' cost. No charge may be made to consider whether an exemption applies or to extract exempt material.[65] For all other bodies, the limit is £450. Costings are based on a staff fee of £25 per hour. Full charge may be made for actual disbursements (not including staff fee) – copying or printing, and sending information. Where the fees levels are exceeded, the authority may respond by providing information and charging the excess, not charging the excess, or refusing the request after responding whether it holds information requested (s. 13). Provision is made to calculate fees in cases of repeat requests or concerted requests within time limits (SI 2004/3244). Where fees are provided under another statute for communicating or giving information, those fees shall apply. This is very important where the latter are higher than under FOIA.

The practicalities

There is detailed advice on the practicalities on dealing with requests.[66] The role of the Clearing House has been described above. Access to information should include access to information in documentary form or in a computer or other memory store – the Act is comprehensive in this regard. Computer printouts, email attachments as well as papers should be available. An FOI office should be established with the necessary staff and facilities in each department, agency and larger PA. The advice covers requests involving personal information. Applications for information could be made personally by email request which is considered to be a request made in writing (s. 8(2)(a)) or by post. Publication schemes containing information published voluntarily by PAs will be published on websites and, as discussed above, these could be documents of vital significance although the evidence on their use has been a little disappointing.[67] Factual and background information behind policy development could be published making them repositories of discussion and debate. They will contain, inter alia, details of information available for a fee. If the government is serious about the virtues of joined-up government and citizen involvement, then these ought to be essential tools in setting up vehicles for dialogue. However, as will be seen, the policy exemption cuts against the government's pleas for 'joined-up policy making' in *Modernising Government*.[68] This spoke enthusiastically about 'getting others involved' in policy 'early on' in the process.

---

[65] EA/2006/0067 and EA/2007/0072.   [66] www.justice.gov.uk/guidance/guidancefoi.htm.

[67] www.ico.gov.uk/upload/documents/library/freedom_of_information/practical_application/ ico_policy_on_publication_schemes.pdf.

[68] Cm. 4310, para. 6.

The government did not, as we saw above, include a duty on PAs to provide indexes for the documents in their possession. If the Council of Ministers and Commission can provide such under their access regimes (see chapter 10), then why not domestic PAs? A request for documents on the rescue of banks, the third Heathrow runway, the invasion of Iraq etc. would cover thousands of documents in a variety of departments and agencies. The absence of duties to provide indexes has been partly met by the publication by departments of IARs (see p. 121 above). The Dacre Review of the thirty-year rule (below) recommended that the government revisit the Civil Service Code to see whether it needs an amendment to include an explicit injunction to keep full, accurate and impartial records of government business.[69]

The FOI office would inform the appropriate division of the request and it would examine the file to see whether exempt information is present. If it is not, the file would be released to the FOI officer, who would inform the applicant of any fees. Assistance should be given to identify which portions are required. If exempt, the file would have the exempt categories clearly identified and marked, and the applicant would only be allowed access to the unexpurgated portion. Where an exemption is not absolute, a decision on the PI must be taken. Specific provision for redacting a document in this fashion is not contained in FOIA but decisions and guidance of the IC and IT have provided guidance on relevant factors and their appraisal.[70]

Appeals will be made to a higher-level officer within the authority against refusal – matters which are covered by the code of practice. The third stage would involve the IC, who would have access to the whole file and whose decision would be binding, subject to appeal to the IT. Exemption decisions would be made at an appropriate departmental level unless the information was politically sensitive, in which case it would be referred to higher authority and to the Central Clearing House if it fell within the appropriate criteria.

Public records[71]

The White Paper envisaged that the provisions concerning access to public records would be brought within the FOIA regime and inconsistent provisions in the Public Records Acts would be repealed. The system for dealing with public records is explained in chapter 9. When a record reaches the end of thirty years after the year in which it was created, it becomes an 'historical record'. They are disclosed, usually to great press attention at the beginning of each year. However, under existing practice, records may be retained in departments and

---

[69] www2.nationalarchives.gov.uk/30yrr/30-year-rule-report.pdf, at para. 8.4.
[70] The IC's guidance is at www.ico.gov.uk/what_we_cover/freedom_of_information/guidance.aspx, and see note 66 above.
[71] See S. Healy 'Freedom of information and its impact on archives' in R. Chapman and M. Hunt (eds.), *Open Government in a Theoretical and Practical Context* (2006). For National Archives see www.nationalarchives.gov.uk/.

not transferred to the National Archives. The idea was that as many records as possible should be disclosed once they are 'historical records' – if they have not been disclosed before under FOIA. Exemptions in ss. 28, 30(1), 32, 33, 35, 36, 37(1)(a), 42 or 43[72] have no application to historical records. Informing an applicant whether it holds historical records is not to be taken to have any of the effects referred to in ss. 28(3), 33(3), 36(3), 42(2), or 43(3) – i.e. prejudicing any of the matters contained in those sections by acknowledging their existence. In the case of s. 37(1)(b) – conferring any honour or dignity by the Crown – the period after which the exemption evaporates is sixty years. In the case of s. 31(1) which lists information relating to the prevention or detection of crime and other matters,[73] compliance with s. 1(1)(a) in relation to *any* record is not to be taken to prejudice any of the items in the section *after* a period of one hundred years.

Information contained in a historical record in the National Archives or Public Records Office of Northern Ireland (PRONI) cannot be exempt under ss. 21 (accessible by other means) or 22 (information intended for future publication). In the case of any information within a historical record in the National Archives or PRONI falling under the exemption in s. 23(1) – information supplied by or relating to the security and intelligence etc. services – a PI disclosure may be made of such 'historical documents' notwithstanding s. 2(3) making it an absolute exemption. Where the records are not in the National Archives, and most are unlikely to be, the absolute exemption still applies. However, where an absolute exemption is contained within s. 2(3) and information is not otherwise provided for as above, the period of closure is indefinite.[74]

Consultation has to take place with the Secretary of State for Justice and appropriate NI minister before a request is refused for an historical record which is a statutory public record held by the authority which is subject to an ordinary exemption. This does not apply to records transferred to the National Archives, PRONI or other authorised place of repository designated by the Secretary of State for Justice.[75] Under s. 66, disclosure of *any* information contained in such records other than 'open information'[76] where there is an exemption other than under s. 2(3) must be made by the PA after being consulted by the PRO etc. Further provisions cover consultation with the Lord Chancellor and NI minister where the record is a transferred public record.

---

[72] Relations within the UK, investigations and proceedings conducted by public authorities, court records, audit functions, formulation of government policy, prejudice to effective conduct of public affairs, communications with Her Majesty etc., legal professional privilege and commercial interests: s. 63.

[73] Apprehension or prosecution of offenders, administration of justice, assessment or collection of tax or duty, operation of immigration controls etc.

[74] This includes ss. 34 (parliamentary privilege), 40 (personal information), 41 (confidential information), 44 (disclosure prohibited by order), and 23(1) where not in the PRO.

[75] And see s. 15.   [76] This is a designation made by the responsible authority.

For the position on public records in Scotland, *An Open Scotland*[77] envis-aged no significant changes to PR management north of the border, which are unaffected by the Public Records Acts.

The Dacre Review of the thirty-year rule was commissioned by the prime minister and reported in 2009.[78] It recommended that the period of thirty years be reduced to fifteen years (see Introduction, pp. 3, 7). It made recommenda-tions concerning full, accurate and impartial records of government business, availability of political advisers' non-political records in a full record, redaction of civil servants names from records and various recommendations on digital records and electronic-record capture. The Government, in consultation with interested parties, may wish to consider whether there is a case for enhanced protection of certain categories of information.

The IT

The role of the IT was added at the bill stage and was not present in the White Paper. There are detailed regulations setting out its procedures including those for national security appeals.[79] It took over the role of the Data Protection Tribunal and added the FOIA and Environmental Information Regulations (EIR) case load. The grounds of appeal against notices are very broad and cover an appeal that the notice was not in accordance with the law, it involved an exercise of discretion by the IC and he ought to have exercised his dis-cretion differently. It may review any finding of fact on which a notice was based (s. 58(1)–(2)). The IT may sit *in camera* and give closed parts to judg-ments. It will be able to take appeals against ministers' 'classifications' under ss. 23(2) and 24(3) concerning classification of security and intelligence and national security but the ground of appeal in the latter case is very narrow.[80] The tribunal is built on traditional tripartite models, i.e. a legally qualified chair and two wing persons (traditionally broadly representative of the interests of authorities and users). The fact that no legal aid will be available will act as a deterrent to those wishing to appeal[81] and the position is not remedied by refusing to allow the IC the power to assist the appellant where the DN was in the applicant's favour. This role for the IC is allowed in other jurisdic-tions. Costs may be awarded against a party to the proceedings. The IT has shown a reluctance to allow the award of costs against a participant (see p. 149 below).

---

[77] Scottish Executive SE/1999/51.

[78] www2.nationalarchives.gov.uk/30yrr/30-year-rule-report.pdf.

[79] SI 2005/14 and 2005/450 and for national security appeals SI 2005/13.

[80] The IT finds, applying the principles applied by a court on an application for judicial review, the minister did not have reasonable grounds for issuing the certificate.

[81] *Freedom of Information Background Material*, Annex A, para. 26.

Promoting good practice and audit by the IC

The IC is under a duty to promote good practice and in particular the requirements of the Act, and the s. 45 and s. 46 codes. The IC will be allowed to conduct
an audit of an authority's practice in relation to FOI where the authority consents to her doing so. There is no right for the IC to do this on her own initiative
as a result, for instance, of unfavourable press reports.

The Data Protection Commissioner as IC

The FOIA is a far from easy regime to comprehend. It is complicated by the
fact that the government fastened various provisions of this scheme onto the
data protection provisions. In fact the DPA seems to have set the mould for
the FOIA in a variety of respects. The use of the Data Protection Commissioner
(formerly Registrar) as the IC did raise an important point of principle. In her
evidence to the select committee in its examination of the White Paper, the then
Data Protection Registrar (DPR) saw herself very much as the champion of
privacy – hardly surprising given her role as DPR. The question is: will she
come with a preconceived attachment to privacy protection rather than towards
freedom of information and openness? In her evidence on the bill, the DPR
expressed the view that perhaps the bill was weighted too much in favour of
privacy. She will be responsible for both areas. In other regimes where both
posts have been held by the same person or where there are two separate posts,
the privacy brief has dominated, although this is not an invariable rule and owes
a great deal to force of personality it seems.[82] The FOI brief is a much wider
brief than the DPA field. Where the provisions of the Data Protection Directive
apply then there is no option but for the FOI provisions to cede pride of place.
The DPR indicated areas where there may be problems by an overlap and where
access to the 'public' aspects of an individual's life may not be sufficiently open
under the FOI provisions. There is a danger that the DPA provisions may make
a file 'secret' where a person's name is attached to it but it is not sensitive or
personal information. As we shall see in chapter 8, such cases have arisen under
a clash of EU access laws and data protection.[83] The problem has been seen
to exist under both EU access regimes and under the FOIA/DPA interface in
England. The approach adopted by the IC has been balanced and appropriate
as will be seen in chapter 8 and it does not reveal a predisposition in favour of
privacy except where justified.

The Commons select committee was alive to the inherent difficulties here and
suggested that the committee should interview any prospective appointment to
the IC's office and that the IC should report directly to that committee rather

---

[82] See R. Hazell, 'The hinge between freedom of information and privacy' in A. McDonald and
G. Terrill (eds.), *Open Government: Freedom of information and privacy* (1998).

[83] *R v Ministry of Agriculture, Fisheries and Food, ex p. Fisher (t/a TR & P. Fisher)* Case C-369/98
(2000) The Times, 10 October; see ch. 8, p. 297.

like the PO. Certainly that committee has been a considerable bulwark to the PO over the years and the IC is likely to need considerable support in tackling such a wide range of bodies. The IC is appointed under letters patent by the Crown, in reality the prime minister, and while s/he enjoys security while in office, the tenure is for five years up to a maximum of fifteen. An effective IC may not be reappointed after the first five-year period. There was also an issue about the IC being based far away from Whitehall in Cheshire where the DPR's office was established. The Lord Chancellor believed that as the range of coverage of PAs extended far beyond Whitehall it was appropriate to have an office other than in London. The initially advertised salary was also considerably below that of circuit judges, let alone senior judges or officials. As this is written the first IC is about to retire. The salary has been increased.

There is also likely to be considerable overlap between the IC, the PO, the Health Service Commissioner and local ombudsmen. In the Lords, this overlap was provided for by the powers of the public-sector ombudsmen and the IC to exchange information which is relevant to their respective investigations.[84] There is likely to be ample scope for constructive co-operation and support. Many ombudsmen investigations involve complaints about inadequate or inaccurate information.

Throughout the events chronicled so far in this chapter, no one had spoken against FOI. To that extent it shows how far we had moved since the orthodoxy of the Thatcher years when legislation enjoining greater openness on central government was regarded as constitutional apostasy. The main points of complaint were that the bill did not go far enough. Various witnesses before the select committee had expressed the view that this was a bill with good points and, more pertinently, could easily be made into a very good bill. Sir Richard Scott felt that it *was* a FOI bill but it required 'stiffening up'. It is, as Tony Wright the Commons committee chair said, a bill that can quite easily be unpacked of some of its undesirable qualities. Lord Woolf's advice to the Committee was basically: 'sometimes one has to be happy with what one can get'.[85] This advice may not have been universally welcomed within the FOI community but the point was reached in proceedings where it was felt that too much opposition to the bill could kill it off. It would be unlikely to reappear for some considerable time.

The FOIA has met with opposition since its enactment. DNs by the IC involving MPs expenses and Cabinet minutes have brought pressure for change. The latter case was supported by the Dacre Review which heard how minutes and records of civil servants were written more cautiously because of the FOIA climate. The IC and IT have not been so impressed by this official sensitivity, as will be shown in chapter 6.

My view has always been that it is better that this bill, with all its faults, was enacted than that it fell. Considerable concessions were made although not on

---

[84] S. 76 and sch. 7 FOIA.   [85] HC 570–ix (1998/99), Qs. 916 and 920 respectively, 14 July 1999.

some of the central features which were seen by the government as undermining 'our way of doing things'. On some vital aspects the Act will need further work or thought on its implications.[86] In the next chapter there will be an examination of the exemptions, and in the following chapter how the exemptions have been dealt with by the IC and IT. At this point there will be an analysis of some important points raised by the terms of the legislation after looking briefly at FOI and devolution.

FOIA and devolution

In the case of FOI covering devolved functions in Scotland, Scotland's executive produced plans, in *An Open Scotland*,[87] for a very ambitious FOIA which would give compulsory powers of disclosure to an IC subject to a collective decision of the Scottish ministers.[88] Information received 'in confidence' from the UK government and departments would be subject to the UK FOIA. The test for withholding information covered by the legislation would be one of 'substantial prejudice' where it was a contents exemption. Class exemptions would be subject to the PI override. In some areas, such as criminal investigation and enforcement, Scottish law would have to gel with UK law. These plans were published in 1999 and, early in 2001, the Scottish bill was published. This has maintained the 'substantial prejudice' test but it has also been inspired by the UK Act. Absolute exemptions are included as in FOIA. The veto as discussed above will apply in some cases of class exemptions but the veto is to be exercised by the first minister after consulting other ministers. However, there is to be no tribunal in Scotland making the Scottish IC (SIC) the means of enforcement, although the IC's decision will be subject to judicial challenge – as in the original White Paper although the Scots have opted for an appeal and not a review. In a case involving the *Sunday Herald* (25/2/07) the SIC criticised the Scottish Executive for treating journalists requests less favourably than those from individuals.

In Wales, a code of practice has been produced by the Welsh Assembly implementing s. 70 of the Government of Wales Act 1998 and Standing Order 17. Part I outlines the provisions under which the Assembly will operate and Pt II sets out exemptions. The code undertakes to operate under a presumption of openness and sets out information it will publish automatically (see www.wales.gov.uk). The response rate set by the code is fifteen working days. Where 'harm or prejudice' are referred to as a ground for not allowing disclosure, these may be outweighed by a greater PI in disclosure. There are nine categories of exempt information.

---

[86] See *Background Material*, note 81 above, pp. 37 and 18 *et seq.* respectively.
[87] See note 77 above.
[88] See The Scotland Act 1998 (Modifications of Schedules 4 and 5) Order 1999, SI 1999/1749 amending the Scotland Act 1998, Pt II, sch. 5.

Some points dealt with by the IC and IT

In the following chapter the exemptions will be outlined. At this stage it will be useful to look at IC and IT decisions on general points raised by the operation of the Act. It should be noted that a reference beginning 'FS' or 'FER' means it is the Commissioner's decision. 'EA' means it is an IT appeal. There have been criticisms of procedures adopted by the IC. In EA/2005/0004 *E. Barber v IC* there was no evidence of the IC contacting the requester to discuss his case personally. EA/2007/0031 *J. Nisbet v IC* saw the IT rule that accuracy and substance of information provided is not an issue for the IT; the important point is whether all the information that is disclosable is disclosed. EA/2005/0003 *E. Simmons v IC* stated that an important point under FOIA is that the law is not concerned with the substantive quality of information held and disclosed but whether it is held and whether it should be disclosed.

Coverage of the FOIA

There has been some important discussion in the case law on sch. 1 to the Act, which deals with those bodies covered by the Act. As seen above there is the possibility of extending the list of 'public authorities' by designation of the Secretary of State under s. 5. From 2005 until 2009, no such orders had been made. A consultation was launched in 2007 on the possibility of extending the range of bodies covered by the Act. This could be very important for instance in relation to government programmes performed under contract by private companies. The Nuclear Decommissioning Authority, for instance, will rely upon private companies to run sites for decommissioning nuclear generating plants.

The schedule makes special provision in relation to some bodies so that they are PAs except for certain items of information – the Bank of England, as we have seen. In some cases a person or body is not scheduled – the Queen or nationalised banks. In other cases a body is present but ony in relation to certain information such as the sub-treasurer of the Inner Temple in relation to information held in his capacity as a local authority.

A particularly contested item has occurred in relation to the BBC. Basically, the BBC is not a PA within the terms of the FOIA where information is held for the purpose of journalism, art or literature by the BBC. In relation to such information, the BBC is not a scheduled body but an excluded body.[89] The complainant in FS50097242 made eleven requests for information to the BBC which included details of the personal shareholding of members of staff who select and present coverage on the Working Lunch programme; details of financial relationships that exist between members of staff working on the programme and the financial experts who appear on it; a record of appearances

---

[89] See FS50103726.

of a financial expert; and a record of the coverage given to a particular company on the programme. The BBC refused to provide all the information requested on the basis that it was not a PA in relation to the complainant's request because the information was held for the purpose of journalism, art or literature within the meaning set out in sch. 1 of the Act. The Commissioner concluded that the BBC misapplied the sch. 1 derogation and that the information requested in part (i), (ii) and (iii), fell within the scope of the Act.

FS50147860 concerned a request for the '10 largest annual claims for expenses by BBC broadcasters in the latest year for which figures are available'. The BBC claimed the information was held 'for purposes of journalism, art and literature' and so the BBC was not a PA under the FOIA for these purposes. Expenses of broadcasters were a part of production costs for programmes whereas management staff were not so classified. The BBC said that if the Act applied they would want clarification of the term 'broadcaster'. Furthermore, even if the Act applied, the cost would exceed s. 12 limits. The IC held in *Sugar v BBC* (below) that some costs were a part of the 'journalistic etc' expenses and so the derogation applied to those. The IT overruled the IC but on judicial review it was ruled that the IC was correct. The 2006 Charter for the BBC established the BBC Trust and Executive Board, the former of which sets overall objectives and strategic direction and oversees the board which implements priorities set by the Trust. The IC believed information was held for multiple purposes and the *dominant* purpose had to be established. Here the dominant purpose was not costs for journalism etc. but for allocation of resources (management). The derogation did not apply. The BBC was in breach of s. 16 in not clarifying what precise information the requester wanted. The BBC would decide what exemptions might apply (see Introduction, p. 6).

FS50070467 saw a request for '20 highest paid entertainers' by the BBC. The request was refused by the BBC because of journalism derogation. What is the dominant purpose where two or more purposes exist? The IC did not believe that 'talent-costs information' possesses enough journalistic etc. quality to qualify for the derogation. Again, there was a breach of s. 16 FOIA by the BBC in failing to clarify the nature of the request.

EA/2005/0032 *S. Sugar v IC and BBC (AP)* concerned a request for the Balen Report on news coverage in the Middle East. The recommendations of the report aimed at improving the BBC's journalism and programme content after some notorious episodes. If the report was held for purposes of art, literature or journalism it could not be obtained under FOIA as explained. The case contains important discussion about public service broadcasters and how freedom of speech was to be protected. The BBC referred to the report as 'management papers' which are to be kept confidential. Journalism per se is excluded but not the 'management of journalism'. The Act did not use the s. 10 Contempt of Court Act terminology of 'journalist's sources' but used a wider concept of journalism. The BBC's argument was that the largest part of what is contained in the report is protected by the proviso. 'This would have the effect of excluding most of the BBC's management information from the remit of the FOIA' (para. 101). However, if a very broad definition were intended there is little point of including the BBC in sch. 1, Pt VI FOIA. 'Functional journalism' is protected (para. 106), which includes collecting, gathering, writing, editing and presenting material for publication and reviewing that material. It is distinguishable from 'direction of policy' within the BBC which is managerial and not essentially journalistic. The bulk of materials in Balen are produced for journalism but their use may be multiple and may vary at different times – sometimes it may be journalistic, sometimes not. What is the *predominant* purpose of holding information: journalistic or non-journalistic? The IT believed the dominant-test is the correct approach intended by Parliament. 'Therefore the application of the dominant purpose test under FOIA will relate to the purpose(s) for which the information was held at the time the request was received by the PA and not at the time the information was created.' Holding it for additional staffing or financial resources would not be journalistic. An output review as used here was for a purpose of governance. The dominant purpose at the time of the request was for purposes other than art, journalism or literature. The IT therefore had jurisdiction to deal with the request (see Introduction, p. 6).

EA/2005/0032 *S. Sugar v IC* was the forerunner to the above where the IT ruled it had jurisdiction to hear the case even though the IC ruled that for the purposes of information sought, the BBC was not a PA. The IT said allowing an appeal to them under s. 57 FOIA was cheaper and more convenient as a challenge and they had more powers than a court on judicial review – the specific power to reverse on the merits. On appeal the High Court ruled that there is no DN to appeal against and so the only option was for S. to bring a judicial review arguing that the 'art etc.' proviso did not apply. In the judicial review, the High Court agreed with the IC, basically holding that the IC's decision is a perfectly rational one and should not have been overturned by the IT. It is a case on jurisdiction where a more relaxed view of jurisdiction was taken than in the leading *Anisminic* decision[90] and *South Yorks. Transport v MMC*[91] was the relevant authority where a wider berth was given to the IC's judgment.

This position was upheld by the Court of Appeal but was reversed by a 3–2 judgment in the House of Lords.[92] The case caused some concern because if the IC agreed with the PA's classification of its status, as he did, there was according to the Court of Appeal no appeal open to the IT to a requester, only the far more expensive route of judicial review. This factor weighed heavily with the majority in the House of Lords who construed the statutory language to provide an appeal, although Lord Hoffmann believed that the IC was thereby effectively given power to determine his own jurisdiction. Nor did Lord Hoffmann approve

---

[90] *Anisminic v FCC* [1969] 2 AC 147.   [91] [1993] 1 All ER 289 (HL).
[92] *Sugar v BBC* [2009] UKHL 9.

the use by judges of the expression 'hybrid authorities' and 'excluded information'. The end result is that the IC's decision on a body's status and relevant information is appealable under the statutory route.[93]

FS50068391 *British Broadcasting Corporation* saw the complainant submit two requests asking for copies of Alan Yentob's charge-card statement and an itemised breakdown of his expense claims. The BBC provided some information in response to both requests, but withheld details of certain payments on the basis that these payments related to activities falling outside the scope of the Act on the basis of the journalism proviso. The BBC argued that this derogation applied broadly and extended to financial information relating to the cost of programme-making. The IC thought that the financial information served a number of purposes, but that it was the dominant purpose which was relevant. The IC considered the information to be held for mainly operational purposes and it thus fell within the FOI provisions. Where the complainant asked the BBC how much their new weather graphics cost, this was treated as falling outside the excluded material.[94] FS50107765 is another request to the BBC; this time for the amount paid to cover the 2006 Winter Olympic games. The familiar rehearsal of the 'held for purposes of journalism etc.' excluding this BBC information from the FOIA was made. The IC held the information fell within the Act. 'Some form of financial cost is necessary to produce programme content' in a majority of cases (para. 18). But the IC relied upon the dual purpose test (above) and what is the preponderant or dominant purpose – journalistic or operational? The charters (both 1996 and 2006) place emphasis on VFM and audit so that the BBC Trust could oversee the Executive Board and so that the Executive Board could manage BBC's financial and operational affairs and provide VFM. The information was held for predominantly operational purposes.

EA/2006/0039 *FoE v IC and DTI* concerned a request for information given to the IC by the DTI as a result of a complaint about DTI by the requester. Section 59 DPA (as amended by FOIA, sch. 2(11) para. 19(3)) was at issue. Prohibition on disclosure by the IC of information under s. 59(1)(b) DPA includes that relating to an identifiable *business*. Does term 'business' cover a PA? The IT upheld the IC ruling that the DTI is correctly classified as a business:

> It is right that in each case the IC should be able to balance the importance of the free flow of information contemplated by the letter and spirit of ss. 58–9 DPA, and the case for disclosure of information relating to the PA which would, in his opinion, be necessary for the purpose of performing his functions, whether or not the consent of the PA is forthcoming. [Para. 42]

Do PI considerations militate in favour of disclosure under s. 59(2)(c)(i) DPA?

---

[93] See EA/2006/0077 G. *Tuckley v IC and Birmingham City Council (BCC)* (28 February 2008).
[94] FS50086077 British Broadcasting Corp.

Section 1 FOIA: holding information[95]

FS50180545 involved requests to the National Audit Office (NAO). The complainant submitted a series of requests to the NAO for information as to the origins of figures contained in a value-for-money for stroke-care report. The main complaints and the IC's responses were that certain information had not been disclosed, because it was held by King's College London (which had been contracted-in). The IC noted that there existed difficulties where information was not held by the PA, but by another body (dealt with by s. 3 FOIA). However in this case the 'other body' was also a PA (being a university). The IC decided that the information was held by the NAO by way of s. 3. The IC directed a search of King's information sources and no undisclosed information was found.

EA/2008/0027 *Home Office v IC* includes a discussion of *Common Services Agency v Scottish Information Commissioner*[96] and barnardising information (see chapter 8, p. 294 below) which concerned the Freedom of Information (Scotland) Act 2002 (FOI(Scotland)A), whose relevant provisions in this case do not differ in any material respect from those in the 2000 Act. The submission of the Home Office was accepted that, in effect, the House of Lords in *Common Services* accepted a submission that the obligations of PAs are limited to information that is truly held by them and that they are not obliged by the legislation to conduct research or create new information on behalf of requesters.

FS50155552 was a request to the Cabinet Office for a list of all documents disclosed under FOIA and EIR and dates of their disclosure. The IC found they were not held in a consolidated list but only as constituent elements. The Cabinet Office argued that to create such a list is not required by FOIA. The IC did not accept this view. The IC requested the Cabinet Office to provide the complainant with the requested information but if it exceeded the appropriate limit under s. 12 to indicate what could be provided within the limit.

In FS50126376 the complainant wrote to the Cabinet Office to request 'Any record or document or extract thereof reporting or evidencing discussions between President Bush and the Prime Minister about the bombing of the Al-Jazeera television office in Qatar or elsewhere. The request additionally sought any document which records comment upon or analysis of such discussions.' The Cabinet Office informed the complainant that a memo it holds recording discussions between President Bush and the prime minister in April 2004 'does not refer to the "bombing of Al-Jazeera television offices in Qatar or elsewhere"'. The IC believed that the Cabinet Office should not have restricted its response to consideration of the April 2004 memo alone. The IC therefore not only investigated whether the Cabinet Office was correct in its assertion in relation to the 2004 memo but also investigated whether it held any other information which contains details of the subject matter requested. Having conducted his

---

[95] Some PAs have repeatedly been in breach of s. 1 and its procedures, e.g. the National Offender Management Service (FS50199479, FS50195955 and FS50198451).
[96] [2008] UKHL 47.

analysis, the IC was satisfied that the Cabinet Office did not hold any information which fell within the scope of the complainant's request. Did the IC act correctly here?

Section 3(2): holding information

Several IT decisions have covered the question of holding information.[97] *Bromley v IC and Env. Ag.* EA/2006/0072 deals with the duty under s. 1 where information is held over a large number of locations. In FS50080369 concerning the *Department for Business Enterprise and Regulatory Reform* (2 October 2008) the complainant requested the names and addresses of respondents in Employment Tribunal applications. The PA refused to disclose the information under s. 3(2)(a), stating that it held the information on behalf of the Employment Tribunal and not in its own right. It claimed that the information was stored only as part of the department's administrative responsibilities. The IC found that the information was held by the PA and that it was not exempt by virtue of s. 3(2)(a).

Quinn v IC and HO EA/2006/0010 featured the Dunbar Prison riot report. '*Quinn*' saw a substituted DN from the IT. The IT held that the IC was wrong to conclude the Home Office did not hold the report. It contained criticism of Home Office document management policies. The IT emphasised that the IT's procedure on an appeal is a rehearing and not a judicial review. The burden of proof (BoP) on 'holding' information is on the Home Office (i.e., the Home Office had to prove it does not hold information despite the notorious difficulty of proving a negative). Regulation 26 of the IT rules places the ultimate BoP on appellant (para. 32). The judgment has a discussion on the s. 12 limits relating to searching for information held. The IC's jurisdiction, says the IT, covers 'information not documents'!! Literally, this is true. But one can ask for documents and the PO and IC have said that quite often the best way to provide information is to provide a document. The Re-use of Public Sector Information Regulations (see chapter 1, p. 16) also refers to *documents* supplied to the requester. The IT was not satisfied on the burden of proof that each copy of the report that was held by the Home Office had been destroyed (para. 40). 'Held' means 'have they got it?' This can present a difficult challenge to PAs.

EA/2006/0085 *M. Johnson v IC and MoJ* concerned information requested on Queen's Bench Division masters and their strike-out orders. The appeal was allowed partly. Paragraph 42 emphasises access is to information not documents (see above). Strike-out rates were not recorded on databases. Information could not be retrieved by a labour-intensive manual process within the cost limit.

EA/2005/0031 *G. Marlow v IC* contains an important discussion on holding in relation to data on a data bank. The appeal concerned the degree to which a PA 'holds' information which is on a subscriber list. The IC's DN was

---

[97] EA/2006/0089 *E. Spurgeon v IC and Horsham DC*. Council did not hold requested information. In EA/2005/009 *R. Austin v IC* the appeal was dismissed but there is criticism of the IC's factual findings re the existence of information. See also EA/2006/0092 *Dr I. Babar v IC*.

substituted (see decision directly below for details). The IC's decision did not refer to an aspect of the complaint which related to a law publisher's terms for the availability of a legislation service. The discussion of 'held', relating to computers, is at para. 20 *et seq*. That information which is downloaded by a PA employee on a PA computer is 'held' because it will be on a PA's PC screen. But what of the publisher's data bank? This would depend upon the terms of the contract. In a 'great majority of cases' information will not be held in the latter case because the access is not unconditional. EA/2005/0031 *G. Marlow v IC* was a continuation of above:

> We have no doubt that in the great majority of cases the total body of information held on a third party's data base and capable of being accessed by a PA under subscriber rights of the type that we have described in the preceding paragraph, should not be characterised as having been 'held' by a PA. [Para. 22]

The situation may be different where a PA has unrestricted rights to access, use and exploitation of a third party's database, so that it may be said that information is 'held' but not in such a case as this where the arrangement is a commercial contractual one for legal materials.

EA/2005/0001 *P. Harper v IC and Royal Mail* (AP) contains a discussion of the powers of the IC to deal with late compliance – either by a s. 48 good-practice recommendation; a s. 49 annual report to Parliament; or a s. 52 EN. The case involved a request for data on the requester that was not held by the PA, it argued, because it was deleted. The PA should have in place data-retention policies. Paragraphs 16 *et seq*. have an interesting discussion of the duty of retrieving 'deleted information' from an electronic system. Information may be 'deleted' and 'emptied' but it is not actually eliminated from the system at that point. Whether such data is recoverable will be a question of fact and degree. Whether it is held will also be a question of fact and degree. See para. 21: the PA should establish whether information is completely eliminated or merely deleted (until overwritten). Computer software can establish this. Paragraphs 22–7 discuss the methods to recover deleted data (para. 27 specifically addresses how far an authority should go to recover data and s. 12 (below) should be borne in mind).

EA/2006/0030 *R. Tatam v IC and General Register Office* concerned a death which had been registered by the partner of the deceased and the requester wanted the registration amended. The request was for relevant documents covering registration. The 'right' is access to information not documents but this refers to the fact that it is *information* that is protected by confidentiality.

Section 12: compliance exceeding fees limits

In FS50123488 *Financial Services Authority* (FSA) the financial regulator possesses very market-sensitive information which could be very damaging if disclosed. The complainant made two requests for information to the FSA for information relating to a managing agency, his syndicate and Lloyd's. The FSA refused to disclose the information in the first request under s. 12 and the information in the second request under ss. 44, 43, 40 and 31. In relation to the first request the IC found that the s. 12 exemption was engaged. Interestingly, he stated that the time limit would not include time spent redacting the information. The IC considered that a PA should ask the complainant to consider refining his request to bring it within the time limit (by way of assistance under s. 16), but that it was not reasonable to do so in the instant case because the time limit would still be exceeded.

EA/2006/0088 *R. Brown v IC and The National Archives* was an appeal from the IC that was allowed. The National Archives (NA) are not relieved of duties under ss.12 and 14 as the IC's DN stated. There was a request for papers on Princess Margaret's affair with Peter Townsend.[98] The NA applied ss.12 and 14 and IC upheld those claims. The IT criticised the procedures adopted by the IC saying the procedures possessed 'no real rigour' (paras. 93–4). In the NA, where records are closed, their descriptor may be closed. There were 637 requests for information; about 350 of these covered closed documents or descriptors. Two hundred and fifty-five were still held within government departments and had not been transferred to the NA. The NA contains in excess of 10 million records housed in over 180 km of shelving. An electronic m-line catalogue is available. The NA wrongly aggregated requests and misunderstood its duties under s. 1 FOIA. The refusal of the NA was due to a belief that the request was not well founded (para. 61). Section 14 FOIA and regulations allow for 'phasing' at intervals of more than sixty days. It covers the same or substantially similar records. The IT treated this as a request for records that are the same or substantially similar and *not* on a similar subject. Section 14(2) (below) is not a safeguard against a large number of requests – s. 12 is.

EA/2006/0093 *W. Urmeni v IC and LB Sutton* concerned penalty charge notices – and information was requested about the number of appeals on certain days. It concerned the question of retrieval, exceeding of the £450 fees limits and s. 12. The IT considered additional information on appeal. 'Where more than one request relates to the same or similar information, there is no obligation on a PA to 'split up' a request and answer each piece individually – it may be different for a single document that includes requests for different sorts of information (para 47). On such a matter s. 16 advice should have been offered.

EA/2006/0067 *J. Jenkins v IC and DEFRA* concerned a request for information from the Veterinary Medicines Directorate (under the Department for Environment, Food and Rural Affairs (DEFRA)) including thirty-seven indexes and catalogues. A European database on serious adverse reactions to medicines would not be supplied and Pfizer who provided the information refused to consent to disclosure. The case contains details of s. 12 calculations for charges (man-hours to retrieve etc.) and considers whether charges may be made to

---

[98] Details in paras. 55–6.

establish whether an exemption applies comes under reg. 6, not reg. 4, of the 2004 regulations.

Section 14: vexatious or repeated appeals[99]

In FS50157445, concerning the Chief Constable of Cheshire Constabulary, the complainant made a request for seven pieces of information relating to the constabulary's coat of arms and logo, the use of these, its policies regarding the recording of conversations and information about the constabulary's Internet domain and service provider. The request was part of an on-going dispute and the complainant admitted that the information was to be used in order to set up a website to publicise the constabulary's perceived shortcomings. The request was refused under s. 14 on the basis that it was vexatious. The IC confirmed the approach of the PA, applying IC Awareness Guidance 22. The IC took account of the complainant's previous 'excessive' behaviour in determining that the request imposed a significant burden on the PA. He also considered that: (1) the request had no serious purpose or value and that there were other means of the complainant giving effect to his intention; (2) the request had the effect of harassing the police; (3) the request could be characterised as obsessive and manifestly unreasonable.[100]

EA/2007/0114 *Gowers v IC and LB Camden* concerned information requested about the Central Complaints Unit of Camden LBC. The request was vexatious under s. 14. The IC's Awareness Guidance Notes state that it is vexatious where, inter alia, it would impose a significant burden on the authority in terms of expense or distraction. The IT believed this may be going too far and s. 12 provides the safeguard in such a case. Being vexatious also had one of the following features – it has no serious purpose or value, it was designed to cause disruption or annoyance, it has the effect of harassing the authority, or can otherwise be characterised as obsessive or manifestly unreasonable. EA/2007/0024 *J. Hossack v IC and DfW&P* again concerned a vexatious request and consideration of the IC Guidance 22. Costs considerations were relevant (these were £11,680 excluding counsel's costs). The Department for Work and Pensions argued that because the request was vexatious, the appeal was therefore vexatious. This was not a legitimate presumption, the IT ruled. The appellant avoided costs award against him on the 'narrowest of margins'. In EA/2006/0070 *V. Ahilathirunayagam v IC and London Met University* a university student was making vexatious requests – s. 14 applied. The IT emphasised the importance of seeking clarification of a request and not making presumptions.

---

[99] See FS50163359.

[100] EA/2007/0109 *Betts v IC* (19 May 2008) contains a discussion was a vexatious request for information about visiting and works policy on highways by East Yorkshire Council. Complaint rejected. Appeal dismissed. EA/2007/0130 *Coggins v IC* – a vexatious request. EA/2007/0088 *J. Welsh v IC* – vexatious request. IC upheld. EA/2006/0088 *R. Brown v IC and The National Archives (TNA)* (see s. 12 FOIA above).

Section 16: duty on authority to provide advice and assistance[101]

In FS50105724 the complainant requested information about parking fines issued over a six-month period. A refusal was based on exceeding the cost limit. However, the IC held that the PA had failed to provide any advice or assistance which prevented the complainant receiving information. In FS50072719 British Nuclear Fuels Ltd was in breach of s. 16 in not advising how it calculated that costs would exceed the £450 limit. EA/2007/0001 *HM Treasury v IC* stated that s. 16 advice etc. is applicant-specific – this was in relation to an exemption claim under s. 35 (see chapters 5 and 6). A Scottish MP could not expect HM Treasury to act as his research assistant and direct him to information available on its website (s. 21).

EA/2006/0046 *C. Lamb v IC* saw a substitution of a new DN by the IT. The request concerned legal advice on the legality of the Iraq war and the advice of Professor C. Greenwood and other lawyers who were not government lawyers. The case shows the importance of getting a requester to specify in his request what he is seeking and to use s. 16 to advance this. The IC found that the Cabinet Office did not hold the information but IC had not taken into account the poorly formulated request of the requester. IT's DN required Cabinet Office to ask requester to particularise items of request.

Section 46 code

EA/2006/003–2007/0007 *G. James v IC, DoT, Cabinet Office and Others* dealt with a request for information provided by Sir N. Bonsor MP (chair of the Select Committee on Defence) to Sir Richard Scott's inquiry into Matrix Churchill. It was believed to be contained in an annex to the reports in the Cabinet Office. Scott was anxious that the public should be allowed access to all materials relating to the inquiry 'save where serious harm to the public interest' would be caused. Nearly ten years after the annex was transferred to the Cabinet Office, not a single file (there were in excess of 10,000) of the annex had been transferred to the National Archives. A document tracking system had been handed over but was now obsolete. Does the Cabinet Office's treatment of annex comply with s. 46 paras 8.4–8.6 of the 2002 code on archives? Or would this be retrospective (see para. 58): 'Preservation of an existing document retrieval system seems to us no more than reasonable compliance with para. 8.5 [of the code under s. 46].'[102]

---

[101] EA/2008/0050 *A. Roberts v IC* on ss. 12 and 16 FOIA, no requirement to use new reporting facilities when they become available – rejected by IT as entitlement to information is at time of request. See FS50086076 where s. 16 was also satisfied. EA/2006/0049–50 *A. Berend v IC and LB Richmond* concerned an appeal which was allowed in part. Documents relating to lease of land by PA. An auditor had investigated the affair. Useful discussion on s. 16 advice and assistance.

[102] And see FS50137528.

Facts and figures

The review of the FOIA on central government conducted by Frontier Economics in 2006 found that the Act cost in total £24.4 million for central government. £8.6 million was on officials' time, the rest on overheads, processing internal reviews, and appeals to the IC and IT.[103] The report calculated that the hourly rate in central government was £34 and not the £25 allowed by the regulations and on average a request took 7.5 hours to deal with. The report found that requesters were of five key categories: journalists, MPs, campaign groups, researchers and private individuals. The report was used as a basis for reform of fee charges under FOIA which the government, after vociferous opposition, shelved in 2007.

The Ministry of Justice publishes annual reports of the FOIA covering central government. In its 2008 report,[104] 32,978 'non-routine' FOI and EIR requests were received for information by monitored departments and bodies – a 2 per cent reduction on 2006. Four per cent of these were subject to a fee and 99 per cent of these involved the National Archives, averaging £57 each. Eighty-four per cent received a response inside the twenty-working-day deadline. Seven per cent were subject to a PI-test extension. Sixty-three per cent were granted in full. Twenty per cent of 'resolvable' requests were fully withheld. The most commonly resorted-to exemptions were s. 30 investigations and proceedings conducted by authorities, s. 40 personal information and s. 41 information provided in confidence. There were 857 requests for internal reviews. Two hundred and twenty-two appeals were made to the IC's office. In 2006, there were 384. There was a 50 per cent reduction in the number of referrals to the Clearing House.

For other PAs it was estimated by Frontier Economics that annually there are about 87,000 requests costing about £11.1 million p.a.

The IC's office itself received 232 requests for information under both the FOIA and DPA. The office received 2,646 FOI complaints concerning PAs in 2007–8 which was marginally up on 2006–7. Over 50 per cent of new cases are closed within thirty days by the office but some take significantly longer. 36 per cent were still open after 365 days i.e. still under investigation or awaiting allocation. In 2007–8, 48 per cent of complaints were informally resolved, 33 per cent were ineligible and a DN was served in 14 per cent of cases. Seventy-five per cent of complaints were partly or completely upheld. Since 2005, there had been 235 appeals to the IT from 922 DNs. The IC had been overturned or varied in 28 per cent of cases, his decision upheld in 53 per cent and 19 per cent were withdrawn.[105]

---

[103] See note 56 above.

[104] *Freedom of Information Act 2000 Third Annual Report 2007*, Ministry of Justice (2008), www.justice.gov.uk. See App. B for the bodies covered.

[105] ICO *Annual Report 2007–8*, HC 670 (2007–8).

The Constitutional Affairs Committee conducted a review of the Act after one year in which it stated that a great deal of information had been released which was being used in a constructive and positive way and that the Act had brought clear benefits. It was described as a significant success but it reported on indefinite delays in internal reviews.[106] The IC's office has published data on the impact of the Act and found that initially FOIA had led to a greater proactive publication of information by PAs but this had decreased by 2007.[107]

Conclusions

There have been attacks on the FOIA and the Foreign Secretary gave a heavy hint of reform to give additional protection to 'sensitive information' in announcing the veto over Cabinet documents in February 2009. There are likely to be changes. FOI did not come easily to the UK and Parliament must uphold the rights which it provides – even in respect of MPs and their expenses. The rights must not be reduced.

The history behind FOI bills going back over twenty-five years in the UK and the amount of work and preparation that went into the present Act are remarkable. The bill was a focal point of attention from numerous groups all of which benefited from the extended Parliamentary scrutiny of the White Paper and the draft bill. The Campaign for Freedom of Information, newspapers, environmental and consumer and other pressure groups, all advocated vigorously the case for reform. The bill was before Parliament for over a year and even on report back to the House of Commons after it passed the Lords, 118 amendments were tabled causing the Home Secretary to apply the guillotine. It is common to have antagonistic sectional interests in the lead up to important legislation – think of hunting, abortion or privatisation. No group spoke against FOI publicly. Lobbying was behind the scenes.

The turnaround from the White Paper produced a vehement sense of betrayal expressed by so many interest groups in a manner not often witnessed in response to bills. Some of this may well have been due to the fact that the information in FOI is 'owned' by the public; it is information about us, or for us or concerning us and our future. It is 'us'. It simply happens to be in the government's possession on trust, as it were.[108] An FOIA is a necessary component in the progress towards a proper participatory democracy. That seemed to be present in the incoming government's rhetoric after Blair's victory in 1997. Since then, of course, the harsh realities of executive power have brought home the necessity for a balance between openness, privacy and confidentiality, or so

---

[106] *Freedom of Information: One year on*, HC 991 (2005–6). Government Reply CM 6937 (2006).

[107] UK Information Commissioner, *Freedom of Information: Three years on* (2008), www.ico.gov.uk/upload/documents/library/freedom_of_information/research_and_reports/foi_report_final_12_may.pdf.

[108] Sir Richard Scott refused to be drawn into a question of ownership of government information which was a 'philosophical question'.

it is claimed. New Labour, and not-so-new Labour, was seen to be protecting and benefiting from old practices.

The government was accused of abandoning internationally recognised standards of conduct in producing its draft bill. Jack Straw denied the existence of such international norms and asserted that the British tradition of government was far more compliant with legal norms than most others. There is truth in both sides' assertions. A good deal of the criticism was exaggerated. The idea of FOI received the highest of judicial endorsements. The bill and the Act contain elements which could too easily lead to over-protection. The disputes over the bill were not confined to the usual Government/Opposition/parliamentary dimensions but produced a clear split in the Cabinet at the highest of levels. There were ministerial scalps. The government's path to FOI provided more than its fair share of drama.

The episode confirms in my mind what has been written for many years: information and its collection and control are the life-blood of government. It always will be as long as we have *government* and the movement towards commercialised, off-loaded, privatised and hybrid government merely compounds the problem – hence incidentally the danger of the breadth of the protection for commercial information in this Act which has been outlined above and to which we shall return.

The extraordinary contents of some clauses of the draft bill were highlighted in the committee hearings before both Houses – the pre-legislative hearings which were a novel feature of Parliament under the 1997 New Labour Government. In the legislative process, the government is invariably in charge but the pre-legislative scrutiny offered enormous opportunities for feed-in at an open and pretty accessible level. The government deserves credit for this. Was the turn-around all a ploy, as Ronnie Campbell suggested to the Home Secretary? Bad bits had been put in so that many could be taken out and the government would get all the credit while leaving it with an Act which clearly left ministers in charge. The Act is much better than the original bill. The swing towards greater emphasis on PI disclosures was balanced by the introduction of absolute exemptions – these are effectively exclusions – and the veto.

Influential figures in the Public Administration Select Committee decided not to fight against exclusions and wide exemptions for security and intelligence matters. This was not a battle they would win. The stinging criticism from that committee was very effectively directed against highly dubious provisions forcing the Home Secretary to promise that he would go away and take a further look. He did, and the bill was significantly improved. If the more offensive provisions had not been removed, the Blair Government would have compromised much of what it had said about the new relationship between government and governed in the new millennium. Had a collective veto been introduced instead of one by an 'accountable person' – how one may ask are they to be made accountable other than by vapid answers to questions in Parliament? – that would have made the Act more acceptable if accompanied by a statutory order for a veto and public statement. That would have left some very wide exemptions that are not necessary in their existing breadth to protect the PI. In the next two chapters we shall see what the IC and IT are making of the 'prejudice' test and what degree of probative material will have to support withholding of information on a contents basis.

Would the bill have been dropped had there been too much opposition? Who would have been the loser if it had been dropped? We would be left with the 1994 code on openness, which although heavily criticised at the time of its introduction gained sudden respect indeed affection when compared with the provisions in the draft bill.[109] Newspapers had started to use the Major code more frequently and alleged they were finding opposition from government in its use.[110] With some amendments the bill was worth saving. Had it been lost, it is unlikely that it would have been reintroduced in any form for many years. It is now up to others to make the most of it. It is also likely that there will be more attacks on the Act by governments in the future.

Access to information legislation began in local government (see chapter 9, p. 366). It was introduced by FOIA into central government and PAs generally. The next step saw it move to Scotland. The interesting question will be to what extent the more liberal regimes operating in devolved government, particularly Scotland – although Scotland's legislation was heavily influenced by the UK model – and Wales will help to act as a counterweight to Whitehall hegemony and its traditional emphasis on secrecy and confidentiality. Northern Ireland is still under the UK FOIA and awaits its own legislation. The role of confidentiality features prominently in the concordats between London and Edinburgh and Cardiff. What opportunities will there be for constitutional pluralism in openness and access?

---

[109] The select committee in its report on the draft bill compared the provisions of the bill and the code: HC 570-I (1998–9), p. lxxxv *et seq.*
[110] See ch. 9, p. 321.

5

The exemptions[1]

Central to any freedom of information (FOI) regime is the existence of exemptions. In this chapter there will be an analysis the case law on exemptions. It sets out the content of the exemptions themselves and provides background analysis. A frequent question is: 'With so many exemptions what's the point of having a Freedom of Information Act (FOIA)'? A brief answer is that it allows access to information otherwise not available and most regimes place the burden of justifying non-disclosure on those seeking to withhold it. While the UK FOIA contains many exemptions that are similar to those present in overseas laws, there are some peculiar characteristics of the UK law. There are twenty-three exemptions (in reality more than this)[2] including ss. 12 and 14 (below). Apart from these two exemptions, all the others are in Pt II of the Act. Eight exemptions are absolute (below). Seventeen are on a class basis.[3] In a class exemption, disclosure of any document within the class is *ipso facto* damaging although PI disclosures may be made under s. 2 where they are not absolute exemptions. In the case of the other exemptions where 'prejudice' or damage would be caused by the disclosure because of their contents, an exemption may be claimed on the basis of the prejudice caused. However, the Commissioner may make a judgement on whether 'prejudice' exists and whether, if it exists, it is *de minimis*. This judgement is not subject to the veto under s. 53, but it is subject to appeal by the authority to the Information Tribunal (IT).

The 'prejudice' test

Virtually all of the exemptions state that an exemption applies if some damage or prejudice would or would be likely to arise. The specific detail differs between exemptions and should be alerted to. The basic test on prejudice was set out in EA/2005/005 *J. Connor Press Associates* and 2005/0066 *Bexley v IC* – the chance of prejudice being suffered should be 'more than a hypothetical possibility: there must have been a real and significant risk'.[4] 'Prejudice must be real, actual

---

[1] The IC has provided detailed and regularly updated guidance on the exemptions, www.ico.gov.uk/home/what_we_cover/freedom_of_information/guidance.aspx#exeguidance.

[2] Where all the subsections within sections are counted the total is larger; see p. 157 above.

[3] See p. 156 *et seq.*   [4] *Connor*, para 15.

and of substance'. Where prejudice would be likely to occur, the likelihood need not be more probable than not, though it should be real and significant; where prejudice would occur, the chance should be greater – it should be more probable than not.[5] EA/2005/0026 and 0030 *C. Martin and Oxford City C v IC* established that there must be a 'very significant and weighty chance of prejudice to the identified public interests (PIs). The degree of risk must be such that there "may very well" be prejudice to those interests, even if the risk falls short of being more probable than not.'[6]

In EA/2005/0026 *Hogan v IC* the IT discussed the formulation 'would or would be likely to' cause damage. This means 'inhibition would probably occur (i.e. on a balance of probabilities, the chance being greater than 50 per cent) or that there would be a 'very significant and weighty chance' that it would occur'. A 'real risk' is not enough; the degree of risk must be such that there 'may very well be' such inhibition, even if the risk falls short of being more probable than not' (para. 53).[7]

I will deal very briefly with the corpus of exemptions and then concentrate on the more controversial. First of all, the concept of 'absolute exemption' has to be examined.

Absolute exemptions

There are eight absolute exemptions. They will be examined in detail below but they cover information that is obtainable by other means; information supplied by or relating to bodies dealing with security matters; court records; information protected by parliamentary privilege; prejudice to the effective conduct of the public affairs of the House of Commons or House of Lords; personal information as explained below; information whose disclosure would constitute an actionable breach of confidence; and information protected from disclosure by law or court order. In most of these cases a public authority (PA) does not have a free hand to disclose in any event. Disclosure is prohibited by existing law or privilege. In the case of personal data, the exemption ensures that applications are dealt with under the Data Protection Act (DPA) or in accordance with the data-protection principles. Applications for court documents are made to the presiding judge. The one exception covers information supplied by, or relating to, security and intelligence services in the possession of PAs. This reflects the continuing governmental perception of these documents as highly sensitive. It should be noted that, even in America, such information is not excluded or given an absolute exemption – although it is afforded a very high degree of protection (see chapter 12).

---

[5] See FS501233488, para. 48.

[6] Following Munby J in *R (Lord) v SoS HD* [2003] EWHC 2073 (Admin). See *Home Office*, note 8 below.

[7] *R (Lord) v SoS HO* [2003] EWHC 2073 cited and EA/2006/0064 *R. Evans v IC and MoD* (para. 21).

Late invocation of an additional exemption

With so many exemptions, an important preliminary question is whether a PA may subsequently raise an exemption not raised in the initial response to a request. Can the Information Commissioner (IC) or IT allow, or are they under a duty to prompt, a PA to claim an exemption. This can be allowed, depending on the particular facts,[8] but the IT has criticised the IC for saying he is under a duty to raise this himself. One may question why not? If there is a question of a prejudice to a PI, should the IC not be able to raise this on his own initiative? In EA/2006/0059 *L. Meunier v IC and Nat Savings and Investment*, a critical IT ruled that the IC is not under a duty to see whether additional exemptions may be claimed. Consideration of an exemption not originally claimed is discussed (para. 81).

In EA/2005/0006 *P. Bowrick v IC and Nottingham CC* the IT discussed the question of whether it can hear argument for an exemption not raised initially. The answer was 'yes', even though outside the s. 17 period but late resort would amount to a breach, nonetheless, of s. 17. The FOIA does not prevent the raising at appeal stage of an additional exemption (para. 42). There is no duty on the IC to raise an exemption for the PA (para. 46). The IC may raise on his own initiative an 'appropriate' exemption (e.g., s. 31 and not s. 30) (para. 48). In this case costs were awarded against the council for 'frivolous, vexatious, improper or unreasonable action'. The case also contains advice on the use of s. 48 powers (practice recommendation) by the IC. The appeal was allowed and the decision notice (DN) amended.

The exemptions

In addition to s. 12 (which covers the situation where the cost of compliance exceeds the appropriate limit[9]) and s. 14 (which concerns vexatious and repeated requests), information that is reasonably accessible to the applicant, other than in accordance with s. 1, is exempt even if a payment is required (s. 21). This will cover information which has to be communicated under any enactment. It will also cover information contained in a publication scheme and any payments required are contained in that scheme. It does not cover information that an authority may release upon request. The words 'reasonably accessible to the applicant' suggest that personal circumstances such as financial means should be relevant.

Information that is held and intended for future publication by the authority or any other person is exempt under s. 22. A notorious event may have the sting temporarily drawn by authorising an internal inquiry to report to the prime minister or another minister. This will then allow the exemption to be invoked

---

[8] EA/2008/0087 *BERR v IC; Home Office v IC [2009] EWHC 1611 (Admin)*.

[9] Under s. 13 the authority may disclose such information under a fee structure peculiar to s. 13. This was a late amendment to allow for expensive disclosures regardless of s. 12.

to prevent disclosure. When the former Treasury Solicitor was summoned from retirement to investigate the events surrounding the intervention by Peter Mandelson's private office in the Hinduja affair (see p. 329 below) this provided a convenient excuse not to disclose information about the affair and in particular whether there were recordings of conversations by the former Northern Ireland Secretary who subsequently became a member of Brown's government. This information may also have been exempted under the 'prejudice to the effective conduct of public affairs' exemption (see below). It does not matter whether the date for publication is determined or not although reports from the IC stipulate that this is not a blank cheque and qualifications will be made (see chapter 6, p. 183). The information has to be held with a view to such publication at the time of the request and in all the circumstances of the case it is reasonable that information be withheld until the future date. This exemption contains a provision which I shall refer to hereon as the non-application of the duty to confirm or deny. Basically, the duty to confirm or deny that the authority holds information does not arise where compliance with s. 1(1) would involve the disclosure of information (whether or not already recorded) falling within the exemption, in this case s. 22(1). It is a response displaying the inscrutability of the Sphinx. In the USA this is restricted to intelligence and criminal law enforcement. This is because of the sensitivity of information relating especially to informers and where confirming or denying whether such information is held could arouse suspicion among the criminal fraternity. Its repetitive refrain throughout this Act suggests overkill. In Scotland, this exemption (s. 22) has a limit of twelve weeks from the date of the request for the period in which publication is to take place (Freedom of Information (Scotland) Act, s. 27).

The next exemption comes under s. 23 and concerns information supplied by, or relating to, bodies dealing with security matters. The bodies themselves are excluded from the provisions of the Act because they are not identified in the schedule to the Act. It is exempt if it was supplied to the PA directly or indirectly by such bodies or the information relates to any of the following bodies: the Security Service; the Secret Intelligence Service; the Government Communications HQ (GCHQ), the special forces and the Serious Organised Crime Agency (SOCA).[10] The duty of confirmation or denial does not apply if it would involve disclosure of such information or it relates to such bodies. A minister may certify that information covered by the certificate relates to, or was supplied by, the specified bodies and this is conclusive evidence subject to an appeal to the IT under s. 60 by the IC or applicant on the grounds the information referred to in the certificate was not exempt information. The IT may, in that case, allow the appeal and quash the certificate applying the principles applied by the court on a judicial review (s. 60(2)–(3)). Appeal is also

[10] Serious etc. Crime Act 2005, sch. 4, 158–60 for SOCA. Other bodies are: the tribunals established under s. 65 Regulation of Investigatory Powers Act 2000, s. 7 Interception of Communications Act 1985, and the Security Vetting Appeals Panel and the Security Commission.

allowed by any other party to the proceedings against a certificate identifying information in general terms as to whether it applies to particular information.

Information not falling within s. 23 is exempt under s. 24 if required for the purpose of safeguarding national security. The duty of confirmation or denial does not apply where exemption from s. 1(1)(a) is required for the purposes of safeguarding national security. This is a familiar exemption and ministerial certificates shall be conclusive evidence although an appeal may again be made to the IT on the same terms as in relation to s. 23.[11] Information may be identified in a 'general sense' and a certificate may have prospective effect. Appeal empowers the IT to quash a certificate where it finds 'on applying the principles applied by the court on an application for judicial review, the minister did not have reasonable grounds for issuing the certificate'.[12] This formulation in other legislation was examined in chapter 2 (see p. 56). National security is an absolute priority but it can be subject to easy exaggeration and its almost unchallengeable status can make it a last refuge for undeserving causes. Section 24 does not provide an absolute exemption but the conclusive nature of a valid certificate offers no prospect of challenge.

Further exemptions cover disclosures which would or would be likely to prejudice defence or the capability, effectiveness or security of any relevant forces (s. 26) and which would, or be likely to prejudice international relations (s. 27). The duty to confirm or deny may be overridden under both exemptions on the grounds explained above. Section 26 could be used to prevent disclosures of tests on, e.g., depleted uranium shells and bombs, controversially used in Kosovo where widespread and serious after-effects were reported and treated. Section 27(1) sets out what is meant by international relations and includes the interests of the United Kingdom abroad, and their promotion and protection. Information is also exempt information if it is confidential information obtained from a state other than the UK or from an international organisation or international court.[13] It is treated as confidential if it was obtained on terms requiring confidentiality or where the circumstances on which it was obtained make it reasonable for the state etc. to expect confidentiality. This will be the norm in international communications that are not meant for public consumption. In confidence means precisely that. It does not mean protected by the law of confidentiality, although in many cases it may be.

Section 28 makes information exempt where its disclosure would or would be likely to prejudice relations between the Government of the UK, the Scottish Administration, the Executive Committee of the Northern Ireland Assembly or the National Assembly for Wales. The duty to confirm or deny may be overridden. This exemption has rarely been resorted to. An important development has taken place in the form of 'concordats' contained in memoranda of understanding 'a multilateral arrangement involving the different devolved

---

[11] See s. 25. A certificate may only be issued by a member of the Cabinet or the Attorney General, Advocate General or NI Attorney General.
[12] See s. 60(4).   [13] See s. 27(5) for state, international court and international organisation.

administrations as well as the UK Government'.[14] Rawlings has written that although the concordats are published, they operate in secrecy and confidentially under UK domination. They result in a lack of transparency and a rule by co-operation which allows Whitehall the upper hand. Essential information is given by Whitehall on the basis that it is treated in confidence. This could prove to be difficult given the different approaches to FOI adopted in the FOI(Scotland)A 2002 (see chapter 4, p. 140).

Further exemptions cover information whose disclosure would or would be likely to prejudice the economic interests of the UK or any part of the UK, or the financial interests of any administration in the UK as set out in the preceding paragraph (s. 29). The duty to confirm or deny may be overridden. The matters excluded in relation to the Bank of England and nationalised banks were noted above (see chapter 4, p. 120 *et seq.*).

Information held by authorities for the purpose of any investigation as defined or criminal proceedings is exempt on a class basis as is information obtained from confidential sources relating to investigations and proceedings as described. I will deal with this exemption in s. 30 in more detail below. The duty to confirm or deny does not apply in relation to information exempt under this section – this is far broader than the usual overriding of this duty which is activated when, e.g., disclosure would prejudice the interests protected by the exemption. Section 31 exempts information the disclosure of which would or would be likely to prejudice law enforcement as defined (see below). The duty to confirm or deny may be overridden on the usual basis.

Information under s. 32 is exempt if held by a PA and it is contained in documents filed with or otherwise placed in the custody of a court for proceedings or created by a court or its administrative staff for the purposes of a particular cause.[15] Similar provisions cover inquiries[16] and arbitrations. The duty to confirm or deny does not apply in relation to information exempt under this provision. This is an absolute exemption but other provisions allow requests for court documents to be made.[17]

Under s. 33, information held by a PA for the purpose of audit and value-for-money (VFM) functions which it carries out in relation to other authorities is exempt on the usual basis of prejudice. The duty to confirm or deny does not arise in circumstances set out in s. 33(3).

Section 34 exempts information where disclosure would breach parliamentary privilege. The Speaker's certificate, or that of the Clerk of the Parliaments in the case of the Lords, is conclusive.[18]

---

[14] See R. Rawlings 'Concordats of the constitution' (2000) LQR 257 and Cm. 4806 on the *Memorandum of Understanding* between the UK Government, the Scottish Executive, the Welsh Assembly and the Northern Ireland Executive Committee.

[15] Presiding judges do have discretion to allow access to documents filed with the court subject to confidentiality or non-disclosure orders. See Sir Richard Scott, HC 570–ix (1998–99), Q. 893.

[16] See s. 32(4) for 'court' etc. It includes any inquest or post-mortem.

[17] E.g., Civil Procedure Rules 1998, r. 5(4).

[18] S. 34(3) and could not be challenged in any other place by virtue of the Bill of Rights 1689.

I pass over, for the time being, information exempt because it relates to the formulation of government policy (s. 35) or information the disclosure of which, in the reasonable opinion of a 'qualified person', would prejudice the effective conduct of public affairs (s. 36). These are controversial measures deserving fuller treatment (see below). They are heavily invoked by PAs (see chapter 6, p. 196).

Section 37(1) protects information concerning communications with Her Majesty, other members of the royal family or household as well as any conferral by the Crown of any honour or dignity. The duty of confirmation and denial may be overridden.

Information is exempt if its disclosure would or would be likely to endanger the physical or mental health of any individual or their safety (s. 38). The duty to confirm or deny may be overridden. Environmental information which the authority has to disclose under s. 74 is exempt (s. 39). This concerns the access regime and exemptions under the Environmental Information Regulations 2004 and will be fully explained in chapter 7.

Personal data are also exempt under s. 40 and will be dealt with in detail in chapter 8. As explained above, most personal data will be protected by an absolute exemption. FOIA has amended the DPA 1998 to extend the definition of data to cover 'recorded information' held by a PA not falling within existing definitions of data. This addition is known as 'unstructured personal data'. Access to personal data thus extended is made under the DPA by the data subject where s/he is requesting his or her own data. Access to information about others takes place under FOIA but subject to various DPA safeguards and exemptions.

Information whose disclosure would constitute an actionable breach of confidence is exempt (s. 41). This covers information from any other person including another PA.[19] A special exclusion covers the duty of confirmation or denial. Note that the term used is 'actionable', not successful action. This connotes something that could be tested in court not something that is certain to be accepted (see, however, chapter 6, p. 219 *et seq.*). Section 81 makes special provision for government departments whereby they cannot claim that a disclosure by one department is actionable by another although they are separate legal entities for the purposes of the Act.

Exemptions also cover legal professional privilege (s. 42), which has been widely resorted to and which covers lawyer/client communications and litigation privilege (see chapter 6, p. 224); trade secrets and commercial interests (s. 43); and that information whose disclosure is prohibited by law (s. 44), including EU law, and court order. These latter two are dealt with in fuller detail below.

---

[19] S. 81 states that 'each government department is to be treated as a person separate from any other government department'. However, this does not allow one department to maintain that disclosure of information by it would be an actionable breach of confidence by another department in order to claim the exemption. The 'Crown' owns the information in any event.

Examination of specific exemptions

Investigations and proceedings conducted by public authorities

Apart from ss. 23–4, the first of the exemptions to cause concern because of its breadth was that set out above in s. 30. In the White Paper the proposal was that law enforcement should be given an exclusion from the Act. In evidence to the select committee in 1998, the Home Secretary stated that if an exemption were substituted for an exclusion it would be so wide as to make it tantamount to an exclusion. Section 30 became the exemption and provides that information held by a PA is exempt information if it has at any time been held by the authority for the purposes of: any investigation which the PA has a duty to conduct with a view to its being ascertained whether a person should be charged with an offence or whether a person charged with an offence is guilty of it; where it has been held for any investigation which is conducted by the authority and in the circumstances may lead to a decision by the authority to institute criminal proceedings which the authority has power to conduct; or, any criminal proceedings which the authority has power to conduct. This is a class exemption and does not relate to any interference with the process of justice or any prejudice to any person, litigant or defendant. The fact that it falls within the exemption is sufficient. It covers information held *at any time*. It is subject to the PI provisions but the protection for s. 30(2) appears limitless when read with the public-records provisions on access (see below).

Under s. 30(2) information is also exempted where it relates to any such investigation or criminal proceedings as set out above, any investigation conducted for the purposes of s. 31(2) (below) under prerogative or statutory powers, or civil proceedings brought by the authority arising from such investigations *and* it relates to information obtained from confidential sources, i.e. informers.[20] The duty to confirm or deny does not arise in relation to exempt information – the breadth of which was noted above. The section defines those who may institute or conduct criminal proceedings in very broad terms and criminal offences includes a variety of military disciplinary offences.[21]

Law enforcement

This exemption is provided for by s. 31. Where information is not protected by s. 30, it will be exempted by this section where its disclosure would or would be likely to prejudice the matters listed in s. 32. This includes the prevention or detection of crime, the apprehension or prosecution of offenders, the administration of justice, the assessment or collection of tax or duty, immigration controls, maintenance of security or good order in prisons or other places of

---

[20] Who are always afforded special protection by the courts: *Marks v Beyfus* (1890) 25 QBD 494; see *Swinney v Chief Constable of Northumbria* [1996] 3 All ER 449.
[21] S. 30(5).

lawful detention, the exercise of functions for the purposes enumerated in sub-s. (2),[22] various civil proceedings and inquiries under the Fatal Accidents and Sudden Deaths Inquiries (Scotland) Act 1976. It requires prejudice and is not as questionable as the exemption under s. 30. It now contains the provision on information relating to accidents, which would cover notorious railway and other accidents, preventing information about causes and shortcomings being disclosed until official 'blessing' had been given to its format unless the PI allows a disclosure.

Formulation of government policy[23]

This section – s. 35 – and s. 36 were the most heavily criticised exemptions in the Act during its parliamentary process. These exemptions feature most prominently in terms of quantity in the case law of the IC and IT (see chapter 6). Section 35 exempts information held by a government department or the National Assembly for Wales if it relates to (note the looseness of that terminology) the formulation or development of policy, ministerial communications; advice or requests for advice by the law officers; or the operation of any ministerial private office.[24] The duty to confirm or deny does not apply to such exempt information – a very broad formulation. Once a decision has been taken, statistical information 'used to provide an informed background' to the formulation of government policy or which relates to ministerial communications may be disclosed. Under a PI disclosure involving this exempt information which is covered by s. 2(1)(b) or 2(2)(b), authorities shall have regard to the particular PI in the disclosure of factual information which has been used, or is intended to be used, to provide an informed background to decision-making. It says nothing about factual information not used and that may have militated against the policy decision.[25] There is nothing about the disclosure of rejected options. Publication schemes will have to be examined to see if they cover this information and if so, in what form.

---

[22] These include the purpose of ascertaining whether any person has failed to comply with the law; whether any person is responsible for any conduct which is improper; whether regulatory action is justified; ascertaining a person's fitness for corporate management or performance of any profession; causes of accidents; protecting charities; securing health, safety and welfare of persons at work; and protecting persons other than those at work against risk to health of safety arising from the actions of people at work. This exemption is on a contents basis and is subject to the public interest test.

[23] J. Relly and M. Sabharwal (2009) 26 *Government Information Quarterly* 148.

[24] S. 35(5) defines this as 'any part of a government department which provides personal administrative support to a Minister of the Crown' and NI Ministers and equivalent support for Welsh Assembly First and Deputy Secretaries. It was a crucial feature in the Peter Mandelson episode leading to his resignation in the Hinduja episode when in return for £1.5 million being donated to the Dome project Mandelson allegedly arranged British citizenship for one of the Hinduja brothers.

[25] In local authority executive arrangements alternative options may be disclosed; ch. 9, p. 371 *et seq.*

'Policy advice', whether from civil servants or special advisers, is not named specifically in this section but it will be covered by the expression 'relates to the formulation of government policy' where advice is central. There is nothing about legal advice from others apart from law officers in the formulation of policy or other expert opinion. The BSE episode which will be examined in chapter 9 (see p. 319 *et seq.*) brought home the enormity of this provision whereby information about the government response to the episode could be protected by this exemption as well as other exemptions. This attracted widespread criticism. Policy itself could be destroyed or seriously undermined by premature publication but this section extends way beyond such protection. government policy includes the policy of the Executive Committee of the Northern Ireland Assembly and the Welsh Assembly Government.

It has to be said that this exemption contradicts the plea made by the prime minister in *Modernising Government* for extensive consultation with 'others', i.e. outsiders, as early as possible in policymaking.[26] Furthermore, the Food Standards Agency and the Advisory Committee on Pesticides both publish advice to ministers, in the former case under statutory authority.[27] These points are equally valid under s. 36.

Civil service organisations generally welcomed the FOI proposals. But they have insisted on an exemption for policy advice: 'information in the nature of, or relating to, opinion or advice or recommendation tended [*sic*] by any person in the course of his official duties for the purpose of the formulation of policy within a department or authority to which this Act applies' said an earlier proposal. The First Division Association (FDA), representing leading civil servants, justified this exemption in the following terms:

> that while the Association wished to enhance the quality of public debate by better informing the public about government operations by timely provision of factual material, policy-making in a goldfish bowl was not to be welcomed.

The FDA had been adamant that identification of individuals will lower the quality of decision-making and could frequently have an adverse effect on the career prospects of the individuals concerned. Identification would cause civil servants to be more compliant with the wishes of ministers, rather than offering independent advice, since they would not wish to be publicly out of step with their ministers. They may be subject to retribution by an incoming government of a different political persuasion where their identity in giving advice can be established. But this is precisely the charge that is made against various senior civil servants today: that they are not sufficiently independent in their advice, they are the PM's people and the present conditions of anonymity help

---

[26] Cm. 4310, para. 6. See *R v Secretary of State for Health, ex p. United States Tobacco International plc* [1992] 1 All ER 212, and the duty to hand over scientific information from a specialist committee to a consultee.

[27] Food Standards Act 1999, s. 19(1)(a). On pesticides, see Pesticides Act 1998.

to conceal this. In Canada, policy advice, although it has wide protection, is not totally exempt, and the consequences so far have not undermined officials' neutrality or efficacy.[28] In other countries, a distinction has been drawn between the deliberative process of decision-making and the post-decision stage. In New Zealand, an exemption protects the confidentiality of advice tendered by ministers and officials and the 'free and frank expression of opinions' *unless* the PI in knowing outweighs the confidentiality. It seeks to protect officials from improper pressure, it requires an objective test of harm and withholding information has to be *necessary*. The Campaign for Freedom of Information have also accepted that this is the world *of real politique* and no government would accept such access without at least a qualification such as in the New Zealand Act. The UK Government was accused of being less liberal. But under the FOIA 2000, s. 35 is subject to a PI override (see chapter 6). It is not absolute. It was seen that the 2009 Dacre Review of the thirty-year rule recommended that the government consider additional protection for 'sensitive information' (see chapter 4, p. 137 and Introduction, pp. 3, 7). The review also recommended redaction of civil servants' names from papers and documents.

The Act states that statistical information is not exempt once a decision as to governmental policy is taken and insofar as the information was used to provide an informed background to the taking of the decision. Where information is not so used, it will be exempt unless it could be argued that in not being used it was not covered by s. 35. It was not a part of the policymaking process. Furthermore, under the section, when making a decision on the PI under s. 2, 'regard shall be had to the particular interest in the disclosure of factual information which has been used, or which is intended to be used, to provide an informed background to decision-taking'. The statistics only come after the decision whereas factual information may come before or after the decision. In previous bills, this has included statistical data and test results; and analysis, interpretation or evaluation of – or any projection based on – factual information, expert advice on a scientific technical, medical, financial, statistical, legal or other matter other than that protected by legal professional privilege. Overseas examples of information that cannot be withheld under such provisions include feasibility studies, plans and budgetary estimates, efficiency studies, environment impact studies, and advice from consultants under contract.[29]

Advice would be caught by s. 36 (below) where in the reasonable opinion of a qualified person disclosure would or would be likely to inhibit the free and frank provision of advice, or the free and frank exchange of views for the purpose of deliberation or 'would otherwise prejudice, or would be likely to prejudice, the effective conduct of public affairs'. This latter formulation would

[28] See ch. 12, p. 480 *et seq*. It does not exempt reasons for decisions affecting an individual's rights, or policy advice from outside consultants/advisers. See FDA evidence, HC 313(i) 1995–6.

[29] Campaign for Freedom of Information, *FOI Bill Briefing No. 3*.

cover infinitely more than control over timing of disclosures of information, which is a matter of understandable protection. Early release could be damaging to legitimate interests of good government. But the blanket exemption of policy advice even after a decision is finished and operative, and even in anonymous form, is disappointing. In the reforms in local government it was seen how policy alternatives were to be disclosed. Such alternatives will be covered by these two sections. They are not absolute exemptions and are subject to the PI test (although both Houses of Parliament are given an absolute exemption under s. 36).

Policy advice and alternatives to proposals must be open in order to inform and improve public debate, unless publicity would harm the proposal to such an extent that its purpose would be defeated *and* the PI thereby injured. This is a question of the timing of release to avoid the defeat or frustration of legitimate plans. The question of identity of an internal adviser should not be fundamental, unless an individual possesses the necessary information that will assist an inquiry into government practice in alleged wrong-doing or cover-up. At that point the veil of confidentiality needs to be broken, and a select committee is the appropriate body to investigate. In the nature of government such matters are likely to involve an abuse of power, a breach of governmental trust, an untruth or high-handed exercise of public power. Only rarely were these matters of governmental right susceptible to legal examination before a court of law although the growing sophistication of judicial review may raise opportunities for such examination.[30]

The policy and advice exemptions under ss. 35–6 go too far and constitute a weakness in spite of their own provisos. Once a decision is made, although it has been authoritatively stated that policy is a 'protean' concept,[31] then what should be missing is the name of the advice-giver alone where s/he is a civil servant. As the exemption stands, it protects not only the identity, but also the content. It should be noted that the exemption applies to 'advice'. Presumably an advisory committee's report would be protected. What of an 'outside adviser' who is not a Crown servant? If formally commissioned, are they engaged in official duties? It would appear so.

These exemptions ultimately affect and belittle a right to freedom of expression – the basic right in democracy. If we lack the means effectively to criticise policy, then our criticism is of little or no consequence. Our position as citizens is to that serious extent undermined. The first exercise by a Secretary of State of the veto power in s. 53 involved s. 35 and the disclosure of Cabinet documents ordered by the IC and IT (see chapter 6, p. 205).

---

[30] See the former Civil Service Department's booklet, *Legal Entitlements and Administrative Practices* (HMSO 1979). They are becoming more familiar before the courts: see *R (Corner House Research and Others) v Director SFO* [2008] UKHL 60; *Bancoult v Secretary of State for Foreign and Commonwealth Affairs* [2008] UKHL 61, and *R (B) v Secretary of State for Foreign Affairs* [2009] EWHC 152 (Admin) – see ch. 11.

[31] Note *Bushell v Secretary of State* [1981] AC 75 per Lord Diplock.

Prejudice to effective conduct of public affairs

Section 36 exempts information not protected by s. 35 and which is held by a government department or information held by 'any other public authority'.[32] It is exempt if, in the reasonable opinion of a qualified person, disclosure of the information under the Act would, or would be likely to, prejudice one of the following:

(a) the maintenance of the convention of the collective responsibility of Ministers of the Crown
(b) the work of the Executive Committee of the Northern Ireland Assembly
(c) the work of the Executive Committee of the Welsh Assembly Government.

What, one might ask, is so precious about collective responsibility? In the formulation of the policy and in drafting the bill on FOI, there were widely publicised disagreements between ministers about the appropriate content of the bill and who should have ultimate responsibility for the bill. No harm was done to the eventual outcome. The law quite rightly recognises a place for confidentiality in Cabinet and ministerial relationships, and between ministers and their servants, and the weakness of the law sometimes causes problems for continuing relationships (see chapter 9, p. 325). Insiders to government are usually adamant (in government) that collective responsibility should be strictly adhered to. Like all absolutes it can produce undesirable consequences such as domination by a small caucus or concealment of inadequate debate over life-and-death decisions. This was the very issue at the heart of the use of the veto in relation to the Cabinet minutes on the decision to go to war in Iraq (see chapter 6, p. 205).

The section continues: '[where disclosure] would or would be likely to, inhibit the free and frank provision of advice or the free and frank exchange of views for the purpose of deliberation . . .'. Clearly there are legitimate reasons why a PA may not wish to divulge advice before a decision is made. Timing could be crucial; early release might sabotage a tactical advantage or a decision itself or might cause damage. People feel inhibited from giving their honest advice if subjected to the glare of publicity and if unpopular or controversial – the government in the goldfish bowl syndrome. The official 'advice' aspect has always been a sensitive issue for FOI reform because it was seen as running the risk of focusing attention on individual civil servants which could lead to 'retribution' by incoming governments who were hostile to such policies on which they had advised. It might also lead to embarrassing publicity where it was clear there was a division between advice and advisers and ministers. To what extent will the authority claim that, even after a decision is made releasing such advice or deliberation, the disclosure will inhibit future decisions because

---

[32] The 1997 WP seemed to confine this exemption to 'government' meaning central government. It was soon developed to have a wider application.

civil servants will be identified and disagreements between them and ministers will be made public putting them in an impossible position?

Last of all, information is exempt where disclosure would 'otherwise prejudice, or would be likely otherwise to prejudice, the effective conduct of public affairs'. Potentially, this could cover just about everything and is truly reminiscent of the spirit of the 1911 Official Secrets Act (OSA). All the exemptions are made out where 'in the reasonable opinion of a qualified person'[33] disclosure would cause the prejudice specified. In the case of statistical information this requirement does not justify exemption so the authority in this case would have to establish the damage that could be caused by disclosure. 'In the reasonable opinion' connotes an objectively justifiable decision and not the residuary *Wednesbury* test of leaving a decision alone unless so unreasonable that no reasonable person could come to such a conclusion.

The duty to confirm or deny does not arise if in the reasonable opinion of a qualified person compliance with s. l(l)(a) would or would be likely to have any of the effects in sub-s. (2). Qualified person is defined in sub-s. (5) and includes officers of the Houses of Parliament where the certificate is conclusive. A list of such persons is available at www.foi.gov.uk/guidance/exguide/sec36/annex-d.htm.

Where a PA is not listed it means a minister of the Crown, a PA authorised by a minister or any officer or employee so authorised. Authorisations may relate to specified person(s) within a specified class, be general or limited and may be conditional.

Commercial interests

Information is exempt under s. 43 where it constitutes a trade secret. This is a common and unexceptional provision in FOI regimes. There is considerable divergence in the various legal systems as to the legal definition of 'trade secret'. 'Trade secret' is a legal term of art *and* has been stated by the Law Commission to cover information which is not generally known, which derives its value from that fact, whose owner has indicated expressly or by implication the wish to maintain it as secret and probably the information is used in trade or business.[34] An amendment in the Lords sought to define a trade secret as: 'confidential trade information which if disclosed to a competitor would cause harm to its owner'. This was unsuccessful.

The second part of s. 43 is drawn in extremely broad terms. It states that information is exempt if its disclosure under this Act would or would be likely to prejudice the commercial interests of any person (including the PA holding it). The duty to confirm or deny is excluded on the usual basis. 'Commercial interests' is very broad – the more usual formulation is commercial confidences,

---

[33] S. 36(5) lists the 'qualified persons' under the section.
[34] Law Commission, *Misuse of Trade Secrets* (1997) No. 150, para. 1.29. See also NCC, *Commercial Confidentiality* (1998).

at least implying some degree of confidentiality. Could commercial interests block access to information about utilities cutting off customers who cannot pay bills? What requests for contractual pricing, tenders, penalty clauses and so on might it cover? What about claw-back provisions, or information on overpayments where the authority has made a bad deal? The IC would have to be satisfied that prejudice would or would be likely to be caused and a threshold would have to be crossed. The Parliamentary Commissioner for Administration has conducted numerous investigations under the 1994 Code on Access where commercial confidentiality has been raised by officials as an objection. So, for instance, tenders or pricing decisions should not be disclosed where that would clearly interfere with the commercial position of an authority. But once contracts were finalised, there would appear less good reason why tenders should be protected by confidentiality unless it could be proved to interfere with future competition against the PI.[35] This is likely to be an important exemption in contracting-out arrangements, under public private partnerships (PPPs) or otherwise. Powerful contractors are likely to stipulate what is to remain exempt in the terms of the contracts. Unless they are designated as PAs, the duty to disclose, if any, is on the PA, not the contractor. It is also interesting to note that provisions in other domestic laws protect information where disclosure could *prejudice to an unreasonable degree* the commercial interests of any person. No such qualification applies here.[36]

Government contractors

We saw how the FOIA applies to a very wide range of bodies. To what extent will it apply to those carrying out public functions or public services under contract? Where such bodies have been designated by the minister for the purposes of the Act, those bodies will then have to disclose information in accordance with the Act's provisions and its exemptions. The commercial interests and trade-secrets exemption under s. 43 is likely to feature widely here. These bodies may only be designated for certain purposes so that FOIA will only apply to such purposes. The public might be interested in the terms of the contract, payments and any special features of a contract delivering a public service. What unfavourable terms allocating risk have been saddled on the PA? Under PPPs, for instance, it was envisaged that contracts should be awarded under the negotiated procedure (the most restrictive or least open) under the European Directives on Public Procurement as implemented. Any other award may be a strong indication that this was not a PPP arrangement.

Designation could become a weapon of traditional secrecy insofar as it may be used as a threat by an authority to comply with its wishes. A very powerful contractor may insist that it is not designated and as many terms as possible

---

[35] See the Parliamentary Ombudsman in Case A9/94, Case A5/96 and Case A1/95.
[36] Clean Air Act 1993, s. 37; Control of Major Accident Hazard Regulations 1999, sch. 8, para. 18, and so on.

remain confidential. Designation will be subject to judicial review. The Government conducted a consultation on designation in 2007.

Section 45 refers to the code of practice making provisions relating to the inclusion of terms in contracts entered into by PAs covering access to information. Will duties exist on such contractors, i.e. companies, to provide information? Only if the contract so specifies. The Nuclear Decommissioning Authority for instance enters into agreements in relation to the release of information with private contractors who are site licensees of those plants which are to be decommissioned.[37] The provisions in the code are somewhat anaemic in this regard and were watered-down from draft versions of the code. PAs should bear in mind their obligations under the Act when entering contracts (para. 31). Reasons for claiming confidentiality should be provided. Confidentiality must be consistent with the Act's exemptions. But for information to have the quality of confidentiality, it must be confidential, even when described in such a way in a contract.[38] The draft code on FOIA 2000 Pt V states that confidentiality should not be guaranteed by a department where information is not confidential. This was removed. An agreement cannot make what is not confidential 'confidential'. The Public Contract Regulations, r. 43, states that information should not be disclosed which is 'reasonably designated as confidential'. Even if a breach of contract took place not to disclose information which was not confidential or commercially sensitive, what would the damage be? Furthermore, if information is confidential there is a PI defence to disclosure under the common law.[39]

Under the 1994 code, as revised, they were under such a duty because they were within the terms of the 1967 Parliamentary Commissioner for Administration Act which governed the operation of the code where contractors performed services for the public. The public-service aspect might attract a complaint of maladministration. Arrangements will have to be made as between the department and contractor as to who should disclose the information and how. Section 75 and sch. 15 of the Deregulation and Contracting Act 1994 allow restricted or confidential information to be handed to contractors on terms that they give it the protection owed by ministers and civil servants. This will be implied

---

[37] See www.nda.gov.uk/documents/upload/NDA_Final_Strategy_published_7_April_2006.pdf.

[38] *Coco v A. N. Clark (Engineers) Ltd* [1969] RPC 41, at 47 drew a distinction between confidentiality under contract and under equity but this is not inconsistent with the presumption that contractual confidentiality can only apply to information which has the quality of confidential information about it irrespective of the parties intent. Parties can agree to call a cat a dog! The law will protect confidentiality under contract providing there is something worth protecting. Cf. *AG v Parry* [2004] EMLR 13. Lord Donaldson stated that courts will enforce agreements not to publish information not of itself confidential (*AG v Barker* [1990] 3 All ER 257) but if not confidential a third party is free to publish and there are likely to be public policy questions where information is the subject of protection by contract but is not of itself confidential and an attempt is thereby made to avoid duties under FOIA: see R. Toulson and C. Phipps, *Confidentiality*, 2nd edn (2006), p. 56 *et seq.*

[39] *London Regional Transport v Mayor of London* [2003] EMLR 4

by the contract as a matter of law. Nothing should require the disclosure of commercially confidential information except a greater PI.

Where services are provided to government, there may well be considerations of intellectual property, commercial confidentiality or management and negotiating positions requiring confidentiality. The guidance on the 1994 code stated that disclosure under the code will have to be decided on a case-by-case basis. This is a situation that ought to be covered clearly by contractual provisions relating to property rights in information or reports and confidentiality.

While the tendency in the law and practice has been to introduce greater openness and transparency into the tendering process, some of these tendencies have been driven by EC requirements implemented into our law, the general position relating to genuine commercial confidences of tenderers and contractors will be maintained. The guidance on the Code on Access stated that the following should be disclosed:

- the identity of the successful tenderer
- the nature of the job, service or goods to be supplied
- the performance standards set (which should be output based)
- the criteria for award of contract
- the winning tender price or range of prices (maximum/minimum) paid.

PAs may be put under pressure to keep confidential the terms of a contract, its value and its performance. Wherever commercially viable, says the code on the FOIA, PAs should endeavour to obtain agreement that confidentiality should not protect such information. Under this lame provision, there is no guarantee that such information will be provided. Except where the contractor is designated, the duty of disclosure falls on the PA. One should not overlook the PI in disclosure where items of fraud, waste or mismanagement occur and the terms of the Public Interest Disclosure Act (see chapter 3, p. 116).

In Australia, contractors with public undertakings – who were supplying natural gas to public utilities – have been equiparated to public bodies, so a less demanding test of 'public confidentiality'[40] protected their 'commercially sensitive information' where it was requested outside an arbitration hearing for which the information was prepared:

Why should the consumers and the public of Victoria be denied knowledge of what happens in these arbitrations, the outcome of which will affect, in all probability, the prices chargeable to consumers by the public utilities.[41]

As noted above, the PI in disclosure has been accepted in PPPs.

---

[40] See *Commonwealth of Australia v John Fairfax & Sons Ltd* (1980) 147 CLR 39.
[41] *Esso Australia Resources Ltd v Plowman* (1995) 183 CLR 10, at 32, per Mason CJ.

Prohibitions on disclosure

The last of the difficult provisions concerns legal prohibitions on disclosure.
These will cover court orders and statutory restrictions. It also includes EU
obligations. This latter carries with it some complications because the regulation
made under Art. 255 EC Treaty seeks to provide an access regime for EU
documents but it has exemptions covering EU-institution documents covered
by the regime which are held by Member States and for Member State documents
held by the institutions. In some Member States, e.g. the Scandinavian countries,
the traditions are much more open than in others including the UK. This could
be a source of conflict. This point is addressed in more detail in chapter 10.
There have been large numbers of cases involving this exemption especially in
relation to the Financial Services Authority (see p. 237).

Removing prohibitions on disclosure

Section 75 FOIA contains a provision allowing the Secretary of State to amend or
repeal by order any enactment prohibiting disclosure of information. There are
numerous such provisions in statutes.[42] The Public Administration Committee
rightly considered this to be a very important provision – these provisions are
also an exemption under FOIA by virtue of s. 44. The committee was concerned that a well-meaning intention might evaporate after initial enthusiasm
and suggested that a parliamentary committee rather like the Deregulation
Committee established to examine deregulation orders under the Deregulation
and Contracting-out Act 1994 should assume oversight for this task. It would
provide the necessary encouragement and discipline. The suggestion was not
taken up by the government. Orders repealing measures prohibiting disclosure
have been made since November 2004 (e.g., SI 3363/2004).

Public-interest disclosures[43]

The focal point under the Act will be the exercise by the authority of its discretion to disclose exempt information when it considers the PI under s. 2. The
authority's discretion overrides the exemption. The exemptions which were
discussed above are contained in Pt II FOIA – apart from ss. 12 and 14. The
IC can determine whether the test for exemption is made out, i.e. whether
the 'prejudice' actually exists or is fanciful or *de minimis* or whether a class
exemption is established. This has been described as a question of fact although
it is in reality a question of law or jurisdictional fact. Once the prejudice does

---

[42] A reasonably up-to-date list is in P. Birkinshaw, *Government and Information*, 3rd edn (2005),
      Annex B.
[43] See M. Carter and A. Bouris, *Freedom of Information: Balancing the public interest*
      (Constitution Unit UCL, 2006) for a detailed commentary examining comparative approaches.

exist, or the class exemption is made out, then the duty in s. l(l)(a) to inform the applicant whether the authority holds information does not apply where an absolute exemption applies, or 'in all the circumstances of the case the PI in maintaining the exclusion of the duty to confirm or deny' outweighs the PI in disclosing whether the authority holds the information. The duty to communicate the information under s. 1(1)(b) does not apply where once again the information is subject to an absolute exemption or in all the circumstances of the case the PI in maintaining the exemption outweighs the PI in disclosure. The case law is discussed in chapter 6.

The wording of the two clauses which allow for a weighing of PIs was amended in the Lords report stage to make sure that where the PIs in disclosure or non-disclosure were evenly balanced or likewise exclusion or non-exclusion of the duty to confirm or deny the holding of the information, the scales would come down on the side of disclosure or non-exclusion. Previously the bias in the bill was the other way in favour of secrecy.

The power of veto comes as an immunity against the enforcement powers of the IC which I discuss below. Under s. 17 FOIA, an authority that to any extent relies upon a claim that an exemption in Pt II FOIA applies in response to a request for information, i.e. to exclude a confirmation or denial of holding information or to justify non-disclosure, has to give the applicant a notice. This must state the fact of their reliance, specify the exemption in question and state (if that would not otherwise be apparent) why the exemption applies. The notice must also contain an estimate of when a decision on the PI involving exemptions that are not absolute exemptions will be made. Guidance is provided on this by the Ministry of Justice and the IC.[44] The IC notes that under the Environmental Information Regulations (EIR) and Scottish Act no reference is made to a period beyond twenty days. The IC recommends that where the PI factors are 'exceptionally complex' a total period should not exceed forty days (i.e. twenty plus twenty) although authorities should aim to respond to all requests within twenty days. The reasons for claiming a PI balance in favour of maintaining the exclusion or non-disclosure must be stated either in the notice or another notice, although not in a manner that compromises any exemption. Along with some other matters, a notice must contain details of internal complaints procedures within authorities and particulars of applying for a decision notice from the IC (below). A notice will have to be served within the first twenty-day period even if the authority has to take longer to determine the PI. If the decision subsequently is not to disclose, a further notice must be issued with reasons for the decision. Although the IC may make a decision on the PI which differs from the authority's, specified authorities may be protected by a veto (below).

---

[44] For the IC, www.ico.gov.uk/what_we_cover/freedom_of_information/guidance.aspx. For the MoJ, www.justice.gov.uk/guidance/freedom-of-information.htm.

Third-party challenges

Very frequently, parties who supply information to departments or authorities will want to be reassured that any confidential or commercially sensitive information will not be disclosed without that party being informed and having a right to challenge that department's decision if in favour of disclosure. The government resisted calls to provide a third-party procedure to facilitate challenge of decisions. Such a procedure was recommended by the Commons Select Committee on Public Administration. The Act simply provides in s. 45 that a code of practice issued by the Secretary of State will advise on good practice to follow. This includes consultation with persons to whom the information requested relates or persons whose interests are likely to be affected by the disclosure of information. It may be necessary to consult such interest directly to determine whether an exemption applies or whether the obligations in s. 1 arise. But in a range of other circumstances, the code advises, it will be good practice to do so; 'for example where a public authority proposes to disclose information relating to third parties, or information which is likely to affect their interests, reasonable steps should, where appropriate, be taken to give them advance notice, or failing that, to draw it to their attention afterwards'. Consultation should take place to assist a decision on whether an exemption exists or on a discretionary PI disclosure. A representative body may be an appropriate consultee. No response from a third party should not determine a decision on disclosure. Where the information is personal information on a data subject the terms of the DPA 1998 will have to be complied with.

When papers are sent in to PAs it will be worthwhile indicating a belief that information should be exempted on grounds of commercial or other confidentiality. This will not be binding on the government/holder in terms of the legal interpretation, but it will send a warning that it should not be disclosed without safeguards.

When information is peculiarly sensitive, companies may wish to warn departments that even disclosure of the existence of the documents containing the information could be damaging. Clearly, an element of 'wolf!' could be associated with this practice but genuine concerns should be communicated.

There is no doubt that the Act and guidance leave third parties in a poor position compared with procedures elsewhere. The original draft code was even weaker. The US FOI did not originally provide for a third-party notice whereby the provider of information, usually a business or company, which has supplied the department, etc. with data on policies, operations or products, seeks to prevent the agency or department that collected the information from disclosing it to a third party in response to the latter's FOI request. This is now provided for by executive order (see chapter 12). More recent access laws in other countries make statutory provision for a 'third-party notice' to advise the provider of information that a request for information it provided has been made and Australian federal law and state laws provide for similar legal procedures protecting the position of a third party.[45] The Code of Guidance accompanying the Code on Access gave much fuller detail on the kinds on information that would attract protection and previous FOI bills have given clearer guidance on what should and what should not be protected. The IC is not given authority to deal with complaints from third parties, only from those who have made a request for information. Third parties will have to seek protection through the DPA actions for breach of confidence or judicial review where an authority is going to disclose information which concerns them or which they have provided. If they are not consulted, they will not know beforehand and so will not be able to prevent disclosure. This is not satisfactory.

In the USA, the 'arbitrary, capricious and substantial evidence' standard is applied to review 'third-party notice' decisions. This entitles the court to examine the whole record of the decision-making and provides discovery (disclosure) rights for a requester to help assess the process. This is distinguished from the *de novo* review where a requester challenges a refusal to hand over documents by the department. This amounts to a new decision on the merits by the court which can examine documents *in camera* if it wishes to assist in its decision.

There is also a practice in the USA which is of great practical importance. This is known as the 'Vaughn index' (see ch 12, p. 464). By this process, agencies have to itemise and justify exemptions claimed for documents; their *ipse dixit* is not sufficient. Departments will have to provide compelling reasons and arguments why documents should be withheld and companies should be prepared to justify to departments, or the IC or IT why they should be withheld. Something like the 'Vaughn index' might evolve from British practice.

Enforcement

A person wishing to complain about the manner in which an application has been dealt with may apply to the IC for her decision on whether their request has been dealt with in accordance with the requirements of Pt V. This will include the general rights of access as well as PI disclosures under s. 2.[46] The IC must specify the steps that have to be taken by an authority, and the time within which they must be taken, to comply with the requirements of s. 1 as well as ss. 11 and 17 of the Act. Section 17 concerns the situation where an authority relies upon an exemption under Pt II as explained above when responding to a request for information. A statement of compliance or non-compliance will be made by way of a DN. The complainant must first exhaust any internal complaints procedure. Before taking a complaint, the IC will have to be satisfied that there has been no 'undue delay' in making the application, that the application is not frivolous or vexatious and that it has not been withdrawn or abandoned. If the

---

[45] See R. Baxter (1997) JBL 199.

[46] Complaints may also include: fees, compliance time, failure to provide particulars of refusal and other matters.

IC makes no decision, this fact must be notified to the complainant together with 'his grounds for not doing so'. Where a DN is made, both the complainant and PA must be informed together with notice of rights of appeal under s. 57. Any period specified in a DN for taking action shall not operate so as to interfere with any rights of appeal. This is also true of steps required to be taken by enforcement notices (ENs) and information notices (INs) (below).

The IC may issue, where satisfied that an authority has failed to comply with any of the requirements of Pt I of the Act, an EN requiring the authority to take such steps as are specified within a timescale as specified. The EN must contain a statement of the requirement(s) under Pt I which the IC is satisfied have not been complied with and the reasons for so finding as well as particulars of a right of appeal. This seems to have a wider remit than a DN and could cover publication schemes as discussed above.

The IC may also serve an information notice under s. 51. This is a formal requirement to provide information as requested to the IC in relation to applications under s. 50, or that is reasonably required for the purposes of determining whether a PA is complying with any of the requirements under Pt I, or to determine whether an authority's practice in relation to functions under the Act complies with the codes of practice under ss. 45–6. The notice may include 'unrecorded information'. It must also contain particulars of any rights of appeal and information does not have to be handed over until an appeal is exhausted. It may not cover information protected by legal professional privilege in relation to obligations, liabilities or rights arising under the Act or in connection with or in contemplation of proceedings arising under the Act (see chapter 6, p. 209). Other information protected by legal privilege is not so excluded but it will be exempt and subject to the PI test. Schedule 3 confers powers of entry and inspection on the IC after a warrant from a circuit judge but not in relation to those items protected by privilege.

Where the authority fails to comply with any of the above notices, the IC may certify that failure by referring the matter to the High Court for it to punish as a contempt. Failure includes knowingly making a false statement or recklessly making a statement which is false in a material respect. The authority and requester may appeal to the IT against a DN and the authority alone may appeal against an EN and IN. The IT has very extensive powers to reverse the IC on appeal.[47]

The veto

Where the Commissioner serves a decision or enforcement notice which concerns request(s) for exempt information and where the authority neither

---

[47] See chapter 4 p. 137. The grounds of appeal are: the notice was not in accordance with the law; or a notice involved an exercise of discretion by the Commissioner and she ought to have exercised discretion differently ie. a merits appeal. Any finding of fact on which a notice is based may be reviewed.

confirms nor denies its existence, nor communicates the information, i.e. the authority believes the PI in withholding the information outweighs the disclosure of the information, the authority may resist that notice. In other words, the power of the IC added as the bill progressed through Parliament to enforce a decision on the PI instead of merely recommending an outcome was compromised by a veto. The provisions are in s. 53. The veto was confined in the passage of the bill to an 'accountable person' who is a Cabinet minister or the Attorney General (or Scottish or Northern Ireland equivalents) and special provisions apply to Northern Irish and Welsh bodies. Bodies covered by the veto are government departments, the Welsh Assembly Executive and any public body designated by order of the Secretary of State. Special provisions relate to consultation where designated bodies are Welsh or Northern Irish PAs. Just before the access provisions became effective in 2005, the Lord Chancellor stated that a veto would effectively be a decision of the whole Cabinet. It was seen in chapter 4 that the first veto has been issued (see chapter 6, p. 205) after consultation with the Cabinet.

Basically, the accountable person may serve on the IC a signed certificate stating that s/he has on reasonable grounds formed the opinion that there was no failure to comply with duties of disclosure in relation to request(s) for information. The certificate must be served within twenty working days of the effective date.[48] Although the IC's powers under the Act are terminated by such a certificate, it is not entirely clear whether the IC or the complainant can seek a judicial review of such a veto (see below). In principle they should be so empowered although the chances of successful challenge would be negligible. Nor is it clear whether alongside the statutory framework, the information could be sought under common law and general powers of disclosure. Under s. 78, it is provided that nothing in FOIA is to be taken to limit the powers of a PA to disclose information held by the authority. These may be statutory or common-law powers. At common law, an authority can disclose whatever it is not unlawful to disclose, which begs questions about self-authorisation which were examined in chapter 3 in relation to the OSA (see p. 101 above) or what it is not against the PI to disclose. It would take a very brave judge to prevent a department disclosing what it had decided to disclose within its sphere of responsibility, as Lord Woolf pointed out in *ex p. Wiley*.[49] In evidence to the Commons select committee, the Home Office felt that the decision of the authority on the PI under cl. 14 – which in the Act has become s. 2 – could be subject to a judicial review. This was because the clause merely dealt with an existing discretion to disclose. Given the detailed treatment of the discretion in s. 2 FOIA, the existence of the IC as a remedial device under the bill and the role of the court on contempt, it is difficult to see what role would be left for

---

[48] S. 53(4) for effective date: either the day on which a notice was given, or if there is an appeal the date of its determination.

[49] *R v Chief Constable of the West Midlands Police, ex p. Wiley* [1994] 3 All ER 420, at 438 b–c.

a judicial review if the statute were the exclusive route to information.[50] The statutory route is exclusive.[51]

It should be noted that under s. 53(6), a complainant has to be given reasons for the accountable person's opinion that a veto should apply, although not in a manner which would disclose exempt information. The IC is only entitled to the s. 53 certificate but she will have access to the information itself (subject to special arrangements as explained above in the case of sensitive information see p. 129) and to the background to the decisionmaking process, so she will be in a good position to assess whether the certificate is supportable. Copies of the certificate have to be laid before both Houses of Parliament and where relevant before the Northern Ireland Assembly and Welsh National Assembly.

The IC would have access to the information herself and so would be in a much better position to judge the cogency of the reasoning and decision of an authority under s. 2 than would say a reviewing court which is usually operating in the dark or at best twilight. The select committee's view was that cl. 14 should be amended so as to include a specific provision coming down in favour of disclosure 'unless there is a compelling argument to the contrary'. This is what s. 2 now does. Authorities would have to give to complainants (but not to the IC) reasons for their decisions refusing access under s. 2. Where a veto is entered complainants might use these to seek judicial review because no other avenue is open to them. Could the IC seek judicial review of a veto, arming herself with the details gathered in her investigation?[52] There seems nothing in principle to rule out such a possibility. The IC was denied the power of litigating on behalf of a complainant. The Home Office believed this would impair the IC's impartiality. Can the IC not properly be regarded as an advocate for openness? The IC does have advisory and promotional responsibilities under the Act. There seems no reason in principle why she cannot seek a judicial review.

The opportunity to seek a ruling under s. 54 on contempt would offer no comfort to the Commissioner because s. 54 only applies to notices that are not complied with, and these cannot be issued in relation to s. 53. The veto is a trump card to that extent. The contempt provisions were originally presented as a central means of enforcing the Act. They will now only be called upon where there is a failure to comply with a notice. Under s. 54(2) the making of false statements by an authority in response to an information notice is taken as non-compliance. Section 54(3), which deals with inquiries by the court where there is an alleged failure to comply with a notice, seems to envisage some judicial investigation into the action of the authority and the court would appear to be able to do more than simply accept the bare assertion of the accountable person. It is not likely that the court would be able to open a window into the mind of that person, however. Section 77 creates an offence of altering,

---

[50] See HC 570–xii (1998/99), Q. 1068.   [51] See also *Sugar v BBC* [2009] UKHL 9.

[52] The Lords committee believed there should be an override power in the Commissioner or at least a power to publish an opinion on the merits that a refusal to disclose on the public interest was wrong. This was before the veto was added to the bill in the Lords.

concealing, destroying etc. records which have been requested and where there is an entitlement to see them.

In the USA judicial deference has been shown to the executive in sensitive areas. In Australia, the minister may issue conclusive certificates in the PI denying access although there were plans to amend this provision (see p. 488). These are not presently reviewable by the Administrative Appeals Tribunal although it may make a recommendation. The position in relation to New Zealand and Canada is noted in chapter 12. A veto power exists in Ireland. Every system of FOI allows the executive to have the final say on the most sensitive of points or affords the executive the greatest deference in such areas; all others, however, do not make the final task of denial as easy for the executive as this Act encompasses. For Jack Straw, to allow the IC the final say would not be 'our way of doing things'. This he displayed when he exercised the first veto.

Copyright and FOI

To a long list of exemptions attempts have been made to add de facto exemptions. An issue has arisen whereby a body covered by the FOIA seeks to withhold access to a document on the basis of copyright and not an exemption under the FOIA. Denying access must be based on an exemption within the FOIA – in this case possibly ss. 21 or 43(2). Copyright is a separate issue regulating the subsequent use of information received. Relevant here is the discussion of the reuse regulations in chapter 1. The Copyright etc. Act 1988 is quite clear.

Section 47 exempts from copyright 'material' which contains factual information open to public inspection pursuant to a statutory requirement (arguably FOIA). It contains a good many other provisions protecting such material from copyright infringement.

Section 50 of the Copyright etc. Act concerns acts done under statutory authority: 'Where the doing of a particular act is specifically authorised by an Act of Parliament, whenever passed, then, unless the Act provides otherwise, the doing of that act does not infringe copyright' (s. 50(1)). The FOIA does not provide otherwise and specifically authorises disclosure. In short, this would appear to cover a situation where documents are produced by the employees of a PA (X) in their employment and which are possessed or held by X even where the copyright is sold to another concern. Obviously specific facts and contexts would need to be addressed to advise further: e.g., are the documents *held* by X? Access cannot be denied in the absence of a relevant exemption. But copyright protects the *use* of what is accessed. Where copyright is owned by a third party the reuse regulations cannot override copyright.

If a PA believes that *any* exemption is made out and that the PI is best advanced by maintaining the exemption then that is the route to follow to claim exemption. If the PA is wrong and challenged successfully, disclosure will have to be made. If the PA decide to disclose in the PI, that is their discretion. In the case of an absolute exemption there is no PI factor under the statute (though cf. the common law and confidence). It is best to keep questions of exemptions and copyright separate.

Copyright is more likely to arise where a party wants access to a document. That the FOIA provides access to information has been covered (see pp. 119, 146 above). An applicant can ask for access to a document. Section 11 FOIA states that an applicant may express a preference for communication by one or more of the following means, and the PA shall as far as reasonably practicable give effect to that preference:

(a) a copy of the INFORMATION in permanent form or other acceptable form
(b) the provision to the applicant of a reasonable opportunity to inspect a record (including a document it is submitted) containing the information
(c) a SUMMARY OR DIGEST of the information in permanent form. (This might reinforce the view that (a) above cannot itself be a filleted form of a document but the document itself subject to any legitimate exemptions.)[53]

---

[53] See *Home Office v IC* [2009] EWHC 1611 (Admin), para. 8 and access to documents.

6

Decisions and appeals on FOI exemptions

'The Act contains a presumption in favour of disclosure.'

(EA/2005/0027 *P. Toms v IC*, para. 2)

The previous chapter set out the general framework of the Freedom of Information Act (FOIA) statutory exemptions and related items including some general
points addressed in the case law. This chapter will concentrate on the case law
of the exemptions themselves under FOIA. The Environmental Information
Regulations (EIR) are dealt with in chapter 7. Excessive cost and vexatious
requests have been dealt with and so we can proceed directly to the main body
of exemptions under FOIA Pt II.

Those contracting with public authorities (PAs) that are covered by the
legislation may attempt to contract out of the legislation's provisions. This is
not possible. In EA/2007 *R. Salmon v IC and King's College Cambridge* the
Information Tribunal (IT) stated 'that no contracting out of basic obligations
safeguarded by FOIA can be permissible' (para. 30). This was given the strongest
of support by the High Court in *Corporate Officer of the House of Commons v IC
et al.*[1] A contractor may attempt to identify information which is 'confidential'
in a schedule and argue that disclosure by a PA would amount to a breach
of contract. Such a schedule would in genuine cases of confidentiality be a
wise practice. However, classification as 'confidential' is not binding on the
Information Commissioner (IC) or IT and if the information held by the
authority does not fall within an exemption, e.g. it is not confidential or a
trade secret, it will have to be disclosed. Otherwise statutory obligations will
be defeated by contractual agreements covering non-confidential information,
which a third party would be free to publish.

One final introductory comment relates to the fact that the IC, assisted
by deputies, constitutes a cohesive team. The IT on the other hand has a
very variable composition. The sections commence with IC decisions and are
followed by IT decisions.

---

[1] [2008] EWHC 1084 Admin, para. 33.

Section 21: information accessible to the applicant by other means[2]

FS50073646 concerned a request for information from the Ministry of Justice (MoJ) about a complaint made by the requester concerning a judge who dealt with the requester's judicial review application and appeal proceedings. Various exemptions applied to protect different bundles of documents. But the IC found that the MoJ were wrong in failing to identify information subject to the s. 21 exemption and therefore were in breach of s. 17(1)(c) and had to provide the requester with an 'accurate and comprehensive list of all documents it holds' to which s. 21 is applicable. In FS50086060 a request was made for information about 'all policies, practices and procedures in the North Yorkshire Constabulary relating to the determination of industrial injury awards and dates and minutes of approval'. Here s. 21 was correctly invoked as the information was available via web addresses.

Appeals

EA/2007/0110 *C. Ames v IC and Cabinet Office* was a request for the identity of the person who redrafted the executive summary of the Iraq Weapons of Mass Destruction dossier. The IC was wrong in law to say s. 21 was correctly invoked by saying the information is available in the Hutton Report – it was not. The IC's decision notice (DN) was substituted.

EA/2006/0077 *G. Tuckley v IC and Birmingham City Council (BCC)* concerned a request for a list of all neighbourhood forums from 1992 and money paid to each by the BCC. The requester subsequently asked for the identity of membership of the Birmingham Association of Neighbourhood Forums (BANF) since 1992 on an annual breakdown. The BANF was a separate entity from the BCC although partly funded by the BCC. From 2004 it was a company limited by guarantee. The BCC said it did not hold the information and the IT queried as to whether it could obtain the information from its own records, e.g. by way of service level agreements. The BANF did not hold information on behalf of the BCC and the BCC did not hold information. Reliance on s. 21 FOIA did not imply the BCC held information and s. 21 was irrelevant on the facts.

EA/2007/0065 *Rhondda Cynon Taff CBC v IC* is a baffling decision on the relationship between the FOIA and EIR (see p. 245 below). This decision seems to make the relationship very complicated between the two regimes. A copy of the Land Drainage Act 1991 was requested. For present purposes IT believed the Act was reasonably accessible and s. 21 rightly claimed by the PA.

---

[2] FS50075171: documents read in open court not necessarily covered by s. 21 – not clear which records applied or whether requester would have access to them. See FS50085775.

Section 22: information intended for future publication[3]

In chapter 5 it was noted how the UK and the Scottish FOIAs differed in their approaches to this exemption. The Scottish version was more qualified and limited the period of publication to twelve weeks. FS50081543 determined that under s. 22 there has to be a settled intention to publish the information at the time of the request; if not, the exemption could not be relied upon.

Section 23: information supplied by or relating to bodies dealing with security matters[4]

FS 50090742: The complainant requested 'the assessment by the Joint Intelligence Committee [see chapter 2, p. 37] of Iraq's declaration of its weapons of mass destruction in December 2002'. The public authority withheld the information under ss. 23(1) and 24(1) (national security). As a result of the IC's investigation the public authority reviewed its original decision and decided to release the information previously withheld under s. 24. The IC accepted an assurance from a senior official that the remaining information had been received from or related to bodies listed in s. 23(1) and that it was therefore exempt. The propensity of the IC to question this statement seems particularly confined. This is also illustrated by FS50134744 involving a requester who asked the Cabinet Office for the contents of a file 'PREM 8/928' listed in the National Archive catalogue. It transpired that he was wrong about the content of the file, but irrespectively wished to pursue the matter. The Cabinet Office concluded that all of the information was exempt under ss. 23 and/or 27 (below). The Cabinet Office later changed its position and stated that the majority of the file was exempt under only s. 23, but that the rest of the file was exempt under s. 27. The IC considered that the s. 23 exemption was invoked in respect of the majority of the information and was satisfied to accept an assurance from the Director of Security and Intelligence in the Cabinet Office to this effect. The IC would only accept such an assurance where the official occupies a position in relation to the security bodies which allows them genuinely to validate the provenance of the information. However the IC decided that the s. 27(1)(a) exemption did not apply because the information was historical and was highly unlikely to provoke a reaction from the foreign state involved.

FS50163794 was a case in which the complainant submitted a request for information held by the Cabinet Office about the so-called 'Shrewsbury Two'.[5]

---

[3] FS50070741: s. 22 wrongly applied because it was not responsible to withhold information from the complainant at the time of the request.

[4] See FS50117046, and FS50154349 on information held on John Lennon.

[5] This involved picketing by a famous actor, Ricky Tomlinson, and subsequent revelations of MI5 involvement. See also FS50177327.

The Cabinet Office explained that a file originating there relating to papers about the 'Shrewsbury Two' had been transferred to the National Archives and was available for inspection. The Cabinet Office also explained that it had retained four pieces of information, but it considered this information exempt from disclosure on the basis of s. 23 of the Act. The IC concluded that the Cabinet Office were correct to withhold this information on the basis of s. 23 because two of the pieces of information were supplied by the Security Service and two were created by the Security Service.

In FS50102023 the complainant requested all the documents held by the Cabinet Office in relation to the bombing of the Rainbow Warrior.[6] The Cabinet Office refused to confirm or deny if information is held under ss. 23(5) and 24(2) of the Act. The IC investigated and upheld the application of ss. 23(5) and 24(2) to neither confirm nor deny if information is held. The IC also found that the Cabinet Office's refusal notice breached s. 17 of the Act.

Appeals

Cases include EA/2006/0053 *M. McCarthy v IC* (see s. 24 below) and EA/2006/0045 *N. Baker MP v IC and Cabinet Office and NCCL*, for which see s. 24 below.

Section 24: national security[7]

Appeals

EA/2006/0053 *M.McCarthy v IC* concerned a request from the Foreign and Commonwealth Office (FCO) of a June 1948 agreement between the UK/USA on signals intelligence. The FCO invoked ss. 24(2) and 27(4) neither confirming nor denying it held such information. The US Government had confirmed its existence. The FCO therefore confirmed its existence. A copy was held by a body to which s. 23 applied. Article 2 ECHR (right to life) was invoked by the requester as a reason to receive the information. The appeal was 'unsustainable' and the IT held that Art. 2 was irrelevant.

The most important discussion about ss. 24 and 23 took place in EA/2006/0045 *N. Baker MP v IC and Cabinet Office and NCCL*. The case of *Baker* concerned information about the tapping of MPs phones and Prime Minister Wilson's doctrine of 17 November 1966 that MPs would not be subject to intercepts and any change of policy would be announced in the House 'at such moments as seemed compatible with the security of the country'. Prime

---

[6] This was the flagship of the Greenpeace movement, sunk by the French foreign intelligence in 1985 in Auckland.

[7] See FS50090742 (s. 23 above), FS50102023 and FS50106800.

Minister Blair announced on 30 March 2006 that that doctrine was being maintained. Additionally, a request was made on how many MPs had been subject to intrusive surveillance or tapping since that date. Had there been a change of policy since that time? Sections 24(2) and 23(5) were claimed. The Cabinet Office responded with a neither confirm nor deny (NCND). The IC took twelve months to issue a DN – 'a very long time' the IT observed (para. 4). The IC agreed with the Secretary of State for Constitutional Affairs that a ministerial notice under ss. 23(2) or 24(3) would only be issued *after* a complaint to the IC had been made. The IT noted that it possessed wide powers to review the merits of the IC's decision and it further observed the wide definition of national security from the Law Lords' decision in *Rehman*.[8] The case for invoking s. 24 is dealt with in paras. 30–3. This included evidence from the director of Security and Intelligence in the Cabinet Office (Mr Wright) who supplied reasons for the NCND response. Basically a response might blow national security cover (para. 34) and so both ss. 23(5) and 24(2) were claimed together. Disclosure of the holding of information would negate the ability of the prime minister to judge at what point it was safe to make any public announcement of change in policy in relation to the tapping of MPs' phones (para. 51(2)). *Baker v Home Office* was prayed in aid but this case (see below under s. 40) was decided under very different circumstances. At issue in *Baker* was: did MI5 hold data on Baker?[9] The present case was very different. Under s. 24, the public interest (PI) favoured maintenance of the exemption.

Section 26: defence[10]

This exemption has attracted very little attention.

Section 27: international relations[11]

The IC has shown a robust approach in challenging claims to this exemption (though see FS50077719 and EA/2006/0040 *Campaign against the Arms Trade v IC and MoD* below). In FS50134744 the complainant asked the Cabinet Office for the contents of a file 'PREM 8/928' listed in the National Archive catalogue (see s. 23 above). The IC decided that the s. 27(1)(a) exemption did not apply because the information was historical and was highly unlikely to provoke a reaction from the foreign state involved. In FS50125539 FCO information was requested from the National Archives about arms sales to Saudi Arabia.

---

[8] *Secretary of State for the Home Department v Rehman* [2002] 1 All ER 122 (HL) and see ch. 11.

[9] Concerning s. 7 DPA and a subject access request: see ch. 8, p. 290.

[10] www.justice.gov.uk/guidance/docs/foi-exemption-s26.pdf.

[11] See FS50086619 and FS50121553. See FS50080115 – s. 27 used to block information on recipients of Christmas cards from the prime minister in 2003 and 2004. The names of foreign leaders and heads of state should be released (ss. 36, 38 and 40 also invoked). See FS 50178057.

Section 27 was properly engaged and PI favoured disclosure (much of the information had already been disclosed). FS50070854 concerned information that was requested from the FCO on the UK/US Energy Dialogue (Cheney Task Force).[12] Sections 27 and 35(1)(a) were invoked. The IC believed that most items were properly withheld but some could be disclosed. Those withheld related to ongoing discussions which were conducted in confidence. Paragraph 24 states that some information related to corruption and political stability in foreign states, comments upon prominent individuals and the potential for countries to be long-term energy suppliers – information that was not shared with the foreign countries and whose disclosure could prejudice UK/US relationships which would not be in the PI. Importantly, the production of a list of relevant documents did not constitute the creation of *new* information, the IC believed. It may be a new task but it did not create new information. The information already exists. It was simply a re-presentation of existing information as a by-product of the initial request.

Case FS500110720 concerned a copy of the letter from the European Commission to the UK Government (Department for Constitutional Affairs) regarding the implementation of the Data Protection Directive (95/46/EC) by the UK. Sections 27 and 35 were invoked. The decision has references to the impact of the Court of Appeal *Durant* decision (see chapter 8, p. 282). Page 8 has a discussion of s. 27 and the PI. The case also dealt with policy formulation and the early stages of infraction proceedings by the Commission under Art. 226 EC. Section 41 was also additionally involved. Section 27(1)(c) was correctly invoked and the PI was in favour of retention (see pp. 11–12). The PI was also in favour of maintaining exemption under s. 35.

FER0081530 involved both EIR and FOIA requests and concerned the FCO and related to information surrounding the Baku–Tbilisi–Ceyhan oil pipeline project. The complainant thought that the information may have been 'sanitised'. During the course of the IC's investigation the FCO supplied a revised schedule of the documents being withheld and the related exemptions under the FOIA and the EIR. This concerned twenty-eight documents under s. 27 and various documents covered by other exemptions. The s. 27 exemptions were engaged because prejudice would have, or would likely to have, been experienced by FCO to the trust and reputation that it enjoyed within a partnership of relevant UK public bodies if it disclosed information that they considered to be embarrassing or a breach of public faith. The PI was found to be in favour of non-disclosure. The s. 35 (formulation of government policy) exemptions were engaged; *DfES v The Information Commissioner and the Evening Standard* was applied by the IC (see s. 35 below). The PI test weighed in favour of non-disclosure. Section 41 was engaged because disclosure would have been a clear breach of trust that could give rise to consequential damage to the confider. No overriding PI in disclosure was found.

---

[12] Cheney was the vice president under George Bush.

Appeals[13]

EA/2006/0040 *Campaign against the Arms Trade v IC and MoD* concerns a request for information relating to a memorandum of understanding with the Saudi Arabian Government about sale of defence weapons. There is a discussion of the use by the IT of special counsel to assist the claimants who were excluded from closed sessions and criticism of the documentation served by the Ministry of Defence on the IT: 'the documentation provided to us was provided without explanation, piecemeal and in an incoherent manner that made it effectively impossible to understand' (para. 21 (d)). The complexity of the documentation required the 'exceptional' resort to a special counsel from the Attorney General's approved list in accordance with CPR Pt 76. The IT found s. 27(1) engaged and the balance of PI favoured non-disclosure. Shortly before this decision the House of Lords ruled that the Serious Fraud Office's cessation of a prosecution for fraud involving Saudi Arabian arms contracts was not unlawful.[14] In EA/2006/0065 *FCO v IC and FoE* the appeal against the IC was allowed. A request was made for information on a US/UK agreement on 'ghost ships' to be dismantled in the UK. Surprisingly, the FOIA and not EIR applied. Details of personnel were not to be disclosed. The information involved activities at the level of Secretary of State, minister or senior civil servants on each side (and US equivalent). Section 27(1) was engaged – a significant risk to US/UK relations was made out, the IT believed. The IT did not consider that s. 27(2)[15] was an option. There was no special deference to the FCOs opinion. An Australian case[16] had decided that similar provisions to s. 27 shall not be changed into a class exemption from a prejudice-to-contents one.

Section 28: relations within the UK[17]

This exemption has attracted little use.

Section 29: the economy

Likewise this has attracted little attention. In FS50105898 a request was made for information to Her Majesty's Treasury fed into the macroeconomic model

---

[13] The most publicised decision to date on the FOIA concerned the Justice Secretary's issue of a veto against a DN in EA/2008/0024 and 0029 (FS50165372) *Cabinet Office v IC and C. Lamb.* This concerned the disclosure of Cabinet minutes in relation to the decision to go to war in Iraq and was focused on s. 35; see below. EA/2006/0053 *M. McCarthy v IC* (see s. 24 above); EA/2007/0071, 0078, 0079 *N. Gilby v IC.*

[14] *R (Corner House Research) v Director SFO* [2008] UKHL 60.

[15] Information obtained in confidence from a foreign state.

[16] *Re Maher v AG's Dept* (1985) 9 ADL 731.

[17] See FS50121252 *Scotland Office.* The Ministry of Justice guidance on s. 28 is at www.justice.gov.uk/docs/foi-exemption-s28.pdf.

used to forecast the performance of the UK economy. The IC was satisfied that s. 29 and s. 35 were correctly claimed.[18]

Section 30: investigations and proceedings conducted by public authorities[19]

In FS50132101 the complainant made a request for the names of the carriers and the details of the investigations that the Civil Aviation Authority (CAA) conducted in ten specific cases, and the names of other carriers it was currently investigating for non-compliance with Council Regulation (EC) No. 261/2004 (compensation and assistance to air passengers denied boarding rights). The CAA withheld the information on the basis of the s. 30(1)(b) exemption, or alternatively the s. 31(1)(g) exemption (below). The IC decided that the information was within the remit of s. 30 and then went on to consider the PI test. The CAA argued that disclosure could lead to the carriers refusing to engage in informal dispute resolution, because the details would eventually be made public; in this respect consumers would be prejudiced. However, the IC decided that there was a significant PI in disclosing the information so as to hold the CAA to account for its conduct of the investigations. Therefore the IC concluded that the information in relation to investigations before the request should be disclosed; however, he thought that investigations which were current at the time of the request would not be suitable for disclosure under the PI test. The IC did not go on to consider the s. 31(1)(g) exemption because where s. 30 was engaged, s. 31(1)(g) would not apply notwithstanding the fact that the PI weighed in favour of disclosure. FS50102203 decided that s. 30(2) was applied correctly. The IC further ruled that information disclosed under FOIA is universally available in principle. FS50106800 concerned the Metropolitan police and a request for files on Special Branch investigations from over one hundred years previously. Section 30(2) on informers was engaged but the PI in disclosure was stronger than in retention – on appeal the names were redacted (EA/2008/0078).

Appeals[20]

EA/2006/0017 *Guardian Newspapers v IC and Chief Constable of Avon and Somerset Police* concerned the papers relating to the investigation of Jeremy Thorpe

---

[18] See also EA/2006/0014 *Derry City Council v IC* under ss. 41 and 43.

[19] FS50118873: Request for information about thefts from private vehicles used to deliver Royal Mail. Ss. 30 and 31 invoked but neither engaged. The information (statistics) was not held for the purpose of an investigation but it was information that could lead (and did lead) to an investigation (para. 41). See FS50139215 *The Com'r of the Met. Police Service* for a request for CCTV footage on 7/7 terrorists.

[20] EA/2007/0013 *Keely v IC and DTI (BERR)* and request about enquiries into company. S. 30 applied and PI in favour of non-disclosure. See EA/2008/0023 *A. Digby Cameron v IC and Beds Police* on s. 30(1)(a)(i).

MP, former leader of the Liberal Party for conspiracy to murder. Sections 30, 38 and 40(2) were claimed. Article 10 ECHR was cited in support of disclosure and the IT[21] emphasised that it examines merits afresh. Even after almost thirty years, the PI favoured maintenance of the exemption under s. 30(1). EA/2006/0022 *E. Alcock v IC and Chief Constable of Staffordshire Police (TP)* deals with a frequent and important point. The requester wanted the identity of a 'malicious informant'. Sections 30, 31, 38, 40 and 41 were invoked. Section 40 applied (see chapter 8, p. 298). Concerning s. 30(2)(b), PI in protecting informers favoured non-disclosure. In EA/2006/0007 *DTI v IC* the IT allowed the appeal and substituted the DN. Information was requested relating to Companies Act investigations into irregularities, disqualification of directors, company liquidation, fraud charges and other related matters. The IC believed that PAs should adequately explain their decisions and transparency should be promoted. What was sought was a 'generalised explanation' which would not reveal identities of witnesses. The DN required DTI to disclose within thirty-five days 'the reason for the investigation in outline terms'. The invariable practice of the PA was not to provide any reasons for a Companies Act investigation. The IC argued that the FOIA had a general presumption of disclosure – a general or public interest to that effect.[22] Paragraph 41 *et seq.* deal with the discussion on balancing of PIs and the general point was made that the balance had to be made on the position at the time of the request although the point of allowing in later evidence was left open. The IT ruled that the PI favoured maintenance of the exemption.

In EA/2005/0023 *Bellamy v IC* (para. 5) the IT stated that not all PI considerations that might otherwise appear to be relevant to the subject matter of the disclosure should be taken into account. What has to be concentrated upon is the particular PI 'necessarily inherent in the exemption or exemptions relied upon.' In para. 21, the IT states that balancing competing PIs does not constitute a 'discretion' – it is a mixed question of fact and law for the IT! Surely, balancing is a JUDGEMENT involving proportionality – and proportionality is a question of law? In the present case, the IT felt, there is no question of discretion! The IC operated PI balancing correctly and the PI favoured non-disclosure. General and specific PIs must be balanced (see chapter 7, p. 264)

Section 31: law enforcement[23]

The complainant in FS50137475 requested from the BBC information relating to the use and effectiveness of television detector vans. The BBC refused to

---

[21] Following EA/2005/0023 *Bellamy v IC*.

[22] See also EA/2005/026 *Hogan and Oxford City C v IC*. The government would not allow a legislative headnote to that effect: see ch. 4. p. 126.

[23] FS50118873 (s. 30 above). FS50140492: the complainant requested the names of three former ministers provided with the use of a government car. One was released. The IC investigated and found that the exemptions were not engaged for the other two. FS50074348: information about numbers and rank of judges disciplined for misuse of departmental computer systems and

disclose the majority of the information, relying on ss. 31 and 42. The BBC pursued several arguments:

1. Information relating to how often the vans were used would reduce the deterrent effect of the vans and thus a significant number of people would decide not to pay their licence fee. It would then have to spend more money on other enforcement activities.
2. Information on technical equipment used in television vans would enable people to find weaknesses in order to evade detection.
3. Information on internal policies in relation to vans would include statistics on how often the vans were used; this could dissuade users from paying the licence fee.

The IC applied the 'would or would be likely to prejudice' test and decided that disclosure would have adverse implications. In considering the PI test, the arguments for disclosure were increased legitimacy and scrutiny of the application of public funds. However, in deciding that the PI lay with non-disclosure, he opined that the use of the equipment is strictly and independently regulated and that disclosure would have a negative effect on the PI for legitimate licence fee payers. FS50138964 concerned a complainant's request for part of HM Revenue and Customs (HMRC) internal guidance on processing tax returns submitted by self-assessment taxpayers under the construction industry scheme. HMRC refused to provide a particular section of this guidance because it considered it to be exempt from disclosure on the basis of s. 31(1)(d) (assessment or collection of any tax or duty). Having reviewed the withheld information the IC decided that HMRC appropriately relied upon s. 31 when refusing to supply the information. However, the IC has also concluded that HMRC breached s. 17 by failing to provide the complainant with an adequate refusal notice within twenty working days of his request.

FS50123489 was the subject of a successful appeal. A request was made to the PA for information on all recipients of anti-social behaviour orders (ASBOs). Sections 31 and 40 were invoked by the PA. The IC ordered disclosure of a full database of ASBOs subject to cases where: redaction of names in cases where reporting restrictions were imposed by the court at original hearing or any hearing into a breach of an order; the ASBO did not progress beyond interim status; the PA is satisfied that the ASBO recipient is 'particularly vulnerable and would be put at real risk by disclosure'; the ASBO has now expired. Key factors for release included an effective media strategy; an effective local publicity strategy; increasing public confidence, deterrence, and awareness of offenders; making orders effective; the offenders will know that the community knows; public reassurance; there was no intention to name and shame; the audience is

those using Internet to view child pornography. NCND under ss. 31 and 36. S. 17 breached as ss.31 and 36 wrongly applied. The PA should confirm whether information is held by it.

primarily within area of 'victims'; and the method would involve the least possible interference with privacy. This decision was successfully appealed against the IC in EA/2997/0021 *LB Camden v IC*. The appeal concerned ss. 31 and 40 and turned on s. 40. The requester wanted information given in open court administering open justice.[24] There was a discussion of s. 40 and IT case law which is dealt with in chapter 8 (see p. 298 below). From the case law and Home Office guidance 'publicity for ASBOs is the norm' (para. 24). Publicity long after the order is made is not the same as publicity when an ASBO is made. Revealing names is not necessary for the purpose of the request (journalism) and sch. 2(6) of the Data Protection Act (DPA) was not satisfied. This schedule is dealt with in detail in chapter 8. The IC's DN was not in accordance with the law and was ruled invalid by the IT.

Case FS50069091 was a request to the Sussex Police for numbers of people (generic not identifiable individuals) subject to Sex Offences Act orders; a geographical breakdown of where they are was requested. The IC emphasised that the request was for generic information not specific and ss.31 and 38 were not engaged. The information was, the IC claimed, available from published information. Courts do not usually impose restrictions on the reporting of an adult defendant's name and address in cases regarding sexual offences in spite of the fact that such information could lead to a violent reaction against the defendant or his family.

Appeals

EA/2007/0085 *P. King v IC and Department for Work and Pensions* concerned a requester who wanted information about a policy insisting that applications to the department had to be made by phone. He queried the safety of this (being overheard) and requested information about security. Section 38 was invoked citing 'safety and security' not health and safety. Late reliance on exemptions under, inter alia, s. 31(1)(a) was not cited in the response. Section 31(1)(a) applied and the PI was against disclosure, the IT ruled. The case contains an interesting discussion of procedures adopted by IC who was wrong, the IT believed, in not finding a breach of s. 1 FOIA.

EA/2007/0041 *R. Hargrave v IC and National Archives* upheld the IC's DN in FS50079972. This was a request for information about a murder in 1954. Sections 31, 40 and 41 were invoked. As explained above, a breach of s. 17 was rectified by the Metropolitan Police. In 1983 there was a seventy-five-year extension of closure under the Public Records Act and the file was held by the National Archives by that time. A murder file cannot be redacted or partially closed under s. 31 – 'it is all or nothing' in this case (para. 23). Evidence was taken in closed session by the IT. Balancing of the PIs is discussed under s. 31(1)

---

[24] See *R (Stanley etc.) v Commissioner of Police etc.* [2004] EWHC 2229.

at pp. 10–11. Section 31 was engaged and the IT found no substantial PI in favour of disclosure.

EA/2006/0060 and 0066 *C. England v LB Bexley and IC* involved a substituted DN. The addresses and ownership details of empty properties that came to the council's notice had been requested. Section 31(1)(a) claimed even though the information had not been collected for prevention of crime (para. 27). It was decided that addresses are personal data for the s. 40 exemption (para. 98). The decision contains a very detailed analysis of the strength of evidence linking s. 31 and preventing the commission of crime. The IT found on the evidence that disclosure would be likely to have a 'significant negative impact on the prevention of crime'. The PI is not in favour of disclosure – it could encourage criminal damage, drug-taking and other criminal activities. The council was allowed to rely on late resort to s. 40. Some scepticism was expressed about the IC raising an exemption on behalf of the PA but this surely must be possible in principle.[25] There is also a discussion of registered property and 'reasonable accessibility' via the Land Registry and s. 21. EA/2006/0071 *Bucks Free Press v IC* was referred to above and the appeal was allowed and the DN substituted. The request was for information of the number of times a notice of intended prosecution has been issued by the Thames Valley Police as a result of alleged speeding offences at two speed cameras. The IC held that ss. 31 and 38 were applied correctly. General figures were sought and connection between disclosure and drivers' behaviour was so 'tenuous' that 'site specific safety factors' did not come into effect and the exemptions were not engaged.[26]

EA/2005/0026 *P. Hemsley v IC and Chief Constable of Northants (AP)* also concerned speed cameras. This was a request for information about speed cameras which are active intermittently at sites. In sunny weather in the early morning a driver in one direction was looking into the sun which would impair vision of speed restriction signs. Section 31(1)(a)–(b) were invoked. The IT identified the information that should be available to the general public about speed cameras (para. 23). But it might be difficult to distinguish between a public-spirited request and one which was less worthy, e.g. 'the creation of a commercial website selling forecasts on the operation of safety cameras'. Disclosure was rightly denied on the facts.

EA/2005/0026 and 0030 *C. Martin and Oxford City C v IC* was a request for vehicle identity numbers from Oxford City Council. Section 31(1) was invoked.[27] A 'very significant and weighty chance of prejudice' to the identified PIs was argued to exist. The degree of risk must be such that there 'may very well' be prejudice to those interests, even if the risk 'falls short of being more probable than not'.[28] Section 31(1) was rightly engaged. PI tests in favour of disclosure are broad-ranging and operate at different levels of abstraction. PI considerations against disclosure are 'narrowly conceived'. The risk of crime

---

[25] See above EA/2006/0059 *Nat Savings*.
[26] See FS50169012.   [27] Para. 27 *et seq.* deal with the prejudice test.
[28] Following Munby J in *R (Lord) v SoS HD* [2003] EWHC 2073 (Admin).

would be greater if the information was disclosed than if not and PI therefore against disclosure.[29]

Section 32: court records

It will be recalled that this is an absolute exemption. FS50150314 involved a request to the MoJ for an audio record of a court hearing in which the requester had been a party. The proceedings were in public. Copies of audio transcript of court proceedings were not covered by ss. 32 or 21 (a right of application to a court does not make it 'reasonably accessible'!) The IT case *Mitchell v IC* (EA/2005/0002) concerning a written transcript of proceedings was cited. In the light of the clear view from the IT, the IC has decided that, like the written transcript, the audio record does not constitute information which is created by a court or a member of the administrative staff of a court. Section 32(1) is not engaged.[30]

Appeals

In EA/2007/0075 *A. Szuchs v IC and UK Intellectual Property Office* there was a request for information relating to a complaint by the appellant. This was information generated by his complaint and related to information held by a person (PA) 'held only by virtue of being contained in any document placed in the custody of the person conducting the inquiry' under s. 32(2)(a) FOIA. The information was therefore protected by an absolute exemption. EA/2005/0002 *A. Mitchell v IC* concerned court documents viz., a transcript produced by a commercial body of case proceedings that had been shredded by the time of the request. Section 32 cannot cover internal notes from the judge to jury or vice versa or orders under the Contempt of Court Act 1981. It does not cover a transcript of the case that is held in public. These are not 'created by a court'! The IC ruled that it was covered by s. 32; the IT found differently overruling the IC.

Section 33: audit functions

FS50095679 was a request to the Office of Government Commerce (OGC) for the 'gateway reviews' which were reports on major information-technology contracts by the Government at five critical stages. These were periodic reviews of a contract's performance for which different colours might be flagged up in a report – Red (immediate action necessary for success), Amber (recommendations to be followed) and Green (all OK) (RAG reviews). Section 33 was invoked: prejudice to the PA's functions in relation to economy, efficiency and

---

[29] Re PI test: para. 53 *et seq.*
[30] Court records: see EA/2005/0002 *Mitchell v* IC, para. 37 and EA/2008/0087 *BERR v IC*.

effectiveness with which other authorities use their resources. The IC was not convinced that disclosure of 'double red' warning reports would discourage co-operation of those asked to provide information to the OGC. Nor is information given purely voluntarily by those persons (para. 23). The IC decided that s. 33 was not engaged. FS50070196 also related to a request for gateways reviews of identity cards programmes and contracts run by the Home Office. Sections 33 and 35 were invoked. The information in question was examined by the IC and his officers in the premises of the OGC. The OGC argument was that disclosure would interfere with co-operation of those interviewees for future gateway reviews and this would damage the PI. The IC was not convinced. Those persons operate in a professional capacity and co-operation is a part of their professional responsibilities.Section 33 was not engaged (see also s. 35 below). This is under appeal to the IT.

Appeals

In EA/2006/0068 and 0080 many large, complex, novel and often IT-enabled civil programmes had missed delivery dates. The OGC had produced a Gateway Process Review Pack. The 'gateway review' process was now mandatory across central government including Ministry of Defence and executive agencies, and local government adopted the reviews on a voluntary basis. They were carried out at key stages of a programme and on a confidential basis. Reviewers are mainly senior civil servants or outside consultants. There are five numbered gateways for the life cycle of a project. Gateway reviews saved the Exchequer £1.5 billion in 2003–5. The case has a full discussion of 'likely to cause prejudice' which repeats points dealt with in chapter 5 (see p. 155 above). Sections 33 and 35 were invoked. 'Misinterpretation' of messages was not a good reason for non disclosure, the IT ruled. The Select Committee on Works and Pensions had recommended publication of gateways reviews[31] and the IT had been influenced by this. The Government did not agree with the routine publication of gateway reviews but did not invoke a 'blanket exemption' for them. Each FOIA request is considered on its merits by the OGC. The Committee on Public Accounts[32] had also recommended publication of gateway reviews – 'Select Committee and PAC reports are historic [*sic*] whereas we believe major IT projects should also be subject to close scrutiny during their development.'[33] If Parliament had meant ss. 33 and 35 to be absolute it would have made them so, the IT believed. Paragraph 51 contains details on the PI factors. Paragraph 64 contains the arguments on the inhibiting effect of disclosure in relation to s. 35 (fourteen arguments were cited). The OGC's arguments regarding both ss. 33 and 35 and PI were not accepted. An appeal to the High Court was made. The High Court allowed appeal because the IT was too influenced in its judgment by a select committee report and this was not something upon which judicial notice could

[31] 3rd report 2004.   [32] 27th report 2004–5.   [33] Quoted at para. 77, EA/2006/0068.

be taken. The IT had made an error of law. But the court did not rule on the merits.[34]

The case was subsequently reheard by the IT in EA/2006/0068 and 0080 (FS50070196 and FS50132936) *Office of Government Commerce v IC*. The IT in this case, decided in February 2009, upheld the publication of two gateways review reports. There was also a discussion of s. 35 (below). The IT emphasised that its ruling was not a precedent for all gateways reviews. Names of those involved in reviews should be redacted but not the grades of functions of parties.

In FS50180545 the complainant submitted a series of requests to the National Audit Office (NAO) for information as to the origins of figures contained in a 'value for money for stroke care' report. The main complaints and the IC's responses were as follows:

(1) Email exchanges between the Comptroller and Auditor General's office and others in the NAO were requested and there were two objective interpretations of the request. The complainant argued that the request was for *any correspondence*. The IC applied the *Berend* case, decided by the IT, and came to the decision that the complainant's purported interpretation was reasonably objective. The NAO then argued that it was exempt information under s. 33. The IC found that the NAO was an 'auditing' body under that section and that the documents were prepared for the purpose of undertaking an audit/examination. However as regards the prejudice requirement, the IC was not satisfied that the documents were of a sufficiently free and frank nature that their disclosure would be likely to inhibit free and frank discussion in the future.

(2) The complainant argued that a request for certain written documentation should have been interpreted more widely. The IC applied *Berend* and found that there were not two objective interpretations (analysis is provided on this point).

(3) The NAO argued that request 9 was a request for an *explanation* which did not constitute a request for information. However the complainant claimed it was a request for information. The IC interpreted the request as clearly asking for information.

Section 34: parliamentary privilege[35]

The exemption has been rarely invoked. The Speaker did not claim the privilege in relation to MPs expenses (*Corporate Officer House of Commons v IC* [2008] EWHC 1084 Admin, para. 2).

---

[34] [2008] EWHC 737 (Admin) and 774 (Admin).
[35] FS50116013 (6 August 2007) House of Commons.

Section 35: formulation of government policy

This has been a very heavily used exemption. It is restricted to central government. Many of the cases involve discussion of the PI. These discussions are set out more fully under this section and the following section.

FS50126011 has an important discussion of the PI under s. 35(1)(a) and (b). A request was made for information concerning Cabinet Office papers in relation to an Asylum and Immigration working group. The papers covered the approach to registration of workers from new (2004) EU accession states – 'A8'. The Cabinet Office claimed s. 35 was operative and the PI favoured non-disclosure. The approach of the IT in *DfES v IC and the Evening Standard* (EA/2006/0006, para. 75) was used. The PI factors were set out. In favour of disclosure were:

i. promoting public understanding behind decisions taken
ii. public participation and debate in policy issues, especially where the subject matter is of a controversial nature
iii. accountability for decisions taken
iv. transparency in decision making
v. information contained within the paper which is already in the public domain.

Against disclosure were:

i. the short period of time that had elapsed between the meeting and the complainant's request, and that the policy in question continues to be kept under review
ii. effects on the principle of collective responsibility for decisions by revealing interdepartmental considerations which may reveal disagreements between ministers and departments
iii. revealing the policy options presented to ministers for collective discussion and decision-making could undermine the process of collective government and inhibit ministers' from having a frank and fully informed discussion in order to reach informed decisions
iv. effects on the comprehensiveness of information provided for consideration in policy making.

At para. 21 the IC set out his reasons for favouring disclosure:

i. Much of the evidence contained within the paper in relation to the labour market can be found in the public domain, most notably in the document: 'The Impact of Free Movement of Workers from Central and Eastern Europe on the UK Labour Market: Early Evidence' (May 2005). It can be reasonably assumed that this information was included in this paper and taken into consideration by Ministers in reaching a decision on the matter.

ii. The government's decision on this matter is considered to be controversial for a variety of reasons, such as with regard to the rules put in place regarding the hiring of labour from the A8; decisions in relation to access to benefits and social services; impacts on immigration and the UK labour market; and the decision not to follow that of many of the pre-existing EU members who chose to delay the opening of their labour markets to citizens of the A8 beyond 2004. The Commissioner believes that this controversy stems, in part, from a lack of public engagement in the process by which the decision was reached. He therefore considers that there is a PI in addressing controversies surrounding the decision, to which the disclosure of this information would assist.

iii. More generally, the factors which accounted for the reasons behind the government's decision are not widely known or understood. The Commissioner believes there is a significant PI in the public seeing the whole picture of the decision making process and he has concluded that disclosure of this information would serve the PI in this respect. This is because it would enable the public to fully understand the reasoning behind the decision taken (in terms of the factors, evidence and analysis taken into account) and enable it to be debated and challenged in a more informed manner.

iv. The Commissioner does not consider that release of this information would adversely affect the ongoing review of the policy. This is because he does not see how ongoing consideration of each of the factors considered in the paper would be undermined if they were placed in the public domain. In addition, the Commissioner believes that the contribution to public debate from which disclosure of the information would result is likely to assist in this review. This is because, in this case, disclosure would enable greater and wider input into the policy making process and assist the government in making a more informed decision, such as with regard to the impact on the UK of the policy to date.

v. The nature of the considerations within the paper would not harm collective Cabinet responsibility as it is difficult to see how the opinions of individual Ministers taking part in the decisions in question could be inferred from this information.

vi. The Commissioner does not consider that the candour of civil servants would be adversely affected by the disclosure of the withheld paper. He believes this to be the case for three reasons. First, in respect of the factors considered in the paper, the Commissioner considers the nature of the analysis to be objective, balanced and reasoned. Secondly, the Commissioner notes that the withheld information does not contain the names of any of the civil servants who produced it and does not attribute any of its contents to individual officials. Finally, the Commissioner considers the case of the Information Tribunal In *DfES v the Commissioner and the Evening Standard* (EA/2006/0006) to be of relevance. That case also related to the application of section 35 in respect of the candour of officials. The

DfES had argued that the threat of civil servants' advice being disclosed would cause them to be less candid when offering such opinions. However, the Tribunal stated that '... we are entitled to expect of [civil servants] the courage and independence that... [is]... the hallmark of our civil service'. It went on to describe civil servants as '... highly educated and politically sophisticated public servants who well understand the importance of their impartial role as counsellors to ministers of conflicting convictions.' In short, it was judged that they should not easily be discouraged from doing their job properly. However, in the circumstances of this case, this factor was not given significant weight. This is also in light of the Commissioner's comments on the timing of the request below.

vii. The timing of the request is an important factor in this case as the request was made after the decision related to the Accession States Worker Registration Scheme was announced. Therefore, the Commissioner believes that the need to protect the space to formulate and develop policy had reduced. That is not say that the PI in protecting the space had completely diminished as the Commissioner acknowledges further policy development might have followed the decision. However, the Commissioner has accorded less weight to this consideration because the decision had been made. The Commissioner notes that in the DfES decision referred to above the Tribunal noted that the timing of a request was of paramount importance to a decision:

The IC continued:

We fully accept the DfES argument, supported by a wealth of evidence, that disclosure of discussions of policy options, whilst policy is in the process of formulation, is highly unlikely to be in the public interest, unless, for example, it would expose wrongdoing within government. Ministers and officials are entitled to time and space, in some instances to considerable time and space, to hammer out policy by exploring safe and radical options alike, without the threat of lurid headlines depicting that which has been merely broached as agreed policy. We note that many of the most emphatic pronouncements on the need for confidentiality to which we were referred, are predicated on the risk of premature publicity. In this case it was a highly relevant factor in June 2003 but of little, if any, weight in January 2005.

In the High Court decision *Office of Government Commerce v the Information Commissioner*[36] (Admin) Burnton J approved the approach taken in DfES:

I accept that the Bill was an enabling measure, which left questions of Government policy yet to be decided. Nonetheless, an important policy had been decided, namely to introduce the enabling measure, and as a result I see no error of law in the finding that the importance of preserving the safe place had diminished.

The PI favoured disclosure.

[36] [2008] EWHC 737 Admin.

In FS50196977 the complainant requested minutes of the meetings of the cross-party group on House of Lords reform from the MoJ. This request was refused under s. 35(1)(a). The complainant argued that the cross-party group was not part of government and was therefore not able to rely on the s. 35 exemption. The IC found that the group was part of government for three reasons: (1) the membership of the group consisted of representatives of the three main political groups, which of course included government; (2) the topic for discussion was House of Lords reform, which was an area of governmental policy making; (3) the outcome of the discussions was to contribute towards the process of drafting the White Papers. The exemption was found to be engaged. The IC went on to consider the PI and found that the exemption should be maintained. He considered the following:

(1) the information itself – it related to a matter of constitutional significance which indicates that there is a significant PI in disclosure, but that very fact also means that it is desirable for the government to be given space to make decisions in order to ensure full and frank discussions

(2) the timing of the request – the PI would be best served while the decision making process remains live, but equally premature disclosure, before decisions have been reached, may be undesirable

(3) information in the public domain – media coverage is significant

(4) wider factors, the likelihood of prejudice – the information was attributable to individuals, which would increase the likelihood of prejudice – if such information was to be frequently released it could hinder full and frank policymaking, this would cause extensive, severe and frequent prejudice.

In FS50153967 the complainant wrote to the Cabinet Office to request records of exchanges between Tony Blair and Rupert Murdoch. The Cabinet Office responded to the request by stating that the information could not be disclosed since the cost of complying with the request would exceed the appropriate limit of £600. During the course of the IC's investigation the Cabinet Office altered its position to say that it no longer believed that the cost of complying with the request would exceed the appropriate limit. Instead, it subsequently disclosed some of the information to the complainant but withheld the remainder under ss. 35, 40, 41 and 43. The IC concluded that there had been procedural failures under ss. 10 and 17 FOIA. In relation to s. 40, the IC thought that the information was personal information, but applied para. 6 of sch. 2 DPA and decided that disclosure was not unfair; it would not constitute an intrusion into the private life of Mr Murdoch (see chapter 8). As regards the s. 35 exemption, the IC was satisfied that the exemption was engaged, and in considering the PI took into account the principles established in *DfES v The IC and the Evening Standard* (EA/2006/0006) (below). He decided in favour of disclosure because: (a) the information was seven years old; (b) it did not identify differences within the government or controversial matters; (c) it did not affect the future candour of officials or ministers; (d) it did not adversely affect future policy formation;

(e) it would help further the public's understanding of government reasoning and promote transparency. The IC decided that the s. 41 exemption was engaged in respect of a small part of the information because it would constitute an actionable breach of confidence. However, he considered that the common law rules on PI in respect of breach of confidence are relevant and decided in favour of disclosure under the common-law test (see below). He lastly considered the section 43 exemption, but made a distinction between any prejudice which would have been caused at the time of the meeting and prejudice which would have been caused at the time of the request. As there would have been no prejudice at the latter time, he concluded in favour of disclosure. The IC ordered disclosure of all of the information within thirty-five days.

FS50121390 is another case concerning prime minister's meetings. The complainant requested a full list of all those who met with the prime minister at 10 Downing Street in June 2005. The Cabinet Office disclosed some information, but withheld the information relating to internal meetings with ministerial colleagues under ss. 35–6 of the Act. The IC concluded that government policy is about the development of options and priorities. Purely operational matters, such as a list of appointments would not come within that definition. Further, it would not be possible to determine the content of any meetings which were held. Therefore the IC decided that details as to the names of officials were not exempt. However, the exemption would apply in respect of references to Cabinet committees under s. 35(1)(a). The IC considered the PI test. The Cabinet Office argued that disclosure could:

1. disenable ministers from discussing sensitive policy issues without inhibition
2. cause individuals with whom the prime minister met to be targeted by lobbyists
3. affect the perceived neutrality of particular civil servants
4. undermine the convention of collective responsibility
5. link civil servants to particular areas of policy.

The IC considered these arguments untenable and decided that it was in the PI to disclose the information. The IC also rejected the Cabinet Office's reliance on s. 36, as he did not think that the opinion of the qualified person was a reasonable one (see below). There was an unsuccessful appeal to the IT, EA/2008/0049, after which the Government disclosed the details. The complainant appealed to the IC about the Cabinet Office's refusal to supply him with the second part of a report produced for the prime minister by Lord Birt on the subject of crime in FS50084358. The Cabinet Office stated that the information was exempt from disclosure under s. 35 (formulation of government policy) and to the extent that the information is not exempt by virtue of s. 35, s. 36 (prejudice to effective conduct of public affairs). However, it confirmed that much of the withheld information is in the public domain as the information is derived from statistics published by the Home Office. The IC has decided that all the information (aside from the statistical information contained within the report) is exempt under

s. 35, but that the balance of the PI test favours the disclosure of this information. This led the IC to further decide that s. 36 cannot be engaged in respect of this information. This is because s. 36(1)(a) provides that s. 36 can only apply to information held by a government department which is not exempt by virtue of s. 35. In addition, although the IC does not consider the statistical information contained within the report to be exempt by virtue of s. 35, he does not consider that prejudice to the effective conduct of public affairs could be caused by its disclosure under s. 36. The opinion of the qualified person under s. 36 was not reasonable or reasonably arrived at. The IC therefore required the Cabinet Office to supply the withheld information to the complainant. The appeal to the IT was successful and substituted a DN but did require statistical evidence to be disclosed. In particular the factors militating against disclosure under the PI included the fact that Lord Birt was commissioned to provide assistance direct to the prime minister with a particular brief to introduce radical 'blue sky thinking' to policy development across a number of sectors and Lord Birt in 2000 (pre-FOIA) would have expected confidentiality: *DfES v IC* EA/2008/0030, para. 36. In FS50088745 a request was made for the minutes and agendas of 'all meetings' between the prime minister and his strategy adviser Lord Birt. Sections 35–6 were again invoked. The project teams for these 'confidential' reports included civil servants and external advisers. The Public Administration Select Committee had drawn attention to the refusal of Lord Birt to appear before the select committee.[37] The requested information in this case goes to the 'heart of the confidential relationship between the PM and a key adviser' (para. 31). The documentation was very limited and between the prime minister and one or two senior advisers – space was required for their deliberations. The PI favoured non-disclosure under both ss. 35–6

The complainant requested Cabinet minutes and records relating to meetings it held 7–17 March 2003 where the Attorney General's legal advice concerning military action against Iraq was considered and discussed in FS50165372. The Cabinet Office confirmed to the complainant that during the period in question, there were two meetings of the Cabinet. However, it withheld the information under s. 35(1)(a)–(b) of the Act ('formulation of government policy' and 'ministerial communications'). The IC accepts that s. 35(1)(a)–(b) is engaged in this case. However, he concluded that (subject to certain specific redactions) the balance of the PI under s. 35 favours disclosure of the information in full. The Cabinet Office was attempting to give overriding force to collective responsibility. Information already made available does not sufficiently enable the public to scrutinise the manner in which the decision was taken. The PI would be advanced by transparency and knowing how decisions were taken.[38] This is a very emphatic case on disclosure. This decision was upheld on appeal but became the subject of a veto under s. 53 FOIA (below).

---

[37] HC 690 (2005–6) but subsequently he did appear after he stepped down as an adviser.
[38] See also on Iraq: FS50062881, FS50073718, FS50069105, FS50064590 and FS50063472.

The OGC in FS50093000 invoked s. 35 in a complaint which concerned all documents relating to a ministerial direction to the Permanent Secretary MoD relating to the sale of Hawk jet trainers and a letter from the chief executive of the OGC to the deputy prime minister. Section 35 was engaged and the PI favoured disclosure for value for money to the tax payer. Arguments that disclosure would interfere with frankness and promote inter departmental rivalries were not successful. Disclosure would assist the public to gauge the robustness of the policy process – future publicity should act as a deterrent against advice which is specious or expedient.[39] At para. 26 the IC stated that the FOIA may make some adjustment to collective responsibility and how that principle of governance was interpreted. Its primary focus is on a decision made, not on a single collective ministerial understanding in the making of a policy decision (para. 26) and the protection of departmental differences. The notice was issued two years before the request, there was a large amount of public money involved and the existence of the NAO and Committee of Public Accounts did not remove the PI in the public knowing directly. The IT has been more circumspect (see below).

The complainant in FS50097518 made successive requests to the Home Office for information relating to the Identity Cards Bill; the memorandum (and drafts) advising on European Convention of Human Rights obligations which were submitted to the Legislative Programme Committee of the Cabinet; and background briefing papers for ministers in response to amendments tabled by opposition parties at the committee stage; and similar information at the report stage. The PA withheld the information, citing s. 35(1)(a) for all of the requests; s. 42 for the first and second requests; and s. 36(2)(b)(i) (free and frank advice) for part of the second request. The IC concluded that all of the information in the second request fell within s. 35 so that s. 36(2)(b)(i) was not engaged. He decided that the information in all three requests had been properly withheld under s. 35(1)(a) because the PI in maintaining the exemption outweighed the PI in disclosure.[40]

FS50119242 concerned a complainant who made a request to the Department of Health (DoH) relating to a report published by the Standing Dental Advisory Committee in November 2003, entitled 'Conscious Sedation in the Provision of Dental Care'. The request covered details of minutes and correspondence for meetings. The DoH claimed the information related to the formulation or development of government policy. The IC decided that the information in question did not relate to the formulation or development of government

---

[39] *Sankey v Whitlam* (1978) 142 *CLR* 1 was cited.

[40] In FS50105954 the complainant requested from DEFRA the release of briefing notes and background evidence advice in relation to the issue of redress in the case of the cross-contamination of non-GM crops by GM crops. He also requested the relevant legal advice and the names of those with whom the legal advice had been shared. The IC decided that the information had been correctly withheld under s. 35.

policy, and therefore he did not believe that the exemption is engaged. However, s. 40(2) was engaged regarding some information and this was redacted.

FS50085775 was a request to the Scottish Office (SO) for proposals for a dedicated Gaelic TV company. The PA invoked ss. 21(1), 35 (1)(a)–(c), 40(2)(a), 41(1)(a)–(b) and s. 43(2). The IC was critical of the way the SO explained the PI test under s. 35 and the manner in which relevant factors were weighed. Some information was properly exempt but other parts inappropriately withheld (eight lever-arch files!). Some of this was generated after the IC started investigation and the IC did not believe the SO was under a duty to disclose this information. There is a helpful discussion of balancing of PIs under s. 35 (para. 17 *et seq.*). The IC believed that policymaking was about developing options and priorities for Ministers – the exemption was unlikely to cover operational or administrative matters. Policy must be government policy and not departmental! It must be 'a political process which requires Cabinet input, or applies across government, or represents the collective view of Ministers' (para. 18). The IC thought it unlikely that policy formulation exemption applied once a policy decision was made.[41] Section 35 does not include the ministers of the Scottish Parliament,[42] drafts of letters (only those communicated), and briefing notes were not covered by s. 35(1)(b) because they are not communications. In EA/2007/0128 *Scotland Office v IC* the IT allowed the appeal in part. Section 35(1)(a)–(b) covered the majority of documents, s. 41 covered one and s. 43 two. The PA disclosed most of the documents, some completely voluntarily, and the disputed documents numbered about forty. The IT noted that there was no evidence post-FOIA or the decision in *DfES* EA/2006/0006 (below) of the 'chilling effect' of disclosure on civil servants. Basically, the PI in disclosure did not equal that of retention under s. 35.

In FS 50086299, ss. 35–6 were invoked. The request concerned meetings between the multinational Chairman's Group, the prime minister and senior officials. Section 17 was breached in that the Cabinet Office did not explain adequately which exemption applied to each element of requested information and why.[43] Paragraph 21 sets out Cabinet Office's reasons for non-disclosure: free and frank discussion on internal and external policy and policy currently under consideration. Lobbyists are unlikely to be inhibited by having comments disclosed, the IC believed. Failure under s. 35 did not mean s. 36 was an automatic fall-back. Disclosure of some documents was ordered. In FS50081525 there was a request for information held by the Treasury about the compatibility of the Financial Services and Markets Bill with the Human Rights Act. The request was refused under ss. 35(1)(b) and 35(3) (refusal to confirm or deny) in relation to Law Officer's advice, and s. 42(1) on legal professional privilege. Additionally, ss. 35(1)(a) and 41 were invoked and the PA breached s. 17(1) by not identifying these exemptions in its refusal notice. The IC narrowed

---

[41] See pp.7–9 on consideration of precedents.   [42] See s. 29 SFOIA 2002.
[43] Similar to the Vaughn index USA; see chapter 12, p. 464.

exemptions to ss. 35(3) and 42(1). Section 35(3) was wrongly applied but s. 42(1) was properly claimed. The ruling on s. 35(3) was subsequently reversed on appeal to the High Court because insufficient weight had been given to the convention relating to law officers' advice and its importance.[44]

FS50070196 has already been adverted to (see s. 33 above). The request was for gateway reviews of the ID cards programmes and contracts conducted by the Home Office. 'Gateways reviews' were discussed above. Sections 33 and 35 were invoked. The IC was prepared to accept that s. 35 is engaged. Paragraph 4.18 arguments for PI disclosure by the requester included the effects the ID cards programme would have on data protection, privacy and civil liberties involving several billion pounds of public money. Disclosure would assist discussion and debate and understanding. Paragraph 4.19 contains arguments by the OGC on PI: these involve a reduction in candour and co-operation, less reliable recommendations by reviewing team, over- caution, the risk of an inaccurate or out-of-context picture, and disclosure undermining still 'live policy development'. Individuals were not directly identified but it may be possible to estimate who did make contributions. The PI in maintaining the exemption did not outweigh the PI in disclosure, the IC ruled.

In FS50104994 there was a request to HM Treasury for information on 'all relevant documentation covering the decision in principle' about the reduction of income tax by 1p in the pound announced in 1999. Section 35(1)(a) was invoked. The PI test is at para. 35 – the test for maintaining exemption was not satisfied by the Treasury. The IC did not accept the PI arguments of the Treasury in relation to s. 35(1)(a). There was criticism of s. 16 aspects in relation to the Treasury and criticism of transfers of requests to other PAs under the s. 45 code. In January 2007, the Treasury released the greater part of the information in compliance with the IC's DN. The DN was appealed in EA/2007/0001 *HM Treasury v IC*.[45] The IT was not impressed by the warnings from the Treasury of 'dire consequences' of releasing information much of which was subsequently released. The undisclosed information was felt sensitive by the Treasury because if disclosed it might confine the range of topics on which Ministers might seek advice from their civil servants. The appeal was allowed in relation to one item of information and a substituted DN was issued. It concerned budget papers. Section 35(1)(a) was invoked. Section 35 is a class exemption but any 'damage' is considered in balancing PI factors. The central question in s. 35(1) is the content of specific information in relation to the exemption. The usual 'chilling effect' factors were recited by the Treasury. The IT believed the chilling effect is inherent in the Act (para. 57(3)). The PI arguments in favour of disclosure are at pp.19–21 and include: the passage of time (the relevant date is 1999); the benefit of participation in government decisions; publication of some information does not remove the desirability of disclosing

---

[44] *HM Treasury v IC and Owen* [2009] EWHC 1811 (Admin). The case was remitted to the IT for reconsideration.

[45] See FS50088619 on tax policy and effect of time on assessing the PI.

more; the possible contribution of rejected options for proposals in the future; and greater transparency, accountability and public debate. The PI was in favour of disclosure except in relation to one item of information (from a perspective in 2005). The IT believed that information generated before the FOIA had no effect on assessing the PI. The underlying assumption of FOIA is that 'disclosure of information held by PAs is in itself of value and in the PI' citing *Guardian Newspapers v IC* EA/2006/0011.

Appeals[46]

EA/2008/0024 and 0029 *Cabinet Office v IC and C. Lamb* (F550165372) saw the application of the Secretary of State's veto in response to the majority decision of the IT upholding the IC's decision to disclose documents (the minutes subject to specified redactions) concerning two Cabinet meetings in March 2003 in which the government committed the UK to the dispatch of troops to engage in hostilities in Iraq. Informal documents accompanying the minutes were protected under s. 35(1)(a)–(b). The IT described the case as 'exceptional' creating very powerful PI reasons for publication. The request for the minutes was made in April 2007. Central to these meetings were papers from the Attorney General outlining his opinion on the legality of using armed force in Iraq without the necessity of a further UN Security Council resolution. Iraq had been in breach of resolutions concerning inspection and information on its alleged weapons of mass destruction (WMD). The background to the case is the fact that no evidence of WMD was found and that the widespread feeling persists that the grounds for going to war were fabricated to comply with US foreign policy. The Butler Review of the use of intelligence on the WMD had made critical findings on the nature of Cabinet proceedings and their management in the period in question leading to hostilities.[47] Briefing papers prepared by officials had not been circulated to the Cabinet but had been replaced by 'unscripted briefings' by the prime minister and Foreign and Defence Secretaries. Discussion took place in detail only between 'a small circle of individuals' for which the Cabinet as a whole would bear responsibility. 'The scope for informed overall political judgement by the Cabinet had been reduced' (para. 28). Discussion of intelligence and its materials by Butler was in closed session, only conclusions were published. The IC had previously issued an enforcement notice (EN) ordering the publication of information supporting the Attorney General's legal opinion dated 17 March 2003. Confidentiality was maintained for information in 'uncirculated drafts' or which were 'preliminary, provisional or tentative' or which might reveal legal risks, reservations and counter-arguments by those involved in giving advice to the Attorney General (para. 32). An agreed disclosure statement of materials to be published was subsequently made. The

---

[46] See *D. O'Brien v IC* EA/2008/0011.
[47] *Review of Intelligence on Weapons of Mass Destruction*, HC 898 (2003–4).

arguments from the Cabinet Office in favour of non-disclosure of the Cabinet minutes (the additional materials were not ordered to be disclosed) were general in relation to collective responsibility and specific in relation to the particular information at issue. Collective responsibility is dependent upon confidentiality. A united face is presented to the public. Differences remain secret. The law and convention of Cabinet confidentiality are examined elsewhere in this book (see chapter 9, p. 328). The IT noted several publications where ministers had publicised events at the meetings in question including their differences of opinion.[48] The former minister Clare Short had subsequently published commentary that was critical of the suppression of debate at the Cabinet meetings (para. 45). That was her view. There had also been leaks and releases to the press by ministers of Cabinet discussions. The minutes revealed no dissent in the Cabinet beyond that contained in other published materials. The IC believed that no member of the Cabinet would face the invidious position of being seen to agree in public but dissent in private.

The Cabinet position was that publishing official documents would damage the PI by undermining a central component of the British constitution. The IC believed that while great respect should be afforded to the conventions of Cabinet governance – it was a 'strong factor' (para. 51) – the decision on *these documents* had to be taken in their specific context bearing in mind the passage of just over four years since the discussion in question. The Cabinet Office gave evidence that if a pattern emerged of publishing minutes where there was no dissent, but not otherwise, that would lead to the obvious presumption that dissent had occurred at those meetings with a weakening of the convention.

The IC's case for PI disclosure included: the gravity and controversial nature of the subject; accountability for government decisions; transparency of decision-making; and public participation in government decisions (paras. 58–9). Expert evidence from Professor Hennessey suggested that the Cabinet had not been sufficiently diligent in testing its leaders' conclusions on going to war. The IT specifically adverted to the fact that publication would not lead to evidence of differences between the discussion at the meetings and subsequent public statements or that publication would significantly better inform the public (para. 69). Some may consider this latter element would weaken the PI.

The majority of the IT were persuaded by the 'compelling' arguments for disclosure in the PI. The decision was 'momentous'. There was the controversy over the fact that only the later version of the Attorney General's advice was given to the Cabinet and not the earlier and longer version. The approaches adopted by those members who knew of the earlier version and those who did not is of 'crucial significance' in understanding recent history and processes of accountability. Enquiries and investigations after the relevant events do not weaken the case for disclosure. The FOIA, as the IC said, has *its own impetus for disclosure*. The very unusual combination of factors reduced any damaging

---

[48] D. Blunkett, *The Blunkett Tapes: Life in the bear pit* (2006); R. Cook, *The Point of Departure* (2003); C. Short, *An Honorable Deception? New Labour, Iraq and the misuse of power* (2004). There were also relevant publications by Alastair Campbell, Lord Levy and John Prescott.

possibility of a precedent being set in ordering disclosure. What the minutes revealed did not sway the PI. The crucial factor was in allowing the public to see and make up its own mind 'on the effectiveness of the decision-making context' (para. 82). The majority ruled that publication, subject to agreed redactions for reasons of diplomatic sensitivity, was in the PI. The IT agreed that additional materials relating to notes taken by civil servants of the meetings should not be published. The minority view of the IT was that publication of the minutes would drive Cabinet governance towards informality and 'sofa government' thereby weakening the public record and undermining good government – I add, representative government.

On 24 February 2009, four weeks after the IT's decision, the Justice Secretary issued his veto under s. 53 FOIA blocking release of the minutes. His decision was one in which he took the view of the Cabinet although Lord Falconer had variously stated there would be a Cabinet decision and Cabinet consultation. Collective responsibility and Cabinet confidentiality do not exist, Straw said, for the convenience of ministers. They are crucial to the accountability of the executive to Parliament and the people. The damage to free debate would be undermined by disclosure of the minutes and that damage to the PI far outweighs any PI in disclosure. At risk was the 'integrity of our system of government' and openness and accountability cannot prejudice that integrity. He concluded by noting that in the Dacre Review of the thirty-year rule for public records (see chapter 4, p. 137 and Introduction, p. 7) a reduction from thirty to fifteen years was recommended. Dacre also recommended that there should be protection under the Act for certain categories of sensitive information (see chapter 9, p. 352).

EA/2006/0006 *DfES v IC and Evening Standard (AP)* contains some important general statements of principle. Section 1 FOIA creates a 'new fundamental right to information' (para. 61). Section 35(1)(a) was invoked. Information about setting of school budgets in England was requested; in particular the minutes of a policy committee. The 'chilling effect' on advice and record-keeping argument was rejected. Some information was published voluntarily. The formulation and development of policy had to be distinguished from implementation of policy and its analysis (p. 13). Witnesses in the case included the Cabinet Secretary. The IT identified the dangers of 'sofa government' by use of specialist advisers. The words 'Relates to formulation and development of policy' in s. 35 are to be construed broadly. There was no need to prevent disclosure of officials' identities. The status of minutes does not automatically exempt documents even though they apply to 'most senior of officials'. 'To treat such status as automatically conferring exemption would be tantamount to intervening within s. 35(1) a class of absolutely exempt information for which the subsection gives no warrant . . .' (para. 69). A decision of the High Court of Australia and the Australian analogue of s. 36 FOIA where the court emphasised the importance of protecting candour and frankness was cited.[49] Paragraph 49 deals with the

---

[49] *McKinnon v Secretary, Dept of Treasury* [2006] HCA 45

grounds in favour of disclosure from the IC and p. 20 *et seq.* deal with the application of the PI test under s. 35(1). In para. 75 the guiding principles in such cases are: the content of particular information. No status is automatically exempt. The protection is against compromise or unjust public opprobrium of civil servants *not* ministers. Timing of a request is paramount. What is highly relevant in June 2003 may carry little weight by January 2005. A Parliamentary statement announcing the policy 'will normally mark the end of the process of policy formulation'. Facts must be viewed carefully, however, and the PI in exemption may not disappear on announcement. Courage and independence are expected of civil servants. But there may be good reason to withhold the names of more junior civil servants. The IT proceeded on the basis that ministers will behave fairly and responsibly to civil servants who may be associated with unpopular advice. A blanket policy of refusing to identify civil servants cannot be justified. There must be a *specific reason* justifying non-disclosure of a civil servant's identity.

There is a general PI in transparency and a better understanding of how the government tackles important policy problems. The 'funding crisis' in schools was of great public concern. The information may not prove to be significant in any public debate but the PI favours disclosure. The IC raised s. 40 on his own motion and DfES objected to this – this was not ruled on. The IC's decision was upheld – the PI favours disclosure.

EA/2005/0040 *Secretary of State for Work and Pensions v IC*[50] concerned a request for the feasibility of the government's ID cards programme and relevant instructions and their full impact, costs and benefits.[51] Sections 35 and 43 were invoked. Paragraph 20 deals with 'statistical information' test under s. 35(2) and also para. 75. There is MoJ (formerly Department for Constitutional Affairs) guidance on 'statistical information'.[52] The test for PI is: does the balance lie in favour of maintaining exemption? Factual information and s. 35(4) are dealt with in para. 71 *et seq.* This application was at a late stage of policy implementation the IT believed and the second stage related to the detailed implementation of the scheme at departmental level. The ID scheme is of an unprecedented scale and complexity incurring costs of several billion pounds. It will ultimately affect the way people access public services (para. 96). There is a PI in knowing what the benefits are. The PI test is the same for this exemption as for other exemptions (para. 103)! The disputed information was introduced at a late stage in the formulation and development of an ID scheme after the decision by government to introduce such a scheme. This was an advanced stage of policy formulation and development of the scheme. The PI was in favour of disclosure and the IT upheld the IC's notice of disclosure although the identities of junior civil servants were rightly redacted.

---

[50] Para. 31 'where required PAs should find that the PI in maintaining exemption is outweighed by the PI in disclosure' – this is wrong; it is the other way around!

[51] Government papers: *Secure Borders – Safe Haven*, Cm. 5387; *Entitlement Cards and Identity Fraud: A consultation paper*, Cm. 5557; *Identity Cards: The next steps*, Cm. 6020.

[52] www.justice.gov.uk/docs/foi-exemption-s35.pdf, p. 9.

EA/2007/0016 *Ministry of Justice v IC* was a refusal to confirm or deny under s. 35(3). Disclosure was sought on the Attorney General's advice in relation to the PI test. Section 35(1)(e) was relied upon. An information notice (IN) was served under s. 51 by the IC (s. 51(5)(a)–(b)). Section 51(5) which provides that no information is required to be given in relation to advice to a PA by a professional legal adviser covers *general* and specific advice from a law officer on advice in response to an FOIA claim. The IT accepted the MoJ's argument that s. 51 FOIA came into play to protect a PA's legal advice on a FOIA claim. It is wider than s. 42 (below) and does not carry a PI test allowing disclosure. There is a strong convention on not confirming or denying law officers' advice (paras. 15 and 42).[53]

EA/2007 *Department for Culture, Media and Sport v IC* saw the IT reverse the IC's decision on disclosure on PI grounds under s. 35. It concerned advice from civil servants to the minister on the list of sporting events that were protected under the Broadcasting Act 1996 from being exclusively pay-per-view. The IC said that encouraging good practice, promoting accountability and understanding, encouraging public debate, and broadening policy input in the age of information were all relevant factors. The IT looked at the material and did not feel these first four items were advanced by disclosure – releasing information just for the sake of it would remove any necessity for s. 35! The grounds for release have to be supportable. The material here was seven years old but disclosure would not assist public debate! There is no fixed cut-off point at which time runs out. Under s. 35(1)(a) there was no PI to match the PI in maintaining the 'private thinking space' of ministers and civil servants – unlike the DfES case above. Likewise under s. 35(1)(b) the case for disclosure has to be as strong as retention and here it was not. This is a troubling case – it is a very important PI question in relation to broadcasting sporting events but the IT felt the evidence for disclosure 'anodyne'.[54]

Section 36: prejudice to the effective conduct of public affairs[55]

For a government department, information which is not exempt under s. 35 may be exempt under this section. It will be recalled that a 'qualified person' may exempt information by making a 'reasonable decision' that disclosure would

---

[53] See FS50093302; EA/2007/0070 (FS50091442) *Scotland Office v IC* and see *HM Treasury v IC and Owen* [2009] EWHC 1811 (Admin), note 45 above.

[54] See EA/2005/0026 *Hogan v IC* below and compare.

[55] FS50121390 (s. 35 above). FS50077877 (s. 38 below). FS50125204: request for names and contact details of all staff at a London Borough. The PI under s. 36 favoured non-disclosure. S. 31 did not protect names of heads of staff and neither did s. 40(2). FS50078471: minutes of meetings between prime minister and Wall-Mart representatives in early 1999. Ss. 36 and 35 wer invoked. Summaries of meetings that were disclosed were not adequate and neither ss. 35 or 36 were engaged. See FS50082251. In FS50104809 the requester wished to see the files generated by his request for information about an MoD contract. S. 36 was invoked. Much of the information was 'mundane' and not protected but personal data of junior officials and some non-public information was protected by the PI. See EA/2008/0049 *Cabinet Office v IC* and FS50155365 in relation to a University's admission tests.

have the prejudicial or inhibiting features as set out in s. 36 (see chapter 5, p. 167). This is challengeable on the basis that the decision is not objectively reasonable.[56] FS50093255, para. 37, provides a website for a list of qualified persons for s. 36 (www.foi.gov.uk/guidance/exguide/sec36/annex-d.htm).

In FS50169313 the complainant submitted two requests for information relating to the 'Parthenon Marbles' and the 'Terracotta Army' respectively. The British Museum released some information but withheld the following:

(1) three covering letters sent with the museum trustees' statement to Greek officials – s. 36
(2) correspondence and emails between the museum and Chinese authorities relating to the Terracotta Army contract – s. 12
(3) correspondence between the director and the Chinese authorities – s. 36
(4) minutes of additional meetings (not available on the website) – ss. 31 and 43.

In relation to (1) the IC found that s. 36(2)(b)(ii) was engaged because the museum director (the qualified person) provided a statement that in his opinion the letters were personal comments made on the reasonable understanding of friendly openness and confidence facilitating the exchange of views freely and frankly; the IC thought that this was a reasonably objective opinion. The PI fell in favour of maintaining the exemption (there is a good PI analysis). In relation to (2), the IC found that s. 12 was engaged because the estimated cost of retrieval would far exceed the £450.00 limit. In relation to (3) the IC found that s. 36(2)(b)(ii) applied in the same way as (1).

In FS50111678 the complainant requested the disclosure of correspondence between the prime minister and Lord Birt (his former strategy advisor). The Cabinet Office refused disclosure initially under s. 35, but later under s. 36. The minister for the Cabinet Office gave his opinion, which was accepted as reasonable by the IC (applying *Guardian Newspapers and Heather Brooke v IC and BBC*). The PI favoured maintenance of the exemption. The IC recognised that there was a PI in transparency of governmental affairs, especially considering the debate on the role of special advisors, particularly Lord Birt, but the information withheld was not of such significance that it would contribute to the debate. However the IC felt it appropriate to clarify that Lord Birt did play an informal role in relation to the appointment of senior staff – that fact should have been disclosed. The IC also 'independently' considered that some of the information requested was exempt under s. 40(2) FOIA and the first of the data-protection principles (see chapter 8, p. 298).

In FS50150598 the IC believed that as far as the advice to a minister was concerned, it was thought that the exemption would apply, because the release

---

[56] EA/2007 *R. Salmon v IC and King's College Cambridge* deals with the situation where there is no 'qualified person' for s. 36 exemption – s. 36 is not thereby engaged! However, the fact that a PA (King's College Cambridge) is largely dependent on private funding does not diminish the nature of its obligations under the FOIA.

of such information would be likely to inhibit such candid and all encompassing advice being supplied to ministers in the future and would make officials less likely to engage in written discussions of such controversial issues. However, the IC in this case considered that the exemption did not outweigh the PI in disclosure. FS50120314 involved a request for a report from the PA that it had prepared on the charging of overseas visitors for treatment received under the NHS. Initially the public authority refused to disclose any of the report but decided to publish with names of PAs redacted. These names were withheld under ss. 36(2)(b)(ii) (inhibition of the free and frank exchange of views), 36(2)(c) (prejudice to the effective conduct of public affairs) and 41 (information provided in confidence). Section 41 was raised subsequently but this was permitted. The IC determined that none of the exemptions were applicable to the information and ordered it to be disclosed to the complainant. Although imparted in confidence, there was no detriment to the PAs (six of whom consented to being identified). Six wished to be anonymous.

FS50117628 dealt with a request to the MoJ for a review carried out by HM Magistrates' Court Service Inspectorate into listing and case management in the Crown Court. The MoJ took seven months to determine the PI followed by refusal citing s. 36 – according to the IC's *Good Practice Guidance 4*, even in complex cases, the time to consider the PI should not exceed forty days. The requested report was only in draft form and contained errors, said the MoJ. The IC found the latter justification irrelevant. The PI favoured disclosure and there were breaches by the PA of s. 17 FOIA. There was a failure to comply with the memorandum of understanding between the IC and government departments in failing to respond to the IC within twenty days and his requests for details about the PI test under s. 36. Section 36 was properly engaged. The views of senior judges were sought and they were against disclosure. There was a possibility that publication would harm relations between the judiciary and government but nevertheless this did not tip the balance of PI against disclosure. Disclosure ordered.

FS50108125 concerned a request about animal experiments in which it was alleged mice had been deprived of water for two days. This would constitute an infringement of experiment licensing conditions. Sections 30, 36, 38 and 44 were invoked. The requester did not challenge the refusal to supply names and addresses under ss. 40 or 38. The PI regarding s. 38 is dealt with at para. 33. Against publication are harassment, jeopardy to health and the publication of anonymous summary reports by the Home Office. In favour were the benefit of public discussion and confidence in robust regulation. A different approach would be taken by the IC in relation to voluntary disclosures by licensees and compulsory ones to the PA. There is a discussion of s. 36 and inspectors' inhibitions. The PI was in favour of anonymous disclosure. Paragraph 62 *et seq.* discusses the 'reasonable opinion' of 'qualified persons' under s. 36 – it must be an objective decision objectively arrived at. Information withheld under ss. 38 and 44 was properly withheld, but not that withheld under ss. 30 and 36.

FS50072316 was another case on Iraq and concerned the unpublished early draft of Iraq's WMD dossier published on 24 September 2002,[57] which was requested from the FCO. Section 36(2)(b) was invoked. FCO took three months to conduct an internal review of a FOI appeal – IC's good practice guide says it should take twenty working days extendible to forty! An error in the IC's office led to a delay of four months before the case was investigated. This dossier was submitted to the Hutton Inquiry but was not discussed or placed in the Annex to the report. The FCO wanted the IC (or his official) with 'suitable vetting' to examine the dossier in the FCO. Ultimately it was sent to the IC at his office. Section 36 was wrongly invoked and material ordered to be disclosed. This DN was appealed in *FCO v IC* EA/2007/0047 and the judgment delivered in January 2008 ordering disclosure subject to a minor redaction.[58] The IT exclaimed that there was no presumption in favour of maintaining the exemption under s. 36(2) as counsel for FCO suggested (paras. 24–5). The qualified person's opinion was not placed before the IT and in future it is preferable for the opinion to be before the IT so its reasonableness may be assessed. Civil servants must expect increased openness post FOIA and the 'chilling effect' generated by that Act. Factors in favour of maintaining exemption did not, at the date when disclosure was refused, outweigh the PI in disclosure. On the chilling effect of disclosure IC took into account some of the arguments from EA/2006/0006 *DfES v IC*. The information was not important in itself but it was important to enhance the 'transparency process' of drafting in such a sensitive issue as this (para. 50).

FS50096973 was a request to DfES for the list of schools suitable for City Academy status. Section 36 was properly invoked. Quoting *H. Brooke v IC and BBC*, 'If the opinion is reasonable, the IC should not under s. 36 substitute his own view for that of the qualified person. Nor should the Tribunal' (para. 13). Disclosure would risk damage to a 'flagship education programme'. It would be difficult to persuade sponsors and authorities to come forward (para. 24). This was 'highly sensitive work in progress' and the PI favoured non-disclosure. FS50073128 was a request for the names and salaries of an MP's staff. The House of Commons invoked s. 36(2) and (7). Section 36(7) is absolute in relation to the Commons and names of staff and its invocation could not be questioned but s. 40(2) did not, of itself, protect the names of assistants.

FS50086128 was a request to the Cabinet Office for information on the dates since 30 September 2002 on which the prime minister met or had conversations with Rupert Murdoch. Sections 36(2)(b)(i) and 36(2)(c) were invoked. The PI was discussed in para. 5.9 *et seq*. Disclosure would not put too much pressure on the prime minister's diary and dates of official meetings should be disclosed.

---

[57] 'Iraq's WMD: The assessment of the British Government' – the Williams' draft.
[58] *The Guardian*, 21 February 2008, was highly critical that the word 'Israel' was removed in a secret hearing under s. 27 FOIA.

There was a breach of s. 17 in failing to provide adequate reasons etc. of exemptions under FOIA.[59]

In FS50098388 the complainant asked the Cabinet Office for (a) drafts of the Iraq Dossier, (b) a covering note with redactions removed, and (c) any comments on the drafts made by the Defence Intelligence Staff (DIS) or anyone else. The Cabinet Office stated that some of the information was not held and the remainder was exempt under ss. 27(1) and/or 36(2)(b)(ii). Regarding request (a) the IC found that the Cabinet had not retained such a draft, other than the dossier available on the Hutton Inquiry website. In relation to (b) the IC found that s. 27 was engaged because the redacted information was of a confidential nature concerning the relationship between the UK and another state, which could undermine the trust within which confidential exchanges between the UK and other governments take place. Upon considering the PI test, the IC ruled in favour of maintaining the exemption because whilst disclosure was in the PI, it would result in significant prejudice to the UK's relationship with other states. Further, he thought that the information would not make any significant contribution to the public debate. There were also some comments on behalf of an international organisation on the dossier to which the Cabinet Office applied s. 27. For similar reasons as above, the IC found that the exemption was engaged and should be maintained in the PI. In relation to request (c), the IC was of the view that the s. 24 exemption was engaged. In relation to comments not from DIS, as the government had published the dossier, the exemption was not necessary in order to safeguard national security. The IC separated the comments by DIS into three types:

(i) drafting comments – s. 24(1) was not engaged; s. 36(2)(b)(ii) was engaged, but the PI fell in favour of disclosure
(ii) technical intelligence assessments – s. 24 was engaged; whilst there were some significant PI arguments in favour of disclosure, the balance fell in favour of maintaining the exemption because intelligence collection methods could have been compromised
(iii) names/designations/contact details – these should be redacted under s. 24.

FS50134653 is linked to FS50098388 (above). The complainant requested information about the identities and/or departments of those who had provided comments on the drafting of the dossier on WMD other than the Defence Intelligence Staff and contributions already in the public domain – between 11 and 16 September 2002. The Cabinet Office stated that they did not have a ready-made list and therefore did not hold the information. However, the IC was of the view that the fact that the Cabinet Office would have to create a list of information that it had would mean that the request was indeed for

---

[59] FS50174491: the PI favours disclosure of information about internal communications relating to the applicant's company's use of the FOIA.

information which was held by the Cabinet Office. In relation to the information, the IC considered that it was disclosable on the same grounds as part of the information requested in FS50098388. He did not therefore consider the applicability of ss. 36(2)(b)(ii) and 24(1).

Appeals

EA/2008/0062 *Home Office and Ministry of Justice v IC* involved a request for disclosure of information contained within internal government departmental communications relating to the company's previous FOI requests. Such non-substantive requests are termed 'meta-requests'. The request was refused on the basis of s. 36. The IC found that s. 36 was engaged because the Home Office had obtained a reasonably held opinion from a qualified person. However, the IC found that the PI favoured disclosure. The Home Office appealed (with the MoJ joined) on the grounds that: (a) the IC had erred in his weighing of the PI and (b) the IC had not taken into account other relevant exemptions, which the Home Office was seeking to raise for the first time before the IT (namely ss. 23, 24, 31, 38, 40, 41, and 43).

The issues raised were as follows:

(a) whether the IC had erred in finding that the s. 36 exemption was engaged (notwithstanding that the parties agreed that it was)
(b) whether the IC had erred in finding that the PI favoured disclosure
(c) if not, whether the appellants could rely on the other exemptions at such a late stage
(d) if so, whether the exemptions applied.

Issue (a)

Whilst the IT found that the s. 36 exemption was engaged, they criticised the IC's approach to this issue; the IC had not seen the submissions to ministers or the ministers' responses. In *McIntyre v IC MoD*, the IT made clear that it was 'unsafe' for the IC to conclude that s. 36 was engaged without seeing those submissions; to do otherwise would make it difficult to consider whether that opinion was reasonable in substance and reasonably arrived at.

In addition, as there was no evidence as to which limb of prejudice the opinion had related (inhibit/prejudice), the lower threshold of prejudice would be adopted. This is significant because the higher threshold requires greater weight to the inherent PI in the exemption being claimed.

Issue (b)

The following PI arguments were made by the parties:

Respondent (IC)

(1) openness and transparency in order to increase accountability

(2) to enable the public to see that decisions were taken promptly and after full consideration

(3) to enable the public to understand the reasoning behind FOIA decisions

(4) the positive effect of increasing the public's confidence in internal procedures for handling requests.

Appellant (PA) General Interests

(1) the procedures for dealing with FOIA requests were published and were therefore transparent without the need for provision of information in individual cases

(2) internal reviews confirmed that the procedures were followed.

Appellant: specific PIs

(1) there would be a chilling effect on the future conduct of those responsible for handling requests – they would not be free and frank in their discussions

(2) there was a resources issue – resources would have to be diverted to meta-requests rather than concentrating on substantive requests; meta-requests circumvented other processes for reviewing such matters (including the IC and the IT appeals); the information contained little of, or no, material value.

The IT found that the PI favoured disclosure and gave strong emphasis to the PI in knowing that public authorities deal with FOIA requests properly and lawfully. Parliament did not intend that meta-requests would be excluded from the scope of the FOIA and therefore such requests are legitimate and should accordingly be dealt with under the Act.

Issue (c)

The IT found that the additional exemptions were claimed too late in this instance, citing the IT case of *Department of Business and Regulatory Reform v IC and CBI*. Issue (d) therefore became redundant, except that the IT decided that minor redaction should take place under s. 40(2). (See *Home Office v IC* [2009] EWHC 1611 (admin) on this point.)

EA/2006/0013 *Guardian Newspapers and H. Brooke v IC and BBC*[60] was a case in which the appeal was allowed and a substituted DN issued. Section 36 was invoked. What should the test of a 'reasonable opinion' of a qualified person under s. 36 be? The case concerned the nature of the IT's appellate powers – these were stated to involve a full rehearing, not confined to evidence available to the IC – a full appeal on merits and on findings of fact. A request was made for the minutes of the Board of Governors of the BBC in relation to the latter's response to the Hutton Inquiry. A central feature was evidence from Greg Dyke. Paragraph 50 deals with the issue by the IC of a preliminary non-statutory DN to the PA, which was not sent to requester. The IT understandably

---

[60] Para. 21 concerns the likely unhappy effect of drafting from the DPA 1998 on the FOIA to produce uncertainty in ss. 57–8 FOIA (DPA ss. 48–9) – 'or' actually means 'and/or'.

raised queries about the perceived independence and impartiality of this in the minds of requesters. *Hogan v IC* EA/2005/0026 saw the IT disagree with the IC's test for 'reasonable decision' (of a qualified person) under s. 36. The IC seemed to repeat the test of unreasonableness in judicial review rather than objective reasonableness. The test must be: is it reasonable in substance and reasonably arrived at? The IT did not think 'reasonably arrived' at entailed a probing examination of evidence considered or not considered but if a higher court thought it did, then absence of evidence on the point would have meant it was not reasonable. So, subject to what any higher court believes s. 36 was properly engaged. Paragraph 81 *et seq.* contain a discussion on how the balance of PI should be weighted. The 'balance' of FOIA as a whole favours disclosure. Disclosure itself is in the PI.[61]

PI factors include passage of time; particular interest to be protected; and the PI itself of transparency, accountability, public debate, better public understanding of decisions and informed meaningful participation by the public in the democratic process (para. 88(5)). Due deference will be given to a qualified person's opinion but the IC has to provide support for his own judgement. The IC favoured the PI in non-disclosure – the IT believed he had wrongly formulated the PI test in agreeing with the BBC. The BBC's evidence was 'unimpressive'. There was 'insufficient attention to relevant details by the BBC and therefore by the IC. PI in maintaining s. 36 exemption did not outweigh the PI in disclosure.' This is a strong case in favour of transparency.

EA/2007/0068 *I. Macintyre v IC and MoD* was a request for the departmental promotion criteria and handbooks by an unsuccessful candidate for promotion. The IC accepted that s. 36(2)(c) was engaged and that the PI favours maintaining exemption. It adds a gloss to the *Guardian and Brooke* cases on whether a decision by a qualified person has to be objectively reasonable and reasonably arrived at. To what extent can an objectively reasonable decision be set aside if a manifestly unreasonable process was adopted?[62] It was not clear which limb of the exemption the minister was using – 'would' or 'would be likely to'. But this did not nullify the opinion.

EA/2006/0064 *R. Evans v IC and MoD* was an interesting case concerning meetings of a minister and an arms lobbying company. Sections 36(2)(b)(i), 35(1), 40, 41 and 43 were invoked. The case examines the question of hearing of fresh evidence by the IT regarding the PI under s. 36. The timing of grounds for exemption is that at the time of refusal – not the IT hearing (paras. 22–3). The PI is that at time of request. The PI was not advanced by disclosing 'notes' of the meeting. *Brook v IC and BBC* determined that the decision of a qualified person under s. 36 had to be objectively reasonable and 'reasonably arrived at'. 'All parties agreed that after Brook "would or would be likely to"

---

[61] See EA/2007 *Department for Culture, Media and Sport v IC* and EA/2007/0070 (FS50091442) *Scotland Office v IC* under s. 36 above for a less-robust attitude to the PI.

[62] Natural justice case law, e.g. *Cinnamond v BAA* [1980] 2 All ER 368.

means that inhibition would probably occur (on balance of probabilities, the chance being greater than 50 per cent) or that there would be a "very significant and weighty chance that it would occur". A "real risk" is not enough.' (para. 21). As a general rule the PI in maintaining an exemption diminishes over time. The IT cannot hear fresh evidence. The witnesses were not able to show evidence of inhibitory effects of disclosure. The PI should not double-count the claim of the minister for the exemption itself. 'Where the information is in a raw unconsidered form the PI in maintaining the exemption is likely to diminish more slowly than where the information is in a finished considered form' (para. 41). Fear of inhibition of disclosure on lobbyists was overstated. In relation to *notes* of meetings and telephone conversations the exemptions were maintained on PI grounds because these were unfinished and incomplete. In relation to 'finished' background notes, there was no such inhibition and the PI favoured disclosure.

EA/2006/0027 *MoD v IC and R. Evans* was another case involving the same reporter as above. The IT substituted an EN. Sections 24, 36, 38 and 40 were invoked. The request was for the complete copy of the 2004 edition of the Directory of the *Defence Export Services Organisation* (DESO). DESO assists in the export of UK military equipment. Information about DESO was limited to MoD and security-cleared members of the UK defence industry. The IC placed a great deal of emphasis on the need for transparency in the defence industry/MoD relations. Disclosure despite s. 36 claims would guard against the risks of 'inappropriate closeness between such companies and MoD' (para. 13). The MoD claimed that transparency was satisfied by publication of redacted copy and names of senior MoD officials. This involved disclosure of senior officials' identities at director-general-level and those who appear in the *Diplomatic Service List*. It would not cover junior rankings unless their names were published in, for example, the *Civil Service Yearbook*. The IT emphasised that this is a one-off decision and does not set a precedent.[63] Anonymity of civil servants is not an 'immutable principle' and civil servants may be made accountable. DPA sch. 2(6) was satisfied here. 'The IT is not minded, however, to sanction the disclosure of all telephone and email details – save for those in *Civil Service Yearbook*' (para. 88).[64]

Section 37: communications with Her Majesty and honours[65]

The case law has been limited.

---

[63] Paras. 53 for arguments for disclosure and 72 for reasons against disclosure under s. 36.

[64] The IT noted that a US judicial decision (4 December 2006) went against disclosure of US officials in US DoD (names and duty stations) Business Appointment Rules.

[65] FS50119029 *House of Lords Appointments Commission*; FS50088853 *HM Treasury*, www.justice.gov.uk/docs/foi-exemption-s38.pdf. See FS 50088853 under s. 40 below and FS50142320 involving the Cabinet Office and requests about the Princess of Wales.

Section 38: health and safety[66]

In FS50082472 the names of individuals, companies and academic institutions holding licences to conduct scientific research on animals was refused under s. 38. The PI under s. 38 favoured non-disclosure. Section 40 was also engaged and allowed exemption.

FS 50108125 (s. 36 above) has a discussion on the PI regarding s. 38 and disclosure of those conducting licensed research on animals (para. 33) (dangers of harassment, jeopardy to health and anonymous summary reports by the Home Office are published; in favour is the benefit of public discussion and confidence in robust regulation). Anonymous disclosure was allowed. FS50077877 shows a not untypical use of s. 38. Information was requested about Tyne and Wear Anti-Fascist Association (TWAFA). Most of the information was disclosed apart from the redacted names and contact details of TWAFA staff and organisations associated with TWAFA. The IC decided that ss. 36, 38 and 40 were engaged. The complainant was not informed of all information held on TWAFA and so there was a breach of s. 1(1) FOIA. The requester was given information about grants given to TWAFA. Under s. 36, the PI favoured non-disclosure. Section 38 was also engaged and the PI favoured redaction of names and contact details.

Appeals[67]

Cases include EA/2006/0071 *Bucks Free Press v IC* (s. 31 above).

Section 39: environmental information

This section is dealt with in chapter 7.

Section 40: personal information or data[68]

This section is more conveniently dealt with in chapter 8 when the DPA is discussed.

---

[66] FS50140492 (s. 31 above); FS50098965 (s. 31 above); FS 50069091 (s. 31 above). See FS 50065053 (s. 41) below and FS 50149373.

[67] See EA/2007/0081 *D. Lawton v IC and NHS Direct* on interesting details on how phone call centres operate.

[68] S. 40 is often cited with other exemptions. FS50075174 (s. 43 below); FS50116589 (s. 41 below); FS 50123489 (s. 31 above). FS 50108122: request for information about a working party examining stakeholder relationships concerning a Country Park including submissions and notes of stakeholder meetings. Some information provided but ss. 21, 31, 36, and 40 were invoked. S. 21 applied and s. 40 had been applied correctly in part. Ss. 32 and 36 were wrongly applied and s. 40 should have applied to some information not identified as personal by the PA. There were inadequate explanations by the PA. FS50066908: CCTV footage covered by s. 40. In FS50179353 the complainant wrote to the FCO to request the names and job titles of the Russian diplomats who were expelled as a result of the diplomatic dispute following the murder of Alexander Litvinenko in London in 2006. The PA refused to disclose the information, relying on the exemption in s. 40 of the Act (personal information). The IC found that the requested information constituted personal data and its disclosure would breach the first data-protection principle which requires that personal data be processed fairly and

Section 41: information provided in confidence[69]

The specific words of this exemption should be recalled – disclosure of information from another, including a PA, where public disclosure would constitute an 'actionable' breach of confidence by that other. It says 'actionable', not winnable. However, MoJ guidance states, 'A breach of confidence will only be "actionable" if a person could bring a legal action and be successful.'[70] 'Could' implies a possibility, not certainty.

FS50111328 involved a request for information about ministerial declarations of interest under the ministerial code. Some information was disclosed but some was protected under s. 41.

FS50088977 involved a request for a copy of an ACAS agreement leading to reinstatement of senior police officer Ali Dizaei. Section 41 was not breached because the information was not provided to the PA by a third party – it was not 'obtained from a third party'. This follows the wording of the section and is narrower than the common law, which will protect information generated by employees of the PA that is confidential. Likewise, FS50065053 featured a request for information about a grievance procedure and settlement of legal claims against employees. The amounts received in settlement were not received from a third party and so s. 41 did not cover these.

FS50123005 concerned a complainant who requested information held by the United Kingdom Atomic Energy Authority (UKAEA) in connection with its meetings with its PR firm. The UKAEA refused to disclose the information, citing ss. 40, 41 and 43. During the course of the IC's investigation, the UKAEA disclosed the information withheld under ss. 40 and 43 but continued to withhold some information under s. 41. The IC found that there had been two procedural breaches under ss. 1 and 10. The IC decided that the s. 41 exemption did not apply because although the information had the necessary quality of confidence, it was not imparted in confidence and disclosure would not have been of detriment to the PR firm. It was for this latter reason that the IC also concluded that the PI weighed in favour of disclosure.

In FS50142318 the complainant requested a copy of a contract agreed by the Somerset NHS Primary Care Trust for the provision of an independent treatment centre. He also requested other additional documents related to the treatment centre. The PA refused to disclose some of the requested information on the basis of the exemptions contained in ss. 41 (confidential information) and 43(2) (prejudice to commercial interests) of the Act. The IC determined that some of the information contained in the contract, relating to how the service provider had calculated its prices, was exempt under s. 41 and a limited amount

---

lawfully. The IC decided that the PA dealt with the complainant's request in accordance with the Act.

[69] FS50088977 (above). FS50141388: an external assessor's report into an academic department was rightly protected by s. 41. FS50153967: request for records of exchanges between Tony Blair and Rupert Murdoch. All information was disclosed apart from two sentences protected by s. 41. FS50188864 on HEFCE. See R. Toulson and C.Phipps, *Confidentiality*, 2nd edn (2006).

[70] www.justice.gov.uk/docs/foi-exemption-s41.pdf, p. 2.

of information in the additional documents was exempt under s. 43(2), as it related to the PA's contract-management strategy. He ordered the remainder of the information that had been withheld to be disclosed.

FS50152888 concerned a complainant who asked Companies House to tell him the identity of an informant who had made allegations, he believed maliciously, about his company that had proved to be unfounded. Companies House had refused the request citing the s. 41 exemption. The IC found that, in refusing the request, Companies House had dealt with it in accordance with Pt 1 of the Freedom of Information Act; he also found no evidence of malicious intent on the part of the informant.

FS50155387 was a request for information on the commission payments made by investment managers on behalf of East Riding of Yorkshire Council. The council supplied the name of its investment manager. However, it claimed that the remainder of the information was exempt on the basis that the exemptions in s. 43(2) (commercial interests) and s. 41 (information held in confidence) applied. The IC decided that the exemption in s. 41 was partially applicable; however the PI defence inherent in the common law of confidence also meant that a disclosure of the majority of the information would not be actionable in law. The exemption was not therefore engaged by this information. The IC's decision was that the information should be disclosed to the complainant, with minor redactions.[71]

FS50146982 was a request for information about an internal inquiry into the death of a patient (Dr A who had committed suicide) and a decision not to hold an independent inquiry. Breaches of ss.1 and 17 were present. Sections 36 and 41 covered much of the information but s. 41 did not apply to all the information. On the question of s. 41 and medical records, the IC ruled that a duty of confidence survived the patient's death. Information obtained from the police was also protected by s. 41.

FS50116589 involved the cost to a PA (Health Trust) of legal proceedings against former employees. Not all the information was covered by s. 40 as not all was personal data. The IC had to serve an information notice (IN) on the PA – the latter argued that without an IN, a disclosure by them would amount to a breach of confidence and they needed the IN for their legal protection (para. 16). The investigation of the case by officials internally may have meant that the PI was sufficiently protected by their results, thereby removing the need for the requester to know directly – i.e., the inquiry and its findings when published would meet the PI. The total cost of the proceedings involved in the inquiry against the former employees was not protected by either section.

FS50105717 was a request to the Commission for Professional and Public Involvement in Health for an internal report about an investigation into the

---

[71] FS50155391 is similar to FS50155387 and is very detailed and one of thirty-six such reports. It was dealt with in the same manner with the same conclusion.

relationship between some NHS Patient Forum members and support organisations. Disclosure was ordered by the IC. Much of the information, including names, was publicly available. The IC made the important point that, in the PI of confidentiality at common law, the burden of establishing the PI, unlike the PI test under FOIA, is on the applicant for the information.

FS50101391 dealt with a request to the National Archives for information from the 1911 census. Despite the fact that there was a government undertaking that the information would be held in confidence for a hundred years, this was not conclusive per se but would be relevant where information was medical, concerned family relationships that would usually be kept secret, or was about very young children who were born in prison and whose birthplace is not recorded, or which is otherwise sensitive. The information here did not reach the *Campbell* criteria[72] (is there a reasonable expectation of privacy?) and was not of a confidential quality although some information was of that quality. The duty of confidence survives the death of a confidor (para. 44). 'Actionable' did not mean that a PA had to identify a personal representative (PR) to act as a plaintiff. Each 1911 census case must be treated on its merits. The point here is that the information was imparted in circumstances of confidence (a promise of confidentiality was not enough (para. 41)) and was protected by the 1889 Official Secrets Act which does reinforce confidentiality) but in most cases the confidence will now have evaporated, the IC believed. This is a strong judgement call by the IC.

Appeals[73]

In EA/2008/0018 *Department of Health v IC* Mr Stimson made a request for a copy of a contract between the DoH and Methods Consulting Ltd (Methods) for the provision of an electronic recruitment service for the NHS. The DoH refused, citing ss. 43 and 41. Much of the contract had been negotiated and specified by the DoH, but Methods had provided the finalised contract. The IC decided that ss. 41 and 43(1) were not engaged, and that whilst the information fell within the s. 43(2) exemption, disclosure was not likely to cause prejudice. The DoH appealed to the IT and the following issue under s. 41 was raised:

(a) whether the Commissioner erred in finding that s. 41 did not exempt disclosure . . .

The public authority claimed that the information fell within s. 41(1) because it had been provided to the authority by Methods and disclosure would amount to an actionable breach of confidence. The DoH argued that the following

---

[72] *Campbell v MGN Ltd* [2004] 2 All ER 995 (HL) see ch. 8, p. 280.

[73] EA/2007/0072 *BERR v IC and FoE*, see under s. 40 above. EA/2007/0105 *McBride v IC and MoJ* refers to *SoS HD v Br Union for the Abolition of Vivisection and the IC* [2008] EWHC 892 (QB). The IT appeal concerned requests for information protected by confidentiality. The appeal was partly allowed. See EA/2008/0059 *I. McLachlan v IC and Medical Research Council*.

factors were relevant: (i) the contract had been provided to DoH by Methods and was thus a proposal presented by Methods; (ii) alternatively all of the draft information was obtained from Methods and that no significant alterations were made, just minor clarifications; (iii) alternatively technical specifications and processes/methodologies were obtained which were certainly provided by Methods. The IT did not accept that the information had been 'obtained' from Methods. The information had been provided by the DoH and its inclusion in a document compiled by Methods at a later date did not transfer 'ownership' to Methods. Therefore s. 41 was not applicable and the question of confidentiality, actionability and the PI test under confidentiality were not considered because the information had not been provided by Methods to the DoH as the rule requires.

EA/2006/0014 *Derry City Council v IC* (see s. 43 below) is a leading case on s. 43 and has important points relating to s. 41. There was a request for the written agreement between Ryanair and Derry City Council for the former to use Derry airport. Sections 29, 41 and 43 were invoked. The contract itself between Derry City Council and Ryanair was not information *received* from a third party and therefore was not protected under s. 41 confidentiality. While this may seem questionable, to put it mildly, it follows the formulation of s. 41. A contract may often contain information received from the other party which they regard as confidential, either in the terms of a schedule or in its stated terms. A 'concluded contract between a PA and a third party [Ryanair] does not fall within s. 41(1)(a) FOIA'. A fax between the parties setting out the main points of agreement must be treated in the same way (para. 32(e)). It may be that some information on technical details in a schedule may be confidential. Commercial terms would usually be regarded as confidential and confidentiality attached to Ryanair's negotiations and contracts with airports (para. 34(c)). Confidentiality did cover the commercial information under s. 41. However, under common law within the confidentiality a PI may override the duty of confidence. Allowing the public to be informed of serious criticism from a reliable source of a value-for-money evaluation was a feature of the PI – 'the human rights highway leads to exactly the same outcome as the older road of equity and common law'.[74] The PI supported disclosure of 'key financial information in a contract, a redacted version of which had already been produced' (35(i)). An attached schedule spelt out the disclosed information which may be added to if an appeal is not made, or made and unsuccessful.

In EA/2007/0103 *Anderson v NI Parades Commission* there was a request from marchers for letters to the Commission criticising conduct of previous marches. The code issued under legislation said comments were treated in confidence. Section 41 applied and letters rightfully refused. Article 11 ECHR was not breached.[75]

[74] *London Regional Transport v The Mayor of London* [2001] EWCA Civ 1491, per Sedley LJ, at para. 35g.
[75] *Tweed v NI Parades Commission* [2006] UKHL 53, ch. 11, p. 454.

EA/2007/0116 *Health Professions Council (HPC) v IC* concerned the HPC which maintains a register of health professionals. The IC served an IN on HPC following a request for information after the requester had made a complaint about a health professional. Sections 30, 40 and particularly s. 41 were invoked. The HPC may investigate a complaint (via a committee) and did not want to disclose information to the IC that had come from health professionals (it argued 'in confidence'). It would undermine the intent of the scheme which was more informal than the previous disciplinary regime. The IT was not persuaded by these arguments (which came 'nowhere near the mark') denying the IC power to issue an IN to allow IC to inspect the documents. The IT noted special arrangement between the IC and MoJ (DCA) for handling of sensitive information and possibly similar arrangements should apply here it queried.[76]

EA/2006/0067 *J. Jenkins v IC and DEFRA* concerned a request for information from the Veterinary Medicines Directorate (under the Department for Environment, Food and Rural Affairs (DEFRA)) including '37 indexes and catalogues'. Sections 41, 43, 12 and 16 were engaged. A substantial amount of documentary information was supplied. The IC said indexes and catalogues should be disclosed. A European database on serious adverse reactions would not be supplied and Pfizer refused to consent to disclosure. There is a discussion of details of s. 12 calculations for charges (man-hours to retrieve etc.). Considering whether charging may be made to establish whether an exemption applies comes under reg. 6, not reg. 4. The IT, following *Hogan v Oxford City Council* said the focus is upon the PI as expressed in the *particular* exemption in question. The IC's decision that the PI did not merit disclosure of withheld information was upheld under ss. 41 (common-law test) and 43.

In EA/2006/0090 *P. Bluck v IC and Epsom etc. NHS Trust* information was requested by the parents about their daughter's death in hospital five years previously. The daughter's spouse refused consent as he was entitled to do. Confidentiality re deceased patient is still protected by s. 41.[77] PRs can bring breach of confidence actions making a claim 'actionable'. EA/2006/0030 *R. Tatam v IC and General Register Office* concerned a death which had been registered by the partner of the deceased and the requester wanted the registration amended. The request was for relevant documents covering registration. Section 41 was invoked. The appeal has some discussion of the jurisdictional basis of the PI under the law of confidentiality as opposed to the FOIA PI but the treatment requires fuller analysis than that given in the decision.[78] Confidence did attach

---

[76] Note *R (Secretary of State for the Home Department) v IC* [2006] EWHC 2958 – these could not stop the investigation but may operate to stop the IC getting information protected by national security. S. 59 FOIA also imposes criminal liability on IC and his office for wrongful disclosure of information (without authorisation).

[77] Para. 18.1 *et seq.*

[78] EA/2006/0084 *B. McTeggart v IC and Dept of Culture, Arts and Leisure* contained some useful discussion about the PI test under confidentially for ss. 41 and 40(2) (i.e., PI in law of

to this information, it was held. The requester argued that a PI overcame confidentiality because of an allegation of an offence of making a false statement by the partner. Paragraph 69 *et seq.* discusses 'actionability' regarding breach of confidence. The right is for access to information not documents but this refers to the fact that it is *information* that is protected by confidentiality.

Section 42: legal professional privilege (LPP)[79]

There have been some important decisions on s. 42 on appeals but FS50069105 concerned a request to the Legal Secretariat to the Law Officers for the final advice from the Attorney General on the legality of invading Iraq together with copies of earlier advice. Section 42(1) and other exemptions were invoked.[80] The advice was leaked, and then subsequently it was published by the Attorney General. Some additional information was also published.

Appeals

EA/2007/0054 *HM Treasury v IC* was an appeal from a DN in FS50081525. This concerned the convention that opinions of law officers of the Crown are not to be disclosed, and nor is the fact that their advice was sought, without their consent. The Treasury claimed this convention was an inbuilt immunity against disclosure. The IC disagreed. The information requested concerned an opinion on compatibility of the Financial Services and Markets Act with the European Convention on Human Rights (ECHR). A number of exemptions were prayed in aid: ss. 42(1), 35(1)(b) and NCND under ss. 35(1)(c), 35(3) and 2(1)(b). The IC found that reliance on exclusion of NCND in s. 35(3) was wrong (para. 54 *et seq.*). There were numerous examples of breach of the convention by governments in the past including the Westland episode, the Scott Report, the advice on the decision in *Factortame*[81] and the war on Iraq (see above).[82] The convention is subject to the FOIA. Neither the convention nor s. 42 provided an absolute immunity although s. 42 is a powerful exemption nonetheless. The IT upheld the IC who determined that s. 35(3) was incorrectly applied and required the appellant to confirm or deny that it held law officers'

---

confidence itself, not under s. 41 because s. 41 is absolute). Accusations of bullying at work and witness statements were requested.

[79] See *BERR v O'Brien and IC* [2009] EWHC 164 (QB); FS50150138 (s. 44 below): s. 42 PI in favour of non-disclosure (discussion of *Bellamy*). FS50081525 (s. 35 above). FS50093501: Ss. 42 and 40 claimed. The impact of *Durant* decision is discussed. Some emails not covered by s. 42 because a legal adviser was not involved. Where s. 42 applied, the PI was in favour of non-disclosure. The requester wanted his data and s. 40 was properly invoked (request should be made under DPA). See FS50193355.

[80] Ss. 35(1)(a)–(c), 40(1) and 27(1)–(2). See Cabinet Office and Legal Secretariat to the Law Officers, *Legality of Military Action in Iraq Disclosure Statement*, www.ico.gov.uk/upload/documents/library/freedom_of_information/notices/appendix_6_disclosure_statement.pdf.

[81] *R v Secretary of State for Transport, ex p. Factortame Ltd* [1990] 2 AC 85 etc.

[82] See para. 117.

advice in relation to the subject matter of the request. The High Court reversed this finding in relation to s.35 (see n 45 above).

EA/2007/0092 *FCO v IC* saw an appeal allowed concerning the Zimbabwean Pension Fund and the FCO legal adviser's opinion thereon. There was a discussion on *Kirkaldie v IC and Thanet DC* and the 'cherry-picking' rule on disclosure which provides that a 'collateral waiver', i.e. partial disclosure, removes the privilege. This only applies says the IT to disclosure in litigation.[83] In EA/2006/001 *Kirkaldie v IC Thanet DC* the IT ruled legal privilege had been waived when a councillor made a public statement about advice from a lawyer. In *Kirkaldie* the IT was not advised on the limits of collateral waiver rule and reliance was placed upon *Kessler v IC* and *Mersey Tunnel Users Assoc v IC* below. The IT mistook the position. The partial-waiver rule only applies to disclosures in litigation. The PI in maintaining legal interest immunity under s. 42 has been emphasised although it is not absolute – there would have to be something unlawful or wilfully wrong about a PAs action to allow PI disclosure and not simply an argument based upon better understanding of the full legal or other basis for adopting a position.[84]

EA/2007/0052 *Mersey Tunnel Users Assoc v IT and Merseytravel* was an appeal about a dispute over access to counsel's opinion concerning the operating costs and financing of the Mersey Tunnel. A complex arrangement had been made to finance loans from income from users and there had been significant increases in charges. The PA argued that s. 42 protected information and the PI was not in favour of disclosure. Disputed information was seen by the requester (shown to him by the district auditor) but on a strict undertaking that it could not be passed on to others. The proceedings were brought to allow him to use the counsel's opinion. The IC and PA resisted the application of the doctrine of partial disclosure of a privileged document. Such waiver only applies to the litigation privilege – not to legal advice more generally. The IT repeated the 'strong in-built PI in s. 42' as a result of case law in the higher courts.[85] But it is not thereby promoted into an absolute exemption. The advice was ten and a half years old (by now almost fourteen years) and the PA pointed out that any legal action by the appellant was now statute barred (para. 46). The IT's concern was with transparency. The inbuilt PI in non-disclosure in s. 42 is a factor but here the PI in disclosure was paramount. A substantial amount of money had gone to one aspect of the public sector instead of to the fee-paying public. There had been no litigation. The countervailing PI arguments in favour of publication were stronger in this case than non-disclosure. The IT raised a query of whether LPP privilege is the same for all areas of law – Criminal, child care and so on – or whether the privilege may be nuanced.

EA/2007/0055 *Dr J. Pugh MP v IC and MoD* was concerned with a request for the response to two judgments of the ECJ on TUPE regulations and the Acquired

---

[83] *Nea Carteria Maritime Co. v Atlantic and Great Lakes Steamship Corp.* [1981] Com LR 139. Cf. other decisions where it was held to apply to disclosure at a council meeting: *Kirkaldie.*

[84] Paras. 29–30.   [85] *Three Rivers DC v Bank of England* [2004] UKHL 48.

Rights Directive. Section 42 was engaged and again found the IT wrestling with the nature of the PI in that section. The PI in preserving LPP is very strong and is reflected in the case law.[86] There is no 'inbuilt weight' automatically attaching to qualified exemptions. 'In the LPP exemption the weight of judicial opinion referred to in [the] cases gives the exemption itself greater weight and to that extent may be described as having an "inbuilt weight" requiring equally weighty PIs in favour of disclosure' (para. 40) – but that is not what the Act says! But the exemption is not 'exceptional' as the IC suggested. It is not converted into an absolute exemption. The PI here was in favour of maintaining the exemption.

EA/2007/0043 *J. Kessler QC v IC and HMRC* is another case concerning a request for information protected by s. 42 FOIA. The request was for the legal advice concerning removal of the 'professional trustee residence rule' given by DTI to HM Revenue and Customs. The PI favoured maintenance of exemption. The requester claimed privilege had been waived. The IT refused a request for an oral hearing. The advice was given by an 'in-house' lawyer and not an outside 'independent' practitioner. *Kirkaldie*, above, was distinguished. 'We are satisfied that the rule that by relying upon part of a privileged document before a court the party doing so waives privilege in the whole document does not apply to partial disclosure of privileged information outside the context of litigation.' 'There is an assumption built into the FOIA that disclosure of information by PAs on request is in the PI in order to promote transparency and accountability in relation to the activities of PAs. The strength of that interest and the strength of competing interests must be assessed on a case by case basis' (para. 57(d)). 'The passage of time since the creation of information may have an important bearing on the balancing exercise. As a general rule, the PI in maintaining an exemption diminishes over time' (para. 57(e)). 'In considering the PI factors in favour of maintaining the exemption, the focus should be upon the PI expressed explicitly or implicitly in the particular exemption provision at issue' (para. 57(f)). 'The PI factors in favour of disclosure are not so restricted and can take into account the general PIs in promotion of transparency, accountability, public understanding and involvement in the democratic process' (para. 57(g)). The factors to be balanced are set out at pp. 23–4. For disclosure:

a. It would further the understanding of and participation in the public debate of issues of the day, specifically an informed debate into the necessity of the measures.

b. It would promote accountability and transparency, oblige PAs to explain the reasons for decisions taken and allow the public to understand decisions made by public authorities.

c. It would allow individuals and companies to understand how decisions are reached by PAs.

d. As the decision has now been taken, disclosure would not impair any current decision making process.

---

[86] See *R v Derby Magistrates Court, ex p. B* [1995] 4 All ER 526 (HL).

e. Obtaining the advice did not involve the provision of confidential information.

f. Considerable damage has been and will continue to be caused to the UK professional trustee business.

g. It is impossible to lobby for change to the legislation without being provided with the advice.

h. There is no suggestion that disclosure would disadvantage the government in any legal proceedings.

i. The advice and legislation do not relate to tax avoidance.

j. The advice was not required with any urgency.

k. The government had made a specific promise to 'share its findings on the viability of tax simplifications with business' in the Pre-Budget Report 2007.

l. HMRC relied on the existence and conclusion of the advice as the sole justification of their decision to abolish the residence rule.

In favour of maintaining the exemption:

a. There is a strong PI in maintaining legal professional privilege. That is, to an individual or body seeking access to legal advice being able to communicate freely with legal advisors in confidence and being able to receive advice in confidence.

b. If legal advice were routinely disclosed, there would be a disincentive to such advice being sought and/or a disincentive to seeking advice on the basis of full and frank instructions.

c. If legal advice were routinely disclosed, caveats, qualifications or professional expressions of opinion might be given in advice which would therefore prevent free and frank correspondence between government and its legal advisers.

d. Legal advice in relation to policy matters should be obtained without the risk of that advice being prematurely disclosed.

e. It is important that legal advice includes a full assessment of all aspects of an issue, which may include arguments both for and against a conclusion, publication of this information may undermine public confidence in decision making and without comprehensive advice the quality of decision making would be reduced because it would not be fully informed and balanced.

f. There is a significant risk that the value placed on legal advice would be diminished if there is a lack of confidence that it had been provided without fear that it might be disclosed.

This does not constitute a simple counting exercise – 'great weight must be attached to the PI in the accountability and transparency of PAs and the decision-making process. A substantial PI would be served by disclosure of fuller reasoning on why the Government reached the conclusions it reached on the State aid' (in relation to abolition of the rule) (para. 69). However,

s. 42 PI was in favour of non-disclosure in this case because the issue was still live.[87]

EA/2005/0023 *C. Bellamy v IC and DTI (AP)* concerned s. 42 (legal profes-sional privilege) and s. 43 (exemptions). The balancing exercise of PI is very fact- and context-specific. Information was requested about two major competitors of the requester. The request was for the brief and evidence for Treasury counsel and the opinion of Treasury counsel including all meetings and correspondence. The IT viewed evidence (requested information) itself. The balancing exercise is a question of law and fact not discretion (para. 34) (again surely this is a question of judgement?). The information was rightly denied.

In EA/2008/0035 *Martin George v IC and the House of Lords Appointments Commission (HOLAC)* Mr Rosenbaum, an executive producer at the BBC, requested information from the HOLAC for minutes, agendas and papers of meetings. The HOLAC provided the information in a redacted form; the redacted passages were excluded on the basis of ss. 36(2)(b), 37(1)(b) and 40(2) (the latter was accepted by Mr Rosenbaum in respect of personal informa-tion). The IC decided that the information was not exempt on the basis of ss. 36 or 37, but considered that s. 42 was engaged in respect of the informa-tion for which legal professional privilege was claimed. The IC found that the PI favoured non-disclosure. The appellant appealed to the IT on the follow-ing grounds: (a) that the information contained nothing to which privilege attaches (b) that the PI was in favour of disclosure. The IT took these as the issues.

Issue (a)

The IT considered the case of *Three Rivers DC v Bank of England* and the IT decision *Jonathon Fuller*,[88] the 'general effect' or 'broad thrust' of legal advice is covered by the privilege. Considering the information involved, LPP was correctly claimed.

Issue (b)

There is a strong element of PI inbuilt into the privilege itself. The IT was 'satisfied that LPP has an inbuilt weight derived from its historical importance, it is a greater weight than that inherent in other exemptions to which the balancing test applies, but it can be countered by equally weighty arguments in favour of disclosure. If the scales are equal disclosure must take place.' The IT considered that the amount of information already in the public domain was of relevance (of which there was enough to inform the debate). However the IT decided that some of the redacted information must be disclosed because the

---

[87] EA/2006/0044 *T. Kitchener v IC and Derby CC (TP)*: s. 42 for barrister's opinion. PI in favour of non-disclosure. EA/2006/0048 *Dr Husbands v IC* saw the IC overruled regarding s. 42. Single-page VAT invoices were not covered by s. 42 but a letter from a solicitor detailing work and charges was covered. S. 41 was not engaged regarding the VAT invoices.

[88] EA/20050023.

decisions of the House of Lords impact upon the lives of the population and the members of the HOLAC have a significant influence on the composition of Parliament and thus its decisions (this being a submission of Mr Rosenbaum – affirmed by the IT).

Section 43: commercial interests[89]

FS50085775 (s. 35 above) contains a powerful statement in relation to s. 43 and the new context of transparency. 'PAs must expect a robust approach to the issue of commercial sensitivity, and be prepared for a greater degree of openness than prior to the advent of the Act' (para. 65).

In FS50168782 the complainant requested details of the budget and operating costs of the council's residential and care homes. The council refused the request on the basis of s. 43(2). It claimed that prejudice would be caused in respect of its purchase of goods and services and that negotiation with the independent care-home sector would be adversely impacted. The IC considered the ('less than well-reasoned') arguments of the public authority and found that the exemption in s. 43(2) was not engaged.

FS50169313 (s. 36 above) concerned a request to the British Museum and costs of loans for two exhibitions concerning the Parthenon Marbles and the Terracota Army. In relation to the fourth issue, the IC had to consider the scope of the request and determine whether it included a request as to the cost of the loan. He applied the IT decision in *Berend* and decided that as there were two objective readings to the request he must provide a response for both readings. He therefore considered whether the information relating to the cost of the loan was exempt under s. 43(2). He found that the information was exempt because there was a real and significant likelihood that disclosure would be likely to prejudice the museum's commercial interests (negotiating future contract prices etc.). The PI fell in favour of maintaining the exemption. Certain other information contained in the minutes was found not to be exempt under ss. 31(1)(a) and 43(2).

In FS50068391 the complainant submitted two requests to the BBC asking for copies of Alan Yentob's charge-card statement and an itemised breakdown of his expense claims. The BBC provided some information in response

---

[89] FS50124423: s. 43(2) does not protect information about a private contractor engaging in vehicle recovery work for a police force and see FS50131138 and the non-protection by s. 43(2) of tendering documents concerning prices quoted. FS50094496: information about a drug used to prevent dietary induced laminitis in horses – s. 43(2) engaged but the PI favours disclosure. FS50066054: s. 43 protects marketing strategies and public-relations information of the Post Office. The PI favoured a level playing field between the PO and its competitors. Disclosure would give an unfair advantage to the latter. Nor does s. 43(1) protect the Student Loans Company's 'Class Training Manual' used to train staff. The information was widely disseminated within the organisation and the SLC was in a monopoly position in providing student loans. FS50141374: the Net Present Value figures (premium paid by bidders to DfT) of unsuccessful bidders for the SW rail franchise were requested. S. 43 (2) was not engaged.

to both requests, but withheld details of certain payments on the basis that these payments related to activities falling outside the scope of the Act – this ground was rejected. The BBC also withheld details of some payments contained on the charge card on the basis of s. 40 because they related to Mr Yentob's personal expenditure. The IC decided that any personal expenditure on the charge card should not be disclosed because it was personal data and disclosure would have breached the first data-protection principle (mainly because he would not have expected the information to be disclosed and it would thus be unfair). The BBC argued that s. 43 applied to the remaining information. However, the IC failed to see how the BBC's commercial interests could be injured. It was thought possible that disclosure of the costs of producing programmes could lead to independent production companies realising they could charge more, but the information in the instant case was too small a part of the overall cost for that to happen. Therefore s. 43 did not apply.

FS50086077 was a case in which the complainant asked the BBC how much their new weather graphics cost. The BBC refused to provide the information on the basis that it was not a PA in relation to the complainant's request because the information was held for the purpose of journalism, art or literature within the meaning set out in sch. 1. This claim was rejected. As an alternative, the BBC applied the exemption under s. 43 to withhold the information. The IC then went on to consider the s. 43 exemption. The BBC argued that disclosure would be prejudicial to both Metra's (the weather graphics system creator) and its own commercial interests. Potential customers of Metra could use the information as a bargaining tool (especially as the system was still being bought at the time of the request), the contract was marked 'commercial in confidence' and Metra had not given its consent. The IC concluded that Metra's commercial interests would be prejudiced. The IC also thought that the BBC would suffer such prejudice because firms would be able to determine how much the BBC was willing to pay for certain systems and future transactions would be very similar. The IC considered the PI test and decided that it weighed in favour of non-disclosure. The BBC had argued that non-disclosure would protect its financial interests (and thus the interests of the public), that there was little PI in disclosure of the cost of such systems and transparency and accountability of the BBC was served by other oversight mechanisms.

FS50094891 centred on the Commonwealth Development Corporation (CDC), a government-owned company, which invests in private equity funds focused on emerging markets in developing parts of the world. The complainant requested the contract between CDC and Actis, one of its fund managers. CDC refused to disclose the contract on the basis that it was exempt under ss. 41 and 43 of the Act. The IC firstly established that CDC is a 'public authority' using ss. 3(1)(b) and 6(1)(a). In relation to the s. 43 exemption he considered CDC's five arguments against disclosure:

1. It would harm Actis' negotiating position when attracting new investors. Competitors would have direct insight into the terms and could thus undercut Actis and potential investors could use the information as a point of reference to negotiate more advantageous terms from Actis. The IC considered it necessary that Actis would enter into contracts with other investors. Because such evidence existed, he thought that the exemption would apply.
2. It would harm CDC's negotiating position when looking for new fund managers. Again the IC thought that CDC must have had a clear commitment to investing with other fund managers; the evidence supported this and the exemption was found to apply.
3. It would harm Actis' negotiating position when acquiring/disposing of investments. Counterparties may have been able to seek a lower price for disposal and would also have a bidding advantage at investment auctions. The IC thought that the exemption would apply for this reason.
4. It would prevent CDC from being able to invest in certain funds. CDC could have been treated as a 'second rate' investor because information on its dealings would be available to the public. The IC decided that the CDC's ability to invest in a number of investment funds would be damaged and its commercial interests would thus be harmed.
5. It would enable rivals to use proprietary information at no cost. The IC considered that there was insufficient evidence to demonstrate that the redacted sections constituted proprietary information which could be used by Actis' rivals to the detriment of Actis' commercial interests.

Overall the IC was of the view that the majority of the information fell within the s. 43 exemption. He considered the PI in relation to the exempted information. The arguments for disclosure were: transparency in government commercial arrangements (particularly as it was controversial and had the potential to create environmental, social and economic impacts) and scrutiny of checks and balances and the application of public funds. The arguments against disclosure were: that the industry was already regulated and subject to suitable disclosure, that the investment of public funds would be undermined, that CDC should be in a position to negotiate best price and that CDC would operate better in the knowledge that confidentiality would be preserved. The PI was deemed to weigh in favour of non-disclosure of the exempted information. As regards the remaining information, the s. 41 exemption did not apply because a contract does not constitute information passing from one party to another (above s. 41). The IC also decided that there had been a breach of s. 12 because CDC had stated that redaction would be too costly, however the s. 12 'cost' criteria do not include redaction.

FS50123488 is one of several cases involving the Financial Services Authority (FSA).[90] The financial regulator possesses very market sensitive information

---

[90] In FS 50106712 the IC rejected the application of the PI test under ss. 31 and 43 by the FSA because the information was now more than ten years old (under Pt V SI 2001/2188, s. 348

which could be very damaging if disclosed – for the market and individuals. The complainant made two requests for information to the FSA for information relating to a managing agency, his syndicate and Lloyd's. The FSA refused to disclose the information in the first request under s. 12 and the information in the second request under sections 44, 43, 40 and 31. The IC considered s. 44 to be engaged because disclosure was prohibited under s. 348 of the Financial Services and Markets Act (below). Vis-à-vis s. 43, the FSA stated that disclosure would: (a) reveal sensitive details as to commercial negotiations; (b) be likely to harm the FSA's efficiency and effectiveness; (c) adversely affect consumer confidence and affect various others' commercial interests. The IC did not consider s. 43 to be engaged. As regards the s. 31 exemption, the IC thought that the FSA performed the functions under s. 31(2), but did not consider prejudice likely. Section 40 covering personal information was considered to be engaged because disclosure would have contravened the fairness element of the first data-protection principle.[91]

In FS50131138 the complainant requested the council to release a copy of the tendering document submitted by the contractor awarded the contract to carry out maintenance work at the council leisure centre. The council responded, informing the complainant that it was willing to disclose a redacted version of the document, with the financial details edited out; it claimed exemption under s. 43. The IC rejected the arguments that disclosure would be prejudicial to the commercial interests of the contractor and/or the council. He concluded that third parties entering into business with a PA should be aware of the FOI decisions; accountability in the spending of public funds is important. Further, the concerns vis-à-vis disclosure did not appear to be raised by the contractor. The council claimed that disclosure could affect the achievement of best prices for future tenders and that disclosure would likely deter other contractors from working with the council. The IC rejected these arguments because the tendering process had finished eighteen months before the request and also no two tenders for work are the same.

FS50114967 concerned a request to the DoH about a procurement programme with Fujitsu. Most information was disclosed but the DoH refused to disclose an Additional Services Catalogue relying upon s. 43 FOIA. Four reasons were advanced and rejected.

operates retrospectively prior to the FSMA). The IC set out the following PI factors under s. 43: the ability of the FSA to have open and candid exchanges with regulated firms, and that any such exchanges (especially involving commercially sensitive information) should remain confidential: 'disclosure would be likely to discourage firms from entering into full and frank dialogue with the FSA; this could lead to a reduction in co-operation with the FSA which would harm the efficiency and effectiveness of the FSA as a regulator; disclosure of the information which was not exempted by section 44 could lead to the obtaining of an incomplete picture and potentially to incorrect conclusions'. S. 44 did protect some of the information but not s. 43(2).

[91] FS50123488 (s. 44 below), concerning the FSA. Some (most) information was protected by s. 348 FSMA but not all. The IC could not see that s. 43(2) was engaged to protect other information.

First, it would be prejudicial to its commercial interests; future prospective contractors may be dissuaded from bidding for contracts because concessions made in the negotiation process may ultimately be revealed to competitors. This argument was rejected chiefly on the ground that businesses should be aware of the assumption in favour of disclosure.

Secondly, disclosure would be prejudicial to its commercial relationship with other local service providers ('LSPs') who had negotiated separate contracts with Fujitsu. This argument was rejected because there was no evidence that the relationship between the DoH and other LSP's would be damaged, or how any such damage would prejudice the DoH. Also, the price schedule was only a small part of the catalogue and it did not contain details as to the negotiations.

Thirdly, disclosure would dissuade Fujitsu from bidding for other public contracts. This was rejected on the same basis as the first.

Lastly, disclosure would provide an unwarranted commercial advantage to competitors of Fujitsu. This was rejected because the information contained no details as to the negotiations, or any other trade secrets.

FS 50107765 is another request to the BBC; this time for the amount paid to cover the 2006 Winter Olympic Games. The BBC argued without prejudice that it was exempt by s. 43. The IC ruled against this exemption. Under s. 43(2), the BBC argued it would provide competitors with valuable price information. Sensitivity of sports information is dealt with at paras. 37–8. Disclosure would be likely to lead to a ratchet effect on offers from rights' sellers. The Olympics must be shown by terrestrial TV (Broadcasting Act 1996). Commercial damage is not 'real or significant', the IC believed. The European Broadcasting Union is the seller of rights in Europe and they already know what the BBC had paid previously. Any damage was no more than 'hypothetical' and s. 43(2) was not engaged.[92] In FS50122723 s. 43(2) was invoked by the Royal Mail in response to a request for information: lost items of mail on a national basis. Competitors were not covered by a similar provision to disclose such information and Royal Mail did submit a report to Postcomm (Condition 8 of its licence). Its competitors could use the information to damage Royal Mail. 'Likely to prejudice' under s. 43 meant more than hypothetical or a remote possibility and that there must have been a 'real and significant risk'. There 'may very well be' prejudice. Postcomm had fined Royal Mail £11.38 million for insufficient protection of mail and a report was published. Disclosure of estimates of loss of special delivery items would assist public discussion. On balance, the PI favoured disclosure.

FS50075174 is an interesting illustration of the balance of interest involved in disclosure or non-disclosure. A request was made for a list of all child-care providers served with notices of intention to cancel registration since September 2001 plus a list of those where notice was subsequently cancelled together with unpublished inspection reports. Section 43(2) correctly applied and disclosure

---

[92] S. 43 was also engaged in FS50067416 (see ch. 8 on s. 40) regarding the John Daly show and the PI arguments were not in favour of publication. By not citing exemptions in its reply the BBC was in breach of s. 17.

would breach s. 40(2). Releasing information on childminders would breach s. 40(2) in circumstances of the case. Section 43 was engaged but information if released might mislead parents rather than assist them so the PI was in favour of retention. Notices were often issued for minor contraventions (late payment of licence fee) but publicity could be very damaging to the providers.

FS50101105 concerned a request to DEFRA for information about a tendering process for a research contract. The PA said s. 43 was engaged. The Refusal Notice failed adequately to explain why the exemption was engaged or why the PI favoured non-disclosure. A breach of s. 17 had occurred. Information detailing the rates charged for specific elements of the project was not commercially sensitive and s. 43 was not engaged even though it would allow insight into a company's internal pricing structure. It comprised a summary of costs, including overall cost, a breakdown of those costs detailing individual tasks, who would perform tasks, the number of days required and rates for a day. DEFRA said disclosing the total number working on a contract and costs per days would allow competitors to assess how the tenderer scoped and costed projects. This would not reveal the company's profit margins, however, which was the crucial aspect of commercial interest. This is a strong decision by the IC.[93]

In FS50163364 the complainant requested a copy of a document from Imperial College London University which was used as an informal guide by some of the public authority's staff to assist with decisions related to the recognition of overseas qualifications when recruiting students. The request was refused on the basis of s. 43(2). The authority argued that its commercial interests would be prejudiced because it was only an informal document which had not been approved by any college body; it therefore did not accurately reflect admissions policy and its release could be misleading and therefore damaging to the recruitment of students. The IC found that the exemption did not apply. He found that there was no real and significant risk of commercial prejudice. Further, potential applicants were of an academic standard to comprehend the nature of the document, provided it was accompanied by an explanatory note of its use and significance.

FS50102474 was a case in which a request for the cost of the 'Children in Need' programme in 2005 was refused (see s. 40, chapter 8). Specifically, how much went to presenters? The BBC said the FOIA did not apply to 'journalism etc.' on the familiar basis but this was rejected (see chapter 4, p. 141 and Introduction, p. 6). The IC therefore asked which exemptions the BBC wished to invoke. Sections 43 and 40 were relied upon. The BBC's relations with independent production companies would be damaged if the financial information was

---

[93] FS50153399 shows that the IC will look for evidence of damage. A request was made for bids received for an informal tender for property sale by the PA. S. 43 was unsuccessfully invoked by the PA and the exemption was not engaged. Details of the winning bid and some other bids were disclosed so IC found it difficult to see how disclosure of other bids would damage PA's commercial interests.

disclosed – competitors could outbid them. The IC was not convinced as bidding seems to operate in the BBC's favour. Some performers publicise their earnings – Jonathan Ross for instance. Section 43 was not engaged and, even if it were, the PI would favour disclosure (pp. 7–8).

FS50081543 involved copies of an invitation to tender issued to four bidders for a major rail franchise. The PA invoked ss. 43 and 22 as it intended to publish the information at a later date. The PA also invoked s. 36 (information likely to prejudice public affairs). The PA did release the information to the complainant once the franchise was awarded. The IC found s. 43 was not engaged at time of the request; s. 36 did apply but the PI was in favour of disclosure (discussion of service levels and/or protecting jobs) and under s. 22 there was no settled intention to publish the information at the time of the request. That was a breach of s. 10. The test for 'likely to prejudice' was: 'a very significant and weighty chance of prejudice: a real and significant risk'.[94] The sensitivity of documents from the PA's viewpoint is explained at para. 21. The IC believed there was no evidence of prejudice to bidders or disruption of the tendering process. FS50093000 (s. 35 above) concerned the Office of Government Commerce (ss. 26, 29 and 35 also claimed) and all documents relating to a ministerial direction to the Permanent Secretary MoD relating to the sale of Hawk jet trainers. Section 35 was not properly applied and, although s. 43 properly applied, the PI favoured disclosure of other parts of the information.

Appeals

EA/2005/0005 *J. Connor Press Associates Ltd v IC* overturned the IC's decision notice in FS50063478. The case concerned a discussion of 'likely to prejudice' commercial interests under s. 43. The applicant requested information and all documentation/correspondence relating to any payments made by the National Maritime Museum to C. Shawcross for an exhibition. The IT followed Munby J's ruling on 'likely to prejudice'.[95] No sufficient risk of prejudice to the commercial interests of the museum was demonstrated to justify the exemption under s. 43(2).

EA/2006/0014 *Derry City Council v IC* is a leading case on s. 41 (above) but deals with s. 43 as well. A request was made for a copy of the agreement between Ryanair and Derry City Council for the use of Derry airport. Sections 29, 41 and 43 were invoked. As noted above, the contract itself between Derry Council and Ryanair was not information received from a third party and therefore was not protected under s. 41 confidentiality. The agreement was made in 1999. It concerned a special deal for Ryanair from Derry Council over charges and fees, building extensions and other commercial spin-offs if it provided a flight service to Derry. The British and Irish governments were involved in discussions. Disclosure of information in 2005 would still have had the effect of giving any

---

[94] See discussion in ch. 5, p. 155.   [95] *Ibid.*

counterparty in negotiations some indication as to what the airport's 'bottom line' was. Section 43 rightly engaged but the PI test was in favour of disclosure because audit would not have provided 'for inspection of the contracts under which particular invoices may have been raised'.[96] The PI at time of request (five years later) was not sufficient to outweigh the PI in disclosure. If s. 43 was not successful, it was unlikely that s. 29 (economic interests) would be.

EA/2008/0018 *Department of Health v IC* was examined under s. 41 above. This was a request for a copy of a contract between the DoH and Methods Consulting Ltd (Methods) for the provision of an electronic recruitment service for the NHS. The DoH refused, citing ss. 43 and 41. Much of the contract had been negotiated and specified by the DoH, but Methods had provided the finalised contract. The IC decided that ss. 41 and 43(1) were not engaged, and that whilst the information fell within the s. 43(2) exemption, disclosure was not likely to cause prejudice. The DoH appealed to the IT and the following issues inter alia were raised:

(a) whether the IC erred in finding that the information was not a trade secret as required under s. 43(1)
(b) whether the IC erred in finding that s. 43(2) did not apply and if it did, whether disclosure was in the PI.

Issue (a)

The DoH claimed that the information was exempt from disclosure under s. 43(1). Whilst the IT accepted that the information was clearly used for the purposes of a trade and the release of the information would cause harm to Methods did not have the highest level of secrecy which a trade secret would appear to merit. Also, it would not have been difficult for a competitor to discover elements of the information and reproduce it.

Issue (b)

The IT considered that any of the information which could constitute a trade secret would more easily be exempt under s. 43(2). The DoH argued that disclosure would prejudice its commercial interests because: (i) its future negotiating position would be weakened; (ii) there would be no incentive for tenderers to be innovative and create products different to Methods'; (iii) other government departments' negotiations may be affected; (iv) there could have been a reduction in quality in respect of the service provided by Methods; (v) a reduction in the number of qualified tenderers would prejudice DoH's commercial position; (vi) other competing websites would have an unfair advantage. In respect of the information's commercial sensitivity, the IT found that some of the information remained secret, but some of the information had also been released (for example on the recruitment website). The IT found that some information should be disclosed in the PI and certain other information should not (a helpful PI

---

[96] On the case for PI in disclosure, see para. 26(a)–(i).

test analysis). A table was provided with reasons for disclosure/nondisclosure for each piece of information. There was also discussion on the impact of *OGC (Civil Procurement) Policy and Guidance version 1.1*. Section 1 of the guidance says that:

> Generally speaking, there is a PI in disclosing information about public procurement to ensure:
>
> - that there is transparency in the spending of public money;
> - that public money is being used effectively, and that public authorities are getting value for money when purchasing goods and services;
> - that authorities' procurement processes are conducted in an open and honest way.

The guidance sets out what should be disclosed and the DoH apparently had not consulted the guidance. Section 2 of the guidance covers information that should not usually be disclosed (see para. 88 *et seq.*).[97]

Section 44: prohibitions on disclosure[98]

This has been a widely resorted to exemption and it is absolute. FS50099223 involving a request to the MoD (above) decided that principles in Art 8 ECHR could not be reduced to a general prohibition under s. 44.[99] This has been attempted on several occasions.

FS50122432 saw the complainant make a request to the DoH regarding the release of details of abortion statistics for 2003, where those abortions had been carried out under 'ground (e)' involving a substantial risk of mental or physical injury to the foetus if born. Some information had already been published by the DoH in the annual abortion statistics for England and Wales. However, it suppressed statistics where the number of occurrences was less than ten, instead marking it as " . . .". The DoH refused to disclose this information, and cited s. 36 of the Act. After carrying out an internal review the DoH upheld the use of s. 36, and also cited ss. 40 and 44, as it believed that the disclosure of this information would be in breach of the Abortion Regulations 1991 for the purposes of s. 44. During the course of the investigation the DoH informed the IC that it was only relying upon ss. 40 and 44 to withhold the information in question. After considering the circumstances of the case the IC decided that the requested information was not personal data, and that therefore s. 40

---

[97] See EA/2008/0047 *FSA v IC and Riverstone Managing Agency Ltd* and EA/2008/0082 *J. Jamal v IC*.

[98] In FS50104541, s. 44 was not engaged by virtue of the Reporting of Injuries, Diseases and Dangerous Occurrences Regs. 1995. In FS50186715 *Legal Services Commission*, s. 38 Legal Aid Act 1998 was correctly invoked to activate s. 44 and maintain the exemption (and see s. 20 Access to Justice Act 1999). FS50213881 *The Office for National Statistics*; FS50181641 *HMRC*. See *Dumfries and Galloway Council v Scottish IC* [2008] SC 327.

[99] EA/2006/0090 *Buck v ICO and St Hellier Uni Hospital Trust*; and EA/2006/0090 *P. Bluck v IC and Epsom etc. NHS Trust*.

was not engaged. He also decided that the disclosure of the withheld information would not be in breach of the Abortion Regulations 1991, and therefore
s. 44 was not engaged. Therefore he required that the withheld information be
released. Additionally the IC also decided that the DoH had acted in breach
of s. 17(1), as it had taken longer than twenty working days to issue a refusal
notice.

In FS50082955 the complainant requested a copy of a draft report prepared
by FIMBRA (Financial Intermediaries, Managers and Brokers Regulatory Association), a predecessor of the FSA concerning events in the 1980s and 1990s in
relation to each building society who ignored risk warnings from the Building Societies Commission on marketing of equity release schemes in the late
1980s.[100] The Financial Services and Markets Act 2000 (FSMA) applied to
FIMBRA and other self regulatory organisations. The FSA withheld the draft
report under ss. 43 and 44 of FOIA (s. 348 FSMA). Section 44 would cover
background information but not 'opinion' information, the IC believed – i.e.,
the opinion of one regulator passed to another represented self-generated information! Section 348 places restrictions on the disclosure by a primary recipient
(FSA) of 'confidential information' as defined which relates to the business or
other affairs of any person and which was received by the 'primary recipient'
for the purposes of the FSA. Information from one regulator to another would
be protected by this provision, it is submitted. Section 349 allows gateways for
disclosure for various public official functions.[101] Opinion information could
be covered by FOIA s. 43 in that it might affect the commercial interests of the
building society involved; it was an unverified report and it had led to proceedings in the High Court leading to an apology from FIMBRA. The requested
report had been leaked and the requester argued it was in the public domain
(s. 180 Financial Services Act 1986). The IC accepted an unauthorised leak did
not put the document in the public domain. The IC investigated the application of these exemptions and found that the FSA was correct to apply both of
them and that opinion information was protected by s. 43 and by the PI in
non-disclosure. This decision notice is currently under appeal to the IT.

FS50137528 was a request for all the sales data for a specified location. The
Valuation Office Agency (VOA) claimed s. 12 applied and some information
was protected by s. 44. The IC found that s. 12 was not in issue as cost would
not be exceeded but s. 44 was applicable – s. 18 Commissioners for Revenue
and Customs Act 2005 prohibited disclosure of information held for a function
of HMRC and also where disclosure would identify a person to whom information relates. The VOA is an agency of HMRC. If a property address were

---

[100] See FS50106712 (s. 43 above).
[101] See also SI 2001/2188. The s. 348 protection is retrospective and protects information received
prior to the FSMA. See *Real Estate Opportunities Ltd v Aberdeen Asset Managers Jersey Ltd*
[2007] 2 All ER 791 [2007] EWCA Civ 197 for a discussion of ss. 348, 349 and 391 FSMA 2000
and *FSA v IC* EA/2008/0061.

disclosed a 'historical title register search' at HM Land Registry would then reveal person's identity. *Slann v FSA* EA/2005/0019 decided that a 'function' under s. 349 FSMA (above) which allows disclosure was one under the parent statute and NOT a disclosure under the FOIA. The same principle was applied here.

FS50074331 was a request to HMRC for correspondence with three tobacco firms which led to a memorandum of understanding between the PA and companies to reduce tobacco smuggling. There is a useful description of the IC's procedures for asking for information from a PA. Section 44 was invoked (s. 182 Finance Act 1989 – which prohibits release of information about an identifiable individual by tax authorities, and s. 18 and 23 Commissioners for Customs and Revenue Act 2005 (CCRA)). Section 182(5) does allow disclosure for lawful authority etc. The FOIA did not provide such and it had to be a disclosure within the terms of the parent statute. Section 18 CCRA prohibits disclosure of information held by HMRC in connection with a function of HMRC.[102]

FS50150138 was a request made for information about an investigation into the requester by the FSA. Some of this was covered by the DPA. The remaining information was protected by ss. 40, 44 and 42. Documents disclosed included letters from former clients with names, addresses and contact details redacted under s. 40; and other items redacted under ss. 42 and 44. Redacted items included material relating to the investigation against the requester and possible regulatory action in relation to the pensions review. In relation to s. 44, the relevant provision was s. 348 FSMA and it protected confidential information obtained for the FSA's regulatory functions. Disclosure of information to carry out a public function of the FSA related to functions under the FSMA and not general duties such as the FOIA (see *Slann* above).[103] This approach was upheld in EA/2007/0136 *J. Calland v IC*.

FS50075781 is another complaint in which information was requested from the FSA. This concerned companies setting inappropriate charges in formulating premiums when selling endowment mortgages. Section 43 was engaged but not s. 44 or s. 31. The summary contains a misleading analysis of the PI test: PI 'in disclosing the information outweighs that of maintaining the exemption'! The FSA argued that much of the information it obtains from companies is voluntary without the use of statutory compulsory powers. Section 171 FSMA allows compulsory acquisition of information. The informal arrangements assist co-operation but the IC was not convinced that s. 31 is engaged. The background to endowment policies meant that there was a good deal of PI in their discussion by informed parties – home purchase is the most important decision in most peoples' lives (para. 54) and the PI is in favour of

---

[102] See FS50168774 in similar vein and EA/2008/0067.
[103] FS50108125 (s. 36 above): disclosure under the FOIA was not a 'disclosure' for purposes of relevant statute and s. 44.

disclosure. Section 44 was invoked by virtue of s. 348 FMSA which provides a statutory bar to information where the information was confidential and the provider has not consented to disclosure. 'The FSA argues that a statutory bar exists because of . . . ss. 207 and 208 FMSA. These require the FSA to issue warning notices to companies about any formal action being considered by the FSA against them . . . Companies receiving such a notice then have a prescribed period to appeal the FSA's decision prior to its enforcement powers actually being used' (para. 56). Disclosing names would circumvent this and undermine due process, it was argued. This, said the FSA, would mean that UK law was not compatible with Human Rights Act rights (Arts. 6 and 8 ECHR). The IC did not agree.

> The IC considers that there is a significant difference between a formal statement of non compliance as published under these sections (207–8) and a disclosure under FOIA. A disclosure under FOIA requires no formal warning procedures and disclosure under this access regime differs from formal statement of non compliance issued by FSA in that information is not being issued by the regulator as a formal sanction under its enforcement powers. Accordingly the IC's decision is that there is no statutory prohibition in place on the disclosure of this information and therefore (leaving aside the HRA) the exemption in s. 44 FOIA does not apply. [Para. 60]

Articles 6 and 8 would not be interfered with by disclosure – Art. 6 because the company had not chosen to exercise its Art. 6 rights (para. 66) or its Art. 8 rights by insisting on a formal process by the FSA instead of the informal one. The companies acquiesced in informality. This seems to be very finely balanced. The IC was upheld on appeal: EA/2007/0093 and 0100.[104]

FS50112347 concerned a complaints file of the Local Government Ombudsman. Section 32(2) Local Goverment Act 1974 (LGA) prevented disclosure by s. 44 exemption. There was, however, a breach in relation to some information under s. 1 FOIA. FS50094124 also concerned the Local Government Ombudsman and a request for information about a complaint. The EIR applied viz. the reg. 12(5)(d) exception (confidentiality – see chapter 7 below) (as well as the FOIA). Section 32(2) LGA 1974 applied to most information and therefore s. 44 FOIA applied.[105]

FS50073646 was a request for information from the MoJ concerning a complaint the requester had made about a judge in dealing with his judicial review application and appeal proceedings. Exemptions in ss. 32, 36, 40, 41 and 42

---

[104] FS50123488 concerned a request to the FSA for information about a managing agent and Lloyds. The s. 348 prohibition covered information received from the regulated bodies (above). The IT held in *Slann v FSA* that the confidor should be asked about consent – here there was no point because they would refuse.

[105] See EA/2007/0094 *Edmunds v IC*: breach of s. 17 by local ombudsman was established but no steps were required to be taken – the IC had supplied reasons (s. 44 and LGA) and this was sufficient.

were invoked for different items of information. In relation to s. 44, s. 139 Constitutional Reform Act 2005 provides for confidentiality of information in relation to judicial appointments. Sections 32, 36 and 42 applied to protect different bundles of documents.

FS50126668 highlighted a problem where the IC is the object of a request – the IC is the PA involved and investigates himself! It concerned the complainant's papers on a DPA reference to the IC by another party. The first part of the request was refused because of s. 44 (s. 59 DPA). The complainant argued that as litigation had ended information was no longer required for that purpose under s. 59(2)(d). This was not relevant and there was no case for a PI disclosure under s. 59(2)(e) DPA. The IC receives regular requests for information about his work under the FOIA.

Appeals[106]

EA/2008/0002 *Craven v IC* concerned a request to the FSA for a report on a building society in the 1990s. The FSA refused relying on s. 44 (s. 348 FSMA) and s. 43. Background information from the building society was protected by s. 44. Opinions of the regulator were protected by s. 43. The IC did not believe opinions were protected by s. 44 because the information did not come from the confidor as required under s. 348, but they were protected by s. 43. The DN was upheld.

EA/2007/0112 *D. Barrett v IC and ONS* was a request for information about relatives from the 1921 census. It was refused under ss. 40(2), 41(1) and 44(1)(a).[107] The Public Records Act 1958 placed an embargo of one hundred years on public access (Instrument 12 1966) following informal undertakings to allow access after one hundred years. Section 44 applied. The IT questioned whether in the circumstances it was reasonable to rely upon s. 22 to withhold information until 2021! The DN was upheld.[108]

EA/2007/0089 *J. Allison v IC and HMRC* was a case in which s. 44 was involved but the IT delivered a warning that the FOIA was not to be employed to obtain 'reasons behind a decision' but was about access to information. It concerned a request by appellant to establish whether a pension fund complied with the Taxes Acts. The appellant was seeking *interpretations* under the FOIA, which is not permissible if not documented. The case involved ss. 18–20 Commissioners for Revenue and Customs Act 2005 which protects tax payers' confidentiality with certain 'gateways' as under the Financial Services Act (above). The DN was upheld.

---

[106] EA/2006/0059 *L. Meunier v IC and Nat Savings and Investment* witnessed a substituted DN. S. 44 was invoked. Information was requested on the premium bond winners for three months. Premium Savings Bond Regs. SI 1972/765 prohibiting disclosure applied.

[107] S. 8(2) Census Act 1921.   [108] Compare the decision in FS50101391 (s. 41 above).

EA/2007/0087 *CLA v IC* was one of the local ombudsman cases. It involved s. 32(2) LGA 1974 and s. 44 FOIA. Information obtained in the course of investigating a complaint by the ombudsman was properly exempt under s. 44. But some information was not obtained as a result of investigating a complaint by the ombudsman. The IT believed that information which does not refer to the complaint itself can be disclosed, including the name of the authority who is investigating, the mechanics of the investigation but which do not refer to substance of complaint, or evidence collected or issues of fact; nor is there protection for information about processes adopted or about ways of proceeding. They were not about the substance or subject of what was complained about. This is quite broad. Only information received from a third party, and not information passed between a Local Commissioner and an officer employed by him, is protected by s. 32(2). How far, one should ask, does this go? The IT was not impressed by the burden on the local ombudsman of separating protected and unprotected information in future cases.[109]

EA/2007/0101 *J. Hoyte v IC and CAA* was a request for a closure report (CR) after a Mandatory Occurrence Reporting Scheme (MOR) to the Civil Aviation Authority (CAA) concerning a hazardous or potentially hazardous flight incident or defect. The MOR was regulated under EC Directive 2003/42/EC and a statutory instrument (Air Nav. Gen. Regs. 2006) and Air Navigation Order. The requester reported his illness (caused, he believed, by contaminated cabin air) as a pilot and wanted access to the CR. Much information was disclosed but not the CR because of s. 44 FOIA (s. 23 Civil Aviation Authority Act 1982). The CAA had a discretion to disclose but refused. The flight operator was treated as a discloser of the incident to the CAA and not the pilot requester. There was no breach of discretion by the CAA and the requester's human rights had not been transgressed (Arts. 2, 6, 8 and 10). Surprise was expressed by the IT that the IC had not inspected the disputed documents himself.

EA/2007/0059 *British Union for Abolition of Vivisection v IC and Secretary of State Home Department* witnessed an appeal allowed in part. The case concerned the licensing of vivisection laboratories. Details have to be provided to the Home Office (HO). The HO decided to publish anonymised abstracts of licences on a voluntary basis. These did not have details of experiments and the IT believed that they contained 'positive spin'. The IC believed the information was given by licensees 'in confidence' to the HO (s. 24 Animals Scientific Procedure Act 1986 and s. 44 FOIA). Other sections were claimed but only s. 44 was dealt with by the IC because he ruled in the HOs favour. The appellants challenged this, arguing that 'in confidence' meant under a legal duty of confidence. If the law of confidence applies, then so does the common-law PI

---

[109] EA/2007/0046 *C. Parker v IC and Parliamentary Ombudsman*: The PO was in breach of s. 17. S. 44 prohibition invoked by virue of s. 15 Health Services Commissioner Act.

test with the onus on the person claiming PI in disclosure. The IT favoured the appellant's case. Not all of the information requested was covered by the law of confidentiality. Much of the information was already available even if it might lead to identification of those conducting experiments. The HO was ordered to review all information received from licensees to see which satisfied the law of confidentiality protection. This was a very strong decision and it was the subject of a successful appeal to the High Court and Court of Appeal.[110] The latter reversed the IT decision and upheld the High Court and IC ruling that 'in confidence' meant under s 24 of the 1986 Act and not under the law of confidentiality, by virtue of the FOIA. The words meant what they said and were not subject to interpretation according to the law of confidentiality.

EA/2006/0057 *M. Dey v IC and Office of Fair Trading (OFT)* was a request for information about a company providing goods via the Internet. Section 44 was invoked. The OFT relied upon s. 237 Enterprise Act 2002. The requester argued that gateways for access under that Act (ss. 239–43) overcome absolute exemption in s. 44. Sections 239–43 referred to disclosures in accordance with the 2002 Act, not under FOIA, repeating the point of other cases. Interestingly, a decision of the Scottish IC was not followed.[111]

EA/2005/0019 *N. Slann v IC and FSA (JP)* has been referred to on several occasions above. Information was requested which included statistics provided by building societies to the regulator (the FSA). Section 44 was invoked – s. 348 Financial Services and Markets Act 2000 and SI 2001/2188 detailing 'gateway' disclosures. Disclosure was allowed for functions under the FSMA or accompanying regulations and not for purposes of the FOIA, which applied generally and which contained dispensing words 'otherwise than under FOIA'. The information was not available to the FSA from any other source and treated as confidential by the FSA and not published. Section 44 applied.[112]

Conclusion

The IC and IT have interpreted and applied the law in a robust manner. No one can accuse them of favouritism towards government or public authorities. Indeed, the government has found their approach too robust in relation to Cabinet minutes and Parliament has been left with a deep sense of grievance in relation to MPs expenses and s. 40. This is examined in chapter 8 (see p. 309). The furore over MPs expenses threatened a constitutional crisis in the spring of 2009. Daily drip-feeds of MPs excesses and greed fomented a fierce public

---

[110] *Secretary of State HD v British Union for Abolition of Vivisection and IC* [2008] EWCA Civ 870 and [2008] EWHC 892.

[111] *D. Reid v Dumphries Council* 210/2006.

[112] In EA/2005/0008 *B. Higginson v IC* there was a request to the Independent Police Complaints Commission for information – denied by s. 44 (prohibition by s. 80 Police Act 1996).

outcry. The exposure of a huge scandal was a direct consequence of the FOIA although the information was leaked to the *Daily Telegraph* several months before the agreed date of publication. More is said about this episode in the Introduction above.

The work of the IT and IC involves the EIR and the DPA as amended by the FOIA. We now turn to these provisions.

7

Access to environmental information

The background

The Environmental Information Regulations 2004 (EIR), SI 2004/3391, form a free-standing provision giving access to environmental information (EI) as defined. Information available under these provisions will be exempt from access under the Freedom of Information Act 2000 (FOIA) by virtue of s. 39 FOIA, although the 'generality' of s. 21(1) FOIA is not restricted by s. 39(1) FOIA. This means that the exemption involving access by other means under s. 21 (see chapter 5) is available under the EIR. The regulations give effect to Council and EP Directive 2003/4 EC and the Aarhus Convention (the United Nations Economic Commission for Europe) on access to information, public participation in decision-making and access to justice in environmental matters signed by the UK in 1998.[1] This is a remarkable example of international agreement on access to information. Section 74 FOIA provides a power to make such regulations in domestic law. A code of practice applies to bodies covered by the regulations. The powers of the Information Commissioner (IC) also apply to the investigation and enforcement of the regulations.[2] Scottish public authorities (PAs), bodies under s. 80, will be covered by Scottish regulations.[3]

The Information Tribunal (IT) has produced some decisions introducing unnecessary complexity into the relationship between the FOIA and the EIR. In EA/2007/0065 *Rhondda Cynon Taff CBC v IC*[4] a copy of the Land Drainage Act 1991 was requested. The IC required the PA to disclose a copy of the Act. The IT believed it was EI. Under reg. 5(1) EIR, a PA that holds EI shall make it available on request. Regulation 5(6) says any rule of law preventing disclosure in accordance with these regulations shall not apply. Section 1(1) FOIA states that as regards 'held' information, an applicant is entitled to have 'that information communicated to him'. Section 21 FOIA deals with (and exempts) information 'otherwise reasonably accessible to the applicant'. Section 39 FOIA exempts EI from FOIA but the IT believed it is nonetheless subject to a s. 2 FOIA

---

[1] See *Aarhus Convention*, Cm. 4736, June 2000.
[2] www.defra.gov.uk/corporate/opengov/eir/pdf/cop-eir.pdf   [3] SSI 2004/520.
[4] See FS50122058 and FER0090259. See EA/2006/001 *Kirkaldie v IC and Thanet DC*

public-interest (PI) test. One may ask why? The EIR have their own PI test. The IC believed the two schemes are 'mutually exclusive' and EIR govern this application. The PA believed that s. 21 still had a role in environmental cases – indeed s. 39(3) FOIA says that s. 39(1)(a) 'does not limit the generality of s. 21(1)'. The two regimes are not 'mutually exclusive' said the IT – they 'run in parallel'. The FOIA provides a 'potential supplementary right of access to environmental information' (para. 32). The PA met its obligations under EIR but it was under an obligation via the FOIA to consider this request because it had not communicated the information to the applicant as s. 1(1)(b) FOIA requires. The IT believed a copy of the 1991 Act was 'reasonably accessible' and s. 21 was rightly claimed by the PA. This seems to make the relationship very complicated between the two regimes. Is it not better – and correct – to treat the EIR as exclusive, as the IC had done? *Quaere* whether this approach of the IT is correct? The two schemes do not run in parallel except for the provision of s. 21(1).

The 2004 EIR came into effect on 1 January 2005 – the same day as the access provisions in FOIA 2000 (see chapter 4). They implement Council Directive 2003/4/EC (OJ L 41/26). Under existing doctrine, where rights under the directive are directly effective they may be enforced through domestic courts if the government has failed correctly to implement the rights. The regulations share features of the FOIA as will be explained. So as well as using the machinery and procedures under the FOIA, the power of ministerial veto under s. 53 FOIA 2000 is retained under the regulations (reg. 18(6)). There are no absolute exemptions. A PI test covers *all* exceptions (exemptions). The detail of the 'exceptions' (exemptions) differs from the FOIA exemptions although there are some generic similarities. Emissions are given special treatment under the regulations (below). A requester for information does not have to make a written request as under FOIA. The EIR cover a wider range of bodies than the FOIA – although here again the IT decisions have been controversial (see p. 250 below). The regulations apply to all information held by a PA covered by the regulations. There is no 'appropriate limit' where the cost of compliance may be exceeded as in FOIA, s. 12 (see chapter 4). Requests must be responded to within twenty working days. This includes those involving PI considerations. An extension from twenty to forty days is allowed for 'complicated and high-volume requests'. There are mandatory provisions for internal complaints and second-opinion procedures on refusal to allow access. 'Working day' and 'historical record' are give the same meaning as under FOIA and DPA provisions may apply.

According to detailed guidance on the EIR published by the Department for Environment, Food and Rural Affairs (DEFRA), available at www.defra.gov.uk/corporate/policy/opengov/eir/guidance/full-guidance/pdf/guidance-6.pdf, 'any request, wherever it comes from, and whatever form it takes, will be a valid request for environmental information so long as the information requested is environmental' (ch. 6.1). The requester does not have to specify which regime a request is made under – this is the responsibility of the authority. Mistakes are frequently encountered. If it is not environmental, then a request under the FOIA should be considered. The authority, and not the applicant, has to identify which regime is operable and relevant where a request is made for information. If the applicant stipulates that the request is under the EIR this has no binding effect on the PA. The guidance offers assistance on who and what are covered by the EIR, what PAs are required to do, handling requests, exceptions, record keeping, offences and monitoring.

There is also a code of practice issued in accordance with EIR 2004, reg. 16 giving advice on 'desirable' practice. Chapters III–V of the code have details on processing applications including charges, clarifying the request and offering advice and assistance to requesters (see www.ico.gov.uk/upload/documents/library/environmental_info_reg/detailed_specialist_guides/environmental_information_regulations_code_of_practice.pdf). PAs must publish their procedures for handling requests. Chapter VI of the code advises on transfers of requests including to the National Archives or NI Public Records Office. Chapter VII provides guidance on consulting third parties. There is also guidance on training, proactive dissemination, public-sector contracts – which mirrors that in the earlier draft FOIA code under the FOIA 2000, s. 45 (see below), receiving information in confidence from third parties, consultation with devolved administrations and on review and complaints procedures. Some of these matters are also covered in the guidance.

The foreword to the code advises that, although not legally binding, failure to follow the code will render it difficult for bodies to comply with their legal obligations. Departures from the code for good reasons will have to be justified to the IC. Authorities are expected to deal with all requests for EI 'regardless of the cost'; there is no equivalent of the FOIA, s. 12 which lays down cost limits (see chapter 4). 'Unreasonable' requests may be refused under an exception (below).[5] The foreword to the code spells out the powers of the IC to issue practice directions and information notices as under the FOIA. The code provides guidance on copyright, which is likely to be very important in some EI.[6]

Contractual arrangements

Contractual arrangements will feature prominently in the EIR – nuclear decommissioning, or new build, for instance will rely entirely upon private contractors to undertake the major construction work. There will be sensitive questions of confidentiality and intellectual property in information associated with such work. The Office of Government Commerce has produced guidance on freedom of information (FOI) and contracting[7] and the s. 45 FOIA code offers advice on FOI and contracting (see chapter 5). The point was made that the

---

[5] There are no provisions dealing with organised campaigns as under the FOIA 2000.

[6] See www.hmso.gov.uk/copyright/managing_copyright.htm and www.hmso.gov.uk/copyright/guidance/gn_19.htm on advice on licensing under FOIA 2000 requests.

[7] www.ogc.gov.uk/documents/OGC_FOI_and_Civil_Procurement_guidance.pdf.

s. 45 code became more contractor-friendly in successive drafts. The EIR code looks and advises more in the spirit of the earlier and more robust and open drafts under s. 45. Authorities are advised that they should refuse to enter agreements that purport to restrict rights of access under the EIR (VIII, para. 47). Confidentiality clauses should be rejected where they relate to contractual terms, a contract's value and performance. The PI test should be explained to contractors. A schedule may be used to identify information which should not be disclosed, a position comparable to that under the FOIA, (see chapter 5). PAs are correctly reminded that such schedules are not immune from the EIR 2004 obligations and rights (para. 48). 'In any event, PAs should not agree to hold information "in confidence" which is not confidential in nature' (para. 49). Where the information relates to emissions, then commercial confidentiality, voluntarily supplied data (below) and other kinds of information (below) are not protected by exceptions. The code is emphatic that PAs should not agree to accept and hold information from third parties 'in confidence' unless it is confidential in nature (para. 51). The EIR regime is mandated by EU requirements and the more robust advice on encouraging openness is in line with the directive's requirements.

Environmental information

To implement the directive's definition of EI faithfully the regulations have to adopt a very wide approach and it is necessary to spell this out in quotation. It includes written, electronic, visual or audio information on:

1. the state of the elements of the environment, such as air, atmosphere, water, soil, land, landscape and natural sites, biological diversity and its components, including genetically modified organisms and the interaction among these elements;
2. factors affecting or likely to affect the environment referred to in 1 above such as substances, energy, noise, radiation or waste, including radioactive waste, emissions, discharges and other releases;
3. measures (including administrative measures) such as policies, legislation, plans, programmes, environmental agreements, and activities affecting or likely to affect the elements and factors in 1 and 2 above as well as measures or activities designed to protect those elements;
4. reports on the implementation of environmental legislation;
5. cost-benefit and other economic analyses and assumptions used within the framework of environmental measures and activities referred to in 3 above;
6. the state of human health and safety, including the contamination of the food chain, where relevant, conditions of human life, cultural sites and built structures inasmuch as they are or may be affected by the state of the environment, or factors, measures or activities affecting the environment referred to in 1 or, through those elements, by any of the matters referred to in (2) and (3) above.

Although extremely broad, there are some limits. The DEFRA guidance (para. 3) states that 'non-existent information . . . which could be created by manipulating existing information' or 'information that does not exist until further research is carried out' is not covered. There is no time limit on historical data. The regulations cover EI 'no matter when the information was created or gathered'. Both the code and guidance assist on the definitions.

Proactive availability

A significant feature of the EIR, like the FOIA, is the proactive and progressive public availability of EI that PAs hold. This will be by electronic means that are easily accessible.[8] PAs must take reasonable steps to organise the information relevant to their functions with a view to the active and systematic dissemination to the public of such information. This duty does not cover excepted information under reg. 12 (below). The information has also to include the facts and their analyses which the public authority considers relevant and important in framing major environmental policy proposals. The information will cover items contained in Art. 7(2) of the directive.[9]

Who is covered?

The definition of 'public authorities' in the directive, Art. 2.2 is broad and goes further than the FOIA. The starting point is to use the definitions of PAs under the FOIA, s. 3 and sch. 1 – with necessary modifications for the Scottish regime set out in the SFOIA and SSI 2004/520. Despite modifications in detail, the general framework is the same for both measures – EIR implementation is an EU requirement. The list of bodies covered by sch. 1 FOIA and that will be covered by EIR, but not including bodies scheduled 'only in relation to information of a specified description', is updated at www.foi.gov.uk/yourRights/publicauthorities.htm.

Designated bodies under s. 5 FOIA – there are none as of writing (see chapter 4) – are given special treatment. Bodies designated and falling within a 'specified description', or only covered by the FOIA in relation to 'information of a specified description', are not per se PAs under the EIR. National security is an exception. Originally the draft guidance stated that the security and intelligence

---

[8] Information collected before 1 January 2005 in non-electronic form is not covered.

[9] This is a comprehensive list covering: texts of international treaties, conventions or agreements, and of Community, national, regional or local legislation, on or relating to the environment; policies, plans and programmes relating to the environment; progress reports on implementation when held or prepared in electronic form; state of the environment reports from national, regional or local bodies which should be conducted at least every four years and which deal with the quality and pressures on the environment; data or summaries of data derived from the monitoring of activities affecting or likely to affect the environment; authorisations with a significant impact on the environment and environmental agreements or a reference to the place where such information can be requested or found in the framework of Art. 3 of the directive (the access provision); environmental impact studies and risk assessments concerning the environmental elements referred to in Art. 2(1)(a) or a reference to where the information may be found.

services were covered. The position is not clear because the exclusions under the FOIA seem to apply but would the services be covered as bodies carrying out 'functions of public administration' (below and EIR 2004, reg. 2(2)(c)). National security certificates would cover the services. The regulations do not apply to any public authority to the extent that it is acting in a judicial or legislative capacity. If a body is covered, there are no geographical restrictions to information.[10]

The breadth in the EU definition of bodies covered by the EIR, itself based on Aarhus, is shown by the inclusion of 'any other body, office holder or person (except a Scottish public authority which are to be covered by Scottish measures: SSI 2004/520) 'that carries out functions of public administration' (reg. 2(1)). The definition includes any other body, office-holder or person (except Scottish PA) that is under the control of a body, office-holder or person falling within the above definitions and that in relation to the environment:

  (i) has public responsibilities
 (ii) exercises functions of a public nature
(iii) provides public services.

Utilities as providers of public services and which are under licence from the state and that are state-regulated would be covered. The words would appear to cover private companies in which public bodies hold majority or controlling shares. They could be broad enough to cover contractors with government who are performing public duties or services, but the precise terms of a contract will have to be noted carefully. These provisions have already been tested before the IC and the IT. The guidance dated 27 July 2004 (which offers 'guidance' and not legally binding instructions) says, in para. 15, that the EIR include private companies and certain public private partnerships (PPPs) engaged in water, waste, transport and energy sectors. Private environmental consultants may be covered. The code of practice also describes 'control' as a 'relationship constituted by statute, regulations, rights, licence, contracts or other means which either separately or jointly confer the possibility of directly or indirectly exercising a decisive influence on a body' (Guidance, para. 2.19). Private companies 'sufficiently associated' with the activities of the government so that they owe similar environmental obligations 'have responsibilities under EIR 2004' (*ibid.*). On transparency and reporting on sustainability issues, see www.defra.gov.uk/environment/business/reporting/pdf/envkpi-guidelines.pdf.

The IC's decision in FER0087031 highlights an important point: Network Rail is not a PA under the FOIA but is such under the EIR. This, however, was successfully appealed to the IT in EA/2006/0061–62 *Network Rail Ltd v IC and NRI Ltd, FoE etc.* The case concerned the EIR 2004, reg. 2. A request was made for information about flooding along a railway line by the requester's home

---

[10] It is not restricted to information about practices etc. in one jurisdiction.

and on other work carried out by Network Rail Ltd. Network Rail Ltd denied it was a public authority for the purposes of the EIR. The IC found against NR Ltd. On appeal, NR Ltd argued information was held by NR Infrastructure Ltd (NRIL) – a wholly owned subsidiary of NR Ltd. The IT treated them as one concern for this judgment. The IT observed that 'The present government shows no sign of wishing to return the railways to public ownership or control' (para. 29). NR Ltd is owned by its shareholders but with government underwriting of loans. The IT believed that case law had established that there was no prospect of a claimant establishing that NRIL was a core or hybrid PA for the purposes of s. 6(3) Human Rights Act (HRA).[11] NR Ltd was not performing 'functions of public administration' and was not covered by EIR 2004, reg. 2(2)(c) (above). The IT felt that NR Ltd was independent despite powers of government to appoint special members and a special director and the fact that government largely finances it or underwrites its loans. These arguments are listed on p. 14–15. The IT described the situation as 'clearly unsatisfactory'. Regulation 2(2)(c) did not apply to NR Ltd and therefore reg. 2(2)(d) did not apply to NRIL; but *quaere* does 2(2)(d) not apply to NR Ltd?

A different conclusion was reached in EA/2006/0083 *Port of London Authority (PLA) v IC and another*. Here there was a request for information about a works licence granted by PLA in 1988 to a company. A request for more detail was responded to and the EIR were specified and a further explanation provided by the PLA. The PLA claimed it was not a PA under the EIR. Some disclosure was made. The IC in the decision notice (DN) said the PLA was a PA and bound by the EIR. Regulation 2(2)(c) was in issue again. Did the PLA engage in 'functions of public administration'? The UN Economic Commission for Europe's implementation guide to the Aarhus Convention and DEFRA's guide were adverted to for guidance. IC said the PLA falls within the EIR in relation to its River Works Licences' functions. The question is: are these functions governmental in nature? Are they part of a statutory scheme; would governmental provision need to be made if they did not exist; is there a statutory basis or is it contractual; is it accountable to government or to shareholders? The PLA is a statutory body. The duties are set out in statute. In performing its functions it must regard its statutory duties. Appointment of the board is heavily influenced by the Secretary of State. It reports to the minister. The minister may require further information. Loans may need approval of the minister. The functions of the PLA align them with a local authority or governmental authority and these include compulsory-purchase powers. It refers to itself in its contracts as a PA! It has powers not shared by the public generally or private bodies. The IT did not believe the commercial functions cited are 'entirely private functions'. Their commercial functions in licensing cannot be divorced from their public administration functions. The relevant function was public and was covered by statute.

---

[11] *Cameron v NRI Ltd* [2007] 1 WLR 163. See also *R (Weaver) v London and Quadrant Housing Trust* [2008] EWHC 1377 – a housing trust is a PA for the purposes of the HRA 1998; see FER0195081.

In FER149772 *Wesley Housing Association Ltd* the complainant made a request to a housing association (HA) under the EIR for access to all documents in relation to the development of specified sites. The HA refused the request on the grounds that it was not a PA for the purpose of the regulations. The IC found that the HA was a PA. The IC considered whether the HA carried out the functions of public administration, the relevant definition of which was 'the development, implementation and study of government policy. Public administration is linked to pursuing the public good by enhancing civil society and social justice.' The HA fell within this definition because its role was to build affordable housing for all needy groups. In this respect the IC considered that the HA was closely connected with the Department for Social Development (DSD). The DSD was responsible for the funding, monitoring, regulation and issuance of guidance and policy objectives. Whilst the HA had independent status and management, the DSD had ultimate control, with powers of intervention. The IC considered that the HA was exercising a public function in respect of the environment; the HA had to comply with various environmental regulations. The IC was also satisfied that the information request fell within the EIR.[12]

Holding information

Environmental information that a PA 'holds' is covered by the regulations and this includes information which it may hold on behalf of another. The definition of holding includes that information which it possesses but which it has produced for, or has received from, another. It includes that held by another person (not only authorities) on behalf of the authority. The guidance states that the EIR do not apply to privately owned papers of a purely personal nature belonging to staff of the PA (Guidance, para. 3.10). Special provision applies to privately owned archives.

Charges

Charges may be made for making the information requested available. Details on charging provisions are contained in the code of practice (pp. 13–14) and in chapter 6 of the guidance. Charges are not mandatory. Where imposed, they should be 'reasonable'. EA/2005/0014 *D. Markinson v IC* has an important discussion on charges under the EIR. Under the EIR, a PA charged £6.00–£6.50 for photocopying a document and 50p per sheet. Guidance from government says 5p–10p per sheet should be charged. The PA's policy was excessive. The PA failed to consider all the evidence. This was not a matter of discretion for the PA but it has to satisfy *Tameside* test.[13] It is not the 'unreasonable' test from *Wednesbury*.[14] A request for an advance payment may be made. The requester

---

[12] See also FS50114241on private companies as PAs.
[13] *Secretary of State for Education v Tameside MBC* [1976] 3 All ER 665 (HL).
[14] *Associated Provincial Pictures Houses Ltd v Wednesbury Corp.* [1948] 1 KB 223; *Secretary of State for Education and Science v Tameside MBC* [1977] AC 1014 has been approved in this context

has to be advised of the amount. PAs must make available a schedule of its charges and information on the circumstances in which a charge may be levied or waived. Where a charge is notified a PA is absolved from compliance with various duties under the regulations until payment.[15]

No charge can be made for allowing an applicant to access any public registers or lists of EI held by the PA. The Sustainable Development Unit (under DEFRA) maintains a register of environmental registers as required by EC law. Charging may not be made where information is made available for examination on the PA's premises.

Procedures for requesting EI

First, it should be noted that any enactment or rule of law such as the Official Secrets Acts (OSAs) that would prevent disclosure of information under these regulations – apart from the exceptions within the regulations – shall not apply.

Public authorities are under a duty to provide EI that they hold on request (reg. 5). Personal data about the requester is to be requested under the Data Protection Act (reg. 12(3) – see chapter 8). Personal data requested that do not refer to the applicant are dealt with in accordance with reg. 13. This mirrors the approach of the FOIA for third-party personal information (see chapter 8).

The duty is subject to provisions set out in the regulations and to the exceptions (exemptions). Information shall be made available as soon as possible and not later than twenty working days after the date of receipt of the request. The twenty-day period may be extended to forty working days where a request is complicated or covers a large number of documents and the PA reasonably believes that it 'is impracticable either to comply with the request within the earlier period or to make a decision to refuse to do so'. The authority has to inform the requester as soon as possible of this and no later than twenty working days after receipt of the request. Information compiled by the authority shall be accurate, up to date and comparable 'so far as the public authority reasonably believes'. Information that covers 'factors such as substances, energy, noise, radiation or waste, including radioactive waste, emissions, discharges and other releases into the environment, affecting or likely to affect the elements of the environment' is subject to an additional duty.[16] Insofar as the PA can do so, and if requested, the PA must inform the applicant of the place where information can be found on the 'measurement procedures, including methods of analysis, sampling, and pre-treatment of samples, used in compiling the information, or refer the applicant to the standardised procedures used'.

The PA must make the information available in the format requested unless it is reasonable to make the information available in another format or form, or it is already 'publicly available and easily accessible *to the applicant* in another form

---

by the IT: see EA/2005/0014 *D. Markinson v IC* above, i.e. all the evidence must be considered and properly addressed.

[15] Payment has to be made within sixty working days after the date of notification of any charge.

[16] Reg. 2(1)(a).

or format'. The guidance states that information may be requested in writing, by telephone, by email, or 'during a meeting or by sign language'.[17] If the request on format is not met, as soon as possible the PA must explain the reason for its decision. The same time limits apply as above. An explanation of the decision and opportunities to make representations and request a reconsideration has to be provided by the PA under reg. 11 (below). Advice must be given on enforcement and appeal provisions in reg. 18.

Under reg. 9 EIR, PAs shall provide advice and assistance to applicants 'so far as it would be reasonable to expect the PA to do so'. A requester may be required to provide more detail where a request is too general and assistance must be provided. The twenty-day time limit applies. Compliance with the code satisfies the duty of assistance.

Regulation 10 deals with transfers of requests. The code of practice and guidance advise on transfers.

Regulation 12 and exceptions from the duty of disclosure

EIR 2004, reg.12 contains the exceptions to disclosure.[18] The exceptions are to be construed 'restrictively', i.e. to encourage openness in accordance with the Directive. Regulation 12(2) states that 'A PA shall apply a presumption in favour of disclosure.' The code of practice also advises that in stating an exception the PAs should not simply 'paraphrase the wording of the exception'. Reasons for exceptions should be clear.

Furthermore under reg. 12(9) where the information relates to an emission, the exceptions in reg. 12(5)(d)–(g) (below) do not apply. These cover confidentiality of proceedings, commercial or industrial confidentiality, the interest of the person who provided that information (where that person was under no legal obligation to supply it and did not supply it in circumstances such that the PA was entitled to supply it to the public apart from the regulations and the person had not consented to its disclosure) and the protection of the environment to which the information relates.

Regulation 20 amends the FOIA, s. 39 to acknowledge the existence of the regulations – subject to exceptions, information available under the regulations is exempt under the FOIA. EA/2007/0065 *Rhondda Cynon Taff CBC v IC* was examined above in which the relationship of the two regimes, and some contestable assertions, were considered.[19]

Under reg. 12(1), PAs are entitled to refuse to disclose EI where an exception identified in reg. 12(4)–(5) (below) is present and 'in all the circumstances of the case, the PI in maintaining the exception outweighs the PI in disclosing the

---

[17] Guidance, ch. 6.   [18] The DEFRA guidance offers comments on the exceptions.

[19] EA/2007/0012 *P. Robinson v IC and ERYC* concerned information about a Tesco development in Beverley, East Yorkshire. The IC dealt with the case under the FOIA but should have dealt with it under the EIR. There was no difference in the circumstances of the case. The PA did not hold information.

information'. The case for secrecy has to outweigh that for disclosure. Where the balance is even, disclosure trumps as under the FOIA. The guidance provides advice on weighing the PIs. Information may be redacted where possible. Human rights under the HRA may be relevant (chapters 8 and 11).

Regulation 12(4)

Regulation 12(4) allows a PA (it possesses a discretion) to refuse to disclose EI on several grounds. These cover: where it does not hold that information when an applicant's request is received (reg. 12(4)(a)); the request for information is 'manifestly unreasonable' (reg. 12(4)(b)). (This last example would suggest a test that is satisfied immediately and which is basically unchallengeable. It would have to be an obvious abuse on the part of the applicant and not simply a difficult request.)

In FER0112249 *Department for the Environment, Food and Rural Affairs* the complainant requested information regarding the distribution of European Union Common Agricultural Policy subsidies. The PA refused disclosure on the basis of regs. 12–13 EIR (see below). The public authority argued that reg. 12 applied because the request was manifestly unreasonable in that it required extensive and costly extraction. However, the complainant had expressed a willingness to extract the information himself; therefore the IC found that reg. 12 was not engaged.

It may refuse disclosure where the request is formulated in too broad a manner and reg. 9 (above) has been complied with (reg. 12(4)(c)); the request refers to documents in the course of completion, that are 'unfinished' or are incomplete data (reg. 12(4)(d)). This covers situations where the documents are premature and need to be finalised. It should be noted that there is no requirement that disclosure would be misleading. The exception is protecting a policy which is still being developed or the statistics or material are not complete. Where information is finalised it may be possible to disclose information although documents are incomplete. There will be difficult judgement calls.

Finally under this group of exemptions disclosure may be refused where the request is for disclosure of 'internal communications' (reg. 12(4)(e)). The exception does not require the s. 36 FOIA qualification of 'the reasonable opinion of a qualified person' to be sought but the FOIA guidance on s. 36 should be followed (see chapter 5). Regulation 12(8) states that 'internal communications' includes communications between government departments.

EA/2006/0073 *FoE v IC and Export Credit Guarantee Dept. (ECGD)* saw an appeal allowed and a substituted DN. Did the EIR properly implement the Directive 2003/4/EC in relation to 'internal communications' in reg. 12(4)(e) above? The FoE requested from ECGD information about the application of credit in respect of the Sakhalin project and specifically correspondence circulating among departments about the 'sensitive' project concerning oil and gas development off an island (Russian) north of Japan and the risk presented thereby to the western grey whale. Evidence to the IT spelt out the huge environmental and social concerns in addition to concern about the whales. The request was denied on the basis of reg. 12(4)(e) to protect confidentiality and collective decision-making in government. The IC in his DN held that internal communications covered communications within a department as well as between departments. He upheld their decision on PI grounds. The IT accepted that the exemption applied to a PA comprising several departments. The IT believed that the PI in withholding the information did not outweigh that in disclosure. The IT did not want to engage in a comparative discussion of s. 35 FOIA and reg. 12(4)(e): 'the onus being to specify clearly and precisely the harm or harms that would be caused were disclosure to be ordered. If no such harm can clearly be made out given the effect and terms of reg 12(2), the balance must fall in favour of disclosure under the test in reg 12(1)(b)' (para. 53). The PI put forward by ECGD included collective responsibility and candour. The former is not a 'trump card'. The 'touchstone is the public interest' (para. 57). 'Life after FOIA has changed and had to change' (para. 61). The minister is accountable but it is not only his final decision which has to be scrutinised. Timing of a request is a factor to be considered. Arguably EIR may set a higher test in establishing an exception [than the FOIA] and a general resort to the 'chilling effect' on record keeping. The IT observed 'officials in all public authorities as well as ministers in government should now be fully aware of the risk that in a given case their notes and records, and indeed all exchanges in whatever form, are in principle susceptible to a request or order for disclosure' (para. 61). The project was not in its infancy or in any way preliminary and there was an undisputed public debate regarding all issues in the project. However, showing disunity in government would be unlikely to add weight to the PI in disclosure. No real prejudice was shown to decision-making and there was a genuine PI in the discussion and the information would enable the public better to understand an important issue. Two years had passed between the request for comments and the request for information. No evidence was presented of harm arising in 2005 of discussions in 2003. The existence of a large amount of published evidence/information was not relevant in this case – the requested information itself was not in the public domain. An appeal to the High Court from the IT was unsuccessful.[20]

EA/2008/0046 *Stephen Carpenter v IC and Stevenage Borough Council* concerned the FOIA and the EIR. Mr Carpenter requested information from the council regarding the council's sale of land to a company which then obtained planning permission and resold the land for a significant profit. The request was refused on the grounds that they were vexatious for the purposes of s. 14 or manifestly unreasonable under regs. 12(1) and 12(4)(b) of the EIR. This was the first IT case involving reg. 12(4)(b). Whilst the council had committed

---

[20] *ECGD v FoE* [2008] EWHC 638 (Admin).

some procedural breaches, the IC decided that it had correctly applied both the FOIA and the EIR. The main issue was whether the requests were manifestly unreasonable. The IT took into account the relevant factors for deciding s. 14 FOIA cases when interpreting reg. 12 (4)(b) (including Awareness Guidance 22). They decided that the requests were manifestly unreasonable because: (i) they were far too frequent – there were ten requests within twelve days; (ii) the requests were very similar in nature – imposing a burden of unnecessary duplication on the council; (iii) the tone of the communications was threatening, intemperate and harassing; (iv) much of the documentation had already been provided and the requests were therefore evidence of an obsessive and unreasonable attitude; (v) despite having made accusations against the council, at no stage did Mr Carpenter institute proceedings.

EA/2006/0043 *Lord Baker v IC and DCLG* saw an appeal allowed and a substituted DN. There had been a request for information relating to officials' submissions made to the deputy prime minister following the report of the inspector in the application to build Vauxhall Tower.[21] The inspector recommended permission be refused. The deputy prime minister allowed permission to build. Advice was received from officials on 8 December 2004 and 28 February 2005 before the deputy prime minister overruled the inspector. The advice was refused under reg. 12(4)(e) – internal communications. The IC said submissions as a whole should have been disclosed but officials' advice should not be. There were familiar arguments about a loss of candour etc. There are differences between s. 35 and reg. 12 but *DfES v IC and Evening Standard* provides broad guidance on these points. Evidence was submitted that, in local government, officials are more anxious to 'get it right' following the FOIA regime. Why should central government differ, queried the IT? Good management must insist on proper advice and recording of advice. *Conway v Rimmer*[22] set the scene for greater openness over forty years ago! In local government planning decisions, the officer's report is published for a meeting that is held in public. Voting takes place in public and reasons must be given. Pre-meeting discussions did not undermine the general requirement for openness. Inconsistencies between local government and central government were noted and questioned. Disclosure of advice and opinions *after* a decision was made public would not undermine to any significant extent the proper and effective performance of their duties. The PI did not weigh in favour of non-disclosure. Any legal challenge under s. 288 Town and Country Planning Act would be likely to be made on the basis of a minister's reasons and not officials' advice, the IT believed. What, however, if the advice had been legal advice?

In FER50092316 the complainant requested information relating to Luton Airport and the South East and East of England Regional Air Services Study (SERAS). Specifically, he requested any information provided to ministers as a basis for decisions on which options to take forward for Luton Airport for

---

[21] Cf. *Bushell v Secretary of State for the Environment* [1981] AC 75.   [22] [1968] AC 910.

appraisal in stage two of the SERAS study, together with any records of the ministers' decisions and the reasons for them. The Department for Transport (DfT) refused to disclose the information and cited s. 35 FOIA. During the investigation of the case the IC informed the DfT that the withheld information was EI, and should have been dealt with under the EIR 2004, and, in that scheme, reg. 14(3)(a) EIR had been breached. Subsequently the DfT informed the IC that it was relying upon reg. 12(4)(e) EIR to withhold the information in question. The IC decided that the information came within that provision, because it was of environmental interest and involved the disclosure of internal communications. The IC then considered the PI as required by reg. 12(1)(b). The arguments of the DfT were as follows:

1. That reg. 12(4)(e) recognised the need for 'self-contained space' for consideration of different policy options; that disclosure would be unhelpful and prejudicial because some of the issues were of a highly sensitive and controversial nature; that disclosure could reveal confidential policy and commercial priorities which might limit impartiality and collective responsibility. All of these arguments were rejected by the IC who acknowledged that the timing of a request is an important consideration (the instant case being four years post-decision). Once a decision has been made, the risk of disclosure prejudicing the policy process is likely to be reduced.
2. That public consultation and debate were only appropriate before policymaking. However the IC thought that disclosure would help inform a necessary continuing debate.
3. That part of the information may have had a doubtful veracity and disclosure could have undermined other government policy. On the contrary, the IC prioritised transparency and the correction of false assumptions.
4. That the information may have misrepresented more contemporary government thinking. This was rejected because the fact that information may be misleading or inaccurate is not a legitimate basis for withholding it.
5. That the commercial interests of both the then current and future airport's operator would be protected by non-disclosure. The lapse of time was considered to negate this.

In para. 41, the IC stated:

> The IC acknowledges that the timing of a request is a very important consideration in this type of situation where different policy options are being examined and debated . . . once a decision has been made on the policy . . . the risk of disclosure prejudicing the policy process is likely to be reduced.

Information relates to meetings occurring in 2001. No detailed evidence was given to the IC of harm from disclosure. Disclosure of information can still be useful after a policy has been announced to inform continuing debate. There is no PI in not revealing information because it may disclose that government assumptions were misplaced. Disclosure would help 'ensure transparency' (para. 48). The IC was unpersuaded that commercial interests of airport operators would be detrimentally affected or that disclosure would lead to lack of co-operation. The IC considered that where government policies could have such wide-ranging and serious implications on people's lives, the environment and the economy, that the PI was clearly in favour of disclosure. Disclosure would allow a 'more informed debate' on important issues (para. 65).

In FS50156849 the complainant requested a copy of the first draft of the Sir Rod Eddington Transport Study. The DfT confirmed that it held a copy of the first draft of the report, but it refused to disclose it, citing ss. 12, 35 and 36 of the FOIA. The DfT also stated that the report contained some EI, which was withheld under reg. 12(4)(e) EIR. The IC, however, was of the opinion that the information was entirely environmental. He looked at the definition of 'environmental information' in reg. 2(1) EIR and concluded that it would include information that would inform the public about the environmental matter under consideration and would therefore facilitate effective participation by the public in environmental decision-making. In light of this, the DfT had breached reg. 14 EIR. The IC went on to consider the possible exceptions. Regulation 4(1)(a) was considered not to provide an exception because it places an obligation on a public authority to proactively make EI publicly available. Regulation 12(4)(d) did not apply because the information was not 'material in the course of completion'; the final version of the study had already been completed. Regulation 12(4)(e) on internal communications did not apply because Sir Rod Eddington was considered to be an external independent advisor. The IC referred to Art. 4.2 of Directive 2003/4/EC on this point ('grounds for refusal . . . shall be interpreted in a restrictive way'). He did, however, accept that in some circumstances information provided by an independent advisor may be an internal communication if there was a contractual relationship or if the advisor was carrying out a function of the public authority.

FER0082566 concerned the Pesticides Safety Directorate (PSD) which is not named separately as a PA under the FOIA but is a part of DEFRA which is covered so the FOIA and EIR apply to PSD. The request was for a copy of advice provided by PSD to ministers following PSD's analysis and consideration of all submissions made during a public consultation into various issues surrounding crop spraying including effects on health. Statistical information in annexes was provided but not the advice itself. The EIR applied. The PA sought an exception through reg. 12(4)(e). The IC decided that the PI is in favour of disclosure. Paragraphs 22 et seq. discuss PI factors: thinking space; public debate; transparency and accountability; and good record-keeping. Disclosure will assist the public to understand how government formulates its decisions in this area.

FER0087774 concerned a request in 2005 for advice to the Energy Minister in 2001 on permission for a wind farm in west Wales. Section 36 FOIA was relied upon. The EIR were the relevant code. The IC held that the PA had not dealt with the request in accordance with regs. 5, 12 and 14. Regulation 12(4)(e) (internal communications) covered information for which s. 36 applied but the PI favoured disclosure. Some information was protected by reg. 12(5)(b) (course of justice) and reg. 13 (personal data). The PA failed to produce reasons for the PI argument. This amounted to a breach of reg. 14. The IC did not think reg. 12(4)(d) (unfinished documents) applied to drafts that were in themselves finished. Paragraphs 36–7 contain a very strong statement of the PI in knowing the range of options considered by the minister in relation to a matter which is the subject of considerable public concern and controversy. The IC did not accept the inhibition argument. Disclosure would give the public a clearer understanding of how decisions are made. It assisted the public to see that decisions were arrived at only after a 'careful consideration which incorporated alternative options'. The reasoning was heavily influenced by *Lord Baker v ICO and DCLG* and the PI in disclosure under reg. 12(4)(e) (above). *Some of the advice was of a legal nature and legal professional privilege (LPP) should be protected and no countervailing arguments overcame the PI in maintaining exception under reg. 12(5)(b) on this ground.*[23] This decision was reversed on appeal to the IT (EA/2008/0052).

FER0178729 concerned a request for a draft version of a subsequently published report (NIREX) on potential radioactive-waste storage sites. The IC believed that reg. 12(4)(d) was like s. 22 FOIA and that where a draft is published reg. 12(4)(d) cannot apply. Regulation 12(4)(e) was applicable (internal communications) but subject to the PI test in reg. 12(1)(b). The arguments were finely balanced and the IC drew on *ECGD v FoE* [2008] EWHC 638 (Admin) and its reliance on two IT appeals (*DfSS* and *SoS for Work and Pensions* – see chapter 6) where it was stated that even in class exemptions arguments were specific to the particular circumstances. The work here represented particularly candid and personal opinions of scientists and the IC was persuaded that the PI in reg. 12(4)(e) favoured non-disclosure.

Regulation 12(5)(a)–(g)

The exceptions in the EIR 2004, reg. 12(5)(a)–(g) are listed as follows. PAs may (again the discretionary nature of this power should be noted) refuse to disclose EI to the extent that disclosure would adversely affect (not it should be noted 'could' so a greater degree of certainty and supporting justification would be required):[24]

(a) international relations, defence, national security or public safety. Regulation 15 makes provision for ministerial certificates stating that an exception is required for national security and the PI does not favour disclosure (see chapter 4). The IT may hear an appeal against the certificate (reg. 18(7))[25]

(b) the course of justice (e.g., law enforcement), the ability of a person to receive a fair trial or the ability of a PA to conduct an inquiry of a criminal or disciplinary nature.

---

[23] See FER0087051 on calling in planning applications by the Office of the deputy prime minister.
[24] 'Would' is used throughout the FOIA.   [25] See FER0162453

EA/2007/0074 *Christopher Boddy v IC and North Norfolk District Council* was an appeal to the IT from a decision of the IC. Mr Boddy sought disclosure of counsel's legal advice obtained by the council concerning the development of certain land in Cromer, Norfolk. The original request for information concerned the properties North Lodge and North Lodge Park. The council refused disclosure, citing s. 42 of the FOIA (the Act). There appeared to be some confusion over the extent of the request; Mr Boddy wanted disclosure of legal advice relating to development of the Rocket House, but this was not explicit in his request. It later transpired that the council possessed legal advices in relation to Rocket House. The IC considered the case and decided that the matter fell within the EIR 2004. However, she stated that the exception in reg. 12(5)(b) would apply; the council was exempt from disclosure by way of LPP. The IT considered the issues as follows:

1. The interpretation of Mr Boddy's request. The IT considered regs. 5(1) and 9 EIR and stated that there is an obligation on the PA to advise and assist the application, which would include advice and assistance on the identity of the information sought so far as is reasonably practicable (an objective test). Therefore it is only if the request is unclear or ambiguous that it should be clarified with the applicant. The IT was of the opinion that the request in the instant case was absolutely clear and unambiguous; it made no reference to Rocket House.

2. Cessation of LPP. The IT applied the House of Lords' case *Three Rivers District Council and Others v Governor and Company of the Bank of England* [2004] UKHL48 on LPP. The IT decided that LPP had not ceased.

3. Application of reg. 12(5)(b). In EA/2006/001 *Kirkaldie v IC and Thanet District Council* reg. 12(5)(b) was applied to information subject to LPP. The test in this respect is whether the course of justice would be adversely affected by disclosure. The IT considered that it would be so affected because the possibility of litigation existed and it would not have been fair for there not to have been a level playing field; disclosure would have revealed the strengths and/or weaknesses of the case to the opposing side and would have adversely affected the course of justice.

4. The PI test. Regulation 12(1)(b) provides for consideration of the PI. It was noted that each case must be considered on its facts and that there is a presumption in favour of disclosure. There were several complaints from Mr Boddy, for example that the council was breaking restrictive covenants and was deceiving the public. However the IT rejected these arguments because they could all be dealt with through private or public legal proceedings. Further, if anybody wished to challenge the council over its actions, they would be able to take their own legal advice.

The IT dismissed the appeal and upheld the IC's decision.[26]

---

[26] EA/2007/0048 *W. Young v IC and DoE NI*, reg. 13 (personal data) and reg. 12(5)(b) (course of justice, fair trial or criminal or disciplinary enquiry by PA).

EA/2007/0022 *M. Watts v IC* was a case involving information requested about a meat supplier in reports by an Environmental Health Officer. Regulation 12(5)(b) was invoked. The requester was attempting to establish a connection with E. coli. For the exception to be engaged the 'effect' must be adverse, the exception must concern that adverse effect, it 'would affect' the course of justice etc. and, lastly, there must be a PI factor to be considered. This is narrower than s. 30 FOIA, which is not confined to information created after a criminal enquiry has commenced. The prospect of a public inquiry was not for criminal or disciplinary matters and so reg. 12(5)(b) and its exception did not apply.

EA/2006/0091 *R. Burgess v IC and Stafford BC* was a case dealing with LPP that had not been waived by the PA. A barrister's report was covered by reg. 12(5)(b) – would disclosure adversely affect a fair trial, the course of justice or inquiries of a criminal or disciplinary nature? *Kirkaldie v IC and Thanet DC* held that reg. 12(5)(b) covered LPP 'particularly where a PA is (or likely to be) involved in litigation'. Was LPP waived by the council giving information to a councillor? The IC believed not. The IT said it had not been waived after a discussion of the case law covered in chapter 6 (see p. 224). Regulation 12(5)(b) did apply. The PI did favour non-disclosure notwithstanding a presumption in favour of disclosure. Errors were noted in the IC's DN.

EA/2006/0037 *B. Archer v IC and Salisbury DC* involved a substituted DN. The case concerned the withholding of a joint report to a planning committee concerning enforcement decisions citing ss. 30, 31 and 42 FOIA. The IC upheld the council's case. The EIR governed the request. The EIR had not been complied with, the IT believed. Neither the PA nor the IC appreciated this. The situation where information was refused under the FOIA but the EIR were then considered on appeal was considered by the IT in *Kirkaldie v IC* where s. 42 was claimed and the IT believed that reg. 12(5)(b) was the relevant exemption and allowed it to be invoked by the council. Things might differ if an EIR exception bore no relationship to an FOIA exemption. Here it is difficult to say that regs. 12(4)(e), 12(5)(b) and 12(5)(d) are all so closely related to ss. 30–1 although there are similarities between reg. 12(5)(b) and ss. 30–1 (investigations) and between reg. 12(5)(b) and s. 42 (legal privilege). *Bowrick* did not appear to take such a strict line on relevance but it could be distinguished, the IT believed. Each case must be decided on its own facts. The IC had not seen the relevance of the EIR. But the regimes were new when the request was made. EIR exceptions may be invoked at the hearing but specific factors in the case plus the fact that requester had been able to make submissions on the EIR allowed them to be invoked and influenced the IT in its ruling. On the facts, the second part of report was covered by reg. 12(5)(b) and the PI favoured non-disclosure. Regulation 12(4)(d) (unfinished documents) was not relevant because it did not apply to the proceedings – and reg. 12(4)(e) (internal communications) favoured non-disclosure on PI grounds.[27] EA/2007/0137 *J. Stewart v IC* was a request for

---

[27] And see EA/2007/0133 *NW etc. Fisheries Committee v IC* (above).

a forensic accounting report commissioned by DEFRA into contractors after the foot-and-mouth outbreak in 2001. Regulation 12(4)(e), (5)(b) and (e) were invoked and the PI justified non-disclosure.[28]

Regulation 12(5)(c): intellectual property rights

EA/2006/0078 *Office of Communications v IC and T-Mobile (UK) Ltd* has been unsuccessfully appealed to the High Court but was partially successful on appeal to the Court of Appeal.[29] Information was requested from Ofcom concerning the location, ownership and technical attributes of mobile-phone cellular base stations. There was concern about radio frequency radiation in the form of electro-magnetic waves. Information had been provided to Ofcom by each company offering a mobile-phone service. The location of the stations can be found by maps on a website. But this did not show the whole database such as address, location and postcode or whether it is mounted on a particular kind of building or structure. The IC's DN in effect ordered these details to be disclosed. At the root of the request were the health aspects of base stations. The Stewart Report in 1999 recommended that a database be set up giving details of all base stations and their emissions. This was to include the name of the company, the grid reference, the height of antennae, the date transmission commenced, the frequency range and signal characteristics of transmission, the transmitter power and maximum legislative power output. This should be 'readily accessible' by the public allowing easy identification of all base stations within a defined geographical area. A voluntary scheme was brought into effect but mobile network operators (MNOs) did not want specific information about precise location, grid reference or address, or if equipment was mounted on a particular building or structure. The IT felt this represented a 'modest dilution' of the Stewart proposals. The MNOs wanted protection of commercially sensitive information arguing this was not detrimental to the Stewart proposals. The information available through the website was also available from local planning authorities. A request was made for information on base stations and Ofcom refused relying on reg. 6(1)(b) (information already publicly available). Grid references were not available. Subsequently Ofcom relied upon reg. 12(5)(a) (international relations, defence, national security or public safety) and reg. 12(5)(c) (intellectual property rights) arguing under reg. 12(1)(b) that the PI favoured non-disclosure. The information was also protected by confidentiality. The IC upheld the complaint of the requester. An appeal was made to the IT on basis that under reg. 12(1)(c) disclosure would have an adverse effect on Ofcom's database right or copyright in data on the website.

---

[28] See EA/2008/0013 *A. J. Maiden v IC abd BC of King's Lynn;* FER0178169.
[29] *R (Ofcom) v IC* [2008] EWHC 1445 and [2009] EWCA Civ 90. See *Home Office and MoJ v IC* [2009] 1611 (Admin).

Ofcom introduced an additional ground of appeal not argued before the IC – s. 44 FOIA and s. 393 Communications Act 2000.[30] Approaches to a new ground of appeal against a DN went both ways but it was decided to allow Ofcom to argue this because of the possibility of criminal proceedings in a breach of s. 393. The MNOs withdrew from the co-operative scheme when the IC found against Ofcom. Recital 10 of the directive was important for helping to define EI. Radio waves are an emission the IT believed thereby introducing the nullification/disapplication of the exception regarding reg. 12(9) – which it will be recalled provides that some exceptions do not apply to protect information about emissions. The names of the MNOs were within the EIR and so subject to a reg. 12(9) disapplication. In other cases the PI favoured disclosure. There were arguments that disclosure would *increase* vandalism etc. Although substantiated to some extent, vandalism was not considerable in itself and did not outweigh the PI in favour of publication advanced by Stewart. The PI, in respecting commercial interests of intellectual property rights, preventing the increase of criminal activity and the withdrawal of MNOs from the voluntary arrangements, were relevant (modification of licences may make voluntary arrangements a 'legal obligation' although MNOs would challenge this). The PI for one exception could not be aggregated and transferred to another exception. The PI in non-disclosure did not outweigh the PI in disclosure. If reg. 12(9) did not apply was information nonetheless 'confidential'? It had been made available to local authorities and it could be published, although to get a sensible picture of the whole would take a great deal of effort. In *Mars v Teknowledge*[31] Jacob J stated that information put into the public domain in encrypted form may still have lost its quality of confidentiality because it could be accessible by anyone with the necessary skill to decrypt! The information here was no longer confidential. Further, the information was not 'easily accessible' for the purposes of reg. 6.

Although there was an unsuccessful appeal to the High Court by Ofcom, the appeal was partially successful in the Court of Appeal ([2009] EWCA Civ 90). That court found that the exceptions could be weighed cumulatively in assessing the PI in disclosure and they did not have to be considered singularly – the sum is bigger than its parts. It disagreed with the IT and Laws LJ on this, and the case was remitted to the IT to reconsider this point noting that the IT could very well reach the same result. Looking at the exceptions in the aggregate would allow the *overall* PI to be assessed. The court did rule in favour of the IT that public benefit from the disclosure can be weighed against possible breaches of third-party intellectual property rights. Such rights to databases set out in the 1997 regulations could not of themselves defeat rights of access. Copyright does not defeat access rights. But using material in breach of copyright is still actionable (see chapter, 5 p. 179). The court also agreed with the IT and High Court that the names of the MNOs were EI and the PI in disclosure extended to these.

---

[30] Concerning general restrictions on disclosure of information.   [31] [2000] FSR 138.

Regulation 12(5)(d): the confidentiality of the proceedings of that or any other PA where such confidentiality is provided by law[32]

FER0086108 was a request for information under the EIR about two contractors cleaning up after a foot-and-mouth epidemic. Exceptions in reg. 12(3), (4)(e), (5)(d) and (e) were cited in relation to one contractor and reg. 12(5)(d) in relation to the second contractor against whom inquiries were proceeding. Regulation 12(4)(e), (5)(b) and (d) were properly relied upon by the first contractor and reg. 12(5)(d) by the second (confidentiality of proceedings). The reg. 12(5)(d) exception concerned a settlement at which information had been prepared exclusively for discussion at the meeting. The PI favoured non-disclosure because DEFRA's trustworthiness would be called into account if it breached the undertaking. It may also leave DEFRA liable to legal action.

Regulation 12(5)(e): the confidentiality of commercial or industrial information where such confidentiality is provided by law to protect a legitimate economic interest[33]

The guidance on contracts was examined above but this exception is not confined to contractual undertakings. Some comments are called for. This seems not as broad as the 'commercial interests' exemption in s. 43 FOIA. The EIR exception covers information protected by commercial or industrial confidentiality protected by law – either legislation, binding agreement or case law (see chapter 5, p. 170). There must be a legitimate economic interest to protect.[34] It might involve costs, prices or insight into a company's operating strategies. Confidentiality per se is not determinative – it must also relate to the protection of legitimate economic interests (Guidance 7.5.6.5). The guidance from the Ministry of Justice on s. 41 FOIA may be relevant but the EIR are not restricted to information obtained by the PA from the other contracting party and a breach of confidence is not referred to as 'actionable' (see chapter 6, p. 219). The environmental implications and impacts of all government contracts will have to be considered including mandatory central-government environmental purchasing policies and procurement practices. The Environmental Protection Act 1990, s. 22 allows information to be kept off a register and this may be a factor to consider. The Procurement Strategy for Local Government covers local government.

---

[32] Para 7.5.5.4 of the guidance advises that exemptions imposed by the local government access laws (see ch. 9, p. 369) do not operate to defeat the EIR 2004. Confidentiality will have to satisfy 'confidentiality' under the law, presumably the common law: See FS50094124.

[33] See FER0184376.

[34] See *Amway Corp. v Eurway International Ltd* Case No. CO/4553/98, [1974] RPC 82 ('the *BNRR* case'): legitimate economic interest also implies that the exception may be invoked only if disclosure would significantly damage the interest in question and assist its competitors' (Guidance, para. 7.5.6.2).

FER0079969 involved a complainant who requested information on a contract signed by the PA with a third-party waste-management company. He requested the price currently payable to the contractor for every tonne of waste dealt with – otherwise known as the 'gate fee'. The council claimed that the information was exempt from disclosure under the exception in reg. 12(5)(e) of the EIR 2004. The IC considered this argument and his decision was that the exception is not applicable. As the decision was finely balanced, the IC also considered, on the alternative assumption that reg. 12(5)(e) did apply, whether the PI in disclosing this information was outweighed by the PI in maintaining the exception. His decision was that it was not.

EA/2007/0133 *NW etc. Fisheries Committee v IC* concerned mussel fishing and a licensing authority and claims for exemption under ss. 41 and 43 FOIA. These were rejected but the IT believed the EIR were the relevant regime. Regulation 12(5)(e) was the relevant exception. Three points were made. Disclosure must have an adverse effect as specified. Secondly, the exception only covers the adverse effect. Thirdly, disclosure 'would' have that effect. The PI must favour non-disclosure and is subject to overriding presumption in favour of disclosure.[35] The information was not confidential and reg. 12(5)(e) was not engaged.

Regulation 12(5)(f): the interests of the person who provided the information

This will apply where the person who provided the information:

(i) was not under, and could not have been put under, any legal obligation to supply it to that or any other PA – the information was volunteered or disclosed to the PA as part of a voluntary undertaking in return possibly as a quid pro quo but without compulsion on the part of the PA

(ii) the person did not supply it in circumstances such that that or any other PA is entitled apart from these regulations to disclose it.

The latter is not free from ambiguity. If the FOIA disclosure applied then the proverbial coach and horses would be driven through this provision. This is another reason why the EIR should be regarded as a separate regime from the FOIA. The EIR are given an exemption under the FOIA so it would not be disclosable under the latter and is covered by the EIR. It does raise the question of whether information may be disclosed by a general discretion residing in a PA. The guidance assumes this may not be the case. Information protected by the law of confidentiality or by a valid agreement would not be disclosable by a PA but is subject to the PI test and the provision on emissions under EIR making it disclosable.

Finally:

(iii) the person has not consented to its disclosure.

[35] *Archer v IC* EA/2006/0037.

The restrictive practices court ruled that information contained in a concession agreement following negotiations between the parties is not fairly described as information 'supplied' by one party to another.[36]

Regulation 12(5)(g): the protection of the environment to which the information relates – where disclosure may lead to environmental damage by theft, pollution, exploitation.

The regulation adds that a PA may respond to a request for the purposes of reg. 12(1) by:

> neither confirming nor denying whether such information exists and is held by the PA, whether or not it holds such information, where that confirmation or denial would involve the disclosure of information which would adversely affect any of the interests referred to in [reg. 12(5)(a)] above and would not be in the PI under [reg. 12(1)(b)].

Such a confirmation or denial is subject to the PI test. In relation to this last point, 'whether information exists and is held by a PA is itself the disclosure of information' (reg. 12(7)).

Emissions

We have seen that special provision is made in reg. 12(9) where the EI to be disclosed relates to emissions. The exceptions above from reg. 12(5)(d)–(g) may not be relied upon by a PA in the case of emissions. Disclosure is the norm.

In FER0085500 the complainant requested a report into an application for a grant towards a proposed biomass generation plant. This was initially refused under ss. 41 (information provided in confidence) and 43 (commercial interests) of the Act. The information withheld fell within the definition of EI in the EIR and the PA should consider what exceptions from the EIR may apply. The PA cited reg. 12(5)(d) (confidentiality of proceedings of public authorities provided by law), (e) (commercial confidentiality) and (g) (environmental protection). The IC found that the information is on emissions and, therefore, reg. 12(9) applied. As reg. 12(9) provides that information on emissions cannot be subject to any of the exceptions provided in reg. 12(5)(d)–(g), the IC found that the exceptions cited by the PA were not engaged. The PA was required to disclose to the complainant the information withheld.

Severance of non-excepted information

Regulation 12(11) stipulates that nothing in the regulations allows EI to be withheld where it is held with other EI that is properly withheld under the

---

[36] See note 34 above.

regulations 'unless it is not reasonably capable of being separated from the other information' so as to make the EI available. Parts of documents not covered by an exception should be disclosed where it is reasonably severable.

Personal data[37]

There is the familiar complexity in relation to personal-data requests involved with other information. As under the FOIA, personal data of which the requester is the data subject must be requested under the Data Protection Act (DPA). Basically, where personal data about another person is sought it shall not be disclosed if the data-protection principles would be breached. These points are dealt with in chapter 8 (see p. 298). PAs may respond by neither confirming nor denying the existence or holding of such data under certain circumstances.

In FER0112249 *Department for the Environment, Food and Rural Affairs* the complainant requested information regarding the distribution of European Union Common Agricultural Policy subsidies. The PA refused disclosure on the basis of regs. 12 and 13 EIR (see above). As regards reg. 13, the PA claimed that the information could not be disclosed under the first data-protection principle. The IC rejected this argument. He accepted that the complainant had a legitimate interest, both as a member of the public and as a member of the press, in knowing how agricultural subsidies were distributed. Further, even though the information related to 'individuals' being paid the subsidy, they were not individuals in a personal capacity; they were individuals in a business capacity. In this case, communicating the details of the subsidy paid to a person in a business capacity was deemed justified.[38]

Refusals under regs. 12(1) or 13(1)[39]

Refusals under these regulations shall be in writing and must be *explained* to the applicant not later than twenty days after the date of receipt of the request.[40] Reasons must be given for a refusal under regs. 12(4)–(5) or 13. The factors a PA considered in making a PI decision have to be included in the reasons. Where a PA has relied on an exception relating to unfinished or incomplete documents (reg. 12(4)(d)), various duties apply including specifying the name of any other PA 'preparing the information and the estimated time within which the information will be finished or completed'. The duty only applies where it knows this information. The refusal notice has to contain advice to the applicant on rights of representation, enforcement and appeal (reg. 18).

---

[37] See FS50106206 and FER0087774.
[38] EA/2007/0048 *W. Young v IC and DoE NI* (see ch. 8).
[39] EA/2008/0054 *De Mello v IC and Environment Agency.*
[40] These provisions are in reg. 14: see FER0087774 (above).

Representations and reconsideration

The PA has to publicise its complaints procedure on its publication scheme. Any written reply from a requester expressing dissatisfaction should be treated as a complaint. A requester can make representations to a PA in relation to his request for EI. This may occur where he believes that the PA has failed to comply with the regulations concerning the request.[41] The representations must be in writing and must be made within forty working days after the date on which the applicant believes that the PA has failed to comply with the regulations. The representation and any evidence must be considered and no charge can be made. A decision on compliance with any requirement is made by the PA. No one who took part in the original decision should undertake an internal review. If this is not possible, internal reviews may have to be abandoned. The guidance and code of practice offer advice on such matters. The code states that, where the outcome of a complaint is that information should be disclosed that was previously withheld, the information in question should be disclosed as soon as possible and within the time limit. Suitable apologies should be made by the PA. A time limit of forty days is given from the date of receipt of a representation to send the PA's decision notice to the requester. The requester has to be informed on certain matters including rights of appeal.

Enforcement and appeal

The requester has appeal rights which again mirror, with some modifications, those under the FOIA (see chapters 4 and 5). These involve the IC and IT. There are offences of erasing, blocking, defacing etc. records by officials with the intent of preventing disclosure either wholly or partly. The provisions in the FOIA referring to exemptions for bodies dealing with security matters and national security are to be treated as a reference to information whose disclosure would adversely affect national security. The veto power under s. 53 applies to the EIR. Section 60 on appeals against national security notices applies to the EIR with modifications.

Costs orders

Costs orders may be awarded against parties for manifestly unreasonable, frivolous, vexatious or improper behaviour. EA/2006/0071 *M. Fowler v IC and Brighton and Hove City Council* saw an appeal allowed and a substituted DN. It concerned the EIR. Information was requested on waste removal and wheeled bins! The case revealed many procedural defects by the PA. The IT made the point that there would be no costs order against a party reasonably pursuing

---

[41] EIR 2004, reg. 11 (any 'requirement').

appeals. EA/2007/0036 *Milford Haven PA v IC and Third Parties* contains a discussion of costs order under IT rules and 'Manifestly unreasonable, frivolous' etc. behaviour under reg. 29 of those rules. The case has discussion of earlier authorities.

Conclusion

Although the EIR derive from an EC and international obligation, as explained, many of the exceptions (not exemptions although the meaning is the same) in the EIR have a broad similarity to exemptions in the FOIA. It will be recalled the two schemes run in tandem and are administered by the Office of the Information Commissioner. Nonetheless, as explained above, there are some significant differences in the two schemes.

The Aarhus Convention was not confined to access rights but also deals with access to justice. The Convention sought to encourage public participation in environmental decision-making. The UK Government believed that no innovations were required in the UK; public inquiries and registers complied with the duties in Aarhus. The access-to-justice right is provided by the internal complaints procedures and the mechanisms of the FOIA. Provisions under international conventions may be invoked but only after all domestic and international remedies have been utilised.[42] It should be recalled that the directive is subject to the usual provisions on direct effect.

The argument in favour of FOI as a human right which I address in chapter 13 is given considerable support by the Aarhus provisions. The courts have emphasised that a promise of 'the fullest public consultation' of the 'adult population of the UK' by the Government on its policy of nuclear new-build had to be matched by reality.[43] The consultation had not been clear on what decision it was leading to – what in fact became a change of Government policy to build new nuclear plants – and had not been accompanied by provision of essential information on economics and waste. Essential information from the Committee on Radioactive Waste Materials had been published after the consultation period was closed and the consultees were not given the chance to comment on this. The court awarded a declaration that the consultees' legitimate expectations had not been met and the decision was unlawful.

---

[42] See Art. 15 UNECE Convention on Access to Information, Public Participation in Decision Making and Access to Justice in Environmental Matters. Note Case C-459/03 *Commission of the European Union v Ireland* [2006] ECR I 4635 on EU law and international law.

[43] See *R (Greenpeace) v Secretary of State for Trade and Industry* [2007] EWHC 311 (Admin), at para. 88 for the quotation.

8

Privacy, access and data protection

The surveillance society

'I'll be watching you' is the motto of the twenty-first century. It is a familiar refrain but as we saw in chapter 1, the past lacked today's technology. In a report in January 2009, the House of Lords Constitution Committee reported on the extent of surveillance in the UK.[1] The following examples were provided (and see pp. 323–41). The National DNA Database (NDNAD) was being expanded and contains 'millions of samples',[2] new databases for a variety of public services were being introduced or developed, and there was a steady increase in the use of CCTV in both the public and private sector. There has been a profound and continuous expansion in the surveillance apparatus of both the state and the private sector. Today, computer databases and data-sharing, the monitoring of electronic communications, electronic identification, and public-area CCTV surveillance are ubiquitous and exert an influence over many aspects of our everyday lives. 'The expansion in the use of surveillance represents one of the most significant changes in the life of the nation since the end of the Second World War, and has been shaped by a succession of governments, public bodies, and private organisations' (para. 3). Widespread surveillance, whether collective or targeted, can be used for unjustifiably discriminatory purposes, it reported. A super database run by a private contractor tracking all phone and internet communications is planned to be operational by 2009. ContactPoint is intended to be a database that stores data on every child in England and Wales. The National Health Service Care Records Service (NHS CRS), a major part of the computerisation project in the NHS, will include a copy of every patient's medical record. The National Identity Register (NIR) will include information on everyone for the purposes of establishing and verifying their identities. A National Identity Scheme Commissioner under the National Identity Cards Act 2006 was to be appointed in 2009.

---

[1] *Surveillance: Citizens and the state*, HL 18 (2008–9); Government Reply, Cm. 7616 (2009).
[2] The Committee observed: 'Whilst a universal National DNA Database would be more logical than the current arrangements, we think that it would be undesirable both in principle on the grounds of civil liberties, and in practice on the grounds of cost.'

There had been 1,600 complaints to the Information Commissioner (IC) on sales of personal data from electoral register rolls – although from 2002 individuals may opt out of having their details on the published version. Data swapping/sharing has been perceived as a problem for decades – blanket powers for departments are contained in the Coroners and Justice Bill 2009.[3] A high-profile episode involved transfer of data to the USA concerning travellers to the USA, a transfer which the European Court of Justice (ECJ) ruled unlawful.[4]

The committee recommended that the government should consider expanding the remit of the IC to include responsibility for monitoring the effects of government and private surveillance practices on the rights of the public at large under Art. 8 of the European Convention on Human Rights (ECHR) (para. 137). But the committee's faith in executive self-restraint does not augur well: the proliferation of surveillance techniques and practices, which are the cause of present disquiet, has either been sanctioned by Parliament or simply 'growed like Topsy' without adequate restraint and safeguards.

Our privacy has gone. Privacy is a much larger issue than data protection. Privacy means the right to be left alone – the maintenance of the integrity of our identity, our private lives, our private information, our image, our physical and psychological integrity and the prevention of anyone making unauthorised invasions into or use of these attributes. In the UK laws have existed to protect personal data since 1984, now superseded by the Data Protection Act 1998 (DPA). The law seeks to protect data containing information about us from unlawful and unfair use. The 1984 Act dealt with computerised personal information. The 1998 Act, as we shall see, is not so confined. The DPA has subsumed the legislation and regulations that covered the topic of subject access to paper files in health, education (schools), social services and housing (known under the DPA as 'accessible information') as well as consumer credit. The DPA appeared a comprehensive provision but it has been amended by the Freedom of Information Act 2000 (FOIA) and has been subject to constant criticism. Questions have been raised as to whether it faithfully implements the EC Data Protection Directive and whether domestic judicial decisions are consistent with EC requirements.[5]

Until the 1998 and 2000 Acts, demands for laws covering paper records held by employers on employees had been stoutly resisted in spite of notorious episodes concerning abuses by self-styled private vetting agencies.[6] In March 2009 the IC issued a press release with details of a database held by a consulting

---

[3] Digital etc. Act 2007; Serious Crime Act 2007; Health Act 2006, ss. 44–55 allow for the compulsory disclosure of documents and matching, profiling, 'mining' are all commonplace.

[4] Case C-317–318/04 (30 May 2006): Europe makes deal with US over flight data details. See http://ec.europa.eu/justice_home/fsj/privacy/workinggroup/index_en.htm.

[5] *Durant v FSA* [2003] EWCA Civ 1746. The European Commission has an Article 29 Working Party comprising DPCs or officials from each member state. In April 2009 the European Commission called for tightening of UK privacy laws to protect Internet surfers as it launched legal proceedings against the UK.

[6] ICO, *What Price Privacy? Unlawful Trade in Confidential Personal Information*, HC 1056 (2006–7). See s. 3 Employment Relations Act 1999 and 'black lists'.

company with details of 3,213 construction workers. Data had been sold to over forty construction companies to vet individuals for employment.[7] Illegal 'blacking' – preventing people obtaining employment – had not disappeared. Reports from the IC's Office have detailed widespread bad practice and breaches of the DPA.[8] Negligent loss of data is commonplace. A notable example was HM Inland Revenue and Customs, which in 2008 lost files on 25 million people. Section 144 Criminal Justice and Immigration Act 2008 amending ss. 55A–E DPA seeks to address such shortcomings (p. 289 below). There are still serious lacunae in legislative protection, as will be explained. The possibilities involving unregulated use of genetic information are startling as indeed are the implications of commercial patenting of such information. The Department of Health sells information on its database that records patient reaction to pharmaceuticals.[9]

The Metropolitan Police, for instance, had refused to destroy 3,500 DNA profiles taken from people questioned but subsequently ruled-out of police investigations.[10] Subsequently the House of Lords ruled that legislation authorising DNA and fingerprint retention of those not convicted or prosecuted was not incompatible with the Human Rights Act (HRA).[11] The European Court of Human Rights (ECtHR) ruled that the blanket and indiscriminate retention of more than 857,000 records of those not convicted or charged without regard to time limits, seriousness or age breached Art. 8 ECHR.[12] The ECtHR has also ruled that CCTV coverage of a man attempting suicide in a public place, which was shown on UK TV, was a breach of his Art. 8 right to privacy.[13]

Privacy protection, human rights and common law

Before examining the 1998 Act as amended by the FOIA, it is important to realise what might be achieved under common law and what protection the ECHR

---

[7] ICO Press Release, 6 March 2009.

[8] *What Price Privacy?*; *Data Protection and Human Rights*, HL 72 (2007–8) JCHR; R. Thomas and M. Walport, *Data Transfer Review* (2008).

[9] See *R v Department of Health, ex p. Source Infomatics Ltd* [2000] 1 All ER 786, CA. A company wanted pharmacists to supply it for payment information about the prescription details of GPs with any personal information anonymised. In cases involving personal confidences, anonymised information, even if not in the public domain, would not be protected where there was no breach of confidence or privacy. The patients did not own the information or documents in question; See *Common Services Agency v SIC* [2008] UKHL 47 and banardising, p. 284 below.

[10] See *AG's Reference (No. 3 of 1999)* [2001] 1 All ER 577, HL where the House of Lords ruled that such DNA material unlawfully retained was admissible as evidence subject to s. 78 PACE. Note the Criminal Justice and Police Act 2001, s. 82 (amending PACE s. 64(1A) allowed for the retention of DNA and finger-print samples even where there was an acquittal or decision not to prosecute.

[11] *R (S) v Chief Constable S. Yorks Police* [2004] UKHL 39. Limits of up to six years for the retention of such data were announced in November 2009.

[12] *S. and Marper v UK*, App. Nos. 30562/04 and 30566/04, 4 December 2008.

[13] *Peck v UK* (2003) 36 EHRR 41. The action had been rejected in the English courts.

offers. For instance, the Council of Europe Convention[14] on Data Protection necessitated the DPA 1984 and though superceded by the EC directive, it is still relevant for second- and especially third-pillar EU activity where the directive does not apply. The Lisbon Treaty will make the directive, or any replacement, apply uniformly to matters across the EU involving data protection although the specific characteristics of national security and judicial co-operation in criminal matters and police co-operation may require derogation or special rules.[15]

The common law witnessed some interesting developments in relation to applications for records where legislation did not apply although today the facts of the case would be covered by the DPA. In the case a health authority was not given an unqualified right to deal with an individual's records as they wished.[16] Limits were put in place by the court. Where personal information is held by 'holders' and is not protected by legislation, and where the possession by such individuals of such information is not otherwise prohibited by the law, it will be well to remember that the possibility of a breach of confidence, trespass or wrongful interference with personal property (documents) under the Torts (Interference with Goods) Act 1977 may have occurred in the manner in which the information was obtained or in which it was used. There may be a breach of copyright involved or some other aspect of intellectual property law.

Where the DPA does not apply, the full effect of the HRA and Art. 8 ECHR should be considered where a person's right to private or family life is compromised.[17] It provides a right to *everyone*. In spite of age-old resistance to the creation of a substantive tort of privacy in our case law,[18] the courts are moulding a right to privacy protection.[19] Such a right is a confluence of the common law of confidentiality and the Art. 8 right to personal and family life. Courts are duty bound to act in accordance with the ECHR under s. 6 HRA and to protect Art. 8 rights against private bodies. The rights have by virtue of that

---

[14] www.coe.int/t/e/legal_affairs/legal_co-operation/Data_protection/

[15] Declarations 20 and 21 to the Treaty, (Schengen, Prum etc.). See Council FD 2008/977/JHA.

[16] *R v Mid Glamorgan Family Health Authority, ex p. Martin* [1995] 1 All ER 356 where an authority offered access but subject to conditions, i.e. not litigating. The court was reviewing the *reasonableness* of the authority's action and this seemed a reasonable offer on the facts including an offer to allow access to a medical adviser nominated by the requester to assess whether and to what extent access could be allowed without causing harm to the requester. On constraints on the authority's action see p. 363j.

[17] See ECHR case law below on Art. 8 and note in relation to companies *Societe Colas Est v France* [2002] 37971/97 (Final 16/7/02).

[18] *Wainwright v Home Office* [2003] UKHL 53 prison strip search was not actionable unless an assault or battery. See *Wainwright v UK* App. No. 12350/04 where the CHR ruled that the facts did not amount to a breach of Art. 3 but they did amount to a breach of Art. 8 and as no action was available in English law a breach of Art. 13. *Wainwright* was decided by the law lords before the HRA took effect.

[19] See notes 22–32 below, but note *Kaye v Robertson* [1991] FSR 62 and *R v Broadcasting Complaints Commission, ex p. Granada Television Ltd* [1995] 7 LS Gas R 36.

duty a horizontal effect. They may be enforced against private parties breaching them.[20] The press do have a Press Complaints Commission Editors' Code giving guidance on privacy – part of the famous self-regulatory framework of the press.[21] For broadcasting, complaints are dealt with by Ofcom which draws up codes.

A new approach to protection of personal information has been a development starting with litigation involving film stars Michael Douglas and Catherine Zeta-Jones where they signed an exclusive right to use photographs of their wedding with a publishing group. A rival publisher published the photographs depriving the parties of the benefit of their agreement. The Court of Appeal felt that their right to privacy had been invaded unjustifiably but an injunction was not awarded to prevent wrongful publication because damages would be an adequate remedy.[22] Subsequently, the Court of Appeal ruled that photographs of their wedding portrayed aspects of their private lives falling within the protection of the law of confidentiality as extended to cover private or personal information. Special considerations applied to photographs in the field of privacy.[23] In *Venables and Thompson v Newsgroup Newspapers Ltd*[24] the High Court was prepared to protect the identity of the murderers of James Bulger after their release from prison in very extensive terms under a combination of Art. 2 (guaranteeing a right to life), Art. 3 (right not to suffer torture, inhuman or degrading treatment) and Art. 8 ECHR (right to privacy). Serious and sustained threats had been made against the youths and the press wanted to reveal any new identities they were given and their whereabouts after their release in accordance with their right to freedom of speech under HRA 1998 and Art. 10 ECHR. Both cases can be explained on the grounds of established principles of confidentiality.

Naomi Campbell v MGN Ltd[25] is the modern *locus classicus* where the majority of the law lords ruled that in publishing information about the famous model attending Narcotics Anonymous, details of her therapy for drug treatment and photos of her leaving the premises of her treatment the defendants had wrongfully published private information on her health and treatment which was protected by a duty of confidence.[26] An assurance of privacy was essential in her

---

[20] Lord Lester and D. Pannick, *Human Rights Law and Practice* (1999), pp. 31–2: 'the state (acting through its courts) is obliged, under the Convention, to protect individuals against breaches of their rights', including those perpetrated by individuals. See *ibid.*, 2nd ed (2004), pp. 44–5.

[21] www.pcc.org.uk/cop/practice.html for the code. R. Shannon, *A Press Free and Responsible: Self regulation and the Press Complaints Commission 1991–2001* (2001). Tony Blair and Prince Philip complained to the PCC in 2008.

[22] *Douglas, Zeta-Jones and Northern Shell Ltd v Hello! Ltd* [2001] 2 All ER 289.

[23] *Douglas and Others v Hello! (No. 3)* [2005] EWCA Civ 595, at 84. See *Douglas and Others* [2007] UKHL 21 on damages for the wronged magazine for breach of commercial confidentiality. See *D v L* [2004] EMLR 1.

[24] *Venables and Thompson v News Group Newspapers Ltd* [2001] 1 All ER 908.

[25] [2004] UKHL 22.

[26] In *Z v Finland* (1999) 45 BMLR 107, orders requiring doctors to give evidence and medical notes on Z who was HIV positive and whose husband was facing criminal prosecutions were

treatment. Disclosure of the information and photographs would be 'distressing and highly offensive' and undermine her reasonable expectation of privacy. The protection of private information fastened upon protection of human autonomy and dignity not solely on a duty of good faith as in the protection of a trade secret or confidentiality, although it was a development of confidentiality. Everything is context-specific and it is notable that there was widespread disagreement between the courts and the judges in this case as to whether the requisite duty had been breached. The fact that she was an addict and that she was receiving medical treatment did not fall under protected categories of personal information. Her drug-taking was illegal and she had denied that dependency (drug dependency by itself would be private information [para. 56 Hoffmann]) and her treatment an understandable response. The press were free to report on these matters. The right to pass on information under Art. 10 ECHR and the right to privacy protection under Art. 8 ECHR have to be balanced one against the other. Neither takes automatic priority. The balance involves what is the reasonable expectation of privacy and what is the public interest (PI) in publicity.

Campbell was decided before *Von Hannover v Germany* which involved the press taking photos of Princess Grace of Monaco with her family in public places and which amounted to a breach of her reasonable expectation of privacy under Art 8 ECHR.[27] The ECtHR was at pains to draw a distinction between comment about political figures in public life especially where hypocrisy, criminality or corruption were involved. The information in the case had no 'watchdog quality: it merely sated the public's curiosity about a famous person. A vital factor is whether the published items contribute to a debate of general interest.'

The decision in *Campbell* and decisions from the ECtHR[28] have encouraged a development in privacy protection under the law of confidentiality which have caused the press anxiety. *Ash v McKennitt*[29] protected the private details of a famous singer's life whose former assistant wished to publish an account of her experience working with the singer. The English courts found argument unconvincing that publication was justified by already being in the public domain and that the singer's lack of sincerity prompted a PI in publishing the information. The fact that someone is a role model does not mean that it has to be publicly demonstrated that they have feet of clay (para. 63) where their

proportionate and justified by PI reasons and there were adequate procedural safeguards and anonymity. Orders naming Z after ten years and revealing her identity in contemporary court proceedings amounted to a breach of Art. 8.

[27] (2005) 40 EHHR 1 and which found German law to be in breach of Art. 8 because its laws provided no adequate remedy.

[28] *Peck v UK* (2003) 13 BHRC 669 and *Von Hannover v Germany* (2005) 40 EHRR 1. In *Murray v Big Pictures (UK) Ltd* [2008] EWCA Civ 446 the Court of Appeal held that it was arguable that a child of J. K. Rowling has a right to privacy and the reasonable expectation that a photo of him would not be published by the press. His action had therefore been wrongly struck out at first instance. See *Wood v Com'r Met. Police* [2009] EWCA Civ 414 police taking and retaining photos of W engaged in political protests at a meeting was a breach of Art. 8.

[29] [2006] EWCA Civ 1714.

conduct is not disreputable.[30] While some public figures may run the risk of exposure of hypocrisy (politicians, journalists and clergy may be favourites – and who else?), the singer had clearly not wanted her life to be treated as an open book. The Court of Appeal upheld her right to privacy in much of the information covering sexual relationships, intimate feelings relating to her fiancé's death, health and diet, emotional vulnerability and a financial dispute. The injunction did not cover 'anodyne' information or that already public. There may be a PI in publishing private information but the courts have not been overly enthused about accepting such a defence.[31] Private life protection and confidentiality are taking different paths.

The litigation involving Max Mosley may come to be regarded as the high-water mark of privacy protection. The case involved notorious events concerning the plaintiff, a famous figure, and events at a private party involving paid hostesses. The thrust of the occasion can be gleaned from the *News of the World* (the defendants) headlines of 'F1 Boss has sick Nazi Orgy with 5 Hookers'. The events were filmed clandestinely by one of the participants and then published in various forms by the newspaper. Mosley sued for breach of confidence and/or unauthorised publication of personal information seeking aggravated and exemplary damages. The confidential information consisted in sado-masochistic practices and sexual activities between consenting adults on the understanding of confidentiality. The newspaper alleged that the event was a mock Nazi parody of Holocaust horrors and involved criminal activity. These amounted to PI justifications for publishing the material. Basically, the judge ruled that none of the allegations was made out and that there had been an intrusion into the private lives of the participants. There was no PI, as opposed to an interest in prurience, in the public knowing. Mosley's status and feet of clay did not justify invasion of his privacy. Damages were assessed at £60,000 and exemplary damages were not awarded.[32]

Decisions of the Court and Commission of Human Rights in Strasbourg have placed limits on a public body's power to refuse access to personal documents or have allowed access to documents in order to make meaningful rights under Art. 8 and these include the famous decision in *Gaskin v UK*[33] where the absence of an independent arbitration to determine requests for access which were contested by the record holder constituted a breach of Art. 8, but not Art. 10. In *Guerra v Italy*,[34] the ECtHR held that not informing local residents of

---

[30] Distinguishing *A v B* [2003] QB 195 and *Woodward v Hutchins* [1977] 2 All ER 751 (CA). See *CC v AB* [2006] EWHC 3083.

[31] *Ass Newpapers Ltd v HRH Prince of Wales* [2006] EWCA Civ 1776.

[32] *Mosley v MGN Ltd* [2008] EWHC 1777 (QB). Mosley applied to the ECtHR claiming that this award was insufficient to remedy the breach of his Convention rights.

[33] *Gaskin v UK* (1989) 12 EHRR 36; also *McMichael v UK* [1995] 2 FCR 718, ECtHR. *Gaskin* concerned social welfare files: see Children Act 1989, ss. 22 (4), 26(2)(d), and 26(3) and SI 1990/2244; Butler-Sloss Report, Cm. 412 (1988) and HMSO, *Working Together* (1999) on consulting and informing in child care.

[34] (1998) 4 BHRC 63.

the dangers of a local chemical plant interfered with their right to enjoyment of privacy and family life under Art. 8 but not their rights under Art. 10 to pass on information. Article 10 did not provide a positive right to be informed. The Commission disagreed on this point. Likewise in *McGinley and Egan v UK*[35] where the UK authorities had exposed servicemen to nuclear-test explosions, the authorities' failure to provide an effective and accessible procedure to allow parties to seek all relevant information and papers constituted a breach of Art. 8. Article 10, however, does not allow a positive right to state-held documents. It prevents the state placing unjustified limits on others passing on information and expressing themselves freely. The Council of Ministers of the Council of Europe has produced a code on access to official documents and as we shall see in chapter 13, movement is afoot to introduce a CoE Convention giving a right of access to official documents.[36] *Oneryldiz v Turkey*[37] saw the Court use Art. 2 ECHR on the right to life to provide a basis for a right to information about dangerously built accommodation from a local authority. As will be seen in chapter 11, Art. 6 has been frequently invoked to rule on breaches of the fair-trial provision where there have been inadequacies in the provision of information to a litigant.

Further, the dealing with inaccurate information which causes harm – financial or physical/emotional – could on the facts amount to negligence as well as defamation. The proximity of the holder to the subject ought to be sufficient to satisfy a duty of care situation in the law of negligence[38] – in spite of recent attempts to limit the range of victims.[39] However, it has to be said that the comprehensive nature of the DPA will make the residual role of the common law less useful in seeking access. Nonetheless the common law and ECHR will have a role to play in protecting information, and conversely in its publication.

This point in relation to publication or openness can be illustrated in chapter 11 when the effect of the ECHR and the need to hold inquiries in public, usually under Art. 2. Article 10 has not been so successful but the inquiry into the notorious murderer Dr Harold Shipman was held in public after a judicial ruling that a private inquiry would be a breach of Art. 10 ECHR but this case has not been followed.[40] In other circumstances inquiries into tragedies, such as child deaths, have been roundly condemned *because* they were heard in public.[41]

While protection of personal information is becoming more of a preoccupation, legislation has increased the range of duties that exist to disclose information on convictions and especially in relation to children, and in law

---

[35] Case No. 10/1997/794/995–996 (1998) 27 EHRR 1.
[36] Rec. No. R(81)19. I. Harden (2001) European Public Law 165.
[37] [2002] EHHR 496.
[38] *Spring v Guardian Assurance plc* [1994] 3 All ER 129, HL: duty between referee and job applicant
[39] See also Malicious Communications Act 1988.
[40] *R (Wagstaff)* v *Secretary of State for Health* [2001] 1 WLR 292; ch. 11, p. 406.
[41] As with the notorious case of Tyra Henry in 1986.

enforcement generally.[42] There are also statutory provisions on information relating to child abuse[43] and copious case law on child-protection registers.[44]

The Data Protection Act 1998 (DPA)

The DPA introduced a statutory scheme to regulate the retention and use of personal data. The DPA is a technical, intricate and difficult statute. It has to be emphasised that although the DPA covers both computerised and manual personal information as explained below, computerised information generally is subject to the same control and availability as manual information. Computerised information does involve additional security measures – encryption has been suggested as a universal method to protect personal data by use of a secret 'key'. If within a government department there is computerised data covered by the Official Secrets Acts and its disclosure is not exempt from prosecution by virtue of the DPA, unauthorised disclosure could result in prosecution. Data that are protected by the law of confidentiality will be protectable by the law of confidentiality. If it is a question of Parliament being informed of the data held by government or its agencies, whatever limitations apply to Parliament's ability to obtain information from the government will apply here also. Data constitutes property, although the complexities involved in the legal classification of concepts conveying appropriate rights and protection have caused, and will cause, legal disputation of a more than usually complex nature.[45]

The DPA was passed primarily to incorporate into British law the provisions of the European Convention on Data Protection 1981.[46] Had the Convention not been incorporated, the flow of data into the UK from other signatory states might well have been prohibited. In July 1995 an EU directive was adopted on data protection which sought to harmonise laws throughout Member States on access to personal data.[47] By virtue of Art. 286 EC and reg. (EC) 45/2001, the directive applies to EU institutions under the first pillar (see above). A 1997 directive was passed on the processing of personal data and the protection of privacy in the telecommunications sector and this has now been replaced by the

---

[42] Rehabilitation of Offenders Act 1974; Pt V Police Act 1997, Criminal Records Agency: *R (L) v Met. Police Com'r* [2009] UKSC 3; Protection of Children Act 1999 and Care Standards Act 2000: *R (Wright) v Secretary of State* [2009] UKHL 3; Sexual Offences Act 2003: *R (F) v Secretary of State* [2008] EWHC 3170 Admin.

[43] Children Act 1989, ss. 19 and 47 and also s. 26. See *Re EC (Disclosure of Material)* [1996] 2 FLR 725; *Re V (Sexual Abuse: Disclosure)* [1999] 1 FLR 267 and *R (A) v Herts CC* [2001] EWHC Admin 211.

[44] *R v Norfolk CC Social Services Department, ex p. M* [1989] 2 All ER 359; *R v Harrow LBC, ex p. D* [1990] Fam 133; *R v Devon CC, ex p. L* [1991] 2 FLR 541; *R v Lewisham LBC, ex p. P* [[1991] 3 All ER 529; *R v Hampshire CC, ex p. H* [1999] 2 FLR 359.

[45] C. Tapper, *Computer Law* (1989); I. Lloyd, *Information Technology Law*, 5th edn (2008); Copyright (Computer Software) Amendment Act 1985.

[46] Convention for the Protection of Individuals with regard to the Automatic Processing of Personal Data, ETS no. 108. There was a commercial necessity in the incorporation by the UK Government of the Convention. See Austin (1984) Public Law 618.

[47] Directive 95/46/EC: OJ L 281/31, 31 November 1995. See D. Bainbridge, *EC Data Protection Directive* (1996).

Privacy and Electronic Communications Directive (European Parliament and Council 2002/58/EC, 12 July 2002 as amended by EC Directive 2006/24/EC) and implemented by SI 2003/2426 and SI 2004/1039.[48]

The basic idea behind the directive and Act is that data subjects (DSs) should have access to personal data (personal information about them), subject to exemptions. Controls should exist over the use that is made of information in personal data and there should be impartial supervision and determination of data holders and disputes involving data-holding. The directive applied to both computerised and manual data and allowed trans-border transfer of electronic personal data to countries without data-protection laws where certain conditions were fulfilled. Countries without data-protection laws, such as the USA, have developed comparable non-legal systems known as 'safe harbours' to protect personal data. The directive applied to public- and private-sector holders of personal information, as did the 1984 Act, and is closer to a privacy-protection law than anything that operated in the UK in that positive duties to inform subjects of the use of data will be established along with rights to object by the subjects to the holding of data. The directive had to be implemented within three years of adoption. The implementing measure was the DPA 1998. The directive was subject to considerable hostility both here and in the USA where opposition continues.[49] The Home Office commissioned studies suggesting that compliance costs will amount to £2 billion. The directive was accused of being a part of the stifling EU bureaucratic over-regulation. It is far from a fully fledged privacy-protection law.

What the Act does

Basically, the DPA provides safeguards in the 'processing' of personal data or information covered by the Act. The definitions come from the directive, and in interpreting the statute interpretations should be adopted consistent with the directive and in a purposive spirit.[50] 'Processing' means the use of data in the broadest of senses and is dealt with below. However, the Court of Appeal has held that the term does not cover the selection of data in order to make a decision concerning a DS. A majority judgment ruled that selection of data is not processing. Not all of the data was automated (below) but it seems very strange to hold that selecting data that will then become automated is not processing.[51] It establishes a regulator of personal data (the IC). But the IC does not provide a complaints service as under the FOIA for requesters for data.[52] The

---

[48] See R. Jay and A. Hamilton, *Data Protection Law and Practice*, 2nd edn (2003); I. Lloyd, *A Guide to the Data Protection Act 1998* (1998). On the electronic communications code see SI 2003/2553 and ss. 109 and 402 Communications Act 2003.

[49] A. Charlesworth, 'Clash of the data titans' (2000) European Public Law 253.

[50] Lord Philips in *Campbell v MGN Ltd* [2003] EWCA Civ 1746, para. 96.

[51] *Johnson v Medical Defence Union* [2007] EWCA Civ 262 – Arden LJ dissenting.

[52] The IC may audit data under s. 42 (below).

Act provides a right of access for DSs (those who are the subject of the personal data) to personal data held by a data controller as specified. If inaccurate, the subject may apply to the court for it to correct, block, erase or destroy the data. There are exemptions from access on the grounds of national security, in relation to crime and taxation and other matters. Data controllers (DCs) will have to register ('notify') with the IC although there will be exemptions from notification. Failure to register where required will be a criminal offence. Subjects will have rights to compensation where there are breaches of the Act. The subject has a right to give notice to a DC to order them to stop processing data which is likely to cause 'substantial damage' or 'substantial distress' to the subject which is unwarranted. These terms are not defined and there are provisos. There is also a right to prevent processing for the purposes of direct marketing.

Breaches of the Act may appear technical and cover apparently innocuous activity and can be met with criminal punishment.[53] The Lords Constitution Committee has, however, re-emphasised the absence of effective powers of regulation and enforcement of the Act.[54]

'Data' and related matters

Section 1 of the 1998 Act defines 'data' and related terms. 'Data' means personal information that is being processed by means of equipment operating automatically in response to instructions given for the purpose – basically electronic or computerised; secondly, information which is recorded with the intention that it should be processed by such equipment; thirdly, information which is recorded as part of a relevant filing system or with the intention that it should form part of a relevant filing system.[55] This embraces 'structured information' which is stored by reference to a code or identifying number for instance. This information covers manual or paper files. The precise scope of what manual files are included has led to conflicting interpretations with the Data Protection Commissioner (DPC) interpreting the provision more broadly than the government.[56] Does it cover a file on which the subject's name is on the front but the information in loosely assorted papers is not readily extractable? If not part of a 'set' it could fall under the personal data added by the FOIA rather than under this heading. It seems it will cover card indexes, rollerdex, and microfiche. The last definition under the unamended 1998 DPA covers manual information not covered above but which forms part of an 'accessible record'

---

[53] Case C-101/01 *Lindqvist* [2004] 2 WLR 1385.   [54] HL 18 (2008–9).

[55] Although not operating automatically, the information is structured, either by reference to individuals or by reference to criteria relating to individuals, in such a way that specific information relating to a particular individual is readily accessible. These would include, as well as filing systems, card indexes.

[56] This was the view of the DPC when she gave evidence to the Select Committee on Public Administration in its inquiry into the White Paper, *Open Government*, HC 398-I (1997–8), Q. 220.

under s. 68 DPA. This covers health records, educational (school) records as defined in schedules and accessible records as defined in sch. 12 which covers housing and social services records. Accessible documents are specified by their governing regulations and not by the terms introduced by the DPA. They will cover a wider range of personal records.[57]

Durant v FSA[58] has given very narrow definitions to the terms 'personal data' and 'relevant filing system' under the DPA. Personal data was interpreted to mean information which is 'biographical' in a significant sense and which goes beyond mere recording of a 'putative data subject's' (PDS) involvement in a life event which has no personal connotations and which does not compromise his privacy. Secondly, the information should have the PDS as its focus rather than another person or body. In *Durant*, D had made a complaint against Barclays Bank which was investigated by the Financial Services Authority. The focus the court held was upon the bank and regulator and their actions, not D. However, the data involved the bank's reaction to D's complaint (paras. 26–31). It seems clear that for whatever reason the court wished to confine the application of the DPA.

The court also confined the meaning of relevant filing system for non-automated files to a system which possesses 'the same standard or sophistication of accessibility to personal data in manual filing systems as to computerized records' (para. 34). Documents would have to be filed in a way that would give easy access to personal information – it is structured in such a way as to make the data 'readily accessible'. Files would have to indicate at the outset that they contained specific information capable of amounting to personal data about the DS and in which files this was held. The files would have to be clearly cross-referenced in a 'sufficiently sophisticated and detailed means of readily indicating whether and where in an individual file or files specific criteria or information about the applicant can be readily located' (para. 50). A temporary replacement clerk could, it has been said, be able to locate the data immediately. The four files in question were ordered in date order, had a sub-divider headed 'Mr Durant', but no further sub-dividers, and a sheaf of papers in a transparent plastic bag. These did not fall under the description of a 'relevant filing system'. The message seems clear for those wishing to avoid the Act's requirements. An Article 29 Working Party on Data Protection from the Commission has investigated the definition of personal documents and has emphasised that the intention in the directive is wide and flexible interpretation of personal data.[59]

The FOIA additions

The FOIA, s. 68 adds to the definitions of data covered by the DPA *recorded* information held by a public authority (PA) which does not fall within any

---

[57] The Access to Medical Reports Act 1988 operates outside the DPA.
[58] [2003] EWCA Civ 1746.
[59] Opinion 4/2007 on the concept of personal data 01248/07/EN, WP 136, 20 June 2007, http://ec.europa.eu/justice_home/fsj/privacy/workinggroup/index_en.htm.

of the above descriptions of data, i.e. it is not computerised or organised in such a way as to be covered by the definitions in the DPA. The DPA rights of subject access and data accuracy are thereby extended to all *recorded* personal information held by PAs. The first four categories apply regardless of whether the data is held by a public or private body. The latter only applies to data held by a PA covered by the FOIA. The additional areas of personal information included by FOIA are not extended to the private sector.

FOIA and data protection

A statutory *legerdemain* allows the FOIA to state that all personal information held by PA is included within the DPA. But it cancels all the effects of being within the DPA for this last category of information apart from subject access rights and accuracy so that the full impact of the DPA will not apply. This disapplies the application of the data-protection principles (DPP) as explained below. Access rights and accuracy will not apply to personal data under the new definition covering the non-public functions of PAs. The effect is that the DPA applies to public authorities' paper records even though they are not part of 'a relevant filing system' and not part of an 'accessible record' as defined in the Act. The sorts of data included would be 'incidental personal information in a policy file' or loosely assembled in papers.[60] Under s. 69 FOIA, where the information is, although not part of a 'relevant filing system' or part of 'an accessible record', nonetheless 'structured to a certain extent by reference to individuals', it is 'relatively structured' for the FOIA. Government guidance advised this would cover a file containing correspondence indexed by dates and headed by a person's name or identifier but which is not a part of a 'relevant filing system'.[61] Such data have to be treated like any other DPA request. It would not have to be a part of a relevant filing system but it would have to be 'personal information' per *Durant* (above).

For data which are 'relatively *un*structured' meaning not 'relatively structured', requesters have to satisfy additional conditions. Unstructured personal data will not be provided unless the request *expressly* describes the information. DSs will not usually have to specify any part of their data to obtain all of that data. The DS will have to describe expressly what is requested for 'relatively unstructured personal information' to be included in response to a subject access request.[62] It should be recalled that under the FOIA generally, requests for additional information from requesters may be made by PAs. For the additional data, applicants will have to be more specific. This may prove to be extremely onerous. Secondly, if allowing access to specified data exceeds a 'prescribed cost ceiling' (see chapter 4, p. 134) the authority may refuse a request.

The effect of s. 70 FOIA is to deprive DSs on whom personal data covered by the FOIA is held of all the rights under the DPA to the group of personal

---

[60] *FOI Consultation on Draft Legislation*, para. 169, Cm. 4355 (1999)
[61] *Ibid.*, para. 170.   [62] *Ibid.*

information introduced under the FOIA apart from rights of subject access and in relation to inaccuracy. The FOIA extended data rights do not apply to personnel records. *Employees* of the PAs identified in the FOIA do not have rights of access to their personnel records under the FOIA extended data definitions; they have DPA rights.

Section 34 DPA provides that where there is a statutory duty to provide information to the public it is exempt from subject access, accuracy and certain other provisions. This is to avoid duplication of other detailed access provisions in public registers, electoral lists[63] and the Land Registry.[64] Special provision is made for the FOIA which is therefore not included within these provisions. If this were not the case, rights under the FOIA could override those under the DPA. The relationship between the FOIA and DPA is complex. The FOIA and FOI(Scotland)A should be construed as liberally as possible but both must be interpreted with regard to the DPA.[65]

Personal data, sensitive personal data and 'special purposes'

'Personal data' are those which relate to a living individual – the DS – who can be identified from that data (or from that data and other information in the possession of the holder of information, or which is likely to come into the possession of the DC) including an expression of opinion about the individual and any indications of the intentions of the data controller in respect of the individual. Previously where opinions on employees were processed and were not exempt, they would have to be disclosed to the employee, but not the intentions of the employer, i.e. to dismiss or to promote. Such data will now be disclosable. The approach of the Court of Appeal to personal data was explained above.

A new category of data known as 'sensitive personal data' is provided for by s. 2. This includes: the subject's racial or ethnic origin, political opinions, religious beliefs or 'other beliefs of a similar nature', whether a member of a trade union, physical or mental health or condition, sexual life, commission or allegation of any offences, any criminal proceedings or sentences against the subject. This is information that is likely to be tradeable and abused.

The House of Lords has discussed the relationship of the FOI(Scotland)A and the DPA in *Common Services Agency v Scottish IC*.[66] At issue were questions of sensitive personal data. This case concerned a FOI request for information to health authorities in Scotland about the incidence of childhood leukaemia

---

[63] See *R (Robertson) v Wakefield MDC* [2001] EWHC 915 Admin on electoral lists. Provision was made for 'dual electoral lists' – abridged and unabridged versions: *R (Robertson) v Secretary of State* [2003] EWHC 1760 Admin.

[64] The price of residential property was made public after 1 April 2000.

[65] *Common Services Agency v Scottish Information Commissioner* [2008] UKHL 47 Lord Hope, para. 4.

[66] *Ibid.*

cases in a postal area by census ward. Numbers of incidents were requested. This area was in close contact with areas where dangerous activities including nuclear reprocessing were taking place. The request was refused on the basis that it could lead to the identification of children because of the small numbers involved and the small area. This meant it would be personal data and protected under the DPA. Disclosure would be in breach of confidence. But, disclosure of barnardised information, it was argued, would not amount to personal information. Barnardisation allows a slight distortion of figures to avoid indentifying individuals. Information to be barnardised was 'held' by the agency, it was ruled for the purposes of s. 1 FOI(Scotland)A (see chapter 4, p. 145) even though barnardisation involved some alteration to figures. But did such an amended form of information amount to 'personal information' because individuals could be identified from that and other information in, or likely to come into, the possession of the DC. That would depend on whether the requester could get access to the 'other information' allowing anonymity to be defeated. If not, or if access would not allow identification, then it is not personal data protected by the DPP (below). This was the approach adopted by the Law Lords, emphatically by Lady Hale, and the court ruled that 'personal data' should be read into the definition of 'sensitive personal data'. Personal data includes sensitive personal data although the latter has additional features. There were differences in the judgments over the interpretation of data and information.[67]

There are also 'special purposes' relating to journalism, artistic purposes and literary purposes (including biographies) which are important in order to ensure added protection to DCs (below) using data covered by the DPA for these purposes. DCs may use personal data for such purposes so as not to allow privacy protection to impede freedom of expression (see below). The DPA seeks to ensure that Art. 8 rights to privacy do not automatically trump Art. 10 rights to free expression. We saw above how the courts have ruled that neither Article trumps the other and balancing is context-specific.

The data controller and processing

The person controlling or processing data is referred to as the 'data controller' (DC) and 'data processor' (DP). Data may be controlled individually or collectively by the use of the IT. A DP is 'any person' who processes the data on behalf of the DC – but it does not include a DC's employee. An example of such a processor is an independent contractor.

---

[67] The case shows again deficiencies in the UK DPA's drafting. If a requester outside the DC's regime requests personal data the real problem is allowing them to identify the DS from other information as specified. The Act does not say that, but that is what the directive implies. There may be reasons when one employee of the DC should not have access because that employee may identify a data subject in contravention of the DPP. This may apply where a DC's departments are clearly separate bodies.

Processing in relation to data or information means, basically, using the data. Because of difficulties in interpretation of earlier legislation the Act specifically covers: obtaining, recording or holding the information or data or carrying out any operation or set of operations on the information or data, including:

(a) organisation, adaptation or alteration of the information or data
(b) retrieval, consultation or use of the information or data
(c) disclosure of the information or data by transmission, dissemination or otherwise making it available
(d) alignment, combination, blocking, erasure or destruction of the information or data.

This is a very wide definition including obtaining and recording data.[68] Although it was felt to be a 'compendious' definition making it is difficult to envisage situations where actions on data would not be covered[69] the Court of Appeal in *Johnson* did find one action which did not amount to processing, selecting information (above), but that decision is widely contested. The wide definition was also necessary to circumvent a decision of the Law Lords[70] which held that where a defendant was charged with using personal data, the act of accessing or retrieving information on a computer so that it could be read either on screen or by means of a print-out was not 'using' the information but simply transferring the information into a different form prior to possible use being made of it, i.e. passing it on to a third party.

General points

DCs have to comply with the DPP in relation to all personal data over which they are the controller. These are explained in the following section. The Act applies to DCs established in the UK, and DCs outside the UK and EEA who use equipment inside the UK for processing the data 'otherwise than for the purposes of transit through the UK'.

As we have seen, the FOIA renames the bodies under the 1984 DPA as the IC and Information Tribunal (IT). A chairman will be assisted by a person representing the interests of information (including DCs) holders and information (including DSs) requesters.

The data-protection principles (DPP)[71]

The principles which govern the processing of data are set out in the DPP. A central feature of the DPA is the protection afforded to DSs. The DPP are central to this task. The DPP are contained in the first schedule to the Act and are to

---

[68] S. 1(2)–(3).   [69] Data Protection Commissioner, *Introduction to the 1998 Act*, ch. 2.
[70] *R v Brown* [1996] 1 All ER545.HL.
[71] The IC has produced detailed guidance on the DPP and other DPA subjects, www.ico.gov.uk/what_we_cover/data_protection.aspx.

be interpreted in accordance with Pt II of that schedule. The following sticks closely to the statutory language. Unless a DC is exempted from the DPP (under s. 27(1)), they are bound to comply the DPP in accordance with s. 4. The DPP are as follows:

(1) Personal data shall be processed, fairly and lawfully and shall not be processed unless (a) one of the conditions in sch. 2 is met (below) and (b) in the case of sensitive personal data, one of the conditions in sch. 3 is also met. 'Fairly' would not include blacklisting, unjustifiably prejudicing or other improper or unreasonable use. Any breach of the law would make processing unlawful, e.g. breaching confidentiality or Art. 8 ECHR.

(2) Personal data shall be obtained only for one or more specified and lawful purposes and shall not be further processed in any manner incompatible with that purpose(s). Obtaining and disclosing under the FOIA is not a 'purpose' that has to be specified according to the IC.[72] Where personal information is confidential a PI disclosure under the common law of confidentiality (below) is not a purpose that has to be specified.

(3) Personal data held shall be adequate, relevant and not excessive in relation to the purpose(s) for which they are processed.[73]

(4) Personal data shall be accurate and, where necessary, kept up to date.

(5) Personal data processed for any purpose or purposes shall not be kept for longer than is necessary for that purpose or those purposes.[74]

(6) Personal data shall be processed in accordance with the rights of DSs under this Act.

(7) Appropriate technical and organisational measures shall be taken against unauthorised or unlawful processing of personal data and against accidental loss or destruction of, or damage to, personal data.

(8) Personal data shall not be transferred to a country or territory outside the EEA unless that country or territory ensures an adequate level of protection for the rights and freedoms of DSs in relation to the processing of personal data. Contravention is an offence and subject to the IC's remedies.

How are the principles interpreted?

Under Pt II of sch. 1 in relation to the first principle, when determining whether personal data were obtained fairly, 'regard is to be had to the method by which they were obtained, including in particular whether any person from whom

---

[72] Below, p. 303.

[73] See the IT in EA/2007/0096 etc. *Chief Constable Humberside and Others v IC* where conviction records including reprimands breached DPP 3 and also 5, below in text. The IT upheld the IC's enforcement notices in that the chief constables had retained data on convictions and other matters in breach of the DPP. See ch. 1 above on the Police National Computer, the Criminal Records Bureau and the Independent Safeguarding Agency.

[74] *Chief Constable Humberside and Others v IC*.

they are obtained is deceived or misled as to the purpose(s) for which they are processed'.

> Subject to para. 2 below, data are treated as obtained fairly under the first principle if they consist of information obtained from a person who:
>
> (a) is authorised by or under any enactment to supply it; or
> (b) is required to supply it by or under any enactment or by any convention or other instrument imposing an international obligation on the UK.

Was full information provided to the subject? Were explanations understood by the subject and was it reasonable for them to be understood? Any uses and disclosures should be explained. All the circumstances behind the obtaining of information to make an assessment on how it was obtained will have to be fully considered by the IC.

Subject to para. 3, para. 2 states that for the purposes of the first principle in the case of data obtained from the DS, data are not to be treated as processed fairly unless (a) the subject has information specified in sub-para. 3 (which refers to the identity of the DC or his representative), the purpose(s) or intended purpose(s) of processing or any further information which is necessary in the circumstances to allow processing to be fair), or (b) the subject is provided with it, or it is made readily available to him 'so far as practicable' and 'in any other case, the DC ensures as far as practicable that before the relevant time or as soon as practicable after that time the DS has, is provided with or has readily made available to him' specified information (in sub-para. 3). The sub-paragraph spells out the 'relevant time'. There are saving provisions if 'disproportionate effort' or legal obligations (other than contract) to disclose or record information are involved.

For the second principle, Pt II states that the purpose(s) for which personal data are obtained may be specified 'in particular' in a notice or in a notification to the DS or IC under Pt III DPA. 'Regard is to be had to the purpose(s) for which personal data are intended to be processed by any person to whom they are disclosed' when 'determining whether any disclosure of personal data is compatible with the purpose(s) for which the data were obtained'.

Part II sets out that no contravention of the fourth principle is to be regarded as occurring 'by reason of inaccuracy in personal data which accurately record information obtained by the DC from the subject or a third party' [and where] 'having regard to the purpose(s) of obtaining and further processing the data the DC has taken reasonable steps to ensure the accuracy of the data', and the subject has notified the DC of the subject's view 'of their inaccuracy and the data indicate that fact'.

The sixth principle is contravened if, and only if, a person is in breach of various provisions of the Act concerning rights of access, processing for direct marketing as well as processing data for automated decision-taking.

The seventh principle concerns appropriate levels of security by the DC considering the nature of the data. He has to ensure the reliability of employees, data processors and forms and terms for processing contracts. The principle has been a focal point of public attention in relation to the DPA because of the dramatic loss of personal data on DSs by Inland Revenue, the Ministry of Defence (MoD) and the Driving and Vehicle Licensing Authority due to a lack of due care in holding, for example, memory sticks, PCs etc. This has led to recommendations by the Constitution Committee of the House of Lords which also has details of the misadventures.[75] The recommendations of the Cabinet Office were noted (chapter 1, p. 15).

The DPA was amended by s. 144 Criminal Justice and Immigration Act 2008 adding a new s. 55A–E to the DPA. These changes allow the IC to serve a monetary penalty order on a DC where there has been a serious breach of the DPP which is of a kind likely to cause serious harm or serious distress. The DC has to know or ought to have known:

(i) that there was a risk that the contravention would occur, and
(ii) that such a contravention would be of a kind likely to cause substantial damage or substantial distress, but
(iii) failed to take reasonable steps to prevent the contravention.

Any sums are payable to the IC and are paid into the consolidated fund. The DC is given procedural rights including a notice of intent to serve and an appeal lies to the IT against a monetary penalty order. The IC may issue guidance.

For the eighth principle, criteria are set out on adequate levels of protection for data transferred out of the UK and include the nature of the personal data. The protection is one which is adequate in all the circumstances of the case having particular regard to: the country or territory of origin of the information contained in the data; the country or territory of final destination of that information; the purposes for which, and period during which, the data are intended to be processed; the law in force in the country or territory in question; international obligations of that country or territory; any relevant codes of conduct or other enforceable rules in that country or territory; and any security measures taken in respect of the data in that country or territory. The eighth principle does not apply where the subject has consented to transfer or transfer is necessary for contractual purposes or for a 'substantial public interest'.

Section 33 covers processing for 'research purposes' including statistical or historical purposes. To be exempt from the second and fifth DPP and s. 7 rights on access, the research must not be targeted at 'particular individuals'. Processing must not cause harm or distress. Individuals must not be identified when data is made available.

---

[75] See note 1 above. Steyn (2009) Public Law 228.

Conditions for lawful processing

Schedule 2 sets out conditions relevant for the purpose of the first principle and one of these must be satisfied for the lawful processing of personal data – they are pivotal in spite of being buried away in a long schedule. The conditions include the situation where the subject has given his consent; and also where the processing is necessary for a variety of grounds such as the performance by the DS of a contract; compliance by the DC with legal obligations other than under a contract; for the vital interests of the DS; for the administration of justice; the performance of a wide range of public functions (statutory, Crown, ministerial or departmental) including those performed in the PI or for the pursuit of the legitimate interests of the DC or a third party except where disclosure is unwarranted because of prejudice to the rights, freedoms or legitimate interests of the DS.

Schedule 3 sets out conditions for the first principle and sensitive personal data (and see SI 2000/417 which adds that processing is in the 'substantial public interest' for a variety of activities). For the processing of sensitive personal data one of the conditions in sch. 3 has to be established.[76] The subject must have given his *explicit* consent to the processing, and processing is necessary for a variety of reasons or is carried out for 'legitimate activities' or, for example, legal proceedings. The list is very detailed and includes the situations where processing is necessary for 'medical purposes'; where processing is necessary because of duties on the DC in relation to employment subject to specified exclusions or further conditions; where processing is necessary to protect vital interests of the DS or another where consent has not been given or has been unreasonably withheld; and where processing is necessary to protect the legitimate activities of non-profit bodies which exist for religious, trade union, political, or philosophical purposes and subject to further conditions including the consent of the DS to third-party disclosure. It covers the situation where processing is necessary for the administration of justice or for the purposes of central government. The Secretary of State may provide for additional safeguards.

Rights of data subjects and others

For DSs, the test of a successful data protection scheme is whether it provides adequate safeguards and rights for the subject. These include rights of access and correction. These rights are contained in Pt II DPA. Section 7(1)(a) provides that an individual is entitled, after making a request in writing and paying the prescribed fee, to be informed by any DC whether personal data of which that individual is the DS are being processed by or on behalf of that DC. If so, the individual shall be given by the DC a description of:

---

[76] Sch. 2 covers *all personal data*; cf. *Common Services Agency v Scottish IC* [2008] UKHL 47.

(a) the personal data of which that individual is the DS

(b) the purposes for which they are being or are to be processed

(c) recipients or classes of recipient to whom they are entitled to be disclosed.[77]

The subject is entitled to have communicated to them in an intelligible form:

(a) the information constituting any personal data of which that individual is the DS (see s. 8(2))

(b) any information available to the DC as to the source of those data.

Under s. 7(1)(d) the subject is also entitled to know the logic involved in decision-making (but not a trade secret) where the data are processed automatically and are likely to form the sole basis for any decision significantly affecting the subject such as work performance, creditworthiness, reliability or conduct.

A DC is not obliged to comply with the request under this section unless the DC is supplied with such information as they may reasonably require in order to be satisfied as to the identity of the requester and to locate the information which that person seeks. It was noted above how the FOIA imposes additional duties on a requester for personal data added by that Act (see p. 283). Where disclosure to a requester would allow disclosure of information about another individual who can be identified from that information, the DC does not have to comply unless the other person consents to that disclosure to the requester or it is reasonable in all the circumstances to comply with the request without consent.[78] Section 7(6) says in assessing reasonableness where there is no consent, particular regard shall be had to any duty of confidentiality owed to the other individual, steps taken by the DC to obtain consent, whether the individual is capable of giving consent and any express refusal or consent by that individual. Another individual can be identified from the information being disclosed 'if he can be identified from that information, or from that and any other information which, in the reasonable belief of the DC, is likely to be in, or come into, the possession of the DS making the request'.[79]

A request must be complied with promptly and in any event before the end of the prescribed period of forty days beginning with the relevant day. Other periods may be prescribed by regulations. Compliance may be ordered by the court. Safeguards exist against repetitious requests. Data supplied must be those held at the time the request is received subject to any deletions or amendments between that time and the time of supply that were going to be made regardless of the request.[80]

Where a request for access is refused under s. 7, a DS who brings an action under s. 7(9) for compensation for breaches of the DPP by the DC may still

---

[77] S. 7(1)(b).   [78] See s. 7(5) on supplying information where the identity can be omitted.

[79] S. 8(7).

[80] S. 9 contains modifications to s. 7 requests where the DC is a credit reference bureau and covers requests under s. 159 Consumer Credit Act 1974 which was an early access right which is now brought within the DPA.

make a claim under the Civil Procedure Rules (CPR) for specific disclosure of the data that was refused.[81] Section 15(2) DPA allows the court to see the data in question where a claim for access is made under s. 7 but not to disclose this to the applicant pending the outcome. It was not a general prohibition against disclosure under the CPR.

Section 10 provides a right to the DS to give a notice to a DC requiring the DC at the end of a period 'which is reasonable in the circumstances to cease, or not to begin, processing data of which the DS is the subject where the processing is likely to cause or is causing substantial damage or substantial distress to him or to another which is or would be unwarranted'. There are exceptions. Within twenty-one days of receipt of the written notice, the DC must give the person sending the notice their own written notice stating that he has complied or intends to comply with the DS notice or stating reasons why the DC regards the notice as unjustified and the extent to which he intends to comply with it. A court has broad powers to enforce compliance. This is likely to be very important in cases of 'blacklisting' and may have special relevance to sensitive information under s. 2.

Section 11 confers a right to stop or prevent processing for the purposes of direct marketing enforceable by court order. 'Direct marketing' means 'the communication (by whatever means) of any advertising or marketing material which is directed to particular individuals'.[82]

Section 12 is concerned with the power to prevent processing by automatic means which involve decisions significantly affecting the DS. This deals with evaluations of the subject's performance at work, creditworthiness, reliability or conduct. They are not exclusive. Common uses are for creditworthiness and psychometric testing. The individual has the right, enforceable through the court, to require the DC to reconsider or take a new decision 'otherwise than on that basis' where such a decision has been made by such processing. There are time limits of twenty-one days from receipt of the notice to set out the steps taken by the DC to comply with the DS notice. These provisions do not apply to exempt decisions which satisfy specified conditions – e.g., entering a contract or where required by statute – or are prescribed in regulations. Certain procedural safeguards for the DS have to be followed.

Section 13 provides that individuals who suffer damage by reason of any contravention by a DC of any of the requirements of this Act are entitled to compensation from the DC for that damage. The Act also provides that distress, by reason of any contravention by a DC of any of the requirements of this Act, may be compensated by the DC if the individual suffers damage by reason of the contravention *or* the contravention relates to the processing of personal data for the special purposes. A defence of taking reasonable care in all the circumstances is available to the DC. The Court of Appeal has ruled that wrongly disclosing

---

[81] *Johnson v Medical Defence Union Ltd* [2005] 1 All ER 87. [82] S. 11(3).

information from police data on the Police National Computer was an offence of misconduct in public office requiring a custodial sentence.[83]

If a court[84] is satisfied that personal data of which the applicant is the subject are inaccurate, the court may order the DC to 'rectify, block, erase or destroy those data and any other personal data in respect of which he is the DC'. This applies whether or not data accurately record information received from the DS or a third party. Additional information may be entered even where it is recorded accurately and the court has power to enforce its orders. Courts may also take steps to prevent further contraventions of the Act. DCs may also be required to notify third parties to whom they have passed inaccurate personal data, where it considers it reasonably practicable – i.e., the extent of the numbers involved (s. 14(6)) – of any rectification etc.

FOIA exemptions and the DPA

The DPA provides exemptions to access. However, personal information is exempt under the FOIA and this subject has to be addressed before dealing with the DPA's exemptions.

As explained in chapters 5 and 6, access to personal data/documents under the FOIA is exempt from the provisions of the FOIA if it is data covered by the DPA. This is because access to such documents by a DS has to be made under the DPA in accordance with that Act's provisions and the exemption under the FOIA is absolute. This will include access to personal data added by the FOIA. Access to records about others has to be made under the FOIA. But an exemption applies under s. 40 FOIA. This exemption is absolute where it constitutes data falling within paras. (a)–(d) of the definition of data within s. 1(1) DPA (p. 281 above) and disclosure to a member of the public would contravene any of the DPP. There is also an absolute exemption in the case of data added by the FOIA where disclosure to a member of the public would contravene any of the DPP but for the exemption in s. 33A DPA (added by s. 70 FOIA). This means that although the DPA does not cover such data, the DPP are 'operative' where disclosure would result in a breach of the DPP. This only applies to manual data introduced by the FOIA and held by PAs. Where a request is for personal data not covered by the DPA or the FOIA, it is not exempt. Where it is data covered by the DPA and the FOIA as described above, but it is exempt from s. 7(1)(c) DPA by virtue of any provision in Pt IV of the same (below), it is then exempt from disclosure under the FOIA, but the exemption is not absolute. It is subject to the PI test (see chapter 5). Where data fall within s. 1(1)(a)–(d) DPA and processing and does not contravene the DPP but processing may be prevented under s. 10 (likely to cause damage or

---

[83] *AG's Reference (No. 1 of 2007)* [2007] EWCA Crim 760.

[84] The jurisdiction is exercised by the High Court or county court in England and Wales and the Court of Session and sheriff court in Scotland. The court has wide powers of inspection but not of disclosure to applicants pending the determination of that question in the applicant's favour.

distress), they are exempt under the FOIA but the exemption is not absolute and is subject to the PI test. The duty to confirm or deny may be overridden under s. 40.

Exemptions

Part IV of the DPA contains the exemptions from the DP provisions. Schedule 7 provides a list of miscellaneous exemptions. Additional exemptions may be made under s. 38 by the Secretary of State. There are two basic exemptions: exemption from subject information provisions allowing access and ensuring certain safeguards, and exemption from the non-disclosure provisions, i.e. from those provisions in the DPP safeguarding processing, preventing disclosure to third parties, allowing rectification and so on. Other exemptions may also apply.

Subject information provisions provide two basic sets of rights. First of all, the DS has the right of access to the personal data. The second is that data may only be treated as processed fairly when certain safeguards are maintained. These are: disclosure to the DS of the DC's identity or that of his representative; the purposes for which the data are to be processed; and any information that would be required to make the processing fair. The DC has to provide this information when the DS has supplied the data. If the DS did not supply the data, the information must be supplied to the DS before the data are processed or disclosed to a third party. If the subject information exemption applies in full, the DS loses both these rights.

The non-disclosure provisions possess three basic features which allow exemptions from DPP as specified 'to the extent to which they are inconsistent with the disclosure in question' (DPA s. 27(3)). If one of the following grounds for exemption is made out, that overrides the rights of the DS as specified in the exemption: that personal data may only be treated as processed fairly if any disclosure of that personal data does not infringe the disclosure restrictions contained in sch. 2 and 3 (processing subject to the relevant conditions); that any disclosure of personal data must take place in conformity with the second to fifth DP principles (see above); that any disclosure of personal data must take account of the right of the DS to object to processing likely to cause damage or distress, the right of the DS to have inaccurate personal data of which he is the subject rectified etc. (see above) and to have third parties to whom the data have been notified informed of that rectification etc.

The above provisions if used in one of the following exemptions will cover the items as set out within the exemption. Exemptions may also override other safeguards in the Act as illustrated in the first ground for exemption – national security.

The exemptions cover national security (s. 28 DPA) which is exempted from the DPP, Pts II (rights of DS), III (notification) and V (enforcement and see s. 28(11)) and s. 55 (which concerns criminal offences of unlawfully obtaining etc. personal data). The exemption of national security amounts to an exclusion from the Act where all the exemptions apply. Under s. 28(2), a certificate signed by a minister of the Crown stating that the exemption from all or any of the above provisions 'is or at any time' was required for national security 'shall be conclusive evidence of that fact'. The certificate may identify the personal data to which it applies by means of a general description. It may have prospective effect.[85] An appeal may be made to the IT by the person affected by the certificate. The IT applies the principles applied by a court on an application for judicial review and may allow the appeal and quash the certificate 'if it finds that the minister did not have reasonable grounds for issuing the certificate'. The powers of the IT are certainly confined.[86] But it is not powerless. The certificate is 'conclusive evidence' of the fact that data are exempt for the purpose of safeguarding national security. The certificate must be related to the statutory purpose; it must not be issued in bad faith or ulterior intent, nor be an abuse of process. Could one add a disproportionate judgement by the executive? At stake is a right covered by Art. 8, so proportionality should be available but there is a reluctance to question 'national security' grounds by the courts (see chapter 11). IT intervention would be less than likely except in the most egregious of cases.

In *Norman Baker MP v Secretary of State for the Home Department*[87] a certificate was ruled invalid because it would allow the security service to respond negatively to a request *regardless* of whether national security was actually involved. Non-committal replies by the security service on grounds of national security to a request for personal data by the DS, neither confirming nor denying their processing of such data and issuing a certificate on the grounds of national security protecting the refusal, was far too broad in the circumstances. The IT had no need to determine the merits of the specific application.

Any person directly affected by the issuing of a certificate may appeal to the National Security Appeals Panel of the IT under s. 28(4).

In *R (Secretary of State for the Home Department) v IC*[88] a certificate was issued under s. 28(2) following a request by a DS for information and the IT allowed the IC's appeal against the award of the certificate. The DC argued that the IC could not appeal under s. 28(4) and the s. 28 certificate prevented the IC issuing an Information Notice to inspect the contested data under s. 43 (below). The High Court ruled s. 28 did not prevent the issue of a notice under s. 43. Once the notice was issued, then s. 28(2) may be invoked and issue would be joined for the tribunal's decision. The DC's suggestion short-circuited the process. The IC was also a person within s. 28(4) and was entitled to appeal against the certificate.

Any other person in the proceedings may appeal against the alleged effects of a certificate in relation to general descriptions of data applying to personal data (s. 28(6)). The IT may determine that the certificate does not so apply. The

---

85 Note the similarity to the FOIA, s. 24(4).   86 See SI 2000/206 and SI 2000/731.
87 [2001] UKHRR 1275.   88 [2006] EWHC 2958 (Admin).

power to issue a certificate must be exercised by a member of the Cabinet or Attorney General or Lord Advocate.[89]

Further exemptions cover processing for the purpose of:

(a) the prevention or detection of crime
(b) the apprehension or prosecution of offenders
(c) the assessment or collection of any tax or duty or of any imposition of a similar nature.

In these cases the exemption covers the subject information provisions and the non-disclosure provisions. The exemption furthermore permits disclosure of such data to bodies like the police in carrying out their statutory functions thereby allowing them to process the data free from the subject access provisions. Provision is made for housing benefit and council tax.

Section 30 covers exemptions for health, education and social work. The Secretary of State has made orders exempting or modifying subject access provisions with regard to physical or mental health or condition of the DS. Data are exempt from s. 7 rights (access) where access would be likely to cause serious harm to the physical or mental health of the DS or any other person. Provision is made for the consultation of relevant health professionals and the receipt of their written opinion on disclosure.[90] There are detailed provisions concerning rights of access of those with parental responsibility. Orders have been made covering past and present pupils of schools making provision for children who have suffered, or may be at risk of, abuse. Exemptions cover social work in relation to the DS or other individuals conducted by government departments, local authorities or voluntary bodies.[91] These records are 'accessible records' (see p. 28) and cover a much wider range of data and documents than the DPA definitions.

Listed relevant functions of a regulatory nature under s. 31 may also be exempted from the subject information provisions. These cover items such as preventing financial loss due to dishonesty, malpractice or other seriously improper conduct by or unfitness or incompetence of persons in banking, insurance, investment or other financial services or in the management of corporate bodies. It covers bankruptcy and professional conduct. Charities and their property are covered. Exemptions to protect people at work and relevant functions are provided, e.g. statutory, Crown or those functions of a public nature in the PI and for health and safety at

---

[89] See also s. 28(8)–(9).

[90] Data Protection (Miscellaneous Subject Access Exemptions) Order SI 2000/419 as amended; and Data Protection (Subject Access Modification) (Social Work) Order SI 2000/415 and amendment SI 2005/467; the Education Order SI 2000/414; Health Order SI 2000/413.

[91] *Ibid.* The social work SI exempts SD access where that would be likely to prejudice the carrying out of social work because serious harm to the physical or mental health of the DS or another would be likely.

work.[92] The public-sector ombudsmen and Office of Fair Trading are likewise provided with exemptions.[93]

In the case of 'special purposes' concerning processing data in connection with journalism, literary and artistic purposes and publications for those purposes, exemptions are allowed from various DPPs where the DC reasonably believes that the publication would be in the PI – having regard in particular to the importance of freedom of speech – and where compliance with the DPP is incompatible with the special purposes. The aim is to protect freedom of speech: it will require an appraisal of the relationship between Arts. 8 and 10 ECHR. In a general sense, neither is absolute and a wide range of factors will have to be considered in seeking a balance. The Act, however, seeks to ensure that the courts cannot be used to obtain a prior restraint against publications using such material by staying proceedings until either the IC has determined that the processing of data is not taking place for the special purposes or the claim is withdrawn (see s. 45). In *Campbell v MGN Ltd* the Court of Appeal ruled that the protection in s. 32 for journalists applied *after* and not only before publication.[94] This reflected the reality that journalism was a continuing and not a fixed process.

Section 34 DPA exempts from subject access and non-disclosure provisions the fourth DPP and s. 14(1)–(3) data which the DC has to publish or allow to be inspected under any other statutory provision and whether free or by charge. This section is amended by s. 72 FOIA so that 'enactment' does not include the FOIA. This was to prevent access rights dominating over data-protection rights. A constantly reiterated fear was that the latter would dominate the former in circumstances where access may be justified. This has been a constant point of contention in IC and IT decisions as well as in decisions of the EU Ombudsman and EU courts (see chapter 10, p. 385). What is the proper balance between privacy and access to personal data? Such a problem arose in *ex p. Fisher*.[95] Where information is refused because it covers personal data, the official reaction all too often is to assert that it is covered by the DPA and in the absence of any other right to examine the information it must be denied. Such denial can cause serious injustice where information is refused as in *Fisher*. Fisher requested information about the status of farmland he had purchased from the DS. The request was refused on DPA grounds.

The case went to the ECJ which felt that it was not possible to apply a blanket rule that stated that data could not be disclosed without the consent of the person who supplied it. The legitimate interests of the applicant for information

---

[92] S. 31(3)(c).   [93] And see s. 233 Financial Services Act 2000.

[94] [2002] EWCA Civ 1373 overruling [2002] EWHC 499 QBD on this point. The House of Lords left this ruling in tact in its decision reversing aspects of the Court of Appeal's decision: [2004] UKHL 22.

[95] Case C-369/98 *R v Minister of Agriculture, Fisheries and Food, ex p. Fisher* (2000) The Times, 10 October, ECJ. See I. Harden (2001) European Public Law 165 and ch. 13 below for the convention. See *Promusicae v T. de E. SAU* Case C-275/06 (2008) 2 CMLR 17.

should be considered. No damage was done to any fundamental interests, rights or privacy of the data provider. Relevant criteria for balancing the interests involved could be found in EC Directive 95/46/EC on data protection. The Court said:

> Article 7(f) of that Directive authorised the disclosure of data if it was necessary for the purposes of the legitimate interests pursued by a third party to whom the personal data were disclosed, except where such interests were overridden by the interests or fundamental rights and freedoms of the data subject which required protection.

It would be wrong to assert that Fisher would not have any right under s. 34 DPA as amended because that section excludes the FOIA. The question is whether disclosure involves a breach of the DPP. This involves a balancing of interests as we shall see in case law below.

Fisher might have rights under s. 35. This provides that personal data are also exempt from the non-disclosure provisions where the disclosure is required by or under any enactment, any rule of law or court order under s. 35. A similar exemption applies where 'disclosure is necessary for the purposes of or in connection with any legal proceedings (including prospective legal proceedings) or for the purpose of obtaining legal advice' or 'is otherwise necessary for the purposes of establishing, exercising or defending legal rights'.

Where data are processed by an individual only for the purposes of that individual's personal, family or household affairs (including recreational purposes) they are exempt from the DP principles and the provisions of Pts I and II.

Confidential references given *by the* DC are exempt from s. 7 if given for: education, training, employment of the DS including prospective employment; appointments to an office; and provision of any service by the DS. The italicised words limit this to references given by the DC.

Subject information exemptions cover the armed forces of the Crown, assessing suitability for judicial appointments including QCs and management forecasts and other items including examination marks and scripts[96] prejudicing negotiations, legal professional privilege and other items.

Section 40 FOIA and personal data exemptions

To recall, s. 40 FOIA exempts personal data from the access provisions. The absolute nature of the exemptions has been discussed although not all personal data are given an absolute exemption (see p. 293). Section 40 is probably the most voluminous exemption in terms of use. It must be recalled that claims by subjects about their own data are dealt with under the DPA provisions; claims

---

[96] This provision is to prevent access before results are published. Some universities have stopped publication of class lists unless those included have consented. This is to avoid receiving notices that processing such data may cause substantial damage or distress in releasing, e.g. an individual's whereabouts.

about others' data are dealt with in accordance with the FOIA subject to DPA protection.[97] Our concern here is with those cases where data are sought by a requester on a third party or where papers requested under the FOIA contain personal data. Clearly, official documents will frequently have names included on them. These may be persons written about or named in the document, authors of the report or officials. Or a requester may simply wish to know about actions of the DS. If simply invoking the DPA could defeat access, it would constitute a major blow to the FOIA.

Most of the cases deal with data which it is claimed could only be disclosed in breach of the DPP thereby making it an absolute exemption. The question is: does it involve a breach of the DPP? A crucial provision in this respect is sch. 2, para. 6 DPA: 'The processing is necessary for the purposes of legitimate interests pursued by the data controller or by the third party or parties to whom the data are disclosed, except where the processing is unwarranted in any particular case by reason of prejudice to the rights and freedoms or legitimate interests of the DS.'[98] The IC and IT have ruled that where a requester seeks to utilise this provision, the burden of proving the legitimate interest is on the requester. Under the first DPP, processing must be fair and lawful. Remember also, that a DS should be consulted about disclosure under the terms of the FOIA code of guidance. In chapter 10 we shall see how the data protection regime has been applied in the operation of EU access to information.

The IT has ruled that the name of an evicted tenant is personal data: EA/2007/0129 *Turcotte v IC and LB Camden*.[99] In FS50133250 the complainant requested information relating to individuals excluded from schools within the local authority area as a result of drug finds. Some information was provided, but the Council refused to provide information at individual school level, citing the exemption in s. 40. Using the definition contained in the DPA 1998, the IC determined that the information was personal data. He then went on to consider under the DPP whether it was fair and lawful to disclose the information. The IC considered that there was a more than slightly hypothetical possibility that an excluded young person would be identified, which, combined with the potentially very serious consequences of disclosure, meant that the Council was entitled to rely on the s. 40 exemption. In FS50145985 concerning the Ministry of Justice (MOJ), the complainant requested detail of the disciplinary action taken against judges including their names, the reasons for the action and dates. The MoJ refused to disclose on the basis of s. 40. The IC found that there had

---

[97] FS50145322: Request for information about events in 1970s and 1980s concerning theft and employment. A breach of s. 17 by failing to specify reason for citing s. 40(5)! As request was for information about the requester, the DPA was involved and the IC dealt with it as a s. 42 DPA issue.

[98] The Secretary of State may, by order, specify circumstances in which this condition may, or may not be satisfied: sch. 2(6)(2)

[99] FS50150598 makes it clear that in relation to the records of a telephone conversation in which names were mentioned, the IC thought that the s. 40(1) exemption would apply, and imported the definition of personal data from the DPA 1998.

been procedural breaches under s. 17, because the response was out of time and no explanation as to reliance on s. 40 was given. As regards substance, the IC found that the information came within the definition of personal data in the DPA. He took into account the following factors: (1) the individuals' reasonable expectations regarding the information; (2) the seniority of the individuals; (3) whether disclosure would cause unjustified damage to the individuals; and (4) the legitimate interests of the public. He found that the information should not be disclosed because whilst (a) the information called into question their suitability for their role and (b) matters in this area should be subjected to scrutiny, they would not expect this scrutiny to be made public. Disclosure would cause unwarranted damage and distress and the MoJ already published broad categories of information in this area. Whilst public confidence might be increased by disclosure, the internal disciplinary procedures in place were sufficient.

FS50177136 concerned a request to the Cabinet Office for information regarding a Cabinet committee that was formed in order to consider data-sharing within the public sector. Some information was provided, however his request for minutes of certain meetings and the name and job titles of the members of the Cabinet committee were refused under ss. 35 and 40 FOIA respectively. In relation to the request for minutes, the IC found that s. 35(1)(a)–(b) was engaged because: (1) Cabinet committees provide a framework for government to consider major policy decisions; (2) the minutes record suggestions and proposals to improve data-sharing and no firm policy decision had been taken at the time of the request; (3) the minutes were recorded for the purpose of providing ministers with an accurate account of the meetings; and (4) s. 35(5) explicitly makes reference to proceedings of any committee of the Cabinet. The PI favoured non-disclosure because it was important to protect the convention of collective responsibility. To disclose the information would lead to government time being spent commenting on, and defending, individual views expressed in a Cabinet committee rather than the position of the government (good analysis on this point: paras. 33–42). As regards the request for names etc, the IC found that s. 40 was engaged and the information was protected under the first DPP.

In FS50178633 the complainant made a request for all correspondence between the General Medical Council (GMC), a named doctor and his employers. The GMC confirmed it held the information. However, the IC found that the GMC was not obliged to respond to the request under s. (1)(1)(a) by virtue of s. 40(5)(b)(i). The IC considered that responding with a confirmation or denial was a disclosure of information which constituted personal data under the first principle of the DPA; the doctor would have a reasonable expectation as to privacy. The PI was in favour of non-disclosure because whilst there was a legitimate PI in ensuring the competence of doctors, the existing mechanisms were sufficient to satisfy it.[100]

---

[100] See EA/2008/0088, *S. M. Butters v IC.*

FS50178913 saw the complainant request information that the Foreign Secretary had received which cast doubt on the evidence given by Ms Proetta in the television programme 'Death on the Rock' (an investigatory programme into the shooting of three IRA members by the SAS in Gibraltar in the 1980s). Ms Proetta gave her witness account of the actions of the SAS. The Foreign and Commonwealth Office (FCO) refused the request on the basis of s. 40(2)–(3), claiming it was exempt personal data. The IC found that the information was personal data. The IC applied the first DPP and considered sch. 3 of the DPA (conditions for processing sensitive personal data). The information could not be disclosed under any of the conditions in schedule 3. Whilst Ms Proetta had been interviewed for the television programme, the withheld information had not been released and she would not have expected or wanted it to be released by the FCO. This case was partly reversed by *A. Brett v IC* EA/2008/0098.

In FS50141015 the complainant requested information from the Department for Work and Pensions (DWP) as to whether there were any compliments or complaints recorded about a doctor employed by a third party. The DWP initially stated that it held no such information and later added that even if it were held by the third party on their behalf, it would be exempt from disclosure by s. 40(5) of the Act. The IC found that due to the contractual relationship between the DWP and the third party any relevant 'complaints' (but not 'compliments') information held by the third party, if it existed, would be held by them on behalf of the DWP, by operation of s. 3(2). However, in accordance with s. 40(5) of the Act, the DWP was correct to neither confirm nor deny the existence of the requested information as to do so would contravene the first of the DPP. The IC considered the consequences of disclosure on the doctor and decided that release of information regarding complaints would be unfair. The type of information requested was of a nature that normally remains confidential between an employee, his employer and possibly a regulatory professional body.

The complainant requested a copy of the winning tender proposal for a particular consultancy post along with details of the scores awarded to all of the tenders which the Department for International Development (DFID) received in FS50088016. While DFID provided the complainant with the overall score awarded to the winning tender and the average score awarded to his tender (the complainant's tender was unsuccessful), DFID refused to disclose: (i) the winning tender proposal (including CV and price bid) on the basis of ss. 40(2) and 43(2); and (ii) a detailed breakdown of the scores awarded to the tenders (score card) on the basis of s. 43(2). The IC found that in relation to (i) the data were personal data, as they contained biographical information; however disclosure would not breach the first DPP. The IC reasoned that any tenderer should have realised that certain details about their bid may have been disclosed and that such tenders are open to public scrutiny. The IC distinguished between information about the tenderer's professional and personal lives, and found that whilst the two were intertwined in places, the details were overwhelmingly about his professional life. In applying sch. 2 of the DPA, the IC thought that there was a necessary legitimate interest in ensuring openness, transparency and accountability, and that disclosure would impose no unwarranted interference (the tenderer's commercial interests were not taken into account).[101] As regards (ii), the score cards, the IC found that s. 40(2) exempted disclosure. The information constituted personal data and because of DFID's policy of not giving tenderers their own cards back, it would have been reasonably assumed that they would not be disclosed to anyone else.

FS50088853 concerned a complainant who sought the background papers relating to the 1993 Memorandum of Understanding (MOU) on Royal Finances under which the Queen and the Prince of Wales would voluntarily pay income tax. The Treasury refused to release the information, citing s. 40 of the Act. The IC made a distinction between private and public finances. Information relating to the former would fall within s. 40(2), which does not attract a PI test. However the factor which swayed the IC against deciding that public finances were involved was that at the time of the MOU there were no FOI provisions and therefore it was not expected that the information would be disclosed.

In FS50130517 the complainant wrote to the House of Commons to request the amounts spent by seven MPs since May 2005 on circulars and reports to their constituents. The IC has decided that the House breached s. 1 of the Act (general right of access to information held by public authorities) by not clarifying to the complainant the information held in relation to the request. He further decided that the information held is not exempt from disclosure under s. 40 and therefore required it to be released.

The complainant requested the names of the doctors who had previously worked in a particular hospital department between the years 2000 and 2004 in FS50119963. The PA initially refused the request on the basis of s. 12 FOIA but in subsequent correspondence confirmed that it was withdrawing its reliance on s. 12 and instead refused to disclose the information citing s. 40 of the Act. The IC concluded that the PA was correct to withhold the information on the basis of s. 40 but had breached s. 17 of the Act by failing to provide the complainant with an adequate refusal notice within twenty working days of the date of her request. The distinguishing feature here was that the applicant had harassed a registrar with correspondence and this was likely again if names were released. While motives of an applicant are not relevant per se, disclosure to the world would include the applicant. But any 'harassment' would be minor – involving correspondence. More crucial was the fact that registrars in the relevant period (2000–4) had a legitimate expectation of confidentiality and no legitimate purpose of the requester was served under sch. 2(6).

---

[101] The IC rejected the arguments of DFID that disclosure was exempt under s. 43 because it would prejudice its commercial interests and that of the tenderers; the IC considered the IT's decision in the *Derry* case (p. 235 above) (interesting discussion).

FS50099223 was a request for information (footage) on Operation Cauldron – sea trials of dissemination of biological warfare agents between 1951–3. In this experiment animals were infected. The footage would reveal images of personal identities and blacking-out would exceed the cost limit. Sections 38, 40(2) and 44 invoked. Disclosure, said the Ministry of Defence (MoD), would breach s. 10 DPA (processing would cause damage or distress). Section 44 was effected through reliance on HRA (Art. 8) but advice was not sought on this by the MoD. The MoD claimed for s. 40 there would be breaches of first and second DPPs and s. 10 DPA (the FOIA, s. 40(3)(a)(i)–(ii)). Section 40 FOIA only applies if disclosure would contravene sch. 1 DPA or s. 10 DPA. The IC was not satisfied that disclosure would be unlawful or unfair. The IC did not feel the second DPP concerning notification for 'specified and lawful purposes' was relevant because the drafter of s. 40 FOIA had in mind that such data could be disclosed and to bar it under the second DPP would effectively bar all claims under the FOIA 'on the basis that data were not originally obtained for that [FOIA] purpose'. This is a significant point in assisting access. It was better to base reliance on the first DPP, which was not contravened. No notifications had been received under s. 10 by the MoD. For s. 40(3) to be breached, a PA must receive such a notice (para. 44: s. 10(1) DPA). Otherwise it cannot make that claim. The IC also believed that the current climate of openness is very different to 1996 when, the MoD alleged, a similar disclosure caused distress.

FS50088977 involved a request for a copy of an ACAS agreement leading to reinstatement of a senior police officer, Ali Dizaei. Section 40 was not active but, in relation to the second DPP, the IC repeated the test in relation to the FOIA above – FOI disclosure it is not a 'purpose' for DPA requirements that has to be identified and stated by the DC. The reliance on DPP six was unsuccessful because that specifically refers to rights in ss.7, 10, 11 and 12 DPA. None was cited. The officer had participated in press and media coverage of his case and he had written a book about his experience (not about the agreement). The Independent Police Complaints Commission had been critical of the agreement and its secrecy. Schedule 2(6) DPA was satisfied here and no clear detriment to the officer was established. Regarding s. 41, the information did not come from a third party – it came from within the Police Authority (from one of its employees and its officers: see chapter 6, p. 219).

FS50110885 was a request for information to Cambridge University about successful applicants to a course: numbers from the same school and their gender were withheld. The IC stated that the 'purposes of processing' for DPA purposes, which have to be stated, are 'broad'. The request concerned the collation of statistics. Disclosure of personal data under the FOIA is not a 'specific purpose for which such information is processed. In responding to a request made under the Act, the IC ruled, the PA is not fulfilling one of its business purposes; it is simply complying with a legal obligation [under FOIA]' (para. 44). It is difficult to argue that compliance with a legal rule would be incompatible with other purposes for which personal data may be processed.

The general question is: is disclosure fair? Schedule 2(6) DPA was satisfied. The IC did not believe in this case that a specific notification to DSs that their data may be disclosed under the FOIA is necessary (para. 47). There was no high expectation of privacy attached to this data (para. 50). To what extent could this last point be generalised?

FS50067416 was a request for the highest earner in BBC NI. The IC stated that while it would breach the DPA to disclose the exact salary, to release the pay band and individual's name would not. Other information related to the cost of producing a show (John Daly) and several presenters ('talents'). The BBC exclusion relating to 'journalism' etc. was invoked (see chapter 4, p. 142 and Introduction, p. 6) and if not applicable, ss. 40, 43 and 41. As in so many BBC cases, the information was held for operational purposes and was not excluded. The question under s. 40 was: is this private or public business? Schedule 2(6) was satisfied in relation to the highest earner in terms of the pay band. It was reasonable to expect that the BBC would keep information about 'talent' fee confidential and s. 40 protected this. The 'talents' were not in a position to influence policy choices affecting expenditure![102]

FS50102474 was a request to the BBC for the cost of the 'Children in Need' programme in 2005 (see s. 43, chapter 6, p. 234). In relation to s. 40, the request was for one payment for a presenter, not a salary. There was a public perception that performers would perform for free:

> The IC considers that individuals who hold such high profile and public facing roles should expect information about them to be available to the public. This is especially so in a climate where the public are constantly alerted by the media to the high earnings of its programme presenters and in a society where the requirement for scrutiny of public spending is increasingly expressed. [Para. 42]

FS50082768 was a request for six pieces of information relating to investigation of serious allegations by relevant police officers against the requester. Section 40(1) was correctly invoked and s. 40(5) (neither confirm nor deny) should have been invoked. Some information had already been disclosed to the requester under the DPA in 2002. The DC breached s. 1(1)(a) in failing to inform the complainant that the whereabouts of the accusers were not held. The IC was satisfied that this is personal data because 'it is information related to the investigation into him, the allegations against him and his arrest and detention' (para. 40).[103] The IC's Awareness Guidance has advice about requests concerning access to information about third parties: would it cause unnecessary or unjustified distress or damage to the person who the information is about?

---

[102] FS50097242 (see sch. 1, ch. 4 above) The IC investigated the BBC's application of the exemptions and found that the information requested is exempt from disclosure under s. 40 of the Act. FS50068026: a request for a report by the BBC into Alan Yentob's expenses. S. 40(2)–(3)(a)(i) exemptions properly applied. See FS50142539: salaries of senior academics at a university withheld and exempt under s. 40(2).

[103] Cf. *Durant v Financial Services Authority* [2003] EWCA Civ 1746 where a FSA inquiry did not place the focus on Durant when investigating his complaint.

Would a third party expect such information to be disclosed to others? Has the person been led to believe that the information would be kept secret? Has that third party expressly refused consent? Furthermore, under sch. 2(6) DPA, it is up to the claimant to prove that it is in the PI for the data to be disclosed (reverses the FOIA PI text). Releasing the name of stations at which serving officers serve would not breach DPP (unless a security aspect is established) but retired officers are entitled not to have data disclosed. Data about the requester's wife and son were also not disclosed because of DPP protection.[104]

In FS50116822 there was a request to an NHS Trust for a copy of an internal report into allegations of financial irregularity made against a former director of research governance. It was entirely appropriate for the IC to consider an additional exemption not considered by the PA.[105] Section 40(2) was invoked. 'Seniority of individual' should be taken into account in deciding whether to disclose.[106] Information about someone acting in an official or work capacity should normally be disclosed unless there is some risk to the individual concerned (from the IC's Guidance) (para. 42). In EA/2006/0074–0076 *Corporate Officer of House of Commons v IC* the IT approved the IC guidance: does it apply to public or private life of the DS (see below). Would disclosure cause unnecessary or unjustified distress or damage to the individual; would s/he expect information to be disclosed to others; was s/he led to believe information would be kept secret; has express refusal to consent been declared? The IC believed disclosure would be fair and lawful. Disclosure of third parties named in the report would be unfair and breach the first DPP but it could be disclosed if anonymised. There was no breach of s. 40.[107]

FS50071451 dealt with requests for information about MPs expenses. It is one of many and the point has been determined in the High Court. The IC took the unusual step of issuing an Information Notice (IN) to the House of Commons! The information was examined at the House of Commons. The request was for the receipts, rental agreements or mortgage interest statements of six MPs under the Additional Costs Allowance (ACA – second homes). The House of Commons claimed that disclosure over and above that in the Publication Scheme would breach the DPA (para. 18). The IC decided that the requested information was personal data and that its fully itemised disclosure would be unfair. However, he decided that it would not contravene the DPP to disclose the information showing the totals paid under specified headings within the ACA. This was ordered to be disclosed. Discussion of sch. 2(6) DPA in paras. 42–9.

---

[104] FS50074144 was a request for the number of complaints received by the agency against a named doctor. He assessed the health of those claiming disability allowance. The information was held by the PA for purposes of the Act (FOIA, s. 3(2)) but s. 40(5) (NCND) applied not only to the doctor's data but also in relation to any complaints against him.

[105] FS50093255: concerned sch. 3 DPA (the conditions for processing 'sensitive data'). S. 40(1) upheld but not raised by PA (i.e., raised by IC). The investigation concerned 'abusive' complainants.

[106] Authorities from IC's DNs cited in para. 41.

[107] See EA/2008/0038 *R. Waugh v IC and Doncaster College.*

The resistance on the part of the Commons is manifest. FS50070469 concerned a request for Tony Blair's ACA (above). The IC asked for information from the Commons on 9 September 2005. An IN was issued on 6 June 2006 and information given to the IC on 14 July 2006! The outcome was similar to the previous case.

FS50067986 is another request to the House of Commons, this time for the travel expenses of MPs including an MP's spouse on official business. The Commons sought to establish motives for the request and use of information. This was impermissible said the IC. If it was possible to establish a pattern of travel (i.e., specific routes) that might constitute a security risk. It was not possible to do so here and sch. 2(6) DPA justifies disclosure, but not however of 'detailed routes, times or dates of those journeys'. See the appeal in EA/2006/0074–0076 *Corporate Officer of the HC v IC* (below).

FS50073128 involved a request for the names and salaries of MPs staff. Section 40(2) did protect relatively junior staff appointments and details of salaries of assistants insofar as disclosure might breach the DPP. The information was 'held' by the House of Commons for the purposes of s. 3(2) FOIA contrary to the arguments of the House. Section 36(7) FOIA is absolute in relation to the House of Commons and names of staff and its invocation could not be questioned but s. 40(2) did not of itself protect the names of assistants.

Appeals

EA/2006/0015–16 *Corporate Officer of HCs v IC and N. Baker (AP)* concerned MPs travel expenses: the total amount claimed for each MP for modes of travel by rail, road, air and bicycle. The expenses involved European, extended and family travel. There had been 167 requests from the public for information on travel by MPs since the FOIA came into effect. Section 40 was invoked. General sums had been published in publication schemes since October 2004. The Scottish Parliament disclosed more information on this topic than Westminster. The DPA's operation had to be affected by a 'culture of openness' argued counsel for the IC at para. 43 *et seq*. Information that is about someone acting in an official or work capacity should normally be provided on request unless there is some risk to the individual concerned. Different considerations would affect family or personal private-life information (para. 63). For the purposes of fair processing, the IC's guidance was accepted by IT: does data belong to public or private life of individual? The interests of MPs not 'necessarily first and paramount consideration in a case such as this' where personal data relate to their public lives (para. 79). Paragraph 6 of sch. 2 involves a balancing of competing interests (the DS and applicant's legitimate interests) not unlike that under a PI balancing of exemptions under the FOIA (even though s. 40 is an absolute exemption).[108] However, because the processing must be 'necessary'

---

[108] *Data Protection Act Legal Guidance* by IC para. 3.1.1 on sch. 2(6) DPA.

for the legitimate interests of members of the public to apply we find that only where (1) (applicant's interests) outweighs or is greater than (2) (DS's interests) should the personal data be disclosed. There is a reversal of the usual PI weightings under exemptions. The PI is in favour of disclosure. This is a very strong decision and has set the standard.

EA/2006/0064 *Rob Evans v IC and Ministry of Defence*[109] was the second decision of an appeal from the IC's decision to allow the MoD to withhold information. The facts are as follows. Mr Evans, a reporter for *The Guardian*, requested information from the MoD about a meeting in June 2005 between Lord Drayson and representatives of Whitehall Advisors Ltd, a lobbying company. The MoD confirmed that it had in its possession three relevant documents: (i) manuscript notes of the meeting; (ii) manuscript notes of a subsequent telephone call; (iii) a background note prepared for the minister before the meeting. The MoD claimed that the information fell within s. 36(2)(b)(i) FOIA or alternatively s. 35(1)(a) and was thus exempt from disclosure. Other exemptions were also claimed for the background note (ss. 40, 41 and 43). Mr Evans appealed to the IC, who considered that s. 36(2)(b)(i) did apply and that the PI weighed in favour of non-disclosure. He also decided that s. 40 would apply to the background note, but that s. 41 would not. Mr Evans appealed to the IT which upheld the decision of the IC to the extent that s. 36(2)(b)(i) applied, but allowed the appeal on the issue of the background note. The substantive decision on that point was given in the instant case.

The first issue with which the IT dealt was that relating to personal data and redaction. The IT concluded that all of the information in the background note was 'personal data' as defined by s. 40(7) of the FOIA. The note could not be redacted, because nothing would be left to disclose. Section 40(2) of the Act was engaged because Mr Evans was a third party requesting information. The question then arose as to whether disclosure would contravene any of the DPP in the DPA. The IT looked at the first principle which was satisfied. It considered that Pt II of sch. 1, para. 2(1)(b) of the DPA was involved and had not been complied with. The issue was whether the data controller ensured *so far as practicable*, before the relevant time or as soon as practicable after that time, that the DS was provided with the information; this had not been done. However the IT circumvented this on the basis that 'where processing has been subsequently requested by a third party, and for a purpose which had not been foreseen at the time of collection, and which was resisted by the data controller, it is not practicable to deliver the information to the DS, before the time of first processing'.[110] Therefore, in respect of Pt II, there was nothing to suggest that disclosure would contravene the first principle.

The IT then considered a possible breach of the first principle on the basis of the conditions contained in sch. 2 DPA. Under para. 6 of that provision, '[t]he

---

[109] See ss. 35–6, chs. 5 and 6 above.
[110] *House of Commons v IC and Norman Baker MP* EA/2006/0015 relied upon.

processing must be necessary for the purposes of legitimate interests pursued by . . . the third party'. It was decided that Mr Evans had a legitimate interest as a reporter, which had to be balanced against the prejudice to the DS (Mr Wood). It was recognised that legitimate interest is not the same as PI, but that in the instant case they amounted to the same thing. The PI in disclosure was minimised as the information would not have been of 'much interest to anyone'. However, the prejudice which would have been suffered by Mr Wood could have been very damaging both for the company and for him personally. The IT therefore concluded that the PI weighed in favour of non-disclosure.

EA/2007/0072 *BERR v IC and FoE*[111] saw a substituted DN. Friends of the Earth wanted information about meetings (lobbying) between the CBI and a government department (DTI) on a variety of subjects with dates, participants, minutes and correspondence. Some information was disclosed but ss. 35, 41 and 43 invoked for other information. Redacted information was requested. Some was disclosed and s. 40 invoked to protect identities. Dates, events, job titles of civil servants and CBI officials and whether there was a record of meetings were disclosed – this covered thirty meetings in a twelve-month period. Ten documents were withheld and a Vaughn index procedure applied.[112] A complaint was made to the IC. The IC decided that six documents should be disclosed and some parts (not all) of others. It was noted that the EIR cover climate change and energy policy on supply, demand and pricing. What is the predominant content of document (i.e., environmental or non-environmental)? If this question fails to produce an answer, the contents will have to be reviewed to see which regime applies! Parliament may not have appreciated the consequences of choosing 'information' rather than documents, the IT opined (para. 29). The cost of redaction should not be taken into account for purposes of SI 2004/3244.[113] Late claims for an exemption may be allowed on a case by case basis. The report contains useful detail on departmental/business relationships and lobbying. Information was not protected by s. 41. The case shows an influence of the Court of First Instance's (CFI) judgment in *Bavarian Lager* case (see chapter 10, p. 385) and s. 40 protection. The reasoning followed the line of the CFI and the IC.[114] EA/2007/0084 *Dundass v IC and Bradford MDC* concerned a request for details of respondents' names and addresses in a consultation exercise. The requester also wanted the last two letters of post codes that could identify an address. This was rightly refused under sch. 2 DPA, paras. 5[115] and 6. The interest of the DS is usually paramount but may be displaced where a public official exercising public functions is involved. The PI test is similar to s. 2 FOIA but the onus here is on the requester not the PA. The information was correctly denied.

---

[111] See also FS50093052.   [112] See ch. 12, p. 464.

[113] The Freedom of Information and Data Protection (Appropriate Limit and Fees) Regulations 2004.

[114] Paras. 101–2.

[115] Processing for administration of justice, official functions or public interest duties.

EA/2007/0061–63, 0122–23, 0131 *Corporate Officer of House of Commons v IC (Leapman, Brooke and Thomas)* was an appeal relating to the ACA payment of fees to MPs (above). The Corporate Officer's appeal was rejected but limits were set to what was disclosable (excludes sensitive personal data of MPs, personal data of third parties but not the name of those in receipt of rents/mortgage interest) and bank statements, loan statements, phone numbers and other matters. The IT ruled that more data should be made public than the IC determined. The rules on which ACA operated were not made publicly available, not even to MPs themselves in case they claimed the maximum! Reservation had not been notable. Lack of transparency did not encourage accountability and transparency in the system which was overseen by the National Audit Office and Commons Committee on Privileges. Pages 17–26 contain discussion on personal data and sch. 2(6). This was appealed to High Court and the IT's decision was confirmed. The questions involved had 'a wide resonance throughout the body politic' bearing on 'public confidence in our democratic system at its very pinnacle'.[116] (See Introduction.)

EA/2006/0074–0076 *Corporate Officer of the HC v IC* is another appeal concerning MPs expenses. An earlier case (EA/2006/0015–0016) led to information on expenses being placed in the publication scheme of the House of Commons. New information sought in this appeal covers (i) spouse, (ii) the number of trips by specific modes of transport, (iii) average costs, (iv) car mileage, (v) taxis (mileage – information on fares not available), and (vi) EU travel. Information was requested about an individual MP (Ms Moffat) and not collective data – the House of Commons held information collectively on MPs. The request was to try and identify 'green and environmental' aspects of travel. There is a useful statement of the reasons not to disclose at para. 63. These cover invasion of privacy and family life; the diversion of MPs and the House from other parliamentary business; the consent of MPs to aggregate disclosure only, not individual disclosure; the subjection of MPs to media scrutiny and so on. Section 40 was invoked by the House (parties agreed that s. 40(3)(a)(i) did not apply). This was about 'public life' not private life and so sch. 2(6) applied. Disclosure of individual's aggregate figures should be made, but not 'disclosure of travel details which could reveal the times, origins and destinations of journeys and the modes of transport likely to be used at particular times and circumstances could be of potential use to malevolent individuals, especially where such information was not otherwise available to them'.

EA/2007/0058 *T. Harcup v IC and Yorkshire Forward (YF)* saw an appeal allowed and a substituted DN. YF promotes business in Yorkshire. Details were sought about business hospitality events including a breakdown of costs. Corporate hospitality information was not provided as this did not cover 'events'! Names were not provided because of the DPA and request for more information

---

[116] *Corporate Officer of the House of Commons v IC, Brooke and Leapman* [2008] EWHC 1084 Admin para. 15.

would have exceeded the £450 costs limit. The complaint was mainly about the use of s. 40(2) DPA. The appellant argued that *Durant* meant this information was not personal data! The IT believed that *Durant*[117] had narrowed the concept of personal data and this was not personal data – merely recording who was at an event. But surely, a 'name' *is* personal data? As a result, s. 40(2) was not breached; had it been personal data, sch. 2(6)(i) DPA would not have made disclosure necessary. But s. 12 prevented disclosure of further information. This decision appears potentially dangerous and mistaken. A name is data and appearing or being at an event is surely 'biographical' even on the narrow understanding of *Durant*.

EA/2007/0056 *K. McCluskey v IC and PPS NI* was a request for information about police officers involved in legal proceedings in which the requester was acquitted. There is a 'fundamental difference between a right to information', as under the FOIA, and the voluntary discretionary disclosure of information by a PA, pursuant to agreement, as took place here (para. 14).[118] Section 40(2) FOIA was applied by the IC. There are also dangers of agreements regarding voluntary disclosure where general access is not made – it could foster or lead to favouritism, abuse and features of corporatism if groups are concerned.

Duty of notification on DCs

DCs are under a duty to notify the IC that they wish to be placed on a register of those intending to process personal data and fees are payable. SI 2000/188 has details on notification (see Introduction and SI 2009/1677). There are exemptions from notification. Data may be processed without registration where it is not 'assessable' under s. 22 – i.e. processing is likely to cause substantial damage or distress to DSs or otherwise prejudice the rights and freedoms of subjects and for which special provisions apply – *and* the processing is not by means of equipment operating automatically in response to instructions given for that purpose or data were not recorded with such an intention, i.e. it is manual data. Section 17(3) allows the Secretary of State to exempt the DC from notification where he believes that data may be processed within a particular category of processing that will not prejudice the rights and freedoms of DSs. Exemption from notification may also be claimed where a DC has a reliable system of self-regulation. A register entry will last for twelve months unless notification regulations vary this period. Even where data are exempt from the notification process, s. 24 stipulates that a DC must make 'relevant particulars' available in accordance with s. 16(1) to any person making a written request within twenty-one days free of charge.

The IC has to make publicly available at all reasonable hours information on the register free of charge in 'visible and legible' form. A fee may be required

---

[117] *Durant*, note 5 above.   [118] FOIA s. 78.

for a copy (see Introduction, p. 4).[119] DCs must ensure entries are as up to date as possible and processing in breach of a registration requirement is a criminal offence. Entries will include the name of the DC and their address or that of their nominated representative, a description of data to be processed and categories of DSs to which it relates, the purpose(s) of processing, recipients of data and non-EEA countries to which data are or may be transferred. The register will allow subjects to assess, in general terms, whether a DC is likely to hold information upon them as, e.g., an employer, retailer or client, customer and so on. The subject may then ask the DC whether the DC has information covered by the Act on the subject. If this is the case, then, subject to exemptions and payment of any fee,[120] the subject has right of access.

Rights of appeal to the IT

There are rights of appeal against notices served on DCs by the IC to the IT. The IT has been described above (see chapter 4).

The Commissioner's duties[121]

Section 53 DPA places various duties on the IC, including promoting good practice by DCs and their observance of the legislation. The IC shall arrange for the publication of information about the Act and good practice as well as advice as appears appropriate. Codes of practice will be prepared and disseminated to guide good practice. The IC may encourage the making of codes by trade associations for their members, may consult on such codes and may advise whether the code promotes the 'following of good practice'. Details of codes may be found at http://www.ico.gov.uk/Home/what_we_cover/data_protection/guidance/codes_of_practice.aspx.

The IC may also, with the DCs consent, assess processing of personal data to see if good practice is followed. The DC will be informed of the results. She may charge for services provided. Annual reports and other reports shall be laid before each House of Parliament as well as any codes prepared under s. 51(3).

Enforcement and other matters

Here we are concerned with protection of DSs. Yet another influence of the DPA on the FOIA may be seen in the area of enforcement. The IC does not make decision notices under the DPA as under the FOIA. The IC, where satisfied that a DC has contravened or is contravening any of the DPP, may serve on that person an enforcement notice (EN) (s. 40(1)). An EN requires the DC to take, or refrain from taking, specified steps within a certain period and/or to

---

[119] The register is available on the IC's homepage, see note 121 below.
[120] S. 26 and note 128 below.
[121] The home page for the Commissioner is www.dataprotection.gov.uk.

refrain from processing any personal data or specified data or processing them in a manner, or for a purpose and after such time, as specified. When deciding whether to serve an EN, the IC must consider, whether the contravention has caused or is likely to cause any person damage or distress. The EN may require rectification, erasure, blocking or destruction of other data held by the DC that contain an expression of opinion which appears to the IC to be based on the inaccurate data – this is in accordance with the fourth DPP (accuracy). Third parties may have to be informed by the DC. An EN must contain various details including rights of appeal and may involve urgent measures. Service of an EN is preceded by a period of informal negotiation, then the possibility of oral or written representations while seeking to establish whether any distress is likely, or has been caused. An EN may be cancelled or varied by written notice.

The IC may receive a request under s. 42 'by or on behalf of any person who is directly affected by any processing of personal data' to make an assessment of whether any processing is being carried out in compliance with the Act. The IC may also, as under the FOIA, serve an IN (see chapter 5, p. 176) to obtain information as well as a special IN. The latter is used in connection with requests under s. 42 as well as in relation to special purposes as set out above, i.e. journalism etc. Section 42 allows the IC to carry out an assessment on a person's request but it is subject to a number of conditions and procedural requirements.[122] It is not as accessible to complainants as the ombudsman function under the FOIA. The IN must contain information on rights of appeal.

A party to actual or prospective proceedings involving special-purposes data may apply to the IC for assistance in relation to those proceedings under several provisions of the Act.[123] The case must involve 'a matter of substantial public importance'. Appeals may be made against notices to the IT as well as determinations on special-purpose data under s. 45 DPA. The grounds of appeal are similar to those to the IT under the FOIA. Appeal lies on a point of law to the High Court or the Court of Session. The IC may apply for search-and-seizure warrants to a circuit judge under sch. 9 including an authorisation to test and operate equipment.

Section 56 contains restrictions on enforced access – forcing others to gain access to their own information to hand it to the 'enforcer'.[124] The former Data Protection Registrar (DPR) had noted an increase in enforced subject access whereby subjects are compelled by prospective employers to gain access to criminal and national insurance records to disclose any period spent in prison or other items.

---

[122] The IC may require information to satisfy herself as to the requester's identity. There are a variety of factors that the IC has to consider. The number of cases received by the ICO in 2008 was 24,851 but assessments are not listed as such. He issued nine DPA ENs and there were eleven DPA prosecutions: Annual Report 2007–8, HC 670 (2007–8).

[123] Under ss. 7(9), 10(4), 12(8) or 14, or by virtue of s. 13.

[124] See ss. 112–13 and 115 Police Act 1997 and s. 163 Serious Organised Crime Act 2005.

Any term or condition in a contract will be void insofar as it seeks to require an individual to produce all or part of a record obtained under data access rights by that individual and which contains information about that individual's mental or physical health made by a health professional in the course of caring for the individual (s. 58).

Those applying for positions with children and vulnerable adults are subject to checks (the 'vetting and barring scheme') involving criminal records from the Criminal Records Bureau and other checks on lists maintained by government departments as we saw in chapter 1 (see p. 14 above).[125] Following the Bichard report[126] into the shortcomings of police management of personal data which led to the murder of two young school girls by a school caretaker Ian Huntley, and where police intelligence was not handed on to relevant parties because of misunderstanding of the DPA requirements, recommendations were made for improvement in police DPA management. By the fourth progress report in 2007, twenty-one of Bichard's thirty-one recommendations had been realised. The top priority was a national police data-sharing facility.[127]

Fees have been set by regulations. These are set at a maximum of £10 for applications under s. 7(2)(b)[128] except where the request comes under regs. 4, 5 and 6 of SI 2000/191. A schedule is attached setting out rates for written documents according to page lengths. The maximum that may be charged is £50.[129] The Act binds the Crown. Government departments shall not be liable to prosecution under the Act but Crown servants may be prosecuted for various matters: unlawfully obtaining and disclosing personal data, unlawfully procuring the disclosure to another person of information contained in personal data, or selling unlawfully obtained personal data.

Problems

In the Constitution Committee's report on *Surveillance*[130] the IC pressed vigorously for a number of changes to the current regulatory regime, 'both in terms of the requirements that should be placed on organisations responsible for handling personal data, and the powers available to the Commissioner's Office to enforce the provisions of the DPA' (para. 225). Five key ways in which

---

[125] See *R (X) v Chief Constable West Midlands Police* [2005] 1 All ER 610 (CA) on fairness in dealing with requests. See *R (L)*, note 42 above.

[126] Bichard Inquiry Report, HC 653 (2003–4).

[127] The fourth progress report is at: http://police.homeoffice.gov.uk/publications/operational-policing/bichard-fourth-progress-report?view=Binary.

[128] See SI 2000/191 and SI 2001/187.

[129] Regulations cover, inter alia, notification by DCs and fees, SI 2000/188 and SI 2009/1677 increases fees for DCs in tier two to £500; Processing of Sensitive Personal Data SI 2000/417 and see SI 2009/1811; functions of designated authority; and designated codes of practice, SI 2000/418 (as amended).

[130] HL 18 (2008–9) and Government Reply, Cm. 7616.

the current legal regime could be substantially strengthened and improved were identified:

(1) mandatory Privacy Impact Assessments (PIAs) by government departments
(2) requirements to have codes of practice under statute in place for proactive information-sharing in the public sector – the Government has agreed to this in their reply to recommendations in its reply to *What Price Privacy?*[131]
(3) proper consultation with the IC before significant new developments
(4) increased audit and inspection powers for the IC
(5) effective penalties for serious disregard for the requirements of the DPP. (Section 77 of the Criminal Justice etc. Act 2008 contains a power to amend s. 55 DPA allowing imposition of custodial sentences.)

The Constitution Committee regretted that the Government had not responded with specific commitments to earlier reports of the Home Affairs Committee on data collection.[132] The committee welcomed the government's decision to provide a statutory basis for the IC to carry out inspections without consent of public-sector organisations that process personal-information systems. However, the proposal would not cover private-sector organisations. It recommended that the government reconsider this matter. 'Organisations which refuse to allow the Commissioner to carry out inspections are likely to be those with something to hide. In addition, the protection of citizens' data may in the absence of legislation be vitiated given the growing exchange of personal data between the public and private sectors' (para. 238).

The committee agreed with the recommendation of the Joint Committee on Human Rights that the role of the data-protection minister should be enhanced and its profile elevated. There was disappointment that the Government's response to that report has not engaged the main point about the need for more effective central leadership:

> The Government should report to the House through this Committee on the feasibility of having Ministry of Justice (MoJ) lawyers working in other departments and reporting to the MoJ on departmental policies with data protection implications, and of certification of legislative compatibility with the Human Rights Act 1998. This should be in conjunction with the current system of certification of compatibility by the Minister in charge of each bill going through Parliament. [Para. 290]

There should be a greater role for IC in advising or warning Parliament of the privacy implications and dangers in legislative instruments on surveillance. It recommended a joint committee be established to oversee the surveillance and data powers of the state and any legislation or proposed legislation which would

---

[131] See note 8 above and note the recommendations of R. Thomas and M. Walport, *Data Sharing Review* (2008).

[132] See note 130 above, para. 436.

expand surveillance or data processing powers should be s
by that Committee.[133] (See para. 376 and Introduction, p.

The European Commission's enforcement action against t
protection of internet privacy was noted above (see p. 272, n

Conclusion

At the start of the millennium it was feared that privacy protection would
outweigh the rights of access to information and that politicians in particular
would be able to use the HRA and Convention rights to prevent access to
personal information that it was in the PI to know. The fear of 'trumping' of
the FOIA by the DPA was noted above. The IC and IT have not allowed this
to happen. Special provisions were built in to protect freedom of speech in the
DPA and the HRA where artistic, journalistic or literary uses are involved.[134]
Rights to access and rights to privacy have to be balanced and the courts have
shown that neither is absolute and that freedom of publication and the right
to pass on information must not be used to damage an individual's reputation
without justification. Any interference with freedom of speech must be shown
to be necessary and proportionate. The courts have been more and more aware
of the importance of this overriding protection for a fundamental human
right.[135] But neither privacy nor freedom of speech is an absolute. Perhaps the
approach is not as robust as that adopted in the USA where those in the public
limelight are not given the full protection as others, in the law of defamation for
instance, thereby allowing inaccurate comments to be made about politicians
with impunity providing they are not knowingly or recklessly inaccurate.[136]
There is no right to privacy protected in English tort law; the considerable
development of confidentiality to cover personal and private information has
been outlined earlier in the chapter. But breach of confidentiality has a PI
defence and Art. 8(1) sits alongside Art. 8(2) qualifying the right to private
and family life on various grounds. One may not agree with the balance that
is struck in particular cases, but balance is inherent in their invocation. The

---

[133] The committee recommend that the government improve the design of the Home Office
Information Charter, and report regularly to Parliament on the measures taken to publicise
the charter and on their monitoring of the public response to it (para. 440).

[134] The 'special purposes data' under s. 3 (see above) and s. 12 HRA 1998.

[135] See, e.g., *Kelly v BBC* [2001] 1 All ER 323 and the cases above p. 273 *et seq*.

[136] Cf. *New York Times v Sullivan* 376 US 254 (1964) and *Reynolds v Times Newspapers Ltd* [1999]
4 All ER 609 where the House of Lords refused to adopt under English common law a qualified
privilege of 'political information'. Note the use in the US of discovery in such trials: 'The
trade-off for the more extensive defence has been the requirement of full disclosure by way of
extensive and onerous pre-trial discovery', per Lord Hobhouse at 659e. The interpretation of
Reynolds subsequently did not inspire confidence in the press and Lord Hutton famously
invoked *Reynolds* to lambast editorial practices at the BBC in the Kelly Inquiry, HC 247
(2003–4), pp. 321–3. *Reynolds* was revisited in *Jameel and Others v Wall St Journal Europe Sprl*
[2006] UKHL 44 and greater protection was given to publications in the public interest which
were not accurate but which were reported and published fairly and responsibly.

English reliance on non-statutory codes on privacy for the press and media, which have often appeared rather toothless, has prompted the judiciary to extend confidentiality.[137] Conversely, the use of 'super injunctions' to protect the 'privacy' of commercial organisations and to prevent reporting of the fact that they are engaged in litigation in controversial circumstances, and even to prevent the reporting of the injunction itself, has been a worrying development (*Financial Times*, 14 October 2009).

Privacy protection, like defamation, is described as a 'rich folk's tort'. It means little to the average punter. Negligence in the holding of personal information, as well as the use of misleading, inaccurate or irrelevant personal information by wielders of power and influence, whether professional bodies or employers or institutions, is a widely documented abuse of power and dereliction of duty.[138] One area which has caused particular problems has been health records. The NHS constitution of January 2009 committed the NHS to protection of confidentiality and privacy of patients and a right to full information on medical treatment, informed choice and involvement in health care.[139] But, like the databases established or to be established elsewhere including national identity cards, there must be a full and effective guarantee for data security. The laws on data protection need strengthening as outlined above. Regulators need enhanced powers to combat arrogant abuse of personal data and privacy. But we have also to realise that effective surveillance has a positive and beneficial aspect – so long as the watchers are watched and are made properly and fully accountable for their actions.

---

[137] In the case of the former Broadcasting Standards Commission, the Court of Appeal has ruled that the code's protection of privacy extends to a company regardless of the position under the ECHR: citing *Nimiety v Germany* (1992) 16 EHRR 97. The case concerned surreptitious filming inside premises of sales of allegedly second-hand goods as new: *R v Broadcasting Standards Commission, ex p. BBC* [2000] 3 All ER 989, CA.

[138] The use by private bodies of information on the political affiliations of prospective employees has been highlighted: HC Debs., vol. 110, col. 1176, and see Introduction, p. 4.

[139] www.dh.gov.uk/en/Publicationsandstatistics/Publications/PublicationsPolicyAndGuidance/DH_093419.

9

Claims and counterclaims

There is a broader context to the subject of information and government. How does government operate alongside the duties to disclose information under the laws we have examined? How does government manage to conceal its operations and activities from public scrutiny? What other provisions are there that place duties on government or others operating under close association with government to disclose their activities to the public, or to bodies operating on behalf of the public interest (PI)?

Principled government

Crisis prompts inquiry.[1] There are numerous sensational events which have provided an insight into contemporary governmental practice and one systemic development which concerns government structure. Previous editions of this book have examined the stormy events surrounding Michael Heseltine's resignation as Defence Secretary from Mrs Thatcher's Government in January 1986 over the Westland helicopter saga[2] – an episode which raised dramatic illustrations of government manoeuverings, internal inquiries as well as select committee inquiries, and leaks in high places. Mr Heseltine felt he was a victim of a conspiracy to end constitutional government because he took his ministerial responsibility seriously in seeking to promote the British defence industry and declared pointedly 'that the case against him was being put by "unidentified sources"'. 'We have no documents, no statements, no piece of paper that we can examine, we have just whispers on the telephone. Now, that is the way British Government is to be conducted . . . '[3]

The affair led to the release of more information than we could usually have hoped for into Whitehall's inner workings. After Westland, governments sought to assuage public anxiety over sensational events in which information was key

---

[1] Public Administration Select Committee, *Government by Inquiry*, HC 51-I (2004–5); Government Reply, Cm. 6481; Lord Hutton (2006) *Public Law* 807.

[2] Heseltine was promoting a British European joint initiative to take over Westland plc which produced helicopters while the prime minister supported an American initiative.

[3] This statement was made in an interview with Brian Walden on *Weekend World*, London Weekend TV, 12 January 1986.

by conducting public inquiries. The first such event was the inquiry into the Matrix Churchill (MC) trial controversy.[4] The inquiry was authorised by the prime minister and was conducted by Sir Richard Scott who had been the trial judge in the *Spycatcher* case. MC was an engineering company involved in exporting what transpired to be dual-use equipment to Iraq which could be put to both civilian and military use. This contravened guidelines on exports made under the Import, Export and Customs Powers Act 1939 prohibiting such export and several executives of MC were charged by Customs and Excise with offences of obtaining export licences by deception. The prosecution collapsed in November 1992 when a minister, under cross-examination, admitted that the government knew that the equipment would be used for the purpose of making armaments. It subsequently transpired that the government had relaxed the guidelines without informing Parliament and that ministers had signed public-interest immunity (PII) certificates (see chapter 11) to suppress vital evidence from the defence. On the advice of the Attorney General these had been signed automatically in most cases without any ministerial judgement on the balance between the interests of officials and the defendants and without any real assessment by each minister of the PI that required protection and whether such certificates were necessary.[5] (The one exception was Mr Heseltine, who had expressed to the Attorney General his reservations about signing PII certificates.) Furthermore, one of the executives had also been used by the intelligence services as an informer to provide vital information. The questions raised by the MC episode go to the heart of abuse by government of secrecy; a failure to notify Parliament of changes by the executive to arm-export guidelines; misleading statements to the House; failure by officials under ministerial bidding to testify before select committees investigating the Iraqi supergun affair[6] and the abuse of PII certificates in a criminal trial with a prejudicial effect on a defence.

These circumstances were the subject of a lengthy inquiry by Sir Richard Scott, which was damning, but the government took comfort from the fact that Sir Richard reported that the government was not prepared to countenance the supply of lethal equipment to Iraq or Iran. Ministers, said the government response to Scott, who signed PII certificates did so without 'impropriety'. There had been no 'conspiracy' to send innocent men to gaol, as alleged on Opposition benches, it was asserted. And there had been no 'deliberate' misleading of Parliament. The factual details were in the previous edition of this book. The Government, through ministers, was found to be seriously at fault by making 'misleading', 'inadequate', 'uninformative' and 'untrue' statements

---

[4] B. Thompson and F. F. Ridley, *Under the Scott-light: British government seen through the Scott Report* (1997); A. Tomkins, *The Constitution after Scott: Government unwrapped* (1998); *The Scott Report*, Public Law (1996) Autumn Issue; P. Birkinshaw (1996) Journal of Law and Society 406.

[5] Scott Report, HC 115 (1996–7), G11.7–11, G13.5, G13.7–9, G13.88–9, J6.67.

[6] Trade and Industry Committee, HC 86 (1991–2).

to Parliament. Sir Richard was critical of government law officers and their conduct in providing advice on PII certificates that was based on a 'fundamental misconception' of PII law.

The government accepted the need for some changes in practices in relation to provision of information to Parliament and the public but lost the general election in 1997.

Sir Richard was given wide terms of reference which he could have requested the prime minister to extend if the former had felt this was desirable. All evidence requested was to be forthcoming, although there were some delays, and ministers and civil servants would present themselves for questioning if requested by Sir Richard. The inquiry was non-statutory and therefore could not take evidence under oath although Sir Richard was assured that any request to convert proceedings to a statutory inquiry would be met. The inquiry was unique when conducted because it took evidence in public from a former prime minister, Mrs Thatcher, who was a central player in the drama and from the existing prime minister, John Major.[7]

The third example concerns the bovine spongiform encephalopathy episode (mad-cow disease), which saw variant Creutzfeldt-Jakob disease (vCJD) transferred to human beings. This disease was caused by the recycling in cattle feed of cattle remains infected with BSE. Cross-contamination in feed mills led to thousands more cattle being infected. By 1995, the first recorded deaths from vCJD had occurred. By 2000, there were eighty-five victims (known) – eighty fatalities – and the disease was spreading throughout Europe. The full extent and effects of the disease will not be 'discernible for many years to come'. In December 1997, the New Labour Government announced an inquiry into BSE and its development until 1996. The chair of the inquiry was Lord Phillips, a Law Lord, and his report was published in sixteen volumes in October 2000.[8] What emerged from this inquiry was that there had been a suppression of the truth and an unwillingness to inform the public of known hazards. In some cases this amounted to positive censorship. Veterinary surgeons and farmers had not been alerted to the symptoms and dangers of BSE. Officials and their scientific advisers were worried about the beef export trade, the adverse public reaction to the purchase of beef and the consequences for domestic cattle farmers. 'A recurring theme in the BSE story has been the growing public suspicion and dissatisfaction that important information was not being shared and discussed openly so that people were denied proper choices in matters that deeply affected them.' A policy of openness is the correct approach, the report says. The government must not appear to be certain where there is no certainty. 'We believe that food scares and vaccine scares thrive on a belief that Government is withholding information. If doubts are openly expressed and publicly explored,

---

[7] *Report of the Inquiry into the Export of Defence Equipment and Dual Use Goods to Iraq and Related Prosecutions*, HC 115-I–V. (1995–6).

[8] HC 887-I–XVI (1999–2000). See B. McHenry on information and evidence gathering for the BSE and other inquiries, (1999) New LJ 1772.

the public are capable of responding rationally and are more likely to [respond to] reassurance and advice if and when it comes.' What appears crystal clear is that the Ministry of Agriculture, Fisheries and Food (MAFF) did not wish to lose control of the research into the diseases if universities and research institutes were informed and developed their own research. Where regulatory measures were devised, the secrecy and haste of their implementation resulted in 'unenforceable provisions'. Secrecy was counterproductive.

The Food Standards Agency (FSA) was established to address some of the questions posed by MAFF's operations (MAFF was replaced by a new ministry) and proximity to the powerful food-production lobby. The FSA possesses a power to publish its advice to ministers and intends to conduct meetings in public.

A public inquiry chaired by a senior judge, Lord Hutton, also inquired into the events surrounding the death of David Kelly after he apparently committed suicide following a grilling before the Foreign Affairs Committee.[9] Dr Kelly had been an expert on biological and chemical warfare and he became embroiled in the media coverage of the Weapons of Mass Destruction (WMD) dossier on Iraq's capability of deploying such weapons within forty-five minutes. He was identified as the source who had expressed scepticism about the veracity of the claims in the dossier to a BBC reporter. The WMD claims had been a central justification for the invasion of Iraq in 2003. The inquiry heard evidence from the prime minister, ministers and the security and intelligence co-ordinator in the Cabinet Office. The report found that the allegations of government exaggeration and distortion were not made out although it was very critical of the BBC and the report's publication was followed by the resignation of the chairman and the director general of the BBC in 2004.

The Butler Inquiry into the Use of Intelligence followed the Hutton Inquiry in an attempt to bring quietus to the remaining anxieties about the use of intelligence leading to the Iraq war which Hutton had not assuaged.[10] It was the widest ranging examination in the UK into the use of secret intelligence. The report used extensive quotations from assessments by the Joint Intelligence Committee and as well as leading political figures. Butler heard evidence in public from the heads of MI6 (as a disembodied voice) and MI5 and from anonymous members of the intelligence service. As I write, inquiries are now sought into the events leading to the war in Iraq. The House of Lords has rejected such an inquiry. The Law Lords rejected the argument that Art. 2 ECHR (the right to life) was breached by an allegedly unlawful war.[11] Inquiries are sought into British involvement in torture (see chapter 11, p. 426). Rumours about an official inquiry into the war which will report after the next election in 2010 are circulating (see Introduction, p. 3).

---

[9] *Report of an Inquiry into the Circumstances Surrounding the Death of Dr David Kelly CMG*, HC 247 (2003–4).

[10] *Review of Intelligence on Weapons of Mass Destruction*, HC 898 (2003–4).

[11] *R (Gentle) v Prime Minister* [2008] UKHL 20.

Sometimes public inquiries assuage anxieties; sometimes they do not. It turns on whether people believe full information is disclosed. The events at the Hillsborough football stadium in April 1989 leading to ninety-six deaths were subject to a public inquiry by Lord Justice Taylor. But there remain widespread reservations about undisclosed information.

From these dramatic *imbroglios* how much light can be shed on the basic principles upon which constitutional government is supposedly conducted in the British state? How much information has to be given about matters of government for claims of governmental power to be legitimated? What are the leading principles of constitutional government? Are they realisable – or only idealistic or rough guides that imperfect men and women are urged to strive towards by tradition, the system or public expectation, knowing that in the world of practical politics their realisation is impossible? Are they mere shams which conceal the actual operation of power in the contemporary state and from which, like Milton's flames in *Paradise Lost*, nothing but 'darkness visible' emerged? The truth is probably a mixture of all of these.

Constitutional principles and central government

In 1992, as part of the Citizen's Charter initiative, John Major launched a White Paper on Open Government followed by a Code on Open Government and Access to Information in 1994 which was revised in 1997. The code ceased to operate on midnight 31 December 2004 when the Freedom of Information Act (FOIA) came into effect but it was notable that the Government refused to accept recommendations of the ombudsman to disclose information to requesters under the code. This practice of refusing recommendations then spread to other complaints of maladministration. One of the subjects of a refused request was information on ministerial interests – in anonymous terms.[12]

In its White Paper from 1997 on Open Government, the Government argued that a FOIA would introduce greater accountability and openness. We have seen some dramatic decisions under the Act. The Information Commissioner (IC) and Information Tribunal (IT) have ordered the prime minister to disclose details of meetings with lobbyists at No. 10. Advice to ministers and the role of lobbyists have also been the subject of disclosure orders (see chapter 6, p. 196 *et seq.*). However desirable openness and accountability are, how far do they or can they go? What counter-arguments can government posit in its own defence for confidentiality in sensitive areas? Even if we accept such principles, who defines 'sensitive'? Is it the *ipse dixit* of the prime minister or minister? Is it Parliament? How 'sensitive' and for whom? The FOIA places the answer firmly

---

[12] *Declarations made by Ministers under the Ministerial code of conduct,* HC 353 (2001–2); *Access to Official Information: Monitoring of the non statutory codes of practice 1994–2005,* HC 59 (2005–6); *Investigations completed on Access to Official Information,* HC 63-I–II (2005–6); Final Report of PCA in 2005 concerned ministerial interests and other complaints where the government refused to accept the PCA's recommendations.

in the minister's court by virtue of the veto under s. 53. This was exercised as we saw above for the first time in 2009.

The Government too has its own arguments. It is unlikely post-FOIA that a government would argue that openness and accountability are not central legitimating principles of its exercise of power. But government has other legitimating principles: namely, efficiency and responsiveness – efficiency in the meeting of objectives, and responsiveness to the claims and needs of its citizens. The demands of too much openness and accountability may hinder these other features of good government. Bentham may have asked for publicity in everything. He also asked for frugality in everything, government might assert. Contrariwise, without openness, it must be asked, how do we know what objectives are and how efficiently they have been met? Without effective accountability, how can we gauge the degree of responsiveness of government?

New forms of governance[13]

Since the first edition of this book, there has been a movement to new forms of government or public management to maintain public service or service to the public. It has extended beyond central government to cover local government and the public–private interface as a whole. In the late 1980s, executive agencies of central government were established to carry out the duties of departments of state accompanied by the apparent relaxation, or redefinition, of ministerial responsibility as a means of achieving accountability in the process of government. Departments will develop overall policy and will continue to be headed by a minister responsible for that policy. Agencies bound by non-legally enforceable contracts established in 'framework documents' will carry out the administration – and to an unavoidable extent develop their own 'local policy' within the parameters set out by the department. Chief executives of agencies will be responsible for operating aspects and their management and for setting and meeting targets, objectives, standards and for monitoring performance. Management responsibility will be devolved within agencies and identifiable officials – employees are still civil servants – will be answerable for implementation. In several respects this constitutes a subversion of the major shibboleths of the British constitution: ministerial responsibility and anonymity of civil servants. There has been a movement to greater reliance upon the private sector to provide public-sector management including the Private Finance Initiative now a part of the Public Private Partnerships. There has been an increased resort to 'task forces' involving recruits from the private sector who will assist in policy development in key areas. Once again we should note that this advice will be exempt from access under the FOIA 2000. Task forces may have disappeared with Prime Minister Blair but reliance upon private consultants and advisers by

[13] HM Treasury and Office of Public Services Reform, *Executive Agencies in the 21st Century* (2002); Cabinet Office, *Executive Agencies: A guide of departments* (2006).

government will continue irrespective of political party.[14] The Committee on Public Accounts was critical of nearly £2.8 billion spent on private consultants in 2006.[15] In 2007, the prime minister in the *Ministerial Code* said there would be annual reports to Parliament on numbers, names and paybands of advisers together with the total pay bill. A reliance upon powerful commercial interests by the Labour Government has been noted, not for private gain – which caused so much damage to the Conservative governments under Thatcher and Major – but for the success of public projects, in particular the Millennium Dome.

In the last two decades, the movement towards new styles of public management and greater reliance upon commercial and market-led practice and private contractors in the delivery of public services or programmes has been seen to be responsible for a degree of abuse in public office and for an appreciable increase in the sleaze factor by ministers and MPs, and in concern over ministerial powers of appointment to quasi-governmental bodies. In 2009, Labour peers were found to be taking considerable payments from commercial companies in reward for advancing the companies' interests in bills. The practice was apparently unregulated and widespread.

Such was the perceived level of public disquiet over the use of public office for private gain that in 1994 the prime minister appointed the Law Lord, Lord Nolan, to head an inquiry into *Standards in Public Life*.[16] Lord Nolan's and his successors' investigations and recommendations and subsequent reports, from what is effectively an informal standing advisory committee, to the prime minister will inform the ethics of the operation of public service for some considerable time to come.[17] It is presently investigating openness and accountability in local and London government and is taking evidence in open meetings across the UK. Its methods involve consultation documents, evidence from experts, formal public hearings and reports. It is instructive to spell out Nolan's seven principles of public life for these restate the desiderata of ethics in public life which must dictate the ethics of all who work in the public sector from the prime minister and ministers down.

---

[14] See NAO, *Government Use of Consultants*, HC 128 (2006–7) and Committee on Public Accounts, HC 309 (2006–7). A *Model Contract* and a *Code of Conduct* exist for special advisers: see Ninth Report from the Committee on Public Standards, *Defining the Boundaries within the Executive: Ministers, special advisers and the permanent civil service*, Cm. 5775 (2003).

[15] Committee on Public Accounts, HC 309 (2006–7), £1.8 billion by central government. Gordon Brown confirmed ten special advisers – a mixture of private and civil service advisers and revoked the Order in Council allowing special advisers to issue executive instructions to civil servants, *The Guardian* , 28 June 2007; NAO, *Government Use of Consultants*, HC 128 (2006–7). See HL 7 (2008–9) on numbers of special advisers.

[16] *Standards in Public Life*, I–II, Cm. 2850 (1995). Lord Nolan's successor was Lord Neill QC who in turn was followed by a former mandarin Sir Nigel Wicks, Sir Alastair Graham and presently Sir Christopher Kelly – a former mandarin. See R. Behrens, 'Openness: A perspective from the Committee on Standards on Public Life' in R. Chapman and M. Hunt (eds.), *Open Government in a Theoretical and Practical Context* (2006).

[17] See R. Behrens, 'Openness'.

His committee stated the seven general principles of conduct underpinning public life as selflessness, integrity, objectivity, accountability, openness, honesty and leadership. No one can expect a paragon of virtue. Rather, taken together, these add up to provide the following: holders of public office should take decisions solely in terms of the PI and not for personal, family or friends' gain. They should not allow financial or other obligations to influence their decisions or public duties. Powers to award contracts (central government procurement was worth about £158 billion in 2006[18] according to the National Audit Office and this does not include local government and the health service), make appointments or bestow honours should be based on merit. They should be accountable and subject to appropriate scrutiny. They should be as open as possible in the decisions and actions they take, giving reasons for decisions and restricting information only when the PI clearly demands. Private interests relating to public duties should be declared and conflicts removed. Lastly, they should lead by example in promoting these principles. Codes of conduct should be drawn up by all public bodies incorporating these principles and internal systems for maintaining standards should be supported by independent scrutiny, and proper induction training and guidance should be given to reinforce standards in public bodies.

It was seen that the Parliamentary Ombudsman (PO) was rebuffed by the government when it refused to publish details of ministerial interests under the code on openness – even anonymously![19] The FOIA has revealed the predations of MPs and publicly funded expenses. The Public Administration Select Committee has reported on *Ethics and Standards in Public Life*. It argued that a rule-based system is not enough and that there should be a statutory standards commission and a constitutional watchdog should have own-initiative powers of investigation. The government would look at this in its plans for constitutional renewal.[20]

Ministerial accountability or responsibility?[21]

By the eighteenth century, ministerial responsibility to Parliament had become one of the focal points of constitutional attention, although the concept lacked precision and is still the subject of ongoing debate. Responsibility in a political sense is what is meant, because after 1689 – and indeed prior to that date, but for a liberal use of suspending and dispensing powers by the Crown – ministers

---

[18] www.nao.org.uk/publications/0506/sustainable_procurement.aspx.
[19] See note 12 above.   [20] Government Reply, HC 88 (2007–8).
[21] Public Administration Select Committee, *Ministerial Powers and Prerogatives*, HC 642 (2002–3) and Government Reply, Cm. 6187. See *Taming the Prerogative* and *The Governance of Britain: Constitutional renewal*, Cm. 7342-I–II (2008).

were never absolved from legal responsibility for unlawful acts.[22] George I stopped attending Cabinet meetings regularly from 1717, reasoning that his ministers now had to answer to Parliament for their advice to him. He could no longer protect them. The difficulties in establishing *individual* culpability led to the convention of collective responsibility of a government for its actions. If they were responsible collectively, then the government should respond and initiate, i.e. govern, collectively. That means unanimously. Disagreement in public could not, would not, be tolerated. Until the late nineteenth century, no minutes were taken of Cabinet meetings, and Asquith stated in 1916 that only the prime minister took notes or a record for the purpose of the letter to the monarch[23] to advise on the collective decisions of the Cabinet. It took until 1975, in the litigation concerning the diaries of the former Secretary of State, Richard Crossman,[24] for the courts to insist that, in law, proceedings within the Cabinet are protected by confidentiality, at least for as long as confidentiality requires.[25] The law proved to be ineffective and rules on keeping confidences were put in place after a report by Lord Radcliffe in 1976 (Cmnd 6386). The subject was revisited by the Public Administration Select Committee in 2006 and 2008 prompted by memoirs from diplomats and private advisers some of which contained embarrassing details aimed at titillation rather than informed debate.[26] There is a real problem. Information may not be legally protected but disclosure of tittle-tattle can be seriously undermining of professional relationships and damaging to those relationships and for which there is no genuine PI in disclosure.[27] Conversely, information from official sources through memoirs may provide a crucial insight into events shaping history. The committee sought to introduce a regime that would give greater control to the Crown but which would provide a robust defence of freedom of speech in the PI. The report wanted features of the scheme to be extended to ministers

---

[22] Note use of *nolle prosequi*. As Charles II observed, while his words were his own, his actions were those of his ministers.

[23] D. G. T. Williams, *Not In the Public Interest* (1965), ch. 2.

[24] *AG v Jonathan Cape Ltd* [1976] QB 752; and Cmnd 6386 on publication by ex-cabinet ministers of memoirs. The Cabinet Secretary would have the final say on information relating to national security and international relations. For background restrictions on civil servants, see K. Middlemas (1976) Pol Q 39.

[25] A point which was also made apropos of civil servants' information. The litigation concerned vol. 1. No injunction was sought for vols. 2 and 3 after it was refused for vol. 1. For non-security-sensitive information, Cmnd 6386 recommended a delay of fifteen years, though in the case of conflict it was up to the ex-minister what to publish – subject to the possibility of an injunction. *Times Newspapers v MGN Ltd* [1993] EMLR 443 deals with the publication of material based on Mrs Thatcher's memoirs, *The Downing Street Years*, without the authorisation of the newspapers who had purchased serialisation rights. An injunction refused as the issue of confidentiality was uncertain in the hands of purchasing newspapers.

[26] *Whitehall Confidential? The Publication of Political Memoirs*, HC 689-I–II (2005–6) and Government Reply, HC 91 (2007–8) and the Public Administration Select Committee, *Mandarins Unpeeled*, HC 664 (2007–8).

[27] *Whitehall Confidential*, HC 689 (2005–6) and Government Reply, HC 91 (2007–8) (*sic*); and *Mandarins Unpeeled*, HC 664 (2007–8); *The Guardian*, 10 August 20007, MoD issues 'gag order' on armed forces after publication of personal details by the press after an incident with Iran.

but it noted that recent problems related to diplomats and special advisers to ministers. The government thought existing practices based on Radcliffe were sufficient.

Once a minister heads a ministry, and it becomes a matter of public record that an area of administration falls within the responsibility of that ministry, the minister at its head assumes responsibility to Parliament for the administration of the ministry, and his servants, conventionally, remained anonymous. The minister has to answer the questions about the ministry's business, though s/he may not always accept the blame for what goes wrong. It depends upon the seriousness of the shortcoming and whether the minister knew or ought to have known of it and whether s/he retains colleagues' confidence. On many crucial items, the minister does not have immediate access to the research resources of his advisers, so s/he cannot ignore their advice.[28] If the minister is to be individually responsible, then s/he must be accountable to Parliament by providing information in debates and at question time[29] and by responding to investigations from select committees: 'A minister does not discharge [an] accountability to Parliament merely by acknowledging a general responsibility and, if the circumstances warrant it, by resigning. Accountability involves *accounting* in detail for actions as a minister.'[30] All departments and agencies must publish annual reports detailing achievements, targets, output and performance and financial information. Government on the Internet has transformed the practice and volume of publications (see chapter 1).[31]

From the 1990s, the government sought to draw a distinction between accountability and responsibility, a distinction which has been necessitated, in its view, by the introduction of executive agencies. Responsibility entails that a minister is directly and personally responsible for particular items, e.g. departmental policy, for the framework through which policies are delivered, resources allocated, and for such matters that s/he has to agree to under the framework documents which constitute agencies' operating manuals. Accountability, it argues, refers to the constitutional duty upon ministers to account to Parliament by way of information provision for the actions of their department and its overall relationship with agencies. Responsibility may be delegated and is increasingly so. Accountability may not be delegated.[32] This is a little too pat. For example, when there is a systemic failure in an agency's programme, where responsibilty has been delegated but where the minister knows of the failure, or ought to know, and fails to act – would the minister not be

---

[28] Very rarely does a minister resign for owning up to the fact that they are not up to the job – Evelyn Morris as Education Secretary is a rare example. There was notable reluctance by Gordon Brown to accept responsibility for the financial collapse from 2007 onwards. Regulation had been 'relaxed' over financial and investment institutions while he was Lord Chancellor but the seeds of light regulation go back to the mid-1980s.

[29] See below.   [30] HC 519 (1985–6), para. 235.

[31] See Committee on Public Accounts, *Government on the Internet*, HC 143 (2007–8).

[32] Cm. 2748, p. 27 *et seq.* and HC 27-I, (1993–4), para. 132 *et seq.* and see Scott, text below.

responsible?[33] By blaming his servants the minister may appear to have lost control of his department.

In his report into Matrix Churchill, Sir Richard Scott noted numerous instances where there had been a failure by ministers to discharge the obligation in what was then para. 27 of *Questions of Procedure* (see below): 'to give Parliament, including its select committees, and the public as full information as possible about the policies, decisions and action of the Government and not to deceive or mislead Parliament and the public' (p. 1799 *et seq.* of the report). If responsibility were to be avoided because of a lack of knowledge or involvement then it was incumbent upon ministers to be 'forthcoming with information about the incident in question'.[34] The obligation of ministers to give information and explanations lies at the heart of ministerial accountability. It depends upon two vital qualities according to the select committee on the Treasury and Civil Service: clarity about who can be held to account and held responsible when things go wrong: confidence that Parliament is able to gain the accurate information required to hold the Executive to account and to ascertain where responsibility lies.

Withholding information means that the obligation is not discharged. This, believed Sir Richard, undermines the democratic process. His subsequent suggestion was for a commissioner to assist MPs to obtain information from ministers especially where it was refused on grounds of PI.[35] This has not been forthcoming. The IC under the FOIA 2000 can make a decision on the PI but the minister or authorised person may invoke a veto over this.[36] Giving the IC the ultimate say on highly sensitive, and politically charged, matters was not the British way, said the Home Secretary.

We need to examine the contemporary practice of government and to compare these practices with the constitutional principles we accept. It will be necessary to look at the position of civil servants and their relationship with ministers and also at the position of Next Steps Executive agencies and how if at all they have been accommodated to the relationship. In the Westland affair, the public witnessed a minister giving information through his civil servants, as it would, he claimed, have appeared improper for him to have supplied it; a minister praying in aid the support of named civil servants; and an invitation by the select committee to the civil servants to come to the committee to tell the story as it really was.[37] In the Kelly episode, the civil servant was 'outed'

---

[33] Note the report of the PCA on the Child Support Agency, HC 199 (1994–5), and of course the notorious events surrounding the dismissal of the chief executive of the Prison Service, Derek Lewis, by the Home Secretary in October 1995 following the Learmont Report on prison security, Cm. 3020. See D. Lewis, *Hidden Agendas* (1997). On becoming Home Secretary in 1997, Jack Straw announced he was to be responsible for prison policy.

[34] Paras. K8.15–16 and p. 877 *et seq.* and see text below.

[35] (1996) Public Law 410, at 426.　　[36] See chapter 6, p. 205.

[37] Note 2 above, para. 240. In the Sandline affair the Foreign Secretary, Robin Cook, diverted blame for arms sales in apparent breach of a UN embargo and an Order in Council onto civil servants but insisted on questions before the FA Select Committee being put to him and not his

and criticised, making little of civil-service anonymity. Practice confuses the division, in other words. The discussion will examine the methods whereby information is provided to the press and media by officials, ministers and MPs; how, in other words, the press officer, the lobby system, the Press Association and 'D notices' operate. Their collective objective is unattributable disclosure which seeks 'to influence without accepting responsibility'.[38]

Collective responsibility

Collective responsibility and Cabinet confidences had been resorted to in some high-profile cases before the IC and IT (see chapter 6). How collective is governmental decision-making? It depends upon the prime minister. Ministers are given a rulebook, the *Ministerial Code*, which Lord Nolan recommended should be renamed *Conduct and Procedure for Ministers*. Its predecessor, *Questions of Procedure for Ministers*, was a secret document until 1992 and Cabinet secretarial staff were issued with *Talking About the Office*[39] although the latter seems long to have fallen by the wayside. The code is a non-legal statement of principles covering not just matters of collective responsibility but also ministerial responsibility to Parliament. The most recent version dates from 2007. A proprietary and ethics team in the Cabinet Office advises on the code. Incoming prime ministers introduce their own code.[40] The code has to be read against the Nolan principles, the duty to comply with the law (including international law and treaty obligations) and the duty to uphold the administration of justice and the integrity of public life. Ministers must uphold the principle of collective responsibility. Ministers are advised that they should not divulge the internal processes through which a decision was made or the level of committee. They must account to Parliament for their actions and those of their departments and agencies. They must give accurate and truthful information to Parliament. Information should only be withheld from Parliament and the public on the basis of the PI test set out in the FOIA. Ministers should require civil servants who give evidence before parliamentary committees on their behalf *and under their direction* to be as helpful in providing accurate, full and truthful information. There must be no conflict between public duty and private interest. Breaches will not be investigated by the Cabinet Secretary but will be referred to the independent adviser on ministers' interests.

---

permanent secretary: HC 1016 (1997–8) for the investigation by Sir Thomas Legg QC into the events. In March 2001, a former BBC reporter wrote that Cook misled the Commons three times in relation to the affair: N. Jones, *Control Freaks* (2001).

[38] Note 5, para. 168.

[39] The *Ministerial Code* dates from 1997. *Questions of Procedure for Ministers*, Cabinet Office, May 1992. See Cmnd 6386 (1976) on ministerial publications. P. Hennessey, *Cabinet* (1986). The Public Administration Select Committee has investigated the code: HC 235 (2000–1); see note 43 below.

[40] PASC, *Ministerial Code*, HC 1457 (2005–6); on the case for independent investigation: PASC, *Investigating the Conduct of Ministers*, HC 381 (2007–8); on constitutional renewal: PASC, *Constitutional Renewal*, HC 499 (2007–8) and *Constitutional Renewal Bill*, HC 698 (2007–8).

Ministers relinquishing office should hand back to their department any Cabinet documents and/or other departmental papers in their possession. Use of detailed diaries as a basis for memoirs is common and these are not official documents.[41] Subject to the Radcliffe rules, a former minister may at any time have access in the Cabinet Office to copies of Cabinet or Cabinet committee papers issued to him while in office. They may have access to departmental papers that they are known to have handled at the time. Except for the prime minister, access is limited to ministers personally (para. 2.9). Conventions govern the use of information from one government to a succeeding one. Each minister will announce and defend his own area of interest once arrived at collectively.[42] It is no concern of Parliament or the public. Collective responsibility of ministers 'requires that they should be able to express their views frankly, in the expectation that they can argue freely in private maintaining a united front . . . [T]he privacy of opinions expressed in Cabinet and ministerial committees and correspondence should be maintained.' In the former editions of *Questions* it was stated that the composition, terms of reference and chairmen of Cabinet committees should not be disclosed. Since 1992, and John Major's declaration of greater openness under the Citizen's Charter programme, the names of Cabinet committees, subcommittees and their terms of reference and membership have been published.

The code has been examined by the Select Committee on Public Administration on several occasions.[43] Its report on the 2007 revisions welcomed the concentration on principle rather than procedural detail and the decision to publish ministers' interests. The committee recommended that the constitutional status of the code be recognised instead of it being treated as a piece of a prime ministerial private rulebook for the 'good fellas' club. The committee supported Nolan's recommendation of a free-standing code and specific highlighting of the seven principles. Nolan's successor had also reported on the code in the sixth report and had pressed that ministers make a record of all contacts with those 'promoting outside interests'. Another recommendation was that ministers have access to an investigator immediately to examine allegations of misconduct and establish the facts to prevent Kangaroo courts dismissing them. The prime minister opted for an independent adviser on ministerial interests. The committee noted that his powers of investigation had been widened and he was to enquire into matters of fact but an assurance that all facts would be disclosed was not given. Whether he investigates a breach of the code is a matter for the prime minister. He is staffed by the Cabinet Office, funded by the

---

[41] See the *Ministerial Code* and Lord Hunt (1982) Public Law 514. A storm blew when the Churchill family sold the papers of Sir Winston Churchill for private gain when it was alleged that many were state papers. See R. Brazier (1996) Cambridge Law Journal 65. For the position in Scotland in relation to papers of a UK minister see (2000) Public Law 309.

[42] Only exceptionally will a decision be announced as a decision of HM Government. Departmental differences should be resolved before referring the matter to the Cabinet.

[43] HC 235 (2000–1). See HC 381 (2007–8) and Government Reply, HC 1056 (2007–8).

Cabinet Office and accommodated by the Cabinet Office. The ultimate arbiter and enforcer of the code is the prime minister but this is not clearly stated. The investigator is not seen to be independent and impartial.

The Cabinet

Nothing encapsulates the absence of law at the centre of British government in the manner of the Cabinet, in terms of its origins and practice.[44] This does not mean an absence of the rule of law as such; it means an absence of legal definition in the structure of government. There are conventions restricting the disclosure by the government of the day of the papers of a previous government within the thirty-year rule without the consent of the previous prime minister concerned and the consent of the Queen.[45] Such matters are now going to be governed by the FOIA and its exemptions and veto (see chapter 6).[46] The Cabinet Office is included as a FOIA public authority (PA) and this covers the Cabinet and its secretariat. A practice also exists whereby government in office denies itself access to a previous government's papers if of a different political party. The conventions on release to third parties cover ministerial minutes; other documents written by a former minister in the course of his duties are not publicly available unless under the terms of the FOIA. The convention on government access to previous papers covers advice to ministers from their officials. Information in the public domain, such as letters to trade associations, trade unions and MPs, is not included in the government's self-denial, nor is information known to a foreign government nor the written opinions of law officers. Lord Hunt believed that commonsense would bridge the gap between this convention and the need to keep present ministers informed where 'continuity of knowledge is important', although clearly the fact that civil servants must possess such continuity of knowledge affords them a certain degree of superiority over ministers.[47]

If it were felt that a previous minister's Cabinet papers should be disclosed to his successor, the permission of the former would be sought. A strong plea

---

[44] See S. Low, *The Governance of England*, 14th impression (1927), ch. II.

[45] Lord Hunt (1982) Public Law 514. Five previous prime ministers were consulted in seeking access to documents relevant to Franks' inquiry into the Falklands War. The inquiry had access to all the secret intelligence papers it required. The Cabinet Secretary has access to the papers of a previous administration.

[46] A government department in s. 84 FOIA includes 'any body or authority exercising statutory functions on behalf of the Crown'.

[47] A pointed episode involved the allegations of MI5's undermining of the Wilson Government by Peter Wright. The allegations were investigated in 1977 when James Callaghan was prime minister. On the conventions just described, Margaret Thatcher denied herself access to the papers. The 'link man' between the Home Office and MI5 at the relevant time was Sir Robert Armstrong, claimed H. Young (*The Guardian*, 19 March 1987). Not so, claimed Sir Robert – the Cabinet Secretary – *The Guardian*, 20 March 1987. The 'link man' was the permanent secretary, who was deceased. On the Scottish Executives' treatment of UK ministerial papers, see (2000) Public Law 309.

has been made for an incoming administration to be supplied with sufficient 'information on potential immediate problems and on the difficulties of implementing specific proposals to ward against initial errors during its first year in office'.[48] Difficulties have been caused over specific projects, e.g. Concorde, or constraints of forward commitments on public expenditure and economic policy.[49] It was felt that greater contact should be encouraged between officials and opposition parties than is practised at present, which is usually restricted to discussion of the machinery of government. Any wider practice has been regarded as 'taboo', although in 1995 civil servants briefed the Opposition leadership on matters arising from their adopted policies more than eighteen months before a prospective election. Unlike the Queen, members of the Cabinet do not receive a full and unabridged set of Cabinet minutes.

A former Cabinet Secretary, Lord Butler, has criticised the 'informality and circumscribed character' of Cabinet meetings on Iraq[50] and Clare Short and Robin Cook made blistering attacks on Blair's conduct and treatment of Cabinet government. In 2006, the *Financial Times* (8 March 2006) reported that Chancellor Brown left colleagues in the dark over axing the 'Operating and Financial Review for Companies', drawing implications for his premiership.

Cabinet committees[51]

The Cabinet is not the only centre for decision-making. For this, or these centres, we must look, inter alia, to Cabinet committees. By November 2008 there were ten committees with twenty-nine subcommittees including four MISC subcommittees. Practice varies enormously. In 1983 Mrs Thatcher identified four main committees.

Hitherto, these committees have been shrouded in secrecy. In 1992, the prime minister disclosed the membership and responsibility of the main standing committees of Cabinet. Gordon Brown published the full details of Cabinet committees, their membership and who may be called to attend. However, Hennessey has commented on an earlier administration that by the winter of 1985–6 there were at least 160 groups within the Cabinet committee network. He identified five types of committee:[52] *standing*, i.e. permanent (for the duration of the prime minister); *ad hoc* or 'single issue';[53] *ministerial*, where civil servants do not participate; *official* for civil servants alone, and *mixed* for both ministers and civil servants.

The actual creation, administration and utilisation of such committees will doubtless vary according to the particular style of the prime minister. Under

---

[48] Dr W. Wallace and Dr W. Plowden, HC 92-II (1985–6), p. 383.
[49] *Ibid.*   [50] Butler Report, p. 320, at para. 611.
[51] www.cabinetoffice.gov.uk/secretariats/committees.aspx.   [52] Hennessey, *Cabinet*, p. 31.
[53] Note Star Chamber to arbitrate on departmental bids for funding before the Expenditure White Paper, replaced by the EDX Committee, and then by the PX and subsequently the PSX committee.

Mrs Thatcher the tendency had been to avoid committees, circulation of Cabinet papers and Cabinet debate wherever possible. Informal ad hoc groups might be stacked against an erring minister,[54] or a colleague might be asked to prepare a paper just for the prime minister with a back-up team of civil servants or outsider specialists. A typical follow-up would have been a meeting at No. 10 with the prime minister and 'her team' – 'a mixture of people from the Downing Street private office, the Policy Unit and Cabinet Office, with one or two personal advisers and sometimes a Treasury minister'.[55] The style is not quite presidential, Hennessey argues, but much of the 'collective spirit' of the Cabinet system has been siphoned off to committees and informal groups – sofa government.[56] This may be simply a more emphatic tendency in what has been happening since the end of the Second World War. Only one decision on nuclear weapons in forty years, for instance, was approved by the whole Cabinet – the decision to proceed with the 'H' Bomb. In Mr Major's premiership, a greater emphasis was placed on government through Cabinet. Tony Blair deliberately pursued a strong centralised style of government while also presiding over devolved government in the UK. While he accepted the convention of Cabinet government, use of 'outside' and special advisers and reliance upon the slick presentation of policies helped create the impression of excessive 'hands-on' government and obsessive control over policy development. The No. 10 Policy Unit had increased significantly in size and comprised mainly special advisers.[57] The proliferation of special task forces operating largely in secret to help the development of policy was widely criticised. These comprised special groups ('experts') and officials.[58] While some Cabinet committees were larger than the Cabinet itself, the committee dealing with the FOI Bill was an example, resort was also made to special inner committees of permanent secretaries operating outside the traditional weekly sessions of all top secretaries.[59] Government by memo, and obsessive control over style and presentation seriously undermined the popularity of Blair's government. The departure of Blair saw what appeared to be a return to more conventional styles of management through the Cabinet.

Our system of Cabinet government is collective in only a very formal sense, as the information and details of policymaking are not presented to the whole Cabinet, but are invariably kept within the narrowest possible range of ministers. So much is no doubt a consequence of more government and more specialisation. It is not the framework for full, free and frank discussion of government policy within the confidence of the Cabinet. But it might be argued

---

[54] Hennessey, *Cabinet*, pp. 102–3, cites Michael Heseltine's report 'It took a riot' on urban deprivation. Mr Heseltine was himself accused of being over interventionist as deputy prime minister in October 1995.

[55] *Ibid.*, p. 102.   [56] *Ibid.*, p. 11.

[57] See Public Administration, *Special Advisers*, HC 293 (2000–1).

[58] A. Barker, I. Byrne and A. Veall, *Ruling by Task Force: The Politico's guide to Labour's new elite* (1999); Public Management Foundation, *In the Public Interest?* (2000).

[59] D. Kavanagh and A. Seldon, *The Powers Behind the Prime Minister: The hidden influence of No. 10* (1999).

that this does not really matter. If the government loses the confidence of the House it must go to the country. That is what is central, along with mute agreement, in collective responsibility. No minister can claim a right to know in detail what another is doing unless the matter touches upon their *own* sphere of responsibility/accountability. Then the minister must provide the information for Parliament to account for their *own* area of responsibility/accountability. Timing of release of information is vital, but while a minister in the Cabinet, with the prime minister's approval, believes it best that Cabinet colleagues are not informed, it is unlikely that Parliament should be. In its response to the Nolan Committee the government, while accepting most of the recommendations, did state that ministers should not be culpable unless they *knowingly* misled Parliament and furthermore ministers should have a right not to inform Parliament where it was not in the PI that Parliament should be informed. Sir Richard Scott noted the Nolan recommendations, the addition of the qualification 'knowingly' to the duty not to misinform Parliament and then the addition of the following words to *Questions* to determine how the PI in withholding information should be determined:

> [only when disclosure would not be in the PI,] which should be decided in accordance with established Parliamentary convention, the law and any relevant Government Code of Practice. [HC Debs., col. 456, 2 November 1995]

He did not feel that the qualification of 'mislead' by 'knowingly' made any material difference to the substance of the obligation on ministers not to mislead Parliament or the public. Withholding information should never be based on reasons of convenience or to avoid political embarrassment but 'should always require special and careful justification'. He also referred to the fact that the PI could be identified from 'established Parliamentary convention'. The numerous subjects on which by convention ministers have refused to answer questions is notorious. The guiding principle today is that information should be provided in accordance with the provisions of the FOIA. Sir Richard believed that the justification for a refusal to answer a parliamentary question on sale of arms or defence-related equipment to other countries should be re-examined and should be the subject of a 'comprehensive review'. 'Commercial confidentiality' should not, in short, be engaged in overkill to suppress information from Parliament and the public.

Sir Richard also pointed to the distinction made between 'responsibility' and 'accountability' by the Cabinet Secretary and others although it has not met with approval from all quarters. If ministers are to be excused blame and personal 'responsibility' *qua* minister:

> the corollary ought to be an acceptance to be forthcoming with information about the incident in question. Otherwise Parliament (and the public) will not be in a position to judge whether the absence of personal knowledge and involvement is fairly claimed or to judge on whom responsibility for what has occurred ought

to be placed. Any re-examination of the practices and conventions relied on by Government in declining to answer, or to answer fully, certain Parliamentary Questions should, in my opinion, take account of the implications of the distinction drawn by Sir Robert between ministerial 'accountability' and ministerial 'responsibility' and of the consequent enhancement of the need for ministers to provide . . . full and accurate information to Parliament. [HC 115, 1995/6, p. 1806]

It has been noted how the *Ministerial Code* and the resolution of the Commons provided for ministerial information to Parliament. How, and when, does Parliament get informed?

Parliament and information[60]

As the 'Grand Inquest of the Nation' Parliament can ask questions. It was the abuse of this ability by some MPs who charged 'clients' for the privilege that was one of the major causes leading to the establishment of the Nolan Committee. Peers have become embroiled in similar venal practices. Parliament can demand debates. It can summon witnesses and call for evidence before its select committees, especially the Public Accounts Committee (PAC), which receives written minutes by the accounting officer of departments where they disagree with a minister on matters relating to expenditure;[61] and the select committees, which are departmentally related. By these processes it holds ministers responsible for their departmental administration. Parliamentary proceedings, like those in courts, are protected by absolute privilege.[62] The mechanisms of parliamentary questions and debates are geared towards the provision of routine information: how many prisoners on remand; how many escapes; how many deportations; how many school closures? – the stuff of parliamentary life. Others see them as opportunities for 'soundbites' and planted prompts whose usefulness will outlive any 'reform' to make parliamentary questions and proceedings more meaningful, as John Major suggested in June 1994 and David Cameron in 2005. The subject of parliamentary questions has been examined by the PAC, which noted that the Government had abandoned the undertaking to cite exemptions

---

[60] See Modernisation Committee, *Connecting Parliament with the People*, HC 951 (2005–6); Procedure Committee, *e-petitions*, HC 136 (2007–8).

[61] These powers were extended during the Nolan Inquiry to cover communications to the chair of the Public Accounts Committee by the accounting officer. They had previously been extended to allow communications to the CAG on an extended range of concerns: *Committee on Standards in Public Life*, Cm. 2850-II, p. 217 (R. Sheldon); and F. White, I. Harden and K. Donnelly (1994) Public Law 526.

[62] A. W. Bradley and K. D. Ewing, *Constitutional and Administrative Law*, 14th edn (2007), ch. 11. See *Prebble v Television New Zealand* [1995] 1 AC 321, PC, where the Privy Council stayed an action when the defendant could not invoke evidence covered by the privilege; *Allason v Haines* (1995) The Times, 25 July; and P. M. Leopold (1995) Legal Studies 204. An amendment to the 1995–6 Defamation Bill moved by Lord Hoffmann allows MPs to waive the privilege and sue for defamation, thereby making an inroad into the Bill of Rights 1689: Defamation Act 1996, s. 13 and *Hamilton v Al Fayed* [2000] 2 All ER 224, HL.

under the FOIA when refusing to answer a question.[63] The more probing investigation exercises are conducted by the select committees of MPs who can have outside specialists advising them.[64]

A development of real significance occurred with the use of select committees to engage in pre-legislative scrutiny of draft bills in addition to White Papers. The FOI Bill and consultation paper were examined by this process. Another development has seen the publication of draft bills with the White Paper. This occurred with the Human Rights Bill and the Local Government Bill enacted in 2000.[65] The PAC had two months to engage in pre-legislation scrutiny of the FOI Bill in the spring of 1999. The Select Committee on Modernisation (HC 1097 (2005–6)) has criticised the reduction in the number of bills going to pre-legislative scrutiny.[66] The recommendation that special committees and standing committees should be called public bill committees with powers to take evidence was accepted; such committees have power to take evidence, see papers and records although there are exceptions to these procedures. Reports from select committees have recommended widespread reforms to Parliament's procedures to revitalise the chamber and the back-bench MP and include parliamentary commissions of inquiry, more scrutiny of draft legislative programmes, pre-appointment hearings by select committees and the prime minister's own recommendation to replace prerogative powers by statute and to publish a draft legislative agenda.[67]

Select committees overseeing departments were created in 1979. Their oversight of finance and expenditure were initially criticised for lacking thoroughness.[68] They were established to oversee and scrutinise the policies, administration and expenditure of related departments, their various agencies and fringe bodies. Members are appointed by the House of Commons, and the party balance usually reflects the balance of the House as a whole, as does the division of chairmen. The Liaison Committee recommended changes in the manner in which members are appointed to select committees. At the time of

---

[63] HC 449 (2004–5) and Government Reply, HC 853 (2005–6).

[64] PASC HC 136 (2002–3), *Ministerial Accountability and Parliamentary Questions*; HC 449-I–II (2004–5), *Ministerial Responsibility and Parliamentary Questions*; Government Reply, HC 853 (2005–6).

[65] Although there were several bills that went through pre-legislative scrutiny from 1997 onwards, there are similar practices going back to the 1970s.

[66] *The Legislative Process*, HC 1097 (2005–6).

[67] First Rep. of SC on Modernisation, *Revitalising the Chamber: The role of the back bench member*, HC 337 [2006–7]; PASC, *Parliamentary Commissions of Inquiry*, HC 473 (2007–8); SC on Modernisation, *Scrutiny of Draft Legislative Programmes*, HC 597 (2007–8); *Pre-appointment hearings by Select Committees*, HC 594 (2007–8); Prime Minister, *Governance of Britain* Cm. 2007 on placing prerogative powers in statute and publishing a draft legislative agenda. On Parliamentary elections themselves, see the Political Parties, Elections and Referendums Act 2000 and the Political Parties and Elections Act 2009.

[68] A. Robinson in G. Drewry (ed.), *The New Select Committees*, 2nd edn (1989); V. Flegmann (1985) *Public Money* 5; see also, John Biffen in D. Englefield (ed.), *Commons Select Committees* (1984).

their report this was controlled largely by party whips. The committee high-lighted good practice in select-committee investigations and some innovations have included the presence of civil servants as aides to the committee to answer questions on specialised points. This practice was adopted by the Select Committee on Public Administration in its investigation into the White Paper, *Your Right to Know* (Cm. 3818 (1997)) and the *Draft Bill and Consultation Paper on FOI* (Cm. 4355, (1999)). The committee also noted the mixed quality of government responses to reports and suggested that the Liaison Committee itself be renamed the Select Committee Panel.[69] Select committees have power to subpoena witnesses and to order presentation of documents. Failure to comply may be contempt of Parliament but that is a decision for the whole House. Nevertheless a memorandum entitled *Departmental Evidence and Response to Select Committees* exists, which was revised in 2005 and 2009.[70] This may not always be applicable to the PAC because of its unique authority. Ministers' views on withheld information must be sought.

Officials who give evidence to select committees do so on behalf of ministers and subject to their directions. Their conduct is subject to ministerial guidance. Ministers are directly accountable to Parliament and civil servants directly accountable to ministers. It would not be appropriate for the House to seek directly to enforce the provision of information from civil servants and below that of departmental head. This would weaken accountability of ministers to Parliament (para. 28). Any refusal to provide information would have to be resolved ultimately on the floor of the House. This, the memorandum states, does not mean that civil servants may not be called upon to give a full account of government policies or their own actions or recollections of events but, in doing so, their role is to facilitate ministerial accountability, not to offer personal views or judgements on matters of political controversy (paras. 41, 55–6).

Committees are advised that they are not to act as a disciplinary hearing and questions concerning the conduct of individual officials should be taken up with ministers and should not be put to officials and should not be answered without further instructions. Presence of witnesses is requested rather than demanded. Ministers decide which officials are to appear. The current memorandum advises that where the presence of a particular civil servant is insisted upon, the House may enforce a formal order for attendance but the 1997 guidance said this was 'unprecedented'. They, and agency chief executives, remain 'subject to ministerial instructions as to how [to] answer questions', a point which somewhat undermines agency 'autonomy'.

Information should, the guidance explains, be provided, subject only to the terms of the guidance and what is necessary in the PI and subject to the FOIA

---

[69] *Select Committees and the Executive*, HC 300 (1999–00); *Government Reply*, Cm. 4737.

[70] Cabinet Office Propriety and Ethics Team, *Departmental Evidence and Response to Select Committees* (2005) now dated 2009. This contains instructions on treatment of classified and confidential information and protective security markings, paras. 80–7.
www.cabinetoffice.gov.uk/propriety_and_ethics/civil_service/osmotherly_rules.aspx.

2000 but without citing details and sections. Requests may also have to be refused where they would 'appear to involve excessive costs'. Previous guidance said the following items should also be excluded: internal advice to ministers; interdepartmental exchanges on policy issues; the level at which decisions were taken or the manner in which a minister has consulted his colleagues; Cabinet and its committees and discussions thereon; advice given by a law officer and other legal advice. Ministerial guidance may offer similar instructions. The 2009 guidance advises civil servants not to be drawn into questions of political controversy and not to offer comments on the advice they gave or would give to ministers. Guidance is given on information supplied in confidence. Guidance is given on avoiding matters *sub judice* and on the conduct of individual officials and this latter is more detailed than in earlier guidance.

Where a 'closed session' is held, there are guidelines on 'sidelining' or expunging classified or confidential information from the testimony. It is inappropriate to take such evidence in public session. Guidance is given on the handing over of classified information and 'top secret' documents must receive the authorisation of the minister. Departmental responses, on which guidance is given, should be made within two months. A refusal to appear or to allow officials to appear occasioned the Leader of the House to guarantee that time will be given to debate the matter on the floor of the House. The director of General Communications Headquarters was not allowed to testify in 1984.[71] Nor were the civil servants in the Westland case and questions were stoutly refused in the Iraqi supergun investigation.[72] Scott was critical of the convention which prevented former civil servants being called to give evidence to committees because they were no longer responsible to a minister.[73] An outright refusal to appear or answer a question might constitute a contempt of Parliament; in reality a vote of censure would have to get a majority in the House, and no doubt ministers could rely upon MPs, of their party at least, being very careful not to encroach upon ill-defined executive privileges. The guidance deals with retired officials and their evidence: 'retired officials cannot be said to represent the minister and hence cannot contribute directly to his accountability to the House'. Evidence should therefore be given by a minister or an official of his choosing. The government is adamant that the confidentiality of relationship between a minister and civil servant shall not be threatened by 'cross-examination' before a select committee of MPs, however much select committees might claim that they are upholding parliamentary supremacy in contradistinction to government's claim that committees only exist by virtue of ministerial responsibility/accountability to Parliament. It is not right, the government maintains, to allow officials to be questioned with a view to establishing the appropriate *locus* of fault in conduct, or the conduct itself, of individual officials. It is claimed that committees have received more useful information from officials than ministers on occasion.[74]

[71] HC 363 (1984–5).   [72] Note 6 above.   [73] HC 115 (1995–6) para. F4.61 *et seq.*
[74] Drewry (ed.), *The New Select Committees*, p. 275.

Pressure has been put on the Leader of the House by chairmen to obtain more information on nationalised industries (a growing family) and to inveigle more information out of government departments and agencies, and committees have a long-standing practice of showing papers and drafts to them for comment and further information.[75] Furthermore, lay witnesses before a select committee have pleaded the privilege against self-incrimination and effectively thwarted the thrust of the committee's investigation.[76]

With the Next Steps executive agencies, the original Ibbs Report, which recommended their introduction to enhance management efficiency, found it difficult to accommodate parliamentary oversight via select committees with the operation of agencies. Agency chief executives are responsible for management and operational decisions and answer to select committees accordingly. Ministers are responsible for overall policy and answer to committees for that. The policy/operational divide is not clear cut, not unlike the responsibility/accountability division, and it has been felt that it shelters ministers and agency chiefs to avoid appropriate levels of accountability as occurred after a series of prison escapes in late 1994 and early 1995 and in the operation of the Child Support Agency where after a highly criticised performance, including one before the select committee, the agency chief resigned.[77] The minister then responsible for the Next Steps initiative informed the Institute of Directors in 1992 that while agency chief executives operated like private-sector managers, nevertheless they could be hauled before committees to answer to them. The Next Steps Initiative (NSI) has produced a wealth of information in the form of framework documents (FDs), performance indicators, reports and specific agreements between departments and their agencies, but it has been felt that committees have not pressed home to advantage the opportunities that this provision could yield and that what is missing, for instance, is greater interplay between the PAC and the departmental committees to assess the information that emerges in a less parochial fashion.[78] Agency chiefs have themselves been disappointed by not being pressed more closely by committees.[79] The government did not accept a recommendation from the Treasury and Civil Service Select Committee (TCSC) in 1994 that agency chief executives should be directly and personally accountable to select committees in relation to their annual performance agreements (which would replace key targets set for chief executives and which are announced to Parliament each year and which are

---

[75] HC 555 (1984–5).

[76] Dramatically by the Maxwell brothers in the investigation by the Social Services Committee into the Maxwell pension scandal: HC 61 (1991–2). Edwina Currie only appeared under great protest to discuss her revelations in the salmonnella in eggs episode: HC 108-I–II (1988–9), p. 185 and Cm. 687 for the Government Reply.

[77] See the Derek Lewis saga, note 30 above and the running battles between Chris Woodhead of OfSTED and the Secretary of State for Education. The *Carltona* principles of delegation apply to the chief executive and agency staff: *R v Secretary of State for Social Services, ex p. Shirwin* (16 February 1996, unreported).

[78] P. Giddings (ed.), *Parliamentary Accountability* (1995).   [79] *Ibid.*, p. 232.

agreed in the context of the business plan which is a more detailed document than the Framework Document and which is not always published in full. The committee recommended that ministers should remain accountable for framework documents and for their part in negotiating the annual agreement and for instructions given to the chiefs and that all such instructions should be published subject only to personal confidentiality and necessary anonymity. The government rejected this recommendation stating that chiefs do appear and committees have all necessary information.[80] A practice has developed after initial confusion whereby questions of an operational nature are addressed to agency chiefs by members and answers are placed in Hansard. Obviously they cannot answer oral questions in the House.

Select committees, like governments, suffer leaks. A particularly notable one occurred in the Health Committee where a draft report was leaked to the department and where pressure was allegedly exerted on the committee. The Foreign Secretary was also leaked a report before it was published by a member of the Foreign Affairs Committee in 1998 leading to the leaker's resignation. The Committee of Privileges has investigated the breach of the rule which prohibits the publication of evidence taken *in camera* or publication before report to the House, or the publication of deliberations of a committee.[81] Members of committees are 'prime misfeasants' and the code contained in the *Notes on the Practice of Lobby Journalism* is not enforced. The press show scant regard for the rules, and the House is reluctant to punish the press, as evidenced in the case of the journalist from *The Times* in 1986 who published details of a select committee's confidential report.[82] The House has power to punish a breach of privilege with imprisonment[83] or withdrawal of a press lobby or press gallery pass. The committee recommended that a pass be withdrawn for certain serious breaches.

MPs themselves are under a duty, by resolution of the House, to disclose private interests in debates or proceedings of the House or its committees or in their official transactions. A compulsory register has existed since 1975 although not all members chose initially to enter relevant details. In the wake of various scandals throughout the late 1980s and the 1990s, Lord Nolan recommended improved clarity of entries and immediate updating with details of all contracts relating to the provision of services in their capacity as members – these would be available for public inspection. He also recommended a new code of conduct for members which would be overseen by a Parliamentary Commissioner for Standards of independent standing. This Standards Commissioner would

---

[80] Cm. 2748, p. 31.

[81] For publication of evidence of the confidential proceedings of the Committee of Privileges by a member, Tony Benn MP, see HC 27 (1994–5). See HC 955 (2006–7) and the publication of the European Select Committee's internal working papers and see HC 529-II (2008-9) and the Culture etc. Committee.

[82] HC 555 (1984–5). The journalist was not punished: HC Debs., 20 May 1986.

[83] Last used in 1880. See House of Commons *Factsheet No. 62.*

have the powers of the PO (also known as the Parliamentary Commissioner for Administration (PCA) and Comptroller and Auditor General and would enjoy the support of a select committee and be able to initiate a complaint under his own discretion. The hearings of the committee (the Standards and Privileges Committee was established to perform this role) are usually in public. The House of Commons voted to require all MPs to disclose earnings from consultancies derived from Parliament and to impose a total ban on paid advocacy in Parliament. The recommendations for a Standards Commissioner and code were also approved.[84] The Standards Commissioner has engaged in some high-profile investigations and, the courts have ruled, is not subject to judicial review because his investigations are primarily for Parliament and not individuals as in the case of the PO.[85] However, when the Standards Commissioner investigated the MP and junior minister Keith Vaz for alleged breaches of the code, the committee criticised the obstruction the Standards Commissioner had met from witnesses who had not been forthcoming with evidence. Vaz had been represented by a leading solicitor in these proceedings. The episode highlighted the limits of parliamentary self-regulation – limitations that were graphically illustrated when the first Standards Commissioner, Elizabeth Filkin, felt impelled to resign in December 2001 because she believed she had been undermined by senior parliamentarians because of her spirited pursuit of inquiries (see Introduction, p. 1).[86] Lord Neill has also reported on a code of conduct and a compulsory register for the Lords.[87] Events in the Lords in 2009 highlighted the serious shortcomings in the absence of any regulatory framework.

Parliament has to assist it the PO, who investigates cases referred to him by MPs alleging maladministration in the conduct of a department's affairs where the complainant concerned has been affected, and as a consequence hardship or injustice has been caused. Some high-profile and potentially very costly recommendations have met with government resistance and delay – a feature which originated with government refusals to accept recommendations under the 1994 Code on Access (above).[88] The PO has also frequently investigated

---

[84] *Standards in Public Life*, Cm. 2850-I, pp. 43–5. The Commons also voted to register details of all contracts with the Commissioner by 31 March, 1996: HC Debs., 6 November 1995. The House of Lords introduced a Members' Register of Interests. See *Erskine May*, 23rd edn (2004), pp. 484–5 and 496 *et seq.*

[85] *R v Parliamentary Commissioner for Standards, ex p. Al Fayed* [1998] 1 All ER 93, CA; In *Hamilton v Al Fayed* [2000] 2 All ER 224, HL, the Lords disapproved *dicta* of the CA that the courts could entertain an action which was the subject of an investigation by the PCS and on which the PCS had reported to the committee. This was a breach of parliamentary privilege and Art. 9 Bill of Rights. The MP had already lost the libel action, which had not been stayed because of the effects of s. 13 Defamation Act 1996.

[86] HC 314 (2000–1), paras. 65–72.   [87] Cm. 4903 (2000).

[88] Refusals have come following reports on occupational pensions, HC 1081 (2005–06), ex gratia payments for those interned in the Second World War by the Japanese, HC 735 (2005–6), and long delay in the *Equitable Life* complaints, HC 815 (2007–8) and HC 41 (2008–9); see also *R (Bradley) v Secretary of State for Work and Pensions* [2008] EWCA Civ 36 on the legal consequences of inadequate response to an ombudsman's report and *R (EMAG) v HM Treasury* [2009] EWHC 2495 (Admin).

cases involving a failure to give advice, or to give inaccurate advice and such errors have been identified as maladministration.[89] He conducts the investigation in private and has access to all the relevant files and documents; he can interview witnesses and demand information, even from a minister, and he can take evidence on oath. Where a minister believes, and issues a notice, that disclosure of information either in content, or as a class of information or documents, would be prejudicial to the safety of the state or otherwise contrary to the PI, the PO must not disseminate the information beyond himself and his officers.[90] He is not allowed access to documents of Cabinet proceedings or of Cabinet committees. A certificate from the Cabinet Secretary approved by the prime minister is conclusive. We shall see that case law has given judges more scope than the PO, although his powers were to be equal to those of judges vis-à-vis investigation and examination. The PO is unlikely to require access to Cabinet papers in any event in his usual complaints role, since his office is shaped to cater for the more routine grievances. They have long attracted complaints about serious regulatory failure of financial institutions. On one occasion the government has found it necessary to issue a certificate on Cabinet documents. This arose out of the PO's investigation into the Court Line episode, which concerned misleading statements made by the Secretary of State in the Commons. The certificate was limited under s. 8(4) of the Parliamentary Commissioner Act 1967 to the actual transactions of a Cabinet committee and did not include drafts of its papers. He was informed of the outcome of the Cabinet committee's discussions and the minister was interviewed.[91] A case involving the local ombudsman, who operates under a very similar regime to the PO although there is direct access to the local ombudsman, has an instructive lesson on the powers of information-gathering given to the ombudsman. In a case involving irregularities in a planning decision in Liverpool where councillors with an interest had voted on a recommendation, one of the reasons why the Court of Appeal allowed an investigation by the ombudsman to stand, in spite of the fact that there was the possibility of a remedy in a court, was because of the ombudsman's access to information and documents. The ombudsman had the means to investigate serious allegations and ordinary litigants were unlikely to be able to acquire the evidence that would be necessary to support a successful application for review.[92] Schedule 2 of the 1967 Act lists those bodies subject to his jurisdiction. His powers of investigation cover those performing services for departments under contract, i.e. 'contracted out', were noted above. It is also notable that there are a wide variety of functions which he may not investigate.

---

[89] See his *Annual Report* (1993) para. 7, HC 290 (1993–4) and P. Birkinshaw, *Grievances, Remedies and the State*, 2nd edn (1994), pp. 203–4, and R. Kirkham *et al.* (2008) Public Law 510.

[90] One reason for insisting that his officers are civil servants.   [91] HC 498 (1974–5).

[92] *R v Local Comm'r for Administration in North and North East of England, ex p. Liverpool City Council* [2001] 1 All ER 462, CA.

The Comptroller and Auditor General (CAG) and the Public Accounts Committee (PAC)

The primary responsibility of the CAG is to examine the accounts of designated bodies and to issue reports for the PAC of the House of Commons. During the first round of hearings by Lord Nolan's committee, the government announced that where a minister was minded to overrule an accounting officer's opinion – usually the permanent secretary or agency chief executive – on the prudent and economical use of public funds, the officer could inform the chair of the PAC.[93] Previously officers informed the CAG and Treasury where they were overruled in more serious matters by a minister involving 'propriety or regularity'. In the Pergau Dam episode in 1994, which concerned the conferral of overseas aid to the Malaysian government in terms which were subsequently ruled ultra vires, there was felt by the civil servants to be no question of irregularity and so the overruling was not communicated to the CAG.[94] He uncovered it when conducting a value-for-money (VFM) audit of the Overseas Development Administration. Following this episode, the government accepted that all overrulings would be communicated to the CAG without delay; there then followed the further concession to the PAC. In the course of the inquiry, it was disclosed that 1,500 Whitehall files were given 'Not for NAO [National Audit Office] eyes' status. This was stopped as a practice after the Labour Government came to power in 1997. These included ministerial private office files containing Cabinet or Cabinet committee papers or minutes and files dealing with the conduct of business with the NAO or PAC usually while they are current. This limitation has been developed from the interpretation of s. 8(1) National Audit Act 1983 which allows the CAG to have a right of access to all such documents as he *may reasonably require* for carrying out an examination and to require the person holding or responsible for a document to give such *information and explanation as are reasonably necessary*. Clearly such a limitation is open to abuse.

Section 8 of the Government Resource and Accounts Act 2000[95] provides that the CAG shall have rights of access at all reasonable times to any of the documents relating to a department's accounts. Those holding or controlling such documents must give the CAG any assistance, information or explanation required. Under s. 25, it is provided that s. 8 will apply where the accounts of a body are to be audited by the CAG by statute or by agreement, i.e. they are not government departments or agencies.

The reports of the CAG have been accused of being 'unambitious', 'constrained' and 'coded', and of failing to explain causes and effects. The CAG

---

[93] F. White *et al.* (1994) Public Law 526. See also F. White and K. Hollingsworth, *Audit, Accountability and Government* (1999).

[94] *R v Secretary of State for Foreign Affairs, ex p. World Development Movement Ltd* [1995] 1 All ER 611: the Secretary of State was found to have acted unlawfully in giving £234 million to the Malaysian government to build a dam as a part of our overseas development programme.

[95] See K. Hollingsworth and F. White (2001) Public Law 50.

cannot examine 'policy' itself, only the impact and expenditure implications and VFM aspects of departmental programmes. VFM audits are a vital feature of CAG investigations concentrating on wider concerns of economy, efficiency and effectiveness of public expenditure and not simply the exchequer audits of accounts. The accounting officer has to appear before the PAC, and the committee has access to all necessary information providing the department possesses it.[96] In defence procurement and pharmaceutical production, the departments do not have all the information that the PAC would like, as will be seen elsewhere.[97] The flow of information often relates to the symbiotic relationship between the department and the trade association or manufacturing company. Elsewhere the PAC has criticised the Ministry of Defence (MoD), in particular, for failing to give information on the accounts of bodies in advance of a proposed privatisation.[98]

The PAC is one of the committees that engages in pre-appointment scrutiny of named public appointments announced by the prime minister in 2007 (*Governance of Britain*, Cm. 7170). The committee's comments are non-binding. Similar hearings with other committees involve appointments of ombudsmen and regulators.

Ministers and civil servants[99]

The following codes set out the code of practice for civil servants: Civil Service Code (2006), www.parliament.uk/commons/lib/research/briefings/snpc-03924.pdf; Civil Service Management Code (CSMC) (April 2008), www.civilservice.gov.uk/about/work/codes/csmc/index.aspx.

The latter is a very straightforward account of the primary duties and responsibilities of civil servants. The latter is a part of the 'contractual relationship' between the servant and the employer (Crown). They must 'handle information as openly as possible within the legal framework'. They must act under the core values: integrity, honesty, objectivity and impartiality. Under the CSMC 4.1.1, civil servants are servants of the Crown and owe a duty of loyal service to the Crown as their employer. Since constitutionally the Crown acts on the advice of ministers who are answerable for their departments and agencies in Parliament, that duty is, subject to the provisions of the Civil Service Code above, owed to the duly constituted government.

The central framework derives from the need for civil servants to be, and to be seen to be, honest and impartial in the exercise of their duties. They

---

[96] A controversy arose when Peter Levene became head of the Procurement Executive for the MoD on terms that he dissociate completely from his former employer with the consequence that he could not answer the committee's questions relating to the placement or operation of government contracts with the company: HC 390 (1984–5), p. v.

[97] See p. 363 *et seq.* below. See National Audit Act 1983, s. 8.

[98] See McEldowney (1991) Mod LR 933.

[99] Institute of Public Policy Research, *Ministers and Civil Servants*, November 2007.

must not allow their judgement or integrity to be compromised in fact or by reasonable implication. In particular civil servants must not misuse information acquired on official duties. Information communicated in confidence must not be disclosed without authority:

> They must not seek to frustrate the policies, decisions or actions of Government either by declining to take, or abstaining from, action which flows from ministerial decisions or by unauthorised, improper or premature disclosure outside the Government of any information to which they have had access as civil servants.

They must not take part in any political or public activity which compromises, or might be seen to compromise, their impartial service to government. 'Civil servants must not misuse their official position or information acquired in the course of their official duties to further their private interests or those of others.' They are advised that conflicts of interest may arise from financial interests and:

> more broadly from official dealings with, or decisions in respect of, individuals who share a civil servant's private interests (for example freemasonry, member-ship of societies, clubs and other organisations, and family). Where a conflict of interest arises, civil servants must declare their interest to senior management so that senior management can determine how best to proceed.

The code has detailed guidance on confidentiality and official information reminding servants of their duties under the Official Secrets Act (OSA) and their confidentiality to their employer. Confidentiality continues after cessation of employment. Further guidance is given on leaked select-committee reports and Crown Copyright. Guidance is given concerning publications and dealings with the media or press for which advance clearance must be given. The Hutton Report into David Kelly had details of the regulations in the MoD. Civil servants and special advisers must seek authorisation of the head of their former department, and the head of the Home Civil Service, before entering into a contractual commitment with a publisher. The government also proposed to clarify the confidentiality and copyright rules for civil servants, special advisers and diplomats – but did not propose their extension to ministers.[100]

Where the civil servant feels that s/he is being required to act in a way which is illegal, improper, unethical, or in breach of constitutional convention, which may involve possible maladministration, or which is otherwise inconsistent with the code or raises a fundamental issue of conscience, s/he should first report the matter internally. If a civil servant had a problem, they should go to the line manager, staff appointed for counselling etc., the police if a criminal matter, or Civil Service Commissioners. 'If you cannot perform your duties in accordance with the code, you should resign.' There have been claims that

---

[100] HC 91 (2007–8) and see HC 689-I (2005–6) and HC 664 (2007–8).

there is widespread abuse of breaches of confidence by civil servants deliberately aimed at frustrating the policies of ministers.[101]

Nolan added a suggested amendment to the code which would allow a servant to utilise the procedures where s/he was not personally involved and is aware of wrongdoing or maladministration – an internal whistle-blowing provision and quite significant – and this the government accepted. He further recommended that, contrary to government proposals, all *successful* appeals should be reported to Parliament and not just those where the government refused to accept the Civil Service Commissioners' conclusions. This would help to ensure wider dissemination of best practice. The government had reservations about this although it accepted that anonymous 'good practice' should be published. He also recommended an informal procedure – 'a servant's friend' – in each department and agency to whom servants could turn in confidence and who would not be part of line management. This was accepted.[102]

The duties and responsibilities of civil servants and ministers has been the subject of a report from the TCSC[103] and the general theme has featured in a variety of subsequent committee reports and government memoranda. It has now also featured in further reports by the TCSC and government responses on the future of the civil service and it was examined by Lord Nolan's committee and by his successor Lord Neill. An initiative to produce a statute for the civil service including a consultation paper and draft bill was published in 2004 (Cm. 6373). This had broad-ranging support but initially found the back burner, although it was subsequently revised in 2008 and 2009 (see Introduction, p. 6). Its purpose was to enshrine independence, impartiality and accountability in law and not prerogative. The background to the 1986 TCSC Report was the low morale in the civil service, the banning of trade unions at GCHQ, the *Ponting* trial, and the *Note of Guidance on the Duties and Responsibilities of Civil Servants in Relation to Ministers* issued by Sir Robert Armstrong which was amended in July 1996.[104] The guidance, which 'was not intended to break new ground' and which has only been slightly modified, reasserted the tradition of civil-service confidentiality and allegiance to the minister, and the responsibility of ministers to Parliament. Its message is expressed in the current codes above.

The committee was surprised that principles of the 1930s were still considered adequate for the late 1980s. It was also uneasy about Sir Robert Armstrong's equation of the Crown with the government of the day. The Crown may be symbolic of the nation, the committee ruminated, to which 'civil servants and others may owe a loyalty higher and more lasting than that which they owe to the

---

[101] The European Policy Forum said of thirty-six serious leaks that had taken place between 'the summer' of 1994 and March 1995 two-thirds were aimed at frustrating government policies: *Financial Times* 17 September 1995. In 2008, there was a notorious episode of leaks from the Home Office to an Opposition front-bencher, which was investigated by the police who gained access to Parliament to search an MP's office via the Sergeant at Arms's consent.

[102] For the Code see HC Deb., vol. 267, col. 234, 23 November 1995.

[103] HC 92-I–II (1985–6).   [104] *Ibid.*, II, pp. 7–9.

government of the day'. The official view stated by the Cabinet Secretary was of an undivided loyalty owed by the servant to the minister. In return the minister should, Sir Robert believed, 'read, mark, learn and digest the information and advice which the Civil Service has to offer . . . and to take that seriously'.[105] Too much, the committee believed, was left to happenstance. What was needed was a set of guidelines promulgated by the prime minister after consultation with other political leaders in the Commons and spelling out the duties and responsibilities of ministers to Parliament and the civil service.

The wider concerns apparent from the 1980s onwards are obviously activated by the 'low morale' which exists when senior civil servants, especially, feel their career prospects are jeopardised if they do not give *politically* acceptable advice to ministers. More immediate was the concern over the accountability of an anonymous civil servant who acted without the authority or knowledge of a minister and for whose actions the minister will not accept responsibility, and the situation where a civil servant feels obliged to reveal what his minister is doing because the latter's behaviour is not in the PI, or so the civil servant believes. On the former situation, the committee, in agreement with the Defence Committee, believed that an internal departmental inquiry which is not fully reported to Parliament cannot qualify as accountability. The latter situation poses several problems.

In the case of a moral dilemma, Sir Robert believed a civil servant could take the matter up as a last resort with the permanent secretary of his department. The Cabinet Secretary, and through him the prime minister, may be consulted. The government has endorsed and acted upon this view.[106] In the case of Ponting and Colette Bowe,[107] these procedures were found defective. More recent leakers have chosen to go public and some faced OSA prosecution. Nolan found that only one appeal to the head of the Home Civil Service had been made in eight years. The First Division Association (the trade union for leading civil servants) has argued for a code of guidance to reinforce the position of the civil servant with possible redress from the PO or resort to the chairman of the appropriate select committee in the Commons or an ethics tribunal. Sir Douglas Wass has called for an 'Inspector-General for the Civil Service' who would be independent of ministers and who could hear civil servants.[108]

In its response to the 1994 TCSC report, the government produced a draft code on ministers and civil servants which draws largely on the Armstrong

---

[105] *Ibid.*, I, para. 3.10. See J. Jacob, *The Republican Crown* (1996); M. Sunkin and S. Payne, *The Nature of the Crown: A legal and political analysis* (1999).

[106] Cmnd 9841. In proceedings before Scott J in which the Attorney General sought a permanent injunction prohibiting newspaper reporting of *Spycatcher's* contents, Sir Robert accepted the possibility, *in extremis*, of a justified leak. See ch., 11, p. 438 *et seq.*

[107] The chief press and information officer at the DTI who effected the leak of the Solicitor General's letter in the Westland affair.

[108] Note 103, vol. II, pp. 43–4. The FDA code is the *Civil Service Code of Ethics* (November 1994). On civil servants who break the law in performance of their duties, see *Legal Entitlements and Administrative Practices*, CSD (HMSO 1979).

memorandum in spite of the widespread criticism of that document being out of touch with the contemporary context of government. The code was amended to take account of the amendments to the Civil Service Code in 1996. Further revisions in May 1999 take account of devolution.[109] Civil servants in the Scottish and Welsh administrations are appointed under the terms and conditions of the Home Civil Service under the devolution Acts. Their primary duties are to 'the administration they serve'. We saw above how these are maintained. The further amendments were explained above.

Credulity would be strained in a serious matter to expect a lengthy process to be gone through and confidences kept. The Defence Committee in 1986 were adamant and probably expressed what the existing position would be: 'Civil servants who leak information should face the sack or internal discipline', not punishment through the courts. If the leak involves items protected by the OSA that Act may be invoked. There have been examples from 2007 onwards of 'misconduct in public office' embracing acts of leaking (below).

Nolan's recommendation, and the government's acceptance, is a big improvement but even so until the Public Interest Disclosure Act 1998, there was nothing by way of official publication which offers scope for debate on what might be a 'justified leak' to the press by a civil servant such as is recognised in other countries.[110] The committee appears to endorse the view that such leaks are never totally defensible, even presumably when informing of evil or criminal acts. The concluding comment in the previous paragraph reinforces what was probably the legal position on the subject of discipline and punishment. Even if the OSA could not be successfully invoked, a civil servant who communicated, in whatever form, information which would embarrass his minister, whom he believed to be acting against the PI, would have no right to claim wrongful dismissal if sacked. For civil servants are not formally under a contract of employment, although such a status may be ripe for legal reassessment and the CSMC sets out 'contractual' terms.[111] The government in fact introduced a provision conferring contractual status, for limited purposes, on Crown servants in the 1988 Employment Act, s. 30 and it planned to put members of the 'new' senior civil service on 'written contracts'.[112] Even if they were under such contracts, as are other employees in the public sector, it seems on the balance of authorities that it may be an implied term of a contract of employment that an

---

[109] CS Code (May 1999) para. 2, now amended.

[110] E.g., US Civil Service Reform Act 1978 and 1989 – the 'Whistleblower' Protection Act. The 1978 Act, strengthened in 1989, establishes the Office of Special Counsel to protect employees and receive 'leaks'. See ch. 3, note 95 and the CIA.

[111] *R v Civil Service Appeal Board, ex p. Bruce* [1989] 2 All ER 907, CA; *R v Lord Chancellor's Department, ex p. Nangle* [1991] ICR 743; *R v Chief Constable of Devon amd Cornwall Constabulary, ex p. Hay* [1996] 2 All ER 711, at 724 d–g; and see S. Fredman and G. Morris (1988) Public Law 58; *The State as Employer* (1989) 61–71; (1991) Public Law 485; and Freedland (1995) Public Law 224.

[112] See *Civil Servants' Employment Rights*, House of Commons Library SN/BT/3698 (2005). The spy George Blake signed an agreement not to publish material gained from his employment with MI6: see p. 45 above.

employee cannot be sued for revealing the confidences of his employer if it is in the PI to reveal such confidences and this outweighs the maintenance of confidentiality. There may be difficulties in suing for wrongful dismissal in such circumstances but the Public Interest Disclosure Act (PIDA) (see chapter 3, p. 116) would be invoked where possible to protect a leaker from reprisals and unfair dismissal.

Leaks outside the terms of the PIDA, even for conscionable motives, are most unlikely to be protected by unfair dismissal legislation. A civil servant who has taken the necessary internal steps by appealing as prescribed without success, and who has not been transferred, could be left with dismissal or damaged career prospects by following his or her conscience and going public where such a course is morally justified.[113] The PIDA seeks to remedy this situation. But its primary emphasis is on *internal* disclosure. While substantial compensation may be awarded under the PIDA, re-engagement or reinstatement is most unlikely in reality, though possible. Prompted by leaks from the Home Office in 2008 to an opposition front-bench spokesman (see chapter 3, p. 115), the Public Administration Select Committee launched an inquiry into Whitehall leaks in the 2008–9 session (see Introduction, p. 6). The leaks involved a very high-profile investigation and arrest of an MP, Damian Green, on charges arising from 'misconduct in public office' by the leaker, a civil servant. The Cabinet Office's guidance to departments states it is appropriate to involve the police in leak investigations when they involve 'a serious and damaging impact on the functioning of a Department and . . . suspicion of leaking sensitive information'. However, the guidance left open the possibility of police involvement without the commission of a criminal offence and the Home Affairs Committee recommended clarification on this (HC 157 (2008–9)). PASC recommended a greater role for independent Civil Service Commissioners in grievances.

Outright lying to Parliament by ministers may indeed be rare, but Sir Douglas Wass described the more usual practice where 'by judicious presentation and omission [the minister] gives an impression to Parliament which is not the impression which would be formed if someone had all the evidence'.[114] Presentation and timing are everything, and these are matters of ministerial

---

[113] Morals are subject to personal interpretation and mischievous leaks are far from uncommon. Before the Public Interest Disclosure Act was passed, secrecy clauses in contracts had proliferated and had certainly been more widely publicised in recent years as an issue of grave public concern. They were common in the NHS (where management practice is still criticised) and increasingly in universities, in nationalised industries, privatised industries and commercial bodies. Of crucial significance, from a breach-of-contract perspective, is whether the clause is appropriately drafted to cover a leak – many were not – and whether the leak occurred during or after the period of employment – dismissal is not possible in the latter case. The 'whistle-blower' is invariably in a weak position when in employment. See: Y. Cripps *The Legal Implications of Disclosure in the Public Interest*, 2nd edn (1994). An action/advisory group, 'Public Action at Work', has been set up to assist 'whistle-blowers': G. Dehn (1993) Public Law 603.

[114] Vol. II, p. 42, note 93.

prerogative. The minister for open government informed the House that government was more like playing poker than playing chess – not all the cards are placed on the table at once – a comment which caused him to be accused of authorising lying to Parliament.[115] The prime minister has stated that where a minister has knowingly failed to give accurate and truthful information to Parliament, they should resign 'except in quite exceptional circumstances of which a devaluation or time of war or other danger to national security have been quoted as examples'.[116]

Sir Robert Armstrong's amended memorandum and government responses promote a duty of confidence into an absolute and inflexible rule admitting of no exceptions. The civil service in the twenty-first century has changed irreversibly from the anonymous monolith of the early twentieth century – a point the government readily accepts. Publications have identified the qualities needed in the civil service to deliver its *Modernising Government* programme.[117] Civil servants have greater pressure of work because of increased and varied duties; they operate under the constant attention of the news media and the press; it is more vociferously unionised and organised around staff associations at all levels; it campaigns far more on behalf of its own causes.[118] On the government side, there is more intervention in senior appointments as well as greater resort to advertising; there have been constant demands for thirty years for more 'activist management and devolved responsibility to more junior line officials' bringing them not infrequently into the limelight.[119] There has also been an increasing resort to 'outside' special advisers by government prompting official inquiries, Nolan Committee investigations and codes of practice. This was necessary after the Employment Appeal Tribunal held that special advisers are not covered by the Civil Service rules on appointments because they are not civil servants.[120]

The identity and level of responsibility of civil servants will become easier to assess, although the Cabinet Office has argued that this development, starting with the financial management initiative and leading to the public service agreements entered into by departments and agencies, will merely strengthen ministerial responsibility or accountability. The public wants more publicity about administration, and the civil service are asked increasingly to advise not only on policy, but on presentation of policies for public acceptance. The IC and IT reports allow senior civil servants to be identified (see chapter 6).

Since the early 1980s, departments have developed ever more detailed information as part of internal management structures. This began with the Department of Environment (DoE) MINIS – the Minister's Information

---

[115] HC Debs., 8 March 1994. In his evidence to Sir Richard Scott, Sir Robin Butler told the former that 'half truths' are necessary. See the evidence of Lord Howe on 'packaging' information to Parliament (HC 115 (1995–6) para. D4. 52).

[116] Cm. 2748, p. 29.

[117] *Modernising Government*, Cm. 4310 and see HC Debs., vol. 341, col. 219 (15 December 1999).

[118] See the memorandum of Nevil Johnson, HC 92-II (1985–6), p. 169.

[119] *Ibid.*   [120] *Lord Chancellor v Coker* [2001] IRLR 116.

System – to provide the minister with information on departmental performance.

Financial management initiatives (FMI) for departments concentrated upon informing managers within departments on the meeting of performance objectives and costs to help ensure their responsibility for the performance of programmes. They originally had little public dimension apart from being within the purview of departmentally related select committees. The TCSC argued for departmental annual reports to explain policies and provide sensible performance indicators and information on FMIs as a back-up for the general annual reviews.[121]

This was instrumental in leading to all departments and agencies publishing annual reports detailing achievements, targets, output and performance and financial information. This was formalised after the cessation of the January Public Expenditure White Paper which had played a crucial role in the budget cycle. Their primary role is to inform Parliament of general performance and expenditure. In addition, framework documents (FDs) and agreements on performance between departments and agencies are published together with other agreements but corporate plans were not initially published although now they are subject to commercial confidentiality. Public service agreements are published. These agreements are said to be 'at the cutting edge of a revolution in the way public services are managed'. These concentrate on outcomes rather than inputs and funding is tied to results. Clear targets for performance have to be set; their realisation will result in extra investment. Targets include information on access to information and citizen redress.[122] The impact of information technology was examined in chapter 1.

Public Records Act

The Public Records Act covers central government. Local authorities maintain archives services as do other public bodies, as do private bodies. The first point to make is that government documents are available, after selection, thirty years after they came into existence.[123] A recommendation may, however, be made for extended closure. The FOIA 2000 aligns FOI and the public records regimes as administered by the National Archives (NA), formerly the Public Record Office (PRO) (see FOI provisions, chapter 4, p. 135).[124]

---

[121] See 13th Report of Committee of Public Accounts, *Financial Management Initiatives* (1986–7).

[122] See N. D. Lewis (2000) European Public Law 201.

[123] Public Records Acts 1958 and 1967. See M. Roper in R. A. Chapman and M. Hunt (eds.), *Open Government* (1987). This legislation does not cover Scottish records. See further A. McDonald in A. McDonald and G. Terrill (eds.), *Open Government: Freedom of information and privacy* (1998) and see the select committee report on the Draft FOI Bill: HC 570-II (1998–9) and S. Healy, 'Freedom of information and its impact on archives' in R. Chapman and M. Hunt (eds.), *Open Government in a Theoretical and Practical Context* (2006), p. 111.

[124] Nat Archives, AR HC 675 (2007–8). On libraries and archives, see Legal Deposit Libraries Act 2003.

Government inquiries frequently produce information in advance of this date, which would otherwise remain undisclosed in any detail – the Hutton and Butler Reports outlined at the beginning of this chapter are examples.[125] The White Paper stated the government's intention to make as many records as possible available after thirty years. Under the Act the thirty-year period may be shortened or lengthened by decision of the Lord Chancellor/Secretary of State for Justice. Scotland and Northern Ireland are not covered by the legislation but administrative arrangements parallel those in England and in Scotland information available for copying and inspection in the NA for Scotland is specifically exempted from the FOI(Scotland)A. The NA has its own fees structure for research activity in lieu of fees under the FOIA. Each department has a departmental records officer who is responsible to the minister in charge of a department. His responsibilities under the Act cover papers from their creation until they are transferred to the NA. In 2008, the NA possessed over a hundred miles shelf space of documents going back to the Domesday Book (http://www.ancestor-search.info/NAT-NatArchives.htm).

The subject of public records was examined by the Wilson Report of 1981.[126] This found that many documents were not available when administrators or researchers needed them. It was impossible to know whether this was by accident, bad judgement or design. About 99 per cent of public records are destroyed because they are regarded as unimportant.[127] Sir John Donaldson MR criticised government apathy.[128] Wilson found 'maximum destruction' at the first review of documents after five years, and only at the second review after twenty-five years were historical factors considered. The White Paper stated that historical grounds were considered at the initial review. The White Paper stated that, in the thirty-five largest government departments, some 155,000 feet (30 miles) are given first review and 23,000 feet (4.3 miles) are subject to second review. The PRO took in about one mile each year. In 1962 it was estimated that departments created one hundered miles of documents each year. Because only one department, Defence, had established a body of academic experts to assist in its selection, the Public Records Act established an Advisory Council on Public Records consisting of lawyers, MPs, senior civil servants and historians. It does not advise on selection – departments do: 'Therefore its members have no means of knowing which records have been withheld, and why.' Where a department is asked for papers which it has retained, and it refuses, the committee may be approached on an informal basis. From 1993, more than 90,000 documents were released by departments.[129] Security papers are not usually transferred. Sensitive information on national security is scrutinised by a Cabinet Office committee.

---

[125] Notes 9 and 10 above.   [126] *Modern Public Records: Selection and access*, Cmnd 8204,
[127] *Timewatch*, BBC 2, 1 January 1986.
[128] See Sir John Donaldson's apprehension on government apathy: Public Record Office, *26th Annual Report* (1985). The Master of the Rolls is chairman of the advisory committee.
[129] HC 570–11 (1998–9), p. 24 *et seq.*

Papers that are recommended for extended closure[130] under present practice include 'exceptionally sensitive papers' whose disclosure would be against the PI; documents containing information supplied in confidence, the disclosure of which would, or *might*, constitute a breach of good faith; and personal documents whose disclosure would cause distress or embarrassment to living persons or to their descendants. In 1971, papers of 'political or commercial sensitivity' were added.[131] Departments may also retain records within the department for administrative reasons, e.g. 'in constant use', and those 'whose sensitivity is such that no date can be put on their potential release' (para. 9.23). These include blanket coverage and cover security and intelligence, personal records of civil servants and various other caregories under review or to be placed under review.

The Lord Chancellor/Secretary of State for Justice has responsibility for public records, and the Ministry of Justice is now answerable to a departmentally related select committee.[132] In 1992 he set in motion a review of the closure criteria. This concluded that disclosure after thirty years should be allowed unless there was harm to national security, international relations, defence, or the economic interests of the UK or its release would distress or endanger individuals and descendants and the information was given in confidence. The protection of documents supplied in confidence to government was added where disclosure might constitute a breach of good faith. *Actual harm* to those interests would have to be proved. Detailed guidance was to be given to departments. For the first group, closure will be reviewed ten years after the thirty-year period. For the remaining categories, seventy-five or one hundred years is the recommended period of closure generally for sensitive personal information. In future, an outline reason for closure or retention will be given, e.g. 'administrative', 'national security' etc. together with appropriate information, providing that will not put the information at risk. The Advisory Council set up under the Act will give advice on applications from departments for retention as well as closure. The White Paper also gave examples of documents released under new relaxed provisions of John Major's Government.[133] These provisions were superceded by the FOIA in 2005. The idea, as seen in chapter 5, was to align the discretionary regime as it now exists with the provisions of the FOIA.

In chapter 4, there was an examination of the Dacre Review of the thirty-year rule in 2009. It will be recalled that it was recommended that the period of closure should be reduced to fifteen years. He also recommended that sensitive documents should be given greater protection under the FOIA exemptions. The

---

[130] For such periods as the Lord Chancellor designates.

[131] The White Paper does not refer to these.

[132] This was the reason ostensibly why the Lord Chancellor was called to give evidence to the select committee on the White Paper, *Your Right to Know* Cm. 3818, which preceded the FOI Bill. He was questioned far more broadly than on public records: HC 198-I (1997–8), p. 80 *et seq.*

[133] The papers of Winston Churchill were sold as a private collection and not as state papers: see R. Brazier (1996) Cambridge Law Journal 65.

timing of the report was very close to the Justice Secretary invoking the veto to stop disclosure of Cabinet documents (see Introduction, p. 7).

Where a Lord Chancellor/Secretary of State has been a member of a government whose papers are eligible for release, a conflict of interest can arise.[134] Such conflicts will increase if the fifteen-year rule is introduced.

Government statistics

Controversy over government's use of statistics has a long heritage. It re-erupted in 2008 and 2009 over the government use of figures for knife crime and stinging criticism on the accuracy of the use of the figures by the chair of the Statistics Authority.

It was claimed that Britain had the worst details on production statistics in the developed world – only 400 items were collected (the Treasury said 900) while in the USA in the same period it was 11,000. The Royal Statistical Society recommended an Independent Statistical Commission upholding the belief elsewhere that effective statistics publicly available are a prerequisite of democratic government. The government was 'reluctant to provide a market researcher for private companies'. Huge numbers of figures are published under the Citizen's Charter initiative and its successor, but not to make up deficiencies in central statistics. *Your Right to Know* (1997), which set out the New Labour plans for FOI legislation, spoke of steps to enhance the reliability of national statistics. In October 1999, a White Paper outlined plans for the publication of a Framework for National Statistics and the appointment of an independent Statistics Commission and a National Statistician.[135]

The Statistics Commission was taken over by the UK Statistics Authority (UKSA) in 2008. The latter was created by legislation in 2007.[136] The chair of the UKSA and his board are at the apex of the national system of statistics and are responsible for ensuring reliable statistics to serve the public good. The chief executive is the executive officer of UKSA and is head of the National Statistics Office. He is the national statistician and head of the Government Statistics Service which comprises statistics staff in government departments. Each department and each devolved administration has responsibility for the collection and retention of statistics relating to their areas of administration. 'National statistics' are those that are compliant with the Code of Practice for Statistics produced by UKSA. 'Official statistics' are those produced by public authorities.

Government communications[137]

A notorious incident involving a specialist adviser Jo Moore to the Transport Secretary who advised that 9/11 was a good day to bury bad news brought the

---

[134] As occurred in 1986–7 vis-a-vis Lord Hailsham and Suez.   [135] Cm. 4412.
[136] United Kingdom Statistics Authority (Statistics and Registration Survey) Act 2007.
[137] See J. Seaton and B. Pimlott (eds.), *The Media In British Politics* (1987): PASC, *Government Communications*, HC 92 (2006–7).

role of specialist advisers and press officers under public scrutiny. The scrutiny continued in the case of Gordon Brown's special adviser, Damian McBride, who was involved in smear campaigns against opposition figures in April 2009. The general importance of press and information officers in presenting ministerial policies in a favourable light has long been acknowledged,[138] as has their role in press manipulation during the Falklands campaign, for example, the Gulf War and the bombing of Kosovo.[139] The criticism of Alastair Campbell, the Downing Street Press Secretary under Tony Blair, who was censured by the Cabinet Secretary Sir Richard Wilson for criticising the Opposition's economic policies in the run-up to the 2001 general election and acting like 'a politician not a civil servant', led to Bob Phillis's *Final Report of the Review of Government Communications* (2004) (interim 2003). This in turn led to the reformulation of government communications in the UK. His report found that government spends £230 million p.a. on communications involving 2,600 individuals (civil servants). The subject had been investigated by the Mountfield review in 1999, the Ninth Report of the Nolan Committee and has recently been examined by the House of Lords Communications Committee.[140] It was criticism of a BBC reporter and government/BBC hostilities that led to the Hutton Inquiry and the severe criticism of the BBC by Lord Hutton.[141] Phillis recommended reforms of FOI laws (before they had come into effect) and a sustained commitment to a long-term programme of radical change in conduct, style and process of government communications. First, there should be a politically appointed Director of Communication. Secondly, there should be a prime minister's Senior Official Spokesperson, a civil service appointment, with management responsibility for No. 10's communications' civil servants falling under that civil service appointment. The Government Information Communications Service, which Campbell had headed, was disbanded and a new communications service, the Government Communications Service (GCS), was introduced, originally with two lead posts as recommended but these were combined with one civil-service appointment. GCS now has 4,000 civil servants as part of its network, 1,376 direct departmental employees and 373 press officers (HL 7, paras. 133–4). These reforms did not prevent abuses of communications by the prime minister's special adviser forcing his resignation in April 2009.

The hope was to make government communications and information more relevant and more local with a communications policy based on openness, not secrecy and spin. The communications involve the media and the public. It

---

[138] R. Crossman, *Diaries of a Cabinet Minister* (1975), vol. 1, p. 497 and the Public Administration Committee's report, note 137 above.

[139] See *The Protection of Military Information*, Cmnd 9112 (1983). Self-censorship was emphasised but official censorship was needed, even in limited conflict. False information should be eschewed, but 'sophisticated measures' to deceive an enemy were permissible: see *The Guardian*, 13 August 1986; and D. Mercer *et al.*, *The Fog of War* (1987); and *The Gulf War*, BBC TV January 1996. See generally on the press: the *Royal Commission on the Press*, Cmnd 6433, and see the reports of the House of Lords Communications Committee.

[140] *Government Communications*, HL 7 (2008–9).   [141] HC 247 (2003–4), pp. 321–23.

wanted to avoid departmental conflicting messages and to promote civil service impartiality. Phillis recommended all major government briefings should be on the record, live on TV and radio with full transcripts available online. They should give daily lobby briefings, which should be televised and those briefing should respond to questions.

In 1984, a century after 'one gentleman of the press was given official permission to enter and remain in the Members' Lobby', the lobby[142] celebrated its centenary. No formal resolution of the House authorised the event of 1884 and informal practice predated that year. The 'famous secret' of the lobby took place twice daily, and lobby journalists used to see the Leader of the House and Leader of the Opposition on Thursday afternoons. Ministerial briefings of the lobby developed, some suggest, from 1926 and a visit to Downing Street during the General Strike. Regular daily briefings emerged only after 1945. Today, these take place with the prime minister's spokesperson twice daily in the Treasury (open to all journalists) and in Westminster (members of the lobby only).

The basis of the lobby was a 'cosy collusion' whereby snippets of information were given on the basis that the source is not identified – unless attribution is permitted. Even the politically uninitiated will appreciate that there are elements of a 'corporatist embrace' in the relationship inasmuch as the press cannot be controlled but they can be compromised if given anonymous 'confidences' by those in the know.[143] The lobby is a voluntary group which regulates itself and operates according to a convention which the government has not wished to see fundamentally altered.[144] The enforced hypocrisy became too much for a growing number of national newspapers. However, securing reform has proved difficult although some changes have been introduced as explained by the Lords Communications Committee,[145] even though it would only establish a more open 'on the record' form of journalism. In 2001, Alastair Campbell agreed to be identified by name in newspaper reports.[146] The House of Lords Communications Committee in 2009 found that information is not to be attributed unless otherwise indicated. Access is 'privileged'. Witnesses to the committee felt that the tradition of unattributed quotations was too deeply embedded in our culture although some witnesses believed the system had become more open. There is still a presumption in ministerial briefings 'that there's not a lot of information that the public and press are entitled to'.[147]

Outside the lobby, leaks unless authorised are subject to the usual process of law. In such cases journalists have been imprisoned for refusing to name

---

[142] M. Cockrell, P. Hennessey and D. Walker, *Sources Close to the Prime Minister* (1984); N. W. Wilding and P. Laundy (eds.), *Encyclopaedia of Parliament* (1968).

[143] See H. Young, *Inside Information* (1982), note 152 below.

[144] *The Guardian*, 9 December 1986.

[145] Note 140. *The Guardian, The Independent* and *The Observer* refused for a period to publish unattributed items of government information. The lobby effectively voted for no change in its practices: *The Guardian*, 14 February 1987.

[146] *The Guardian* 14 March 2000.   [147] Nick Robinson, BBC Political Editor, to the committee.

their sources in disclosing incompetence in Whitehall.[148] Successful prosecution followed the publication of military intelligence information by Duncan Campbell *et al.* in 1978 in the ABC trial – even though the information was otherwise published. In 1987, the offices of the BBC in Glasgow were raided following publication of an article on the 'Zircon' satellite intelligence system.[149] The offices of *The Observer* and *The Guardian* were objects of police requests for confiscation orders in July 2000 in order to seize correspondence from the MI5 renegade David Shayler. Parliament was raided in 2008 following leaks to a Conservative front-bench spokesperson from the Home Office. And so on. Powers of search under the OSAs 1911–89 are subsumed under those in the Police and Criminal Evidence Act 1984.

The *Ministerial Code* is more relaxed than previously about official and private broadcasts, interviews and articles. 'The policy content and timing of all major speeches, press releases and new policy initiatives should be cleared in good time with the No. 10 Press Office as should all major interviews and media appearances' (8.2). In all other communications ministers must uphold collective responsibility. Those wishing to broadcast in a private capacity should get clearance from another minister if the latter's responsibilities were involved. Those wishing to practise journalism regularly must obtain prior approval from the No. 10 Press Office.

Formal rules govern the lobby and are issued by the Parliamentary lobby journalists.[150] Breach is most unlikely to lead to exclusion.[151] The lobby has often been used to discredit and to disinform, but it is a practice, notwithstanding the 'attribution' reform in 2000, that will outlive any FOIA reform, as witness General Alexander Haig's description of his character assassination in the US by 'Reagan's henchmen' in his book *Caveat*. To achieve this, the president's men opened that 'great smithy of information' – the government – to the press. They 'escorted reporters inside in a way hitherto unknown in Washington'. The press had 'never had sources like this' – it told them everything. 'And of course, it would not risk losing these sources by offending them, so it wrote what it was given.'

The year 1939 saw the establishment of the Central Office of Information headed by a minister of information.[152] The office, but not the minister, survived the Second World War. It is now responsible for government marketing and communications and promoting information campaigns. It produces an annual report.

---

[148] This followed the Vassall Tribunal of 1963.   [149] Zellick (1987) New LJ 160.

[150] HC 555 (1984–5), pp. 92–4.

[151] Lobby journalists rejected a proposal that each should swear an oath of secrecy, but tied on a proposal that those who broke the confidentiality of lobby statements should be barred from the lobby.

[152] H. James in A. May and K. Rowan (eds.), *Inside Information: British government and the media* (1982). The office is an executive agency seeking to 'enhance the effectiveness of government's communications': see HC 496 (1994–5).

Previous editions have examined the specific relationship between the BBC and the government. The most important development was the Hutton Report and the introduction of a new management structure for the BBC.[153] The attack by Blair and Campbell on the lack of impartiality of the BBC reporting the invasion of Iraq was as vitriolic as anything from the Thatcher government and its ministers.

D notices

Yet another corporatist embrace is illustrated by the D-notice system (now known as DA notices).[154] Originally established in 1912 and entitled the Admiralty, War Office and Press Committee, the relevant body is now known as the Defence, Press and Broadcasting Committee (http://www.dnotice.org.uk/). Established on a voluntary basis and deriving no legal basis from OSA or other Acts of Parliament, its membership comprises senior civil servants from the relevant departments,[155] representatives of certain press and publishers' agencies, societies and associations, and latterly the BBC and Independent Television News. Media and press representation heavily outweighs official membership. The secretariat and expenses are borne by the government. The secretary must be fully informed of the facts behind a DA notice, which is issued to limit or prevent publication of information which would be against the PI. The secretary applies and interprets the scope of DA notices, i.e. what is detrimental to the national security of the country. According to the memorandum of the committee submitted to the Franks Committee in 1972[156] it is not otherwise concerned with the national interest, although the secretary 'is instructed to bring to the notice of the chairman of the committee (or his deputy) any cases which lie at or beyond the border-line of the D notice system for consideration as to whether ministers should be informed of what other action should be taken'. The system is 'designed to protect national security while at the same time safeguarding the freedom and independence of the press and is based on mutual trust and confidence'.[157] There are six in operation covering, e.g. defence plans; defence equipment; nuclear weapons; radio and radar transmissions; cyphers (codes) and communications; civil defence and photographs of defence establishments. Ad hoc notices may be agreed and issued and more formal procedures may operate in time of war.[158] Adding addresses of ministers' second homes in the country for security reasons was discussed in 1999. They are issued personally to editors of the national and provincial

---

[153] W. Runciman (ed.), *Hutton and Butler: Lifting the lid on the workings of power* (2004) G. Dyke, *Inside Story* (2004); A. Campbell, *The Blair Years* (2007).

[154] See 'The Defence Advisory Notices: A review of the D notice system', MoD Open Government Document, No. 93/06; N. Wilkinson, *Secrecy and the Media* (2009).

[155] Home Office, Foreign Office, Ministry of Defence: Cmnd 5104-II, p. 241 *et seq.*

[156] Vol. II, p. 242.   [157] *Ibid.*

[158] L. Lustgarten and I. Leigh, *In from the Cold* (1994) p. 276 *et seq*

press, various news agencies and relevant publishers as well as the BBC and ITV and advice is sought on their content from the secretary of the committee. However, a large number of editors said they would follow the advice of their lawyers rather than the secretary.[159] In 1992 the then secretary of the committee stated that he gave 'positive advice' urging editors not to publish about a dozen times a year. There were about a hundred inquiries a year from editors and publishers.[160] A D notice was used in 1994 to stop publication of names of MI5 officers killed in a helicopter crash at the Mull of Kintyre; in 1999, the press were served with a D notice to stop publication of the names of MI6 officers revealed on a website and the website address itself. They have been issued in relation to SAS activities in 2001 and covert operations and in 2003 not to publish recent photos of F. Scappaticci – an IRA officer who was an informer.[161] Most recently, a notice was issued in relation to the inadvertent leaking of details of an anti terrorist operation by the Assistant Commissioner of Police outside No. 10![162]

The corporatist element is emphasised in that these notices are not creatures of law but are voluntary, represent an exclusive relationship between the state and private or quasi-governmental organised interests, and are self-regulatory, although they cover some similar areas as the OSA and breach could, but not necessarily will, involve a prosecution. Indeed compliance itself is not a *legal* guarantee of immunity. This was evident in December 1987 when the government invoked the civil law of confidentiality to prevent the broadcasting of a Radio 4 programme on the security services, although it had been cleared by the secretary to the committee[163] Failure to agree to DA notices may mean exclusion from the circle of trusted recipients of information. The close interrelationship between the press and government made any significant alteration of the D-notice system by the reform of s. 2 OSA less than likely, though we shall have to see how it operates alongside the law of confidentiality. In fact, throughout the late 1980s and 1990s the system was under strain because the government had effectively bypassed it on several occasions but it is still resorted to. The system would be used to prevent what occurred in the USA in 2006 when the identities of 2,600 CIA officers were revealed.

This takes us to another facet of the contemporary state – the public/private interface and the corporatist tendencies in the distribution and exercise of power. What do we know of the networks through which contemporary government chooses to influence, and what ought we, or our representatives, to know? What are the consequences of government seeking to achieve public ends via private or quasi-public institutions?

---

[159] *Ibid.*, p. 275   [160] Fairley (1991) 10 Oxford JLS 430.
[161] See *The Guardian*, 10 November 2001 and 17 May 2003.
[162] See *The Guardian*, 10 April 2009 for a list of high-level inadvertent leaks including that by Bob Quick.
[163] The same allegedly occurred in the case of *Immediate Action* written by a former SAS soldier.

Government, non-departmental bodies and private organisations – quasi-government[164]

Openness and accountability are two of the legitimating principles of our governmental system, though they have to be weighed against other principles such as efficiency, responsiveness and security. Collective and individual ministerial responsibility are predicated upon the former. If we set these claims upon which legitimacy is dependent against actual practice, the constitutional principles are invariably suborned. Democracy is based upon voting and representation for all those whose personal attributes do not disqualify them. In order to vote meaningfully, I must know what I am voting for. My representative must convey what the parliamentary elite have done in their stewardship of the 'gubernatorial power' and what, in return, he or she has done, or the legislative assembly has done, to investigate that stewardship. It comes to this: we cannot guarantee that we will know all that is relevant, and the system of government has not been devised in which we could. But we can ensure that vigilance and suitable pressure have been applied to ask the right questions, and get the best answers.

Openness and accountability cannot be taken as absolutes, because we do yield to countervailing pressures that are present in appeals to efficiency, responsiveness and security, and which are duties of government. In the fictional TV series *Yes Minister*, the senior civil servant's advice to young Bernard, a junior civil servant high-flier concerning open government, 'My dear boy, it's a contradiction in terms. You can be open, or you can have government',[165] is far too strong, but there is a scintilla of uncomfortable truth for the advocate of open government. The lines between openness and accountability, and efficiency, responsiveness and security, represent clashes between degrees of participatory and representative forms of democracy. But make no mistake, they are clashes over forms of democracy. The lines are always shifting as encroachments are made on the nature of the government prerogative and its assertion of the absolute supremacy of executive power and politics and policy in government and administration. The encroachments demand justification for the exercise of collective power in the purported furtherance of the PI through reasons, rational explanation, debate and institutional structure. That area of pure politics will never disappear entirely; far from it unless we require stultifying uniformity and oppressive, perhaps irresponsible inertia. Our present task is to confine it to its legitimate realm and not to allow it to rule arrogantly and rudely where it does not belong.

The chapter so far has concentrated on Whitehall. What about government beyond Whitehall that is not subject to the democratic pressure of our high politics? We all know who can vote; less easy to assess is on what issues we can vote.

---

[164] See Cabinet Office, *Public Bodies* (annual); Cabinet Office, *Public Bodies: A guide for departments* (2006).
[165] 'Open Government' in the BBC TV series *Yes, Minister*.

The points which follow are complex, but they involve the following themes.[166] Outside the formal and constitutional structure of government emerge bodies that are created by government/Parliament by a variety of devices. These bodies are responsible for particular areas of administration that fall outside a department's specific responsibility to administer directly, but which might be under the direction or guidance of a ministry, which can be achieved by a variety of devices.[167] Ministerial power of appointment is an obvious means of control and one that has caused sensational press and media coverage. This was an area which was addressed by Lord Nolan who made a variety of recommendations to deal with appointments to quangos. It must be said that the FOIA 2000 has as one of its distinct and positive features an enormously broad remit of bodies covered by the duties on access. To these bodies, which are in sch. 1 of the Act and which include many advisory bodies and non-departmental executive bodies, may be added bodies designated by the Secretary of State to be covered by the Act's provisions. This may occur where they perform public duties or provide public services under contract with a PA and it is appropriate to designate them as a PA (see chapter 4, p. 121). They will of course be protected by the Act's exemptions. It has been seen that no bodies have been so designated since the Act came into force and that the government conducted a consultation on designation.[168]

If public expenditure is involved, either by way of grant in aid from the sponsoring department or by direct vote from Parliament, then the CAG would have the duty of scrutiny and inspection of accounts.[169] In their evidence to Nolan, the CAG and chairman of the Public Accounts Committee (PAC) outlined difficulties they had encountered with non-departmental bodies and the CAG provided a list of bodies whose accounts he did not audit. A report from the PAC detailed shortcomings in financial regularity concerning many non-departmental bodies and executive agencies 'representing a departure from the standards of public conduct which have mainly been established during the past 140 years'.[170] Among the faults identified were poor monitoring of expenditure; failure by departments to establish effective monitoring of non-departmental public bodies that they fund and sponsor; failure to obtain information by those in authority; infrequent meetings, which were improperly recorded; concealing information; and failure to secure arms' length relationships with private-sector consultants.[171]

---

[166] See: P. Birkinshaw, I. Harden and N. Lewis, *Government by Moonlight: The hybrid parts of the state* (1990).

[167] Issuing codes of guidance, statutory regulations, departmental regulations or by allowing an appeal or complaint to be made by an aggrieved party to the Secretary of State; see Birkinshaw, *Grievances, Remedies and the State*, ch. 4.

[168] Ministry of Justice, *Consultation on Designation of Additional Public Authorities under the Freedom of Information Act 2000*, Consultation Paper CP 27/07.

[169] See White etc., note 93.   [170] *The Proper Conduct of Public Business*, HC 154 (1993–4).

[171] NAO, *Government Use of Consultants*, HC 128 (2006–7); PAC, HC 309 (2006–7), criticism of £2 billion spent on consultants in 2006.

What concerns us is that these bodies themselves become repositories of vast amounts of information, and secondly they establish relationships with sponsoring departments which are not on the record of any public document. The subject of nationalised industries in the past – and the public corporations which manage them, and indeed the boards of privatised industries, and the relationships of these bodies with ministers, was and is a case in point. Since 2007, there has been a re-emergence of nationalisation, or massive state under-writing, of banks in the UK and USA in particular. In the UK, nationalised banks are not scheduled in the FOIA and are not therefore covered by it. The relationship between these bodies and ministers is of a confidential nature, and it is impossible to fathom whether such bodies are under a greater degree of political control than the arm's length statutes establishing them would suggest.[172] The poor performance of the privatised rail system led to the re-nationalisation of what is now Network Rail – with apologies from the Secretary of State for Transport for misleading the House of Commons over the episode. It will be recalled that the IT ruled this body was not a public authority for the purposes of the EIR (see chapter 7, p. 250).[173]

The powers of regulators of utilities and to some extent consumer representative bodies were beefed up by the Competition and Services (Utilities) Act 1992 which, inter alia, provided a legal duty to provide complaints procedures for privatised industries' consumers. From 2000, statutes for gas and electricity, water, the post office and rail transport have made regulatory agencies commissions and not one-man bands, and have introduced additional duties to publish information. The Communications Act 2003 made provision for the communications industry. The legislation has also strengthened consumer representation and complaints procedures.

In gas and electricity consumer councils are placed under increased duties to publish more information, to assist consumers and to name and shame reluctant energy companies and to protect vulnerable consumers such as the disabled or chronically sick, those of pensionable age or those residing in rural areas.

More generally, if a government hives off to an independent agency executive powers to regulate, license or control an aspect of commerce or finance in the PI, how do we or our representatives know that the PI is being maintained? Indeed, does the government know that the PI is being maintained? In deciding whether to assume a responsibility for regulation or supervision of a sector or activity, the government has to make a political decision. These decisions are made through the traditional channels of government decisions, followed by legislation, royal charter or whatever.

---

[172] See Treasury Committee, *Banking Reform*, HC 1008 (2007–8) and Government Reply, HC 1131 (2007–8) and HC 144 (2008–9).

[173] See Joint Committee on Human Rights, HL 77 (2006–7) on the meaning of 'public authority' under the Human Rights Act.

When the state enters into close working relationships with private concerns, the problems posed for the constitutional 'watcher' include establishing what has been devolved on to the private body by way of public responsibility. A classic case of this kind was the administration of the civil legal aid scheme by the Law Society now devolved onto a statutory commission. A further example is the state's reliance upon the accountancy profession to formulate appropriate standards of good practice in the keeping of accounts and the supervision of audits. A prolonged process of bartering involved the government's desire to extract undertakings from the Institute of Chartered Accountants that the latter would take a much more active role in ensuring that its members provide information to the Bank of England and regulators on the financial affairs of banks and financial institutions whose books its members audited. The profession initially managed to avoid the incorporation of these duties in legislation on the undertaking that satisfactory *internal* criteria were met.[174] A series of scandals including the BCCI collapse and the subsequent Bingham Report forced the government to place these duties in statutory regulations.[175] Audit came under sustained attack throughout the world leading to legislation in the USA under the Sarbanes Oxley Act 2002 following the Enron, WorldCom and other scandals. The UK regulatory body on corporate governance and reporting is the Financial Reporting Council and its operating bodies. This is a non-statutory body comprised of members of the corporate community and the chair and deputy chair of its board are appointed by the Secretary of State. The financial crisis of 2007 onwards was not confined to audit failures but to regulatory failure and three decades of light-touch regulation by government and regulators. The tri-partite structure of Treasury, Bank of England and Financial Services Authority for regulating the financial markets under the Financial Services and Markets Act 2000 was widely criticised for obscuring regulatory responsibility in the UK.

Who makes decisions? How? Where? Under what controls? With what publicity? With what accountability and to whom? If we do not know what is going on, we cannot hope for answers. It must be conceded that this is not so much a right for individuals, unless their lives are directly affected by such decision-making, as for Parliament. Parliament knows little of what goes on in this twilight world – indeed, one of the benefits of privatisation from the government's perspective is that Parliament's interest ought thereby to be reduced. In his second

---

[174] S. 47 of Banking Act 1987 and SI 1994/524.

[175] See now Financial Services and Markets Act 2000, ss. 341–6 and The Financial Services and Markets Act 2000 (Communications by Auditors) Regulations 2001, SI 2001/2587. On duties of confidentiality owed by banks to clients, see *Tournier v National Provincial Bank etc.* [1924] 1 KB 46; *Bank of Tokyo v Karoon* [1986] 3 All ER 468; *Robertson v Canadian Imperial Bank of Commerce* [1995] 1 All ER 824 PC; *Christofi v Barclays Bank plc* [2000] 1 WLR 937, CA; and *Jackson v Royal Bank of Scotland* [2005] UKHL 3. See also *Barclays Bank plc v Taylor* [1989] 3 All ER 563; Police and Criminal Evidence Act 1984, s. 9(1) and sch. 1; and *Bank of Scotland v A* [2001] 1 WLR 751.

report on *Standards in Public Life*[176] Lord Nolan observed how in local public bodies such as Training and Enterprise Councils there was invariably too much 'hands on' control by central government.

It is quite clear that in dealing with mighty client groups, not even the government is always fully informed. Corporate taxation and overseas havens has been an area of concern. The CAG has commented adversely upon the failure of the companies within the armaments industry to supply adequate information of profit levels and pricing to the Treasury. Many of the important contracts are not open to competitive tender.[177] The Review Board for Government Contracts – a joint non-statutory CBI/MoD nominated body – annually reviews the appropriate profit formula for non-competitive contracts. Its recommendations are used as a basis for discussion between the CBI and the government. It also reviews individual contracts referred to it. The CAG has criticised the industries for failing to reveal the details behind the information which they provide to the Board: 'I question whether this denial of information is consistent with the government's responsibility to Parliament to account for the basis on which they have accepted the recommendation.' The Treasury did not know how to get this information while still retaining the 'co-operation' of the industry. It is a big money-earner and a big employer. It cannot be told, it has to be persuaded, to adopt suitable approaches after *quid pro quo* bartering. It is impossible to know whether this is in the PI. Steps have been taken to make armament procurement more efficient and cost-sensitive from the government's perspective but not even the Public Procurement Directives of the EC apply to such contracts so none of the advertising publicity and non-discrimination or 'transparency' provisions apply.[178] The lack of transparency was illustrated by the cessation of the prosecution for bribery involving BAE systems and leading figures in Saudi Arabia – a decision which left an indelible stain on Britain's role in upholding the rule of law (chapter 2, p. 34). In September 2009, the Serious Fraud Office seemed likely to proceed with prosecutions of senior figures in BAE for corruption.

A similar theme concerns the Department of Health (DoH), the devolved administrations pharmaceutical companies and the Pharmaceutical Price Regulation Scheme (PPRS) which is regulated by the department and which is voluntary and non contractual scheme although referred to in s. 261 NHS Act 2006. Companies which are not exempt from the scheme have to submit accounts and production and sales figures to officials. Scheme members with total home sales of NHS medicines of £35 million in its financial year have to

---

[176] Cm. 3270-I–II.

[177] www.mod.uk/NR/rdonlyres/4D92E10F-2AA2–4DCE-9CE2-B1EF30F5A256/0/ 2006_Annual_ Profit_Formula_Review_Report.pdf.

[178] The MoD has undertaken to publicise details of every major contract just signed or going to tender. The minister undertook to notify the chairman of the PAC of security-sensitive defence contracts in excess of £250 million. He was not informed of the Zircon satellite system, which was estimated at £500 million. The £250 million threshold has been reduced to £25 million.

provide an annual financial return. Companies may be asked to reduce *over-all* profit rates if these are considered too high. There is no enforcement but 'negotiation' for scheme members who can complain to a complaints panel of any view taken by the department on profits. Non-members are subject to statutory controls under the 2006 Act and they can appeal decisions to a tribunal. The PPRS does not apply to individual drugs but to overall levels of profitability, which allows a variety of accounting sleights of hand by drug companies to distort the real profit level. It has been reported in the past that the department lacks adequate information and inside knowledge on costs and did not know 'whether they had played a good hand or had been the victim of a bluff'.[179] The chairman of the PAC has asked officials whether 'the Department . . . [is] really serious about wanting to get a good deal for the taxpayer'.[180] The PPRS was last revised in 2008 coming into effect in 2009 and the scheme and annexes provide far more detail than earlier versions on what should be provided by way of information. Whether this is 'adequate' information from the drug companies is not known.

What is really at issue here are the methods by which government governs. Anyone with an interest in FOI and open government must understand that the topic is not exhausted by allowing individuals to have access to public documents. It is centrally concerned with knowing how these dense public/quasi-public and private networks operate. Only when we have a reasonably clear idea of this can we hope to know what questions to ask and whom to put them to.

In *Quangos: Opening the doors*[181] the government set out its proposals for about 1,100 non-departmental public bodies (NDPBs) spending over £22 billion p.a. There should be annual public meetings 'where practicable and appropriate' and other public meetings where these would help consultation. Where practicable, they should release summary reports of meetings. Evidence should be invited from members of the public to discuss matters of public concern and widespread consultation should be exercised by such bodies. There should be consideration of bringing more bodies within the jurisdiction of the PO. The FOIA would apply where relevant (see chapter 4). Select committees should have oversight and codes and registers of interests should apply for members. They should publish annual reports and possibly efficiency reports and make greater use of the Internet. Bodies will be removed where no longer required and will be subject to periodic reviews. The remit of the Public Appointments Commissioner will be extended (below). The Select Committee on Public Administration recommended that there should be an annual publication covering all bodies 'carrying out its policy' possibly accompanying the government's annual report. It recommended a greater role for select committees, including receipt

---

[179] P. West in A Harrison and J. Gretton (eds.), *Health Care UK* (CIPFA, 1985); see HC 551 (1983–4)

[180] HC 551 (1983–4), chairman, PAC.

[181] Cabinet Office (1998), following *Opening up Quangos*, November 1997. See D. Lewis *Efficiency in Government: The essential guide to British quangos* (2005).

of minutes of meetings between Ministers and NDPBs and audit of all executive NDPBs accounts by the CAG although this would have to be considered by the PAC. Local bodies should report to scrutiny committees of local authorities as a condition of any funding agreement. Regional structures of accountability should exist for those bodies which operate regionally or locally. Any vacancies to be filled on boards should be placed on the Internet as should reports from the Prior Options Reviews which examine whether a function should be exercised by a NDPB.[182]

The role of NDPB and NHS accounting officers should emphasise formal responsibility for all aspects of propriety. The Audit Commission should be authorised to publish PI reports on NHS bodies at its own discretion. A member of the board of the NHS executive body should act as a complaints officer for internal complaints from staff raised confidentially and outside the usual management structure. Anonymity should be guaranteed.[183]

Public Appointments Commissioner[184]

A Commissioner for Public Appointments has been in existence since 1995; s/he may be one of the Civil Service Commissioners. Departmental appointments procedures would be monitored and regulated by the Commissioner. Ministers should only be involved in the planning and decision-making stages of appointments. The Tenth Report from the Committee on Standards in Public Life recommended further reconsideration of ministerial involvement. The Commissioner publishes an annual report and the Office of the Commissioner for Public Appointments comes under the Commissioner's control and not the Cabinet Office. All secretaries of state would have to report annually on public appointments made by their departments and candidates would have to declare 'significant political activity' in the previous five years – but what about political contributions direct or indirect? – and the Commissioner publishes a code (in fact guidance) for the operation of relevant procedures, and reasons for departure from the code on the grounds of 'proportionality' should be documented and capable of review. The government should seek to produce a more consistent legal framework governing propriety and accountability in public bodies. A code of conduct for members of public bodies and their staff should be mandatory and compliance should be a condition of appointment. The Commissioner deals with complaints, ensures independence in appointments after appropriate scrutiny and audits practices.

---

[182] HC 209-I–II (1998–9) and Government Reply, HC 317 (1999–2000).

[183] See the former Public Service Committee, HC 168 (1995–6).

[184] Office of the Commissioner for Public Appointments, *Code of Practice for Ministerial Appointments to Public Bodies* (2005); Cabinet Office, *Making and Managing Public Appointments: A guide for departments*, 4th edn (2006); Appointments Commissioner AR, HC 716 (2007–8); PASC, *Public Appointments*, HC 731 (2006–7) and Government Reply, HC 515 (2007–8). See *The Guardian*, 14 February 2008, 'North left in cold in quango packing by Londoners'.

Others have suggested a role for select committees in approving appointments and this was taken up by the prime minister in 2007 for ombudsmen and regulators.

In 1998, the Commissioner's remit was extended to cover nationalised industries, public corporations, certain utility regulators and advisory NDPBs, although the procedures would not be applied with full rigour in the case of the latter because many of the positions are unpaid. The remit does not extend to task forces (see chapter 4). Lord Neill examined the operation of the Commissioner and task forces in his report in 2000 and found a concern over 'disproportionality' in the way the procedures worked in the case of non-remunerated appointments and posed the question whether 'expert' positions should be occupied by reference to criteria that might not concentrate on competition, balance and fairness. In 2007–8 there were 2,621 appointments to positions covered by the code but some are exempt.

Local government, the public and information

Since the Poor Law Reform Act 1834, a system of compulsory local authority audit has existed in England and Wales. The Municipal Corporations Act 1835 opened up the books of the corporations to inspection, in the legislature's attempts to ferret out corruption that had been rampant in the commercial oligarchies administering the cities. Duties to provide information to ministers and auditors increased as the century developed and as central government became more and more jealous of its powers of supervision over local administration. Public knowledge of local authority affairs did not appear to become an issue until later in the nineteenth century when local government administration became more widespread and more coherent. Following a judicial decision that reporters were not allowed as of right to attend and report council meetings, an Act of 1908 was passed allowing press access to council meetings, but it could be avoided by delegating business to a committee. Nor were agendas circulated in advance under the Act.

In 1960, Margaret Thatcher MP secured the passage through Parliament of the Public Bodies (Admission to Meetings) Act, which opened up council meetings to the press and public. Minutes of councils and committees[185] had to be published. Even after the 1972 Local Government Act, which opened up committees to the press and public, problems remained. The legislation did not cover subcommittees, though local authorities were urged to be open in their administration. Research conducted in the 1980s showed that while many authorities opened up their subcommittees, with exceptions, to the public, a substantial number of those who replied did not.[186] Other studies found

---

[185] Only where they had referred and not delegated powers: *Wilson v Evans* [1962] 1 All ER 247.

[186] P. Birkinshaw, *Open Government, Freedom of Information and Local Government* (1985).

authorities adamantly refusing to provide information which they were under a legal duty to provide.[187]

Politics, members and information

The 1989 Local Government and Housing Act disqualified persons from being members of authorities where they hold politically restricted posts within s. 2. By early 1991, over 36,000 had been disqualified under this provision. An adjudicator supervises and grants exemptions under the Act.[188] A monitoring officer in the authority acts as an internal 'whistle-blower' and reports to the authority where s/he believes that an unlawful or 'maladministrative' act has taken place including a breach of a code within the authority. A chief finance officer was placed under similar duties in relation to unlawful expenditure which had been or was about to be incurred and the official's duty included reporting to the auditor where necessary.[189] Controls were established over staff appointments including ensuring the confidentiality of staff records,[190] the voting rights of members of various committees and subcommittees etc., and the political balance of committees and subcommittees according to political representation on the council.

The Local Government Act 2000 in introducing new styles of 'executive arrangements' to local authority administration sought to modernise local authority governance, enhance public involvement and make policymaking more transparent. These points will be addressed shortly. While political minorities faced increasing alienation, the courts developed the common-law rights of elected members.

Members of the council have a common-law right to inspect the books and papers of the council. Conflicts over the scope of the right produced an explosion of litigation.[191] Two opposing positions are present in the case law: the corporate responsibilities and duties of members of the corporation to the corporation, and the duty and responsibilities of members as representatives of a wider range of community interests which they are elected to represent.

Members do not have a 'roving commission' to examine the documents of a council.[192] They must establish a 'need to know' in order to perform their duties as councillors, and any irrelevant motivation or any ulterior, indirect or improper motive may be raised as a bar to their inspection.[193] Where a member is also a member of a specific committee, he or she has the right to inspect the committee's documentation, barring improper motive etc., on the part of the

---

[187] P. McAuslan, *The Ideologies of Planning Law* (1980).
[188] *Ahmed v UK* [1999] IRLR 188, ECtHR.
[189] Ss. 114–15 Local Government and Housing Act 1989.
[190] Because the Local Government (Finance) Act 1982 unwittingly gave access to them it was believed.
[191] Birkinshaw, *Open Government*.
[192] *R v Hampstead Borough Council, ex p. Woodward* (1917) 116 LT 213.
[193] *Ibid.* and *R v Lancashire County Council Police Authority, ex p. Hook* [1980] QB 603, CA.

member, though this ought not in principle to be easy to establish on the part of the committee or council because of the strong *prima facie* right of the member to inspect.[194] Where a member is not a member of a committee, he or she has to establish a 'need to know' a committee or subcommittee's documents. The claim of such a member is not as strong as that of a member of the actual committee, although the courts will be reluctant to second-guess a council's decision to allow inspection to a non-committee member.[195] A member of a parent committee will, even though not a member of the subcommittee, usually have a right to see documents of its subcommittee, and even a right to attend the subcommittee.[196]

Case law has developed these principles. At common law it has been established that, *pace* the standing orders of the authority, which under the 1989 Act may contain items by order of the Secretary of State, and which must be followed if they cover the subject area unless *ultra vires*, a ruling party can appoint *only its members* to the committees of the authority.[197] This is now altered by the 1989 Act but the restrictions on membership do not apply to new-style executives. In *R v Sheffield City Council, ex p. Chadwick*,[198] it was held that it was *ultra vires* for a policy committee to delegate functions to a subcommittee of ruling party members alone *simply to avoid* informing opposition members of decisions in the formulation of the budget. It was unlawful to use a subcommittee for purely party-political purposes. The case involved alternatives to the actual budget recommendation that was made and could support a suggestion that a 'need to know' will cover alternative policy options. The councillor was entitled to attend the meeting and see the documents, although strictly speaking the meeting was only operating in a recommendatory capacity in settling the budget.[199] Where the leaders of a party group met informally with officers and made what, in effect, were decisions *on behalf of the* council, they were acting in an executive capacity and were covered by the common-law 'need to know' principle. The meetings were within the formal framework of the council structure, and not outside it, and the councillor could establish a need to know and a right to attend.[200] There seems no reason in principle why a 'need to know' might not exist in relation to the papers and documents of a working group etc. if they are council papers. It would depend upon the facts.[201]

---

[194] *Ibid.*　　[195] *Birmingham City District Council v O* [1983] 1 AC 578, HL.

[196] *R v Hackney London Borough Council, ex p. Camper* [1985] 3 All ER 275, subject to veto in exceptional instances.

[197] *R v Rushmoor Borough Council, ex p. Crawford* (1981) The Times, 28 November.

[198] (1985) 84 LGR 563.

[199] Widdicombe recommended that recommendatory committees and subcommittees should be removed from this duty.

[200] *R v Hyndburn Borough Council, ex p. Strak* (CO/918/85, 17 December 1985). If operating in a purely advisory capacity, it was doubted whether a right to attend would exist, though surely a 'need to know' may still be established for access to documents.

[201] E.g., officers cannot be members of committees and so on. They can now be a member of an executive (see p. 371 *et seq.* below).

Local Government (Access to Information) Act 1985 (ATIA)

The law relating to members' rights and the public's rights to information in particular was reformed by the ATIA. This Act constitutes an FOIA for local government, and there is an immediate irony in the fact that it was passed with the approval of the government, which had steadfastly refused such legislation for itself. That legislation had to wait until the FOIA 2000 (see chapter 4). Regulations heavily influenced by the 1985 Act, but with some significant alterations, apply to the new executive arrangements under the Local Government Act 2000 (LGA). The 1985 Act does apply to oversight and scrutiny committees of authorities which are established under the LGA and which will have a central role in holding new-style executives to account. Provision is made where functions are delegated to individual councillors under s. 237 Local Government etc. Act 2007 (SI 352/2009).

The 1985 Act provides for greater public access to the meetings and documents of principal councils, i.e. essentially county, district and London borough authorities, and regional and district authorities in Scotland and unitary authorities. It opens up council, committee and subcommittee meetings to the public, and provides for access to local authority information. 'Information' in the Act includes an expression of opinion, any recommendations, and any decision taken. Meetings must be closed to the public, and information will not be available where 'confidential' items, as specifically defined, are dealt with.[202] This is where a government department provides information upon terms which forbid public disclosure. It may also be protected under the OSA, if one of the six protected areas. It includes cases where publication is prohibited by court order or statute.[203] Under the terms of the Act, an item is not confidential simply because a party gives the information 'in confidence'.

Information can be exempt under the Act if it falls under one of a list of categories. If exempt information is involved, the authority can exclude the public from its meetings and refuse access to information containing such items where the PI is in favour of this. They are required to consider the PI in disclosure as under FOIA. The list of exempt categories were modified by SI 2006/88 making some amendments to exemptions, simplifying language and introducing a PI test amending the ATIA for local government. The exempted items cover: information relating to any individual; information that is likely to reveal the identity of an individual; information relating to the financial or business affairs of any particular person (including the authority holding that information); information relating to any consultations or negotiations, or contemplated consultations or negotiations, in connection with any labour relations matter arising between the authority or a minister of the Crown and employees of, or office-holders under, the authority; information in respect of which a claim to legal professional privilege could be maintained in legal proceedings; and information which reveals that the authority proposes:

---

[202] As defined by the Act, not common law.   [203] It includes the Data Protection Act 1998.

(a) to give under any enactment a notice under or by virtue of which requirements are imposed on a person or

(b) to make an order or direction under any enactment.

Finally, exempted items also include information relating to any action taken or
to be taken in connection with the prevention, investigation or prosecution of
crime. Information is not exempt where it has to be registered under a variety
of Acts or where the PA is awarding planning permission to itself under the
terms of reg. 3 TCPA Gen. Regs. 1492/1992. Modifications are made for Wales
on the same basis as above by SI 969/2007 W. 86.

Unless the 'proper officer' believes it to contain confidential or exempt information, the public will have access to officers' reports for items on the agenda
of meetings and advance notice of agenda, meetings, their place and time. A
reasonable number of copies of reports and agenda must be available at the
meetings. The provisions requiring public notice may be waived where the
chairperson is of the opinion that the item should be considered at the meeting as a matter of urgency 'by reason of special circumstances' which *must be
specified* in the minutes.[204]

An important dimension to the Act concerns 'background papers', namely
those documents relating to the subject matter of the report which 'disclose any
facts or matters on which, *in the opinion of the proper officer*, the report or an
important part of the report is based and have, *in his opinion*, been relied on to a
material extent in preparing the report' (emphasis added).[205] The information
is available for specified periods before and after the meeting.[206] Minutes are
open for inspection. Additional information has to be published.[207] Interference
with rights under the Act is a criminal offence.

The Act covers a wide range of principal councils and has been extended to
cover joint consultative committees of health and local authorities and community health councils.[208] The Act also extends members of authorities' rights of
access to information in the possession or under the control of local authorities
and relates to any business to be transacted at a meeting of the council, its
committees or subcommittees. A member does not need to establish a 'need to
know' as under the common law where he or she is not a member of a specific
committee, but some of the exemptions will apply to requests, especially those
relating to employees, recipients of housing or services, children, contracts, the

---

[204] Does this reduce the safeguards available under the 1972 LGA? Standing orders of authorities
dealt with urgent business.

[205] See *Maile v Wigan MBC* [2001] Env LR 11: use of a report from a database does not give a
right of access to the whole database. Background papers do not include published work from
a database.

[206] Including written summaries of proceedings where exempt information is excluded from the
minutes and this exclusion prevents a 'reasonably fair and coherent record of the whole or part
of the proceedings'.

[207] Names and addresses of councillors, rights under the Act etc.

[208] Health Service Joint Consultative Committees (Access to Information) Act 1986.

legal immunities apropos of advice and the prosecution, prevention or investigation of crime. These exemptions would *not apply* to a request at common
law. However, the rights of a council member under the Act are more extensive
than those of the public, as the right to go through background papers is not
restricted to those papers which the 'proper officer' believes formed the basis
of the officer's report to a material extent.[209] The 2006 regulations made some
adjustments to members' rights.

The legislation leaves important matters of judgement in the hands of the
'proper officer'[210] and the chairman of a meeting although a PI test is now
included. This includes selection of items or reports which are exempt, materials
in background papers which were relied upon to a material extent, and in the
case of the latter those items which as a matter of urgency require incorporation
without the statutory notice of five clear days.[211] No specific procedure for
challenging such decisions is contained in the statute, so it will be a matter
of pressurising councillors or seeking relief via the local ombudsman or the
courts.[212]

One further point concerns the fact that the Act preserves the right to exercise
a power of exclusion to suppress or prevent disorderly conduct at a meeting.[213]
It has been decided that a chairperson can exercise this right in advance of a
meeting; this would prevent the public seeing how members voted when it came
to a subsequent ratification of the chairperson's decision.[214]

The 1985 legislation will apply to committees and council meetings but the
LGA 2000 sought to reduce the number of committees and place greater reliance
on executive arrangements. They will also apply to oversight and scrutiny
committees established under the LGA 2000. Local authorities will be covered
by the FOIA 2000 which I examined in chapters 4–6. Executive arrangements
will fall under provisions in the LGA 2000 which are examined below.

The LGA 2000 and new executive arrangements for authorities

In *Modern Local Government: In touch with the people*,[215] the government set
out its plans for modern local government and appropriate forms of executives
for such authorities. Such executives were to be built on a 'culture of openness
and ready accountability'.[216] Pointing out the pathetically low turnout at local
elections, the paper believed that councillors did not sufficiently reflect their
communities (only a quarter of councillors were women) and that the structures
within which local authorities operated were the result of nineteenth-century

---

[209] See P. Birkinshaw, *Government and Information: The law relating to access, disclosure and regulation*, 3rd edn (2005), ch. 5.

[210] LGA 1972, s. 270(3).

[211] This has been amended under the LGA 2000, s. 98 to allow for an extension.

[212] See 2nd edn of this book, p. 140, note 13 and accompanying text.

[213] *R v Brent Health Authority, ex p. Francis* [1985] QB 869; Cf. *R v Secretary of State for the Environment, ex p. Hillingdon LBC* [1986] 2 All ER 273.

[214] *Ibid.*   [215] Cm. 4014 (1998).   [216] Para 1.2.

legal philosophy. The committee structure, which has been outlined above, was 'inefficient and opaque', with councillors spending 'too many hours on often fruitless meetings'.[217] 'Above all, the committee system leads to the real decisions being taken elsewhere, behind closed doors, with little open, democratic scrutiny and where many councillors feel unable to influence events.'[218] It set forth an agenda for change involving new organisational frameworks to run councils, the creation of opportunities for giving local people a greater say in the running of the council and its service provision – by establishing 'beacon councils', improving local services, reforming business rates, improving local financial accountability, capital finance and providing a new ethical framework. The subject of standards and organisation had been heavily influenced by the Nolan Committee on Standards report on local government.[219] These themes were developed in *Local Leadership: Local choice*[220] and are now in the LGA 2000 and regulations as amended.

The way forward was for councils – which under new arrangements will remain single legal entities – to consult the local community on how they wish to be governed with referenda on whether there should be a directly elected mayor as in London. Detailed guidance on local consultation has been provided.[221] This referendum could be initiated by a petition of 5 per cent of the electorate or a proposal from the council. Statutory guidance would provide details on content and timing of referenda and regulations would contain the rules of conduct for a referendum paying regard to the Neill Report (Nolan's successor) on party-political funding.[222] A majority decision in favour of change would be binding on the council. If the proposal is not supported, it cannot be implemented.

The two (originally three) models of management are (i) a directly elected mayor with a Cabinet and (ii) a council leader with a Cabinet. These models will seek to provide a 'clearly identified and separate executive to give leadership and clarity to decision-taking' and 'powerful roles for all councillors to ensure transparency and local accountability'.[223] Such forms of governance will provide for a separation of the executive and will be efficient, transparent, and accountable:

> All councillors will have powerful roles, acting together in the council, or as members of the executive or powerful overview and scrutiny committees. People will know who is responsible for decisions, and communities will have a clear focus for leadership. Decisions will be scrutinised in public, and those who take them and implement them will be called publicly to account for their performance.[224]

---

[217] Para 1.15.   [218] *Ibid.*   [219] Cm. 3702 (1997).   [220] Cm. 4298 (1999).
[221] DETR, *Modern Local Government: Guidance on enhancing public participation* (1998). DETR, *The Local Government Act 2000 New Council Constitutions: Guidance pack* (2000) contains Consultation Guidelines for English Local Authorities.
[222] Cm. 4057 (1998).   [223] *Local Leadership etc.*, note 220 above, para. 3.1.
[224] Para. 3.3.

Authorities operating executive or alternative arrangements must publish a constitution and standing orders and a code of conduct must be publicly available. Guidance in two volumes on the LGA 2000 New Council Constitutions was published in 2000 and includes a code on recommended practice for local government publicity.[225]

The details on these points are contained in Pt II LGA 2000. They are supplemented by regulations and guidance.[226] A resolution of an authority is required in order for the executive arrangements to operate, which must be available for inspection at principal offices for public inspection.[227] Standard provisions apply in terms of notices in two newspapers circulating in the area providing the details of arrangements.

Before adopting its new constitution, a council should address a variety of themes relating to the model of its new constitution and the executive's functions and whether they should be limited. All councillors will agree or approve key plans and decisions. Regulatory responsibilities such as licensing and planning will not be functions of the executive but will be carried out by the full council or delegated to committees. Section 236 Local Government etc. Act 2007 allows the delegation of functions to single councillors in relation to their wards and a written record must be maintained and publicly available on this (SI 352/2009).

All new forms of local governance must have one or more overview and scrutiny committees (OSCs) (see s.22 LGA 2000). They are to have the same political balance as the full council and will meet in public with the current rules on public access applying (see p. 369 *et seq.* above). Details on size, number etc. would be for local choice. They would be required to cover all aspects of the executive's responsibilities. The constitution would provide for details such as co-opted members (non-voting) and chairs, and requesting a full debate in council before a decision is taken or implemented. Constitutions of authorities will be required to provide that OSCs: (i) would be able to require members of the executive and officers to attend their meetings and to invite others to attend; required to meet and examine these people in public (the current rules on access to meetings and information to apply); (ii) would be able to have all necessary support and information and training to discover what their local community wants and to represent them effectively; (iii) would be required to ensure the standing orders protect minority interests on the committee to get their concerns onto the agenda.

The executive is the driving force of new arrangements and will take the lead on all policy and strategy issues, including the budget, searching for best value under the LGA 1999 (see p. 380 below) and decisions on resources and priorities. The executive will be the focus for forging links and partnerships outside the council. The expected size will be 15 per cent of the council or ten councillors whichever is the smaller. They may be smaller but where there is a

---

[225] DETR, May 2000. See also DETR, *Modular Constitutions for English Local Authorities* (2000).
[226] See notes 221 and 225 above.   [227] LGA 2000, s. 29.

Cabinet with a leader or elected mayor there should be at least three members. The constitution would set out membership but the executive would not usually reflect the political balance on the council – unlike other committees and subcommittees of the authority. It will comprise majority or coalition members. Specific members would be given portfolios – this was the preferred option with the government because it 'speeds up decisions and clarifies responsibilities, improving accountability'.[228] Decisions would either be taken by the whole Cabinet, in subgroups, as individuals or as combinations of these. In a Cabinet with a leader, appointments would be made by either the leader or the council, and in the latter case the council would by majority vote decide the make-up of the Cabinet under its constitution.

Formal co-option would not be allowed but a mayor could benefit from a political adviser paid for by the council in addition to those advisers serving the three largest groups. S/he could attend but not vote at executive meetings. Where there is an elected mayor, policy would be implemented via a council manager – 'typically' the chief executive.

Executive meetings and access to information

Any provisions on access to information will need to comply with the FOIA (see chapter 4). An executive must ensure that a record of all decisions taken, and the reasons for those decisions is produced, and that record, along with factual and background papers[229] (excluding that information which is currently exempt under sch. 12A LGA 1972) relating to those decisions must be made public. Once a decision is taken by an individual, the record of that decision and the reasons for the decision and additional items must be made public. In the case of executive decisions and decisions by individuals ('individual decisions') officers must ensure the public availability of the record of the decision and the reasons for it, any alternative options considered and rejected (note the FOIA, chapter 4) and other matters such as an interest in a decision. The 1972 legislation (as amended by the ATIA 1985) will continue to apply to meetings of the full council, committees and subcommittees including the OSCs. The same provisions on openness that apply to committees will apply to cases where the executive consults with an OSC. The OSCs will also have the right to see, but not make public, any information relating to their responsibilities that would be exempt to the public by virtue of sch. 12A LGA 1972 although the regulations spelt out qualifications (see below). The OSC is also within the provisions of s. 15 Local Government and Housing Act 1989 (duty to allocate seats in relation to the size of representation of political groups). Political advice to the executive remains private. Meetings of the executive may be open to the public or press, or be private (see below and s. 22(1) LGA 2000).

As explained above, the OSC would have the right to demand the attendance of the mayor or leader, along with members of the executive or council officers

---

[228] Note 220, para. 3.41.   [229] See *Maile v Wigan MBC*, note 205 above on background papers.

to answer questions or to contribute to a debate on policy with an implied right to call for papers from those parties. The government was originally minded to make advice from officers public along with factual material. This would have created an anomalous position vis-à-vis the FOIA 2000 (see chapter 4, p. 167). The government realised that officers might be placed in a sensitive position when it was seen that their advice was not being followed and the regulations excluded access to their advice. Reports and background papers will be provided as explained below. The duty to create a record of decision and the reasons would lie on an officer when it is the decision of all or some of the executive. If made by an individual member of the executive, it is their responsibility to create the record and to make it available to the proper officer who is under a duty to ensure it becomes public available as described above and failure to create or make it available is a criminal offence. OSCs will also be able to ask for any additional factual information they require to support their work.

In s. 22(1) LGA 2000, meetings of the executive or its committees, joint committees and subcommittees may be held in public or private. The decision on openness is taken by the executive. This seems at first to cut across the thrust of the 1985 legislation on access but that legislation has been used as a basis for the regulations on openness and access (see below). A written record must be kept of *prescribed* decisions made by executives and their committees held in private and by individual members which must include reasons for decisions. Prescribed suggests obviously not all decisions. These records, together with 'such reports, background papers or other documents 'as may be prescribed' must be made available to the public in accordance with regulations made by the Secretary of State. These bear some similarities with the provisions in the 1985 legislation and have been amended to simplify language and to allow a PI test allowing access on the same basis as the FOIA. The whole or any part of a document may be held back on specified grounds. The regulations may make provision as to the circumstances in which meetings are to be held in private in whole or in part; the information to be included in written records; on the reasons to be included; those responsible for the records; on the requirement that such records may be made available to members of authorities and to the OSC; their availability by electronic means; on the regulations' ability to confer rights on members of the public, members of local authorities or the OSC in relation to records or documents; and to create offences in respect of rights or 'requirements' under the section. Further regulations may be made concerning access to joint committees or written records where held in private etc. (see s. 22(12) LGA 2000).

Regulations made under this section[230] while containing rights for the public to see papers relating to forthcoming decisions require executive meetings or

---

[230] Local Authorities (Executive Arrangements) (Access to Information) (England) Regulations 2000, SI 2000/3272 and SI 2002/716. See SI 2006/69 which made some amendments to exemptions, simplifying language and introducing a public interest test in line with SI 2006/88 amending the 1985 access act for local government (see p. 369 above).

part of meetings to meet in public when taking 'key decisions' and on other occasions. These cover the situation where an officer is present during a discussion but not where the officer (who is not a political adviser, assistant or council manager) is present for the 'principal purpose' of briefing the decision-maker on matters connected with an executive decision. The public may be present where items in the forward plan (below) are to be discussed and a decision will be made on such items within twenty-eight days of that meeting.[231] The requirement for a public meeting is subject to reg. 21 concerning confidentiality and other matters (below). Meetings held in public must have reports, agendas and background papers published five clear days in advance.[232]

'Key decisions' is a pivotal feature of these arrangements and these are basically decisions which in the opinion of the decision-taker are likely to result in significant financial implications. In determining such decisions, 'significant', regard shall be had to guidance issued by the Secretary of State. The intention may be good but the regulation (reg. 8) bristles with subjective judgements. This does not prevent *discussion* of key decisions by executives in secret (a 'private meeting') where the officer is not in attendance or is offering advice. Executives will decide what is a key decision. Where it is not a key decision, or otherwise not within reg. 7, the authority can meet in private and papers will not have to be available in advance. Key decisions may be delegated to individuals and only discussed at meetings and this will produce less publicity although reports on decisions taken by individual executive members must be publicly available in advance for at least five clear days before making a key decision. The member or officer shall ensure it is publicly available as soon as possible after the member or officer receives it. This is subject to confidential and other items in reg. 21 (see below). Background papers must also be available for reports or part of reports in sufficient number. In standing committee, the minister stated that 'an executive may meet as a group of executive members, each of whom will have personal responsibility for an area of decision taking'.[233] If a decision is based on a *draft* report are these excluded from the publicity provisions? One would expect that a decision based on a *draft* report converts the report into a final report. The regulation states that 'report' does not include a draft report and 'document' does not include a draft document. Reports submitted to an individual executive member or officer with a view to it being considered when he makes a key decision must be sent by the person submitting the report to the chair, or every member in the absence of the former, of a relevant OSC.

Executives must publish 'forward plans' (FPs) with details of key decisions due to be taken in the coming four months (reg. 13(2)) the documentation available about them, and the proposed consultation arrangements. A plan, other than the first plan, shall have effect from the first day of the second month

---

[231] 'Principal purpose' may be interpreted in the light of guidance issued by the Secretary of State. The third ground involves a situation where a reg. 15 notice has been given concerning a key decision and the matter is 'impracticable' regarding inclusion in an FP.

[232] SI 2002/716, reg. 9.   [233] Standing Committee A, 23 May 2000, col. 269.

for which the immediately preceding plan has effect – they are updated on a monthly basis. Regulation 14 concerns the contents of plans. These include the matter in respect of which the decision is to be taken, details of individual decision takers, dates or periods of decisions, all those to be consulted and the means of such consultation,[234] steps and details to be taken by those who wish to make representations to the executive about decisions to be taken, and a list of documents submitted for consideration to the decision-taker but not those only available in draft form.

The taking of a 'key executive decision' must be preceded by the publication of a regulation 12 notice. Regulation 12 provides for an instruction to be given to the proper officer to publish a notice of key decisions; that an FP with particulars of those decisions has been prepared; the period for which the FP is to have effect; that the FP may be inspected free of charge, and at all reasonable hours, at the authority's offices; that the FP contains a list of documents submitted to the decision-takers for consideration in relation to the matters in respect of which decisions are to be taken; addresses from which copies of listed items are available; that other relevant documents may be submitted; procedures for requesting those documents (if any) as they become available; and the dates in each month in the following twelve months on which each FP will be published and made available to the public at the local authority's offices. This must be published in one newspaper circulating in the authority's area not later than fourteen days before the first day on which the FP is to have effect.

There is a general exception to this requirement in reg. 15 – where publication is 'impracticable' – but, subject to reg. 16, no decision shall be taken until the decision-taker, either an individual or a chairman of a body, has informed the chair of a relevant OSC or each member thereof of the matter to which the decision is to be taken (reg. 15(1)(a)). Various formalities must be complied with. There is also an exception on the grounds of 'urgency'. Once again, a variety of safeguards exists to attempt to prevent abuse of the provisos. Where an executive decision has been taken and it was not treated by the decision-maker as a key decision, the OSC may require a report to be submitted by the executive to the local authority within such time as specified. This must include details of the decision and reasons for it, the body or individual who made the decision, and reasons for the executive's opinion that it was not a key decision. The executive leader or appropriate person must submit a quarterly report on decisions taken under reg. 16 in the preceding three months, the number of such decisions and a summary of their subject matter. Obstruction of rights of public access is an offence (reg. 23).

In the final stages of the LGA Bill the government made it clear that executives would be open to the public when discussing 'key decisions' made by authorised individuals and not simply when making a collective decision. They will be

---

[234] *R (Partingdale Lane Residents Assoc.) v Barnet LBC* [2003] EWHC 947 (Admin) on an executive's duties to consult.

open unless the public are excluded under reg. 21(1), i.e. whenever it is likely that if the public were present, confidential items would be disclosed to them 'in breach of the obligation of confidence'. Nothing requires the disclosure of information which in the opinion of the proper officer is confidential, is advice of a political adviser or assistant, or which is 'exempt information'. The definition of confidentiality is that available under the ATIA 1985. Exempt information is that defined in the reformed sch. 12A and now includes a PI test. The public may also be excluded to maintain public order. Further provisions on resolutions, public notice ('five clear days') and public attendance and facilities for 'duly accredited members of the press' echo those in the 1985 legislation. These provisions also cover meetings of committees of executives.

Regulations make provision for the inspection of documents after executive meetings of authorities and executives' committees, as well as inspection of background papers and additional rights of access to documents for members of local authorities that are similar to some of the provisions contained in the ATIA. Nothing in the regulations confers a right of access to confidential or exempt information (above) or to 'advice provided by a political adviser' (reg. 21). Where a copy of a report or part of a report accompanying agenda items at a meeting is withheld, the report shall be marked 'not for publication' and a statement to that effect specifying that it contains confidential information, by reference to the descriptions in sch. 12A of the LGA 1972, the description of exempt information applicable to that report; or that the report contains advice of a political adviser or assistant. The public may be excluded from meetings on similar grounds as above by resolution, which has to identify the part or parts of meetings from which the public are excluded. Records and reports must be publicly available for six years beginning on the date on which the decision relating to the record or report was made. Background documents are available for four years from the date of the meeting; any longer period is discretionary.

The additional rights of members to access covers 'any document, which is in the possession, or under the control of the executive of a local authority and contains material relating to any business to be transacted at a public meeting' other than a document which is in the form of a draft (reg. 2). In relation to private meetings certain exemptions under sch. 12A are grounds for refusing access to documents and parts of documents. Amendments were made in 2006 (SI 69/2006). The above rights are in addition to any other rights, e.g. common law, or under the 1985 Act (see p. 367).

The regulations add a new exemption: 'advice from political advisers'.[235] Although such advisers may participate in discussions of political groups, they can take no role in formal meetings. As the Campaign for Freedom of Information state the point, 'by formally encouraging the involvement of political advisers – but allowing all traces of their advice to be deleted from the

---

[235] Reg. 7(3)(c) and see s. 9 LGHA 1989.

published record – the government may be undermining its own claim that the new arrangements will provide greater transparency and accountability than at present'. [236]

Standards

A power to issue a code of conduct for members was conferred on the Secretary of State under s. 50 LGA 2000. This is now contained in Local Authorities (Model Code of Practice) Order SI 1159/2007.[237] This deals with general principles, the scope of the code, general obligations, declarations of interests, registers of interests, gifts and hospitality and dispensations, financial interests to be registered. Guidance is given on discrimination, bullying, use of confidential information, improper influence, gifts, family relations, interests, declarations of interest, gifts and hospitality and other items including conduct related to work. Reference is made to the Code of Recommended Practice on Local Authority Publicity (2001). Principles governing the conduct of local government members may be specified by order under s. 49. These build on the general Nolan principles and the 1990 code and were developed in subsequent revisions. Authorities will have to produce their own codes of conduct, which are to be available for inspection. Authorities must also establish standards committees[238] and ethical standards officers to promote high standards of conduct by members and co-opted members. A Standards Board is established for England to promote and maintain high standards of conduct and to refer cases to ethical standards officers for investigation. There are detailed provisions on investigations and reports. Cases may be referred to an Adjudication Panel. Part 10 of the Local Government etc. Act 2007 makes certain amendments to these provisions. In Wales, the functions of the Standards Board are performed by the local ombudsman or a monitoring officer and there is a Welsh Adjudications Panel.

The law provides for the disclosure of pecuniary interests by members – the code seeks to cover other interests which may interfere or conflict with a councillor's public duties. Breach of the code could constitute maladministration.[239] Section 19 of the Local Government and Housing Act 1989 introduced a compulsory register for members' pecuniary interests but not other interests.[240] The code seeks to widen this. Section 19 has now been replaced by s. 81 of the 2000 Act and s. 82 empowers the Secretary of State to issue by order a code for local government employees.[241]

---

[236] Campaign for Freedom of Information, *Local Government Bill: Briefing for report stage*, (2000).
[237] SI 2008/708 W82 for Wales.
[238] Standards Committee (Eng) Regs. 2008 SI 1085 – see SI 2001/2812, SI 2003/1483.
[239] And see Cmnd 5636 and Cmnd 6524.
[240] The draft 2001 code states that ministers believe that members should declare membership of freemasons and 'similar organisations': para. 5.6.
[241] Model Code of Conduct for Local Government Employees Consultation Paper 2004.

Other duties

There are numerous and important statutory duties imposed on authorities to provide information to central government, the Audit Commission, the Local Government Ombudsman, members of authorities and the public.[242] Many authorities have been innovative in engaging and informing beyond statutory duties. The arrangements for the Greater London Authority repeat many of the general provisions in local authority legislation as well as providing for some statutory innovations such as the mayor's annual report, the annual state of London debate and a People's Question Time. In relation to audit of local authorities this is now governed by the Audit Commission Act 1998 (as amended by the LGA 2000 and Pt 8 LG etc. A 2007). This is an area of vast importance. The Audit Commission is responsible for audit and also for ensuring value for money. It carries out, or arranges under legal duties, comparative studies to make recommendations for improving the economy, efficiency and effectiveness of authorities' services or financial or other management practice and these are usually publicly available. Auditors' reports under these provisions must be considered at a public meeting from which the public may be excluded under the terms of the AITA 1985. The Audit Commission is given wide powers to publicise relevant matters including contravention of the duty to collect and publicise information. These, of course, flow from the Citizen's Charter but similar legal duties do not affect central government.[243] Such provisions are unlikely to generate much public feedback. There are numerous and considerable powers and procedures in relation to audit and the Audit Commission published a *Code of Audit Practice* (2005). The Audit Commission's remit extends to health bodies and social housing.

The LGA 1999, which introduced 'best value' (BV) in the provision of public service in local government, envisaged widespread local consultation with local communities in establishing BV. A central government code of practice on consultation has existed since 2001 and its present version dates from 2005 (Cabinet Office, Better Regulation Executive, *Code of Practice on Consultation* (2005)).[244] Changes were made to best value by the LGA 2000. However, the Local Government and Public Involvement in Health Act 2007 will remove the requirement of performance indicators and standards and the duties to produce BV plans and reviews – to remove unnecessary regulatory burdens. But they have been supplemented by devices which have similar objectives through local area agreements.

---

[242] See ch. 4 of Birkinshaw, *Government and Information.*
[243] The provisions which do apply here are internal and administrative.
[244] V. Lowndes and N. Rao, *Enhancing Public Participation in Local Government* (2000).

10

Secrecy and access in the European Union

Introduction

The European Union which makes binding laws for the UK has often been criticised because it has effectively enhanced the powers of the national executives
vis-à-vis democratic assemblies. The EU's origins as an international organisation, whatever Community jurists may say of the contemporary order, have
ensured that maximum secrecy and sensitivity attended its diplomatic relationships. International organisations have been heavily criticised in the past
because of excessive secrecy.[1] The United Nations has adopted a very open policy
for meetings and documents although the Security Council has adopted more
private preliminary meetings. The Council of Europe has a recommendation on
access to documents from 2002 which replaced earlier recommendations and
it has produced a convention for signature on access to official information.[2]
Regional and international developments are examined in chapter 13.

In its own operations and practices the institutions displayed a 'democratic
deficit', it is commonly alleged, insofar as the directly elected European Parliament does not have overall control of the legislative process, although its
position has been enhanced by procedural changes introduced by revisions to
the Treaty of Rome.[3] The absence of effective oversight of EU laws by national
assemblies[4] has been a further cause of concern as the legislative impact from
the EU assumes ever-growing importance in terms of domestic influence. The
aborted EU Constitution Treaty was replaced by the Lisbon Treaties on the EU
and the Functioning of the EU and provisions in these treaties on greater access
and transparency will be addressed later in this chapter. Those provisions also
contain procedures to enhance the position of national parliaments by increasing their information about, and their influence upon lawmaking in the Union.
The Lisbon Treaty (there are two treaties) awaits final approval by the Czech

---

[1] D. Curtin and H. Meijers (1995) CMLR 391, at 395.
[2] Council of Europe Committee of Ministers Rec. R (2002) 2 *Access to Official Documents*, 21
February 2002; the convention is Council of Europe Treaty Series/205 18.VI.2009.
[3] The co-decision procedure introduced under Art. 251 EC.
[4] P. Birkinshaw and D. Ashiagbor (1996) 33 Common Market Law Review 499; C. Kerse (2000)
European Public Law 81; Amsterdam TEU Treaty Protocol No. 13.

Republic following the Irish and Polish ratification of the Treaty in October 2009.

Prior to the present regulation on access to documents, a code on access existed allowing access to the documents of the Council and Commission.[5]

Amsterdam, Article 255 EC and the Regulation on Access to Information

The Amsterdam Treaty in Art. 1 of Title 1 TEU stated, as one of the general principles of the European Union, that 'This Treaty marks a new stage in the process of creating an ever closer union among the peoples of Europe, in which decisions are taken *as openly as possible* and as closely as possible to the citizen.' The italicised words were added at Amsterdam. They herald a greater emphasis on openness as well as subsidiarity – taking decisions at as local a level as possible. Subsidiarity was strengthened in the Lisbon Treaty. The immediate development came in an amendment to the EC Treaty and Art. 255 which provided for the introduction of a regulation on access to documents covering the Council of Ministers, Commission and Parliament. It is restricted to those institutions. The regulation was adopted on 30 May 2001 after completing the procedure in Art. 251 – the co-decision procedure. Each institution must also establish specific provisions regarding access to its own documents in its rules of procedure.

The regulation was something of a victory for the supporters of transparency. The European Parliament engaged combatively with the Commission 'emboldened by the role it had played in the collapse of the Santer Commission a couple of years earlier (1998–9) and the concomitant difficulty that the subsequent Commission had in resisting calls for greater transparency.'[6] The Council was also swayed by the criticism of a lack of transparency in the EU and accepted many of the proposals from Parliament for a document that was less executive-minded in its final shape. Drafts of the regulation had met with critical responses from the EU Ombudsman.[7] In a valuable report, the House of Lords Committee on the EU reported on the draft regulation.[8] It was critical of the Commission's failure to consult before the adoption of the draft regulation. 'Extensive external consultation would have demonstrated a commitment to openness' (para. 46). It criticised recital 12(15) which states that 'Member States shall take care not to hamper the proper application of this Regulation.' It was seen as going far beyond the requirements of co-operation in Art. 10 EC and seems to impose a requirement on Member States (MSs) freedom of information (FOI) laws not to be more liberal than the EC regime. Sweden and Scandinavian countries

---

[5] See P. Birkinshaw, *Freedom of Information: The law, the practice and the ideal*, 3rd edn (2001), ch. 8.

[6] I. Harden (2009) EPL 239.

[7] See *Wall Street Journal*, 24 February 2000, p. 11 and reply from Romano Prodi, same journal, 9 March 2000.

[8] *Sixteenth Report*, HL 109 (1999–2000).

pride themselves on their openness and many MSs are seeing the benefits from greater transparency. The 'Community system should not create any unnecessary restrictions, especially where national FOI regimes are more liberal' (para. 53).

Regulation 1049/2001

The recitals to the regulation repeat the movement to greater transparency within the Union and state that its purpose is to give 'the fullest possible effect to the right of public access to documents' laying down general principles and limits to access. The regulation should give guidance to access to documents in the Euratom and Coal and Steel Communities,[9] access to legislative documents was exhorted to 'the greatest possible extent' while preserving institutions' effectiveness. This covers delegated legislation and would involve the comitology committees. It covers second- and third-pillar documents held by the institutions and 'all agencies' should apply the principles laid down in this regulation. In 2003, the regulation was extended specifically to all executive agencies. 'Highly sensitive documents' were to be subject to special treatment. The regulation covers documents drawn up by the institutions and also those received by them. MSs should take care not to hamper the proper application of the regulation while respecting the security rules of the institutions. It is expressly stated that 'it is neither the object nor the effect of the Regulation to amend national legislation on access to documents'. However, the regulation does contain provisions that apply when an institution holds documents originating in a MS and vice versa. In the UK, the general right of access is under the FOIA and exemptions in the FOIA would have to apply to stop access to documents within the UK but the regulation seeks to influence the decision on access as will be seen.

In short, the regulation seeks to ensure the widest possible access to documents, to ensure the easiest possible exercise of the right, and to promote good administrative practice on access to documents.

By virtue of Art. 255 EC, citizens of the Union and any natural or legal person residing or having its registered office in a MS enjoy the right of access. The institutions 'may' grant access to other natural and legal persons. The institutions' rules allow for this.[10] Those applying for access do not have to provide reasons.

'Document' is defined broadly so as to include any content, whatever its medium, concerning a matter relating to the policies, activities and decisions falling within the institution's sphere of responsibility.

---

[9] The latter Community has now gone.

[10] Council – Annex II of the Council's Rules of Procedure [2004] OJ L 106/22; Annex to the Commission's Rules of Procedure and OJ L 345/94 (20 December 2001); European Parliament's Rules of Procedure, r. 97, 16th edn (2008).

The exceptions

Article 4 of the regulation governs exceptions (exemptions). If only parts of the requested document are covered by an exception, the remaining parts of the document must be released. Furthermore, in a particularly robust case the Court of First Instance (CFI) dealt with the situation where the Commission ruled that there were exceptions that prevented access. As the file was excessively long it would require a great amount of time to conduct a detailed review of documents thereby preventing partial access to documents which was also denied. The court ruled that the regulation required the institutions to conduct a concrete assessment of the documents requested except where it was manifestly clear that access should be denied or allowed. A refusal to conduct any examination was 'manifestly disproportionate'.[11] The ability to balance the workload implications of a request against the interest of good administration had to be respected but non examination was exceptional. The norm was a right of access and an examination (para. 101 *et seq.*). The Commission's decision was annulled.

Settled case law of the courts states that the exceptions must be interpreted and applied 'restrictively' so as not to defeat the right of access.[12]

If an exception applies, the institution 'shall' refuse access; the exception is to that extent mandatory. However, the condition 'disclosure *would* undermine' a specified interest is used suggesting some degree of proof. The draft version of the regulation had 'could'. Would is more certain and emphatic. Furthermore, application of the exceptions requires the exercise of judgement because they all involve a harm test and some are also subject to an overriding public interest (PI) in disclosure. The mere fact that a document concerned a protected interest did not *ipso facto* justify application of the exception. Such an application only applied if the institution had previously assessed and explained whether access to the document would specifically and actually undermine the protected interest and whether there was no overriding PI in disclosure where such a test applies (below). The risk of a protected interest being undermined had to be 'reasonably foreseeable'. The institution would have to provide reasons for the findings of its concrete examination.[13] Reasons, however, are context specific.

Provision is made for documents coming from third parties – 'third party' means any natural or legal person other than one of the three institutions. The institution must consult the third party with a view to assessing whether one of the exceptions is applicable, unless it is clear that the document shall or shall not be disclosed.

Article 4(1) provides that the institutions shall refuse access to a document where disclosure would undermine the protection of:

---

[11] Case T-2/03 *Verein für Konsumenteninformation v Commission*, judgment 13 April 2005.
[12] Case T-211/00 *Kuijer v Council* [2002] ECR II-485, para. 55; Case T-194/04 *Bavarian Lager v Commission* [2007] ECR II-4523, para. 94.
[13] Case T-237/02 *Technische Glaswerke Ilmenau Gmbh v Commission* [2007] 1 CMLR 39; see *Turco*, note 17 below.

(a) the public interest as regards:
  – public security,
  – defence and military matters,
  – international relations,
  – the financial, monetary or economic policy of the Community or a Member State;
(b) privacy and the integrity of the individual, in particular in accordance with Community legislation regarding the protection of personal data.

It should be noted that Art. 4(1) does not provide for an overriding PI in disclosure as regards the relevant exceptions.

Under Art. 4(1)(a) (specifically ruling on indent 1 and 3) the European Court of Justice (ECJ) has ruled that the Council must be recognised as enjoying a 'wide discretion' for the purpose of determining whether the disclosure of documents would undermine the PI.[14] The review of the legality of such a decision was limited to verifying whether the procedural rules and duty to state reasons had been complied with, whether the facts had been accurately stated, and whether there had been a manifest error of assessment or misuse of powers. In assessing the exceptions, the Council was not obliged to take account of the applicant's particular interests in seeing them (para. 43). Even though the reasons were brief for the decision in question they were 'adequate' (para. 81). A statement of reasons under Art. 253 EC must be appropriate to the act in issue.

Article 4(1)(b) has been the subject of considerable debate and litigation. In *Bavarian Lager*, the CFI ruled that the Data Protection Regulation (45/2001) does not trump the access regulation to prevent disclosure of personal data.[15] In this case a meeting took place between EU officials, British civil servants and representatives of a beer-brewing trade organisation which discussed matters relevant to the applicant who was not allowed to attend the meeting. The meeting took place after proceedings commenced against the UK under Art. 1226 EC for alleged breaches of Art. 28 EC. The applicant requested the names of those from the association who had attended the meeting and other names of companies who had made submissions to the Commission. In order to determine whether Art. 4(1)(b) applies, 'it is necessary to examine whether public access to the names of the participants at the meeting . . . is capable of actually and specifically undermining the protection of the privacy and the integrity of the persons concerned' (para. 120). The participation of the names as 'representatives' of organisations did not affect their private lives (para. 125).

Under Art. 4(2) institutions shall refuse access to a document where disclosure would undermine the protection of:

---

[14] Case C-266/05 P *Sison v Council of the EU*, judgment 1 February 2007. The case concerned specific restrictive measures directed against certain persons and entities to combat terrorism in Decision 2002/848/EC.

[15] Case T-194/04 *Bavarian Lager v Commission* above; see Case C-465/00 *Österreichischer Rundfunk and Others* [2003] ECR I-4989.

- commercial interests of a natural or legal person, including intellectual property,
- court proceedings and legal advice,[16]
- the purpose of inspections, investigations and audits, unless there is an overriding public interest in disclosure.

Under Art. 4(2) an overriding PI in disclosure may also be applied even where a harm test is made out. In *Turco*, the ECJ ruled that an overriding PI need not be distinct from the general principles of openness and transparency that underlie the regulation.[17] The institution must identify any overriding PI and *explain* whether an overriding PI justifies disclosure (para. 49). In *Turco* the harm test was not established (para. 66). Where a harm test is made out by an institution then applicants have to argue for the PI but their arguments unavoidably face the considerable difficulty of not having seen the relevant document. The EU Ombudsman's office does not know of a case where officials have identified a PI in disclosure where a harm test has been established.[18]

In the UK requesters are assisted by placing the burden explicitly on those seeking retention rather than disclosure where the PI applies. *Turco* has assisted applicants but where a harm test is established they are still in a difficult position.

The Secretary General to the EU Ombudsman has suggested the following reform to assist applicants:

> The . . . problem could perhaps be addressed by giving the Ombudsman an additional role . . . If an applicant whose initial application was refused wanted to argue that there is an overriding PI in disclosure, he or she could have the possibility of turning to the Ombudsman at that stage. The Ombudsman could inspect the document, formulate an independent view and report to the institution and the applicant (without, of course, disclosing the document or its contents to the applicant). The applicant could then make a confirmatory application, if he or she so wished and eventually contest a refusal either in Court or before the Ombudsman, as at present. However, at that stage the Ombudsman would not deal again with the question of overriding public interest. If a case turned on that issue, it would therefore be more likely that the applicant would go to Court, which would have available to it the Ombudsman's view, based on his inspection of the document and the institution's reaction to that view in its reply to the confirmatory application.[19]

In relation to the legal advice and opinion exception involving the institution's own legal service a general and abstract argument from an institution that disclosure would lead to doubts as to the lawfulness of a legislative act did not suffice to establish that the protection of legal advice would be undermined. Independence would not be compromised by disclosure of

---

[16] Case T-237/02 *Technische Glaswerke Ilmenau Gmbh v Commission* [2007] 1 CMLR 39 where a strict test in favour of disclosure was applied by the CFI.

[17] Joined Cases C-39/05 P and C-52/05 P, *Sweden and Turco v Council*, judgment of 1 July 2008, paras. 67 and 74.

[18] See I. Harden, note 6 above.   [19] *Ibid.*

legal opinions where there were no reasonably foreseeable – as opposed to purely hypothetical – risks of frank and reliable advice being undermined. The institution had to make an assessment of where the PI lay. Disclosure of an institution's legal advice documents from its legal service on legal questions arising when legislative initiatives were being debated increased transparency and strengthened the democratic right of European citizens to scrutinise the information forming the basis of a legislative act. Non-disclosure may be justified in cases of particular sensitivity or where it went beyond the legislative process but such a case required a 'detailed statement of the institution's reasons'.[20]

Protecting decision-making

The decision-making process of the institution is protected by Art. 4(3). Provision is made for pre-decision and post-decision stages of decision-making. Exceptions apply to access to documents relating to either stage. Before a decision is made (pre-decision), the exception applies both to documents drawn up by the institution for internal use and to incoming documents. After a decision is made, the exception covers only documents containing 'opinions for internal use as part of deliberations and preliminary consultations within the institution'.

The grounds for withholding information are the same, i.e. that public access would *seriously* undermine the institution's decision-making process. A test of 'overriding public interest' applies (see above).

There is therefore no exclusion of the deliberative stage of decision-making. Access may be had to documents containing internal discussions. Where access to such documents is requested, access must be allowed unless the institution can show that serious harm to its decision-making process is reasonably foreseeable and not purely hypothetical[21] and the requester cannot establish that there is an overriding PI in disclosure.

---

[20] Case C-39/05 P *Sweden and Turco v Council of the EU* [2007] ECR I-11389. See also Case T-36/04 *Association de la Presse Internationale ASBL v Commission* [2007] CMLR 51.

[21] In Case T-403/05 *MyTravel v Commission*, judgment of the CFI of 9 September 2008 the court stated that disclosure of that document in this case would carry the risk not only that the possibly critical opinions of Commission officials might be made public, but also that the content of the report – which is a preparatory document containing the views and recommendations of the working group – could be compared with the decisions ultimately taken on those points by the Member of the Commission responsible for competition matters or within the Commission and, accordingly, that that institution's internal discussions would be disclosed. That would risk seriously undermining the decision-making freedom of the Commission, which adopts its decisions on the basis of the principle of collegiality and whose Members must, in the general interest of the Community, be completely independent in the performance of their duties [para. 51]. See paras. 52–4.

Documents originating from a Member State and held by an institution

In Art. 4(5) the regulation makes provision for documents originating from a MS which are held by an institution. It provides that a 'Member State may request the institution not to disclose a document originating from that MS without its prior agreement'. 'Loyal co-operation' should exist between the MSs and the Union, and the CFI has ruled this as meaning that, where a MS makes a request, access is governed by national measures and not by the regulation.[22] The ECJ did not follow this judgment.[23] The ECJ ruled on the following: a 'document originating from a Member State' covers any document that a MS transmits to an institution regardless of the author. Article 4(5) does not give the MS a 'general and unconditional right of veto to access'. Furthermore, the Article gives a MS an opportunity to participate in a decision by the institution.

Decisions should involve a 'genuine dialogue' discussing the possibility of invoking exceptions in Art. 4 above, the ECJ ruled. There should be no delay in commencing dialogue and time limits (below) should be observed. If, following such dialogue, the MS objects to disclosure, it must state reasons for that objection with reference to the exceptions set out above in Art. 4(1)–(3). If the MS does not provide reasons for its refusal upon request, the institution should allow access where it believes none of the exceptions above applies. Where a reasoned refusal is given, permission for access should be denied by the institution which has to explain the reasons for the MS refusing access under one or other of the exceptions above. The EU Courts may review the validity of reasons provided by a MS.

The exception could produce serious problems were it not for the Council's practice of treating the written positions of delegations and documents summarising the oral statements by member states of the Council, or those held by one of its preparatory bodies, as Council documents and thereby within the regulation.[24]

There is no EU provision allowing access to documents submitted by Member States to institutions within those Member States. National provisions would have to apply. Not all Member States have access to information laws – Spain for instance. The EU Ombudsman has suggested measures to approximate principles on access within the Union.[25]

Documents held by a Member State originating from an EU institution

Article 5 governs this position:

---

[22] Case T−168/02 *IFAW Internationaler Tierschutz-Fonds* v *Commission* [2004] ECR II-4135. See para. 61.
[23] Case C-64/05 P, *Sweden (IFAW)* v *Commission* [2007] ECR I-11389.
[24] See Bart Driessen, 'The Council of the European Union and access to documents', 2005 European Law Review 675, at p. 687.
[25] Cited in Harden, note 6 above.

unless it is clear that the document shall or shall not be disclosed, the Member State shall consult with the institution concerned in order to take a decision that does not jeopardise the attainment of the objectives of this Regulation.

The Member State may instead refer the request to the institution.

As Harden says, it is not clear which law determines whether it is clear whether a document should or should not be disclosed.[26] The meaning of this provision is not entirely obvious. In particular, it is debateable whether the phrase 'unless it is clear that the document shall or shall not be disclosed' refers to national law, Community law, or both. 'However, the intention seems to be that the Member State is entitled to apply national law but, in so doing, must comply with the general obligation under Article 10 of the EC Treaty, to "abstain from any measure which could jeopardise the attainment of the objectives of this Treaty".'[27] The MS has a power to refer the request to the institution.

Procedure

Article 6 deals with applications that may include discussion about 'very long documents' and provision of information and assistance in making requests. Applications must be in any written form. A time limit of fifteen working days is allowed to provide access or to give a reasoned refusal. For very long or very numerous documents an extension of fifteen days is allowed. A 'confirmatory application' (second request) may be made within fifteen days on total or partial refusal. Article 8 governs procedures on confirmatory applications. Failure to notify a decision within the time schedule (fifteen days extendable as above) shall be considered a negative reply. An express refusal, or failure to make a decision, allow the applicant to seek judicial review via the CFI or to complain to the ombudsman. The ombudsman is a free service to complainants and they have emphasised the duties on openness and transparency in their complaint investigations and publications.[28]

Sensitive documents

Article 9 governs 'sensitive documents', i.e. classified.[29] Classification has a legal consequence unlike the position under the UK Official Secrets Acts where classification is used for internal security. The originator of such documents

---

[26] (2009) EPL 239.

[27] Harden, note 6 above, citing para. 70 of the ECJ's judgment in *Sweden (IFAW) v Commission* (above).

[28] In his 2008 Annual Report, at p. 10, he wrote: 'By far the most common allegation examined in inquiries opened in 2008 was lack of transparency (36 per cent of inquiries). Whether in contractual cases, requests for access to documents, infringement complaints, or selection procedures, refusal to provide information or documents was a recurring theme.'

[29] For Council documents see Council Decision 2001/264/EC OJ L 101/1 (11 April 2001); for the Commission, Commission Decision 2001/844, OJ L 317/1 (3 December 2001).

appears to have complete control over their publication and placement on the register under Art. 11(2). This includes power to refuse to allow public notice of the *existence of* a document.[30] Those handling such documents that relate to defence, public security and military affairs require appropriate security vetting. Arrangements to inform Parliament of these documents should be made by 'interinstitutional agreement'.

The Articles make provision for access following an application, maintenance of publicly available and up to date registers of documents held by the institutions, electronic access, including to legislative documents and publication of a range of materials in the Official Journal under Art. 13.

Further details may be requested by the institution to help identify documents. The duty to hold a register will be invaluable. Applicants may be consulted where there are repetitive requests or where large (voluminous) files are sought. Access may be had by either consulting documents 'on the spot' or by receiving a copy and the cost of access may be charged to the applicant. Documents will be supplied in the available language version, account being taken of the applicant's preference. There are no charges for on-the-spot access, less than twenty pages of A4 paper, electronic access or via the register. Copyright in documents is protected.

The duty to maintain registers of documents was a big advance on the British approach under the FOIA (see chapter 4). Staff should be trained for the tasks involved in access requests and existing procedures for registering, filing, archiving and clarifying documents. The institutions must also take steps to inform the public of their rights. While the Commission has taken great steps to inform the community of its policies, actions and plans, there is no named equivalent of publication schemes as under UK law to provide information on a voluntary basis. The final version of the regulation increased the information that has to be published under Art. 13. The Commission has recommended that there should be a new obligation on the institutions to define in their rules of procedure which categories of documents are directly accessible to the public so that requests under the regulation do not have to be made. The proposals, which are dealt with below, said nothing about improving the provision and use of registers although this has been a comment of the Commission in a paper from 2004. The EU Ombudsman has made suggestions on improving the register and also suggested more specificity on what is a 'document'. What kind of emails, for instance, should be registered? The number is vast and clearly not all are appropriate for registration, but some are. In its response to the 2008 Green Paper from the Commission suggesting amendments to the regulation (below), the EU Ombudsman recommended reforms to the system of registration. What are the defining criteria?[31] In an investigation reported in 2009, the EU Ombudsman criticised the Commission's register for not being

---

[30] *Sison*, note 14 above, para. 97.
[31] Case 3208/2006/GG, www.ombudsman.europa.eu/recommen/en/063208.htm.

'comprehensive'. He deplored the Commission's failure to (i) deliver on its commitment to further develop its registers with any convincing action in that direction and (ii) provide any concrete indications as to the exact scope of the new centralised system, which seemed to be intended to be operational only by 2010. The Commission rejected a draft recommendation in which the EU Ombudsman asked it to include references to all of its documents in a register, as required by the regulation. However, as a parliamentary committee had taken the matter up through motions, the EU Ombudsman considered that a special report was not necessary.[32]

Article 17(1) of the regulation stipulates that each of the institutions covered by the access law has to publish annual statistics on request.

The institutions of the EU that are covered include: the Parliament, the Council of Ministers, the Permanent Representatives Committee, working parties and departments and committees set up by the treaty or by the legislator to assist the Council; the Commission includes members of the Commission as a collective body, individual members and their private offices, directorates general and departments,[33] representations and delegations together with committees set up by the Commission and committees set up to help it exercise its implementing powers. This would cover the comitology committees, which have become an object of considerable academic interest.[34] A list of such committees of both the Council and Commission shall be drawn up in implementing measures. The regulation applies to EU agencies created for a variety of specific purposes as they 'should apply the principles laid down in the Regulation'. Bodies in the third pillar such as Europol and Eurojust have adopted their own decisions on access. The European Council – the body comprising the heads of state or their representatives – is not covered. Nor are the courts.

The Commission's 2004 report

The Commission published a report in January 2004 on the implementation of the regulation.[35] This has details of the operation of the regulation noting that the greatest users are academics and lobbyists. Journalists were not big users of the law. There are details of applications and results to the institutions and the figures on use of the exceptions. Parliament used legal opinion exceptions in more than half of its negative decisions. The main use of the Council was to protect intergovernmental relationships and the deliberative process. The Commission's use of exceptions related very notably to investigations, inquiries

---

[32] Complaint 3208/2006/GG against the European Commission.

[33] There are twenty-seven Commissioners and forty-one directorates general and services at present.

[34] See P. Craig, *EU Administrative Law* (2006), ch. 4.

[35] Report from the Commission on the implementation of the principles in Regulation (EC) No. 1049/2001 regarding public access to European Parliament, Council and Commission documents, COM(2004) 45 final, 30 January 2004.

and audits. The report is a requirement of Art. 17(2). The report was positive on the initial operation of the regulation, noting that any reform would have to work in the context of treaty reforms that have been active for over six years. The right of access should be located more clearly within the wider issue of public participation in the democratic life of the Union which is rather ironic given the eventual Commission's proposals. This was followed by a European Parliament resolution,[36] calling for a proposal for legislation which would strengthen Community legislation on transparency. In 2007, the Commission commenced a public consultation on access to documents.[37] This was followed by a Commission proposal to 'recast' the regulation.[38]

The Commission's proposals for reform[39]

The Commission proposes that *all* natural and legal persons should have the right of access. This would end the existing distinction between citizens and residents (who enjoy the right of access) and other natural and legal persons (who 'may' be granted access – see above).

The Commission has proposed amendments to assist applicants in applying for documents where these are not clearly stated or they cannot be identified. Time only starts to run from the time clarification is received. If they are precise requests but the document cannot be identified, is this not a problem with an institution's indexing?

The Commission also proposes extending the normal deadline for handling a confirmatory application to thirty working days, with a possible further extension of fifteen working days. The Commission has argued that the fifteen-working-day deadline is far too short, amounting to an impossibility.

Crucially, the Commission proposes amending the definition of document which would mean that no application for access to a document drawn up by an institution could be made unless that document had been 'formally transmitted to one or more recipients or otherwise registered'.[40]

A document that was not so formally transmitted outside the institution would not fall under the regulation as a 'document' unless it was 'registered'. This would give the Commission wide powers of inclusion and exclusion. The Commission's proposals would also exclude access to investigation files or proceedings of an 'individual scope' until they were closed or an act had become definitive, i.e. completed. Documents obtained or taken from natural or legal persons in the framework of such investigations should be permanently

---

[36] 4 April 2006, P6TA(2006)0122, A6–0052/2006.

[37] Public Access to Documents Held by Institutions of the European Community: A review, COM(2007) 185 final

[38] COM(2008) 229 final. Recasting is a special legislative technique which Harden believed was not best suited to the regulation in that it placed constraints on Parliament's manoeuvrability. For Parliament's initial proposals, see note 57 below.

[39] I lean heavily on Ian Harden's article, note 6 above, in what follows.   [40] Art. 3(a).

excluded even if any harmful effect had been removed by the flow of time.[41] This change would remove the PI consideration overriding an exception.[42] Harden suggests that a literal reading of the proposed new text would allow a whole document to be permanently excluded 'even if the relevant information were contained only in a footnote'.[43] There are also implications for the use of databases and data search engines and how the expression 'documents' is defined. Such engines might have been designed with internal management needs only in mind and may need to be designed with the needs of transparency in mind specifically with respect to 'the design and content of electronic databases'.[44]

The exceptions

Proposals are put forward for two new exceptions, some recasting and some new wording.

Protection of the environment

A new exception would cover the protection of 'the environment, such as breeding sites of rare species', with no possibility of an overriding PI in disclosure.[45] This is in line with the Aarhus Convention examined in chapter 7.[46] Further alignment of the access regulation and the environmental information regulation are proposed including those involving emissions into the environment (see chapter 7).

Court proceedings and legal advice

Court proceedings and legal advice are currently protected in Art. 4(2). To these would be added 'arbitration and dispute settlement proceedings' by way of 'clarification'. The EU Ombudsman has ruled that the WTO dispute resolution[47] is not covered by this exception so it may not be a clarification but a considerable extension.

The Commission's proposal preceded the ECJ decision in *Turco*.[48] The ECJ, as we have seen, reversed the ruling of the CFI and ruled that the regulation imposes an obligation to disclose the opinion's of the Council's legal service in connection with a lawmaking process. This would cover the situation where the service had expressed doubts about a draft legislative measure. The Commission believed that this would basically place the service in an invidious position if it subsequently had to advise on the measure's legality. Such a sensitivity could

---

[41] Art. 2(6).   [42] In particular, Art. 4(1)(b), Art. 4(2), first indent and Art. 4(3).
[43] Harden p. 246.   [44] *Ibid.*   [45] Art. 4(1)(e).
[46] See Regulation 1367/2006 European Parliament and Council of 6 September 2006 and application of Åarhus Community institutions and bodies 2006 OJ L 264, p. 13.
[47] See Case 582/2005/PB, www.ombudsman.europa.eu/decision/en/050582.htm.
[48] Joined Cases C-39/05 P and C-52/05 P, *Turco v Council*, judgment of 1 July 2008.

not justify an exception to openness within the regulation, the ECJ ruled. Any improper pressure on the service to colour its published advice should be dealt with by the Council and should not act as an excuse for non-transparency. Harden has suggested that a new obligation should be included, possibly in the recitals, to disclose the opinions of the institutions' legal services concerning legislative processes.[49]

Privacy and integrity of the individual

The Commission proposed a change to the exception concerning privacy and integrity of the individual in Art. 4(1)(b) at present. This reform has been drafted in the light of the ruling by the CFI in the *Bavarian Lager* case.[50] The amendment in a new Art. 4(5) seeks to allow the names, title and functions of public-office holders, officials and PI representatives in relation with their professional activities to be disclosed unless, in the particular circumstances, disclosure would adversely affect those persons (see chapter 8 above). It continues:

> Other personal data shall be disclosed in accordance with the conditions regarding lawful processing of such data laid down in EC legislation on the protection of individuals with regard to the processing of personal data.

This quotation suggests that for 'other personal data' the governing provision should be reg. 45/2001 on the regulation of personal data and not the regulation on access. *Bavarian Lager*, in fact, decided the opposite and that the access regulation should be the governing provision.[51] This view on reg. 45/2001 has been a long-standing view of the Commission.[52] The CFI judgment stresses that the Art. 4(1)(b) exception only applies to data that are 'capable of actually and specifically undermining the protection of privacy and the integrity of the individual'. It does not apply to all personal data.

The proposal has been criticised by the European Data Protection Supervisor (EDPS).[53] Harden shows that in the view of the EDPS, the quoted sentence above from the proposal 'does not do justice to the need for a right balance between the fundamental rights at stake'.[54] The Data Protection Regulation provides no clarity on when public access should be allowed. The European Parliament's proposals for reform in response to the Commission are addressed briefly below (see p. 396) but the proposal on data protection is influenced by the EDPS:

---

[49] Note 6 above.   [50] Case T-194/04, *Bavarian Lager v Commission* [2007] ECR II-4523.
[51] See especially paras. 98–100 of the judgment.
[52] And this is the Commission's position in its appeal to the ECJ against the decision of the CFI in *Bavarian Lager*. Pending case C-28/08 P. See also, European Data Protection Supervisor, *Public Access to Documents and Data Protection*, Background Paper Series (July 2005), No. 1.
[53] Quoted in Harden, note 6 above. Opinion of the European Data Protection Supervisor on the Proposal for a Regulation of the European Parliament and of the Council regarding public access to European Parliament, Council and Commission documents, 30 June 2008, available at www.edps.europa.eu.
[54] Harden, note 6 above, p. 249.

6. Personal data shall not be disclosed if such disclosure would harm the privacy or the integrity of the person concerned. Such harm shall not be deemed to be caused:

- if the data relate solely to the professional activities of the person concerned unless, given the particular circumstances, there is reason to assume that disclosure would adversely affect that person;
- if the data relate solely to a public person unless, given the particular circumstances, there is reason to assume that disclosure would adversely affect that person or other persons connected with him or her;
- if the data have already been published with the consent of the person concerned.

Personal data shall nevertheless be disclosed if an overriding public interest requires disclosure. In such a case, the institution or body concerned shall be required to specify the public interest. It shall give reasons why, in the specific case, the public interest outweighs the interests of the person concerned. Where an institution or body refuses access to a document on the basis of paragraph 1, it shall consider whether it is possible to grant partial access to that document.

Decision-making

Further proposals would widen the exception for the decision-making process by extending the range of papers protected to include *all* documents in that process. Together with the narrowing of 'documents' that are covered by the regulation (above) and the exclusion of documents which are part of the administrative file of an investigation or of proceedings concerning an act of individual scope these would considerably extend the scope of exceptions.

Member State documents

Furthermore, an amendment to the exception in Art. 4 concerning multi-level governance states that a Member State may give reasons to an institution for withholding documents based on exceptions in reg. 4(5) 'or on specific provisions in its own legislation preventing disclosure of the document concerned'. The 'adequacy of these reasons . . . shall be appreciated by the institution . . . insofar as they are based on exceptions laid down in this regulation'. The *IPAW* judgment of the ECJ ruled that while national laws may identify an interest deserving protection, an exception had to be consistent with reg. 4. The institution had to rely on an exception within the regulation.[55]

Miscellaneous

Further revisions are outlined for selection procedures for contracts seeming to make it easier to refuse documents opening up decisions involved with

---

[55] Case C-64/05 P *Sweden (IFAW) v Commission* [2007] ECR I-11389. See paras. 83–4 and paras. 86 and 88.

awarding contracts. Changes are proposed for staff selection procedures. Suggested amendments to copyright run the risk of extending the exception to protect papers covered by copyright from access. The proposal is not clear in its ambit but seems to see copyright as a means of defeating access and not simply reuse of information (see chapter 5, p. 179).

The Commission's suggested reforms place overall emphasis on lessening the administrative burdens of access regimes by introducing exclusions in relation to investigations and increased time limits. Such an objective is understandable, especially if inadequate resources are allocated to make access and transparency more realistic. If a right is given, its realisation should be adequately resourced. Many, though not all of the suggested reforms, appear somewhat defensive, revealing a spirit of secrecy and 'we know best' that does not accord well with the glowing praise for transparency accompanying the EU Constitution and Lisbon Treaty fanfares. As Harden argues, they do not fit well with the Commission's 'European Transparency Initiative' which was launched in November 2005, which it described as a 'drive towards more transparency' and which included a review of the regulation.[56] The additional exclusions and widening of exceptions run the real risk of enhancing the opportunities for networked corporatism and reducing a wider public involvement in administration. The Commission has consistently taken a less-than-positive approach to genuine transparency and access. The European Parliament in its proposed amendment to the regulation has placed in a recital to the regulation a statement that an inter-institutional register of lobbyists and interested parties is a 'natural tool for the promotion of openness and transparency'. The European Parliament has its role cut out to promote that wider interest.

The Cashman Report and the European Parliament's proposals

The European Parliament debated the proposals for reform following a report by Michael Cashman[57] on 11 March 2009. The recommendation on personal data was outlined above. The Parliament's proposals are far more consistent with the principles of transparency and openness than the Commission proposals. A new recital 4, for instance, states:

> Transparency should also strengthen the principles of good administration in the EU institutions as provided for by Article 41 of the Charter of Fundamental Rights of the European Union ('the Charter'). Internal procedures should be defined accordingly and adequate financial and human resources should be made available to put the principle of openness into practice.

---

[56] Minutes of the Commission's meeting no. 1721 of 9 November 2005.

[57] The Committee on Civil Liberties, Justice and Home Affairs, 2008/0090 COD 5 January 2009, www.europarl.europa.eu/sides/getDoc.do?pubRef=-//EP//NONSGML±COMPARL±PE-415.164±02±DOC±PDF±V0//EN&language=EN.

The proposals can be viewed at www.statewatch.org/news/2009/mar/eu-access-reg-cashman-11-march-adopted-ver2.pdf.

They are very detailed and frequently diverge from the position of the Commission. Access rights are not confined to citizens or residents. 'Document' is not as confined as in the proposals examined above. The legislative process should be open allowing wide access to documents 'the widest possible access to their activities . . . including delegated activities' and the exceptions 'shall not apply to documents transmitted within the framework of procedures leading to a legislative act or a non-legislative act of general application'. There is no specific exception for pre- and post-decision-making within the institutions as at present. The new recital (28) states that 'In principle, all documents drafted or received by the institutions and relating to their activities should be registered and accessible to the public. However, without prejudice to the European Parliament's scrutiny, access to the entire document or to part of it could be postponed.' Procurement and staff selection processes are excepted until final decisions. MSs:

> shall seek to ensure that an equivalent level of transparency is granted in relation to national measures implementing acts of the institutions of the European Union, in particular by clearly publishing the references of the national measures. The objective is to give citizens a clear and precise understanding of their rights and obligations deriving from specific EU rules and enable national courts to ensure that those rights and obligations are respected in accordance with the principles of legal certainty and the protection of the individual.

In relation to documents originating from a MS they shall be consulted and 'documents provided to the institutions for the purpose of influencing policymaking should be made public'. Exceptions claimed for MS and third-party documents would have to be consistent with those in the regulation. In relation to the PI test:

> a strong public interest in disclosure exists where the requested documents have been drawn up or received in the course of procedures for the adoption of EU legislative acts or of non-legislative acts of general application. When balancing the public interest in disclosure, special weight shall be given to the fact that the requested documents relate to the protection of fundamental rights or the right to live in a healthy environment.

Information Officers should be appointed to ensure compliance within each directorate general.

The Lisbon Treaty

Battle is clearly drawn between the Commission and the Parliament. The Commission seeks to increase its discretionary powers to control dissemination of information in a variety of respects and seeks new provisions to exclude information from access. How do these square with the provisions on openness and transparency made in the Lisbon Treaty?

Reform of the treaties governing the European Union has engaged the institutions and Member States since 2001. There was a sense of profound disappointment in many quarters when the proposals for a treaty on the European Constitution were abandoned following its rejection by the Dutch and French in referenda in 2005. The plan B involved the Treaty of Lisbon which comprises two treaties. Virtually all the important features of the Constitution are in these treaties, particularly the first treaty on the EU. These treaties do simplify the structure and operation of the European Union in many ways. The three pillars will be absorbed into one body and the EU will have legal personality. The treaties await final approval depending upon ratification by the Czech Republic. Ratification has now taken place.

Under Art. 6 TEU, the Union recognises the rights, freedoms and principles set out in the Charter of Fundamental Rights of the European Union of 7 December 2000, as adapted at Strasbourg, on 12 December 2007, which *shall have the same legal value as the treaties*. It continues that the provisions of the charter shall not extend in any way the competences of the Union as defined in the treaties. Under Art. 42 of the Charter of Fundamental Rights there is a right of access to the documents of the institutions, bodies, offices and agencies of the Union. This is a fundamental right in international law, and much broader in its effect than existing rights, and on the coming into force of the Lisbon Treaty it will become a legally binding part of the treaties and not simply a matter of intergovernmental agreement.

Within the charter are rights to good administration and a right of access to documents – they will become legally binding 'fundamental rights'.

Under Art. 10 TEU every citizen shall have the right to participate in the democratic life of the Union. Decisions shall be taken as openly and as closely as possible to the citizen. The latter repeats provisions in the existing Amsterdam EU Treaty in Art. 1 and in Art. 1 of Lisbon.

Article 11 provides that the institutions shall, by appropriate means, give citizens and representative associations the opportunity to make known and publicly exchange their views in all areas of Union action. The institutions shall maintain an open, transparent and regular dialogue with representative associations and civil society. The European Commission shall carry out broad consultations with parties concerned in order to ensure that the Union's actions are coherent and transparent. Citizens (not less than a million) may invite the Commission to submit proposals for laws for the purpose of implementing the treaties.

In the Constitution the provision on access to documents was in the first part of the treaty which dealt with constitutional basics (Art. I.50). It is now (apart from its presence in the charter above) in the second part of Lisbon: the Treaty on the Functioning of the EU (TFEU).

Under Art. 15 TFEU (replacing Art. 255 EC) it provides that in order to promote good governance and ensure the participation of civil society, the Union institutions, bodies, offices and agencies shall conduct their work as openly as possible. After provisions about Parliament and the Council meetings being in public, the latter when considering and voting on a legislative act, it states:

> 3. Any citizen of the Union, and any natural or legal person residing or having its registered office in a Member State, shall have a right of access to documents of the Union institutions, bodies, offices and agencies, whatever their medium, subject to the principles and the conditions to be defined in accordance with this paragraph.
>
> General principles and limits on grounds of public or private interest governing this right of access to documents shall be determined by the European Parliament and the Council, by means of regulations, acting in accordance with the ordinary legislative procedure.
>
> Each institution, body, office or agency shall ensure that its proceedings are transparent and shall elaborate in its own Rules of Procedure specific provisions regarding access to its documents, in accordance with the regulations referred to in the second subparagraph.
>
> The Court of Justice of the European Union, the European Central Bank and the European Investment Bank shall be subject to this paragraph only when exercising their administrative tasks.

The first point to note is that this measure does not confer rights on those who are not citizens or resident in the EU. The position at present is that non-citizens and residents are covered. Secondly, it applies to all institutions of the EU. This will include the European Council which is now made an 'institution' under Lisbon. Because of the collapse of the pillars into one EU edifice there will be no formal distinction between what were EC and EU concerns. The coverage of this measure would appear to be much broader than the existing regulation.

11

Openness, information and the courts

The role of the courts in helping to create a more open society is vital. Greater openness depends upon the mutual co-operation of the executive, Parliament and the courts. In the early 1990s, the High Court observed that it could not create a freedom of information (FOI) statute.[1] Parliament did by enacting the government's bill. The courts' role in the Freedom of Information Act (FOIA) is limited, though important, to appeals on points of law. The Information Commissioner (IC) and the Information Tribunal (IT) were deliberately introduced to avoid litigation and save cost. Some important judicial decisions have emerged on the FOIA and EIR as we saw in chapters 6 and 7. Courts could be called upon to make crucial decisions on review and numerous recent judgments have raised questions relating to openness. These decisions exist alongside the reforms brought about to administrative adjudication by the Tribunals, Courts and Enforcement Act 2007, which has established a two-tier system of tribunals. Some important judgments have involved the Special Immigration Appeals Commission (SIAC) and its use of secret proceedings and special counsel.[2] There is no doubt that after years of indifference, English courts have displayed a greater awareness of the benefits to be gained from openness and freedom of expression. The common law was recognising such a fundamental right – and not simply a state concession – and it has been boosted by the Human Rights Act 1998 (HRA). Lord Bingham's eloquent dicta from *Shayler*[3] provide evidence of how far the courts have travelled in twenty years:

> The reasons why the right to free expression is regarded as fundamental are familiar . . . Modern democratic government means government of the people by the people for the people. But there can be no government by the people if they are ignorant of the issues to be resolved, the arguments for and against different solutions and the facts underlying those arguments. The business of government is not an activity about which only those professionally engaged are entitled to receive information and express opinions. It is, or should be, a participatory process. But there can be no assurance that government is carried out for the people unless the facts are made known, the issues publicly ventilated.

[1] *R v Secretary of State for Defence, ex p. Sancto* (1992) The Times, 19 September.
[2] J. Ip (2008) Public Law 717; see note 282 below. [3] [2003] 1 AC 247 para. 21.

Sometimes, inevitably, those involved in the conduct of government, as in any other walk of life, are guilty of error, incompetence, misbehaviour, dereliction of duty, even dishonesty and malpractice. Those concerned may very strongly wish that the facts relating to such matters are not made public. Publicity may reflect discredit on them or their predecessors. It may embarrass the authorities. It may impede the process of administration. Experience however shows, in this country and elsewhere, that publicity is a powerful disinfectant. Where abuses are exposed, they can be remedied. Even where abuses have already been remedied, the public may be entitled to know that they occurred. The role of the press in exposing abuses and miscarriages of justice has been a potent and honourable one. But the press cannot expose that of which it is denied knowledge.

Section 12 of that Act's emphatic instruction that the 'Court must have particular regard to the Convention right of freedom of expression' in order to ensure a free press unhampered by unnecessary restraints indicates legislative support for Art. 10.[4] The important place of s. 12 in protecting press freedom was recognised by the House of Lords in *Cream Holdings* (see p. 444 below);[5] the Privy Council has overturned death sentences where there had been a failure to disclose materials to petitioners for mercy;[6] courts have emphatically declared the importance of obtaining documentation concerning an individual's possible innocence in terrorist proceedings even though the production was opposed by the US Government which threatened not to co-operate in passing intelligence to the UK Government if the information were disclosed (see p. 426 below). There has been a remarkable litany of case law concerning an enhanced appreciation of openness.[7] Conversely, the Law Lords, reversing the Divisional Court ruled that a decision by the director of the Serious Fraud Office to stop criminal inquiries into arms sales, in which corruption was said to be instrumental, was not against the rule of law. The investigation was at the point of discovering vital information but its revelation could have damaged national security.[8] Placing a limit on the disclosure of information about the environmental impact of a cement plant in regulatory management of the environment was not seen as an error which vitiated the grant of a permit for the plant and the agency had not breached its duty of consultation by failing to provide enough information.[9]

Since 1967 courts, following earlier administrative concessions, have been prepared to assist litigants in dispute with state institutions in England and Wales, to the extent that, on exacting conditions, they will allow access to documents in the possession of state bodies or allow cross-examination of

---

[4] *Derbyshire CC v Times Newspapers Ltd* [1993] 1 All ER 1011, HL; *R v Secretary of State for the Home Department, ex p. Simms* [1999] 3 All ER 400, HL, and Lord Steyn in particular; and *Kelly v BBC* [2001] 1 All ER etc. and the older *Hector v AG of Antigua* [1990] 2 AC 312.

[5] [2004] UKHL 44.   [6] *Lewis v AG of Jamaica* [2000] WLR 1785 PC.

[7] *Greenpeace* [2007] EWHC 311; *R (Eisai Ltd) and NICE v Shire Pharmaceuticals Ltd* [2008] EWCA Civ 438.

[8] *R (Corner House Research) v Director Serious Fraud Office* [2008] UKHL 60; J. Jowell (2008) 13 JR 273.

[9] *R (Edwards) v Environment Agency* [2008] UKHL 22.

official witnesses. This topic, discussed in more detail later in this chapter (see p. 450 below), is known as public-interest immunity (PII).

When discussing openness and the courts, it must be appreciated that the theme is subject to various interpretations. It may refer to the openness of courts themselves: 'Publicity is the very soul of justice';[10] their being open to the public; and their proceedings being in the public domain – the ultimate form of openness being live broadcasts.[11] The principle of openness applies to tribunals although many sit in private because of the sensitive and personal details they have to deal with.

In a second sense, the phrase can refer to the role of the courts in helping to achieve openness or fuller provision of information: by insisting on information being provided as evidence supporting an assertion; by way of reasons being afforded for decisions that affect our lives; or by giving greater access to those claiming a right to information. A further element in this second sense would involve the role of the courts in advancing freedom of speech; protecting and enhancing our civil liberties such as demonstrating peaceably; and developing, without unjustified interference, our intellectual and personal lives even in the absence of a First Amendment entrenching a right to freedom of speech as in the USA.

A third sense of the expression can refer to the role of the courts in resolving disputes between parties over property rights in information or over the use of information acquired in a variety of circumstances. Typically, a confidential relationship creates certain obligations and entitlements over the use of information. While the courts have developed the law of confidentiality to protect information irrespective of a pre-existing relationship,[12] especially in relation to personal privacy, it has remained for the legislature to give fuller definition to the law relating to copyright and patents,[13] copyright of information held on computers and computer misuse.[14] Copyright does not protect ideas per se.[15] I briefly address confidentiality, but my overriding concern is with the first two senses. I will not be able to deal in any detailed manner with freedom of

---

[10] *Scott v Scott* [1913] AC 417, Lord Shaw, p. 477. See *Pretto v Italy* (1984) 6 EHRR 182 and Art. 6 on publicity. On decision in public see *Campbell v Fell* (1985) 7 EHHR 165.

[11] The Criminal Justice Act 1925 prohibits the use of cameras in courts. There has been discussion of live broadcasts of trials but not those involving juries or magistrates. See *BBC, Petitioners (No. 2)* 2000 SLT 860 and broadcasting of the Lockerbie trial. Broadcasts of proceedings in Scottish courts have been allowed to a limited extent. There has been experimental filming of proceedings in the Court of Appeal, and filming of the delivery of judgments by the Law Lords. The former Lord Chancellor Lord Falconer was keen to film court proceedings but after his replacement the initiative was side-lined: *The Guardian* 10 March 2008. The new Supreme Court established under the Constitutional Reform Act 2005 may be filmed if the president agrees, which he has done.

[12] See p. 445 below.   [13] Copyright, Designs and Patents Act 1988.

[14] Computer Misuse Act 1990 and Police and Justice Act 2006 ss. 35–8; see also Copyright (Computer Software) Amendment Act 1985 and note *Intellectual Property and Innovation*, Cmnd 9712 (1986). See generally J. Phillips and A. Firth, *Introduction to Intellectual Property Law*, 4th edn (2001); W. R. Cornish and D. Llewellyn, *Intellectual Property*, 5th edn (2003).

[15] *Baigent and Leigh v Random House Group Ltd* [2006] EWHC 719 Ch – the *Da Vinci Code*.

speech or demonstration or censorship. These are detailed topics well provided for elsewhere.[16]

The 'Golden Met-wand'

Publicity for the law, and public information about the rules of conduct of society that are to be implemented through its courts and that may account for deprivation of liberty, property, and – until 1965 in the UK – one's life,[17] are vital components of the rule of law.[18] So too is a judiciary free from executive or other interference. Developed markets and commercial and financial enterprise require an extended law of property and intellectual property, contract, corporations law, regulatory law, and securities and investment law. The fact that most of dispute resolution, guidance through rules or standards, or the establishment of dispute procedures and policy-initiating bodies, do not involve the use of courts is not to deny the fact that courts are ultimately the final arbiters of law. Unless, that is, Parliament has definitively and successfully excluded the courts from a province of decision-making,[19] or where practice has effectively excluded the courts, as in judgments on the interests of national security (see below). Deliberate exclusion by Parliament is comparatively rare, and usually jealously scrutinised by the courts – or subject to attack from senior judges.[20] The stirring words of the judgments in *Scott v Scott*[21] tell us that what goes on

---

[16] E. Barendt, *Freedom of Speech*, 2nd ed, (2007); G. Robertson, *Obscenity* (1979); T. Gibbons, *Criminal Justice and Public Order Act* 1994; D. Feldman, *Civil Liberties and Human Rights*, 2nd edn (2002); J. Beatson and Y. Cripps (eds.), *Freedom of Expression and Freedom of Information* (2000).

[17] The death penalty still survived for treason and some military offences until the Human Rights Act 1998, s. 1(3), sch. 1, Pt III, Art. 1. It may be revived in time of war or imminent threat of war, *ibid.*, Art. 2.

[18] L. Fuller, *The Morality of Law* (1964). *R (Anufrijeva) v Secretary of State* [2003] UKHL 36.

[19] *Anisminic Ltd v Foreign Compensation Commission* [1969] 2 AC 147 on the enforced casuistry in which the courts engage to insist upon all errors of law being of a jurisdictional nature. Cf. *Page v Visitor of the University of Hull* [1993] 1 All ER 97, HL. In *R v Security Service Tribunal, ex p. Harmon and Hewitt* QBD 14 February 1992, Kennedy J questioned the efficacy of the provision seeking to prevent judicial review of decisions of the Security Service Tribunal, s. 5(4) Security Service Act 1989.

[20] The most dramatic incident in England in recent years concerned Lord Woolf's protestations against the removal of judicial review in immigration decisions: see *de Smith's Judicial Review* (2007), 1–051. In America, after some limp-wristed cases involving suspected terrorists the Detainee Treatment Act 2005 sought to remove the federal courts' jurisdiction from cases before the military commissions involving suspected terrorists. Greater sophistication was shown in *Hamdan v Rumsfeld* 126 S Ct 2749 (2006) where the Supreme Court held that the Geneva Convention was not removed in hearings before military commissions and the federal courts' jurisdiction was not removed by that Act. The Military Commissions Act 2006 (MCA) sought to prevent suits before the Military Commission being removed to the courts. The Supreme Court, however, ruled that the MCA had not removed the right of those detained in Guantánamo to seek habeas corpus before the federal courts and the inadequate and ineffective procedures in use before the Commissions meant the MCA operated as an 'unconstitutional suspension of the writ': *Boumediene and Others v Bush and Others* No. 06–1195, 12 June (2008).

[21] [1913] AC 417. Freedom of the press to report proceedings of a court was a 'strong rule' said Lord Steyn in *In Re S. (FC)* [2004] UKHL 47. There has been prolonged debate concerning secrecy of proceedings in family courts:*Improving Transparency and Privacy in Family*

in the courts is public business, even if it concerns private parties. There are numerous exceptions which are noted below.

There is no rule of statute law that judges must give reasons for their decisions although the Court of Appeal has stated Art. 6 European Convention on Human Rights (ECHR) requires reasons for a judicial decision.[22] Poor reasons are unlikely to withstand appeal.[23] Yet judges operate within a tradition, spreading back as far as the common law, which *insists* that the reasons for their decisions are, unlike juries, publicly expressed or published. Their decisions have to fit into the body of established precedent and be reasoned to conclusions that will be publicly contested and rigorously analysed in academic work and subsequent judicial proceedings. A good judge feels the pressure of his peers to 'pass muster'. If he does not, his reputation as a lawyer, though not his judicial salary,[24] will suffer. Indeed, the alleged secrecy of Star Chamber proceedings was the cause of vitriolic attacks on that body in the seventeenth century. The attack was politically motivated by common lawyers, but it struck a deep and pervasive chord of sympathy in influential circles.[25] The law must be known after hard argument and testing. Being allowed to utter forth truthfully on the law without a reck as to consequences is one thing and has a centuries old tradition behind it. Being instructed, on the other hand, that certain matters are reserved issues for politics alone, is another tradition and one that was deeply ingrained in our political and legal consciousness.[26]

Freedom of governmental information has been reserved business. Unlike freedom of speech or a right to life, it has not been perceived as a human right.

Courts – Confidence and Confidentiality, Cm. 6886; see DCA, Cm.. 7036; *Confidence and Confidentiality: Openness in Family Courts – a new approach*, Cm. 7131; and SIs 857, 858/2009. See Practice Direction [2009] 2 FCR 606. The use of 'super injunctions' to prevent the identities of commercial litigants being indentified on grounds of privacy protection has caused alarm among the press. Attempts were even made to suppress reports about parliamentary questions being asked about the organisations but information had been widely disseminated through Twitter on the web: *The Guardian*, 14 October 2009

22 *Anya v University of Oxford* [2001] EWCA Civ 405; *Flannery v Halifax Estate Agencies Ltd* [2000] 1 All ER 373, CA: 'The duty to give reasons was a function of due process and, therefore, of justice in all cases . . . transparency should be the watchword.' Henry LJ. Cf. s. 10 Tribunals and Inquiries Act 1992.

23 The advice of Lord Mansfield CJ to magistrates was not to give reasons, for while their decisions would doubtless be correct their reasons would often be wrong and thus reviewable: J. Campbell, *Lives of the Chief Justices* (1874), vol. 4, p. 26.

24 Prospects of promotion will doubtless be blighted if there is an ostentatious record of successful appeal.

25 Both G. R. Elton in *The Tudor Constitution*, 2nd edn (1981) and Kenyon in *The Stuart Constitution* (1966) believe that Star Chamber was much maligned and unjustly so: it administered 'the Common Law by means of a different procedure', including written depositions, exchange of evidence and cross-examination of the accused under oath (Kenyon, p. 117). Allegations of secrecy were fabrications. For criticism of the view that it was the Privy Council in another guise, see W. Holdsworth, *History of English Law*, vol. 5, ch. IV (1924).

26 *R (Gentle) v Prime Minister* [2008] UKHL 20 Art 2 ECHR did not create a right not to be exposed to death in an unlawful war thereby requiring an inquiry into the circumstances leading to of the cause of war. 'The draftsmen of the European Convention cannot, in my opinion, have envisaged that it could provide a suitable framework or machinery for resolving questions about the resort to war.' Lord Bingham, para. 8.

Even when confronted with cases concerning freedom of speech, courts traditionally disclaimed any constitutional dimension to their decisions, holding that the prevention of a meeting or a public address was simply a corollary of the police apprehending a breach of the peace, a concept which has been stretched to breaking point.[27] The wind of change has made its presence felt. In *Derbyshire County Council v Times Newspapers*[28] the House of Lords unanimously ruled that a local authority, and indeed even central government, could not sue for defamation. Such an action for the 'organs of government' would be contrary to the public interest (PI) because it was of the 'highest public importance' that a public body should be open to uninhibited public criticism and a right to sue would place an undesirable fetter on freedom of speech. What was striking was that the House of Lords chose to make their ruling on the basis of the common law and not under the provisions of Art. 10 ECHR, which was a prime factor in the Court of Appeal's decision denying such an action.[29] The Law Lords' decision is a particularly robust assertion of the role of the common law in protecting human rights and it presaged a longer-term change in judicial sentiment. This change was evident before the HRA 1998 came into effect and it is worthwhile repeating Lord Hope's words from *DPP v Kebelene*[30] where he said that 'it is now plain that incorporation of the ECHR into our domestic law will subject the entire legal system to a fundamental process of review and, where necessary, reform by the judiciary'. In *ex p. Simms*, the Law Lords ruled that it was unlawful to interfere with a prisoner's right of access to a journalist who was contemplating writing an article about the possibility of a wrongful conviction. The journalist had declined to sign an undertaking not to publish such an article. The interference, which regulations could not justify in the absence of specific authorisation in legislation, amounted to an invasion of the prisoner's 'fundamental or basic right' to freedom of expression.[31] Lord Steyn emphasised the point graphically: 'freedom of speech is the lifeblood of democracy. The free flow of information and ideas informs political debate. It is a safety valve . . . '[32] Article 10 lay behind the decision to open up the inquiry into Dr Harold Shipman, the mass murderer, to the public – a secret

---

[27] E.g., *Duncan v Jones* [1936] 1 KB 218; *Thomas v Sawkins* [1935] 2 KB 249; *McLeod v Met. Police Com'r* [1994] 4 All ER 553, CA. For graphic evidence on the 'right' to demonstrate and its development under common law and Art. 11 ECHR, see *DPP v Jones* [1999] 2 All ER 257, HL and note *Austin v Met. Police Commissioner* [2009] UKHL 5 on the legality of crowd 'containment'.

[28] [1993] 1 All ER 1011, HL.

[29] *Oberschlick v Austria* Case No. 1990/197/257 (1991) 19 EHRR 389, E Ct HR; see *Re W* [1992] 1 All ER 794, CA and allowing publication of an article about a ward of court because of a real public interest in the case which involved two homosexual male foster parents: Art. 10 invoked in support and *Kelly v BBC* [2001] 1 All ER 323. See *In Re S. (FC)* [2004] UKHL 47 and *A Local Authority v W* [2005] EWHC 1564 (Fam). See also *AG's Reference No. 3* [2009] UKHL 34. On use of criminal libel, see *Lingens v Austria* (1986) 8 EHRR 407 and *Oberschlick* above; and *Prager and Oberschilick v Austria* (1995) 21 EHRR 1.

[30] *DPP v Kebelene* [1999] 4 All ER 801, at 838h–j. Not all are happy with this prospect of what John Griffith's has described as 'celestial jurisprudence'.

[31] *R v Secretary of State for the Home Department, ex p. Simms* [1999] 3 All ER 400, HL.

[32] At 408d.

inquiry would have interfered with freedom of expression and a right to pass on information.[33] *Wagstaff* was the high point of Art. 10 and openness. In *Pro Life* it was emphasised by Lord Hoffmann that Art. 10 does not provide a right of access to information or a right to a means of broadcasting.[34] Attempts to use Art. 10 to obtain a public hearing into a variety of matters have failed on a similar basis.[35] Article 2 – the right to life which carries with it the right of independent investigation and inquiry into the circumstances of death – has been used to obtain a public inquiry and legal assistance for the next of kin of a victim of violence or alleged negligence.[36]

Various international declarations seek to protect freedom of expression, opinion and information. Article 10 ECHR proclaims that:

> Everyone has the right to freedom of expression. This right shall include freedom to hold opinions and to receive and impart information and ideas without interference by public authority and regardless of frontiers.[37]

But the right, because it carries duties and responsibilities, is subject to qualifications:

> as are prescribed by law and are necessary in a democratic society, in the interests of national security,[38] territorial integrity or public safety, for the prevention of disorder or crime, for the protection of health or morals, for the protection of the rights, authority and impartiality of the judiciary.[39]

This body of qualifications has to be seen in the context of case law of the European Commission and European Court of Human Rights (ECtHR), which has stressed that the restrictions *must be* prescribed in law,[40] are *necessary*, are proportionate to legitimate objectives and subject to strict interpretation. The restrictions must be predicated by a 'pressing social need'[41] that is proportionate to the means of safeguarding it; in short, the authorities must not engage in

---

[33] *R (Wagstaff) v Secretary of State for Health* [2001] 1 WLR 292.

[34] *R v BBC, ex p. Pro Life Alliance* [2003] UKHL 23, [2004] 1 AC 225. The Law Lords also ruled that a ban on political advertising (animal rights) did not breach Art. 10. *R (Animal Defenders International) v SoS Culture, Media and Sport* [2008] UKHL 15; and s. 321(2) Communications Act 2003 and *VgT v Switzerland* [2001] 34 EHRR 159.

[35] *R (Persey) v Secretary of State* [2003] QB 794 and *R (Howard) v Secretary of State* [2003] QB 830.

[36] *Khan* [2003] 4 All ER 1239; *Amin* [2003] UKHL 51 but cf. *R (Scholes) v Secretary of State for the Home Department* [2006] EWHC Civ 1343 where an inquiry under Art. 2 was refused and which concerned the death of a youth in a detention centre. See *R (AM) v Secretary of State* [2009] EWCA Civ 219 and Art. 3.

[37] Art. 10(1).   [38] I. Cameron, *National Security and the ECHR* (2000).

[39] Art. 10(2). Cf. *Leander v Sweden* (1987) 9 EHRR 433, A 116; and *Z v Austria* No. 10392/83 (1988) and *VW BLUF v Netherlands* (1995) 20 EHRR 189. See *Hadjianastassiou v Greece* (1992) 16 EHRR 219 and *Informatsionverein Lenlia v Austria* (1993) 17 EHRR 93. *Segerstedt-Wiberg v Sweden* (2007) EHRR 2 (CCHR) – breach of Art. 8 by not allowing access to secret police files. Also a breach of Art. 10 because there was an interference with freedom of speech, Arts. 11 and 13.

[40] In a body *of published* rules considered *binding* and formulated with sufficient precision to regulate one's conduct: *Silver v UK* (1983) 5 EHRR 347 and discussion of the proviso in Art. 8(2); *Sunday Times v UK* (1979) 2 EHRR 245. See *R v Advertising Standards Authority Ltd, ex p. Matthias Rath BV* (2001) The Times, 10 January.

[41] The *Sunday Times* case, note 40 above.

overkill or exaggerated reaction. We saw a balancing or rights under Art. 10 and under other Convention Articles, especially Art. 2 and the right to life and Art. 8 in the case of the notorious murderers of Jamie Bulger (see p. 275 above) when the courts ordered anonymity for identity and whereabouts.[42] Furthermore, the Convention allows judges to strike a note of fundamentalism that had been absent from our legal traditions until the last fifteen or so years. In *Handyside*, for instance, it was noted how:

> Freedom of expression constitutes one of the essential foundations of a society, one of the basic conditions for its progress and for the development of every man [*sic*]. Subject to paragraph 2 of Article 10, it is applicable not only to 'information' or 'ideas' that are favourably received, but also to those that offend, shock or disturb the State or any sector of the population. Such are the demands of that pluralism, tolerance and broad-mindedness without which there is no democratic society.[43]

Judges have been criticised for their inherent conservatism, for practising a politics that affects neutrality but which is far from neutral.[44] Why should they assume the right to promote social and political change? Such change, many argue, is a democratic responsibility not a judicial function. Who assesses the quality of those who practise the judicial function? How are judges appointed?

Judicial appointments[45]

The system for appointing judges was transformed by the Constitutional Reform Act 2005 (CRA). There is now a statutory Judicial Appointments Commission (JAC),[46] which is an executive non-departmental body sponsored by the Ministry of Justice. It has a lay chair and fourteen members comprising five judges, one barrister, one solicitor, five lay members, one tribunal member and one lay justice. The JAC selects candidates for recommendation for appointment to judicial offices set out in sch. 14 of the Act and the senior judges. Separate arrangements will exist for judicial appointments to the new Supreme Court. The power is recommendatory although the Justice Minister cannot put forward alternatives. The statutory criteria of appointment are merit, good character, and diversity through fair, open and effective procedures which are subject

---

[42] Similar protection was given to Mary Bell, the child murderer, and Maxine Carr, the partner of Ian Huntley.

[43] *Handyside v UK* (1976) 1 EHRR 737, *Silver v UK* (1983) 5 EHRR 347. In *Leander*, note 39 above, refusing access to information on a national security register was neither a breach of Art. 8 – right to privacy – nor Art. 10, the Court held; see *Rotaru v Romania* 8 BHRC 449 and failure to provide redress where security services hold erroneous information about individuals. See *Fressoz and Roire v France* (2001) 31 EHRR 28 for a striking example of the influence of Art. 10.

[44] See John Griffith (2000) Mod LR 159, criticising Sir John Laws (1993) Public Law 59 and (2001) LQR 42 criticising Sir Stephen Sedley; Sedley's response at (2001) LQR 68. See S.Sedley, *Freedom, Law and Justice* (1999).

[45] See HC 1703 (2005–6) from the Constitutional Affairs Committee. C. Thomas and K. Malleson, *Judicial Appointments Commissions: The European and North American experience and possible implications for the UK* (1997).

[46] Annual reports available at www.judicialappointments.gov.uk/annual/annual.htm.

to constant review. The criteria are explained in published guidance. The JAC describes itself as listening and learning. Most posts are widely advertised. There is a Judicial Appointments and Conduct Ombudsman[47] to deal with complaints from candidates although complaints first have to be made to the JAC. In 2007–8 there were thirty-nine complaints to the JAC and fifteen to the ombudsman. None of the latter was upheld. Under the CRA, the Lord Chancellor has become the Secretary of State for Justice. The Lord Chief Justice has assumed the mantle of spokesman for the judiciary in the political dialogue with the government. A memorandum of understanding between these figures sets out the key principles and arrangements of the new scheme.[48] Although many of the details were contained in the statute, the legislation was not 'comprehensive'.[49] The reforms brought about a chilling of relationships between the senior judiciary and the government and fears for the maintenance of the rule of law itself. This led to the inclusion in s. 1 CRA a provision stipulating that nothing in the Act affected the operation of the principle of the rule of law!

The erstwhile process had ensured that only the 'safe and the sound' and almost exclusively white and socially privileged males were appointed.[50] For an appointment to the High Court, a barrister is expected to have displayed the necessary ambition and dedication not only to have mastered the most difficult briefs, but to have mastered the system. For appointments to QC, level of income was important though by 2001 no longer described as 'decisive'. A new system for appointing QCs was agreed between the Bar Council, Law Society and Lord Chancellor in 2004 and involves the Queen's Counsel Appointments and Complaints Committee, which has a lay member (with one senior judge and two lawyers) appointed jointly by the Chairman of the Bar and President of the Law Society. The published competency framework makes no reference to income. Any injudicious, intemperate or outspoken public statements would doubtless be damning. The background of the vast majority of individuals concerned and the remarkable absence of notoriety among the judiciary, certainly the higher judiciary, testify to that. In January 2008, *The Guardian* noted that the first ten appointments to the High Court under the new system all looked remarkably like former appointments. Data information on judicial appointments is one of the exempted items under the Data Protection Act.

Once in office, judges no longer serve under a 'voluntary' code of silence known as the 'Kilmuir Rules'. These were written in 1955 by the then Lord Chancellor stating that generally judges should not make public utterances on subjects in the media.[51] Their application was relaxed over the years as Law Lords appear to have been excluded from their provisions. In his first press conference as Lord Chancellor, Lord Mackay announced that the 'Kilmuir Rules' were ripe for reform. He would encourage more discretion on the part of

---

[47] AR HC 632 (2006–7)   [48] See www.dca.gov.uk/consult/lcoffice/judiciary.htm.
[49] House of Lords Committee on the Constitution, HL 151 (2006–7). See HM Courts Service Framework Document, Cm. 7350 (2008).
[50] See J. Rozenberg, *In Search of Justice* (1994), ch. 2.   [51] (1986) Public Law 384.

judges so long as interviews did not prejudice their judicial work.[52] Measured judicial comments have become more overtly critical of government policies and legislative reform. Lord Woolf has attacked the removal of a right of appeal in the Asylum Bill which had existed for over twenty-one years. The former Lord Chief Justice, Lord Taylor, criticised the Criminal Justice Act 1991 for attempting to restrict judicial discretion in sentencing and his predecessor spoke out against reform of the legal profession. On this latter point, the judiciary collectively went on strike in 1989.[53] Lord Woolf openly led the attack on government proposals to remove judicial review from immigration. Lord Taylor appeared on *Question Time* and delivered the Dimbleby lecture on TV. Press conferences have been called by Lord Taylor and Lord Woolf, in the latter case on a subject – imprisonment – which drew a fierce retort from the Home Secretary and which prompted the Lord Chief Justice to write to all High Court judges advising them to think twice before speaking to the media. On becoming Lord Chief Justice in 2006, Lord Philips spoke at a press conference on the dangers to judicial independence by government policies. Lord Steyn criticised American actions in Guantánamo Bay while still in office but Lord Bingham waited until retirement before crticising the war in Iraq as contrary to international law. Sir Richard Scott's engages with the government after the publication of the Matrix Churchill Report (see chapter 9) were particularly vitriolic. There have been very interesting judicial observations in academic and professional journals on the waning of judicial independence, including in the latter case an attack on the previous Lord Chancellor Lord Mackay for seeming to interfere with the independence of the President of the Employment Appeal Tribunal, Wood J.[54] There are numerous judicial comments of a less weighty nature which have placed the judiciary in a very poor light or put them on a par with 'new wave comedians'.[55] The contribution made by greater openness has been welcome but the words of Viscount Kilmuir had some sound advice: 'So long as a judge keeps silent', opined Kilmuir, 'his reputation for wisdom and impartiality remains unassailable.' By greater openness, they expose both strengths and weaknesses. They will also lay themselves open to increased accusations of prejudice. This aspect has been reinforced by Art. 6 ECHR and the HRA which provide that everyone has the right to a fair trial. If judges speak publicly on controversial subjects, they are ill-disposed to judge disputes involving those subjects.

The openness of the courts

In *Scott v Scott*[56] it was stated as a general principle of constitutional signif-icance that justice should be openly administered, although proceedings in

---

[52] *The Guardian*, 4 November 1987.   [53] Rozenberg, *In Search of Justice*, pp. 71–2.
[54] Sir F. Purchass, 'Lord Mackay and the judiciary' (1994) NLJ 527.
[55] Judge Pickles describing Lord Lane CJ as a 'dinosaur': *The Guardian* 28 November 1990.
[56] [1913] AC 417; see *Re X* [1975] Fam 47 and *Re Z* [1995] 4 All ER 961, CA, See *Storer v British Gas plc* [2000] 2 All ER 440 and *R v Bow County Court, ex p. Pelting* [1999] 4 All ER 751, CA. See J. Jaconnelli, *Open Justice: A critique of the public trial* (2002).

chambers were an exception to this. The High Court has ruled that even though proceedings were in chambers, that did not mean that a judgment had to be secret: 'The concept of a secret judgment is one which I believe to be inherently abhorrent' declared Jacob J.[57] The openness of the courts is not to satisfy public curiosity or to stimulate debate, but to keep the 'judge while trying under trial'.[58] Secrecy would depend upon the nature of the proceedings and their subject matter. Trials concerning prosecutions under the Official Secrets Acts and security-sensitive information have been the obvious occasions where secrecy has been invoked,[59] as are cases where justice itself would be defeated by disclosing trade secrets or confidential information. The SIAC may sit in secret and give secret sections to judgments. SIAC procedures, and control-order cases, may involve use of the special counsel procedure (see below). The use of anonymous witnesses in criminal trials was declared unlawful by the Law Lords but was reversed by legislation.[60] The Court of Appeal has also prevented the publication of the identities of witnesses (former paratroopers) involved in the Bloody Sunday shootings in Derry in 1972 when they gave evidence to the inquiry under Lord Saville.[61] Sufficient weight had not been given to the safety and right to life of the former soldiers by the tribunal. Screening of security or undercover officials giving evidence may take place as an alternative to *in camera* proceedings.[62] And what is said in court is protected by absolute privilege in any subsequent defamation proceedings.

The Woolf reforms on civil procedure led to a new rule under Pt 39 Civil Procedure Rules 1998. This provides under r. 39.2 that 'the general rule is that a hearing (trial) is to be in public'. Special arrangements do not have to be made for accommodating members of the public. Hearings, or parts of hearings, may be in private where, inter alia, publicity would defeat the object of the hearing, the matter involves national security, confidential information, or it is necessary to protect the interests of children or patients. A private hearing may also be held where the court believes this is necessary in the interests of justice. The courts also possess powers to prevent reporting of details such as names of those involved in proceedings or witnesses.[63] Breaching orders may be a contempt.

The Contempt of Court Act 1981 (CCA) sought to balance freedom of press reporting and the administration of justice. Section 4(2) provides a court with a power to order postponement of publication for such periods as it thinks necessary to prevent a substantial risk of prejudice to the administration of

---

[57] *Forbes v Smith* [1998] 1 All ER 973; and see *Hodgson v Imperial Tobacco Ltd* [1998] 1 WLR 1056.
[58] Per Lord Diplock in *Home Office v Harman*, below.
[59] As in parts of Clive Ponting's trial; OSA 1920, s. 8. PII (below) was not claimed in Ponting's trial, but was in *Matrix Churchill*. See *Re A and Others* [2006] 2 All ER 1 (CA) – *in camera* proceedings for national security.
[60] Criminal Evidence (Witness Arrangements) Act 2008 and *R v Davis* [2008] UKHL 36.
[61] *R v Lord Saville of Newdigate, ex p. A* [1999] 4 All ER 860.
[62] Richard Dearlove, Head of MI6 gave evidence to the Hutton Inquiry as a 'disembodied voice'. See *Re Officer L* [2007] UKHL 36.
[63] See *Re S*, note 29 above.

justice in those proceedings, or any other proceedings, pending or imminent.[64] Knowledge of the order must be proved to establish contempt (and see below).[65]

Section 11 allows the court to give directions prohibiting the publication of names or evidence where these were not disclosed in open court. The section does not give instruction on when such matters may be withheld.[66] The widespread use of the section to protect the anonymity of witnesses led to challenge in the European Commission of Human Rights and a right of appeal was provided against ss. 4(2) and 11 orders and other orders restricting publication of reports of trials on indictment and access to such trials and ancillary matters.[67] Brooke J has urged caution in accommodating the legitimate interests of the media and that judges should 'think long and hard' before banning contemporaneous reporting under s. 4(2);[68] courts had a discretionary power to hear representations from the press or media before considering whether to make a s. 4(2) order and they ought normally to hear representations when a request for such was made and the court anticipated that their representations would be of assistance.[69] The Court of Appeal has ruled that a judge should only withdraw into chambers to consider a s. 4(2) order where this is appropriate and s/he must resume sitting in open court 'as soon as it emerges that the need to exclude the public is not plainly necessary'.[70] It has also ruled that the court must be satisfied that in reporting the proceedings a substantial risk of prejudice to the administration of justice is present and, if so, whether it was necessary to make an order postponing publication in the circumstances of the case. Secondly, the court must balance the considerations which supported the need for a fair trial by an unprejudiced jury and the requirements of open justice on the one hand and a legitimate PI on the other.[71] Judges should also not be over-protective of juries and must credit them with intelligence.[72] Nonetheless, the *New Law Journal* has claimed that in the Central Criminal Court up to 20 per cent of all cases 'on some days' are covered by s. 4(2) orders.[73]

Statutes allow the names of witnesses and other evidence to be withheld by restricting reporting,[74] and courts have a common-law power to withhold

---

[64] *Re Central Independent Television plc* (1991) 1 All ER 347: court postponed all TV and radio reports so the jury would not hear news items; the Court of Appeal said this was 'overkill'. See also *Ex p. Telegraph plc* [1993] 2 All ER 971; *Re Times Newspapers* [2007] EWCA Crim 1925 on the limits of s. 4(2) (and s. 11) but possibilities under common law.

[65] *Re F* [1977] 1 All ER 114, CA; and *Re L* [1988] 1 All ER 418. Cf. *AG v Leveller Magazines Ltd* [1979] 1 All ER 745, HL.

[66] *R v Evesham Justices, ex p. McDonagh* [1988] 1 All ER 371; and *R v Westminster City Council, ex p. Castelli* [1996] 2 FCR 49. See *Re Times Newspapers* [2007] EWCA Crim 1925.

[67] S. 159(1) Criminal Justice Act 1988.   [68] *AG v Guardian Newspapers Ltd* [1992] 3 All ER 38.

[69] *R v Clerkenwell Magistrates' Court, ex p. Telegraph plc* [1993] 2 All ER 183.

[70] *Re Crook's Appeal* [1992] 2 All ER 687.

[71] *R v Beck, ex p. Daily Telegraph plc* [1993] 2 All ER 177, CA.

[72] *Ex p. Daily Telegraph* (1993) The Guardian, 15 March. See (1992) New LJ 957.

[73] Above. And see the comments of the court in *R (Binyam Mohamed) v SoS FA* [2009] EWHC 152 (Admin).

[74] Children and Young Persons Act 1933, ss. 39 (amended by s. 45 Youth Justice and Criminal Evidence Act 1999) and 49; Administration of Justice Act 1960, s. 12; Sexual Offences

identity and information where its revelation would frustrate the cause of the action, such as breach of confidence or patent. The House of Lords has noted the long list of such statutory prohibitions and in the exercise of the court's inherent jurisdiction agreed that an injunction preventing the disclosure of a defendant's identity in a murder trial should be lifted.[75] The defendant had murdered her young son and the original aim of the order was to protect the victim's sibling, her other child. Here, Art. 10 and publicity won the balancing exercise.

Section 6(c) CCA preserves as contempt that which intentionally impedes or prejudices the administration of justice. Such contempt was discussed in *AG v Newspaper Publishing Ltd*[76] which was part of the *Spycatcher* episode (see p. 438 below).

The subject headings of contempt have been developed by judicial precedent, and as they are based upon 'the broadest of principles' they can occasionally be put to novel and unexpected use. Where, on an application for discovery,[77] documents which had been handed to a solicitor who was representing a prisoner in a highly controversial prison control centre regime, the solicitor was found guilty of civil contempt when she allowed a reporter sight of the documents. Most of these had been read out in open court and were handed to her by the Home Office by order of the court on the basis that they were used for the litigation and not for other general purposes of the National Council for Civil Liberties, her employer. It was generally accepted that she had acted without improper motive.[78] A 3–2 majority in the House of Lords upheld the finding of contempt declaring that the case had nothing to do with human rights. It was a straightforward breach of an undertaking to the court.[79]

Had the reporter copied all the evidence given in court orally as the trial proceeded, no breach of law would have ensued as long as the public were admitted. He could also have 'bargained privately' to obtain a copy of the mechanically recorded speeches in court. He was a feature-article writer, not a reporter producing an accurate account of the proceedings for the quality press,[80] so his sight of the documents was not *de minimis* and a mere breach of technicality, but a serious contempt.

Lords Scarman and Simon believed that once documents had been read out in open court, the obligation of protection of confidentiality ceased; potentially inadmissible documents should be filed separately; anything else marked as

(Amendment) Act 1976; Magistrates Courts Act 1980, ss 8 and 71; see Children Act 1989, s. 97 (as amended by the Access to Justice Act 1999): see *Kelly v BBC* [2001] 1 All ER 323 and the impact of Art. 10 ECHR; Criminal Justice Act 1988 and rape victims; and Criminal Justice and Public Order Act 1994, s. 44 which repeals s. 8(8) Magistrates' Courts Act 1980. JPs cannot withhold their own identities from the public: *R v Felixstowe Justices, ex p. Leigh* [1987] QB 582.

[75] *Re S* [2004] UKHL 47. See *AG's Reference*, note 29 above, and rape trials.

[76] [1987] 3 All ER 276. See also *AG v Punch Ltd* [2002] UKHL 50, at p. 452.

[77] *Williams v Home Office (No. 2)* [1981] 1 All ER 1211.

[78] Though cf. Lord Denning in the Court of Appeal [1981] QB 534.

[79] *Home Office v Harman* [1983] 1 AC 280.   [80] Which might involve some question-begging!

exhibits should be available for inspection as part of the public record, as occurs in the USA, whether read out or not. The documents had become public knowledge, and after objecting to discovery the Home Office had not subsequently objected to publication on grounds of PII. Lord Scarman favoured the American practice of a judicial record and a public right to 'complete information' as a common-law right.[81] *Per contra*, Lord Roskill observed that, at that time, we had no FOIA in this country. Under the FOIA, an absolute exemption covers court documents. This is because courts possess their own powers to disclose court documents and application is made to the courts.

The Civil Procedure Rules (CPR) came into effect following the recommendations of Lord Woolf. Part 31(22) CPR governs the subsequent use of disclosed documents. The court still has the power to order the restriction or prohibition of the use of a document which has been disclosed, even when read to or by the court or referred to in a public hearing. The courts, however, have shown a greater degree of flexibility in establishing when documents have entered the public domain.[82] Unlike the amended rule in 1987, the 1998 version will have to be read in the context of Art. 10 ECHR: that freedom of speech or passing on information should only be restricted where there is a pressing social need or to advance some other important objective.

Protection of sources of information in litigation[83]

Section 10 CCA states:[84]

> No court may require a person to disclose, nor is any person guilty of contempt of court for refusing to disclose, the source of information contained in a publication for which he is responsible unless it be established to the satisfaction of the court that disclosure is necessary in the interests of justice or national security or for the prevention of disorder or crime.

[81] See *Re Application of NBC, USA v Meyers* 635 F 2d 945 (1980); *US v Mitchell* 551 F 2d 1252 (1976); *Nixon v Warner Communications inc.* 435 US 589 (1978). See Lord Hobhouse in *Reynolds v Times Newspapers* [1999] 4 All ER 609, HL.

[82] *SmithKline Beecham plc v Generics UK Ltd* [2003] 4 All ER 1302 (CA); *SmithKline Beecham Biologicals SA v Connaught Laboratories Inc.* [1999] 4 All ER 498, CA; in *McCartan Turkington Breen v Times Newspapers (NI)* [2000] 4 All ER 913, HL the House of Lords held that a press conference called on private premises was a 'public meeting' for the purposes of attracting qualified privilege under legislation. It did not decide that the public had a right to attend. What limits may be placed on journalists on information imparted at such meetings being further disseminated because it is argued it is confidential? Lord Bingham said at 922 c–d: 'It is very largely through the media, including the press that [citizens] will be informed. The proper functioning of a modern participatory democracy requires that the media be free, active, professional and enquiring.'

[83] R. Costigan (2007) Public Law 464. See the Johannesburg Principles on National Security, Freedom of Expression and Access to Information adopted by the NGO Coalition (1998) 20 HRQ, No. 18: protection of national security may not be used as a reason to compel a journalist to reveal a confidential source.

[84] For the background to s. 10 see *British Steel Corp. v Granada Television Ltd* [1981] AC 1096 and Y. Cripps (1984) Camb LJ 266.

This section gives an immunity from contempt proceedings to those who do not reveal the identity of a source of information contained in a publication for which they are responsible, unless the person seeking the identity proves to the court that disclosure is *necessary* for one or other of the stated grounds. This is a crucial provision in relation to leaks of information that result in 'publications' because if the identity of the 'leaker' is revealed the full wrath of the 'injured' party will be visited upon the former. At common law, courts may order an individual to reveal the identity of a source of information and this involved a straightforward balancing exercise.[85] No First Amendment freedom-of-speech protection has been afforded to journalists and their sources in the United States when they report on wrongdoing. In US litigation, a leak to a reporter involved identities of CIA operatives – an illegal act – and its source was a senior presidential adviser and chief of staff to the vice president, Scooter Libby, who had leaked the information to damage an opponent. Libby's identity had to be revealed.[86]

Under s. 10 the court may not order disclosure unless one of the grounds is made out, and even then it must exercise a discretion before ordering disclosure and must regard a broad array of factors. These may include the means of obtaining the information, and the public importance of disclosing the information from the source when balancing competing claims.[87] Disclosure of the source must be necessary for one of the four stated objectives before the discretion is exercised, not desirable or conducive towards the objectives.[88] Of especial importance is the need to maintain confidentiality of the source of supply, inter alia, of information to the police,[89] voluntary or public bodies promoting the welfare of vulnerable individuals,[90] or licensing or regulatory authorities promoting the PI.[91] Prior to s. 10 being enacted, the courts had given no immunity to protect the revelation of a source of information where national security was allegedly involved.[92] Nor had courts given much succour to claims of immunity where the 'interests of justice' *are* advanced by disclosure, in allowing a wronged party to obtain necessary information and evidence from a party who had become innocently involved in the tort.[93] Immunity may be given

---

[85] *Alfred Crompton*, note 243 below, whether or not contained in a publication.

[86] *In re Grand Jury Subpoena Judith Miller* 2005 US App LEXIS 2494 DC Circuit, Feb. 15 2005. See *Brandzburg v Hayes* 408 US 665 (1972). Libby was subsequently convicted of criminal offences and fined and sentenced to imprisonment but his prison sentence was commuted by President Bush.

[87] *X Ltd v Morgan Grampian (Publishers) Ltd* [1990] 2 All ER 1, HL.   [88] *Ibid.*

[89] *Marks v Beyfus* (1890) 25 QBD 494; Cmnd 6542, para. 287. See *ex p. Wiley* [1994] 3 All ER 420, HL.

[90] *D v NSPCC* [1977] 1 All ER 589, HL.

[91] *R v Gaming Board for Great Britain, ex p. Benaim and Khaida* [1970] 2 QB 417; *Rogers v Secretary of State for the Home Department* [1972] 2 All ER 1057.

[92] *AG v Mulholland* [1963] 2 QB 477, and *AG v Clough* and [1963] 1 QB 773.

[93] *Norwich Pharmacol Co. v Customs and Excise Comrs* [1974] AC 133, a case involving discovery against a third party. Note also *Ashworth Hospital Authority v MGN Ltd* [2001] 1 All ER 991 (below). See, incidentally. Consumer Safety (Amendment) Act 1986, s. 1.

where investigation of crime, or the possibility of investigation, is advanced, as in the case of police informers or where information relates directly to law enforcement, e.g. collection of customs and excise revenues, or taxes.[94]

Section 10 introduced a rule of law concerning disclosure of sources of information in addition to the judicial balancing of competing interests, which appeared previously to be the case. The section was considered *in extenso* in the litigation[95] involving *The Guardian* newspaper, the arrival of cruise missiles and, as it transpired, Sarah Tisdall.

A 'secret' memorandum was prepared by the Ministry of Defence (MoD) relating to the installation of cruise missiles at a Royal Air Force base in the UK. A copy of the memorandum was sent to the prime minister, and six copies were sent to senior members of the Cabinet and the Cabinet Secretary. A junior civil servant photocopied the memorandum and anonymously handed it to *The Guardian*, which subsequently published the memorandum. The Secretary of State for Defence was furious[96] and demanded the return of the documents in order to identify the source of the leak from markings on the copy and to take appropriate action. The claim of the Crown was basically that it was their property and they were entitled to its return under the Torts (Interference with Goods) Act 1977 in an undamaged form. Although successful in the lower courts, this point did not succeed in the House of Lords.[97] The Crown also argued that recovery was necessary in the interests of national security. While publication of this particular document was not a security risk, but merely a political embarrassment since its publication warned the Opposition in Parliament of the time of arrival of the missiles, the fact remained that a civil servant in a position of trust and confidence had betrayed a loyalty to the minister, and this did constitute a security risk for future, more important potential leaks. Section 10 was prayed in aid by *The Guardian*.

The House of Lords established that s. 10 places the onus of proof on the party seeking the order of disclosure of identity, viz. the Crown. Identity will remain a secret unless the court is satisfied that 'disclosure is necessary in the interests of justice or national security or for the prevention of disorder or crime'. Lord Diplock was emphatic that the discretion involved in balancing the interests between the PI in being informed of events of public importance and the PI in maintaining a confidence did not occur. The immunity applied *until and unless* one of the four grounds of release was established on the balance of probabilities to the satisfaction of the court. This is a question of fact, not

---

[94] *Alfred Crompton*, note 243 below.
[95] *Secretary of State for Defence v Guardian Newspapers Ltd* [1984] 3 All ER 601, HL.
[96] He had hoped to outflank the Opposition by revealing the information to Parliament at the last possible moment.
[97] Griffiths LJ did not concur on this point with the majority in the Court of Appeal. See Cripps *The Legal Implications of Disclosure in the Public Interest*, 2nd edn (1994), at pp. 284–5 on the effect of s. 8(4)–(5) of the OSA 1989.

a question of discretion or of 'constitutional right', an evocative phrase which Lord Diplock would repudiate:

> if it is intended to mean anything more than that in ascertaining the extent of the rights which it confers the section should give a purposive construction and, that being done, like other rights conferred on persons by statute, effect must be given to it in the courts.[98]

It is important to appreciate that the case came to the Law Lords as an appeal against an interlocutory order, i.e. a preliminary procedural point. By the time the Law Lords had to decide the construction of s. 10 and its application to the case, the identity of the 'leaker', Sarah Tisdall,[99] had become an issue of national notoriety. The Court of Appeal and three of the Law Lords thought that the affidavit evidence of the principal establishment officer of the MoD, to the effect that disclosure of the document was necessary to discover the source of the leak, established that disclosure was necessary in the interests of national security. This was further supported by the affidavit evidence of the editor of *The Guardian* and, for the Law Lords, the notorious events concerning Sarah Tisdall, who pleaded guilty to a charge under s. 2 of the Official Secrets Act (OSA) 1911, and of which judicial notice could be taken. Taken together, these factors *just about* established the case for the Crown. As Lord Diplock noted, however, there was evidence in existence *at the time the affidavit from the principal establishment officer was presented to the High Court* that would have put beyond all doubt that it was necessary to establish the identity of the leaker. Two Law Lords, and the judge who heard the application for the order of disclosure, did not think that the Crown had made out their case at the time of the application under s. 10. The two dissenting Law Lords did not think that it was permissible to take judicial notice of events subsequent to the application. It is not unknown for judges to give instruction to officials on how they *should have* drafted affidavits to put forward a more plausible case in order to avoid such difficulties in the future. This Lord Diplock obligingly provided,[100] as well as applying 'the necessary mental gymnastics' in order to feel satisfied that the interests of national security required the release of the document to establish the identity of the source. 'The evidence', said Lord Fraser to the contrary, 'may have caused a little political embarrassment to the Government', but it contained nothing of military value. 'Without more information than he had, the judge could not properly have been satisfied that disclosure' by *The Guardian* was 'necessary' – not necessary and expedient, but necessary in the interests of national security. Any other interpretation, agreed Lord Scarman, would not have done justice to the rule, which in its structure 'bears a striking resemblance' to the way

---

[98] Cf. Lord Scarman, below. See *X Ltd v Morgan Grampian (Publishers) Ltd* [1990] 2 All ER 1, HL, where the Law Lords held that a balancing of interests will take place even after it is established that revelation is necessary.

[99] A junior clerk in the registry of the private office of the Foreign Secretary.

[100] See pp. 608 h–j and 610 g–h.

in which the articles of the European Convention are drafted, viz. 'a general rule subject to carefully drawn and limited exceptions which are required to be established, in case of dispute, to the satisfaction of the European Court of Human Rights ... It is no part of the judge's function to use his common sense in an attempt to fill a gap which can be filled only by evidence.'[101] On the contrary, Lord Bridge's common sense dictated, 'it is surely unthinkable that the Government should have embarked on the present litigation without taking the elementary step ... of an internal interview' to establish the identity of the 'leaker'. Lord Bridge could infer from his involvement in governmental responsibilities[102] that a lack of urgency in the government's demand for the document[103] was not due to sloth on its part. Judicial notice could be taken of the fact 'that important decisions in Government are rarely taken without time-consuming consultation and deliberation'.[104]

On one point, however, the Law Lords rejected the Crown's arguments, accepted by the judge at first instance and the Court of Appeal by majority, that its right of property in the documents and information thereon defeated, *ipso facto*, the immunity from disclosure under s. 10. The Crown could not use its proprietorial claim to get access to information from the document, thereby allowing it to pursue its contractual, tortious or equitable claims against the 'leaker' in order to pursue the 'interests of justice':

> Having regard to the emphatic terms in which s. 10 of the 1981 Act is cast, I have not found it possible to envisage any case that might occur in real life, in which, since the passing of the Act, it would be necessary *in the interests of justice* to order delivery up of the document .... [on a proprietal basis alone].[105]

In more fundamental terms, Lord Scarman declared:

> [Since] it is in the 'interests of all of us that we should have a truly effective press' (per Griffiths LJ) rights of property have to yield pride of place to the national interest which Parliament must have had in mind when enacting the section.

In subsequent case law the Court of Appeal and the House of Lords have ruled that 'in the interests of justice' meant nothing more august than vindicating a right by pursuing an action[106] opening up the possibility of the section being used to assist a plaintiff in a breach of confidence action. This occurred in a case concerning a journalist named Goodwin who had obtained confidential information about the financial position of an engineering company and who sought the comments of the company for its views. It responded by obtaining

---

[101] The evidence of dangers to the security system, he believed, was 'meagre and full of omissions'.

[102] As chairman of the Security Commission?

[103] The story was published on 31 October; proceedings were commenced on 22 November.

[104] Lord Bridge had been responsible for review of telephone taps; see *The Guardian*, 18 March 1986.

[105] Emphasis added; see below. Note, *X v Y* [1988] 2 All ER 648 and s. 8(4)–(5) OSA 1989.

[106] *X Ltd v Morgan Grampian (Publishers) Ltd*, note 98 above. On website service providers, see *Totalise plc v Motley Food Ltd* [2001] NLJR 644.

a breach-of-confidence injunction against Goodwin and by seeking an order for the disclosure of his source. This would clash with a journalist's first commandment – 'Do not reveal your sources'. Both the Code of Practice of the Press Complaints Commission and the Code of Conduct of the NUJ state the moral obligation of a journalist to protect sources. The company convinced the courts that the information must have come from a stolen copy of a company document and it needed the source's identity to obtain further protective injunctions and to trace the thief and take appropriate action. The source had been involved in a serious breach of confidentiality, the Law Lords believed, and the interests of justice outweighed the statutory protection. There had been no 'iniquity' on the part of the company and there was no great PI value in the information and the company could suffer serious damage if unable to identify who had passed secrets to the press. The journalist was subsequently fined £5,000 for failing to obey a court order.[107]

Although the Law Lords appeared to conduct some sort of balancing exercise, this is a worrying precedent for independent and investigatory journalism because it does seem to place a premium on proprietorial rights over the ethical considerations of a journalist. Robertson and Nicol have suggested that a possible amendment might restrict the exception to the 'interests of criminal law'. In 1994, the European Commission of Human Rights ruled by eleven votes to six that the court order in *Goodwin's* case was in breach of the Art. 10 ECHR. The government has suggested that a possible solution before the European Court of Justice (ECJ) would be to argue that journalists should offer sources a warning before receiving information: 'I must warn you that anything you say or give' etc.[108] Subsequently, the Commission's view of *Goodwin's* case was upheld by the ECtHR by an 11–7 judgment. The rulings of the English courts were not *necessary* in a democratic society in the interests of justice – they were disproportionate.[109] This judgment appeared to place serious question marks over s. 10 of the CCA. Goodwin was awarded legal costs and expenses but received no compensation. His story never ran. Under the HRA s. 2(1), the ECtHR judgment will now have to be taken into account by domestic courts.[110] The Court emphasised that protection of journalists' sources was vital for press freedom. The absence of such protection would have a 'chilling' effect on sources and would undermine the 'vital public watchdog role of the press'. Their ability to provide accurate and reliable information may be adversely affected.[111] The ECtHR adopted a similar line in defence of press freedom in hearing the case of a reporter who had written stories about irregularities in EC institutions on the

---

[107] He was lucky not to have been imprisoned.

[108] See *Broadmoor Hospital v Hyde* (1994) The Times, 18 March: information of no great importance and no attempt internally to establish the identity of a 'leaker'; disclosure not ordered.

[109] *Goodwin v UK* (1996) 22 EHRR 123, ECtHR.

[110] As will the jurisprudence of the Commission and Council of Ministers.

[111] *Ibid.*, at para. 39.

basis of leaks allegedly from OLAF, the anti-corruption office of the Union. His action before the CFI claimed that OLAF's action to uncover the leak resulted in an invasion of his privacy. His application before the ECtHR was successful on the grounds that the Belgian authorities (acting on a complaint from OLAF) had breached his Art. 10 rights by searching his home to attempt to identify his source thereby interfering with the 'right to information'. The reasons offered by Belgium were not sufficient to interfere with the right.[112]

The decision in *Goodwin* was followed by the Court of Appeal's judgment in *Camelot*[113] where the national-lottery operator wished to obtain disclosure orders to establish the identity of an employee who had disclosed documents to a journalist. Fearing, the plaintiff claimed, that future leaks could involve the disclosure of the identity of a lottery winner, the court awarded the orders for disclosure as there was no overriding PI involved in exposing a 'spin on accounts'. A source, Schiemann LJ believed, would always have to run a risk in disclosure. The Court of Appeal subsequently came down on the side of the journalist and the PI in protecting the confidentiality of his sources and these outweighed any legal professional privilege that might apply. The case involved the leak of a barrister's draft opinion. The chambers had not assisted themselves in that they had failed to conduct an internal inquiry to try and establish the identity of the leaker. Legal privilege did not outweigh the interest in protecting the source on the facts of the case.[114]

Where a case has no merit, and confidential information about a patient is leaked in unjustifiable circumstances, the House of Lords has been swift to order disclosure of the source. Any 'chilling effect' was worthwhile, the court believed, in a case concerning Ashdown Security Hospital.[115] The protection of confidential patient information was 'vital' and the case was 'exceptional'. It concerned allegations of irregularities in the Moors murderer Ian Brady's medical treatment. The Court of Appeal subsequently refused a further order forcing the disclosure of Ackroyd's (the journalist) source on the grounds that there was a real prospect of it being established at trial that the confidentiality of maintaining medical confidentiality did not override the PI in non-disclosure of a journalist's source.[116] When the case was heard on the substantive issue the impact of the HRA and the human rights context was fully felt.[117] The High Court refused to order the journalist to disclose his leak. There was no pressing need to reveal the identity of the leak although any motive of leaking in the PI was misguided. Seven years had passed between the leak in question and the

---

[112] Case T-193/04 *Tillack v Commission* (4 October 2006) and *Tillack v Belgium* App. No. 20477/05 (27 November 2007). The European Ombudsman investigated a complaint by Tillack and found no basis for the allegations made by OLAF and errors on the part of OLAF: Complaint 2485/2004/GG May 2005.

[113] [1998] 1 All ER 251; see, however, *Saunders v Punch Ltd* [1998] 1 All ER 234, ChD.

[114] *John v Express Newspapers plc* [2000] 3 All ER 257.

[115] *Ashdown Security Hospital v MGN Ltd* [2002] 4 All ER 193 (HL).

[116] *Mersey Care NHS Trust v Ackroyd* [2003] All ER (D) 235.

[117] *Mersey Care NHS Trust v Ackroyd* [2006] EWHC 107 (QBD).

judgment. Disclosure would not be proportionate to the basic PI in maintaining freedom of the press. The case was upheld on appeal.[118]

The House of Lords has ruled that prevention of crime meant crime in general, not only a specific crime, in denying a journalist the immunity.[119] Other case law has established that 'in order to prevent crime' meant that a crime had to be possible or be likely to be committed and not a breach of confidentiality.[120] Doctors and journalists have codes of practice protecting the identity of confidential information and sources of information in the latter case and the problem is not going to disappear.[121]

Wide powers to demand information exist under the Police and Criminal Evidence 1984 and under the Terrorism Act 2000. Provisions under earlier terrorism legislation featured in a sensational case involving a Channel Four documentary broadcast alleging large-scale collusion and conspiracy between members of the Royal Ulster Constabulary and loyalist terrorist groups in Northern Ireland resulting in over twenty murders and numerous conspiracies to murder. When the journalists refused to hand over material under a court order because it would reveal a source who had been promised anonymity and the identity of a junior researcher whose life would be endangered, contempt proceedings were initiated. The programme could easily be labelled as unreliable because it relied heavily on the evidence of one uncorroborated and unidentified witness, but it was in the best tradition of investigative journalism. The Divisional Court achieved a compromise of sorts because it recognised the 'moral stance' of the journalists impelling them not to reveal identities and the court did not impose sequestration orders as sought by the Attorney General which would have bankrupted the respondents, but imposed a fine of £75,000. In future, however, companies would not be treated so leniently.[122] The Stevens Inquiry subsequently found widespread collusion between paramilitaries in Northern Ireland and the security services. In the inquiry into the Bloody Sunday shootings by paratroopers in 1972 conducted by Lord Philips, journalists refused to reveal sources. Lord Philips decided that punishment would not be constructive.[123]

Now we can look at the role of the courts in insisting upon if not complete openness then at least the provision of information. Our first consideration returns to the discussion of national security.

National security

There is nothing new about litigation concerning national security in English law. In 1637 the famous case of *Ship Money* heard argument about the Crown's

---

[118] [2007] EWCA Civ 101.   [119] *Re an Inquiry etc.* [1988] 1 All ER 203 (HL).
[120] *X v Y*, note 105 above.
[121] See Public Interest Disclosure Act 1998, s. 43G and stringent conditions for protection of disclosures to the media.
[122] *DPP v Channel Four Television Co. Ltd* [1993] 2 All ER 517; cost to company £750,000.
[123] www.bloody-sunday-inquiry/

prerogative powers to raise taxes in the defence of the realm.[124] We shall see that in *Rehman* (see p. 423 below) the terrorist threat has given an international dimension to national security – undermining the security of countries far away may undermine our national security.

For years before the *Zamora* case[125] and for years afterwards courts accepted unquestionably the sentiments of Lord Parker that:

> Those who are responsible for the national security must be the sole judge of what the national security requires. It would be obviously undesirable that such matters should be made the subject of evidence in a court of law or otherwise discussed in public.

However, there should be evidence of national security. More recently, in a case involving the Terrorism Act 2000 and the search and seizure powers under ss. 44–7, Lord Bingham said:

> In the result, therefore, the House has before it what appear to be considered and informed evaluations of the terrorist threat on one side (based on secret security intelligence) and effectively nothing save a measure of scepticism on the other. There is no basis on which the [Crown's] evidence can be rejected.[126]

As evidenced by *Chandler v DPP*, although the courts might not associate ineluctably the interests of the state with the interests of the government of the day,[127] on national-security matters they were ready to defer to the judgment of the Crown and would not allow evidence on national security from its witness to be shaken in cross-examination. In the *Hosenball* litigation, deportation of an American citizen in the interests of national security precluded the usual tenets of fair play and knowing the details of the case that one's accusers were making. 'In national security cases,' declared Lord Denning, 'even natural justice must take a back seat.'[128] National security 'is par excellence a non-justiciable question', said Lord Diplock. National security is a question of fact, said Lord Hoffmann more recently. 'In the interests of national security' is a question of judgement, he continued, ill-suited to the judicial branch as we shall see. These are familiar fare to the public lawyer, given added interest by judicial decisions in which the national-security blanket has been spread over executive action in the war on terror.

The first such judicial decision that attracts our attention concerned the controversy surrounding events at General Communications Headquarters (GCHQ). The government in January 1984 announced that it was banning

---

[124] *R v Hampden* (1637) 3 State Trials 825.   [125] [1916] 2 AC 77.

[126] *R (Gillan) v Met. Police Com'r* [2006] UKHL 12.

[127] Cf. McCowan J in *R v Ponting* [1985] Crim LR 318, and ch. 3 above, p. 87 *et seq.*

[128] *R v Secretary of State for the Home Department, ex p. Hosenball* [1977] 3 All ER 452; the 'Three Advisers' who were resorted to have now given way to procedures under the Special Immigration Appeals Commission Act 1997: see p. 430 below. Sedley J had ruled that in refusing admission of an alien to the UK on grounds that presence was 'not conducive to the public good' the applicant must be given the opportunity to make representations: *R v Secretary of State for the Home Department, ex p. Moon* [1996] COD 54.

trade union membership among civil servants at GCHQ in Cheltenham.[129] There had been minor disruptions through industrial action at GCHQ, the last occasion being in 1981, and for some years the government had been conscious of the sensitivity of serious disruption in the information-gathering responsibilities of GCHQ. The government was studying the possibility of lie detectors (polygraph security screening) on the staff at GCHQ, and the Cabinet Secretary told union leaders, prior to the government's announcement about banning unions, that there would be further consultation after the results of pilot schemes were known. In the event, the right of the GCHQ civil servants to belong to a trade union was taken away without any consultation with their representatives (the right was restored in 1997). On the government side it was claimed that what was done was performed on the grounds of national security. A contrary belief is that the prime minister wished to implement lie detectors without any objection from unions and that the UK Government had acted under pressure from the US Government. The claim of a threat to national security was not made in substance at the hearing in the High Court when the Council of Civil Service Unions challenged the legality of the government's action. It was argued on the government's behalf that consultation upon matters affecting national security would be so circumscribed as to be practically useless. Glidewell J rejected this, holding that the decision was one that should be taken fairly, and that the failure to consult rendered it unfair and a denial of a legitimate expectation of consultation because of the serious implications involved in depriving an individual of union membership.[130] The Court of Appeal accepted the government's claim that consultation *could have* interfered with the interests of national security, and so did the House of Lords,[131] holding that, on the facts, consultation was not necessary as a matter of law.

In the House of Lords much attention was given to the role of the courts in assessing claims involving the invocation of national security. Courts, the Law Lords unanimously believed, were ill-suited to assess the national-security requirements of state affairs. However, if action affecting individual rights, interests or legitimate expectations were based upon national security, whether in consequence of a statutory or prerogative power, the courts would look for evidence to support a claim that the action was, as in the instant case, for the purpose of avoiding disruption injurious to the national security. The court must act on evidence, said Lord Scarman. 'Evidence', reiterated Lord Roskill, 'and not mere assertion must be forthcoming.'

---

[129] For GCHQ, see ch. 2, p. 36 *et seq*. The decision was not announced to the Cabinet.

[130] [1984] IRLR 309.

[131] *Council of Civil Service Unions v Minister for the Civil Service* [1984] 3 All ER 935, HL. To the limited extent that courts require some evidence of possible injury to national security when action affects individual rights, they have accepted that such issues are justiciable, i.e. susceptible to the judicial process. Usually such topics are catered for and allocated by a constitution: *Baker v Carr* 369 US 186 (1962) esp. Brennan J. See also L. Lustgarten and I. Leigh, *In from the Cold* (1994), ch. 12.

The evidence relied upon was an affidavit of Sir Robert Armstrong, the Cabinet Secretary, sworn on 6 April 1984. His affidavit recorded the apprehension that consultation would have caused disruption. Two months prior to this, the Foreign Secretary, in giving evidence to the Commons Foreign Affairs Select Committee, did not mention this matter, but spoke of the necessity of keeping the activities of GCHQ out of the public eye.[132] Nor was the matter mentioned in legal argument at first instance before Glidewell J. It may be, as Griffith has suggested, that the real reason for banning union membership without warning was one of political expediency and not national security.[133] Certainly, the courts accepted without question the affidavit evidence. It was not tested; it was not probed; it was not examined. The case was an application for judicial review, and this procedure is not meant to be a process for clarifying disputes of fact by allowing cross-examination of the witnesses – the prime minister, the Foreign Secretary, the Secretary to the Cabinet – nor allowing frequent applications for discovery of documents.[134] The courts wanted evidence of a national security risk; the evidence had to be more than a bare assertion; but the court was not prepared to weigh it. Some evidence was given, and in the circumstances it would take a brave person to predict that disruption injurious to national security would not have occurred had the unions been forewarned.[135] One may suspect the duplicity of the government, but, as our law stands, it would be difficult to come to a conclusion other than that decided if one were put into a neutral seat and asked whether was there a possibility of such disruption, and if so would it be likely to affect adversely national security? The criticism of the GCHQ decision was directed at the manner in which courts are structured in Britain to avoid asking the most pressing questions in cases relating to national security. Should we require evidence of a clear and present danger to national security? The argument also concerns the issue of whether we need to give fuller definition to what the 'national security' and the interests of national security actually are and what their proof require (see chapter 2, p. 34).

Since GCHQ, the strongest statements from the courts on the non-justiciability of claims to be acting in the interest of national security came in *Rehman*.[136] The SIAC had found that the Secretary of State did not have sufficient evidence to form a judgement that Rehman's deportation in the interests of national security had been made out to a high civil balance of probabilities. Rehman was a Pakistani national who was resident in the UK. The Security Service alleged he had been involved in directing terrorist activities in the Indian subcontinent and training young people in England in military activities. The opinions emphasised that although the SIAC had powers of review, due weight had to be given to the assessment and conclusions of the Secretary of State in

---

[132] See J. A. G. Griffith (1985) Public Law 564.   [133] *Ibid.*

[134] See below for discovery (now disclosure), p. 450 *et seq.*

[135] The European Commission of Human Rights rejected as inadmissible an application from the union under Art. 11(2): App. No. 11603/85, Decision 20 January 1987.

[136] [2001] UKHL 47

the light of his responsibilities, the means at his disposal of being informed, and his understanding, of the problems. He was in the best position to judge what national security required.[137] For Lord Hoffmann, our constitution requires that issues of national security are issues of judgement and policy for the executive branch of the state and not for judicial decision. A court should not therefore differ from the opinion of the Secretary of State on such a matter provided his opinion is based on evidence:[138]

> This brings me to the limitations inherent in the appellate process. First, the Commission is not the primary decisionmaker. Not only is the decision entrusted to the Home Secretary but he also has the advantage of a wide range of advice from people with day-to-day involvement in security matters which the Commission, despite its specialist membership, cannot match. Secondly . . . the question at issue in this case does not involve a yes or no answer as to whether it is more likely than not that someone has done something but an evaluation of risk. In such questions an appellate body traditionally allows a considerable margin to the primary decision-maker. Even if the appellate body prefers a different view, it should not ordinarily interfere with a case in which it considers that the view of the Home Secretary is one which could reasonably be entertained. Such restraint may not be necessary in relation to every issue which the Commission has to decide. As I have mentioned, the approach to whether the rights of an appellant under article 3 are likely to be infringed may be very different. But I think it is required in relation to the question of whether a deportation is in the interests of national security. [Para. 57]

Hoffmann emphasised that the need for restraint was not based upon any limit to the Commission's appellate jurisdiction. The wide nature of that jurisdiction was demonstrated by the express power to reverse the exercise of a discretion. 'The need for restraint flows from a common-sense recognition of the nature of the issue and the differences in the decision-making processes and responsibilities of the Home Secretary and the Commission' (para. 58).

On other occasions the courts have refused to accept that national security deprives them of jurisdiction but they have been reluctant to do anything that would resemble either a challenge on the merits of a decision made on the grounds of national security or to investigate a procedure leading to a decision concerning national security where the very procedure itself was adopted on grounds of national security. In *ex p. Hodges*, an employee at GCHQ had his positive-vetting security clearance withdrawn when he revealed to his supervisors that he was a sexually active homosexual. He had volunteered full details of his activities. So while the courts would not contest the merits of the decision itself they would investigate the question of his being denied access to the notes of interviews, although his challenge here was unsuccessful.[139] *R v Ministry of*

---

[137] See Lord Slynn of Hadley at para. 26 and Lord Steyn at paras. 28 and 31.

[138] See paras. 50–4.

[139] *R v Director of GCHQ, ex p. Hodges* (1988) The Times, 26 July; see *R v Secretary of State for the Home Department, ex p. Ruddock* [1987] 2 All ER 518.

Defence, ex p. Smith[140] held that exercise of the prerogative power in defence of the realm was justiciable in all but the rarest of cases, i.e. those involving a clear issue of national security where in addition, *per* Simon Brown LJ, the court lacked expertise or material for a judgment. In this case the court could do nothing to overrule a ban employing homosexuals in the UK armed forces. *Smith* took his case to the ECtHR in Strasbourg and was successful in claiming a breach of Art. 8.[141] The scrutiny before the domestic courts was not 'anxious enough'. The domestic threshold of judicial review had been set too high and did not provide a sufficient safeguard. However, even in national-security cases, a failure to follow a fair procedure may be upbraided by the courts.

The courts have ruled that a bare assertion of national security cannot prevent the courts investigating a plea of unlawful telephone tapping (prior to legislation on interception).[142] For a court to remain silent 'would be to say that the court should never inquire into a complaint against a minister if he says his policy is to maintain silence in the interests of national security'.[143] But what sort of answers or reasons do they insist upon to justify the exercise of power? In *Cheblak*[144] the Court of Appeal virtually abandoned all but the most exiguous forms of controlling the Home Secretary's power of deportation on the grounds of national security and assumed that the latter had acted in good faith unless the contrary were proved and, as he was under no duty to give any reason other than deportation was on the grounds of national security, this was an impossible task. In fact, this area generally is one where courts in other countries are reluctant to tread.[145] But Cheblak was the nadir of judicial abnegation and subsequent rulings from the ECtHR and the incorporation of the HRA have introduced some procedural constraints over executive action.

The procedures involved in the *Chahal* case, where Chahal was detained subject to decisions on his status as an asylum seeker whose presence was not deemed conducive to the public good, were referred to in chapter 2 (p. 46 *et seq.*). Under the relevant provisions of the Geneva Convention, a refugee requesting asylum could be deported where their presence was a danger to the security of the host nation. The Home Secretary decided Chahal was such a danger. The court could not review the evidence on which the Home Secretary based his decision although it was satisfied that he had balanced the welfare of the refugee and national security. Chahal successfully applied to the ECtHR[146] which established breaches of Arts. 3 (degrading and inhuman treatment), 5(4) (detention without judicial authorisation) and 13 (lack of an effective remedy

---

[140] [1995] 4 All ER 427: On appeal [1996] 1 All ER 257.

[141] *Smith and Grady v UK* (1999) IRLR 734.

[142] *R v Secretary of State for the Home Department, ex p. Ruddock,* note 39 above; see I. Leigh (1987) Public Law 12.

[143] Any change in guidelines on tapping should have been publicised, Taylor J believed.

[144] [1991] 2 All ER 319.

[145] See L. Lustgarten and I. Leigh and their discussion of *Australian Communist Party v Commonwealth* (1951) 83 CLR 1.

[146] *Chahal v UK* (1996) 23 EHRR 413.

in relation to Art. 30) because the procedures involved in the UK only allowed an exiguous form of review of such an important matter and the High Court had refused relief.[147] In *Chahal*, the ECtHR stated that national authorities cannot be free from 'effective control by the domestic courts whenever they choose to assert that national security and terrorism are involved.' But the Court nonetheless appreciated that some evidence may have to be withheld from the claimant on PI grounds and relied heavily of procedures adopted in Canada to deal with evidence against suspected terrorists. These influenced the SIAC procedures and I examine them below.[148]

Once again, the HRA will be felt even in these sensitive areas. Where fundamental human rights are involved, the ECtHR has expected a more probing procedure to test the case and this has had its impact on national courts. They engage in 'anxious scrutiny review' and have to set aside the inherent limitations of judicial review as a remedy in human rights cases. The ECtHR has held in the past that judicial review in England was an effective remedy under Convention law (Art. 13).[149] But that decision has subsequently been subjected to sustained analysis when judicial review was seen as an inadequate remedy for purposes of Convention law (Art. 6) where bias was alleged.[150] The basic approach today is that Art. 13 will be breached where there is not an independent and effective review of questions of primary fact and, although legitimate grounds may exist for not disclosing evidence, there must be adequate safeguards.[151] Judicial review has had to develop to meet these criticisms where human rights are involved so that a more probing scrutiny takes place. Proportionality will be used to examine the factors engaged in a decision. As Lord Steyn said, the finding by the ECtHR in *Smith and Grady* – that the claims of breach of Art. 8 were justified – showed that the English courts had not been anxious enough in their examination of the exercise of the power to ban them from the armed forces.[152] But in some cases, scrutiny may be anxious but it is conducted with essential evidence missing, or by secret procedures.

Binyam Mohamed[153] concerned a non-national British resident, at the time in Guantánamo Bay, who had allegedly been tortured overseas with the involvement of British intelligence officers. The Secretary of State accepted there was an 'arguable case of torture' on behalf of the applicant (para. 2). Through

---

[147] *R v Secretary of State for the Home Department, ex p. Chahal* [1995] 1 All ER 658. See also *Tsfayo v UK* (2007) HLR 19 for criticism of the inadequacies of English judicial review in safeguarding ECHR rights and Art. 6 ECHR.

[148] See also *Tinnelly & Son Ltd v UK*, ch. 2 above, p. 46.

[149] Cf. *Vilvarajah v UK* (1991) 14 EHRR 248. Art 13 is concerned with the provision of an effective remedy.

[150] *Kingsley v UK* (2001) The Times, 9 January (ECtHR) App 35605/97. See also *Tsfayo v UK*, note 147 above.

[151] *Chahal v UK* (1996) 23 EHRR 413; see *Smith v UK* (1999) 29 EHRR 493.

[152] *R (Daly) v Secretary of State for the Home Department* [2001] 3 All ER 433 (HL).

[153] *R (Binyam Mohamed) v SoS FA* [2009] EWHC 152 (Admin).

proceedings in the English High Court Mohamed sought disclosure of forty-two secret files to assist his case against charges before a Military Commission at Guantánamo Bay.[154] This led to various hearings in which the files were ordered to be disclosed to his lawyers subject to any PII plea by the Crown.[155] The relevant judgment of the court contained seven paragraphs that related to *in camera* proceedings. These paragraphs provided a summary of reports by the US Government to the Security Service and the Secret Intelligence Service (SIS) on the 'circumstances of BM's incommunicado and unlawful detention in Pakistan and of the treatment accorded to him by or on behalf of the United States Government'. The summary was highly material to Mohamed's allegation that he had been subjected to torture and cruel, inhuman or degrading treatment and to the commission of criminal offences referred to in para. 77 of the first judgment on the case. Special advocates (below) represented him in the absence of his legal advisers. These paragraphs formed part of a secret annex to the judgment. The Foreign Secretary's certificates to the court made clear that if the redacted paragraphs were made public the US Government would re-evaluate its intelligence-sharing relationship with the UK with the real risk that it would reduce the intelligence provided. The Foreign Secretary's judgement was that the US Government might carry that threat out, causing serious prejudice to the national security of the UK.

The court heard evidence from Witness B, an officer of the Security Service, MI5, both in private and *in camera*.[156] Some proceedings in private were conducted before counsel and lawyers for Mohamed. Some were not. The court was asked to make the transcript of the examination in private (as distinct from the examination *in camera*) available to the media and to the public. This was granted unopposed. The court, in its judgment and by letter to the Press Association dated 7 November 2008, invited representations from the media on questions raised by the case.

> We did so in the light of the fact that the media had had no opportunity to make representations on an issue of such importance to them, as the argument had taken place in camera, and it would not be just to arrive at a decision on keeping the redacted paragraphs out of the public domain without hearing from them.[157] As the Editor of the Law Reports has pointed out in his submissions to us, there has been a marked increase in the number of hearings held in secret, with the court being closed to law reporters and the press; consequently they have often been denied the opportunity of making submissions.

---

[154] Under principles established in *Norwich Pharmacol* [1974] AC 133.

[155] [2008] EWHC 2048 (Admin); [2008] EWHC 2100 (Admin); [2008] EWHC 2519 (Admin).

[156] The reasons for the evidence being given in private were explained at para. 53 of the first judgment ([2008] EWHC 2048 Admin).

[157] Cf. the practice of hearing submissions from the media in relation to reporting restrictions. See *C v CPS* [2008] EWHC 854 (Admin), at para. 4; the judgment of Brooke LJ in *Ex p. Guardian Newspapers* [1999] 1 WLR 2130, at 2147H; and r. 16 of the Criminal Procedure Rules.

We understand from the Editor of the Law Reports that it was the practice some time ago to allow law reporters to listen to argument in camera so that they might produce a record of the argument addressed to the court. A record of the argument forms an important part of the report of each case reported in the Law Reports. Nowadays, given the issues in many cases heard in camera, attendance of a law reporter is no longer possible, unless that reporter had security clearance. However it is important that the argument be recorded and in this case it is particularly important that the argument made by the Special Advocates be made public in view of its novelty and significance. We will therefore summarise it without referring to the facts and matters set out in the redacted paragraphs and closed evidence and judgment. [Para. 26]

Special counsel argued that there is no absolute bar to the use of PII certificates (below) in cases involving officials in serious crime. In other words, nothing supported a departure from a balancing test in other common law jurisdictions where such issues of PII arise: the PI in secrecy and the PI in justice being done. There was no support in international law for such an exclusion. The court believed that openness should apply to the allegations amounting to serious breaches of the rule of law. 'It is the upholding of the rule of law in this way that is a factor of the greatest PI in this case, given the allegations against officials of the United States Government and the role of officials of the Government of the United Kingdom in facilitating what is alleged' (para. 41).

Second, facts relating to issues of public interest which would not otherwise emerge are brought into the public domain. The public sittings of the courts and their public decisions are one of the means through which, in a democratic society information enters into the public domain. Such information can be important in a democracy as forming the basis of free speech that promotes political debate or as a means by which the government can be held to account. [Para. 42]

Publicity would allow for public debate helping to end uninformed speculation. It would allow for discussion of US Government reports on detainees and whether they were treated humanely and in accordance with international law. It would allow for discussion of information provided to the UK Government by the US Government in 2002 and 'what was actually known about such techniques by officials of MI5 at the time'. There was emphatic support for the freedom of the press 'the watchdog of the public' as described by Lord Steyn and as illustrated in *Spycatcher*.[158] 'The requirements of open justice, the rule of law, free speech and democratic accountability demonstrate the very considerable interests in making the redacted paragraphs public' (para. 54). Special advocates argued the case vigorously against the UK Government that despite real threats from the US, the passages should be made public. The position of the US, they argued, was 'irrational and unreasonable', merely wishing to avoid political

---

[158] *AG v Guardian Newspapers* [1990] 1 AC 109, at 183, and *Observer and Guardian v UK* [1991] ECHR 1385, at para. 13. Lord Steyn in *Re S. (A child)* [2005] 1 AC 593, at pp. 602–4; *McCartin, Turkington Breen v Times Newspapers* [2001] 2 AC 277.

embarrassment (para. 76). To publish the passages, which was Mohamed's wish, would vindicate the vital PI in the open administration of justice. However:

> Nor can the principle that there is no confidence in wrongdoing be relevant to the assessment of the likely damage to national security. Nor can we accede to the submission that the Foreign Secretary should resist the threat made. It is both irrelevant and unrealistic. It lies solely within the power of the United States to decide whether to share with the United Kingdom intelligence it obtains and it is for the Foreign Secretary under our constitution, not the courts, to determine how to address it. [Para. 76]

So despite the criticism, the court ruled that the judgement of the Foreign Secretary had been made in good faith and was based on evidence that the threat is real; the motives of the US Government were irrelevant. 'It is the actuality of the threat that is alone relevant to national security.' (See now Introduction, p. 6.)

The court noted various alternatives to publication.[159] The Intelligence and Security Committee (ISC) had published two reports on these subjects in March 2005 (Cm. 6469) and July 2007 (Cm. 7171). It was clear that the forty-two documents disclosed as a result of these proceedings were not made available to the ISC. The court found that their reports could not have been made in the terms they were had the ISC possessed the documents. The evidence was that earlier searches had not discovered them. The forty-two documents, Witness B's closed and open evidence and the closed passages in the judgment had been given to the ISC and the prime minister had extended their remit to cover 'particular cases' (see chapter 2, p. 48 *et seq.*). Though important, the ISC cannot publish redacted material by virtue of s. 10 of the Intelligence Services Act. Convention case law established that the state was under a duty to investigate and punish those guilty of breaches of Art. 3.[160] References could be made to the Attorney General – as I write, they have been made but not all are comforted by the independence of that office from government.[161] The court noted that any possible trial would be *in camera.* In *Shayler,* it will be recalled that Lord Bingham also set out the possibility of the director general of MI5 conducting inquiries. These were not deemed appropriate safeguards.

On balance, it was not in the PI to expose the UK to the real risk of a loss of intelligence. As Lord Hope said in *A v Secretary of State,*[162] the first responsibility of government in a democracy is to protect the lives of citizens and it is the court's duty to assist. It is up to the US Government to put the information into the public domain. So judges may be outspoken but in national security they know their place. In *R (Corner House Research) v Director of the Serious*

---

[159] As set out in *R v Shayler* [2002] 2 All ER 477 (HL).
[160] Lord Lester and D. Pannick, *Human Rights Law and Practice* (1999), para. 4.3.17 and *Assenov v Bulgaria* (1999) 28 EHRR 652.
[161] See Home Affairs Committee www.parliament.uk/parliamentary_committees/home_affairs_committee/hacpn090224no28.cfm.
[162] [2004] UKHL 56, para. 99.

Fraud Office[163] it was again emphasised that the duty of decision in relation to national security and foreign relations lay with the executive branch of the state. The highly controversial circumstances of this case concerning the cessation of a prosecution by the director general of the Serious Fraud Office into alleged corruption in arms sales were noted above (see chapter 2, p. 34 and chapter 9, p. 363).

Special Immigration Appeals Commission, control orders and special advocates

The subject of secret trials and non-disclosure to a defendant of evidence to be used against him have been a pre-eminent feature of the proceedings before the SIAC and before courts dealing with 'control orders' to place those suspected of terrorist activities under a form of house arrest. These exclusions are statutory and differ from PII certificates although information is 'closed' on PI grounds.[164]

The SIAC was created by the Special Immigration Appeals Commission Act 1997 in response to the observations in *Chahal* (above). The object of that Act was to provide as effective a remedy as possible for those challenging immigration decisions that involved information which the Secretary of State considered should not be made public because disclosure would be contrary to the PI. The Act has been amended.[165]

Normally, immigration appeals go to the Asylum and Immigration Tribunal (AIT). One ground of appeal is that removal would be incompatible with the appellant's Convention rights. However, appeal is precluded to the AIT where the Secretary of State's decision was taken wholly or partly on grounds of national security or wholly or partly in reliance on information which in the Secretary of State's opinion should not be made public in the interests of national security, the interests of the relationship between the UK and any other country, or otherwise in the PI.

An appeal so precluded is, however, appealable to the SIAC. Grounds of appeal include not only breaches of law but that a discretion should be exercised differently. Schedule 1 to the Act provides for the appointment of members to the SIAC by the Lord Chancellor. The SIAC is deemed to be duly constituted if it consists of three or more members, at least one of whom holds or has held high judicial office, and at least one of whom is or has been a legally qualified member of the AIT. Usually the SIAC sits in a panel of three – and the third member appointed is a person with experience in security matters. This membership has

---

[163] [2008] UKHL 60.

[164] Disclosure may be total (to special counsel) but restricted only to them; in PII disclosure may be limited but not restricted by reference to parties. See also SI 3085/2008 on financial restrictions under the Counter-Terrorism Act 2008.

[165] E.g. Nationality, Immigration and Asylum Act 2002. See SIAC and the Special Advocate, HC 323-I–II (2004–5); Government Reply, Cm. 6596 (2005); SI 2003/1034 for SIAC's rules of procedure; for Canadian practices, see paras. 71–4 of the judgment of McLachlin CJ in *Charkaoui v Minister of Citizenship and Immigration* [2007] SCC 9. See D. Dyzenhaus (ed.), *The Unity of Public Law* (2004).

been commended by senior judges for giving the SIAC a firm basis in relevant expertise.[166]

The Lord Chancellor (Minister of Justice) is given the power to make rules under s. 5 of the 1997 Act. Particularly relevant are:

> (3) Rules under this section may, in particular –
>> (a) make provision enabling proceedings before the Commission to take place without the appellant being given full particulars of the reasons for the decision which is the subject of the appeal,
>> (b) make provision enabling the Commission to hold proceedings in the absence of any person, including the appellant and any legal representative appointed by him,
>> (c) make provision about the functions in proceedings before the Commission of persons appointed under section 6 below, and
>> (d) make provision enabling the Commission to give the appellant a summary of any evidence taken in his absence . . .
>
> . . .
>
> (6) In making rules under this section the Lord Chancellor shall have regard, in particular, to -
>> (a) the need to secure that decisions which are the subject of appeals are properly reviewed, and
>> (b) the need to secure that information is not disclosed contrary to the public interest.

The Special Immigration Appeals Commission (Procedure) Rules 2003 (SI 2003/1034) have been made. These rules have been amended (SI 2007/1285). Rule 4, which was headed 'General duty of Commission', provided as follows:

> 4(1) When exercising its functions, the Commission shall secure that information is not disclosed contrary to the interests of national security, the international relations of the United Kingdom, the detection and prevention of crime, or in any other circumstances where disclosure is likely to harm the public interest.
> (2) Where these Rules require information not to be disclosed contrary to the public interest, that requirement is to be interpreted in accordance with paragraph (1).
> (3) Subject to paragraphs (1) and (2), the Commission must satisfy itself that the material available to it enables it properly to determine proceedings.

Rule 34 provides for the appointment of special advocates. These are security-vetted lawyers. Rule 35 provides for the manner in which the special advocate is to perform his function of representing the interests of an appellant to SIAC. These include cross-examination of witnesses and making submissions to the Commission at any hearings from which the appellant and his representatives are excluded. Rule 36 provides that the special advocate may

---

[166] *RB (Algeria) v Secretary of State for the Home Department* [2009] UKHL 10.

communicate with the appellant or his representative up to the time that he is served with 'closed material' but not thereafter unless authorised so to do by SIAC. 'Closed material' is defined by r. 37(1) to mean material upon which the Secretary of State wishes to rely in any proceedings before the SIAC, but which the Secretary of State objects to disclosing to the appellant or his representative. Such material may only be relied upon if a special advocate has been appointed to represent the appellant's interests (r. 37(2)). If the Secretary of State wishes to object to disclosure to the appellant of any material upon which he proposes to rely ('closed material') he must give notice to the special advocate (r. 37) and, after hearing submissions from the special advocate and the Secretary of State's counsel, the Commission must then decide whether disclosure would be contrary to the PI and, if it is, uphold the objection, or if disclosure is not contrary to the PI, overrule the objection (r. 38). If the objection is upheld, the closed material is put before the tribunal in a private session from which the appellant and his advisers are excluded (r. 43) although the special advocate will be present. When serving closed material upon the special advocate, the Secretary of State must also serve a statement of the material in a form which can be served on the appellant, if and to the extent that it is possible to do so without disclosing information contrary to the PI (r. 37(3)(c)).

If the SIAC overrules the objection, it may direct the Secretary of State to serve on the appellant all or part of the closed material which he has filed with the SIAC but not served on the appellant. In that event, the Secretary of State shall not be required to serve the material if he chooses not to rely upon it in the proceedings.

A wide search is carried out for 'exculpatory material', namely material that will advance the case of an appellant or detract from the case of the Secretary of State. Exculpatory material is disclosed to the appellant save where this would not be in the PI. In that event it is disclosed to the special advocate. Rule 38 applies to such material.

Section 7 of the 1997 Act confers a right of appeal to the Court of Appeal against a final determination of an appeal made by the SIAC in England and Wales 'on any question of law material to that determination'.

In *R (Roberts) v Parole Board*[167] the Law Lords considered the extension of the special advocate procedure to parole hearings for prisoners guilty of the most serious of crimes. Lord Woolf CJ, for the majority approving the extension, said that in cases where special advocates were used the task of the court was to decide, looking at the process as a whole, whether a procedure had been adopted which involved significant injustice. Lord Bingham believed that denying an applicant information not even disclosed in outline to him or his representatives, and which they could not challenge, could not meet the

---

[167] [2005] UKHL 45; [2005] 2 AC 738, para. 83(vii). See *M v Secretary of State for the Home Department* [2004] EWCA Civ 324 on the assistance of special advocates.

fundamental duty of fairness. For Lord Steyn, such a practice was contrary to the rule of law. However, the 'closed procedure' involving special advocates has been extended to claims for damages; it was 'a firmly established principle of our legal system' (*B. Al Rawi v The Security Service* [2009] EWHC 2959(QB)).

Control orders were introduced under the Prevention of Terrorism Act 2005 and replaced the powers of executive detention under the Anti-terrorism, Crime and Security Act 2001 when such powers were ruled a breach of the ECHR by the Law Lords.[168] They basically involve periods of house detention for fixed periods in a day which are continuous as well as other restrictions on movement, contact etc.[169] These procedures (civil not criminal) may also involve the use of a special advocate whose role has been described above. The procedures are contained in sch. 1 to the 2005 Act and in the CPR Pt 76. For present purposes they operate in a very similar fashion to the SIAC procedures. However, the High Court is the body that deals with judicial aspects of the orders because they involve both British nationals and non-nationals, unlike the SIAC. Orders may be of two kinds: derogating (from Art. 5 ECHR made by a judge) or non-derogating (in simple terms made by the Secretary of State and subsequently reviewed by the judge).

The important point to emerge in *MB*[170] was were the procedures in which evidence was not given to the defendant or his lawyers but only to the special advocate in breach of Art. 6? To recall, Art. 6 protects the right of a fair trial before an impartial judge and in open court in the protection of an individual's civil and political rights and criminal charges. Provision is made for exclusion of the press and public on the familiar grounds including national security. The schedule to the 2005 Act (e.g., paras. (2)(b), 4(3)(d)) and Pt 76.2 of the CPR make provision for non-disclosures in the PI and also anonymity of subjects of the orders. As Lord Bingham expressed the point, the case illustrates 'The problem of reconciling an individual defendant's right to a fair trial with such secrecy as is necessary in a democratic society in the interests of national security or the prevention or investigation of crime is inevitably difficult to resolve in a liberal society governed by the rule of law' (para. 25). His conclusion was that a fair procedure consistent with Art. 6 had not been conducted where evidence had been denied. 'The right to a fair hearing is fundamental.' For Baroness Hale, a trial in which evidence had been withheld from parties was not automatically unfair. It depends upon the justification and safeguards:

---

[168] Following the declarations of incompatibility in *A v Secretary of State for the Home Department* [2004] 3 All ER 169 (HL) and subsequently *A v UK* 3455/05 [2009] ECHR 301, note 181 below.

[169] For the relevant ECtHR case law on disclosure to a litigant and Art. 6 ECHR, see Baroness Hale in *Secretary of State for the Home Department v MB* [2007]UKHL 46, at para. 62. See also on control orders: *Secretary of State for the Home Department v JJ* [2007] UKHL 45 and *Secretary of State for the Home Department v E* [2007] UKHL 47.

[170] *Secretary of State for the Home Department v MB* [2007] UKHL 46 and *Secretary of State v AF* [2008] EWCA Civ 1148. See also *A v HM Treasury* [2008] EWCA Civ 1187 and *R (Malik) v Manchester Crown Court* [2008] EWHC 1362.

It would all depend upon the nature of the case; what steps had been taken to explain the detail of the allegations to the controlled person so that he could anticipate what the material in support might be; what steps had been taken to summarise the closed material in support without revealing names, dates or places; the nature and content of the material withheld; how effectively the special advocate had been able to challenge it on behalf of the controlled person; and what difference its disclosure might have made. All of these factors would be relevant to whether the controlled person had been 'given a meaningful opportunity to contest the factual basis' for the order. [Para. 65]

Everyone involved will have to do their best to ensure that the 'principles of judicial inquiry' are complied with to the fullest extent possible. The Secretary of State must give as full as possible an explanation of why she considers that the grounds in section 2(1) are made out. The fuller the explanation given, the fuller the instructions that the special advocates will be able to take from the client before they see the closed material. Both judge and special advocates will have to probe the claim that the closed material should remain closed with great care and considerable scepticism. There is ample evidence from elsewhere of a tendency to over-claim the need for secrecy in terrorism cases: see Serrin Turner and Stephen J Schulhofer, *The Secrecy Problem in Terrorism Trials*, 2005, Brennan Centre for Justice at NYU School of Law. Both judge and special advocates will have stringently to test the material which remains closed. All must be alive to the possibility that material could be redacted or gisted in such a way as to enable the special advocates to seek the client's instructions upon it. All must be alive to the possibility that the special advocates be given leave to ask specific and carefully tailored questions of the client. Although not expressly provided for in CPR r 76.24, the special advocate should be able to call or have called witnesses to rebut the closed material. The nature of the case may be such that the client does not need to know all the details of the evidence in order to make an effective challenge. [Para. 66]

If the judge has no effective option but to confirm an order when crucial evidence has been withheld that would amount to a breach of Art. 6. The solution which the majority adopted was to read para. 4(3)(d) of the schedule to the 2005 Act, and to give it effect 'except where to do so would be incompatible with the right of the controlled person to a fair trial'. This would then bring into play the equivalent of CPR r. 76.29(7). The Secretary of State can serve the closed material. When pushed, authorities often become more flexible. He cannot be required to serve it. 'But if the court considers that the material might be of assistance to the controlled person in relation to a matter under consideration, it may direct that the matter be withdrawn from consideration by the court. If the Secretary of State proceeds with his order it will be quashed if the material is crucial to his decision.' This solution is Convention-compliant, requires no derogation and still allows informer and infiltrator evidence and avoids reliance upon torture evidence, which, although inadmissible in UK courts and tribunals, places the burden upon the controllee to establish that torture has been used. Her belief was that special advocates are not in themselves always a solution.

A different approach characterised the House of Lords in *RB* where conjoined appeals concerned questions of deportation of aliens on the grounds of national security.[171] It was v not a control-order case (see Lord Phillips in *RB* at paras. 94–7). The House accepted that deportation does not involve Art. 6 rights.[172] Article 13 requires an effective remedy to protect Convention rights and this, it is submitted, would involve common-law fairness. Control orders involved Art. 6 rights and, potentially, Arts. 8 and 5 rights – the latter involving the right not to be detained except after judicial process. The applicants in *RB* were not detained but on bail and so Art. 5 was not involved. Proceedings had gone before the SIAC under the SIAC Act (above). The complaints alleged that they were to be deported to countries where they were either likely to be tortured and thereby breaching Art. 3 or they faced the prospect of trials in a country where evidence obtained by torture would be led thereby breaching Art. 6. The basic conclusion of the judgments was that the SIAC is the guardian of primary fact and findings of fact could not be interfered with by the Court of Appeal in the absence of an error of law. The appeal to the latter on a point of law was similar to a traditional judicial review on the basis of *Wednesbury* unreasonableness, illegality or procedural impropriety. Although proportionality was accepted as a principle of law, it is quite clear it had no place in the appeal but it would feature in the SIAC's considerations on appeal from the Home Secretary. Basically, the SIAC satisfied the requirements of effective legal protection of Convention rights. The fact that an additional appeal had been provided by Parliament was neither here nor there, although the SIAC must act fairly. Otherwise facts were not to be reassessed on appeal. The SIAC resolved the primary facts and conducted painstaking procedures; its judgment in one case was 136 pages and hearings took place over five days. Their examination of all materials was exhaustive, the Law Lords held. These included memoranda of understanding between the relevant prime ministers and heads of state assuring the UK that the appellants would not be tortured were the appellants to be returned to the respective countries. There was no independent monitoring of these.[173] Closed evidence had been resorted to and involved these communications. The full detail of the assurances was not disclosed but the parts relied on by the UK Government were disclosed to the appellants. This evidence did not concern national security but diplomatic and international relations. Arguments that

---

[171] *RB (Algeria) etc. v Secretary of State for the Home Department* [2009] UKHL 10.

[172] Lord Hoffmann in *RB*, at para. 172, citing *Maaouia v France* 33 EHRR 1037, Lord Hope at para. 222 and Lord Brown at para. 255. Lord Phillips, at para. 88, accepted this but suggested the level of procedural protection would be the same.

[173] Anthony Lester QC wrote in *The Guardian*, 20 February 2009 that the UK Government had made an agreement with a human rights centre to carry out the monitoring but the Law Lords said there were reservations on Jordan's part because of sensitivity about its word being doubted. There was no independent monitoring of the prisoners in Algeria. In *AS and DD v Secretary of State for the Home Department* [2008] EWCA Civ 289, the SIAC ruled that a MoA with Libya offered no sufficient guarantee that the claimants would not be tortured. Lord Steyn (2009) Public Law 228.

the vires for the rules of procedure only covered national security grounds were not accepted. The SIAC had conducted hearings in a fair manner and its use of closed material was lawful. The Law Lords only referred to the evidence in the open case in making their judgments – they refused to view the closed material. There was no need to apply the safety provisions as explained in *MB*. To repeat, Art. 6 was not directly engaged in the procedure to deport in *RB*. It arose consequentially.

In the case of the evidence in Jordan being obtained through torture, the law in Jordan allowed a defendant to challenge evidence on such grounds but the onus was on the defendant to prove as much. This was consistent with the judgments in *A v Secretary of State* where torture evidence was ruled inadmissible in legal proceedings in the UK.[174] A trial conducted as one might be in Jordan would render a Member State of the Council of Europe in breach of Art. 6. But the test was: was there a flagrant and total denial of a fair trial? The House of Lords, moved by diplomatic sensitivities, did not find this test satisfied. There were no substantial grounds for believing that there was a real risk to the Convention rights of the appellants:[175]

> The issue before SIAC was whether there were reasonable grounds for believing that if Mr Othman were deported to Jordan the criminal trial that he would there face would have defects of such significance as fundamentally to destroy the fairness of his trial or, as SIAC put it, to amount to a total denial of the right to a fair trial. SIAC concluded that the deficiencies that SIAC had identified did not meet that exacting test.

Lord Phillips did not find that in reaching this conclusion the SIAC had erred in law (para. 154).

After the decision in *MB* and before *RB*, the Court of Appeal had to decide whether in a control-order case there was an irreducible minimum of information to which a subject was entitled. The majority held, saying there were no rigid principles:

> There is no principle that a hearing will be unfair in the absence of open disclosure to the controlee of an irreducible minimum of allegation or evidence. Alternatively, if there is, the irreducible minimum can, depending on the circumstances, be met by disclosure of as little information as was provided in *AF*, which is very little indeed.

Sedley LJ, dissenting, ruled that it is unfair to use wholly undisclosed evidence even if a judge believes it is unanswerable.[176] The Court of Appeal decision was reversed in the House of Lords (see Introduction p. 5).

---

[174] [2005] UKHL 71. See P. Birkinshaw in B. Clucas, G. Johnstone and T. Ward (eds.), *Torture: Moral absolutes and ambiguities* (2009), ch. 6 on the shortcomings in *A*.

[175] *Saadi v Italy* App. No. 37201/06 28/2/08 CHR.

[176] *Secretary of State for the Home Department v AF* [2008] EWCA Civ 1148 on appeal to the House of Lords.

Courts in the UK, said Lord Bingham in *Shayler*, are not alone in having to ensure that those charged with serious offences of terrorism or serious crime are tried in a fair manner, but in a process that does not compromise disclosure of information that could damage security or endanger informers or the lives of security personnel.[177] The courts have been vigilant to check that powers of executive detention are not used for discriminatory or disproportionate purposes and have ruled such powers ultra vires even when exercised after a derogation from the ECHR under state-of-emergency provisions. A declaration of incompatibility was issued against the offending statute.[178] Evidence obtained by torture by overseas officials is not admissible in British courts including the SIAC.[179] But the burden of proving that it was obtained by torture rests on the shoulders of the person making the allegations. In the secretive procedures of the SIAC this may be an impossible task.[180] In *A v UK* the ECtHR accepted that although there may be good reason to limit the evidence disclosed on grounds of national security those subject to detention had to have an effective opportunity to challenge the decision. The ECtHR ruled that there had been breaches of Art. 5(4) ECHR and the guarantee of procedural fairness when four detainees had been denied a fair hearing before the SIAC when 'open material' did not contain important incriminating evidence. Secrecy had denied them an effective opportunity to challenge the detention. In the case of five other detainees the open material was specific and allowed an effective challenge so no breach occurred under Art. 5(4).[181]

EC law has also had an impact. In *Johnston*[182] a woman police officer challenged a non-renewal of a contract of employment because of a policy in the RUC not to allow women to be armed on service which meant they could not perform 'general police duties'. In the industrial tribunal where she alleged a breach of domestic laws outlawing discrimination a ministerial certificate was issued stating that the action was taken in the interests of national security and public order effectively barring further inquiry by the tribunal. It was argued that this denied her rights under the directive on the implementation of equal

---

[177] *R v Shayler*, at para. 33.

[178] *A v Secretary of State for the Home Department* [2005] 3 All ER 169 (HL).

[179] *A*, note 174 above.

[180] See Baroness Hale in *MB* [2007] UKHL 46, at para. 73. See *Secretary of State for the Home Department* v AF [2008] EWHC 689 (Admin).

[181] 3455/05 [2009] ECHR 301.

[182] *Johnston v Chief Constable of Royal Ulster Constabulary* [1986] 3 All ER 135. In *R v Secretary of State for the Home Department, ex p. McQuillan* [1995] 4 All ER 400, Sedley J stayed proceedings involving a challenge to an exclusion order under the Prevention of Terrorism (TP) Act 1989 pending the outcome of other references before the ECJ on the question of the impact of Art. 8a(1) of the EC Treaty and Art. 9 of Directive 64/221, which allows derogation from freedom of movement (Art. 48) with safeguards: *R v Secretary of State for the Home Department, ex p. Adams* [1995] All ER (EC) 177. In *Gallagher* the ECJ found that in the case of the Irish nationals the UK was in breach of EC law because of the absence of an independent competent authority to hear the deportee's appeal: *R v Secretary of State for the Home Department, ex p. Gallagher* [1996] 1 CMLR 557 and SI 892/1996, introducing a right of interview for the deportee with persons nominated by the Secretary of State.

treatment under EC law. The ECJ held that even though stated to be conclusive evidence of the reason for derogation from the treaty, the certificate nonetheless sought to deprive an individual of her rights and to deny the principle of effective judicial control over the power of derogation. On the facts of the case, the derogation was not justified because it did not confer a general proviso covering all measures taken for reasons of public safety and had to relate to specific factors which were not made out by the chief constable and government. *Svenska Journalistförbundet* saw the Court of First Instance (CFI) of the EC rule that the Council's reliance on public security to deny access to documents by Swedish journalists was unlawful as there had not been a proper reliance on Art. 190 and its requirement to provide a reason for a decision. The case was important for stating that third-pillar documents were within the scope of the decision and codes of the EC on access and that public order was not an automatic ground for excluding judicial examination.[183] In *Kadi and Al Barakaat*[184] the ECJ, overruling the CFI, held that UN Security Council resolutions seeking economic sanctions against terrorism are binding only in international law. It subjected the contested EU regulations to full review under EU human rights standards and found them in breach of the right to a hearing, the right to judicial protection and the right to property. It is a very important judgment on the relationship between international law and EU law in which the ECJ expressed some scepticism about adequate safeguards in the operation of international law.[185]

A few more points on the use of 'national security' to preclude examination in the courts of matters of PI are apposite.

A Wright mess

Peter Wright was a former member of the British security services who wished to publish his memoirs.[186] In these he made, often repeating, serious allegations against senior officers of MI5 of treasonable wrongdoing and criminal activity. The allegations were based on 'confidential' material gained while in Crown employment. He sought to publish his book in Australia. The English Attorney General sought to restrain publication by commencing proceedings in New South Wales. He also commenced proceedings in England against *The Observer* and *The Guardian* newspapers, which had published details of the allegations which they claimed to have received from other sources as well as the author.

---

[183] Case T-174/95 [1998] All ER (EC) 545.

[184] Joined Cases C-402 P and 415 P (3 September 2008). On freezing funds and combating foreign terrorism, see *PMO v EU Council* Case T-248/08 CFI 4/12/08 and *A v HM Treasury* [2008] EWCA Civ 1187 (CA).

[185] T. Tridimas (2009) Fordham J of Int Law (forthcomimg).

[186] See *AG v Observer Newspapers Ltd* [1986] NLJ Rep 799, CA upholding the order of Millett J. Approval must be given for publications of memoirs by civil servants. For CIA agents, see *Snepp v US*, ch. 12, note 85, p. 477, above.

Further proceedings were commenced against other newspapers. In the English proceedings,[187] the Attorney General sought injunctions restraining further publication. This is referred to as 'prior restraint'. Its use in the USA has been heavily circumscribed because of the First Amendment to the Constitution guaranteeing freedom of speech.[188] It had a much wider scope in England, where courts were not so prepared to allow publication, while reminding the 'injured' party that he may sue for damages. This position has now been affected by the HRA 1998, s. 12 (see below). The absence of 'prior restraint' may, conversely, help freedom of speech; it can also be easily abused by a powerful and irresponsible press.

No one suggested in the case of *The Observer* or *The Guardian* that they were acting irresponsibly.[189] In fact they gave an undertaking that they would exercise their own judgement carefully before publishing anything relating to the security service. This would permit, said Sir John Donaldson, 'the disclosure or publication of information whether or not in the public domain, about serious criminal misconduct or other serious wrongdoing by members of the British security services'. This was too much. While accepting that there was a PI in knowing of grave malefactions by senior officers, there was a competing PI in maintaining a confidentiality that was not simply a private 'contractual' confidentiality but a confidentiality relating to 'public secrets':[190] 'The Attorney-General is not personally the beneficiary of the right to confidentiality which he asserts, nor is the executive. His claim is made on behalf of the state, that is the general community.' When assessing the competing PI of knowing, and maintaining a duty of confidentiality by preventing the public from knowing, it 'might lead a court properly to conclude that, in the context of the confidentiality of the work of the security service, the proper approach is that the conflict . . . should be resolved in favour of restraint unless the court is satisfied that there is a serious defence of public interest which is *very likely*[191] to succeed at the trial'. It *was* in the PI to discover wrongdoing in the security service, and the greater the wrongdoing, the greater the right to know; but Sir John could not agree that, given 'a sufficiently serious *allegation*', publication of the allegation with a view to forcing an investigation 'was justified'. Sir John reasoned:

> Where there is a confidentiality, the public interest in its maintenance has to be overborne by a countervailing public interest, if publication is not to be

---

[187] *AG v Guardian Newspapers Ltd* [1987] 3 All ER 316, Ch D, CA and HL. For the European Convention and confidentiality of state secrets, see Application 4274/69 *X v Germany* 35 Recueil 158; 9401/81 *X v Norway* 27 DR 228; *Leander, VW BLUF!*, note 39 above; and *A v UK*, p. 437 above.

[188] E. Barendt, *Freedom of Speech*, 2nd edn (2007).

[189] The allegations had been published elsewhere. *The Independent*, 27 April 1987, and other papers published extracts in defiance of the injunction. The Australian courts had issued orders restraining publication of the book pending the trial.

[190] *AG v Jonathan Cape* [1976] QB 752. See *Fairfax*, p. 446 *et seq* below.

[191] Emphasis in original. This was questioned in particular in the Court of Appeal in *Spycatcher No. 2* by Bingham LJ.

restrained. In some cases the weight of the public interest in the maintenance of the confidentiality will be small and the weight of the public interest in publication will be great. But in weighing these countervailing public interests or . . . those countervailing aspects of a single public interest, both the nature and circumstances of the proposed publication have to be examined with considerable care. This is sometimes referred to as the principle of proportionality – the restraint or lack of restraint proportionate to the overall assessment of the public interest. Thus it by no means follows that, because the public interest in the exposure of wrong-doing would justify the communication to the police or some such authority of material which has been unlawfully obtained, it would also justify wholesale publication of material in a national newspaper.[192]

Publication through a newspaper, 'the widest and most indiscriminate' form of publication, was not justified. However, the papers were free to publish accurate reports of legal proceedings in New South Wales (although the House of Lords subsequently enjoined such discussion) or England, or proceedings before Parliament. One matter which had not been enjoined was a TV programme by Ms Cathy Massiter – a former security official – which contained an appearance by Mr Wright. No action was taken against Ms Massiter in England, yet it was taken against Mr Wright in Australia. In those latter proceedings, the British Government admitted the veracity of Wright's allegations as a tactical ploy to avoid a confrontation with Mr Wright and Ms Massiter. This left the British Government with the unenviable task of persuading an Australian court that it was in Australia's national interest to maintain Wright's confidence to the Crown. PII of documents was sought by the Crown for relevant documents in the New South Wales proceedings. This was refused, and the Crown's case was presented in evidence by the Secretary to the Cabinet, who was subjected to rigorous, indeed hostile, cross-examination. His performance was poor. He had to take the witness box a second time to retract a statement alleging that the decision not to prosecute previous 'leaks' of MI5 secrets was taken by the Attorney General. It was not so, Attorney General Sir Michael Havers stated in Parliament. The senior civil servant who had performed so adroitly before the Defence Select Committee in the Westland episode[193] was made to look implausible and totally unconvincing. The New South Wales court refused the injunction sought by the Crown, undermining all the Crown's assertions unequivocally.[194] The court also criticised Sir John Donaldson's judgment preventing by interim injunction reporting in newspapers in England of allegations of unlawful conduct. A different view of such matters was taken in Australia.[195] The Court of Appeal of New South Wales rejected the government's appeal. 'National security' did not allow the government to conceal that it had acted

---

[192] [1986] NLJ Rep 799, at 800. *Unlawfully* here means in breach of confidence.
[193] HC 519 (1985–6).
[194] See M. Fysh (ed.), *The Spycatcher Cases* (1989). He who comes to equity . . . !
[195] *Commonwealth of Australia v John Fairfax & Sons Ltd* (1980) 147 CLR 39. See note 217 below.

without honour and capriciously. The High Court of Australia also rejected the appeal.[196]

The injunctions issued against *The Guardian* and *The Observer* were subject to further proceedings when three English newspapers published extracts from Peter Wright's memoirs. Sir John Donaldson in his judgment had warned that other newspapers were not free to republish, and the Lord Chancellor had chipped in with his own warning. In proceedings initiated by the Attorney General, Sir Nicolas Browne Wilkinson held that a contempt of court for breach of the precise terms of an injunction could only be committed by a party enjoined by the injunction – *The Guardian* or *The Observer* – or by a party who has aided and abetted those bound by the injunction.[197] In the absence of such elements, it would only bind those who were parties to the initial litigation: it operated *in personam* not *in rem*. Sir Nicolas was at pains to dissociate himself from the necessity of the law protecting a public secret as a public right, as Sir John had endeavoured to do. '[T]he basic right protected by the 1986 injunction was exactly the same as the right of a manufacturer to stop an employee disclosing trade secrets or of one spouse to restrain the other from revealing "pillow talk".' It was for Parliament and not the courts to create a public-law remedy protecting public rights to confidentiality of state secrets, he believed. This, however, is what Scott J did but not in terms which extended the law.

This reasoning did not prevail in the Court of Appeal, which overturned the Vice-Chancellor's decision, paving the way for contempt proceedings against the respective newspapers. However, the judgment of the Master of the Rolls was particularly receptive to some of the Vice-Chancellor's criticisms. The case was not about national security, nor about a state interest (as he had formerly suggested), but about confidentiality protecting an employment relationship, he believed! The Attorney General was now seeking to protect a right to confidentiality by contempt proceedings against publication which was 'intended or calculated to impede, obstruct or prejudice the administration of justice' – specific intent. Contempt would be established where the party was shown to have published with knowledge that the material was subject to a court order prohibiting publication and that it was the subject matter of a pending action. Publication would destroy that most evanescent of rights, confidentiality. The courts, and no one else, would decide to what extent the right should be protected, regardless of who asserted it.[198] This seems understandable in basic principle. The similarity to a 'gagging writ' should not be overlooked, especially where, as in Wright's case, the publishers allege that the government acquiesced in prior publication of similar 'confidential' information. The House of Lords effectively endorsed this judgment in subsequent

---

[196] See Fysh (ed.), *The Spycatcher Cases.*
[197] *AG v Newspaper Publishing plc* [1987] 3 All ER 276.
[198] [1987] 3 All ER 276, at 289. See *Re X* [1984] 1 WLR 1422.

proceedings.[199] *Contra mundum* orders have been used by the courts to restrain the 'whole world' from prejudicing the court's orders.[200] This is an extremely convenient gagging device for government and represents one of the only unqualified victories from the *Spycatcher* episode. The position of s. 12 HRA would today have to be considered (below).

Wright's case became a matter of international notoriety. After publication of his book in the USA, and further publication of extracts in the *Sunday Times*, the government's attempts to protect the confidentiality of information acquired by its servants appeared forlorn. Government efforts concentrated on seizing the profits emanating from Wright's breach of duty, as well as maintaining the injunction. That such a confidentiality existed was accepted, though it was unclear whether it was a private- or public-law right protecting public or private confidences. That, however, did not prevent the House of Lords from upholding the interim injunction, and even extending it to cover legal proceedings in New South Wales concerning Wright's allegations.[201] The real motive of the majority of the Law Lords appears to have been the desire to use an injunction against the newspapers to punish Wright and to deter other security officers, rather than to protect a confidence. The public could not read reports of what was publicly available. Two of the dissenting Law Lords, Lord Bridge and Lord Lloyd, both addressed the judicial freneticism in the English litigation with some considerable degree of foreboding. Lord Bridge, former chairman of the Security Commission, believed that for the first time in his life he had seen the necessity of the incorporation of the ECHR into English law given the executive excesses he had been witness to.[202] In further proceedings, the BBC was enjoined from broadcasting a serious discussion on the security services on Radio 4.[203]

Some judicial sanity was restored to these events when Scott J refused to award a permanent injunction against the newspapers at the suit of the Attorney General. In a judgment distinguished by its clarity and grasp of legal principle, the judge held that the secret was out and the PI dictated it be reported upon. Any damage to the PI had been done; a court order was unnecessary and not justified. Confidentiality was not the same as copyright in the case of the

---

[199] [1991] 2 All ER 398, HL. On the worrying implications of the interlocutory and contempt proceedings from *Spycatcher*, see Lord Oliver writing extra-judicially in 'Spycatcher, confidence, copyright and contempt' (1989) 23 Israel LR 409.

[200] For *contra mundum* injunctions see *Venables and Thompson v News Group Newspapers Ltd* [2001] 1 All ER 908. Note, *Punch*, below.

[201] The injunction was lifted in the High Court, restored with amendments in the Court of Appeal and extended in the House of Lords in a 3–2 judgment, *AG v Guardian Newspapers* [1987] 3 All ER 316. Cf. the First Amendment to the US Constitution and *New York Times Co. v US* 403 US 713 (1971). Note *US v Progressive Inc.* 467 F Supp 990 (1979). On prohibition of library loans of *Spycatcher*, see *AG v Observer Ltd, Re Application by Derbyshire Country Council* [1988] 1 All ER 385.

[202] [1987] 3 All ER 316, at pp. 346–7.   [203] *AG v BBC* (1987) The Times, 18 December.

newspapers.[204] The government appealed unsuccessfully to the Court of Appeal and to the House of Lords.[205] The court upheld the right of the press to report on what was in the public domain. Two appeal court judges agreed with Scott J that the newspapers were correct to publish the initial serious allegations because it was in the PI that they should be reported and this was supported in the House of Lords. This would seem to go against the thrust of the House of Lords majority judgment in the interlocutory proceedings. Neither Wright himself nor his agents or servants could publish his book because this remained a serious breach of confidence.

It is now reasonably clear that, should the Attorney General seek an injunction to protect confidences owed by officials in security or intelligence or related civil servants or indeed others, the court will only award an injunction to prevent publication by a third party where there is a risk of *additional* harm to national security or public order or to the PI where that information is already in the public domain. The duty owed by security and intelligence officers themselves is lifelong unless it falls within the iniquity category recognised by Scott J and which was given some degree of support by two of the Law Lords and the Court of Appeal in the *Spycatcher* litigation or where possibly, as Scott J suggested, it is no longer confidential or comprises trivia. In *Lord Advocate v Scotsman Publications*, however, the Law Lords accepted the duty of confidentiality owed by such officers was lifelong and it was assumed that this was the holding in *Spycatcher*. Is the duty lifelong irrespective of the material or is it only lifelong where the material remains confidential? The latter accords with better sense. The subsequent history shows that such officers must not go public with any disclosures on information gleaned in service although the courts have refused to prevent publication of extracts from memoirs originally published overseas (chapter 2, p. 45).

But even where disclosure may be justified, the means adopted must be appropriate. Publication, Scott believed, may take place where the matter is 'trivia' – but who is to judge, and might it well be an offence under the OSA? – or where publication is duly authorised. Where information is published by third parties where the source is a security or intelligence official there may well be criminal offences under the OSA 1989 (see chapter 3). Where all possible damage has been done, an injunction will not be issued to prevent third parties

---

[204] *AG v Guardian Newspapers Ltd (No. 2)* [1988] 3 All ER 545, ChD, CA and HL. In the House of Lords, Lord Griffiths dissented on two points from the other judges including on the question of *The Guardian's* breach of confidence in reporting Australian proceedings; he felt they were in breach of confidence.

[205] See Lords Goff and Griffiths giving qualified support to the general proposition although there was no public interest in Wright's disclosures concerning operations of the service. Lord Goff doubted whether Wright could be prevented from publishing the book but he was alone on that point. Scott J raised the point of whether in equity the Crown owned the copyright to the book because it recorded events which took place while he was in Crown service; see Lords Griffiths and Jauncey in *Guardian Newspapers (No. 2)*, note 204 above. This point has been taken up in subsequent proceedings.

publishing. That may well be the case at an application for a permanent injunction as in the proceedings before Scott J but on an application for an interim injunction different considerations are bound to come into play. There the court is concerned to hold the ring and to ensure that no damage is done to either party in what are often uncertain circumstances. Section 12 HRA is relevant. With two competing versions of the PI it would be a brave judge who preferred the word of an editor or whoever against that of the government on where the PI lay. Even the ECtHR held in *Spycatcher*, when that case inevitably made its way to Strasbourg, that the original injunctions were not in breach of Art. 10 ECHR; it was only *after* publication in the USA that the continuation of the injunctions constituted a breach of that Article.[206] While s. 12 HRA may make a crucial difference in applications for orders prohibiting interim injunctions in the future where serious evidence of possible damage to national security is present, no court will second guess the government's claims. Section 12 will help root out the clearly bogus claims.

The terms of s. 12 are that relief should not be granted to restrain publication before trial unless the court is satisfied that the applicant is likely to establish that publication should not be allowed at the full hearing. The wording is emphatic and does not seem to contain a discretion unless the court is so satisfied. Damages may be an appropriate remedy. If the court is not satisfied, relief should not be granted. The courts will, however, be sensitive to well-grounded claims of national security or personal danger. In s. 12, there are safeguards against the non-representation or attendance of a respondent to prevent abuses of *ex parte* (absence of the publisher/author) claims. In the case of material which is journalistic, literary or artistic, the court must have particular regard to the importance of the Convention right of freedom of expression in Art. 10 ECHR, the PI in publication and any relevant privacy code or the extent to which the material has, or is about to become, available to the public. After some doubt it is clear that '*likelihood* [emphasis added] of success at trial' is essential. This is context based. 'There can be no single, rigid standard governing all applications for interim relief.' The court must not award an injunction unless the prospects for success for the claimant are 'sufficiently favourable'. 'The general approach should be that courts will be exceedingly slow to make interim restraint orders where the applicant has not satisfied the court that he will probably ("more likely than not") succeed at the trial.' This is the general test to apply before exercising a discretion to make an award but a less demanding test may be necessary where potential consequences of disclosure may be 'particularly grave'.[207] The press have argued that judges hearing applications for interim injunctions have been over-ready to award orders to protect the 'privacy' or confidentiality of commercial organisations in sweeping terms. Clear guidance will have to be given by the new Supreme Court.

---

[206] *Observer and Guardian* v *UK* (1991) 14 EHRR 153, ECtHR.
[207] *Cream Holdings v Bannerjee* [2004] UKHL 44, at para. 22.

The emergence of the Internet and the globalisation of publishing make the efficacy of prohibition orders all the more questionable. In July 2001, the High Court dismissed an application by the Attorney General to prevent publication by a 'renegade MI6 officer' Richard Tomlinson of extracts of his book, *The Big Breach: From top secret to maximum security*, because of publication elsewhere in the world (in this case, Moscow) (and see chapter 2, p. 45).[208] The Master of the Rolls also held that the editor may decide what is in the PI to publish without seeking the prior approval of the authorities. Consultation was 'desirable' but the Attorney General's permission was not required. This aspect cannot survive the Law Lords decision in *AG v Punch Ltd* where it was ruled intent to harm national security on the part of the editor did not have to be proved to establish contempt on the part of an editor who had published Shayler's articles in breach of a court order.[209]

The House of Lords in *AG v Blake*[210] gave the government cause for hope in this area when it ruled that MI5 and MI6 officers and former officers do owe a lifelong duty of confidentiality to the Crown ('an *absolute* rule against disclosure, visible to all, makes sense'). Furthermore, if such officers do publish in contravention of their written undertakings under the OSA not to divulge any material acquired in the service in the press or in book form, and which is not otherwise confidential or damaging to the PI to disclose, such officers must account for any profits acquired from the breach of the undertaking. As Blake was an escaped prisoner outside the jurisdiction and not amenable to the criminal courts and an indictment for breaches of s. 1 OSA 1989, nonetheless, Blake's position, if not a fiduciary in relation to this information, was analogous to a fiduciary and an account of profits was the appropriate remedy, the court believed.[211] Armed with this decision, it was subsequently argued that Tomlinson also had to account for profits in that. in addition to the breach of undertaking, he had assigned copyright to the Crown.

There was no need for the Law Lords to rule on the compatibility of s. 1 OSA with Art. 10 ECHR. Such compatibility was ruled to exist in *Shayler* (chapter 3, p. 106). Furthermore, *Blake* does not decide that information from a source such as Blake cannot be published by another – although that is the effect of the Law Lords judgment in *AG v Punch Ltd* where there is a breach of court orders. *Blake* decides that the wrongdoer in breach of his promise will have to account for ill-gotten gain.

Judges and confidences

The law recognises a duty to maintain a confidence which has arisen from a contractual relationship, or in circumstances where information is acquired and from which an obligation of confidence can be inferred. In the absence of

[208] *AG v Times Newspapers Ltd* [2001] 1 WLR 885.
[209] [2003] 1 All ER 289 (HL) overruling the Court of Appeal.
[210] [2000] 4 All ER 385, HL.   [211] Lord Hobhouse dissented.

an express or implied contractual undertaking, most common in employment and trade-secrets cases, the law looks for some relationship where it would be inequitable not to protect the confidences or 'secrets' which exist within a relationship,[212] or a situation in which confidentiality or privacy should be protected (chapter 8, p. 273). The fact that information is stamped 'confidential' does not make it so for legal purposes, nor is every secret protected by the law.

In the Crossman diaries litigation[213] it was held that the law of confidentiality could protect by injunction not only domestic or trade/commercial secrets, but 'public' secrets, that is information emanating from state or public business, not information which has been made public.[214] The case concerned Cabinet and Cabinet committee discussions, which are buttressed by the convention of ministerial collective responsibility, a convention which the court saw it as its duty to maintain to protect the confidentiality owed in law to Cabinet discussions and details of decisions. The period of time for which it had to be maintained was a matter of judgment on the facts of the individual case. The litigation involved the diaries of the former Cabinet minister, which revealed information about Cabinet business while in office obtained from other Cabinet ministers and civil servants. The Crown was seeking to restrain publication by injunction – by prior restraint. On the facts, an injunction was not necessary, because the events happened over ten years before the litigation.[215] As we have seen, the concept of 'public secrets' was extended in *Spycatcher*[216] to protect on an interim basis the confidentiality of the 'public secrets' attaching to operations of the security services. In the proceedings for a permanent injunction, Scott J and the higher courts were very influenced by an Australian decision in which the Australian government sought to prevent publication of a book containing confidential government information.[217] Mason J explained how the equitable principle of confidentiality was fashioned to protect personal, private and proprietary interests of the citizen 'not to protect the very different interests of the executive government'. Equity will protect government information but it has uppermost in mind that government is operating in the PI not in a private interest:

> It may be a sufficient detriment to the citizen that disclosure of information will expose his actions to public discussion and criticism. But it can scarcely be a relevant detriment to the Government that publication of material concerning its

---

[212] *Argyll v Argyll* [1967] Ch 302. See Sedley LJ in *Douglas v Hello! Ltd* [2001] 2 All ER 289, CA.

[213] Ch. 9 p. 325.

[214] Though damages or an account of profits would then be appropriate if disclosure followed a breach of the obligation. The Wright episode led to some startling measures from the courts to protect information already in the public domain or public knowledge – see note 202 above and G. Jones (1970) LQR 466–70; and further (1990) 42 Current Legal Problems 48.

[215] An injunction was not sought to prevent publication of vols. II and, especially, III. Since then, publication of ministerial memoirs has become the norm.

[216] *AG v Guardian and Observer* (1986) The Times, 26 July and [1987] 3 All ER 316. See *AG v Turnaround Distribution Ltd* [1989] FSR 169.

[217] *Commonwealth of Australia v John Fairfax and Sons Ltd* (1980) 147 CLR 39.

actions will merely expose it to public discussion and criticism. It is unacceptable in our democratic society that there should be a restraint on the publication of information relating to government when the only vice of that information is that it enables the public to discuss, review and criticise Government action . . . Unless disclosure is likely to injure the public interest, it will not be protected.

The judge continued:

If, however, it appears that disclosure will be inimical to the public interest because national security, relations with foreign countries or the ordinary business of government will be prejudiced, disclosure will be restrained.[218]

This sets out quite clearly the different tests to be applied in private and public, i.e. state, relationships. Confidentiality remains a protean but uncertain concept protecting information. When the courts are concerned with relationships between individuals and a legal remedy is sought to protect confidentiality, the courts are on more familiar territory where they can assimilate the concept with property – though this can be taken too far. This is especially important for trade secrets and freedom of trade, and according to the majority opinion in the interlocutory *Spycatcher* litigation for 'damaging' disclosure of Crown secrets.[219] The law was once on less certain ground where it sought to protect confidences arising from relationships when breach of confidence would allegedly be inequitable. This is not true today and confidentiality has been extended to protect personal information as was seen in chapter 8. Confidentiality alone is insufficient reason to withhold information where the interests of justice require its release.[220] In sex and race discrimination cases, for instance, the tribunal chairman can examine papers on other employees to assess whether discrimination has taken place against the plaintiff in promotions or appointments.[221]

In cases involving public bodies, the PI is advanced by healthy debate and criticism of government. Measures inhibiting freedom of speech and freedom of the press move on thin ice. Under public private partnership (PPP) initiatives, a common feature is the categorisation of information as confidential or commercially secret. Sedley LJ has reminded us that Art. 10 ECHR is not just about freedom of expression. 'It is also about the right to receive and impart information, a right which (to borrow Lord Steyn's metaphor in *ex p. Simms*

---

[218] *Ibid.*

[219] See, e.g., *Faccenda Chicken Ltd v Fowler* [1985] 1 All ER 724, and [1986] 1 All ER 617, CA which deal with the position of 'trade secrets' in employment; note *Crowson Fabrics v Rider* [2007] EWHC 2942 Ch – employees as a class do not owe general fiduciary duties to their employer – the question is fact-sensitive. In *Wright's* case, the Crown sought to vindicate a right *in personam* to the profits of his breach of confidentiality and a right *in rem* to the confidential information itself, above. See also *AG v Blake* [2001] AC 268; and *Re Z* [1995] 4 All ER 961 and ss 1(1), 3(j) and 8(1) Children Act 1989.

[220] *Alfred Crompton,* note 243 below.

[221] *Science Research Council v Nassé* [1980] AC 1028; note *West Midlands Passenger Executive v Singh* [1987] ICR 837.

at 126) is the lifeblood of democracy.'[222] The courts have held that the PI may justify a leak that would constitute a breach of confidence or copyright, and a defence to an application for an injunction could be made by establishing that it was in the PI for the public to know, for instance, that the police were using unreliable instruments to assess the level of alcohol in motorists' blood, as in *Lion*.[223] However, to be protected, one disclosing the information has to show that the breach was in the PI and not merely interesting to the public, and that the chosen method of publication is appropriate. Illegal or other wrongdoing that is effected by a breach of confidence may be more appropriately published by informing the police or respective authorities, rather than by detailing the contents of a conversation, obtained by an illegal tap, in the national press.[224] In *Lion*, the Court of Appeal believed that plaintiffs seeking an injunction prohibiting publication would have to establish that the defendant could not show that there is a serious defence of PI which *may* succeed at the trial. In *Lion* the plaintiffs could not establish this, so the injunction was refused.[225] Where a defence of PI can be raised, the courts can involve themselves in a familiar balancing act of weighing the PI in maintaining confidentiality, against the PI of informing the public of matters of *real* public concern. Donaldson MR has insisted that there should be a 'moral imperative' to publish openly, rather than informing the authorities before an injunction restraining publication would be refused. In the *Spycatcher* case, Scott J believed it was of real public concern that there should be reporting of allegations of serious misconduct by MI5 officers. Section 12 HRA should be recalled and how this will place the onus on those who are seeking to prevent publication.

It was seen in chapter 8 how the courts are developing confidentiality to give fuller expression to the Art. 8 ECHR right to privacy and family life and how protection of the legitimate expectation of privacy has emerged (see p. 273 above). However, the police were correct to inform the owner of a caravan site that two occupants were convicted paedophiles, information that caused the owner to order the two occupants to leave. The police had disclosed the information in the PI to protect local children and 'vulnerable' adults. The information was already in the public arena. Although it would have been desirable to have interviewed the two occupants before disclosing the information, a course which the police did not adopt, the police had not acted unlawfully because any information provided by the occupants would have

---

[222] *London Regional Transport v Mayor of London* [2001] EWCA Civ 1491, para. 55,

[223] *Lion Laboratories Ltd v Evans* [1984] 2 All ER 417. CA. This was not a publication of a wrongdoing as such.

[224] *Francome v Mirror Group Newspapers Ltd* [1984] 2 All ER 408.

[225] Note the test on the defendants in *AG v Guardian and Observer* above, pp. 438–9. Cf. *Schering Chemicals Ltd v Falkman Ltd* [1982] QB 1. See *Bonnard v Perryman* [1891] 2 Ch 269; *Gulf Oil (GB) Ltd v Page* [1987] 3 All ER 14. See Cmnd 8388 and remember that bribing employees, e.g., to disclose information is a crime: Prevention of Corruption Act 1906 and 1916. And see Law Commission Paper No. 313, *Reforming Bribery* (2008).

made no difference to the situation.[226] Laws have placed increasing obligations upon sex offenders to disclose their wrongdoing in order to warn the public but we have not yet adopted the practice of some US states whereby the names of such offenders are publicly displayed.[227]

The law will protect a confidential, original and commercially promising idea. There can be no breach of copyright in a creative idea unless it is reduced to material form and used without permission. Copyright cannot protect ideas as such; that is within the realm of plagiarism.[228] It is beyond the scope of a work such as this to describe the emerging law relating to intellectual property, copyright and patents.[229] Judicial law is inadequate to provide appropriate protection to such ideas and information and had given way to a succession of unsatisfactory statutes.[230] A 1986 White Paper led to The Copyright, Designs and Patents Act of 1988. There were fears that it would unjustifiably extend authors' proprietorial rights in a manner which would substantially interfere with freedom of speech. As an endnote it is interesting to observe in the *Fairfax* decision referred to above, although the court issued a judgment that became the basis of the present law concerning the inapplicability of the private law of confidentiality to the world of government, publication of the work in question was prevented by injunction because it breached copyright.[231] Courts in England have seemed to believe that the PI defence under copyright law is not as broad as under confidentiality and Art. 10 ECHR is no defence against a breach of copyright.[232] It was seen in the cases on freedom of information that copyright has been claimed as an exemption against disclosure under the FOIA. This, as was explained, was misconceived (p. 179 above). While Art. 10 is not an absolute, there is a danger that exercise of property rights may defeat a 'fundamental right'. However, as is clear from litigation involving

[226] *R v Chief Constable North Wales Police, ex p. AB* [1998] 3 All ER 310, Home Office Circular 39/1997; *Woolgar v Chief Constable of the Sussex Police* [1999] 3 All ER 604; cf. *Hellewell v Chief Constable of Derbyshire* [1995] 4 All ER 473.

[227] Known colloquially as 'Megan's law'. Under the Police Act 1997, Pt V, the Protection of Children Act 1999 and the Care Standards Act 2000 and Safeguarding of Vulnerable Groups Act 2006 there are compulsory vetting and disclosure provisions relating to those who work with children and other activities: *R (L) v Met. Police Com'r* [2007] EWCA Civ 168 [4 All ER 128] and disclosure of non-criminal matters under s. 115 Police Act. Relevance was the key and this could include non-criminal information. See *R (Wright) v Secretary of State etc.* [2009] UKHL 3 and breaches of Art. 6 ECHR; *Trent AHA v Jain* [2009] UKHL 4 – no common-law liability under the relevant Act. See the Education Act 2002 and Sexual Offences Act 2003, Pt 2 and *R (F and Thompson) v Secretary of State for the Home Department* [2008] EWHC 3170 QB – notification requirements for an indefinite period breached offenders' Art. 8 ECHR rights.

[228] *M. Baigent and R. Leigh v Random House Group Ltd* [2006] EWHC 719 (Ch) concerning the *Da Vinci Code.*

[229] J. Phillips and A. Firth, *Introduction to Intellectual Property Law*, 4th edn (2001); W. R. Cornish and D. Llewelyn, *Intellectual Property: Patents, copyright, trade marks, and allied rights*, 5th edn (2003).

[230] The first Copyright Act was passed in 1709.   [231] Note 217 above.

[232] *Hyde Park Residences Ltd v Yelland* (2000) the Times, 16 January; and *Ashdown v Telegraph Group plc* [2001] 2 All ER 370.

the copying and publishing of the secret diaries of the Prince of Wales a PI defence is available under the 1988 Act under s. 171(3) together with a defence of fair dealing under s. 30.[233] These were not available on the facts which involved a breach of confidence and no countermanding PI in copying and publication.

Public interest, immunity and information

This somewhat arcane subject, unknown to any but a small band of litigation and academic lawyers, was projected into public notoriety by events surrounding the collapse of the Matrix Churchill prosecution where 'gagging orders', as the press and media called them, were slapped onto documents which proved to be essential for the defence. It was a central subject in Sir Richard Scott's inquiry and report where a detailed analysis of the law is contained (see chapter 9). A public body,[234] a term now given an identification in the FOIA 2000[235] may wish to withhold documents, or not to have officials answering questions in a court, because the PI demands that the information should not be made public. A claim is made for PII. PII protects the interests of the state as a whole and not just the executive branch of the government.[236] A claim used to be made, misleadingly, for Crown privilege.[237] The Crown possessed a prerogative immunity at common law against orders for discovery (the former term for disclosure) of documents. This was abolished by s. 28 of the Crown Proceedings Act 1947, subject to two provisos: any rule of law survived that authorised the withholding of information in the PI because disclosure would be injurious to that interest;[238] and disclosure of the very existence of a document was not to be enforced if in the opinion of the minister it would be injurious to disclose whether it existed.[239] The first proviso related to the doctrine of Crown privilege (given extensive definition by a unanimous House of Lords in 1942)[240] whereby, having regard to the contents of the particular document(s), or if the document belongs to a class which, on the grounds of PI, must as a class be withheld from production, they should be withheld. This grouping of documents as a 'class' was used in the FOIA 2000 as was seen in chapter 4. The judgment of

---

[233] *Ass Newspapers Ltd v HRH PoW* [2006] EWCA Civ 1776.

[234] While it is clear that PII may be invoked by bodies that are 'private' in a legal sense to protect the confidential aspects of work which they perform on the public welfare (*D v NSPCC* [1978] AC 171), the courts will circumscribe the circumstances in which it may be invoked: *SRC v Nassé* [1980] AC 1028. In another context, see: *Re D* [1995] 4 All ER 385, HL, *Re G (a minor)* [1996] 2 All ER 65. See *Secretary of State for Children etc. v JN* [2008] EWHC 1199 and non disclosure of external expert reports.

[235] Ss. 3–7 and sch. 1.   [236] *R (Binyam Mohamed) v SoS FA* [2009] EWHC 152 (Admin) [32].

[237] 'Privilege' is misleading in so far as the minister, and the court, are under a *duty* not to allow disclosure of information *injurious* to the PI.

[238] RSC Ord. 24, r. 15 now CPR 1998, Pt 31.3(1)(a).

[239] RSC Ord. 77, r. 12(2) now CPR 1998, Pt 31.19.

[240] *Duncan v Cammell Laird & Co. Ltd* [1942] AC 624, per Viscount Simon.

the minister sufficed although Viscount Simon insisted that the minister must exercise a proper judgment.[241]

Administrative concessions were made by the government, and in 1968 the House of Lords overruled the wider aspects of *Duncan v Cammell Laird* in *Conway v Rimmer*.[242] Against the claim of the Crown that the candour[243] of communications between officials required protection, the Law Lords maintained the court's right to inspect the documents for itself; to make its own judgment on whether they should be protected; and if not, whether they should be disclosed to the other party if relevant. The decision was regarded as epoch-making, albeit daunting. Judges were to be the arbiters of the PI in what could be highly sensitive areas of official confidentiality. Professor de Smith thought that if 'There are some things that English judges are poorly equipped to do', this was certainly one of them.[244] Examination of the judgments in *Conway v Rimmer*[245] shows how cautious the Law Lords were. Cabinet documents were excluded, as were diplomatic dispatches and even the non-disclosure of papers coming before junior ministers concerning advice and formulation of policy at a low level met with judicial approval. 'The business of government is difficult enough,' opined Lord Reid, 'and no government could contemplate with equanimity the inner workings of the government machine being exposed to the gaze of those ready to criticise without adequate knowledge of the background and perhaps with some axe to grind.'[246] These were all examples of 'class documents'.

On the contrary, Lord Keith, in the *Burmah Oil*[247] decision, believed such an opening up might lead 'not to captious or ill-informed criticism, but to criticism calculated to improve the nature of that working [of government] as affecting the individual citizen'. In *Burmah Oil*, the House of Lords held that a certificate from a Secretary of State that the documents were of a high-policy content, and related to ministerial discussions with senior officials,[248] was not conclusive. The courts could balance the PI of preventing harm to the state or the public service by not ordering disclosure, and the PI of doing individual justice in the courts by ordering discovery if that would assist a

---

[241] The *breadth* of the decision was not supported by previous authorities, and was not accepted totally in Scotland or the Commonwealth (for the US, see *US v Reynolds* 345 US 1 (1952)). The 'contents' claim was used extensively after 1947, especially to protect inter- and intra-departmental communications and communications between outsiders and officials.

[242] [1968] AC 910. A judicial reaction had already set in against the full impact of *Duncan*; see D. G. T. Williams, *Not in the Public Interest* (1965). On statutory privileges for information, see I. Eagles (1983) Camb LJ 118; see *Sethia v Stern* (1987) The Times, 4 November.

[243] Confidentiality by itself is not an adequate ground to prevent discovery: *Alfred Crompton Amusement Machines Ltd v Customs and Excise Comrs (No. 2)* [1973] 2 All ER 1169, and cf. *SRC v Nassé*, note 234 above.

[244] *Judicial Review of Administrative Action*, 4th edn (1980) p. 40, note 57.

[245] See note 242 above.

[246] In *Burmah Oil Co. Ltd v Bank of England* [1980] AC 1090, Lord Wilberforce declared that 'it is not for the courts to assume the role of advocates for open government'.

[247] *Ibid.*   [248] And communications with the senior officials of the Bank of England.

litigant to vindicate his claims in law. If necessary, the court could examine the documents if they appeared likely to be relevant to the cause in action.[249] The case extended the principle of *Conway v Rimmer* and was doubtless influenced by case law in Australia and the USA.[250] The Law Lords' insistence that courts had a power to review the certificate of the minister concerning documents of a 'high policy content' in the highest levels of government, subject to national security or considerations of an equally important dimension,[251] is quite startling, albeit welcome. The impact of this approach can be seen in a case from as long ago as 1981, *Williams v Home Office,*[252] where disclosure was ordered to a former prisoner of discussion documents between high-level officials and a minister on the merits of the control unit at HM Prison Wakefield. The plaintiff did not win his eventual action, but the documents revealed a clash at the highest level on the merits and propriety of the form of punishment implemented within the unit, and confusion in the aims of penal policy. Its impact was seen also in litigation concerning haemophiliacs who had been infected by HIV-contaminated blood purchased by the NHS from the USA. In their negligence action they successfully overcame government arguments seeking to withhold necessary documents because the latter claimed they related to the formulation of government policy of self-sufficiency in blood products by ministers and briefings for ministers for which the department claimed PII.[253]

But *Burmah Oil* was perhaps too emphatic. The grounding of the argument by some of the judges in terms of the rhetoric of constitutional principle could not, at that time, remain unamended.[254] A 'more considered' approach characterised the majority ruling in the subsequent *Air Canada* litigation.[255] This concerned the test judges should apply before they examine documents and before they make their balancing decision on disclosure or confidentiality. Air Canada and other airlines complained of the exorbitant landing and user charges at Heathrow Airport. It was claimed on their behalf that the charges imposed by the British Airports Authority were ultra vires inasmuch as they were not exacted for the purposes contained in the statute,[256] but to pursue an ulterior governmental economic policy of reducing public-sector borrowing.[257] On

---

[249] They did examine but decided that they were of no assistance to Burmah Oil's claim for an unconscionable transaction.

[250] *Sankey v Whitlam* (1978) 53 ALJR 11; *US v Nixon* 418 US 683 (1974); *Env Defence Soc v SPA Ltd* [1981] 1 NZLR 146; *Auditor General of Canada v Minister of Energy Mines and Resources* (1985) 23 DLR (4th) 210. In the first two cases, evidence was required for criminal proceedings.

[251] e.g. diplomatic and foreign affairs.

[252] [1981] 1 All ER 1151; cf. *R v Secretary of State for the Home Department, ex p. Herbage (No. 2)* [1987] QB 1077, CA.

[253] Re HIV Haemophiliac Litigation [1990] NLJR 1349.

[254] The reaction in some quarters was not unlike the response to the education of the children of the masses in the nineteenth century: the expletives were now written closer to the ground!

[255] (*No. 2*) [1983] 2 AC 394.   [256] Airports Authority Act 1975.

[257] By setting strict financial targets for the British Airports Authority to meet.

general disclosure[258] the minister refused to disclose documents which comprised communications passing between government ministers and the preparatory drafts used by ministers of their meetings, and which related to the formulation of government policy regarding BAA and the limitation of public-sector borrowing. PII was claimed. At first instance, the judge ordered production, subject to his inspection, even though the documents might not assist the plaintiffs case because the information 'would substantially assist the court to elicit the true facts regarding the plaintiffs' case' and would thereby affect the court's decision. This was a sufficient PI justification for their discovery, subject to judicial inspection and exhaustion of appeals before inspection by the applicants. This decision was overruled in the Court of Appeal and by a majority in the House of Lords.[259]

The majority decision of the Law Lords held that, before a judge exercises a discretion to examine documents for which immunity is claimed, plaintiffs must establish that they will assist their case or damage their adversary's, and that they are necessary for disposing fairly of the case or saving costs. Not only is the onus on the applicant to convince the judge that they will assist the applicant, but s/he will also have to convince the judge as to *how* they will assist. If a requester cannot be precise on this point, stating with conviction and specificity what they will contain, then the danger is that the arguments will appear speculative and part of a 'fishing' expedition. In cases against a public authority (PA), Fox LJ held in the Court of Appeal, a plaintiff must have prima facie evidence of his own without the aid of disclosure, 'save in the most exceptional of cases'. The case must be able to 'take off' without assistance said a Law Lord. The 'interests of justice', the majority held in the House of Lords, meant that the task of the court was to decide the case fairly on the evidence before it, and 'not to ascertain some independent truth by seeking out evidence of its own accord'. The minority felt that the court could inspect where disclosure *might* assist the plaintiff, or defendant, *or the court*, in determining the issues, with the onus of proof on the applicant for discovery. If this onus is discharged, then there is strong authority to suggest that even Cabinet documents can be inspected by the judge to establish whether disclosure to the applicant is necessary.[260] Without a doubt, the onus on the applicant to get the judge to inspect is a very heavy one. The more probing a judicial inquiry is, the more likely it is that there will be material to establish ultra vires or unlawful considerations or action. Courts are not there to inquire; they are there to decide on the basis of what the applicant can give them.

This was especially true of judicial review cases, which are meant to be speedy and expeditious and, save in rare circumstances, a review on the affidavits as filed and not by way of disclosure and cross-examination of

---

[258] Which involved the exchange of lists of relevant documents. The certificate was actually signed by a senior civil servant.

[259] Lords Scarman and Templeman dissented.

[260] See Lord Fraser in *Air Canada* for the majority. He referred to cases of 'serious misconduct'.

witnesses.[261] Case law formerly suggested that disclosure should only be allowed where there is a mistake or something unsatisfactory in the affidavits.[262] This was subject to any PII claims. What is conventionally under consideration is the surface of the decision-making process, not the contents of documents or the decision-maker's state of mind. It is unlikely that the limited approach has altered with the replacement of Ord. 53 by Pt 54 of the CPR, which now deals with judicial review and which is no longer exclusively available in London. Other developments have brought about a relaxation in practice. Pre-action protocols provide guidance on information and reasons for decisions and action. The Bowman Report acknowledged that cases brought under the HRA might require more frequent applications for disclosure in order to ascertain whether action was 'necessary under Art. 8 or 10 ECHR'.[263] It might also prove necessary to establish an effective remedy under Art. 13 ECHR, which although not part of the Convention incorporated under the HRA, is nonetheless a potent factor in the ECtHR's assessment of alleged breaches. Courts had shown a relaxation on restrictions in cases involving sensitive questions which required examination.[264] The Court of Appeal[265] accepted that public bodies who are challenged over the matter of the exercise of a discretion or power can expect that the burden of establishing a case will be upon the applicant; however, once the case is accepted for hearing, it becomes the duty of the respondent council 'to make full and fair disclosure'.[266] It is, said the Master of the Rolls, 'a process which falls to be conducted with all the cards face upwards . . . and the vast majority of cards will start in the authority's hands'. Courts have demanded more rigorous and exacting scrutiny where human rights are involved.[267]

The approach to disclosure on judicial review was re-examined by the House of Lords in *Tweed*, a case on appeal from Northern Ireland that concerned the banning of a march by the Northern Ireland Parade's Commission.[268] The claimant argued that the ban breached his Convention rights (Arts. 9, 10 and 11). A request was made for documents containing the views of the police and others on the proposed march. Lord Bingham noted that in the minority of judicial review applications in which the precise facts are significant, procedures

[261] Lord Wilberforce in *Zamir v Secretary of State* [1980] AC 930; Lord Scarman in *IRC v National Federation of Self Employed and Small Businesses* [1982] AC 617; Lord Diplock in *O'Reilly v Mackman* [1983] 2 AC 237; and cf. *R v Liverpool City Council, ex p. Coade* (1986) The Times, 10 October; and *R v Secretary of State for the Home Department, ex p. Gardian* (1996) The Times, 1 April. See the *Bowman Review of the Crown Office List* LCD (2000), which led to CPR 1998, Pt 54.

[262] *R v Secretary of State for Foreign Affairs, ex p. WDM Ltd* [1995] 1 All ER 611.

[263] This would appear to be reinforced by the case in note 268 below.

[264] *R v Secretary of State for the Home Department, ex p. Herbage* [1987] QB 872 QBD.

[265] *R v Lancashire CC, ex p. Huddleston* [1986] 2 All ER 941; and see *R v Secretary of State for Transport, ex p. Sherriff & Sons Ltd* (1986) The Times, 18 December.

[266] Not by disclosure, but by a 'voluntary' explanation of events.

[267] See *Smith* and *Chahal* etc., see note 151 above. Note *R v Secretary of State for the Home Department, ex p. Turgut* [2001] 1 All ER 719, CA.

[268] *Tweed v NI Parades Commission* [2006] UKHL 53.

exist for disclosure of specific documents to be sought and ordered. 'Such applications are likely to increase in frequency, since human rights decisions under the Convention tend to be very fact-specific and any judgment on the proportionality of a public authority's interference with a protected Convention right is likely to call for a careful and accurate evaluation of the facts.' But disclosure should not be automatic. The test will always be whether, in the context, disclosure appears to be necessary in order to resolve the matter fairly and justly. Lord Carswell believed it would now be 'desirable to substitute for the rules hitherto applied a more flexible and less prescriptive principle, which judges the need for disclosure in accordance with the requirements of the particular case, taking into account the facts and circumstances' (para. 32). Most judicial review cases will not require disclosure for the reasons explained above. It will not be routine in judicial review. Even where proportionality is raised 'disclosure should be carefully limited to the issues which require it in the interests of justice. This object will be assisted if parties seeking disclosure continue to follow the practice where possible of specifying the particular documents or classes of documents they require . . . rather than asking for an order for general disclosure.' [para. 33] In determining the extent of such disclosure or inspection the court will take into account all the circumstances of the case and in particular the overriding objective in Pt 1 of the CPR and the concept of proportionality.[269] Where a proportionality challenge is made, disclosure may be allowed to assess the balance that was struck between a stated PI and the claimant's rights, the relative weight to be accorded to relative considerations and the desirable intensity of review. This will be subject to any necessary redaction or consideration of PII claims. Lord Carswell was quick to point out that this will not transform judicial review into a merits review.[270]

The case law on PII is legion and represents one of the most delicate areas of judicial judgment in contemporary law. Out of the abundance, three points can be made briefly. One is that it has been extended to criminal cases, which could cause extreme difficulties for the defence. The courts and the Attorney General had given guidance on such cases.[271] Scott's recommendation for use of PII certificates in criminal trials was that they should not be used on a class basis to protect information. '[I]f PII class claims are sanctioned, Whitehall departments will inevitably seek to bring within the recognised classes an increasing range of documents. I do not believe that the instinctive Whitehall reaction to seek to withhold Government documents from public inspection is likely to change.' Only a contents claim should be made and if the evidence is relevant and

---

[269] *Civil Procedure 2006*, vol. 1, para. 31.12.2.

[270] *Tweed*, note 268 above, at para. 35, quoting Lord Steyn in *Daly* [2001] 2 AC 532, at para. 27: there has not been a shift to a merits review. See also Lord Carswell at para. 32 and Lord Brown at para. 57.

[271] (1981) 74 Cr App Rep 302. See Home Office, *Disclosure*, Cm. 2864 (1995) and *R v Ward* [1993] 2 All ER 577; *R v Keane* [1994] 2 All ER 478; *R v Brown (Winston)* [1994] 1 WLR 1599.

material and may, the court believes, be of assistance to the defence, it should be disclosed. If there is a risk of the PI being seriously damaged by disclosure, then the trial should be halted. In that respect, Sir Richard did not believe it was correct to talk of a balancing of interests as had previous cases – the PI of doing justice as against the PI of protecting public security. Justice demanded the provision of information or the withdrawal of charges.[272]

Following several critical cases in Strasbourg and breaches of Art. 6 ECHR by the courts in England, the House of Lords provided detailed guidance on PII claims in criminal prosecutions.[273] Lord Bingham ruled that:

> Fairness ordinarily requires that any material held by the prosecution which weakens its case or strengthens that of the defendant, if not relied on as part of its formal case against the defendant, should be disclosed to the defence. Bitter experience has shown that miscarriages of justice may occur where such material is withheld from disclosure. The golden rule is that full disclosure of such material should be made. [Para. 14]

Special advocates had been employed to assist the court in determining claims for PII in criminal trials but their use should be a last resort and never routine and 'no other course will adequately meet the overriding requirement of fairness to the defendant' [para. 22]. They should only be used in cases of exceptional difficulty. If material does not weaken the prosecution case or strengthen that of the defendant, there is no requirement to disclose it (para. 35). When any issue of derogation from the golden rule of full disclosure comes before it, the court must address a series of questions including the specific facts of the case and nature of material withheld: does material weaken or strengthen a case as stated above; is there a real risk to an important PI by disclosure? If 'yes', can the defendant's interest be protected without disclosure or can disclosure be ordered to an extent or in a way which will give adequate protection to the PI in question and also afford adequate protection to the interests of the defence? Can there be disclosure short of full disclosure by summaries or extracts or edited or anonymised documents? The judge would have to approve disclosure. Does the limited disclosure represent the minimum derogation necessary to protect the PI in question? If 'no', the court should order such greater disclosure as will represent the minimum derogation from the golden rule of full disclosure. If limited disclosure is ordered may its effect be to 'render the trial process, viewed as a whole, unfair to the defendant? If "Yes", then fuller disclosure should be ordered even if this leads, or may lead, the prosecution to discontinue the proceedings so as to avoid having to make disclosure.' This last point should be continually addressed as the trial progresses.

The defence should be involved to the 'maximum extent possible'. Very rarely will some measure of disclosure to the defence not be possible:

---

[272] HC 115 (1995–6).
[273] *R v H* [2004] UKHL 3. On special advocates see *Edwards and Lewis v UK* (2003) 15 BHRC 189.

even if this is confined to the fact that an ex parte application is to be made. If even that information is withheld and if the material to be withheld is of significant help to the defendant [quaere assistance but less than significant], there must be a very serious question whether the prosecution should proceed, since special counsel, even if appointed, cannot then receive any instructions from the defence at all.

The ECtHR has ruled that where the prosecution withheld information from the defence without informing the trial judge, a subsequent review of the evidence by the Court of Appeal in the absence of the defence lawyers did not remedy a breach of Art. 6(1) and (3)(a)–(b) ECHR.[274]

A major problem was the non-disclosure of material the prosecution did not intend to use. New procedures covering disclosures were introduced by the Criminal Procedure and Investigations Act 1996, Pts I and II along with a code of practice. This was heavily criticised because too often full and reliable schedules of unused documents were not produced by police disclosure officers.[275] The Criminal Justice Act 2003, Pt 5 amended the 1996 Act. The Act together with codes of practice in 1997 and 2005, a revised Attorney General's guidelines and a protocol from the judges, *Disclosure: Protocol for the control and management of unused material in the Crown Court* (20 February 2006), now set out the responsibilities of disclosure officers.[276] The 2003 Act removed the subjective basis for assessing what has to be disclosed to an objective one. There were now to be 'initial' duties of disclosure and 'continuing' duties of disclosure – and the amount of documentation involved will often be voluminous. As shown in *R v H* the House of Lords has confirmed that where fairness requires 'full disclosure' that should be the 'golden rule' with regard to information which assists the defence or undermines the prosecution. Clearly, abuse of the duties would run the risk of breach of Art. 6 under the HRA, but one first has to know that the material exists and what it contains. Here, the FOIA will be of little use, given the exemption in ss. 30–1 (chapter 6, p. 188 *et seq.*). Indeed, PAs generally are likely to view certain FOIA information requests with a view to possible litigation causing them to invoke an exemption.

Secondly, it emerged in *Matrix Churchill* – and largely from a judgment of Bingham LJ – that ministers were advised by the Attorney General to sign PII certificates virtually as an automatic response without considering whether such was really required. On the contrary, it is up to the minister to exercise his own judgment. The fact that a judge makes the ultimate decision on disclosure does

---

[274] *Rowe and Davis v UK* 2890/95 (2000) 30 EHRR 1; and cf. *Jasper v UK* (2000) 30 EHRR 1 where proper procedures were followed; see *Dowsett v UK* [2004] 38 EHRR 41. See *Hugh Jordan v UK* ECtHR 4 May 2001 and breaches of Art. 2 where there were inadequate investigations into the shooting of Catholics in Northern Ireland. This breach included use of PII certificates and inadequate provision of information.

[275] See M. Zander, *Cases and Matreials on the English Legal System*, 10th edn (2007), p. 292 *et seq.*

[276] *R v K* [2006] EWCA Crim 724. The 1996 and 2003 Acts also changed the law in terms of defence disclosures to the prosecution.

not absolve the minister of his duty.[277] Last of all, where national security is impleaded the courts will rarely wish to look behind the minister's appropriately drafted certificate although there must be a residuary discretion in the court.[278]

Sir Richard Scott was critical of the use made by the Attorney General of PII certificates in his report into the *Matrix Churchill* trial. He was clearly of the view that ministers must read the certificates for themselves and formulate their own opinion and not simply act as a rubber stamp, an approach which is neither 'necessary nor appropriate'. He followed the judgment of Lord Templeman in *ex p. Wiley* to that effect. A court is unlikely to second-guess a minister who believes disclosure should be made, which was the advice of Lord Woolf in *ex p. Wiley*. In other words, the minister must exercise judgment before signing and must not be dictated to by another official. Appropriate advice must of course be sought and considered.

Following the Scott report, the Major Government announced that PII would only be claimed in future on a contents basis.[279] This was confirmed by the incoming Labour Government.[280] The undertaking would only be binding on Crown bodies including the Crown Prosecution Service. It would not be binding on local government or the police and non-Crown public bodies.[281] Furthermore, the undertaking did not prevent class exemptions applying in a profligate manner in the FOIA 2000.

The concluding point concerns the increasing resort to 'closed procedures' involving special advocates. This has been extended to actions in private law notwithstanding the criticism of the procedures by the law lords in *AF* (Introduction, p. 5). In these cases the evidence is not disregarded by the court as in PII; it is used by *one* side.[282]

---

[277] The decision of Bingham LJ was *Makanjuola v Met. Police Com'r* [1992] 3 All ER 617, CA. In his report on Matrix Churchill, Sir Richard Scott criticised the use by the government of PII certificates on a class basis in criminal trials. The government did not initially accept this criticism which drew forth further criticism from Sir Richard.

[278] *Balfour v FCO* [1994] 2 All ER 588, CA and see Lord Scarman in *Burmah Oil*, note 246 above. See *McQuillan's* case, note 182 above, and questioning of whether national security was at issue or a question of protection of informers. See, generally, Simon Brown LJ 'Public Interest Immunity' (1994) Public Law 579.

[279] HC Debs., vol. 287, col. 949; and HL Debs., vol. 576, col. 1507, 18 December 1996.

[280] HC Debs., vol. 297, col. 616, 11 July 1997.

[281] In care proceedings, see s. 42(3) Children Act 1989 and *A Met. Borough Council v S.* [2003] EWHC 976 (Fam) and *Re W (children) (care proceedings: disclosure)* [2003] EWHC 1624 (Fam).

[282] *B. Al Rawi etc. v The Security Service* [2009] EWHC 2959 (QB).

12

Freedom of information: overseas experience[1]

This chapter will focus upon the role of legislation in other countries, as well as their political practice, in providing and protecting information, whether to or about individuals or, in the case of the USA, committees of the legislature overseeing the operation of legislation and expenditure. I will concentrate on the USA, Canada, Australia and New Zealand.[2] These are countries that, in spite of their enormous differences both between themselves and with Britain, nonetheless possess certain legal cultural similarities with the British system, either through common-law inheritance or through direct or indirect constitutional influence. This chapter will allow us to assess the contribution which overseas practice has made to opening up government, or otherwise, and will also act as a benchmark for our own practice. It should be noted that freedom of information (FOI) laws have faced reactions from executives and legislatures seeking to rein in what are regarded as excesses. We start by examining America where this is certainly true, but in Ireland the FOI Act of 1997 was subject to modification in 2003, which also illustrated a constraint on openness.[3]

Today, over seventy countries possess FOI laws. In addition there are multinational regimes such as the EU laws examined in chapter 10. Germany is a recent recruit with a law coming into effect in 2006. China introduced a law by State Council decree in 2007 to come into effect in 2008. The law in South Africa covers private entities where they affect the human rights or rights of individuals. The laws are being introduced in Islamic states – Egypt was planning to introduce laws in 2008. Sweden had its freedom of the press law from 1776. But the modern story begins in the USA.

---

[1] Useful figures on FOIA overseas is contained in R. Hazell *et al.*, *Estimating the Likely Volumes, Sensitivity and Complexity of Casework for the IC under FOIA 2000 and EIRs* (Constitution Unit, UCL, 2004). See also Open Society Justice Initiative, *Transparency and Silence: A survey of access to information laws and practices in fourteen countries* (2006).

[2] For civil law systems, see HL 97 (1998–9), p. 35. See also generally N. S. Marsh (ed.), *Public Access to Government-held Information: A comparative symposium* (1987) and R. Vaughn (ed.), *Freedom of Information* (2001).

[3] M. McDonagh, *Freedom of Information Law*, 2nd edn (2006).

USA

'Freedom of Information cases are peculiarly difficult' (*Miscavige v IRS* No. 92–8659 (11th Cir. 17 September 1993).

The USA has possessed a Freedom of Information Act (FOIA) since 1966. Previous statutes had only allowed public access to government documents if a 'need to know' was established,[4] and they allowed agencies to withhold information for 'good cause'. The Supreme Court has observed that a priority of the Act is to 'ensure that the Government's activities be opened to the sharp eye of public scrutiny'.[5] That court had decided almost thirty FOI cases between 1966–2008.[6] All agencies in the executive branch of the federal government, including administrative regulatory agencies, are subject to the FOIA. Excluded from the operation of the Act are the judicial and legislative branches of government. So too are members of the president's *immediate personal staff*, whose sole function is to give advice and assistance to the president. This exclusion includes the vice president. State government and local and city government are not included in this legislation.[7]

The aim of the Act, as amended in 1974, is to provide public access to an agency's records if it is covered by the Act. An applicant does not have to demonstrate a specific interest in a matter to view relevant documents – an idle curiosity suffices. The legislation provides a presumptive right of access to documents and files to *anyone* – it is not restricted, it should be noted, to American citizens. The legal onus is on those denying access to justify denial. In 1993, both the president and the Attorney General made highly publicised statements emphasising their commitment to making the operation of the Act more effective to enhance openness and participation. The opposition has not been slow to laud these virtues also to enhance the role of the consumer vis-à-vis government. In 1996, the FOIA was amended by the Electronic FOIA amendments (see below). However, secrecy became a characteristic of George Bush's presidency and in 2001, the Attorney General issued a memorandum to all departmental and agency chiefs. This contains advice on a presumption of non-disclosure under FOIA: 'Any discretionary decision by your agency to disclose information protected under FOIA should be made only after full and deliberate consideration of the institutional, commercial, and personal privacy interests that could be implicated by disclosure of the information.' They will be defended by the US Department of Justice unless the department's decision lacks a 'sound legal basis'. Decisions on classification of (making secret)

---

[4] The Housekeeping Statute of 1789. The Administrative Procedure Act 1946 allowed inspection unless 'good cause' required confidentiality. This provision was widely invoked by agencies.

[5] *United States Department of Justice v Reporters Committee for Freedom of the Press* 489 US 749 (1989).

[6] *Collaboration on Government Secrecy*, www.wcl.american.edu/lawandgov/cgs/.

[7] Many have their own FOI laws. See P. Birkinshaw, *Freedom of Information: The US experience*, Hull University Law School Studies in Law (1991).

documents can be taken by over 4,000 federal officials.[8] Informal classification of documents by departments and agencies has increased since 2001. The Critical Infrastructure Information Act 2002 made serious inroads into the FOIA (below). The Intelligence Authorization Act 2003 contained prohibitions on complying with intelligence requests from foreign governments and George Bush, by Executive Order 13233, restricted access to the records of former presidents. The war on terror brought high-profile assaults on transparency, none more famous than Guantánamo prison and secret rendition.

However, in 2007, Congress enacted Public Law 110–175, grandly entitled the Openness Promotes Effectiveness in Our Government Act maintaining the cycle of ten-yearly reforms to the FOIA. This amended the provisions on awards of attorney fees where complainants substantially prevail – a position which now favours requesters. Fees provisions were amended to take account of agency delay and the FOIA is extended to cover federal contractors, i.e. those contracting with federal entities. An Office of Government Information Services is established as an overseer of the FOIA and offers mediation services. The Act also codifies the president's Executive Order 13392 (2005) encouraging all federal bodies to respond positively and timeously to FOI requests and to establish more coherent administrative arrangements for the FOIA. The Attorney General reports annually on the impact of the order on agency administration. The Department of Justice has an on-site regular report on the FOIA at http://www.usdoj.gov/oip/foiapost/2009foiapost1.htm.

Finally, although the Bush administration made widespread resort to secrecy and secret practices, the incoming president, Barak Obama, in a memorandum on 21 January 2009 (day one of his presidency) to the heads of all executive branch departments and agencies declared his firm commitment to government transparency.[9] The memorandum has the effect of an executive order. 'My Administration is committed to creating an unprecedented level of openness in Government. We will work together to ensure the public trust and establish a system of transparency, public participation, and collaboration . . . Government should be transparent.' This unprecedented presidential directive calls upon federal agencies to 'harness new technologies' to make information about their operations 'readily available to the public' and to 'provide . . . information for citizens about what their Government is doing in their name.' The president directed officials at the White House, the Office of Management and Budget (OMB), the Department of Justice and the National Archives and Records Administration immediately to begin co-ordinating recommendations by 21 May 2009 for an 'Open Government Directive' to be issued by the Director of the OMB 'that instructs executive departments and agencies to take specific actions implementing the principles set forth in this memorandum'. A companion

---

[8] Information Security Oversight Office 2007 Report to the President, www.archives.gov/isoo/reports/2008-annual-report.pdf. See D. Metcalfe, 'The nature of government secrecy' (2009) *Government Information Quarterly* 305.

[9] *Transparency and Open Government*, 21 January 2009.

directive on the FOIA instructs the Attorney General in the same period to issue new guidelines to the government implementing the same principles of openness and transparency in the FOIA context (see Office of the Attorney General Memo for Heads of Executive Departments and Agencies, *The Freedom of Information Act*, 19 March 2009).

Basic FOIA requirements

Each agency covered by the FOIA has to publish in the *Federal Register* details of its organisation: the employees from whom and the methods whereby information may be obtained; details of its procedures *including* informal ones; rules, policies or interpretations of general applicability; and rules of procedure and instructions as to the scope and contents of all papers, reports or examinations. The agency cannot rely in legal proceedings upon any matter that it is bound by law to publish and which it has not, and of which the litigant has not had 'actual and timely notice'. Agencies are also undertaking 'affirmative information disclosure' via the Internet and so on whereby information is released before a specific request. This has now become a legal requirement. One point that awaited final clarification is that the federal FOIA, as opposed to some state and city FOIA laws, does not spell out the types of information sources, other than documents, which are covered by the Act. However, it is taken to cover information in documents in whatever form it takes. The 1996 Electronic FOIA makes it absolutely clear that the FOIA covers electronic records.[10]

Exemptions

Although the basic thrust of the Act is positive and supportive of openness, there are nine exemptions from the FOIA, which include national-defence or foreign-policy information that is properly classified as confidential, secret or top secret by presidential executive order. National security tends to be seen in terms of defence and foreign policy and is not as widely drawn as in the UK (see chapter 2). An executive order of 1982[11] reversed the trend of relaxation of security classifications and 'broadened the discretion to create official secrets'. Many of the safeguards against over-enthusiastic classification were removed. So, mandatory secrecy requirements rather than permissive ones became more common, the 'balancing test' requiring the weighing of public access against the government need for secrecy was eliminated, and systematic

---

[10] See Electronic FOIA Amendment Act 1996 and note 24 below.

[11] EO 12356 (47 FR 14874 – April 1982). In 1983, there were 17,141,052 derivative classification decisions made: this is the act of incorporating, paraphrasing, restating or generating in a new form classified source information.

declassification was cancelled.[12] The order allows for its own mandatory 'review requests' of classified information as an alternative to FOIA actions. A new executive order took effect in October 1995 which liberalised the 1982 Reagan order.[13] This is still the governing provision although it was amended in 2003 by EO 13,292, which pushed back de-classification dates. The 1995 order hoped to ease the process of declassification in several ways: the period of classification has been shortened in most instances to ten years; automatic de-classification has been introduced for records over twenty-five years old unless information is 'especially sensitive'; systematic declassification is reintroduced in other cases which establishes a programme to review classification; the balancing test is restored in amended form to 'determine whether the public interest (PI) in disclosure outweighs the damage to national security that might reasonably be expected from disclosure'. It removes presumptions against automatic classification in some areas, e.g. foreign-government information; concise reasons must be given on the documents for classification; and a Security Classification Appeals Panel and a Policy Advisory Council are established. The objectives of the 1995 order have not been matched by developments in practice. The orders are co-ordinated by the Information Security Oversight Office, which receives its policy and programme guidance from the National Security Council.[14] Its annual reports have details of numbers of classification and de-classification decisions. The White House has claimed that the National Security Council (NSC) is a personal adviser to the president and is therefore not covered by the FOIA.[15]

Under the FOIA, the internal rules and practices of an agency will be exempt but not the manuals and instructions on the interpretation of regulations. Other important exemptions include: trade secrets; commercial and financial information obtained by the government that is privileged or confidential; inter- or intra-agency memoranda or letters which are not available by law;[16] information protected by other statutes especially concerning the CIA and also taxation; personnel or medical files disclosure of which would constitute a clearly unwarranted invasion of privacy; and investigatory records compiled for law enforcement purposes if disclosure would result in certain types of harm. Some law enforcement information is excluded from the FOIA. An exemption covers agency information concerning supervision or regulation of financial institutions and information concerning wells. Reliance by an agency on an

---

[12] The National Co-ordinating Committee for the Promotion of History believed EO 12356 had caused a 'massive' restriction on previously available information.

[13] EO 12958.   [14] US Dept of Justice, *FOIA Update XVI No. 2* (1995).

[15] *Armstrong v Executive Office* 25 March (DC Circ 1995). On exemptions under FOIA for exports' licensing (armaments) see the Scott Report, HC 115 (1995–6), para. D4.5.9.

[16] *Department of the Interior and Bureau of Indian Affairs v Klamath Water Users Protective Ass'n* US Supreme Court No. 99–1871, 5 March 2001 (decided): the FOIA introduced a 'general philosophy of full agency disclosure'. 'Congress had to realise that not every secret under the old law would be secret under the new.'

exemption is discretionary and not mandatory and so exempt information may be disclosed.[17]

The courts can be robust in applying and limiting exemptions. In *ACLU v DoD*[18] disclosure was ordered of photographs and videos depicting abuse of detainees at the *Abu Ghraib* prison in Iraq. The court ruled that the application of the s. 7F exemption concerning withholding of information necessary to protect the safety of a wide range of individuals is subject to a balancing of interests. The court determined that the risk of violence to US troops and others as a result of disclosure is outweighed by 'core values of FOIA'.

Challenging a refusal

Where there is a refusal to supply information, appeal procedures are specifically provided in each agency's FOIA regulations. A denial letter will inform the applicant of a right of appeal – usually within thirty days.[19] The official refusing the appeal must be identified, and the exemption and reasons for refusal must be given. The requester must be informed of his or her right to apply to the federal court where there is a complete rehearing with the burden of proof on the agency. Attorney fees are recoverable where an applicant 'substantially succeeds' and although the FOIA cases no longer receive a *de jure* automatic priority in federal court dockets they do receive such treatment *de facto*.

After the Federal Court of Appeals decision in *Vaughn*,[20] trial courts may, on a motion by a plaintiff, require the government to itemise the documents, to provide a detailed justification of claimed exemptions, and to index by cross-reference the itemisation to the justification. A justification requires 'a relatively detailed analysis in manageable segments'. An itemisation must 'specify in detail' which parts the agency believes to be exempt. An index cross-references the itemisation and the justification, allowing easier identification of the information required.[21] This is particularly helpful where the applicant does not know what the contents of the documents are, where classification is obscure, or where it is difficult to meet a government claim without a clearer description of the documents. Informal practices have developed whereby *inter partes* meetings will take place between applicants to discuss documents and exemptions. The process is known as an 'oral *Vaughn*' affidavit, so named after the case introducing the itemised exemption practice and proceedings are used as a form

---

[17] See *Chrysler Corp. v Brown* 99 S Ct 1705 (1979).   [18] 389 F Supp 2d 547 (SDNY, 2005).

[19] The 1974 Act provides for internal disciplinary measures where refusal was arbitrary or capricious.

[20] *Vaughn v Rosen* 484 F 2d 820 (CA, DC, 1973).

[21] See B. Braverman and F. Chetwynd, *Information Law* (1985) for a copious treatise; R. G. Vaughn, *Explanation of Federal FOIA etc.* (1981). See also K. C. Davies, *Administrative Law Treatise*, 2nd edn (1978), vol. 1, ch. 5 and 1982 Supplement and works cited in note 1 above. The Department of Justice publishes a *FOI Caselist* and and a *FOI Guide* and *Privacy Act Overview* each year.

of bartering or negotiation with benefits for both sides – 'litigotiation' as it is called.[22]

The court can engage in *in camera* inspection of documents. If a third party wishes to stop an agency handing over information concerning him to a requester, he may seek judicial review of an agency's decision. This is known as a reverse FOIA suit (see below).[23] Third-party practices in other jurisdictions are more sophisticated but operated with the benefit of hindsight.

1996 FOIA amendments

The 1996 FOIA amendments[24] expand the type of records that must be published without request to include all those that are likely to be the subject of more than one request. Agencies will also have to make many records available online; electronic reading rooms must be established in all agency reading rooms by 1 November 1997. Agencies also have to produce guides for requesters containing an index of all major information systems of the agency, a description of 'major information and locator systems' maintained by the agency,[25] and a handbook on obtaining information from the agency. Indexes also have to be produced of previously released records that are likely to be the subject of future requests. The traditional cameo of a paper request and a long wait for reply is now, because of the technology-driven developments, untenable.[26] However, there has been some resistance to the index requirement by the agencies.

Agencies are given twenty days to respond to requests for documents (this was doubled from ten days which was felt to be unrealistic). Negotiations may take place around the modification of a request. Unreasonable refusal to modify a request may justify an agency delay. However, expedited requests and responses may be made in two cases: where requesters can show that failure to obtain the records on an expedited basis will pose an immediate threat to life or physical safety of a person; or requesters who are primarily engaged in the dissemination of information to the public (press and media) where they can show that their request involves matters on which there is an urgent need to inform the public concerning 'actual or alleged federal government activity'. The agency must rule on the request for expedited processing within ten days and provision must be made for expedited appeals. No set time limit is provided for the response which must be made as soon as practicable.

In March 2001, the General Accounting Office issued a generally favourable report on the 1996 Act and its operation. Most agencies examined had established 'electronic reading rooms' but 'data quality issues' limited the usefulness

---

[22] AG's Advocacy Institute, Dept of Justice, *FOIA for Attorneys and Access Professionals*, (1987), p. V 57.

[23] Under Administrative Procedure Act 1946, s. 10.

[24] M. Tankersley, 'Recent developments: Electronic FOIA' (1998) Admin Law Rev 339–458.

[25] *Ibid.*, p. 421.   [26] *Ibid.*, p. 430.

of some reports on the Act.[27] Subsequent reports have detailed information on target rates and performance under the president's executive order of 2005 seeking to ensure more responsive compliance with the order.[28]

General impact of the FOIA

The FOIA is often hailed as the great initiator of open government. We should not be blind to the fact that there has been considerable opposition to it in the USA. In 1979, Dresner[29] spoke highly of the FOIA's impact upon government accountability, scrutiny and improved decision-making, as well as on inhibiting corruption. From 1980, however, the executive presented repeated proposals for reform of the FOIA because of the cost of its administration, the quantity of case law, and because the Act was being used in ways which Congress never intended.[30] The business community has long lobbied for reform which would facilitate businesses' opportunity to challenge requests for information about them and a reform was introduced in 1987 by executive order improving the position of third parties. The law enforcement agencies were not satisfied with the exemption which covers their operations, and in 1986, 'after years of deliberation',[31] Congress passed a major FOIA reform which extends the exemption available to law enforcement practices. In fact, the 1986 Act actually *excludes* certain categories of documents from the FOIA.[32] Further, the records or information no longer have to be investigatory, and may be withheld when they *could* (not would) reasonably be expected to interfere with enforcement proceedings; could deprive a person of a fair trial; could reasonably be expected to constitute an unwarranted invasion of privacy; could reveal the identity of a confidential source which furnished information; could disclose techniques and procedures for law enforcement investigations or prosecutions; or could reasonably be expected, if disclosed, to endanger the life or physical safety of *any individual* (not only law enforcement personnel) – which is understandable.[33]

The exemption which has been the subject of most litigation concerns inter- and intra-agency memoranda and letters not available by law. Basically, this exemption seeks to protect deliberations in the policymaking process. The exemption is meant to cover advisory opinions, not factual information, although 'pre-decisional memoranda expressly incorporated by reference in a final decision must be disclosed'.[34] Since the earlier case law the judiciary have

---

[27] US GAO 01–378 March 2001, *Information Management*.

[28] www.fas.org/sgp/foia/ag101606.pdf.

[29] S. Dresner, *Open Government: Lessons from America* (1980).

[30] By 'information brokers' for example, seeking commercially confidential information.

[31] US Dept of Justice, *FOIA Update*, vol. VII, No. 4 (1986); and vol. VIII, No. 1 (1987), for details.

[32] S. 552(7)(c) – 'live proceedings' and informants.

[33] See *US Department of Justice v Landano* 113 S Ct 2014 (1993).

[34] For the exemption to apply the documents must be protected from discovery in civil suits: *Federal Open Market Committee v Merrill* 99 S Ct 2800 (1979). In *NLRB v Sears, Roebuck* 421 US 132 (1975) the Supreme Court drew a distinction between post-decision documentation

extended the breadth of this exemption in a series of decisions.[35] In 1993, the Attorney General declared a policy guideline to the effect that this exemption should be defended in the courts only where an 'agency reasonably foresees that disclosure would be harmful to an interest protected by that exemption'.[36] Where only a governmental interest would be affected by disclosure there is a far greater scope for discretionary disclosure than in the case of personal privacy or commercial confidentiality and detailed guidance is given on factors to consider. The memorandum of 2001 was outlined above.

The 1986 Act was a major success for the executive, and other reforms include the Paperwork Reduction Act 1980, which seeks to minimise the extent and cost of the 'paperwork burden' on small businesses and state and local government although the executive order 12356 imposing greater secrecy has been largely superseded.[37] Further, the federal government has employed the Espionage Act to punish unauthorised disclosure of information even though the cases did not concern spying to which it was commonly thought to have been restricted. In the past, the executive has also taken steps to placate the British Government since Crown documents not available in the UK may well be available in the USA under the FOIA. UK departments mark such documents 'UK Confidential', although this, by itself, would not ensure exemption in the USA.[38]

There are positive and well-recorded benefits to the legislation.[39] Relyea has described how a civil service acceptance of the Act has been fostered within the agencies. Specialists are responsible for FOIA requests and 'brokerage' thereon.[40] Training programmes, publications and information about the Act are first class.[41] There is a marked degree of professionalism on the government side and the requester side.[42] However, charging fees without justification, refusing to act until money is 'upfront', intentionally understaffing FOI departments, forcing litigation, indiscriminate censorship, and other

---

(not protected) and pre-decision documentation (protected). The exemption also protects information covered by legal professional privilege.

[35] *Wolfe v HHS* 839 F 2d 768 (1988); *Access Reports v Department of Justice* 926 F 2d 1192 (1991); *Mapother v Department of Justice* No. 95–5261 DC Cir 17 September 1993; *Quarles v Department of Justice* 893 F 2d 390 (1990); *Petroleum Info. Corp. v US Department of Interior* 976 F 2d 1429 (1992).

[36] US Dept of Justice, *FOIA Update*, vol. XV, No. 2 (1994).

[37] R. Ehlke and H. Relyea (1983) 30/2 *Fed Bar News and Journal* 91.

[38] Examples covered documents relevant to the Sizewell 'B' proposals for a PWR nuclear generator. See incidentally *de Zeven Provincien* [1986] 3 All ER 487, HL and use of American courts in English proceedings to get pre-trial discovery of information. Embarrassment was caused when records on President Clinton relating to his residence in the UK as a student were released to the US Government in 1992.

[39] Campaign for Freedom of Information, *Secrets*, No. 22 (1991).

[40] H. Relyea, 'A comparative review of the Access to Information Act (Canada) and the US FOIA' (1986, unpublished paper).

[41] These include manuals published by the Department of Justice, the *FOIA Update* and also excellent publications on the use of the legislation published by Congress. *FOIA Update* was replaced by *FOIA Post* in 2001 and is available at www.usdoj.gov/oip/foiapost/mainpage.htm.

[42] See Birkinshaw, *Freedom of Information: The US experience*, p. 23.

unhelpful practices have all been well-known occurrences. So too is ignoring time responses which should take ten days for an initial response. One FOIA suit has taken eleven years to resolve through the courts.[43]

More effective procedures have been in place giving third parties notice and allowing opportunity for challenge when documents relating to them are sought. The business and commercial community were anxious for such safeguards. The commercial confidentiality exemption has placed the burden on those claiming the exemption to prove it but in *Critical Mass Energy Project v NRC*[44] the Court of Appeals upheld this rule – so that, for instance, if an agency states that disclosure would impair its ability to obtain similar information in the future it would have to prove such – but added a new exemption. Where information had been volunteered to agencies and was not 'customarily' made available to the public by the supplier of the information, it attracted the exemption.

The 1986 FOIA has amended the basis for charging fees for complying with duties under the legislation. Requests for commercial purposes will be charged the actual cost of document review and search time (i.e. employee-hours involved and documents are reviewed line by line) and duplication fees, though requesters may still be entitled to a fee waiver if, for instance, their request is for information that it is in the PI to disclose 'because it is likely to contribute significantly to public understanding of the operations of Government'. Search and review fees will be waived for educational, non-commercial scientific organisations and requesters from the news media.[45]

The FOIA has generated a vast industry in the USA among the business community.[46] The Department of Justice has publications of annual reports with detailed figures on requests.[47] In 2008, the Department of Defense (DoD), as an example, reported 71,699 processed requests for records under the FOIA. In the processing of these cases, the DoD granted in full 28,451, partially denied 14,901, and denied in full 2,554 on the basis of FOIA exemptions. The total DoD operating cost associated with the processing of requests during this report period was $70,755,178. The average cost of processing a single case during this period was approximately $986.00. Fees collected amounted to $617,878. The Department for Health and Human Services received 66,583 requests and granted almost 47,000 completely. Full denials based on exemptions were 1,824. The total cost to the department was $28,137,346.29. It collected fees of $967,877.60. The CIA received 1,935 requests. Two hundred and thirty-seven were granted totally, 532 partially. The Department for Homeland Security received 108,952 FOIA requests. The cost was reported at $24,085,616.68.

The Coalition of Journalists in 2006 reported that over 60 per cent of requesters are from commercial bodies, many seeking information on

[43] *Gulf Oil Corp. v Brock* 778 F 2d 834 DDC (1985).
[44] 975 F 2d 871 (DC Cir 1992); cert denied 113 SCt 1579 (1993).
[45] Birkinshaw, Freedom of Information: The US experience, p. 8.
[46] Relyea, 'A comparative review', see note 40 above.   [47] www.usdoj.gov/oip/fy08.html.

business competitors. However, it has been stated that this does not generate any significant amount of litigation; far more significant as a generator
of litigation are PI groups seeking information about companies' compliance
with the law.[48] Use of professional data brokers to make requests is common.
Requests from 'private citizens' amount to about a third of the total. The press
accounts for only about 6 per cent of the total. In 1983, there were 262,265
requests under FOIA; by 2008 there were, according to the former director of
the FOIA programme in the Department of Justice, Dan Metcalfe, 'millions'.[49]

In 1983, the US General Accounting Office estimated the cost of the Act in
1981 at $61 million, 'although costs cannot currently be measured with any
precision'. This is comparable with the price of maintaining the armed services'
marching bands or golf courses on military bases. Estimates of the cost of
government self-promotion and public-relations exercises run to about $1.5
billion per annum at 1989 prices. 'Thus, it is considerably less expensive to
provide the public with the information it seeks via the FOIA than it is for the
Executive to provide what it determines the public should know about agency
activities and operations.'[50] By 2008, the three departments outlined above
reported a cost of $122,978,140. Seventy-one departments and agencies have
their figures reported. Figures for 2001 show that the total cost for administering
FOIA was $287,792,041.08.[51] One further factor is that government publications
in the USA are not protected by copyright laws as are government publications
in the UK.[52]

The FOIA is one of four major statutes facilitating open government in
the USA. The FOIA is primarily concerned with individuals gaining access to
agency records. Since its inception, however, a large number of professional
organisations, known, inter alia, as 'data brokers or 'surrogate requesters', use
the FOIA to gain information that they can market and sell to those with an
interest. A private foundation, the National Security Archive, has been used by
government officials because its files are better indexed than the departments'
files.

Critical Infrastructure Information Act and Homeland Security Act (2002)

The Critical Infrastructure Information Act of 2002,[53] was passed on 25 November 2002 as part of the Homeland Security Act. The Act regulates the use and
disclosure of information submitted to the Department of Homeland Security

---

[48] R. Stevenson, 'Protecting business interests under the Freedom of Information Act: Managing
Exemption 4' (1982) 34 Admin Law Rev 207.

[49] Note 8 above. In 2001, the total number of requests was 2,246,212: US Department of Justice
Office of Information and Privacy, *Privacy Conference 2003*.

[50] Relyea, 'A comparative review'.   [51] US Department of Justice, note 49 above.

[52] Copyright etc. Act 1988, s. 163. The position in the UK has become more relaxed on an ex
gratia basis.

[53] 6 U.S.C., §§131–4.

(DHS) about risks and threats to critical infrastructure. Section 1016(e) of the USA Patriot Act defines critical infrastructure as 'systems and assets, whether physical or virtual, so vital to the United States that the incapacity or destruction of such systems and assets would have a debilitating impact on security, national economic security, national public health or safety, or any combination of these matters'.

The implications of this legislation are massive. The US government is asking private organisations to share information about the nation's critical infrastructure assets. A President's Critical Infrastructure Protection Board was established shortly after 11 September 2001, which in 2002 produced a 'clear roadmap to protect a part of its infrastructure so essential to our way of life'. The board was abolished in 2003 but the legislation was brought into effect by regulations. Part of the roadmap was an 'unprecedented partnership between federal government and private organisations' in which a voluntary sharing of information with the government has been requested. It is suggested that up to 90 per cent of the nation's infrastructure is controlled by private industry. Companies were concerned that such information may be released under the FOIA. Federal government was concerned that, without such information, the USA may be more vulnerable to further terrorist attacks.[54]

Critical infrastructure information (CII) is therefore excluded from the FOIA, the details of which are finalised in regulations; criminal sanctions are imposed for unauthorised disclosures for CII under the latter (reminiscent of Official Secrecy laws in the UK); the provisions in the Act override state and local FOIA laws. CII includes physical and cyber-based systems and services essential to national defence, government or economy of the US, including those systems essential for telecoms (including voice and data transmission and the Internet), electrical power, gas and oil storage and transportation, banking and finance, water supply, emergency services (including medical, fire and police) and the continuity of government operations. In public private partnerships more information is required from the 'traditionally private functions' of energy and telecoms relating to risk assessment, risk prevention and security testing amongst other items. *Voluntary* sharing of information by the private sector companies will be protected under the FOIA by the Homeland Security Act, s. 5(a)(1)(A). A provider has to mark information with an *express* statement of its CII status. Just think about the Enron, Andersen and Worldcom scandals or police corruption. Enron filed a suit against the state of California when the state attempted to *subpoena* Enron's record of electricity sales. After the collapse, the Enron documents showed that the company had rigged electricity markets, created power shortages, raised prices and artificially boosted its own profits. Under s. 724 Homeland Security Act, CII includes the identity of the provider. The legislation overrides agency rules specifically on rule-making,

---

[54] J. Summerill (2003) The Federal Lawyer 24. See further: G. M. Stevens, *Homeland Security Act 2002: Critical Infrastructure Information Act* (Congressional Research Service, 2003).

judicial case law on *ex parte* contacts – i.e., access given to privileged parties only in lawmaking – and disclosure under the Act does not waive legal professional privilege or trade-secret privilege. The effect is to reverse the presumption of disclosure in the FOIA. Challenge could only be on a jurisdictional basis – this information is not CII. Opponents argued vigorously that existing exemptions covered such information adequately especially exemptions one and four of the FOIA on trade secrets and commercial confidentiality.

The Act and regulations[55] only cover information given to the Department of Homeland Security.

Federal Advisory Committee Act (FACA)[56]

The FACA, which is accompanied by regulations, is within the FOI mould but has its sights set more firmly on the real target of bureaucratic decision-making. The Act, enacted in 1972, has six basic objectives: to establish standards and uniform procedures to govern the creation, operation and termination of federal advisory committees; to ensure that whenever possible advisory committee meetings are open to the public and accessible; to reduce their cost; to avoid specific interest-group domination and rubber-stamping of prior decisions; to keep the public and Congress advised on all aspects of advisory committees; and to ensure they remain advisory and not executive. In 1970 it was estimated that as many as 3,200 such committees existed with a membership of 22,000[57] and in 1990 there were 1,071 committees comprising 22,391 persons. There is a concern that subjective preferences of organised interests could easily influence official decision-makers.[58] An early indication of its potential utility was given in *FCN Inc. v Davis*,[59] when a newspaper editor wished to be present at meetings between Treasury officials and consumer groups which were recommending whether labelling should be required for chemical additives in liquor. He obtained a court order prohibiting the closure of future meetings.

The FACA gives a broad definition to the advisory committees, or their subcommittees or subgroups, of agencies and departments whose members are not full-time officers or employees of the agency.[60] The Act covers such bodies if they have a fixed membership; if they have a defined purpose of providing advice to a federal agency; if they have regular or periodic meetings; and if they have an organisational structure. Committees have a two-year lifespan and those rendered otiose are terminated. A designated official will chair the meetings or attend, and the FACA requires a 'balanced representation of points of view'. In a famous example, a 'task force' established to advise Hillary Clinton on health reforms and policy was held not to be a committee under the

---

[55] See Federal Register, vol. 71, No. 170, Friday, 1 September 2006, Rules and Regulations.

[56] B. W. Tuerkheimer, 'Veto by neglect' (1975) 25 *AMULR* 53; Vaughn, note 21 above.

[57] HR Rep No. 1731 91st Congress, 2d Sess 14–15 (1970).

[58] S Rep No. 1098 92nd Congress, 2d Sess 6 (1972).   [59] 378 F Supp 1048, DDC (1974).

[60] For meetings of these officials, see 'The Sunshine Act' below.

Act.[61] The Supreme Court has declined to apply the FACA to the American Bar Association's Committee on Judicial Appointments, which advises the president on potential nominees for federal judgeships. The Supreme Court[62] has subsequently ruled that the president and vice-president may successfully claim executive privilege to protect documents requested in litigation more easily than was previously thought to be the case, distinguishing *Nixon v US*.[63] The Federal Advisory Committee Act has been narrowed considerably by litigation arising from these events so that in establishing a National Energy Policy Development Group within the Executive Office of the president, formally with only federal employees as members but on which it was alleged that non-federal employees fully participated, FACA did not apply.[64]

Adequate advance notice of the meetings must be given in the *Federal Register*, and subject to reasonable regulations any member of the public is given the right to attend, file a written statement or make an appearance. Detailed minutes with a complete description of the discussion must be kept, along with conclusions, and they must be available for inspection and copying.

The FOIA exemptions apply with some modifications. The agency head to whom the committee reports determines in writing whether an exemption will apply, and these have to be explained in detail. Reports have to be made out by the agency head on the extent to which he has accepted committee recommendations as well as on the latter's activities, status and membership.

It will be appreciated that, on paper, the FACA could go to the nerve centre of many of the essential decisions in the interface of public–private relationships and state regulation of private interest groups. That being the case, it is not surprising that its reception was marked by 'non-administration, non-use and ingenious bureaucratic techniques of evasion'.[65] In the first year of its operation there was widespread closure of meetings, often without citation of the exemption, or with citation of exemptions that courts had ruled did not apply. Setting up of 'informal ad hoc groups' has been resorted to, although in *Aviation Consumer Action Project v Yoke*[66] the District Court ruled that an ad hoc Civil Aviation Bureau meeting with airline representatives was covered by the FACA, though not where the president consulted informally with various groups as part of a publicity exercise.[67] Other evasive tactics have included holding meetings abroad, even on a private yacht! Domination by private interest groups was not uncommon, e.g. the National Petroleum Council carried out much of its work in subcommittees convened without public notice and often in oil-company offices.

---

[61] *Assoc. of American Physicians and Surgeons v Clinton* 997 F 2d 898 (DC Cir 1993). This reversed an earlier decision.
[62] *Cheney v US District Court for the District of Columbia* 542 US 367 (2004).
[63] 418 US 683 (1974) below.   [64] *In re Cheney and Others* 406 F 3d 723 (2005).
[65] Tuerkheimer, 'Veto by neglect'.   [66] Civ No. 73–707, DDC, 24 June 1974.
[67] *Nader v Baroody* Civ No. 74–1675, DDC, 23 June 1975.

Some of the recommendations to strengthen the safeguards – including over-sight of FACA by an agency other than the Office of Manpower and Budget,[68] effective enforcement sanctions, quick and informal appellate procedures to challenge closure, and a verbatim transcript of meetings which are closed for subsequent judicial review purposes – have been accepted.

The Sunshine Act

The Sunshine Act (SA) of 1976 is an 'open meeting' law allowing access to the meetings of those agencies within its scope. Its aim is to open up to the public portions of the 'deliberative processes' of certain agencies. It does not provide a right to participate in decision-making, nor can it be invoked to insist that a meeting be held.[69]

The Act applies to all multi-headed agencies, that is 'agencies headed by a collegial body composed of two or more individual members, a majority of whom are appointed by the President, and sub-divisions of agencies appointed to act on its behalf.' Certain internal advisory meetings are not covered, nor are departments headed by a single person.[70] The Act covers the deliberations of the requisite number of agency officials 'where such deliberations determine or result in the joint conduct or disposition of official agency business'.

One week's public notice of the date, time, place and topic of the meeting must be given. A named official with a publicised telephone number must be appointed to answer queries. The law requires more than notice in the *Federal Register*. The federal law does not, however, require the keeping of minutes or verbatim transcripts – unlike many state sunshine laws – though regulations adopted by an agency may themselves require minutes. Records do have to be kept of closed meetings. To close a meeting a majority of agency members must agree, not simply a majority of the quorum of a meeting. The FOIA exemptions, with modification, apply. The inter/intra-agency communication exemption does not apply but meetings may be closed to protect information where disclosure would be likely to frustrate the implementation of a proposed agency action and to protect information concerning litigation.

Where judicial review of a closure of a meeting is sought, the burden of proof is upon the agency concerned. A failure to exhaust internal agency remedies – internal review – does not preclude the opportunity for relief via the courts. The courts will usually only interfere with a failure to pursue the procedures under the law if the breach was intentional, repetitive or prejudicial. The courts have, however, been reluctant to allow parties to use their transcript of agency proceedings under the Act to supplement the record of other agencies' decisions

---

[68] OMB had stated that fifteen days' notice of meetings was adequate, whereas the courts had ruled that thirty days was the requisite period. OMB works under a presidential brief.

[69] Vaughn, note 21 above.

[70] E.g. Treasury, Labor, Defense, Interior, and Food and Drug Administration.

or rule-making in judicial proceedings. The Act provides for 'reasonable attorney fees and other litigation costs reasonably incurred' against any party (not simply the government as in the FOIA) where the requesting party substantially prevails in the application.

As under the FOIA, agencies submit annual reports to Congress on the SA and the Congressional Research Service compiles an overview to discern trends for Congress as it does also for the FOIA.

The Privacy Act

The Privacy Act (PrA) was passed in 1974 and has been subject to numerous amendments and a good deal of criticism. It regulates the collection, control, content, dissemination and use of certain categories of government information and focuses upon 'systems of records' established, controlled or maintained by an agency.[71] This means in those circumstances where information may be retrieved by a name or other identifying symbol. It allows individuals on whom executive federal agencies have documents, files or data to examine the documentation after a written application. A *Citizens' Guide*[72] describes in detail the procedures to follow to obtain information about oneself, and it spells out in simple terms the kinds of information that agencies are likely to possess on individuals, adding that this was 'just a fraction of the information held on individual citizens'. An individual may write to an agency head or PrA official, who both have a duty to inform the individual whether files are held on him or her. Or a more thorough check may be made by consulting the compilation of PrA notices published annually by the *Federal Register*. This contains details of all federal records systems, the kinds of data included, and the categories of individuals on whom the information is held. Retrieval procedures and relevant officials are identified, and the notices are available in reference, law and university libraries. The compilation is, however, poorly indexed and difficult to use.

Unlike the FOIA – and that Act is used frequently in conjunction with the PrA – only the subject of the data or records can apply for sight of them. It confers rights on US citizens or aliens lawfully admitted – not 'any person' as the FOIA. The subject can seek amendment of the records which he or she believes to be inaccurate, irrelevant, untimely or incomplete. Copies of the record, in a form comprehensible to the applicant, must be provided and he or she must be told who, outside the agency, has had access. The Act provides criminal and a variety of civil sanctions.[73] There is no standard procedure for retrieval,

---

[71] It does not cover information owned or possessed by private institutions, it should be noted, unless it is held by a federal body covered by the Act; of the Data Protection Act 1998 and the UK and the 1995 EU Directive on data protection, see ch. 8.

[72] Report by Library of Congress, CRS, 20 September 1985.

[73] Enjoining access, amendment, and damages for 'improper maintenance' of the contents of records or for other breaches of the Act or regulations adversely affecting the individual.

unlike the FOIA, but agency regulations prescribing procedures are common; rejections must be accompanied by a letter specifying the appeal procedures. If appeal is refused, the agency must refer to the exemption it is invoking and must also state why it is not available under the FOIA. The authority for the collection of information must be specified, as must the use to which it is to be put. Information should only be collected where it is relevant or necessary for carrying out lawful duties. Information must be accurate, timely, relevant and complete, an obligation which does not apply to the FOIA.

Disclosure of any record covered by the PrA to a third party without the written consent or request of the subject is prohibited unless the third-party request falls under one of eleven exceptions.[74]

If an agency seeks to rely upon an exemption, however, and is challenged, a *de novo* review can take place in the courts with the burden of proof on the agency to establish one of the exemptions. These fall into two categories: 'general' and 'specific'.

General exemptions cover CIA systems of records and criminal law enforcement systems of records, though the latter only cover criminal investigation records, records compiled to identify criminal offenders or alleged offenders, or compiled at any stage of law enforcement after arrest. This information is only exempt if rules state the reasons for exemption of a system of records from each provision of the PrA. If an individual challenges the exemption before the courts, the courts must determine that a system of records properly falls under the exemption and that all exemption procedures have been followed.[75]

Specific exemptions cover information classified by executive order as under the FOIA; law enforcement material not falling under the general exemption; secret service material; civil or military service employment or promotional suitability information; and information relating to suitability for federal contracts. The exemptions are discretionary, and, for an agency to invoke them, all necessary procedures must be followed. Under specific exemptions, an agency head may exempt his agency's records from fewer of the provisions of the Act than under general exemptions, and challenge through the courts is allowed.

The PrA is one of a number of statutes protecting the privacy of personal information, including the disclosure of information identifying certain US intelligence officers, agents and sources/informants.[76] In the 98th Congress over thirty bills on privacy-related matters were introduced into Congress.[77] Such a frenzied activity may suggest that all is not well with the PrA, and certainly

---

[74] E.g. where records are used internally by employees of the agency in performance of their duties, 'routine' use, or where it is required and is not exempt under the FOIA.

[75] If they have not been, the records may be subject to the PrA. If discretion to exempt is exercised, only a few of the Act's safeguards apply.

[76] Right of Financial Privacy Act 1978; Foreign Intelligence Surveillance Act 1978; Intelligence Identities Protection Act 1982 (USA), which punishes disclosures that the authorities *have reason to believe* would harm US intelligence operations by naming officials.

[77] House Committee on Government Operations: H Rep 98–455 (1983).

there are apparent incompatibilities between the PrA and the FOIA.[78] The PrA has an 'old feel' to it. Bills are frequently presented to Congress to give greater protection to consumers and their privacy. There has also been a significant rift between the US authorities and EU institutions concerning the inadequacy of data protection in the USA when compared with the EU (see chapter 8).[79] A safe-harbour policy and agreement is in place with the EU and other countries that allows a self-certifying data-protection framework for US companies.[80]

The General Accounting Office reviewed the PrA in 2003.[81] This found that the Office of Manpower and Budget – a nerve centre in federal government – had to set new standards in leadership, good practice and compliance. As far back as 1983 in Congressional *Oversight Hearings* of the PrA, it was stated that the current US federal system for data protection was seriously deficient because it lacked an adequate monitoring mechanism to ensure compliance and enforcement.[82] Our own Information Commissioner (IC) might come to mind in this context. There was no overall regulatory body for privacy laws in the USA. Serious malpractices such as computer matching were common, it was felt. This is where whole categories of people may have their records screened to see if they belong to a separate, supposedly incompatible category such as 'welfare recipient'.[83] Computer-matching amendment laws were passed in 1988 and 1990, which authorise computer-matching agreements between agencies and gives the public procedural protection before agreements are finalised. In 1998, President Clinton called upon all federal agencies to take further steps to ensure privacy protection. These included identification of specific senior officials within agencies with responsibility for privacy protection and consistency in the application of privacy principles.

The USA has a constitutional background which takes privacy seriously. The First, Fourth and Fifth Amendments to the Constitution protect freedom of speech, security of property, protection against self-incrimination, and due process of law and have all been regularly invoked to protect the inviolability of an individual's privacy. A federal law protects individuals against invasions of privacy.[84] The Privacy Protection Act 1980 prohibits government agents from making unannounced searches of press offices and files if no one in the press office is suspected of a crime. As befits a privacy-conscious society, many complaints are made to the Office of Management and Budget – which compiles the annual reports on the PrA from agencies – about agency breaches of PrA provisions. The tradition of privacy protection was however, disturbed in the war on terror. The Foreign Intelligence Surveillance Act 2000 as amended extended the use of warrantless intercepts as we saw in chapter 2, p. 68, to much public disquiet in the USA.

---

[78] Vaughn, note 21 above.   [79] A. Charlesworth (2000) European Public Law 253.
[80] www.export.gov/safeharbor/eu/doc_eg_safeharbor_eu.asp.
[81] www.gao.gov/new.items/d03304.pdf.   [82] Rep 401–59 (1983).
[83] This is also a vexed issue in the UK.   [84] Restatement 2d Torts, para. 652A.

FOI and constitutional and administrative practice

The constitutional history of the USA has been more jealous in its protection of freedom of speech, its insistence upon informed debate and freedom of information, than has our own.[85] Executive excesses have been investigated including the notorious episode concerning illegal arms sales to Iran and payments to Nicaraguan rebels in the 1980s and CIA torture in the war on terror. In the Iran arms case President Bush senior did not raise the plea of 'executive privilege' in these proceedings to protect documents, but it has been frequently invoked.

'Executive privilege' as a term was only coined in 1958, although feuds concerning the 'President's claim of constitutional authority to withhold information from Congress' go back to the eighteenth century.[86] In *US v Nixon*[87] the Supreme Court rejected an absolute claim to executive privilege by the president although the case concerned the investigation of serious *criminal* charges against senior executive officials. The courts are the final arbiters in judicial proceedings and law enforcement on what the president and his officials must produce in the interests of justice.[88] *Nixon* was subsequently distinguished by the Supreme Court as *Nixon* concerned a *criminal* and not a *civil* matter.[89]

At the height of the impeachment process against President Clinton, it was decided that government lawyers were not able to be protected by the plea of attorney–client privilege to protect their advice to the president when a grand jury was investigating possible commission of federal crimes.[90] As the Federal Court of Appeals said in an earlier case, 'openness in government has always been thought crucial to ensuring that the people remain in control of their

[85] See *New York Times Co. v US* 403 US 713 (1971) and the First Amendment protection of freedom of speech and the press; although see *Snepp v US* 444 US 507 (1980), where the Supreme Court held that an agreement by CIA employees not to publish *any* information acquired as an agent without specific prior approval was judicially enforceable vis-à-vis classified *and* non-classified information, and all profits accruing from publication were held on constructive trust for the CIA, and see *US v Marchetti* 466 F 2d 1309 (1972). See *AG v Blake* [2000] 4 All ER 385, HL. Cf. *Reading v AG* [1951] AC 507, HL; and *Haig v Agee* 453 US 280 (1981) inter alia. See, generally, E. Barendt, *Freedom of Speech*, 2nd edn (2007).

[86] R. Berger, *Executive Privilege* (1974).

[87] 418 US 683 (1974). In *Nixon v Administrator of General Services* 433 US 425 (1977), the court upheld as constitutional a congressional statute requiring the former president to hand over his presidential papers to an executive agency prior to their eventual disclosure to the public. Burgher CJ and Rehnquist J dissented.

[88] *US v Nixon* above, the Watergate tapes. There was an uncanny familiarity to that event when the Royal Ulster Constabulary refused to hand over their tapes recording events surrounding the shooting of two youths in Armagh in 1982 to the investigating officer, John Stalker. When pressurised into giving access, it was announced by the RUC that they had been lost. A written transcript would be made available, but only on the condition that it was not used for any report. Unlike the Special Prosecutor, Stalker never got his tapes! See J. Stalker, *Stalker* (1988).

[89] *Cheney v US District Court for the District of Columbia* 542 US 367 (2004).

[90] *Re Bruce Lindsey* 148 F3d 1100 (1998 US App).

government'.[91] This episode brought into dramatic focus the role of the office of independent counsel in investigating the president.

The position is not paralleled vis-à-vis Congressional committee demands for information. They do not have the same power as courts. Because Congress has no specific power to demand information, and because of the separation of powers doctrine as well as the equality and independence of each branch of government, presidents have sought to refuse Congress the right to control and demand executive information. *Per contra* 'Congress as the arm of the Government responsible for making and overseeing the operation of the nation's laws, has the power to inquire into and review the methods by which those laws are enforced.'[92] Claims to such a privilege for the executive increased markedly after 1954.[93] The courts have not supported an unqualified Congressional right to demand information from the president, and Congress would have to establish a strong need to fulfil its constitutional responsibilities of oversight, and that such fulfilment was only possible with access to the president's papers, before the courts ordered access. Where such a right was claimed by a Senate committee – in the Watergate episode – the need was not established,[94] although at that time the House Judiciary Committee possessed most of the relevant information and was about to make available its findings on impeachment proceedings against the president. A statute giving Congress the right to demand information in global terms would, in all probability, be ruled unconstitutional.[95]

In November 1982, a White House memorandum for the heads of executive departments and agencies stated that executive privilege could only be claimed 'in the most compelling of circumstances' where after 'careful review' an assertion of privilege was necessary. Brokerage between Congress and the White House would minimise the need for the invoking of executive privilege. Within a month, there was an explosive clash between the Environmental Protection Agency (EPA) and a Congressional committee when the head of the EPA's hazardous waste programme was holding back information on toxic waste sites and their clean-up. She was cited for contempt of Congress. The Justice Department unsuccessfully sought judicial exoneration of the head as she was acting under the direction of the president in refusing to hand over information. The court pressed the parties for a friendly settlement without further judicial intervention.[96] The committee eventually obtained its

---

[91] *Re Sealed case (Espy)* 121 F3d 729, at 749 (DC Circ 1997).

[92] R. L. Claveloux (1983) Duke LJ 1333.

[93] R. Berger, *Executive Privilege* (1974). A famous example involved President Eisenhower's refusal to cede to the demands of Joseph McCarthy who was inquiring into the army's loyalty and security programme.

[94] *Senate Select Committee on Presidential Campaign Activities v Nixon* (CADC) 498 F 2d 725 (1974).

[95] See *Nixon v Administrator of General Services*, note 14 above.

[96] *US v House of Representatives of the US* 556 F Supp 150 (1983). See 'EPA Document Agreement' (26 March 1983) *Congressional Quarterly* 635.

information.[97] Sauce was added to the fare when it was disclosed that the head of the EPA's hazardous waste programme had frequently met, informally and socially, with representatives of companies whose activities she was regulating, although similar opportunities were not offered to environmental lobby groups.[98] In the presidency of George W. Bush the privilege was frequently resorted to stop *subpoenas* from Congressional committees including that involving his senior adviser Karl Rove over the dismissal of federal prosecutors in 2007.

It would take another book to describe the interrelationship between administrative process and law; the requirement of a full record of administrative hearings and rule-making proceedings; the opportunities for interested parties to participate in policy formulation and to be adequately informed about the subject matter; and the resort to courts for 'hard-look', or a very probing, judicial review of an agency's decisions or regulations in order to establish an adequate evidentiary basis for such decisions and regulations – in other words, that an agency has taken a 'hard look' at all the evidence.[99] And it would require a further volume to examine the reaction against excessive secrecy.[100] Nevertheless, safeguards combine together to put administrative policymaking through a series of tests and justifications based upon informed criticism that are largely unparalleled in the UK, although one must be careful not to exaggerate. For instance, in the desire of the White House to deregulate wherever possible, the executive has set a cost–benefit analysis that has to be satisfied before new regulations can be passed. Executive Order 12498 instructs agencies to notify the Office of Manpower and Budget of *all* agency research with links to possible regulation. The desire to deregulate is met with some counterproductive consequences.[101] The ascendancy of the 'New Right' in US politics allowed a populist outcry against big government to be matched by anti-regulatory sentiment. Soft regulation and an absence of reliable information were blamed for the credit crunch commencing in 2007. In his first days in office in 2009, President Obama signalled an initiative undertaking wholesale regulatory reform. The past thirty years have seen the pendulum swing between information and secrecy, between less regulation and better regulation. The substance of the major laws has been remarkably consistent.

[97] A claim of privilege was made over the appointment of W. Rehnquist as Chief Justice. The claim was withdrawn on the understanding that only senators, and not their staff, might see the relevant documentation.

[98] There are specific provisions allowing access to environmental information in the US: see P. Birkinshaw in E. Lykke (ed.), *Achieving Environmental Goals* (1992).

[99] W. Funk *et al.*, *Federal Administrative Procedure Sourcebook*, 3rd edn (2000). J. Lubbers, *A Guide to Federal Agency Rulemaking*, 3rd edn (1998); and the annual J. Lubbers (ed.), *Developments in Administrative Law and Regulatory Practice.*

[100] S. Katz, *Government Secrecy: Decisions without democracy* (1987). A. Roberts, *Blacked Out: Government secrecy in the information age* (2006).

[101] A. B. Morrison (1986) 99 Harv LR 1059, who argues that agencies are placed in a straitjacket and the rules that do satisfy OMB tests are more easily attacked in the courts. See, *ibid.*, p. 1075, for OMB staff reply.

Canada[102]

The Canadian constitution is a written federal constitution, but it has within its operation many features of the Westminster model of government, most notably a developed sense of ministerial responsibility and parliamentary government. The FOIA in America saw a hostile executive, and direct advisers to the president are exempt from the Act although such communications may not be protected by executive privilege or attorney–client privilege (see above). The American law was generated by law reformers, good-government advocates, journalists and Congress. It is a frequently cited criticism in the USA that the FOIA laws do not apply to Congress and the judiciary and alleged connections between some members of those bodies with organised crime. In Canada, Crown privilege and Cabinet confidentiality had to be expressly incorporated into the legislation; the legislation was far from independent of executive influence, and the press impact for reform was minimal.[103] In the USA, the FOIA was developed largely without executive assistance, frequently in the face of executive opposition; in Canada, the Access to Information Act (AIA) was 'drafted by the administration and developed through amendments it perfected'.[104] The AIA has eight or nine times as many exemptions as FOIA. Unlike the AIA, the FOIA did not provide for an information ombudsman or commissioner. Congressmen were jealous of their role as citizens' representatives and Americans like litigation.[105]

The AIA was passed in 1982 and is part of a broad constitutional package reflecting a wish for a new constitutional structure as Canada sloughed off the last vestige of control from Westminster.[106] The Act was amended in 1992 and in 2006. Access is allowed to federal government records and includes 'letters, memos, books, plans, maps, photographs, films, microfilms, sound recordings, computerised data and any other documentary material regardless of physical form or characteristics or any copy thereof'. It has been held by the IC to apply to email and that bodies under the Act should keep email correspondence for two years.[107] It is specific in a way the US FOIA is not. An access register exists which contains descriptions of government records, their probable locations, and other information which 'will likely assist you in identifying precisely which records you wish to see'. Instructions are provided on how to identify, as precisely as possible, the information an applicant is looking for, how to get assistance and how to apply for access. Government departments have access co-ordinators who assist free of charge. A request must be in writing, and there is an application fee of $5 with additional fees for time in excess of five hours

---

[102] See M. Drapeau and M. Racicot, *Federal Access to Information* (2002).

[103] Relyea, 'A comparative review'. The Canadian Bar Association was very proactive.   [104] *Ibid.*

[105] See R. B. Stewart, 'Reform of American administrative law: The academic agenda vs the political agenda' (unpublished paper for Conference on Comparative Administration and Law, 1984).

[106] Canada Act 1982; E. C. S. Wade, A. W. Bradley and K. D. Ewing (eds.), *Constitutional and Administrative Law*, 10th edn (1985), pp. 730–3, for a pithy and lucid account.

[107] IC, *Annual Report 1994–5*. See IC, *Annual Report 2006–7*, p. 39 on email archives.

spent on a request and for computer processing and copying time. Originally an applicant had to be a citizen of Canada or a permanent resident.[108] In 1989, the right of application was extended to any individual or corporation present in America. An agency has thirty days to respond to the initial request, though this may be extended where a request is complicated. The head of each government institution covered by the Act must submit an annual report to Parliament on the administration of the Act. If a body claims that information is exempt, it has to justify that it is exempt. Government institutions are required to remove exempt information from disclosable information and to disclose the latter. The Act does not apply to Crown commercial organisations. As well as the provisions of the Act, information may be classified for internal security purposes under a Treasury Board Manual of 1991.

There has been evidence of official tampering of documents to hinder access; in particular to prevent access to documents relating to intrusive practices by the Canadian peacekeeping forces in Somalia.[109] It is further felt that the law lacks specific guidance on openness and that such guidance and direction need to be spelt out. Since 1997, the IC has rated bodies covered by the Act on their FOI performance annually. One positive effect seems to be that reports of delay in responding to requests fell from 50 per cent of requests in 1997, to 14.5 per cent in 2003–4 and to 23 per cent in 2006–7. The gradings are published in annual reports of the IC.

Excluded material

Excluded material includes Cabinet secrets or confidences of the Queen's Privy Council covering such items as policy proposals, background options and discussions, agenda of Privy Council meetings and minister–adviser discussions on policy briefings and draft legislation. Discussion papers may be released if, inter alia, the decision to which they relate has been made public.[110] The first IC believed she had a right to determine whether they have become public, although the IC's decisions cannot be enforced. The Standing Committee on Justice and Solicitor General described this blanket exclusion as unjustified. It has not been followed in all provincial access statutes.

Exemptions

The Act provides for mandatory and discretionary exemptions. The former include classes of documents such as information from foreign, provincial

---

[108] See *IC v Minister of Employment and Immigration* in IC, *Annual Report 1984–5*, p. 124, for a bizarre interpretation of this provision.

[109] See R. P. Gillis in A. MacDonald and G. Terrill (eds.), *Open Government: Freedom of information and privacy* (1998), ch. 8, p. 155.

[110] *Or* if the *decision* was made at least four years before a relevant request, or if the papers have been in existence for more than twenty years.

or municipal governments; certain confidential information from the Royal Canadian Mounted Police; personal information; and information supplied by outside sources (*sic*).[111] The discretionary exemptions are extensive and include those which might harm federal/provincial affairs, international affairs, Canadian defence or the detection or prevention of 'subversive or hostile activities', lawful investigations, or those which might facilitate the committing of a criminal offence if released. If release would threaten trade secrets, legal privilege or personal safety it may be exempted. Also exempt is the 'advice or recommendations developed by or for an institution or a minister' that would disclose accounts of their deliberations and consultations apropos of negotiating plans or positions – an exemption which has the 'greatest potential for routine misuse'. Third-party information covering trade secrets, competitive ability, contractual matters or other confidential information may be waived from exemption without consent where 'the disclosure would be in the public interest and it relates to health, public safety or the protection of the environment'. Safeguards ensure third-party notice and right of challenge.

Data-banks covering personal information may be made exempt where they contain exempt files which consist predominantly of personal information held for law enforcement or reasons of national security. They are made exempt under an order of the Privy Council. Use of this block exemption is carefully scrutinised by the courts.

Basic provisions

Citizens are urged to use 'existing informal channels' to obtain information and access. This may be a way of institutionalising brokerage as the access co-ordinator has responsibility for all internal aspects of the administration of the Act and has to be informed of all direct requests from the public.

Departments must introduce reading-room facilities within two years of the introduction of the Act. An access register, available in approximately 700 libraries and 2,700 post offices, is constantly checked to ensure accuracy and that it is up to date. The register is organised in chapters, one covering each federal institution and related agencies, and each chapter contains:

1. a description of the organisation and responsibilities of the institution, including details on the programmes and functions of each division or branch
2. a description of all classes of records under the control of the institution in sufficient detail to facilitate the exercise of the right of access under the Act
3. all working manuals
4. titles and addresses of appropriate officials.

[111] Trade secrets are specifically referred to. When information relates to defence, international affairs or an 'exempt data bank' – see text – additional safeguards are adopted in the courts concerning level of judge, *in camera proceedings* and so on and are provided in the legislation: see *Reyes v Canada* (1985) 9 Admin LR 296; *Russell v Canada* (1990) 35 FTR 315 and *X v Canada* (1992) 46 FTR 106

The Information Commissioner

An ombudsman – the IC – to deal with complaints concerning access has been established and the IC has access to information which is exempt under the Act. The first IC declared her intention to construe the exemptions as narrowly as possible. Complaints must be made within a year of the initial request, and they must be in writing unless this requirement is waived. The IC's decision cannot be enforced against departments although the IC may select for judicial scrutiny points which require judicial interpretation, even when the applicant cannot afford the cost of litigation and where she has consented to the suit's proceeding after a department's refusal. Individuals have access to the courts following refusal. The IC may participate in proceedings brought by others, receive information that the complainant will not – unless successful – and may be heard *ex parte* by the court.[112] Courts may review decisions on exemptions on a 'reasonableness' basis. Where the IC supports a complaint but a remedy is not negotiated, a report is made to the minister. Investigations are conducted in private.

It must be said, however, that examination of the IC's annual reports produces a less sanguine perspective of the Act's operation and this tone has pervaded IC reports throughout the nineties. The *Annual Report 2005–6* complained of the government's failure to abide by its promise and Parliament's wish to strengthen the AIA. The government's actions were in fact contrary to widening access. The IC did report on the new government's plans to produce an Open Government Act. The IC has criticised the absence of publicity or explanations of the Act. Indeed, no clause was incorporated providing for public education and enlightenment on the Act and no funds are provided for such. The IC has reported that the 'FOIA cannot be improved upon nor can it serve a country well if its very existence is kept secret'. In the *Annual Report 1984–5*, the IC remarked that access co-ordinators were becoming demoralised and isolated and were subject to criticism from colleagues when they pursued the objectives of the Act too vigorously. Where a co-ordinator was absent, there were no temporary fill-ins, so phones and correspondence were not answered. The *Annual Report 1985–6* was even gloomier in its tone, and it noted how the most frequent users were journalists, academics and researchers although the largest group now is the business community. This gloomy tone has continued and subsequent reports state that his budget had decreased by 10 per cent since 1991 but applications had increased by 56 per cent. In that year he dealt with 1,016 complaints. He reported desultory responses from some departments but also found more constructive approaches among officials. Funding problems have been persistent and have prevented the IC performing his 'watchdog functions' (*Annual Report 2005–6*, p. 3). The IC 'audits' on departmental information practices were noted above. In 2006–7 he opened 1,257 complaints, down from 1,319 in 2005–6. The *Annual Report 2006–7* had a particularly critical tone: 'Too often, responses to access requests are late, incomplete, or overly censured.

---

[112] See, e.g., *Annual Report 2006–7*, p. 53.

Too often, access is denied to hide wrongdoing, or to protect officials or governments from embarrassment' (p. 11). He also has investigators who specialise in national security work and they have access to the Canadian security and intelligence service premises and files. The Canadian IC's report in 2008 was entitled *Review and Streamlining of the OIC Complaints Handling Process – Final Report.*

The Canadian Parliament keeps the operation of the Act under review.[113] In 1993–4, the IC issued a ten–year anniversary report which recommended the appointment of a parliamentary committee to recommend reforms and he then made forty-three recommendations for reform or change in government practice. He recommended repeal of the exemption which removes access rights to documents under the Act which government is under a duty to publish at a fee and for which it charged exorbitant rates (p. 12). He recommended that he have a binding power of decision and that there should be access to government contracts and details of bids. The role of MPs has, however, been criticised in that they have left too much to the IC and have not provided a continuing momentum for development of openness.[114]

The Privacy Act

One of the most commonly invoked exemptions under AIA is that relating to personal information. A Privacy Act was assented to in 1982 which allows access to personal individual records of scheduled government departments by the individual subjects concerned where these records are held by the department. It does not cover private-sector bodies. A Privacy Commissioner (PC) shares premises and general staff with the IC, although they are different individuals and they have different legal advisers because the interests of the two may clash, e.g. access to personal information may be sought by a 'client' of the IC and challenged by a 'client' of the PC. Personal information is given a wide interpretation and safeguards are imposed on the use, purposes, collection and dissemination of material. Personal information banks and a personal-information index are published, setting out all personal information held, who has control of it, the purposes for which it is used, etc. The same criteria apply to applicants for access as obtain under the AIA. They can request correction and notice of unsuccessful requests for correction. The general scheme of the Act, including exclusions, exemptions and reviews of indexes, is similar to those under the AIA. It has carried out some useful studies on e.g. *Genetic Testing and Privacy* (1993 Privacy Commissioner of Canada).[115]

---

[113] Especially the 'confidentiality' clauses in existing statutes (about thirty had such); Office of IC, *Main Brief to HC Standing Committee on Justice and Legal Affairs* (May 1986).

[114] See Gillis, note 109 above, p. 159.

[115] PC of Canada (1993). Success rates for complainants also differ between the Commissioners in the same subject areas. In some cases the PC may be complained against in relation to the

Most provinces have created FOI and privacy rights in one statute and have also combined the commissioners into one office-holder. It was felt that FOI tended to dominate privacy protection.[116] Specific statutes on privacy protection are also appearing in the provinces: Ontario has introduced a Personal Health Information Privacy Act 2000.

Conclusion

In 1981, a commentator upon the FOI movement in Canada noted:[117]

> It has been the experience of public interest interveners such as the Consumers Association of Canada that regulated companies have tended to overwhelm them with information, and as a result the challenge has been to build up expertise so as to be able to interpret this mass of information . . . Is the information coming in a digestible form or in an uncontrollable manner?

This raises a general problem about obtaining information. Raw information can be next to useless. What information do we want? In what form is it most useful? Who is going to use it? For what purpose is it going to be used and how is it going to be most usable? The Act has according to Roberts fostered 'adversarialism' between officials and requesters and has produced official responses to manage 'sensitive requests' and contentious issues in requests. Special attention is given to identities and 'especially interesting' requests despite the Act's premise of equal treatment. Rules on handling requests are not publicly available.[118]

The Canadian statute is less biased towards disclosure than the American one and is more mindful of past practices of confidentiality.[119] In fact, the original proponents of the FOI Bill were the Canadian Bar Association, whose bill was far more adventurous and forthright than that which the government accepted.[120] A review of the two Acts by the House of Commons Standing Committee on Justice and Solicitor General has made some important recommendations on the legislation.[121] In particular, it recommended that Cabinet confidences be brought into the exempt categories and that they should no longer be excluded. This was not accepted and the recommendation was repeated in the 1993–4 report of the IC. This provision was included in an Open Government Bill drafted by the IC's office in 2005–6. Also included was a provision that all exemptions should be subject to a PI test, should contain a requirement of

---

manner in which a complaint was dealt with, but the IC may not be the subject of such a complaint.

[116] Gillis, note 109 above, p. 151.

[117] H. Janisch in J. McCamus (ed.), *FOI: Canadian perspectives* (1981).

[118] A. Roberts in C. Hood and D. Heald (eds.), *Transparency: The key to better governance?* (2006), ch. 7.

[119] J. McCamus (1983) 10 *Govt Publications Review* 51.   [120] Janisch (1982) Public Law 534.

[121] *Open and Shut: Enhancing the right to know and the right to privacy* (March 1987). See specifically ch. 3 on exemptions. This report was rejected by the federal government in *Access and Privacy: The steps ahead* (1987).

injury for non disclosure and be discretionary. Officials should have to keep full records of their work and governance in an oral culture should be consigned to the past. The coverage of the Act should be 'comprehensive' covering excluded bodies and all those spending public funds or performing public functions. Mandatory secrecy provisions in other statutes should not be allowed to exist in perpetuity.

As well as the above provisions under access legislation, the Charter of Rights has been invoked to attempt to obtain government information, including that in the hands of the ombudsmen. The Supreme Court in Canada has heard argument that the right to free expression conveys a right to access to information as a constitutional right.[122]

Australia[123]

Official reports in Australia, prior to their FOIA, placed the blame for excessive secrecy in government on the residue of the influence of the English tradition and its association with Crown prerogative.[124] The FOIA enacted in 1982 has to be set against an ostensibly impressive range of reforms in Australian administrative law that straddle the Administrative Review Council (ARC), the Administrative Appeals Tribunal (AAT), the establishment of a Federal Ombudsman, and a reformed basis of judicial review of administrative action.[125] These seek to advance: openness, fairness, participation, impartiality and rationality in decision-making. In 1983, an FOI Amendment Act was passed to cover certain deficiences in the 1982 legislation, including access to documents up to five years old at the time of the commencement of the 1983 Act. Further reforms took place in 1986, 1988 and 1991, which introduced third-party notice requirements, as well as clarifying and simplifying various procedures.

In a 1983 report on the Act by the Federal Attorney General in Australia he spoke in hopeful tones about the benefits of the Act, which included the improvement of official decision-making, a better-informed public and a truer democratic political process as well as giving individuals information held on themselves or influencing the decisions 'fundamentally affecting their lives'. He was a little surprised, therefore, that much less use of the Act had been made than anticipated.[126] The Act has helped to strengthen and not weaken ministerial

---

[122] On appeal from *The Criminal Lawyers Assoc. v Ontario (Public Safety and Security)* (2007) ONCA 392.

[123] M. Alhadeff, *Denying the Public's Right to Know: A critique of the operation of the FOIA 1982* (2006). J. McMillan *Law and Policy Paper No. 21*, Australian National University/CIPL (2002).

[124] *AG for New South Wales v Butterworth and Co. (Australia) Ltd* (1938) 38 SRNSW 195; and Report by the Senate Standing Committee on Constitutional and Legal Affairs on the FOI Bill (1978), ch. 4.

[125] See, for instance, the annual reports of the ARC; and M. Partington in P. McAuslan and J McEldowney (eds.), *Law, Legitimacy and the Constitution* (1985), pp. 199–207.

[126] *FOIA 1982 Annual Report by the Att-Gen* (Aust. Govt. Publishing Service, 1983). The Department of Social Security anticipated 100,000 requests; it received 1,177.

responsibility in Parliament. The Act has been the subject of a further review by the Standing Committee on Legal and Constitutional Affairs in 1987 and in 1994 the ARC and Australian Law Commission issued a detailed discussion paper on the Act at the request of the Attorney General leading to a 1996 joint Australian Law Reform Commission and ARC *Open Government Report* recommending proposals for change and extension of the Act's provisions.[127] This followed reports from the ombudsman who found increased departmental resistance to the Acts in the form of delays and unnecessary secrecy. In 2008, the prime minister reported that it was his plan to implement these reforms![128] Between 1982 and June 2006, there had been 766,080 requests for information under the Act to federal bodies. In 2004–5 there were 41,430 requests and 85 per cent of these were for personal information. In 2007, responsibility for the 1982 Act and 1988 Privacy Act was transferred to the prime minister and Cabinet Office and away from the Attorney General.

The legislation

The 1982 Act places a duty on the responsible minister to publish, not later than 12 months after commencement of the Act, particulars of the organisation he heads, its functions and powers; arrangements allowing public participation for non-official persons or groups in whatever form in the formulation of policy; the organisation's administration; the categories of its documents; and details on access procedures and officers. Ministers have to publish in the *Federal Gazette* all documents – including computerised records – which may be used to make decisions or recommendations affecting rights, privileges, benefits, obligations, penalties or other 'detriments'. Every person has a legally enforceable right to agency and ministerial documents which are not exempt. A decision on access has to be given within sixty days, and refusal must be accompanied with reasons. As with Canadian and US legislation, there is a third-party notification procedure.

Exemptions[129]

The Act provides access to documents not information as such – unlike the UK FOIA 2000 (see chapter 4). Documents are exempt where 'disclosure . . . would be contrary to the public interest', viz. it 'could reasonably be expected to cause damage to: the security or defence of the Commonwealth; international relations; federal/state relations'. The AAT has formulated principles to help tease out the formulation of PI although these have not been universally acclaimed. The principles seek to protect high level communications, the policymaking

---

[127] Following an interim report published in March 1995 – Australian Law Reform Commission and ARC, *Discussion Paper 59*.

[128] www.pmc.gov.au/foi/docs/annual_report_0708/FOI_annual_report_2007–2008.pdf.

[129] Contained in ss. 32–47.

process, the frankness and candour of deliberations in 'future pre-decisional communications'.[130] The Attorney General's Department has listed a variety of features both in favour and weighing against a disclosure in the PI.[131] The Attorney General's Department, in fact, could find no examples of release of policy documents against the wishes of the government.[132] Cabinet and Executive Council documents are exempt, as are internal working documents where disclosure would reveal advice or deliberations relating to the 'deliberative functions of an agency or minister or of the Commonwealth Government' and would be against the PI. A certificate from the minister covering these exemptions is conclusive evidence on the PI. This decision cannot be reviewed by the AAT; it can determine whether there is a reasonable basis for the exemption claim. If it does not believe there is, it may *recommend* revocation.[133] The AAT has held that it would be cautious about entering into an unfinished course of policymaking and negotiation and the benefit of the doubt, even in cases where there were very strong grounds in favour of disclosure, would lie with the minister where he had a 'relevant reasonable ground for non-disclosure'.[134] This exemption does not apply to purely factual information, reports on scientific or technical experts expressing an opinion on technical matters, or to reports of a prescribed body or organisation *within* an agency. Other exemptions cover familiar territory: law enforcement; public safety; Commonwealth financial interests; documents the disclosure of which would involve unreasonable disclosure of personal information; legal privilege; trade secrets; disclosure that would detrimentally affect the national economy; or disclosure that would constitute a breach of confidence. This last exemption would seem to be very wide in scope.

The ARC found that decision-makers were unclear about how to apply the exemptions and nothing like the *Vaughn* index (see p. 464 above) seems to have appeared. There are also four forms of PI balancing tests applicable in the range of exemptions which does not make application easy. These are open unless access is contrary to the PI; balancing of interests involved to establish where preponderant interest lies; modified – i.e., disclosure in the circumstances would cause unreasonable risk or damage etc; and finally 'closed' – i.e., never open.

In addition to the above exemptions, information may be refused where it relates to 'all documents, or all documents of a specified class, that contain information of a specified kind or relate to a specified subject matter' and would 'substantially and unnecessarily interfere' with the other functions of the agency or minister. Reasons must be given for refusal, but again this exemption seems to allow ample scope for refusal.

---

[130] *Re Howard and the Treasurer of the Commonwealth of Australia* (1985) 3 AAR 169; see Terrill in McDonald and Terrill (eds.), *Open Government*.

[131] Terrill in McDonald and Terrill (eds.), *Open Government*, p. 106.   [132] *Ibid.*, p. 111.

[133] For figures, see Australian Law Reform Commission and ARC, *Freedom of Information* Issues, Paper 12 (1994), p. 46; also *Re Howard etc.* (1985) 3 AAR 169.

[134] *Re Rae and Department of Prime Minister and Cabinet* (1986) Admin Review 136.

Amendment and review

Part V of the Act allows the subject of personal documents to apply to have the records amended. Part VI covers the review of the agency's or minister's decision. Departments are given thirty days to process a request – a reform introduced in 1991. An internal review will take place upon request within fourteen days after the day of notification of refusal. Three months is not an unknown period. Alternatively, an application may be made to the AAT if no decision is notified within thirty days.[135] Initially about 300 complaints were made to the AAT each year but when the application fee was increased from AUD 200 to AUD 500 the numbers dropped dramatically. Another route is via the Commonwealth Ombudsman who, although s/he cannot investigate decisions taken by ministers, may examine the whole context of the decision. The AAT has power to make any decision that could be made by the agency or minister and can, in some cases, review whether disclosure would be contrary to the PI.[136] Its remit is to review on the law and on the merits. *In camera* proceedings are possible for inspection of 'exempt' documents by the AAT if it is not satisfied with the minister's certificate. If a minister does not accept a finding of the AAT that is adverse to his classification, it is not binding upon him, but he must notify the applicant of his reasons and place a copy of these before both Houses of Parliament.[137] From the AAT there is an appeal on a point of law to the Federal Court. The AAT, in spite of its introduction to reduce formality in state/citizen conflict has not escaped criticism for being over formalistic.[138]

The Commonwealth Ombudsman

The annual reports of the ombudsman have been notable for his own complaints that he receives inadequate funding to perform his responsibilities under the FOIA. Several persons who wished to be represented before the AAT were turned down because of a lack of funding.[139] He received no additional staff for his FOIA responsibilities. The 1983 legislation not only added the representational role to his responsibilities: he now has to monitor the Act and recommend improvements in access. He claimed that his treatment by the government

---

[135] As from 1 January 1987. A downpayment of AUD 300 at that time had to be provided for registration; it is now AUD 682.

[136] Different departments have taken different attitudes on the same documents as to whether exemption should be claimed: *Re Dillon and Department of Treasury* and *Re Dillon and Department of Trade* (1986) Admin Review 113. Under the Act, the AAT cannot insist on access to exempt information.

[137] A minister has responsibility for administering the FOIA, and he has access to all necessary documents. *Quaere* collective responsibility?

[138] See Australian Law Reform Commission and ARC, *Freedom of Information*, Issues Paper 12 (1994), p. 74.

[139] The 1983 Amendment Act allows the AAT to make a recommendation for payment of a successful applicant's costs to the Attorney General.

was both 'unfair and demonstrably discriminatory' and that lack of resources meant that he had been unable to monitor the Act as required. In the period after 1984–5, the position had not improved and in 1991 the ombudsman lost the role of counsel before the AAT.[140]

The ombudsman is beset by other problems. It has been decided that his records of complaints investigations are not exempt, under s. 38[141] of the Act, from an FOIA request. All ombudsmen would invoke the protection of complete confidentiality for their investigations – a confidentiality usually protected by law – so the decision does appear anomalous.[142] It will be recalled that the UK IC is the subject of many FOI complaints (see chapter 6). To gain exemption, the ombudsman may well have to rely upon the general confidentiality provision in the 1982 Act and other exemptions.

The ombudsman has access to disputed documents, including those for which exemption is claimed.[143] In 2001–2 he received 266 FOI complaints, and the AAT received 99. The ARC has noted that the ombudsman has not played as significant a role in FOI as anticipated[144] and in 1995 it identified the absence of an 'advocate for FOI to oversee the Act and monitor compliance' as a deficiency.[145] The lack of a single unified advocate for FOI in Australia has been a source of criticism. There is no single focal point for advocacy, investigation, giving guidance and monitoring the Act. The coverage of FOI material in the annual reports of the ombudsman is very thin – he has a large number of other responsibilities. The ombudsman also addressed these issues in a paper *Designing an Effective FOI Oversight Body – Ombudsman or independent Commissioner?* to the 5th International Conference of Information Commissioners in November 2007. The paper is available on the website (www.ombudsman.gov.au).

The prime minister's annual report on the legislation announced in 2008 that a review of the legislation was being planned and consultation on a bill would take place in 2009. Among proposals would be a unified IC Office, implementation of the 1996 ARC report *Open Government* and free access for personal information.

Some reaction to the legislation

The courts have ruled that the legislation is applicable to some private institutions carrying out functions in the PI, for example a law society and universities, although documents of university council meetings have been held

---

[140] In that earlier period, the Commonwealth Ombudsman resigned.

[141] *Kavvadias v Commonwealth Ombudsman (Nos. 1 and 2)*; see CO, *Annual Reports* (1983–4), pp. 30–2 and (1984–5), pp. 165–8. Requests came mainly from former complainants.

[142] *Kavvadias* has not been followed by Victoria State vis-à-vis its own FOIA and their ombudsman.

[143] Unless a certificate under s. 9(3) of the Ombudsman Act 1976 is issued.

[144] Tenth Annual Report, para. 76.

[145] Australian Law Reform Commission and ARC, *Discussion Paper 59.*

to be properly classified as exempt by the AAT as they were compared with Cabinet documents.[146] Boldness in some areas is not reflected in others. The High Court of Australia has held that there is no general rule of common law or principle of natural justice that required the giving of reasons for administrative decisions.[147] Another judge, however, adverting to this issue and the FOIA generally, spoke of the need for legislation to 'deal with the real problems and not the symbols and to preserve democratic values' of society.[148] Information rights, he argued, must extend from the public sector to the private one. I should mention that one of the areas singled out for special attention by the ARC in its 1994 report was the extension of the legislation to the private sector, especially given the impetus for privatisation and corporatisation and government business enterprises. Coverage of private bodies performing public tasks is patchy. In the USA, for instance, public-disclosure laws place duties on private bodies to disclose information to the public through annual inventories about designated toxic material and hazardous materials.[149] But the US FOIA imposed no *direct* duties on private bodies themselves until the 2007 amendments to the FOIA covered government contractors.

In the first full year of the FOIA's operation, there were almost 20,000 requests involving 152 agencies; of these 1,105 were refused, 500 were reviewed internally and 27 formed the subject of a complaint to the ombudsman; 168 were referred to the AAT. More recent figures for 2001–2 were given above and in 2007–8 the ombudsman received 206 complaints.[150] These mainly concerned delay. In that year there were 29,019 requests for information to federal bodies – a 25 per cent decrease on the previous year. The media have been criticised for not making greater use of the Act. PI groups are 'reasonably frequent users'. Commercial use appears to be limited. The ARC found that some agencies did not support the 'Culture of openness' more than ten years after the legislation was introduced.[151] In 2006, the ombudsman's own-motion report *Scrutinising Government: Administration of the Freedom of Information Act 1982 in Australian Government agencies* (Report No. 2/2006) covered many of the relevant issues including the concern over falling standards.

It is interesting to observe that departments are differing in their attitudes towards the FOIA. Such differences seemed to be anticipated by the Attorney General, who wrote to all relevant agencies in 1983 asking them to inform his secretariat of FOIA requests which were being taken to the AAT, so that *consistency* in approach could be achieved. In the early stages of the legislation

---

[146] *Re Burns and Aust NU* 1 February 1985; *Cf. Sankey v Whitlam* (1978) 142 CLR
[147] *Public Services Board of New South Wales v Osmond* (1986) 159 CLR 656
[148] Kirby J (1986) Admin Review 1023.
[149] Birkinshaw in E. Lykke (ed.), *Achieving Environmental Goals*, p. 98.
[150] www.pmc.gov.au/foi/docs/annual_report_0708/FOI_annual_report_2007–2008.pdf.
[151] Australian Law Reform Commission and ARC, *Discussion Paper 59*, p. 11.

there was some evidence of informal bartering by federal and provincial government to secure opposition to a federal agency's liberal attitude to disclosing information.[152] However, every state and the Australian Capital Territory has FOI legislation and, in some cases, echoing the situation in the USA, such laws are more advanced than the federal model.

The Australian Act has been used to make some dramatic disclosures about, e.g., disputes before the Chief Justice and the Prime Minister's Department concerning litigation involving indigenous Australians' land rights.[153] However, the fact that the Act is enforced by individuals and ultimately rests upon governmental goodwill for enforcement is seen as a serious weakness by Terrill.[154]

New Zealand[155]

New Zealand enacted an FOIA – the Official Information Act (OIA) – in 1982. The Act makes provision for the publication of internal rules and has many distinguishing characteristics from the Australian laws. The legislation also repealed the NZ Official Secrets Act 1951. It would be pointless running through similar provisions once more, but it is worth pointing out that an Information Ombudsman has been created, the New Zealand Ombudsman in fact, to deal with information complaints. His recommendations *are* mandatory on the minister or department concerned and take effect from the commencement of the 22nd day after the day on which his *recommendation* is made to the department, unless, originally, the responsible minister otherwise directs or decides by order in council. The ministerial veto was replaced by a Cabinet veto by way of an order in council in 1987, which has never been exercised. There is a PI override on some exemptions including 'the constitutional conventions protecting policy advice'.

The Act also created an Information Authority which was a body mandated to review the Act and access practices, to enlarge the scope of the Act, to recommend procedural reforms in the Act, to invite public as well as official comment about the Act, to make suggestions for extension of the Act and to seek advice from and to conduct investigations into all appropriate authorities. For this latter duty, access to necessary documents is given subject to veto on account of national security and to prevent crime. The Information Authority could meet in public or in private, and it reported to Parliament. It has a life-span of five years. Its term of office was not extended so the Act lacks an independent champion apart from the ombudsman.

The two areas causing initial difficulty were those relating to personal and private information and competitive commercial contracts. Policy advice became a

---

[152] *Re State of Queensland and Department of Aviation* (1986) Admin Review 138
[153] Terrill in McDonald and Terrill (eds.), *Open Government.*   [154] At p. 112.
[155] I. Eagles, G. Liddell and M. Taggert, *Freedom of Information: New Zealand* (1992).

problematic area. Exemptions most commonly relied upon were the protection of confidentiality of advice and the internal working documents exemption protecting the 'free and frank' opinions of officials. The ombudsman has found the former exemption too expansive and has sought to restrict its scope. He heard evidence that a failure to maintain full and frank discussion neutered or hindered the civil service, and similar views had emerged from Australia.[156] Tendering for government contracts had been kept confidential, and the ombudsman has suggested that commercially confidential information should be separated from other information in tendering.

After the ombudsman there is the possibility of judicial review of ministers' decisions; the ombudsman has been successfully challenged before the courts. As in Canada, there is a separate Privacy Commissioner supervising the operation of the Privacy Act and a Privacy Act of 1993 covers both the public and private sectors. Specific codes are produced which are binding and tailored to individual industries. An Official Information Amendment Act was passed by Parliament in 1987 and in that year a Local Government Official Information and Meetings Act was enacted. Under s. 7 of the NZ Bill of Rights Act 1990, everyone has the right to freedom of expression including the freedom to seek, receive and impart information and opinion in any kind or form. The existence of the OIA has led to provision of more information in relation to the Public Finance Act, the Fiscal Responsibility Act (part of the former by virtue of reforms in 2004), the Privacy Act covering all holders of data and the consultation provisions of statutes like the Local Government Act 2002.

What is interesting about the New Zealand legislation is that it concentrates attention on the PI in disclosure rather than a class or contents exemption as is the case with the UK FOIA (see chapter 6). There are also no excluded categories of information such as Cabinet documents. *A Policy Framework for Government-held Information* (1996) has recommended greater resort to the intent of making information available in advance of FOI requests. Readers are reminded of the situation in the USA and should compare the use of publication schemes in the UK.

Conclusion

In the previous edition the examples examined revealed different approaches adopted by countries operating in a liberal democratic tradition and at broadly similar stages of economic development. Now very different traditions are engaging with freedom of information and transparency. The different socio-cultural and political backgrounds of the countries have ensured variations in

---

[156] *Report of the Chief Ombudsman*, (1984) and *Murtagh v Com'r of Taxation*. See *Police Com'r v Ombudsman* [1985] 1 NZLR 578, on a challenge to the ombudsman's powers.

their approaches to FOI, although all have reacted to the growth of government and bureaucracy, the escalation of information gathering and control by executive agencies – and in some cases private bodies – and the inability of democratic institutions of representative government to oversee these developments effectively, albeit in different ways. It is notable for instance that the draft law in Egypt and the South African law cover the private sector in their terms. In the liberal democratic traditions, the 'state' is the object of attention and not the public–private interface. Such an interface will be the next development in FOI.

It might be pertinent to ask whether the legislative developments constitute an acknowledgement of the failure of representative government and the first faltering steps towards a more substantial participatory form of government. If this is claimed, then the legislation we have examined has a long way to go – which has been acknowledged in Australia and Canada. In Australia, the veto power has been exercised frequently. Even in New Zealand, often regarded as a model of FOI practice, problems have been identified.[157] The most recent recruit to FOIA excluding the UK has been the Republic of Ireland where Official Secrets Acts still operate under the influence after so many years of former British rule.[158] The amendment to the 1997 FOIA in Ireland took place in 2003 and amounted to a retrenchment.[159] One might say that public disquiet has been bought off rather cheaply in the countries we have examined. The legislation can only operate with full effect within a cultural framework that is already in existence – a governmental attitude which accepts it *might* have to undergo change as the legislation works inwardly upon government, and a public attitude that, although perhaps unfamiliar with the use of information to challenge governmental presumptions, is nonetheless prepared to acquire that expertise. Expectations that the legislation by itself will achieve the goals that many FOI advocates hope for are pie in the sky. Different public attitudes and different governmental institutions are necessary for the real success of FOI legislation. Transition has to operate beneath the surface as I explain in chapter 13. The laws also have to address the context of governance as it now exists – not as it existed decades ago.

The overseas legislation was also very instructive when the UK FOI Bill was first presented to the Commons Select Committee on Public Administration for the latter to scrutinise (see chapter 4). Many of the glaring deficiencies in the draft bill compared badly with overseas legislation and the most objectionable of the provisions seemed to represent an effort to break with internationally

---

[157] N. White, *Free and Frank: Making the Official Information Act work* (2007).

[158] See M. McDonagh, *Freedom of Information Law in Ireland*, 2nd edn (2006). The OSA 1963 was amended by the FOIA to prevent proper disclosure under FOIA being punished under the OSA.

[159] M. McDonagh, 'Freedom of information in Ireland: Five years on', *freedominfo.org*, posted 22 September 2003; and Irish Information Commissioner, *Freedom of Information: The first decade* (2008).

accepted norms of conduct. The Acts in Australia, Canada, Ireland and New Zealand all possessed long titles or opening purpose clauses that afforded a central importance to openness and access in the way in which the legislation was interpreted. This was denied in the UK FOIA (see chapter 4). The Acts also displayed other ways of dealing with complaints and compromising government prerogative.

13

Conclusion

The UK Freedom of Information Act (FOIA) has been in effect in relation to individual access rights for almost five years. Any assessments of the effects of the Act are at this stage likely to be exploratory and qualified.[1] However, there are signs of optimism. The first Information Commissioner (IC) has had a robust and positive influence in advancing openness and transparency. The IC, and the Scottish IC, have been focal points not only in enforcing the Acts but in championing the era of freedom of information (FOI), the legislation and what they represent. The Information Tribunal (IT) under the UK model is producing a steady stream of jurisprudence on the legislation including the Environmental Information Regulations (EIR) and the Data Protection Act. The courts have been supportive of the principles of openness and transparency in their judgments concerning appeals. 'FOIA introduced a radical change to our law, and the rights of the citizens to be informed about the acts and affairs of public authorities . . . in the absence of a public interest in preserving confidentiality, there is a public interest in the disclosure of information held by public authorities.'[2] A powerful legal culture of openness and transparency has been developed. FOI has gained strong support across all spectrums of the press. Attempts by government and Parliament to remove features of the Act that were deemed hostile or unhelpful – and it must be remembered that Parliament has felt the impact of the Act in the decisions leading to reform of MPs expenses – were thwarted.

In a short time, the FOIA has become a fixture of public life in the UK to such an extent that any attempt to remove it by a future government would be nigh impossible, although modifications may come. Crucially, the momentum for the Act does not rely upon one figure. If a new IC were to take a low profile in promoting and enforcing the Act, the IT with its varied membership is there to

---

[1] The Constitution Unit at UCL is engaged in a series of research initiatives aimed at assessing the impact of the Act and realisation of its objectives in its short operation and, as I write, these studies are not published in final form. See M. Glover and S. Holsen 'Downward slope? FOI and access to government information' in R. Hazell (ed.), *Constitutional Futures Revisited: Britain's Constitution to 2020* (2008), ch. 11 and R. Hazell *et al.*, *Does Freedom of Information Work? The impact of the Freedom of Information Act 2000 on central government* (forthcoming).

[2] *Office of Government Commerce v IC and Another* [2008] EWHC 737 (Admin), paras. 68–9.

hear appeals on a wide basis. The first IC supported a new statutory commission of several individuals to reduce dangers of one person domination.[3] And above the IT are the courts. There is an institutional dynamic in the UK model that is not present in some of the more obvious models overseas where the legislation lacked momentum and champions. New Zealand has one of the most liberal models in terms of access to Cabinet documents – where change in the UK seems likely (see chapters 5 and 6) – yet it has no champion of FOI as such and the Information Authority disappeared after its initial phase of existence.

There were wider objectives in government introducing FOI legislation. There were the questions of increased openness and transparency which have become universal features of good governance. There was enhanced accountability – again a universal indicator in promoting and assessing good governance. There is the objective of explaining how government works to enhance the public's trust in government. Further objectives listed by the Constitution Unit involved bringing government closer to the people and involving people in government by helping them to understand government better and to participate when they so desired. Improving the quality of government decision making, improving advice to government, removing waste and unnecessary expenditure and helping to fight corruption were seen as objectives – anticorruption objectives are very prominent in states with poorer economies but are not confined to such states. Putting government-held information to profitable use by reuse by the private sector is a relatively new addition (see chapter 1) but an important feature in strategies for economic promotion. Enhancing service delivery and performance of public authorities are two further objectives. The realisation of these objectives will be subject to constant study.

There has also been criticism from influential thinkers and academics about the benefits of increased openness and transparency.[4] Scepticism has been expressed about the real virtues of these qualities in achieving greater accountability and efficiency. Providing more and more information in response to requests or proactively simply allows the real picture to be concealed. An FOI presumption is the proactive provision of reliable, useful and accurate information. In relation to requests, an authority can only hand over what is requested. If that is inaccurate that will lead to further questions.

At the heart of the FOI debate is a question of value: in the absence of compelling reasons to refuse, which are independently determined, should individuals have a right of access to the information held by their governments? If not, why not? No one has made a convincing public case denying such a right. There is none. Blair's Government should be applauded for promoting the FOIA. Sections of the government and Parliament came to resent it. It can be a nuisance for those in power or privilege. That is a part of its importance. By giving people information of importance to them, otherwise of little significance

---

[3] R. Thomas and M. Walport, *Data Sharing Review* (2008).
[4] See many of the contributions in C. Hood and D. Heald (eds.), *Transparency: The key to better governance* (2006).

and, on the whole, for nothing, the Act is an irreplaceable part of democratic and responsive government.

The story is unfinished. The fact that FOI laws are now in existence in over seventy states with many others preparing the way for access regimes is widely known.[5] These as one would expect differ widely in their content and effectiveness. Several questions from the FOI explosion remain.

The first of these is whether FOI should accompany those rights that are regarded as human rights – rights that deserve to be designated as fundamental because of their intrinsic importance.[6] They are rights that override other rights or, as in the UK system, are virtually indispensable instruments in the interpretation of laws. Existing rights under Art. 19 Universal Declaration of Human Rights, Art. 13 International Covenant of Civil and Political Rights, Art. 13 American Convention on Human Rights and Art. 9 African Charter on Human and Peoples' Rights include freedom of speech and a right to seek, receive and impart information. It has been seen in the European Convention of Human Rights (ECHR) case law concerning Art. 10 on freedom of speech that this right which includes a right to receive and impart information has not been interpreted as conferring a right of *access* to government information whereas Art. 8 on protection of private and personal life has provided such a right (see chapter 8, p. 273). Other ECHR rights, such as the right to life and justice, have conferred rights to information. In *Claude Reyes v Chile*[7] the Inter-American Court on Human Rights found that Art. 13 American Convention conferred a general right of access to official information and states must provide a system for exercising that right. Freedom of speech is universally applauded. What is the point if the speech is badly informed?

The governing institutions of the international conventions have adopted statements and declarations on access to information. The UN Convention against Corruption calls on states to ensure effective access to information and OECD is promoting initiatives of rights to information. Closer to home a draft Council of Europe Convention on Access to Official Documents has been under discussion but there are criticisms that this Convention is too confined to be an effective instrument in conferring adequate access.[8] The European Parliament in proposing amendments to the existing EU regulation on access to documents has provided that, in assessing the public interest (PI) in disclosing documents

---

[5] D. Banisar, *Freedom of Information Around the World: A global survey of access to government information laws* (2006) – the number has increased.

[6] P. Birkinshaw (2006) 58 Admin LRev 177.

[7] Case 12.108, Report No. 60/03, Inter-Am. C.H.R., OEA/Ser.L/V/II.118 Doc. 70 rev. 2, at 222 (2003).

[8] www.aip-bg.org/documents/coe_convention_eng.htm. The Council of Europe's Draft Convention on Access to Official Documents provides for 'everyone' to have access: no distinction is made between citizens, residents or others. For critical comments from the Parliamentary Assembly of the Council of Europe on the draft convention (see http://assembly.coe.int/Main.asp?link=/Documents/AdoptedText/ta08/EOPI270.htm). The convention has been agreed and opened for signature among Council of Europe members: CoE Treaty Series/205 18.VI.2009.

over an exception, 'special weight' shall be given to the fact that documents relate to fundamental rights (see chapter 10).

Numerous non-governmental organisations and PI groups have taken up the cause of freedom of information and transparency. The support for a fundamental right of access to information as a universal requirement was debated at the Carter Center in 2008, which produced the Atlanta Declaration and Plan of Action for the Advancement of the Right to Access to Information.[9] This document makes some rather sweeping claims about the universality of access to information in 'all cultures and systems of government' that are not the case (see chapter 1) but the document does note that the poor, women, the marginalised and vulnerable suffer disproportionately from a lack of access to information. The powerful or privileged invariably have access. The right which is stated to be a fundamental right would extend to:

> all intergovernmental organisations, including the United Nations, international financial institutions, regional development banks, and bilateral and multilateral bodies. These public institutions should lead by example and support others' efforts to build a culture of transparency.

The right would include the features of good practice with which the UK law is largely consistent although it does provide that all exemptions should be subject to a PI override and subject to what is permitted by international law. Our law would have difficulty here in terms of information that is effectively excluded (see chapter 5) and where national security is involved (see chapter 2). There should be institutional support for access with 'procedures designed to ensure the full implementation and ease of use, with no unnecessary obstacles (such as cost, language, form or manner of request) and with an affirmative obligation to assist the requester and to provide the requested information within a specified and reasonable period of time'. States and international organisations should have systems ensuring full and effective implementation. Access should cover all branches of government including the judiciary – the IC has commenced an investigation into access to information about disciplined judges but there would be real difficulty about personal information on appointments (see chapter 11). Furthermore, in advocating a repeal of official secrecy laws s. 2 of the 1911 Act would have been an easy target. The 1989 reforms, despite their potential breadth, which has been criticised above, are limited to areas affecting security, defence, international relations, crime and special investigation powers (see chapter 3).

The Atlanta Declaration is also important in setting its range of institutional coverage beyond the nation state. It sets forth a detailed plan of action for states and non state bodies. The inclusion of private bodies within an access regime is the next important item to consider for future development. But what limitations should exist? The Atlanta Declaration states that intergovernmental

---

[9] www.cartercenter.org/documents/Atlanta%20Declaration%20and%20Plan%20of%20Action.pdf.

organisations, the OECD and international financial institutes, regional development banks and trade bodies should give effect to the principles stated in it. Furthermore:

> The right of access to information also applies to non-state actors that: receive public funds or benefits (directly or indirectly); carry out public functions, including the provision of public services; and exploit public resources, including natural resources. The right of access to information extends only to the use of those funds or benefits, activities or resources. In addition, everyone should have the right of access to information held by large profit-seeking corporations where this information is required for the exercise or protection of any human right, as recognized in the International Bill of Rights.

The power of designation of private bodies in the UK FOIA was referred to (see chapter 4) but that power has not been exercised (see Introduction, p. 7). The South African Promotion of Access to Information Act 2 of 2000 allows access to information in the possession of private bodies in order to exercise or protect an individual's rights (s. 50). Exemptions relating to commercial information and confidentially may be overridden where the PI in disclosure 'clearly outweighs' the harm (s. 70).[10] A draft decree on access to information laws in Egypt in 2008 also included access to private organisations' documents.

For 'multinational corporations', or transnational corporations (TNCs as they are called in the discourse of globalisation), and 'large domestic businesses', they 'should establish voluntary commitments to proactively disclose information in the public interest, and such efforts should be encouraged and supported'. The dangers or weaknesses of voluntarism are all too apparent. However, companies are used to duties to disclose information under health and safety and environmental regulation and under corporate management and ownership. Regulators are subject to FOI laws and will have voluminous amounts of information on private companies although there may well be wide exemptions and statutory prohibitions on disclosure. The abuse of power of TNCs in pharmaceutical pricing, in Third World production and exploitation of unorganised labour and the denial of rights for children and the economically weak is a well-recounted story. The countries in which abuse takes place do not have effective FOI laws, or FOI laws at all. There are difficulties in using laws in countries where companies are registered – either because of a lack of resources or wide exemptions where there are laws, or secrecy laws and practices, in the registering state. The latter bring to mind tax havens, for instance, protected by privacy.

The future would indicate that providing FOI as a human right in internationally agreed conventions and in providing for coverage of private bodies as outlined in the Atlanta Declaration would be a start in tackling abuse of economic power. No one will underestimate that power. Global financial markets were under forms of regulation, but a heady cocktail of complexity, opacity,

---

[10] I. Currie and J. Klaaren, *Promotion of Access to Information Act Commentary* (2002).

greed and cowardice prevented governments and regulators understanding or stopping the maelstrom that unfolded. An essential feature in preventing abuse of power is knowing how that power operates and what it is doing.

The primary responsibility for good government and good regulation falls on government. Good regulation may entail levels of self-regulation or soft-touch regulation. Whatever, government cannot absolve itself of the duty of knowing how power affecting the general welfare is being exercised and it cannot avoid the duty of informing society of its own exercise or non-exercise of powers in response to events involving markets, professions and business. FOI is a central feature of responsible and responsive government. But the law has to be effective. This involves a complex array of factors. I conclude with words from a previous edition setting out these factors as a reminder, now that FOI has adopted an international dimension:

> No one should expect that an FOIA will change the nature of government or the behaviour of the governed overnight. Much work, effort, goodwill and education will have to be provided. Progress and democratic development will take time. They are worth striving for. Unless, however, there is a change in attitude and ethos in our public administration and in the public/private interface, FOIA by itself will be something of a confidence trick. It is an inescapable development in democratic and responsible government. But an FOIA must be accompanied by more widespread changes in attitude and in major institutional reform if we are to be better informed and more open. Those are the necessary conditions to help reduce the abuse of power. The forces and the sources operating against such conditions should never be underestimated or overlooked.[11]

[11] P. Birkinshaw, *Freedom of Information: The law, the practice and the ideal*, 3rd edn (2001), p. 482.

Index